*Academic Charisma and the Origins
of the Research University*

GUSTAV SEEBERGER'S VORHALLE DER MÜNCHENER UNIVERSITÄT, 1846,
NOW GESCHWISTER-SCHOLL-PLATZ, UNIVERSITY OF MUNICH, FROM MÜNCHENER
STADTMUSEUM. REPRODUCED WITH PERMISSION.

# Academic Charisma *and the* Origins *of the* Research University

*William Clark*

THE UNIVERSITY OF CHICAGO PRESS

CHICAGO AND LONDON

The University of Chicago Press, Chicago 60637
The University of Chicago Press, Ltd., London
© 2006 by The University of Chicago
All rights reserved. Published 2006
Paperback edition 2007
Printed in the United States of America

16 15 14 13 12 11 10 09 08 07      4 5 6
ISBN-13: 978-0-226-10921-3 (cloth)
ISBN-13: 978-0-226-10922-0 (paper)
ISBN-10: 0-226-10921-6 (cloth)
ISBN-10: 0-226-10922-4 (paper)

Library of Congress Cataloging-in-Publication Data
Clark, William, 1953–
Academic charisma and the origins of the research university / William Clark.
p. cm.
Includes bibliographical references and index.
ISBN 0-226-10921-6 (cloth : alk. paper)
1. Education, Higher—History—18th century.  2. Education, Higher—History—19th century.
3. Universities and colleges—History—18th century.  4. Universities and colleges—History—19th century.  I. Title.
LA179.C53 2006
378´.009´033—dc22
2005015152

# Contents

# Prologue

# 1

## Charisma and Rationalization

Befitting the subject, this is an odd book. It traces the development of the academic from medieval forms up to modern incarnations. The latter inhabit the research university, the origins of which this book seeks to illuminate. To do so, it casts light on bureaucratization and commodification—the twin engines of the rationalization and the disenchantment of the world. The research university forms part of this modern order, in which the visible and the rational triumphed over the oral and the traditional. But through the cunning of history (or something) the rationalized academic world that we now enjoy spared academic charisma.

The period covered stretches from the Renaissance to Romanticism, with attention to the 1770s to 1830s. The research university originated in Protestant German lands and diffused globally in the nineteenth and twentieth centuries. German academia thus provides the focus, to which English and Jesuit academics will offer interesting points of contrast. The book deploys microanalyses of academic practices, not as a sop to palliate postmodern queasiness about grand narrative (which I plan to tell and especially of a Protestant Ethic), but in earnest.

The origins of the research university lie in a transformation of academic manners by ministries and markets. German ministers of state and avatars of the market worked, as they saw it, to reform and modernize benighted academics. As a consequence of their efforts, a joint bureaucratization and commodification of academic practices took place, from which the research university emerged.

A German Protestant academic had to pass muster with bureaucratic or rationalized criteria for appointment, which included productivity in publication, diligence in teaching, and acceptable political views and lifestyle. But to achieve success, one also had to acquire fame, be in fashion, and display "originality," a spark of genius, in writings. This became a new sort of academic charisma tied to writing for "applause" and "recognition." The modern academic emerged, I shall argue, from the cultivation of this new legible charisma. But, despite the dominion of writing in modern academia, aspects of traditional oral culture persisted and, among other things, played an important role in fabricating reputation.

A word now about the time periods under analysis here. By the "early modern era" historians typically mean the time from about 1450/1500 to 1780/1800—the Renaissance, Baroque, and Enlightenment. Historians typically set the modern era per se as beginning with the French Revolution (1789) and the Romantic era or Romanticism. This book concerns the great transformation of academic charisma and the gradual emergence of the research university from the Renaissance to Romanticism. A crucial time, as noted, was around the 1770s to the 1830s—the late Enlightenment and Romantic era, the onset of the modern era.

I shall use "traditional" versus "modern" to contrast two academic regimes or orders. The modern is the research university. The traditional is what came before and endures in some ways and places. I intend the terms only descriptively. No simple opposition obtains between the modern and the traditional. Elements of traditional academic practices persist in the modern academic regime of research, for example, voting for academic appointments, as well as the use of personal connections to achieve academic ends of all sorts, licit or not.

The rest of the chapter will discuss the analytical framework of the book, the empirical base of the book, and finally the structure of the book in its parts and chapters.

## THE ANALYTICAL FRAMEWORK

### Material Practices

Figure 1.1 is from a famous sixteenth century work by Sebastian Münster. The illustration appears in that work at least twice, used for two different universities. The scene depicted is thus conventional, as opposed to anyone's lecture in particular. The windows and walls suggest a castle or a church. European academia had only metaphorically a tower, one of ivory. Its architecture was actually ecclesiastical in origin—and remains so for universities with nostalgia and the cash flow to accommodate it. The space thus has rather more spiritual than secular overtones. And, while relatively small, the space offers little intimacy.

The lecturer sits in a *cathedra,* a chair. The notion of a professorial chair stems from this. The cathedra had been, at first, where a bishop sat to teach.

1.1. An academic lecture, from Sebastian Münster, *Cosmographey;
das ist/Beschreibung Aller Länder* . . . , Basel, 1598 [1592].

The church where his chair resided became by synecdoche a "cathedral."
Later canons, that is, high officials at cathedrals and other churches, also acquired what was called a cathedra or chair. From there it passed to professors, as the funding of professorships originated in medieval canonries.

The professor sits in the chair here, symbolizing his chair. He lectures
from a book to eight visible students, some by no means youths. Only the
professor's chair has a backrest. The students sit on simple benches. The
lucky ones have a wall to lean against. Only one appears prepared to take
notes. A few others look at papers or a book . . .

We shall be interested in material practices, such as illustrated in figure
1.1, apropos the emergence of the research university and the transformation of academic charisma. What is the difference between the layout and
the intimacy of a lecture hall versus a seminar room? When did German academics, if ever, begin to have conversations in a setting called a seminar?
Have academics always conducted master's and doctor's exams at tables?
What was the provenance of these academic tables? When did students begin the practice of writing? Writing notes in lectures? Writing exams at
desks? Writing papers for a seminar?

Interest in the material practices of academics reaches back at least to the German *Kulturgeschichte* of the nineteenth century. More recently what anthropologists and archaeologists have called "material culture" has received greater attention in regard to academia and science. Works by Michel Foucault, Jack Goody, and Bruno Latour, among others, have endeavored to illuminate epistemic practices from their material bases. Peter Becker and I have used the notion of "little tools of knowledge" to designate such studies.[1]

Material practices will be studied in this light in the chapters that follow. The transformation of academic charisma came about with or even through an armory of little tools—catalogues, charts, tables (of paper), reports, questionnaires, dossiers, and so on. Such things comprise the modern, mundane, bureaucratic repertoire of paperwork and much of the power of the modern academic comes from such trifles. Foucault wrote, "The constitution of tables was one of the great problems of scientific, political and economic technology in the eighteenth century . . . The table of the eighteenth century was at once a technique of power and a procedure of knowledge."[2]

One can learn much from the material practices of academics—about the nature of academic work from the transformation of the lecture catalogue, about the constitution of the research library from the battle over its catalogues, about the commodification of academics from tables evaluating them, about the appointment of academics from the layout of the paperwork, about the doctor of philosophy from the iconography of title pages of dissertations, about the nature of exams from the nature of tables as wooden or paper.

## Modern Metaphysics

At least since Hegel's *Philosophie der Geschichte*, a tradition of thought has held that the essential dialectic of the Middle Ages was that between Church and State, while that of the modern era is or was between State and Society, between the public and the private. The latter two terms, to be sure, are fraught with the weight of history, but cannot be avoided.

Karl Marx's notorious "On the Jewish Question" (*Zur Judenfrage*) gave the modern distinction between the public and the private, vis-à-vis the traditional opposition between Church and State, a most piquant formulation. Political emancipation of religious minorities had become possible in Europe, he held, because religion had been moved from the public sphere of the state into the private sphere of civil society. Science and academia had lost their old ecclesiastical or theological foundations as part of this transformation. Religion should now concern an academic or scientist only in their private persona, thus not qua academic or scientist. An academic or scientist now embodied a disinterested professional persona. In this sense, academia first lost its theological, transcendental mission in the Enlightenment.[3]

In the modern metaphysics of research, a cool, objective, meritocratic, professional self suppresses the passionately interested, collegially motivated, nepotistic, old-fashioned, traditional academic self. This modern schizophrenia is demanded of many professionals in the modern era. Max Weber saw it as willed by both bureaucratic and capitalistic interests.

> Bureaucracy, in its perfection, stands in a specific sense also under the principle *sine ira ac studio* [without anger or interest]. Its specific quality, quite welcome to capitalism, develops itself all the more perfectly the more it "dehumanizes," the more perfectly, that is, that its specific feature, prized as its virtue, succeeds: exclusion of love, hate, all the purely political and above all the irrational emotional elements resisting calculation . . . Instead of personal interest, favor, grace, and gratitude motivating the lords of older [traditional] orders, modern culture, the more complex and specialized it becomes, demands all the more the personally disinterested, so strictly "objective" *expert* (*"sachlichen" Fachmann*).[4]

The modern bureaucratic distinction allowing the formation of a public-professional, expert self, and its insulation from the interests and hobbies of the amateur, private self, lies in the distinction between the office and the home. That distinction is largely absent in traditional societies or groups, in which nepotism, bribery, cheating, and other violations of office space, abhorrent to modern bureaucratic and academic regimes, are a way of life.

Many fraternities at American universities resemble traditional groups in this sense. Student culture long resisted—still resists—the separation of public and private selves and spaces, understandable since most students make love and study in the same room. The modern schizophrenia must be forced on each generation. Those who work at home, including academics in the low-tech, humanistic disciplines, fall prey to archaic behavior all the time, confusing themselves with their work. The expansion of laboratories in the nineteenth century, and the massive scale that many acquired in the twentieth century, made the separation of the office or workplace from the home somewhat easier for most scientists.

Marxists called this "alienated labor": when one is at home, one is not at work, and when one is at work, one is not at home. There were many good things about alienated labor, including the meritocratic practices that allowed excluded groups in Europe—especially women and Jews—into the academic world. But bureaucratic and entrepreneurial interests did not generally advance this alienation and rationalization of academic life (making it rather academic labor, as life was now a private matter) for egalitarian reasons, such as integrating excluded groups. German managerial or bureaucratic capitalism, working with the "Protestant Ethic," had other objectives in the modern metaphysics of the office and the professional persona that produced the research university and the new academic charisma.

But back to Hegel. One aim of this book is to illuminate the transformation of the traditional or medieval juridico-ecclesiastical academic world into the modern politico-economic regime of research. The juridico-ecclesiastical mentality reflects a society in which Church and State predominate; the politico-economic mentality one in which State and Society, the public and the private, do. Many chapters to follow have, thus, a twofold goal.

First, to set out the originally juridico-ecclesiastical understanding of academic life and practices: traditional academia was invested with a theological or religious as well as with a juridical or legalistic cast. Such a juridico-ecclesiastical academic order fused the public and the private. Second, to elucidate the transformation of academic practices into our politico-economic world: it is here that the public and the private become separated, here that the study becomes the office, here that things like nepotism and patronage give way to merit.

The politico-economic (or "cameralistic") world is that of ministries and markets. The study becomes the office, but with a window on the market. In the traditional academic order, charisma had inhered in the juridico-theological cast of academic life. In the modern politico-economic regime, academic charisma comes much from certain labors loved by the market.

## Tradition and Rationalization

This study employs Weber's notion of three sorts of legitimate authority: the charismatic, the traditional, and the rational. Weber uses the German word *Herrschaft*, which he specifies in one place as being equivalent with the Latinate word *Auctorität* (authority). One usually follows Weber's suggestion and speaks in English of the three sorts of legitimate authority, although the German *Herrschaft*, which is "lordship" in old-fashioned English, more precisely means dominion. I shall largely follow general practice and speak of legitimate authority here. But I shall often reduce the notions elliptically to substantives: charisma, tradition, and—in place of rationality—rationalization. As part of the analytical framework, these notions help elucidate how medieval and early modern academics became "modern."[5]

In this section, I shall discuss tradition and rationalization in a general way, and then discuss the latter more specifically in reference to a few historical examples of German practices. Much of this book centers on exhibiting the older juridico-ecclesiastical academic order as one legitimated by traditional authority, while the politico-economic regime of modern research legitimates itself by rational authority—or, rather, it rationalizes. The next section will take up the matter of charisma and its persistence in modern academia.

As a paradigm of traditional authority one could take groups whose structure, despite many complexities, is family-like. Chapters to follow will show that early modern academic faculties and colleges, like craft guilds and kindreds, had a family-like structure at base. The collegial manners—the practices and institutions—of academic faculties and colleges embodied traditional authority. Early modern academic appointments, for example, were largely governed by nepotism, favor, seniority, gifts, and other such collegial practices which, unlike the family strictly taken, usually included voting as a central practice.

Academics typically obtained positions via a vote by a faculty or college or group of electors. A vote manifested the collegial will of the body. By dint of the traditional authority vested in such collegial will, legitimately ascertained and manifested, an academic held his office legitimately, even if the office had been won chiefly in view of nepotism or seniority or gifts—all traditional academic manners in a world that fused the public and private.

Most chapters of this book will exhibit the traditions or manners of early modern academics, and then show how ministries and markets worked to rationalize such practices—how bureaucratic and entrepreneurial interests worked to alter or subvert the traditional authority of faculties and colleges. In place of the traditions of academics, reformers wished to install the "rational" authority of ministries and markets—to instill their rationalizations.

Weber says, "Bureaucratic administration means: authority (*Herrschaft*) by dint of *knowledge*—that is its specific fundamental character." Rationalization or rational authority substitutes supposedly adjudicated knowledge for the simple will of traditional authority.

> Bureaucracy has a "rational" character: rule, aim, means, "objective" (*sachliche*) disinterestedness dominate its behavior. Its emergence and diffusion has thus had everywhere . . . a "revolutionary" effect, just as the march of Rationalism tends to do generally in all domains.

Rationalizing charisma, fashioning experts, stems not only from bureaucratic bodies.

Superior to the bureaucracy in knowledge—expert knowledge and acquaintance with facts within the relevant sphere . . .—is usually only the
profit seeker, that is, the capitalist entrepreneur. That is the only really (at
least relatively) immune instance in the face of the inescapability of the
bureaucratic rational domination of knowledge. All other instances have
fallen inescapably into mass organizations under bureaucratic domination,
just like mass production under the domination of . . . precision machines.[6]

Rationalizations by bureaucratic and capitalist precision machines have
recast academic life. The two great engines of rationalization have thus been
the ministry and the market—in their modern forms, state bureaucracy and
managerial capitalism. If one wishes to grasp the origins of the research university, freed of Romantic and other contemporary ideologies, then one
must be prepared to reconsider an old grand narrative with fresh ears.

THE MINISTRY. In chapters throughout this book, we'll find the visible hand of German state ministries in projects to reform academic practices. As noted, ministers aimed to substitute their agenda and putative
rational authority for the traditional authority of academic groups. The
genesis of the modern researcher lies, in part, in such ministerial reformations. The diffusion of this bureaucratic persona into other national contexts is another matter. In the epilogue, we shall consider the matter but,
alas, only outline its contours there. Here we'll consider the ministerial or
bureaucratic mentality that drove German academic reformations.

To that end, let us inquire whence bureaucrats and take Brandenburg-
Prussia as a handy example. Friedrich Wilhelm and Friedrich I reigned
there from 1640 to 1713.

> The "new bureaucrat," as a social type, was well represented by the aides of
> Frederick Wilhelm, the Elector, and of his immediate successor. These
> restless, intensely selfish men played their cards with cold-blooded effi-
> ciency. They were ardent collectors of tips, bribes, and valuable gifts. They
> had to be unscrupulous, ever suspicious, sharp-witted careerists to come
> out on top for a while in the turmoil.[7]

Thus they were typical Baroque courtiers, traditional aristocrats, like the
modern mafia.

Friedrich Wilhelm I and Friedrich the Great thereafter ruled Brandenburg-
Prussia from 1713 to 1786. They tried to turn the cold-blooded courtier ca-
reerists and collectors of tips, bribes, and gifts from the previous two reigns
into enlightened public servants. The Prussian kings considered the virtue
of meritocracy over aristocracy for public service.

The famous edict of 20 December 1722 on the Prussian General Directory said of such servants, "They must be as talented as can be found far and wide, and of evangelical-reformed or Lutheran confession, who are loyal and honest, who have open minds, who understand economics and engage in it themselves." Rational authority was in the air here and the king was seeking to cultivate a distinction in his ministers between their private lives and interests, as opposed to their public duties and offices—which was hard to do in aristocrats.[8]

Friedrich Wilhelm I militarized the ministry, so to speak. He looked for competence in the field. He preferred the middle-class citizen with talent to the noble with none. He put the notion of meritocracy onto a courtly system that was still essentially one of patronage. In 1723 for the General Directory, he even set office hours on the four days per week when ministers met. In summer they were to be at the "office" by seven o'clock in the morning and in winter at eight. Upon their complaints, the good king reset the first morning hour to nine o'clock. The king did not set the time at which ministers' service ended each day. But given his stipulations about their noontime meal, he presumed they would usually only work to one or two in the afternoon.

This being-at-the-office was, moreover, not yet the bureaucrat's office as specialized and insulated space from which private life and personal interests might be kept distant. Ministers rather worked with the king in one large room, each ministry or department given only its own separate table— a crucial little tool. Despite the qualifications, the above "indicates a turning point in the external position of high officeholders. From a part-time occupation of well endowed gentlemen . . . a profession with fixed office hours has arisen."[9]

The king's son, Friedrich the Great, said, "The king is the first servant of the state." But his ministries took a return in the direction of aristocracy, where a distinction between public and private became cloudy again. The new king, at least before 1760, did not heed the advice of the cameralists— to whom we turn soon—on meritocracy in public service.

After 1763, two systems arose. There was an aristocratic, courtly system, based on connections, gifts, and favors, and mostly for higher subjects and offices, versus a bourgeois, bureaucratic system, based on examination, work, and merit, and mostly for mid- to lower subjects and offices. This second system fit the rationalizing winds blowing over academia. In Prussia and elsewhere in the German lands, the rationalization of academic life took place within the framework of bureaucratization and good policing, as it was called.[10]

THE CAMERALISTS. The theorists of this were the cameralists. That is what or who the Germans had instead of the British political economists or the French physiocrats. "A cameralist must be an economist and an expert on policing," said Johann Justi, who held that the end of good policing lay in promoting the "culture of the lands." Justi and others considered an essential part of cameralism to be what they called police science, *Policey-Wissenschaft*.[11]

Good policing faced a three-fold task by Justi's lights: to see that useful arts, sciences, and crafts were learnt; to insure that resources were not wasted; and to make sure there was no idleness. Sonnenfels, an Austrian cameralist and police scientist, said, "The sciences constitute an important part of education, and so considered become a subject of police provision." The Prussian cameralist Zincke agreed that schools were "actually a police institution (*Policey-Anstalt*)." The culture of the lands thus entailed the good policing of schools and academic institutions which, despite reservations, the enlightened cameralists and police scientists treated like any other form of social and economic production.[12]

Justi was the Adam Smith of police science, so his views on the administration of academia are worth some time. Cameralist analyses and ideologies not only help to explicate the origins of the research university, but also historically helped solidify and diffuse its rational practices. Justi's views below follow from general principles of police science.[13]

The state, he holds, must set up inspectors for wares, as well as a system of seals or labels to indicate ranges of excellence in products. When the state notices that some products, including academic ones, are inferior, then prizes and payments ought to be instituted to encourage invention. External experts should also be brought in, "since for money one can obtain everything," even academics (or, if not, one needs to manufacture that sort).

Good policing insures that the state's religion is not subverted and sees to the diligence of subjects. So a regulation of holidays is important, for there must not be too many. Guilds are old-fashioned groups. "One tends to call the improved sort of occupations that have first been introduced in modern times 'manufactures' and 'factories.'" Guilds (like academic faculties) are inefficient due to odd ceremonies, archaic production methods, and conservatism. Mastership too often comes from connections, and is given on the basis of "sumptuous masterpieces, never useful for normal life, and not at all given in view of diligence and true talent." But the rational state should not try to manage everything.

Ministers should facilitate entrepreneurs who undertake ventures on their own. Mines provide a good example. The sovereign should supervise mines as well as universities. But to stimulate mining, there must be a free mining industry, so individuals will hunt for minerals. Miners, like academics, need some freedom of action, and the sovereign should give up mining per se, even though the industry works under sovereign auspices.

The point of universities for Justi and other cameralists is to make students useful as future tools—servants of the state and upright citizens. If universities had merely the goal to improve citizens' understanding and widen human knowledge, then one would need no public funding for institutions of such little benefit to the state and common good. Police science advises ministers to stamp out pedantry. Academics who teach at state institutions must be chosen from the best and most famous, and chosen not in view of connections or gifts, but rather for their talent and merits. The ministry will take care that all the chief sciences are taught and that professors lecture in a fluid and pleasant manner.[14]

The state gets more from academics if it offers them moderate amounts of money and, as compensation, accords them largely ceremonial honors. The wise minister manages academics through their vanity. One gives them "a gracious audience, a short chat," and if an academic is "in the list of the king's little entourage," this has a greater effect than "when great sums of money go out of the treasury for the promotion of science." And like miners, academics need some freedom. "When we consider the nature of the sciences, as well as the history of learning from all times and lands, we find that sciences ever grow when they [academics] have reasonable freedom to think." That is cameralist-capitalistic policy.[15]

THE MARKET. Within the superstructure of policing ministerially imposed, cameralists and police scientists called for an insulated infrastructure of entrepreneurial activity. Academia was treated like mining, and vice versa. Cameralists favored the cultivation of a sphere of academic freedom within the broader sphere of state supervision. This academic freedom was not posited in view of any Romantic notions about academia as a realm of culture. The cameralists were thinkers of the Enlightenment, that is, cold-blooded pragmatists.

The insertion of academia within the market or, rather, the cultivation of a market in academia, was by no means self-evident. And it was above all a Protestant phenomenon. Such a commodification of academia did eventually penetrate German Catholic lands (and in the nineteenth and twentieth centuries, the "free world"). But some resisted it for a time. The Austrians, for example, did so. Good pupils of the Jesuits, the Austrians at first favored a radical rationalization of academic practices, based wholly on meritocracy. Irrational things such as the fame won by publication in the very poorly policed Republic of Letters—which the cameralists saw as, in fact, a market—had no real place in an academic meritocracy.[16]

In chapters to follow, we'll look at the emergence and character of market phenomena in German academic practices. We'll see that the market insinuated itself between the home and the office. It called forth a new side or self within the academic. Let us call the "public" self that which is supposed to inhabit the office, striving for objectivity, impartiality, impersonality, and the public good, and distancing itself from private interests. Call the "private" self that which inhabits the home, thus able to cultivate private, personal, intimate interests. Given such definitions, the market induced a private-public self, a sort of third man or body mercantile, fraught with oxymoronic and odd qualities, as well as much charisma.[17]

German Protestant ministries demanded that academics obtain "applause" and achieve fame in order to be appointed or advanced at the university. But, as one of the great riddles of history, German Protestant ministries decided that, while they recognized academic applause and fame, they did not manufacture it. They left that feat not only to expert or peer review, a mysterious modern institution, but also to instruments of the market, such as the review press, where the new private-public self or the academic's third body circulated. A new sort of academic charisma radiated from that circulation.

## Academic Charisma

Charisma provides a counterpart to the motifs of rationalization and disenchantment. The notion of charisma comes from Weber. I'll give a brief sketch of it. Then, using the example of professorial charisma, I'll indicate the sense and scope of charisma in this book.

WEBER'S CHARISMA. Weber never wrote a treatise about it, but the notion appears in important works and crucial places. This allows for learned disputes about Weber's theory of charisma and whether such a thing exists, as opposed to a congeries of perhaps contradictory notions developed over time in different contexts. I shall thus present salient and relevant aspects of Weber's notion of charisma, without refereeing scholarship about it, and without worrying about the orthodoxy of my sketch and later use of "charisma" regarding academics.[18]

Weber's writings on religion and his writings on politics and economics provide the two major contexts for grasping Weberian charisma. In the realm of religion, charisma, for him, bears evident traces of magic. The original charismatic religious figure was the sorcerer, then later the priest and especially the prophet, the herald of a new cult. Regarding academia, part of academic charisma sprang from this topos—the teacher as spiritual or cultic leader. In the sphere of politics and economics, the original charismatic figure was the warrior, then later the general or king. Part of academic charisma sprang from this topos—the martial, agonistic, polemical cast of academic knowledge as it developed in medieval Europe.

A charismatic figure possesses above all power. For sorcerers, the power consists in their supposed ability to control nature or humans. The modern scientist as a "wizard" in popular culture disposes over traces of this charisma. Other figures, such as athletes and actors, display more nebulous sorts of charisma. But, in general, a person exudes charisma because he or she succeeds as a leader, a hero or Führer, in religious, martial, or other arts. Charisma thus emerges from and inheres in a social relation. A group of people ascribes certain extraordinary abilities or powers to a person. That person has charisma in relation to the ascribing group, whose members become active or passive disciples or followers or fans.

There is an historical trajectory from charisma, to tradition, to rationality only perhaps in Weber's analysis of the sorcerer. In this context, charisma collapses mostly into magic and may inhere, seemingly properly, in objects as well as in persons. Charisma here resembles a fetish.[19]

But, on the whole, Weber holds that charisma inheres properly only in persons. When it crystallizes in things—such as in a professorial chair, for example—the object is not a fetish, but only a means to convey charisma, which is always exercised or exuded by a person or group. Moreover, every society in every time and every place interweaves a complex fabric of charismatic, traditional, and rational authority. The anthropologically and historically primary sort of authority is not the charismatic, but the traditional, which, to put it crudely, most resembles the patterned behavior of animals: progeny or descendents behave the way they do because their progenitors or ancestors behaved that way. In relation to the traditional, both the charismatic and the rational represent disruptive or revolutionary forces.

In the extreme case, a charismatic figure arises to oppose and overturn the tradition. A Jewish prophet announces a new covenant. A Roman general marches his army on Rome. Charismatic authority thus faces the dilemma of the next generation. Permanent revolution will obtain, unless one finds a way to convey charisma from the leader to the disciples. In the latter case, words or blood or titles or offices often come to convey charisma. To secure stability, charismatic authority thus transmutes to an extent into traditional authority, which in a backhanded way indicates the charismatic base of some or much traditional authority.

The rational shares with the traditional the virtue of stability. Rational authority or rationalization—such as embodied in state bureaucracies and managerial capitalism—have the power to alter or even revolutionize a traditional social order, but achieve relative social stability at the same time. Rationalization replaces simple historical or inherited or brute patterns of behavior with other patterns; it can, however, rationalize and legitimate them by appeal to reason: it is more "efficient" or more "productive" or more "politically correct" or simply more "rational" to behave this way, instead of what traditions dictate.

In Europe at least, historical development since the Middle Ages has expanded the sphere of rational authority, at the expense of the traditional, and perhaps the charismatic, too. Weber's thesis of the disenchantment of the world—since Europe came to dominate it after the Middle Ages—forms the obverse of the thesis of the expansion of rationalization in Europe. The notion of "disenchantment" puts the decline of magic at center stage here. If one associates charisma with magic, then one tends to conclude that the trajectory of history has led to the decline of the charismatic in modern society. But rationality can be charismatic. The Enlightenment epitomized and liquidated itself here: "the charismatic transfiguration of 'reason' (which found its characteristic expression in the apotheosis of reason by Robespierre) is the last form that charisma has taken altogether in its fateful path."[20]

In the most general sense, charisma is not magical. It is, rather, the opposite of the quotidian, the normal, the routine, the mundane, the profane. As noted a few times above, a charismatic figure has and exudes something extra-ordinary. The appearance of a figure such as Hitler (or Robespierre) indicates that a bureaucratized society can fall under the sway all too easily of the charisma of a demagogue or tyrant. One of this book's aims is to consider to what extent we should see the emergence of the Romantic cult of personality at the modern university, including the rise of the notion of the academic or scientific "genius," in terms of a Weberian charismatic transfiguration of reason.[21]

PROFESSORIAL CHARISMA. This book treats professorial charisma at length. The research university stems from the German university system, as opposed to, for example, the English. The German university was a professorial university; the English was a collegiate university in which professors played a marginal role until the twentieth century. In the pre-Germanic period of Oxford and Cambridge, other academics—such as the heads of houses, the tutors, the fellows, later the dons—played a more important role than the professors, as the collegiate university was centered around colleges and their masters. In this book, we shall look at academic charisma in general. But, because the German research university provides the second major theme, the particular academics who governed it receive more attention.

At the traditional university, as we'll see in detail in chapters to follow, a professor embodied traditional authority. For example, as noted above, one became a professor usually in good part thanks to the vote of some committee or electoral college. Voting represented no rational process, but was simply traditional in certain societies for obtaining consensus and expressing the will of a group. The vote expressed more about the committee or college than it did about the elected person. The person would reproduce the group and uphold tradition.

At the research university in its original German form, a professor was to embody rational authority. The ministry decided who would become a professor. It based its decision, officially, not on a vote, but rather on informed consideration of the advice of relevant specialists and the ministry's knowledge of the field and available academics. In this case, the professor would reproduce not a group in the first instance, but a system.

That is, however, not the end of the story. This book aims to illuminate the charisma embodied in the traditional university and, more importantly, the charisma preserved or newly created by the research university. A central thesis here is that, like modern capitalism, the research university achieved an amazing "dynamic equilibrium" (M. Norton Wise) by the cultivation of charismatic figures within a broader sphere of rationalization. As noted, the entrepreneurial domain of activity within a bureaucratic superstructure, envisaged by the cameralists, constitutes one aspect of this dynamic stability.[22]

But we turn here first to the traditional university, which abhorred charismatic individuals. Charisma functioned on the whole to uphold and validate the tradition, and thus realized itself largely as routinized or crystallized charisma, vested in clothing, chairs, books, offices, titles, and the like. For example, as we'll see, professors and lecturers at the traditional university tended to use the textbooks used by their teachers, who had used the textbooks used by their teachers, and so on. In other words, curricula did not change much, at least officially. When charismatic individuals appeared such as William of Ockham or René Descartes, who assailed the curriculum, its sacred nature as a canon became manifest.

Like the liturgy, the academic or scholastic canon embodied crystallized or routinized charisma. To assail it and succeed made one a hero of knowledge, founder of a new canon. A charismatic figure succeeds, as noted, by finding disciples, who establish a new tradition or canon. To assail the canon and fail usually made one an academic or actual heretic.

The traditional university usually reacted decidedly hostilely to prophets or heroes who departed from the script, that is, the canon. The juridico-ecclesiastical regime, discussed above, instantiated the charisma. Academic degrees, such as the doctor of medicine, academic titles, such as professor of history, and academic offices, such as dean of the Law Faculty, conveyed charisma to their bearers in a framework on the model of clerical orders and chivalrous knighthood. The section on material practices above noted the professorial chair or cathedra. This conveyed substantial charisma to its holder, for very few could legitimately sit in this chair and teach with recognized authority on canonical texts.

In short, as vested in clothing, books, furniture, titles, and so on, charisma at the traditional university served to uphold authority by sanctifying traditions and differentiating academics as a group from other groups in society. The traditional university resisted the charismatic individual for the sake of a charismatic collective. And when an Ockham or a Descartes appeared on the scene, the effects mirrored those of successful prophets or revolutionaries. The strength of the modern research university consists in its ability to rationalize and routinize such prophecy and revolution, to make equilibrium dynamic.

The politico-economic cast of the modern university dissolved most of the charisma vested in juridico-ecclesiastical institutions and mentalities. German academics, for example, cast off academic costume by the eighteenth century and began to dress like the bourgeoisie. Traditional academic costume came out of the closet only on highly ceremonial occasions. Some academics find parts of the curriculum canonical thus sacred to this day; but academics at many universities began changing textbooks virtually at will in the eighteenth century. Over time, only bureaucratic inertia stood in the way of curricular change. Chapters below will consider how academic degrees and titles survived and what they came to mean in the modern academic world. Certain offices, such as the deanship, can convey an impressive bit of charisma to this day. But much academic business became and is just bureaucratic.

Alongside the vestiges of academic charisma from the traditional university, new sorts appeared, and many chapters to follow undertake to explicate them. For example, at German universities collegial voting no longer appointed professors, nor did civil service examinations appoint them, as one might expect in a fully rationalized meritocratic system. Above, we noted the role of the market in modern academia. But the ministry made the final decision on appointments. It grasped the process as one of "recognition": the ministry recognizes the "right person" for the position. This notion of recognizing the right person was fundamentally new in academic appointments, but harkens back to notions of the recognition of the successor to a charismatic leader, which itself requires charisma to accomplish. At places like Harvard University, the process eventually developed to recognizing not only the right but also the "best person," presumably on earth.[23]

Academic charisma at the research university inheres more in individuals than in collective, corporate, collegial bodies—that is the scandal of the research university from the perspective of traditional academia. A professorial chair conveys much of its traditional charisma to this day. But, if an Isaac Newton or an Immanuel Kant has sat in a particular chair, then the ghost or spirit of that individually famous academic infuses the chair. One of Stephen Hawking's many claims to fame today is that he occupies "Newton's chair." Moreover, an academic enhances charisma not collectively or collegially, but rather by directing an institute or having a center through which to realize academic projects. In many chapters to follow, we'll have occasion to observe the modern cult of academic personality.

## Narrative and Calculation, Irony and Nostalgia

"From its origin, science has been in conflict with narratives," as Jean-François Lyotard has written. By "narratives" he means oral storytelling. This dictum can be taken to mean that science has been trying to turn the oral world into the visual. Modern science and academic knowledge generally seem to be subversive of oral culture and of narrative. In our Weberian terms above, narrative typically serves as a resource or tool of traditional authority, a tool to which, for complex reasons, modern rational authority appears to be rather hostile.[24]

In chapters to follow, we shall see that many ministerial rationalizations of academic labor deployed—appropriately so—a "ratio": devices for calculation, broadly conceived. Thus, as noted above, the modern academic and bureaucratic world avails itself of an arsenal of little tools, such as lists, tables, charts, graphs, maps, and so on. These calculating devices not only offer the instruments for the rationalization of life and labor, but they also appear to supplant or subvert or even destroy traditional narratives and oral cultures. In a number of chapters, we shall thus consider the apparent intolerance of calculators for narrators.

Despite the modern programmatic hostility to narration or oral culture, Hayden White sees narrative as a protean and nearly omnipresent force, an ineluctable disposition, present at all times and places, and in all groups, including those of modern scholars and scientists. Lyotard perhaps would have argued the same, at least in *La conditione postmoderne*, where narrative played an important role in forging the social bonds of groups, something that tools of calculation seem unable to do. In other words, even the radical rationalizers tell stories.[25]

In that spirit, some chapters below will look for stories and "read for the plot" in a number of perhaps unlikely places. I shall be concerned in particular, on the one hand, to examine how certain ministerial or academic tools achieve and enforce the separation of public and private selves. But I shall also attend, on the other hand, to illuminating how other ministerial or academic devices serve as narratives to effect the same separation. So in chapter 9, for example, I shall read a ministerial diary or journal as a narrative device that accomplished the suppression of a private, domestic self from a professional, public one.

That analysis, like many here, will be full of irony. The modern academic regime of research seems to be more or less as hostile to that as it is to narration. Irony and nostalgia play fundamental roles in this study of academics and their charisma. Each offers an antidote to the other. But each serves a separate purpose, and I could not delete the one without deleting the other. This book contains criticism of the sort of academic life and labor that has descended upon us from the German university system. Part of this critique may be motivated by a vague nostalgia for a golden age of college life. Such nostalgia can perhaps lead one to the antipodes of the Germanic university as potential resources to help remedy the ills of contemporary academia. But that is another matter and exceeds the rationale of this book, albeit desiring to offer a history of the present, but still a history, and not a manual of action. Nostalgia must thus be leavened with irony.

The presence of that trope is overdetermined in this work. Irony expresses and conceals a love-hate relationship with most of the principal entities involved in this study: the Germans and the Austrians, the English and the Jesuits, the Enlightenment and Romanticism, rationality and charisma, academia and me. The productivity of such ambivalence has been an important theme since Freud. Irony also itself became important in the time and place on which this study most focuses—the German cultural space in the 1770s to 1830s.[26]

Despite the apparent hostility of the ethos of research, irony is for me, moreover, an essential academic attitude about academia, that is, the essence of reflexivity. I do not know when this became so. We probably do not have this attitude from Akademos, the legendary hero whose name we bear. But perhaps it is as old as Socratic epistemic self-reference.[27]

On the subject of alleged academic corrupters, I shall end this part with one of my favorite anecdotes. It well illustrates the sorts of materials and mentalities with which I have immersed myself quixotically for several decades, and from which this study and its irony arose. In the mid 1750s, Austrian elites and academics had had enough of being dominated by the Jesuits. Empress Maria Theresa thus allowed ministers and academics outside the order to take charge over Austrian educational and cultural affairs. In the spirit of the Jesuits, however, the Austrians produced their own catalogue of forbidden books, which they published as *Catalogus Librorum rejectorum per Consessum Censurae* in Vienna in 1754.

A revised catalogue appeared from the commission on censorship annually from 1755 through 1757. The composition and publication of the catalogue of forbidden books became thereafter rather complicated, as new editions of it appeared alongside supplements and revisions, some issued by the commission's press and others by private publishers. In the 1760s and 1770s, various editions of the catalogue forbade works by Gottsched, Lessing, Moser, Mendelssohn, Wieland, Voß, and of course by Goethe, whose *Die Leiden des jungen Werthers*, a best seller, made the Austrian index of forbidden books, which itself soon became popular.

It is not clear whether it became a sort of honor to be in the Austrian catalogue of forbidden books. But it does appear that the catalogue and its many revisions caused heated competition in the market among publishers of different editions. The catalogue also afforded a means for a certain sort of academic and author to discover companions in the devil's advocacy. In 1777 the official Austrian catalogue of forbidden books thus forbade itself.[28]

## THE EMPIRICAL BASE

Parts of the discussion above have implicitly indicated elements of the empirical base—aspects of the material culture of academics, such as chairs and books; practices of traditional academia, such as protocols of voting; bureaucratic innovations, such as ministerial surveys to recognize the right academics; the cult of academic personality, as vested in citations, institutes, and so on. Here I shall discuss a sort of ethnographic empirical base.

As noted, the German lands constitute the center of the analysis, for which Jesuit and English academics offer interesting points of comparison and contrast. In the plot of this book, the Jesuits will play the most radical rationalizers, while the English strive to uphold the tradition. This casting puts the Germans and their ilk in the middle of things.

## The English

The fellows or monks of my time [at Oxford] were decent easy men who supinely enjoyed the gifts of the founder. Their days were filled by a series of uniform employments: the Chappel and the Hall, the Coffee house, and the common room, till they retired, weary and well-satisfied, to a long slumber. From the toil of reading or thinking or writing they had absolved their conscience, and the first shoots of learning and ingenuity withered on the ground without yielding any fruit to the owners or the public.[29]

Until the nineteenth century, England had only two universities—the large and rather well known ones at Oxford and Cambridge, collectively called "Oxbridge." Some might find that this book has royally skewered Oxbridge. But the fact of the matter is that the seeming skewering here rather results from effects of irony in masking nostalgia. The latter naturally attends Oxbridge as an academic paradise lost—or, rather, as a utopia fantasized by alienated labor. Oxbridge possesses a long academic tradition, but on the whole an inglorious one. Relatively few academics seem to be aware of that. It would appear that most academics even believe the opposite, a false belief of which, during visits to Oxford or Cambridge, one is usually not disabused by friendly fellows, most of whom doubtless know much better.

Why has Oxbridge enjoyed such a wildly inflated reputation, essentially undeserved, at least between 1500 and 1900? "Architecturally, by the end of the sixteenth century, the colleges were the most striking feature of Oxford and Cambridge. Visitors usually remarked on their size and sumptuousness." As they still do. The most common word out of the mouths of Anglophone academic tourists is "quaint." (I wonder often what that is in Japanese.) The colleges are quaint, and their fellows not nearly so odd now as they once were. Like Mad Ludwig's royal Bavarian castles, modern Oxbridge's fame grew from the tourist industry and, now, is a great beneficiary of the nostalgia induced by our modern Germanic regime.[30]

The modern marketing of Oxford began as early as the late seventeenth century. In view of the traditional naiveté of its fellows, it is possible that they knew not what they had wrought. The Germans would have. Three nice publications emerged from Oxford from 1674 to 1675, thus barely missing an *annus mirabilis*. The first was Anthony Wood's *Historia et antiquitates oxoniensis*, and the second was Thomas Hyde's *Catalogus impressorum librorum bibliothecae bodleianae*, both of 1674. David Loggan's *Oxonia illustrata*, in which the colleges were depicted in all their quaintness, appeared as the third work in 1675.[31]

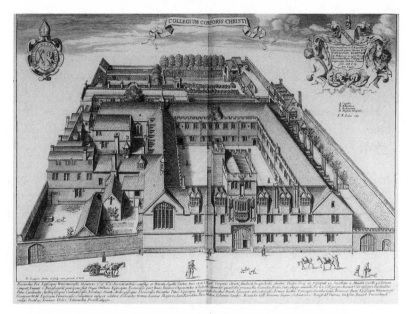

1.2. Corpus Christi College, Oxford, from David Loggan, *Oxonia illustrata*, Oxford, 1675.

Figure 1.2 shows Loggan's illustration of Corpus Christi College. The unfortunate vertical line down the middle comes from the fact that the illustration occupies two whole pages in Loggan's already large format volume. Such buildings were and are still magnificent. If not marketing, it is hard to see what the point of the Loggan's sumptuous publication was— institutional narcissism? It proved, however, a clever ploy and drove that other university to commission *Cantabrigia illustrata*, published by Loggan in 1694.

Historians of Oxbridge sometimes cite remarks of Zacharias Conrad von Uffenbach, based on his visit to Oxford and Cambridge in 1710. His travel memoir contains much of interest that only an outsider would notice. But, as he sang no praises to the sacred cows of English academic culture, one sighs at his tone. "In general I must report about Cambridge that the place itself is not so big, and is as poor as a small village . . . and, if the fine colleges were not in such abundance here, it would be the most miserable place in the world. One is also poorly accommodated." Oxford, as he noted, was indeed larger but, save its fine colleges, only a larger version of Cambridge.[32]

What of the most numerous of the early modern Oxbridge academics themselves? A twentieth century historian echoed Gibbon's withering depiction from the eighteenth century.

Much has been written about the Fellows of the eighteenth century, and most of it is not to their credit. They stand accused of wasting their time and opportunities . . . But the Fellows can be reproached with more than lack of scholarship and industry. Far too many of them led frankly self-indulgent lives and did not trouble to conceal their shortcomings . . . Indeed the pleasures of the table loomed large in their lives, and, even when they did not grossly exceed, they were disinclined to curb their appetites.[33]

The eighteenth century is usually taken as the nadir of Cambridge's history, as it is of Oxford's, too. I suspect, however, that the college fellows of the sixteenth and seventeenth centuries were given neither less to leisure and pleasure, nor more to work and study.

Thus it is that the English and Oxbridge have been chosen to embody paradise lost, a nostalgic foil to Jesuitical and Germanic rationalizations. It remains to be seen in chapters to follow whether Oxbridge will play the ultratraditionalist role for which I have cast it.

## The Jesuits

"If I see white, I would believe it to be black, if it were so defined by the Church hierarchy," as reads Rule 13 of Loyola's *Exercitia spiritualia,* perhaps one of the more famous dicta of the early modern era. Few secular academics seem to exhibit nostalgia for Jesuiticism. The Jesuits were fierce figures. They bore some striking similarities to English academics.[34]

Figure 1.3 is Matthäus Merian's seventeenth-century depiction of the Jesuit college and church in Munich. Smaller and more regular in the growth of its additions than Corpus Christi Oxford, the Jesuit college exhibits the same monastic quad at base. A well-traveled visitor, exaggerating a bit, said in 1644 of the Munich college, "Of all that the Jesuits' possess in the whole world, this college is the most magnificent." Few academic structures in the entire German lands could rival this college until the nineteenth century.[35]

The Jesuits once loomed largely over academic Europe. They were kicked out of France in 1762 and Spain in 1767, then temporarily abolished in general by the pope in 1773. Before that, if the Jesuits had not run the educational system of early modern Catholic Europe, they had dominated it. By 1700 they had more than seven hundred institutions of higher learning, with over two hundred in Central Europe. In the German Catholic lands, there was little the Jesuits did not control, till their suppression in 1773. Only in Erfurt and Salzburg did German Catholic universities remain entirely free of Jesuits. And, where they did appear, they eventually wrested control of the the-

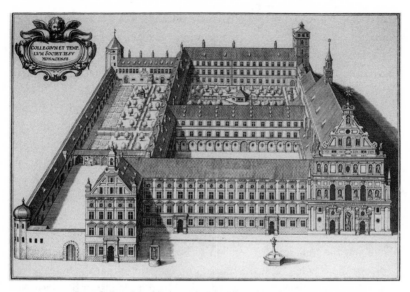

1.3. Jesuit College, Munich, from Matthäus Merian, *Topographia Germaniae.*

ology and arts and philosophy (and sciences) faculties—the Jesuits did not do law or medicine. Despite some efforts at accommodation with Protestants and others, the Jesuits oversaw a rival academic world until 1773.[36]

Like the English, the Jesuits centered their academic system on the college—and a college lodged in the sort of building shown in figure 1.3, but generally less imposing. Like English college fellows, Jesuit instructors remained celibate and clerical in habits. The typical Oxbridge fellow, unless a hopeless slacker or hardcore academic, was headed one day for a vicarage or parsonage. And in that sense, the fellows formed part of the Anglican civil service in the countryside, the secular-clerical pillars of the English state in the provinces.

The Jesuits pursued this sort of clerical civil service more radically. Weber noted,

> The monk, the exemplary religious person, was also the first who lived in a methodical fashion, scheduled his time, practiced continuous self-control, rejected all spontaneous enjoyments, in order to do his duty . . . He was thus the first professional and destined to serve as the principal tool of bureaucratic centralization and rationalization.[37]

The Jesuits were "the last word, the *ne plus ultra*, in the organization" of the monastic or "regular" and secular religious orders that had appeared during the Middle Ages—the Benedictines, Cluniacs, Cistericians, Augustinians, Hospitallers, Templars, Franciscans, and Dominicans. The Jesuits emerged late, in the sixteenth century. They served as the tools and shock troops for the Catholic Counter-Reformation against the Protestant Reformation.[38]

As David Knowles noted, "In the traditional monasticism all postulants were received for membership of a single undifferentiated community . . . In no case was there an oligarchy of talent," until the Jesuits came on the scene. As we'll see, the concept of meritocracy does not stem from traditional academia. Even in the Protestant lands, the notion of academic appointment and advancement by merit would have to be imposed on the whole by ministers and cameralists on reluctant academics. The Jesuits in fact helped pioneer the bureaucratic notion of meritocracy in academia. They play the arch-rationalizers in this book.[39]

It was no accident that the most thorough attempts at the bureaucratization of academic labor took place in Catholic lands with a Jesuitical past—Austria and France. "The bureaucratic spirit is a thoroughly Jesuitical . . . spirit. Bureaucrats are the Jesuits of the state, the state-theologians . . . Bureaucracy is a circle from which no one can escape. Its hierarchy is a *hierarchy of knowledge.*"[40]

## The Germans

The Germans, especially the Protestant ones, pursued a mediate way, a *via media*, between the English as the upholders of traditional academic mores and the Jesuits as the purveyors of a radical rationalization of academia. This characterization aims not to make the Protestant German way appear somehow the most sensible. To the contrary, as noted, most of the critique, veiled or not, in this book will grace this mediate path leading to the "Germanic" research university. The characterization rather aims to make central issues crystal clear.

By the German lands, which I shall also call the "Germanies," I mean the amorphous sociocultural space in Central Europe in which the German language held sway. That was not the political entity that would be known as Germany or the Second Reich after 1871. Until the Second Reich came on the scene, the political landscape of Central Europe, especially before the nineteenth century, appeared as the most diverse in all Europe. Some parts, such as Austria, Bavaria, and Brandenburg-Prussia, were as large as large lands or even empires. Others, such as Canton-Basel, the Free Imperial City of Frankfurt am Main, and the once Free Imperial City of Straßburg (Strasbourg), were small city-states.

I shall refer to all such entities collectively as the "Germanies." For variation, I'll refer at times to the Austro-German lands or German lands. Such terms also lack precision, since by the Late Middle Ages the German Swiss provinces, for example, were not part of those lands. One might refer to the Holy Roman Empire (*Reich*) of the German Nation(s), that old political entity to which most of the Germanies belonged, until Napoleon terminated it in 1806. The problem with the "Empire" or the "First Reich" is that things like German-speaking Canton-Basel did not belong to it, while Czech-speaking Prague and Bohemia did, while German-speaking Königsberg and Prussia per se did not, and so on. Whence the line from Goethe's *Faust*, "The dear Holy Roman Empire [of the German Nation], what keeps it still together?" (*Das liebe heil'ge Röm'sche Reich, / Wie hält's nur noch zusammen?*)[41]

Thanks to their chaos, the Germanies formed the only large cultural or linguistic space in Europe in which both major early modern Christian confessions—Catholicism and Protestantism, chiefly the Evangelical and Reformed Churches, that is, Lutheranism and Calvinism—were represented in significant numbers. The confessional differences had ramifying academic differences. That makes the Germanies particularly propitious as an object of study, above and beyond the fact that the research university originated there.

All too many universities populated the German cultural space—the land of universities and academics from the Late Middle Ages to the modern era. There is a list of the relevant (and some irrelevant) universities in appendix 6. Most will be mentioned here and there in chapters to follow, as examples of this or that. A few will prove to be most important for the story. But it seems better to let those become apparent simply as they do.

The early modern English and German universities present pretty much the realm of the academically possible in Europe, which provides another ground for the decision to include Oxbridge in the analysis here. The English and German academic models embody polar opposites of a sort. If one understands those two chief academic systems, one can situate most—but not all—other early modern universities on a spectrum between them.

Here's why. Historians of universities typically see two medieval models, the University of Bologna and the University of Paris, based on which other European universities evolved. North of the Alps, the University of Paris proved most influential. By 1500 France had about sixteen provincial universities, on the whole rather small, and one monstrous university in Paris with sixty-eight colleges. England and the Germanies pursued alternate ends of the Parisian-French model. By 1500 England had only two universities, Oxford and Cambridge, which between them had about twenty-two colleges, neglecting the monastic ones. The German lands, however, had about seventeen universities (and many more than that by 1800), mostly small, and each with only one, two, or a few colleges.[42]

The English universities of Cambridge and Oxford became centered on colleges during the early modern era, while the German universities or, rather, the Protestant ones, became centered on faculties. The typical medieval and early modern faculties were only four: theology, jurisprudence or law, medicine, and, finally, arts and philosophy, which included essentially the sciences too. At German universities, the one or two colleges at each university became more or less identified with the arts and philosophy (or sciences) faculty.

But the real power at German universities was vested in the faculties and their organs, such as the academic senate. The chief administrative organs at Oxbridge drew rather on the heads of houses, that is, the heads of the colleges. Oxbridge colleges were assemblies of master, doctors, and fellows. German faculties were assemblies of professors and lecturers. The Jesuit colleges and universities exhibited a rather strange mixture of the collegiate and professorial university, but on the whole actually most resembled Protestant Oxbridge. In other words, the Reformation had very different academic impacts in England and the German lands, as the English system came to have most in common with a Catholic one.

The modern research university grew from the faculties of German Protestant professors. The North American system, for example, had been based on the model of the Oxbridge colleges. It began grafting the German professorial university onto itself in the second half of the nineteenth century. At American universities, the undergraduate college remained essentially a descendant of the Oxbridge college, while the graduate schools emerged as a superstructure of German faculties or departments that were added on to the undergraduate college. After the 1870s, the new graduate schools cultivated research, while the college had a traditional pedagogical mission. Confronted with the German research university, Oxbridge itself began to change then, too; and, in the 1890s, so did the French.

The German research university had achieved a canonical form by the 1830s, first, in what would later become the Second Reich. From there, it had spread to other German-speaking lands. In the first half of the nineteenth century, the conquest had spread already to Northern, Eastern, and Southern parts of Europe—to Scandinavia, Russia and Greece. In the second half of the nineteenth century, as just noted, the German research university colonized academia in the United States, Britain and, by the end of the century, France.[43]

The nineteenth century witnessed as well the second phase of European colonialism. Parts of the globe that had remained largely immune from penetration and control—Africa and Asia—fell now to the new European science-based military, medical, and industrial technologies. The spread of European science to those continents had little thereafter to do with any philosophical or theological attraction of European science or culture. It had to do, rather, with the simple power of European science-based military and related technologies. The vehicle for spreading European science and academics globally became the German research university, the final and the most insidious phase of European colonialism.[44]

This book was written with that, among other things, in mind.

## THE STRUCTURE OF THE BOOK

The book falls into two unequal parts. The first traces essential processes and effects of the rationalization of academic life and labor. The second part examines resistances and oddities.

The first part focuses on the rise of the visible and legible in defining academic labor and charisma. In rudimentary statement, this consists in the triumph of the eye over the ear. Some agreement seems to obtain that this happened. Disagreement attends the question of when and to what extent. To avoid most of the polemics about the when, this study locates the triumph of the eye—the dominion of the visible and legible in academia— over a long period. The question concerning to what extent is addressed by part two of this book.

The first part, however, examines the gradual process whereby the visible, especially forms of writing and recording, overcame and, to good extent, eclipsed the traditional oral culture of academia. The rationalization of German academia wrought by ministries and markets aimed to substitute writing in place of speaking and hearing. Academic charisma would be manufactured by publications and written expert or peer review, instead of by old-fashioned academic disputational oral-arts, unsubstantiated rumors, and provincial gossip.

The first part comprises chapters 2 to 8. Chapters 2 and 3 continue in an introductory vein, while chapters 4 to 8 examine central aspects of the new academic regime definitive of the research university: graded written examinations for undergraduates, seminar papers for graduate or postgraduate students, doctoral dissertations as the rite of passage into professional academic life, "publish or perish" for a professorial appointment, and the constitution of the library catalogues recording and referencing such publications.

Academic oral culture appears in most of those chapters, but usually as vestigial or incidental—a marginal step or stage leading to the cultivation and exhibition of modern charisma in paperwork. The second part of the book, comprising chapters 9 to 11, recurs to such vestiges of academic oral culture. These chapters consider, in part, whether orientation on the market facilitated the persistence of the ear and the tongue. A certain, odd sort of noise and voices did continue to haunt or inform academic charisma. The themes of narrative, reputation, and the voice, not neglected in part 1, receive more attention in part 2.

Finally, the epilogue will recur to some of the motifs of this prologue. In a largely descriptive way, and based primarily on contemporary secondary sources, it will recount the consolidation of the German research university in the nineteenth century and its diffusion.

## Part One

# Tradition, Rationalization, Charisma

## On the Dominion of the Author and the Legible

# 2

## The Lecture Catalogue

A source of information and disinformation, of propaganda and publicity, the lecture catalogue is an epitome and emblem of the modern academic order. It is the single most condensed academic document, the royal road to the academic subconscious.

But universities did not commonly publish lecture catalogues until the seventeenth century. And many did so with little consistency until the eighteenth century, or even later. Given the nature of teaching at Oxford and Cambridge, those universities and their colleges do not appear to have needed or wanted a university publication like the lecture catalogue until the modern era. Information about tutorials and other classes, in so far as it needed to be advertised, typically appeared on bulletin boards in college butteries and the like.

The *Cambridge University Calendar* did not begin appearing until 1796. And Oxford does not seem to have had a university publication until 1870, when the *Oxford University Gazette* appeared for the first time. In the sixteenth century, Jesuit colleges and universities published a number of lecture catalogues, but then appear to have published such catalogues at best occasionally. The history of the published lecture catalogue seems to be largely a Continental Protestant one until the late eighteenth century.[1]

The catalogues considered below come from the German cultural space. The chapter has sections on parades, paperwork, and publicity. It aims to sketch the framework for the book more concretely than chapter 1 could, while also attending to this most condensed academic genre as an important bit of modern material culture.

### PARADES

The niceties of parading epitomize traditional academic mentalities. Hierarchy and precedence were central to them. In this section, we'll commence by comparing and contrasting parading practices at the University of Cambridge and the University of Basel, as examples. This will swiftly bring us to the central place of the professorate in the German as opposed to the English academic system. The centrality of the professor in the German system will find itself reflected in the lecture catalogue. The latter will in turn help illuminate traditional professorial practices of musical chairs, pluralism, and nepotism. The relation of the professorate to the calendar and the curriculum may then be seen through the lecture catalogue, which will bring us, finally, to the ordinary or full professors and their chairs.

## Cambridge on Parade

Behold the University of Cambridge on parade: figure 2.1 from David Loggan's *Cantabrigia illustrata* of 1694. Attention to real parading will be repaid with elucidation of parading in the lecture catalogue. The traditional lecture catalogue was at base the university on parade—how it formally presented itself as a collegial body.

In figure 2.1 from *Cantabrigia illustrata*, students and academics stand in the order of inverted academic precedence from the top left down to the bottom middle. That is how they would probably march in a parade. Remember that, in many parades, the best come last, and the least first. Beginning at the left in the top row, the first figures embody the lowest sorts of students in ascending order. The middle figure is the bachelor of arts, followed by the bachelor of law and medicine, who have the same costume, followed by the three sorts of masters of arts. The first row ends with the figure whose clothing signifies the highest sort of a master of arts as well as a bachelor of theology, who also have the same costume.

From this first row, we see some of the niceties of academic manners in the ivory tower. Students of arts (and philosophy and sciences) are the least. Students of theology are the best. And those of medicine and jurisprudence occupy the middle and face each other, locked in potential conflict. Should physicians or jurists march nearest the theologians? Early modern jurists spilt much ink to legitimate their proximity to the theologians, for the latter had the highest socioacademic status in traditional European society.[2]

Rows two to four mix a few nonacademics, perhaps playing servants (*famuli*), crashing the parade. The third from the right in the second row gives us our first doctor, the anomalous doctor of music. Following figures trace out a spectrum of degrees and sorts of other doctors. These end in the third row, left to middle, with the highest sorts of doctors of law or medicine, embodied in the one costume for both, followed by the highest doctor of theology. Other than the doctor of music, no doctors of philosophy or lit-

2.1. The order of academic precedence and costumes, University of Cambridge, from *Cantabrigia illustrata*, by David Loggan, Cambridge, 1694.

erature or arts or sciences existed at Cambridge or Oxford or most other universities at this time (an issue to which we'll return in chapter 6). In the third row, the last two figures embody, respectively, a noble and a university officer. The fourth and final row is reserved for the most important persona, the prochancellor of Cambridge. He stands alone in the middle, flanked to the left by an honor guard, and to the right by unnumbered but labeled servants.[3]

The parade exhibits a hierarchy of disciplines and of degrees. Theology claims pride of place as the loftiest discipline. Arts and philosophy (and sciences) remain the lowliest. And medicine and law occupy the middle. An order of degree-holders, complexly articulated, crosscuts this order of the disciplines. A master of arts (number 7) stands superior to a bachelor of law or medicine (number 6), but inferior to a bachelor of theology (number 9). We see the hierarchy from the order of marching. Note, by the way, the absence altogether in this Cambridge parade of anyone called a professor. That will soon prove important for us.

From the parade we also see a hierarchy of clothing. Costumes become in general more elaborate and expensive from the top left down to the bottom middle. Thanks to the rather ascetic dress of Protestant theologians, however, this forms another complex system. Alas, we have no time at the moment for the philosophy of clothes. Dwelling on this Cambridge parade, however, intimates the importance of academic precedence.[4]

Early modern German academia had nothing to compare with this Cambridge fashion show, most charming and even homoerotic in its own way. But matters of academic precedence and hierarchy remained more than virulent in the Germanies. (Indeed, the Germans still call an academic and bureaucratic hierarchy "an order of clothing," *eine Kleiderordnung*.) In traditional society, hierarchy rules and is embodied.[5]

The order in the parade and the charm of the clothing indicate the traditional authority and charismatic elements of an academic regime still medieval at base. Charisma vested itself not in the individual's body, but rather in corporate and collegial bodies, such as faculties, as well as in the legal or juridical persona, such as given by academic degrees. To comprehend the nature of traditional charisma, one must not discount the clothes as a charm.

## Basel on Parade

Behold now the University of Basel on parade—or some of it. Figures 2.2 and 2.3 show Basel lecture catalogues from 1690/91 and 1712/13, respectively. At the time, the University of Basel, situated in the German-speaking part of Switzerland, was medium-sized and well known. In short, it offers a good place to begin. These catalogues give us snapshots of the university, taken at about twenty years apart.

Notice, first, that the catalogues are in Latin. Like its academic costume in figure 2.1, this is how the medieval and early modern university presented itself. Traditional authority and academic charisma were as much vested in the charm of Latin as in elaborate costumes.

Production of the catalogue came under the auspices of the rector or prorector, the head of a university in the German cultural space. The actual editing of the catalogue usually fell to the professor whose Latin skills were supposed to have been best. The best Latinist, theoretically, at a university would have been the professor of eloquence and poetry, or the professor of Latin. The former professorship, by the way, meant Latin eloquence and poetry, since the academic study of vernaculars emerged very slowly. The professor of eloquence and poetry usually served as *os academicum*, the academic mouth. This professor typically had to pen or at least edit documents published in the name of the university, for example, encomia on the sovereign's birthday and, later, the lecture catalogue.[6]

The next thing to notice is that the entire teaching staff and all their classes fit on one page. Academia amounted only to a cottage industry until rather recently. It was a collegial and "moral" community, one where private and public life fused. Academic life resembled village life, a nearly communal life. These men all knew each other, for better or worse.

We'll notice that they are all indeed men simply in passing, and return to the issue of gender in a later chapter. At the moment, we shall examine, rather, the men's academic status. The top line of figure 2.3 (neater than figure 2.2) reads: Catalogue of Professors. Figure 2.1 from Cambridge showed us a parade of scholars, masters, and doctors. A lecture catalogue shows, rather, a parade of academic staff, so students perforce fail in figures 2.2 and 2.3. The early modern German academic staff, moreover, no longer centered on masters and doctors and their order of costumes. It centered, rather, around professors and the order of faculties and chairs. In early modern German academia, charisma became professorial.

Next we see, after a few lines in figure 2.3, the most important academic persona by office: the rector, Emanuel Zaeslin. As the highest officer, his name appears in bold type, reflecting the great charisma of office in a traditional society. The two catalogues show different rectors. Like the deanship in each faculty, the rectorship rotated. So in figure 2.2, the rector, Lukas Burckhardt, is a professor in the faculty of jurisprudence. In figure 2.3, the rector is a professor in the philosophy faculty. The rectorship typically rotated over the period of four years or semesters through all four faculties and, within each faculty, usually but not always through all full or ordinary professors. Most professors probably wanted to be rector at least once. But, as with many academic administrative offices, the amount of labor and time demanded often exceeded the power and prestige acquired.[7]

Above or below the rector's name, we see the length of time that the catalogue covers. At Basel from 1610 to 1818, the rectorial year extended from summer solstice to summer solstice, while the academic or teaching year began in the autumn. The catalogues here match not the academic year but rather the rectorial year. This ties these documents above all to the rectorship. Each of the catalogues covers a full year. The transition to an academic year of semesters took shape only slowly throughout the German cultural space and elsewhere. Some universities produced catalogues divided into semesters in the sixteenth century, while others first made such a division in the eighteenth century or later. Oxbridge developed a rather idiosyncratic system of trimesters very early on.[8]

# CATALOGVS
## PROFESSORVM ACADEMIÆ BASILIENSIS
### CVM SERIE EXERCITIORVM OMNIVM
#### PVBLICE PRIVATIMQVE AB IISDEM
#### DEO ADJVVANTE
#### HABENDORVM.

*A Solſtitio Æſtivo Anni M DC XC.*
*Ad idem Solſtitium Anni M DC XCI.*

# LVCA BVRCKHARDO IC.
## RECTORE.

---

### IN THEOLOGIA.

IOHANNES ZVINGERVS, S. Theol. D. & Novi Teſt. Profeſſ. Facult. Senior, Deo vires valetudinemque conſervante, alternis Septimanis, horâ III. pomeridianâ, in explicatione *Epiſtola Pauli ad Hebræos*, ſolitâ methodo perget, abſolutoque *Capite ſecundo* aggredietur *tertium.* Collegia ſua *explicatoria & examinatoria* nec non *Diſputatorium* in univerſam Theologiam continuabit; alia quoque, ubi id petierint Studioſi, illis adjuncturus.

PETRVS WERENFELSIVS, S. Th. D. V. T. Profeſſ, Eccleſiæ Paſtor, Fac. h. t. Decanus, in Pſalmorum explicatione perget, horâ III. pomerid. alternis ſeptimanis, privatim quoque Studioſorum conatus juvare paratus.

JOH. RODOLFVS WETSTENIVS, Fil. S. Th. Doct. Locor. Comm. & Controverſ. Prof. diebus Mercurii & Sabbati horâ X. locum de *Peccato* exponit, controverſias ſuccinctè tractat: in Collegiis privatis examinatoriis & diſputatoriis, Studioſorum conatus promovere quotidie pergit.

*Diſputationes Theologica* ordinariæ diebus Jovis, & præter eas etiam extraordinariæ & ſolennes, ſatis frequenter habentur. Sunt quoque inter Miniſtros Verbi Divini, qui Studioſis noſtris *Collegia*, ut vocant, *pratica* indulgent, quibus ſe concionando exercere poſſint.

### IN JVRISPRVDENTIA.

LVCAS BVRCKHARDVS, J. V. D. Facult. Senior, operam ſuam in Studio Juris experientibus non denegabit.

NICOLAVS PASSAVANT, J. V. D. Pandect. Prof. perget horâ X. in Lectionibus ſuis publicis; privatas quoque Explicatorio-examinatorias continuabit.

JACOBVS BVRCKHARDVS, J. V. D. & Codicis Juſtin. Prof. horâ II. *Codicem* ejusque ſingulas Leges explicare perget, & præmiſſâ accuratâ uniuscujusque tituli diviſione, una cum ratione ordinis, attemperabit captui Auditorum, ita ut omnium tàm juniorum quàm provectiorum utilitas promoveatur; privatim verò coepta Collegia continuabit, & alia nova examinatoria & diſputatoria, pro deſiderio & voto Studioſorum, adjunget.

SEBASTIANVS FESCHIVS, J. V. D. Inſt. Imp. Prof. ac Decan. Libellum hunc, quâ fieri poteſt brevitate ac perſpicuitate, exponere, principia Juris Civilis ex Legum Romanarum libris eruendo, & ad Juris Naturæ fontes lumine digitum intendendo, publicis prælectionibus horâ IV. perget. Præterea ſi vel hoc, vel alio Juris genere docendo commodare poſſe Studioſæ Juventuti videbitur, privatam operam requiſituris pollicetur.

### IN MEDICINA.

JACOBVS ROT, D. Pract. Prof. Collegii Senior, & p.t. Decan. in Aphoriſt. Hipp. doctrina explicanda, & Patholog. Fernelii particulari obſervationibus & exemplis illuſtranda pergit alternatim horâ X. pronus ad deſideria Studioſorum impertienda.

NICOLAVS EGLINGERVS, Med. Theor. Prof. diebus Lunæ & Martis Aphoriſmos Hippocratis Mercurii & Veſſeris Inſtitutiones ex mente veterum & recentiorum explanabit horâ IV. p. m. Collegia explicatoria, examinatoria, Practica, Conſultatoria & Chymica petituris, operam ſuam non denegabit.

JOH. JACOBVS HARDERVS, Phil. & Med. Doct. Anat. & Botan. Prof. horâ II. æſtivâ in plantarum officinalium viribus uſuque ad affectus humani corporis nobiliore; hyberno verò tempore in partium cerebri functionibus ulterius explicandis perget: publicis quoque privatiſvè ſectionibus cùm hominis, tùm aliorum animantium, ſtructuram oſtendet. Collegiis denique varii generis, Anatomicis, Practicis, Explicatoriis, Examinatoriis, aliiſvè, Studioſis inſervire non detrectabit.

### IN PHILOSOPHIA.

JOH. JACOBVS HOFMANNVS, Hiſtoriar. P. P. in *Epitomes* ſuæ *Hiſtoriæ Univerſalis* curſu, diebus Lunæ & Mercurii, in *Tacito* verò Lectionibus *Hiſtorico - Politicis* illuſtrando, Martis & Veneris, pergit, utrumque horâ IX. matutinâ. Cæterùm privatim ac publicè Studioſæ Juventuti porrò, pro gratia divinitus conceſſâ, inſerviet, in quibus opera ejus deſiderabitur.

SAMVEL BVRCKHARDVS, J. V. D. Log. Prof. & Ord. Senior, donec convaleſcat, ſuum habet Vicarium.

BONIFACIVS FESCHIVS, J. V. D. Ph. Pract. Prof. in prælectionibus ſuis horâ I. pomeridianâ Ariſtot. lib. 5. Eth. Nicomach. exponere perget: Operam inſuper ſuam in Collegiis privatis examinatorio-explicatoriis & diſputatoriis ſtudioſæ Juventuti pollicetur.

JOHANNES WETSTENIVS, J. V. D. Linguæ Græc. Prof. p.t. Decanus, diebus Lunæ ac Mercurii *Novum Teſtament.* Martis verò & Veneris horâ IV. p. m. *Homerum* tractabit, eumque notis Grammaticis, Mythologicis, Practicis illuſtrabit. Privatim coepta Collegia, quâ Philologica, quâ Philoſophica Explicatorio-Examinatoria cum Diſputatorio *v.9.* continuabit; aliaſque nova petituris inchoabit.

THEODORVS ZVINGERVS, Phil. & Med. Doct. Phyſices Prof. Ord. Lectionibus horâ IV. habendis ad Explicationem Meteororum perget. Privatis etiam Collegiis tam Philoſophicis quàm Chymicis, ſuam qualemcunque opem Studioſæ Juventuti offert.

JOH. GEORGIVS MANGOLT, Phil. & Med. Doct. Rhetoricæ Profeſſ. P. in elucidanda & ad uſum ducenda Rhetorica Lucii pergit horâ I. pomeridianâ: privatim Philoſophiam docet explicando, diſputando, etiam in experimentis Philoſophicis operam ſuam impertit.

M. JOH. JACOBVS BVXTORFIVS, Ling. Heb. Pr. alternis diebus horâ octavâ legendo & examinando pergit: in Lectionibus quidem exponit Prophetam *Amos*, in Examinibus verò Analyſin Gramm. *Pſalmorum* exigit. Cæterùm privatam ſuam operam in his literis, uti hactenus, ita porrò non negabit.

M. SAMVEL WERENFELSIVS, Eloquent. Profeſſ. horâ II. pom. Epiſtolas Ciceronis explicare pergit, ad Orationes ſubinde rediturus; alia exercitia Oratoria privatim petentibus aperiet: Collegia Philoſophica & Philologica continuabit.

M. JACOBVS BERNOVLLI, Mathem Pr. P. Geometriæ penſo nuper abſoluto, telam Aſtronomicam publicè exorſus eſt: privatim verò univerſam Matheſin, cùm Theoreticam, tum Practicam docere pergit.

*Collegium Experimentale Phyſico-Mechanicum* hebdomadatim diebus Jovis, horâ III. in coenobio D. Leonhardi magnâ Spectatorum frequentiâ celebratur.

JOH. JACOBVS BATTIERIVS, J. V. D. Logices Profeſſor. Vicar. coeptam à ſe non ita pridem Syſtem. Burgersdiciani explicationem continuabit. Cæterùm ſi quid in Philoſophiæ Philologicæque Studio, Juris etiam Naturalis diſciplinâ, juventuti commodare poſſe videbitur, Studiis illius inſervire nunquam ceſſabit.

\*\*\*   \*\*\*   \*\*\*

*Muſicam* docet Muſicus & Organiſta ordinarius.

*Gallica Lingua* diſci poteſt ex Concionibus Gallicis, in æde Prædicatorum haberi ſolitis; ut & ex inſtitutione Magiſtrorum hujus Linguæ complurium.

*Lingua Italica* Studioſis ſuam operam offert M. JOHANNES TONJOLA, Concionator Italicus & alii.

Præterea *Geometriam Practicam, Architecturam Civilem & Militarem* apud nos diſcendi, egregiam harum rerum Studioſi invenient occaſionem.

*Bibliotheca* etiam Academica die Jovis hebdomadatim ab horâ I. ad III. in uſum Studioſæ Juventutis aperitur.

---

BASILEÆ TYPIS JACOBI BERTSCHII.

2.2. *Catalogus Professorum*, University of Basel, 1690/91.

# CATALOGUS PROFESSORUM
# ACADEMIÆ BASILIENSIS
cum deſignatione Diſciplinarum, in quibus docendis atque
explicandis DEO JUVANTE ſinguli verſabuntur.

*RECTORE*
## EMANUELE ZÆSLINO,
*A Solſtitio Æſtivo Anni* MDCCXII.
*Ad idem Solſtitium* MDCCXIII.

## IN THEOLOGIA.

SAMUEL WERENFELSIUS, S. Theol. Doct. N.T.Prof. Lectionib. publicis concionem Chriſti in monte habitam explicabit, privatam interea operam Studioſis navare perget.

HIERONYMUS BURCARDUS, S. Theol. Doct. Eccleſ.Paſtor. V.T.Prof. Fac.p.t.Dec.h.III.pomerid. diebus Martis, & Mercurii difficilior V. T. Loca explicabit; Privatam quoque operam ſtudioſæ Juventuti pro virili commodabit.

JACOBUS CHRISTOPHORUS ISELIUS, Th.D. Loc. Comm.& Contr.Th.Prof. pro cathedra quidem novas Pontificiorum *Methodos* excutere & confutare perget, privatim ſuſceptos in explicanda ſana doctrina labores, porro V.D. urgebit; neque alia ulla in re, qua poterit, ſtudioſæ Juventuti prodeſſe ceſſabit.

JOH. LUDOVICUS FREY, S.Th.D. ejusdemque Prof. Extraord. & Hiſtor.Ord. Die Martis Librum H.Grotii de Verit.Rel.Chriſt. explicat, hor. IX. mat. Privatim Inſtitutiones S. Theolog. ejus ſtudioſis tradere pro gratia divinitus conceſſa perget.

*Diſputationes Theologicæ* ordinariæ diebus Veneris, & præter eas extraordinaria ac ſolennes, ſatis frequenter habentur. Sunt quoque inter Miniſtros V.D. qui *Studioſis noſtris* Collegia, ut vocant, Practica indulgent, quibus ſe concionando exercere poſſint.

## IN JURISPRUDENTIA.

JACOBUS BURCARDUS, J.U.D. Pandect. & Jur. Canon Prof. Univerſit. Senior, p. t. Decanus, h. X. diebus Lunæ, Mart. & Mercurii Pandectas methodo conſueta explicare perget, & præmiſſa accurata titulorum connexione, attemperabit ſe captui Auditorum, ita ut omnium tam juniorum quàm provectiorum utilitas promoveatur. Die Ven. autem explicationem Can. Jur. ac privatim cœpta Collegia continuabit, & alia explicatoria atque diſputatoria pro deſiderio & voto Studioforum adjunget.

BONIFACIUS FESCHIUS, J.U.D. Cod. Juſt.& Jur.Feud. Prof. hora II. pomerid. in expoſitione *Codicis* diebus Lun. Mart. & Merc. ita verſabitur, ut ad uſum hodiernum omnia ſit relaturus; jus vero *Feudale* die Vener. dilucida & fuccincta tradet methodo: nec non Collegia privata examinatoria & diſputat. continuabit.

JOH. JACOBUS BATTIERIUS, J.U.D. Inſtit. Imp. & Jur. Publ. Prof. diebus quidem Lunæ, Martis & Mercurii Inſtitutiones; die Veneris autem Jus publicum breviter & ad captum Studioforum hora IV.exponet. Collegia quoque privata examinatoria, atque diſputatoria continuabit: & in *H.Grotii Libros de Jure Belli & Pacis* iterum volentibus aperiet.

## IN MEDICINA.

THEODORUS ZUINGERUS, Medicinæ Pract.Profeſſor, Aphorismos Hippocr. h. X. practicè explicare, atque obſervationibus illuſtrare perget. Privatim autem Collegia varii generis examinatoria, explicatoria, ac diſputatoria diligenter continuabit.

EMANUEL KÖNIG, Med.D.& Theoret.Prof.Theoriam verè Medicam non ex fictis hypotheſibus,ſed veris Obſervationibus conſpirantem Hor. IV. Auditoribus prælegere incipiet, eumque in finem *Baſilicam* ſuam *Medicam* publico olim promiſſam & ex perpetuis rationis & experientiæ nexibus exſtructam, nova eaque perſpicuâ methodo exædificatam aperiet, ſicque *Inſtitutionibus* hucusque deſideratis completiſſimis Studioſos (commonſtrando ex principiis mechanicis veram Theoriam eſſe mutam praxin,& veram Praxin mutam theoriam) manuducet.Nec iis

## IN PHILOSOPHIA.

JOHANNES WETSTENIUS, J. U. D. Philoſ. Mor. ut & Juris Nat. & Gent. Profeſſ. Facult. Jurid. Adſeſſor, Ord. Philoſ. Sen. publicè diebus Lunæ, Mart. & Merc. *Pufendorfii lib. de Officio Hom.& Civ. die* Ven. autem *Grotii lib. de Jure B. & P. h.* III. Σ. θ. explanare; privatim verò Collegia Philoſophicis atque Juridicis, & quocunque officiorum genere poterit, Studioſæ Juventuti commoda promovere perget.

JOH. RODOLPHUS BECK, Phil. & Med.D. Phyſ.Prof. h. t. Decanus Med. h. I. pom. Cosmologiam continuabit. Collegiis porrò Theor. pract. examinat. explicator. ſtudioſæ Juventuti pro Virib. prodeſſe ſtudebit.

EMANUEL ZÆSLINUS, P. & M.D. Rhet. Prof. Rhetoricam docere, ac ſubindè ſacra poëmata Buchanani & profana Ovidii de triſtibus alternis vicibus explicando, ejus uſum monſtrare perget; privata quoque collegia Philoſoph. & Philologica petituris aperire paratus.

JOHANNES BERNOULLI, Ph.& Med.Doct. Math.P.P. hora II. pom. Aſtronomiæ uſum & applicationem ad Chronologiam docere perget. Collegia privata tam diſputatoria quam explicatoria in varias Matheſeos & Philoſophiæ partes habet habebitque diſcendi cupidis.

SAMUEL BATTIERIUS, Phil. & Med. Doct. Gr. Ling. Prof.Publ. in Lectionibus ſuis hora IV.pom. diebus Mart. & Merc. textum Græcum Novi Teſt. Studioſis explanabit; die Ven. autem ad lectionem Homeri eos ducet. Privatim quoque Collegia varia Philologica, Philoſ. Phyſico - Med. habere perget.

JOHANNES BUXTORFIUS, Ling. Hebr. Profeſſ. Fac. p. t. Dec. diebus Lunæ, Mart. & Merc. hora II. pom. analyſin Pſalmorum Gramm. exiget, die Veneris autem miſcellanea philologica auditoribus ſuis proponere perget, iisdem privatam quoque operam pro virili impenſurus.

JOH. LUDOVICUS FREY, S.S.Th.D. ejusdemq; Prof. extraord. Hiſtoriar. ordin. die Lunæ, Mercurii & Veneris h. IX. Hiſtoriam explicat; Privatim etiam Diſciplinis Philoſ. operari volentibus lubens operam ſuam commodaturus.

NICOLAUS HARSCHERUS, Phil. & Med. D. Orator. P.O. in lectionibus publicis hora I. Epiſtolas Ciceronis ad Familiares tractare perget, nonnunquam etiam ex ſelectis ejusdem Orationibus, ad captum auditorum exponere ſuſcipiet. Privatim quoque in collegiis variis, diſputatoriis & declamatoriis exercitiis habendis operam ſuam, pro ut occæpit facere, lubens commodabit.

JOH. RODOLPHUS ZUINGERUS, Phil. & Med.D. Logic. Profeſſ. Horâ IX. Lectionibus publicis Syſtema Logicum explicare, atque privatis Collegiis ſtudioſæ Juventutis commodum promovere perget.

Muſicam docent *Muſici & Organiſtæ varii. Sed & ſinguli ſeptimanis ex liberalitate Ampliſſ. D. D. Scholarch. duo Collegia Muſica in ſuperiori Colleg. habentur, in quibus ſtudioſa Juventus in Muſica tam Vocali quam Inſtrumentali, gratis informatur & exercetur.*

*Gallica Lingua diſci poteſt è Concionibus Gallicis in Æde Prædicatorum haberi ſolitis, ut & ex inſtitutione Magiſtrorum hujus Linguæ complurium, inprimis autem* LUDOVICI VINCENT, *Campani. &* CLAUDII DE LA CARRIERE *ex Epiſcop. Metenſi.*

*Linguæ Italicæ Studioſis ſuam operam offerunt* VINCENTIUS PARAVICINUS, *Gymnaſii Mariani Corrector, &* JOH. PUSTERLA, *Mediolanenſis.*

*Bibliotheca etiam Academica Die Jovis hebdomadatim ab horâ I. ad III. in uſum Studioſæ Juventutis aperitur.*

BASILEÆ, *Typis Friderici Lüdii, Univerſ.Typ.*

ANNO MDCCXII.

2.3. *Catalogus Professorum,* University of Basel, 1712/13.

The professors appear in the main body of the catalogues. The order here inverts the order of the Cambridge parade. It is the normal or uninverted order of academic precedence, where the best come first. From the top left to the bottom right, the faculties have their traditional order of academic precedence in the German cultural space and elsewhere: first comes theology, second jurisprudence or law, third medicine, and last and least arts and philosophy (and sciences)—here called the philosophy faculty. The mere lecturers in music, French, and Italian fall to the end or run across the bottom of the page. This indicates that the few modern languages and other subjects taught had not been fully integrated into the curriculum or, rather, into the system of professorial chairs.[9]

## The Order of Academic Precedence

The order in the faculties was also important. A glance at the catalogues shows that within each faculty the names of professors structure the list, and the listing is not alphabetic. What then determines the order? In traditional academia at least four possible considerations or criteria might play a role in setting academic precedence.

(1) In terms of the sorts of academic degrees, as in the Cambridge parade.

(2) In terms of the dates of when academic degrees were received. Here precedence or seniority accrued in the order of the length of time a degree had been held. The longer one had been a doctor or master, the more seniority one had. The latter could be measured (a) absolutely: no matter where one had graduated, only the respective degree dates mattered. Or it could be measured (b) relatively: degree-holders from other universities had lower status relative to degree-holders teaching at their alma mater (*Doctor sive Magister Noster*).

(3) In terms of the dates of when professorships were received. Here precedence or seniority accrued in order of the length of time a professorship had been held. The longer one had been a full or ordinary professor in the faculty and/or university, the more seniority one had. That latter could also be measured (a) absolutely: seniority carried over intermurally and/or between faculties. Or professorial seniority might be measured (b) relatively: seniority only accrued intramurally and/or within a faculty.

(4) In terms of a complex calculus of (1) to (3).

We shall return to matters of academic precedence many times in this book. A little reflection would show, for example, that the absolute versus relative methods of setting precedence bore directly on the mobility, or lack of it, of professors between universities, given how much precedence mattered in a traditional social group such as academia.

The conception of the modern professorate hinged on the transformation of differential status from seniority to salary: where one marched in the parade became less important than how much one was paid. And ad hominem salary offers—a technique actually designed for the case of the extraordinary (that is, not a full) professor—one day became the means facilitating professorial mobility. But that would be the modern system. The early modern one, where hierarchy ruled, generally worked against academic mobility.[10]

Basel adhered on the whole to 3b above: precedence by length of time a professorship had been held in the faculty. The three "superior" faculties—theology, law, and medicine—each had here three ordinary or full professorships, that is, three chairs. In each faculty, the three chairs formed a hierarchy, also in part designated by differential salary. By standard early modern practices, professors tended to move up the faculty hierarchy upon the departure or death of a colleague. In universities where chairs in the superior faculties had ordinal names (*primarius, secundus, tertius, etc.*), the senior professor in each usually had the *primarius* professorship, the next senior the *secundus*, and so on. In figure 2.2, the senior professor in each superior faculty has styled himself "Facult. Senior" or something similar.[11]

Professors in the superior faculties in the catalogues here thus appear in order of the length of time they had been a professor in the respective faculty. In eighteenth century catalogues, the same would be true in the philosophy faculty. However, the catalogue from 1690/91 (figure 2.2) shows a more articulated order of precedence in the philosophy faculty. Close scrutiny of biographies shows that the professors in the Basel philosophy faculty in 1690/91 oddly replicated the overall order of academic precedence—theology, jurisprudence, medicine, arts and philosophy—within the faculty itself. That was possible since many of them had academic degrees in one of the superior faculties. We'll return to that matter later.

Early modern professors moved through and between faculties and chairs. In figure 2.2, J. J. Battier is at the bottom of the philosophy faculty. Twenty years later in figure 2.3, he has moved into the law faculty, where he is its junior member. The next from the bottom in figure 2.2, Jakob Bernoulli, died in 1705, so he is not in figure 2.3. Third from the bottom in figure 2.2, S. Werenfels, made it all the way to being the senior of the theology faculty in figure 2.3. Fourth and fifth from the bottom in the first catalogue, J. J. Buxtorf and J. G. Mangold, died in 1704 and 1693, respectively, thus are not in the second catalogue here. In figure 2.2, fifth from the top in the philosophy faculty, T. Zwinger, survived the latter two colleagues and was the senior professor in the medical faculty in figure 2.3. Fourth from the top in the first catalogue, J. Wettstein, remained in the philosophy faculty in the second catalogue and was now its senior, as he styled himself. In 1714 he became a professor in the law faculty. Third from the top in figure 2.2, B. Faesch, was the second professor in the law faculty in figure 2.3. Second in figure 2.3, S. Burckhardt, died in 1705, so was not in figure 2.3. Finally, the philosophy faculty senior in figure 2.2, J. J. Hoffmann, died in 1706, so was absent from figure 2.3. So much for the philosophy faculty in figure 2.2.

What do we see from this? Of the ten individuals in figure 2.2 from 1690/91, five did not move up to one of the three superior faculties, while the other five did. We shall soon discuss why, but you can take this as a fact: many or even most early modern academics had their eyes on a chair in one of the superior faculties. That explains why so many professors in the philosophy faculty had doctorates in theology, law, or medicine. By the way, three of the five, who did not change faculties above, died between the time of our two catalogues, so we cannot be sure about their aims. But one of them at least, Mangold, had already obtained a doctorate in medicine, which of course would have allowed him to move into that faculty.

This brings us to the subject of academic musical chairs. It is a modern, bureaucratic notion that salary might increase over time by seniority or merit to someone remaining in the same position. In the early modern era, advancement came by way of changing positions in a sort of musical chairs—opting up—or by academic pluralism, a hallowed ecclesiastical practice. Indeed, the practice of musical chairs itself stems from canonical practices. Opting up in the canonical hierarchy was called *jus optandi* in canon law. In the German academic system, opting up or musical chairs was called *Aufrücken*. Alongside pluralism, it formed an essential part of traditional practices of advancement.

Early modern Protestant professors much resembled canons at cathedrals, because a professorial chair much resembled a canonry; indeed, the former originated in the latter during the High Middle Ages. Like medieval canons, professors usually began at the bottom of the hierarchy—here in the arts and philosophy (and sciences) faculty—and tried to move up. The subjects of the chairs had not much importance. The powers and privileges and monies tied to the respective chairs (or canonries) gave, rather, the essence of the matter. What counted was a place in the hierarchy and ways to enhance it. The charisma of office came, as it did at the cathedrals, from the place of one's chair in the canonical hierarchy.[12]

Professors in the arts and philosophy faculty not only tried to move into a superior faculty and, then, to move up. They also tried to move between chairs in the arts and philosophy faculty. Some chairs in the faculty paid more and/or had more prestige than others. In Basel, for example, the nine chairs in the philosophy faculty were de facto divided into two classes, higher and lower, between which professors often tried to move. One opted up from the lower to the higher class of chairs for more money and prestige.[13]

List 2 in appendix 1 will make such practices clearer (lists and tables are in appendices at the rear of the book.) List 2 shows that in 1558 the three least well-paid arts and philosophy professors at Leipzig—those of dialectics, grammar, and elementary mathematics—could make 80 to 100 percent more by opting up to the chair of rhetoric, or poetics, or physics, if one of them became vacant. The top chair—for Greek, Latin, ethics, and politics—looks like an ad hominem joint chair of Greek-Latin and ethics-politics. The 300 florin salary might not have survived the demise of its pluralistic holder.

## Nepotism and the Professorate

The difference between medieval canons and early modern Protestant professors lay in the more thoroughgoing professorial practice of the third thing they had in common besides opting up and pluralism: nepotism. Note the most salient information from our two Basel catalogues. Of the Bernoullis, Buxtorfs, Faesches, Werenfels, and Wettsteins, we find two each, as well as three Battiers and three Zwingers. The clear winners are the Burckhardt family with four faculty members. These men stood in relations of grandfather, father, son, grandson, uncle, nephew, great-uncle, and so on.

For lack of space and time, we cannot pursue a social history of these men. But bear in mind that the little list of common surnames above does not consider sons-in-law who became faculty members. Study of the professor's daughter has been much hampered by a failure of biographical and prosopographical sources on academics to record maiden names of professors' wives, if they record wives' names at all. Failing such information, it is hard to tell which professors at Basel were maternal nephews and/or sons-in-law of someone in the faculty. What we see from common surnames in catalogues is only the tip of an iceberg.

Basel was known for nepotism. In fairness one should say that Basel probably proved but the best known, if not most notorious case, of standard academic practice. In seventeenth-century Basel, there were altogether about eighty professors, of whom 60 percent came from just fifteen families. The winners then were the Burckhardts, who had eight professors, followed by the Faesch family with six. The eighteenth century saw other and more families—such as the Bernoullis—enter the lists, as the university and town took measures to make appointment less nepotistic. Still, in the end, town and gown formed a more or less coherent endogamous group or incestuous kindred of academics and aldermen.[14]

We have been considering the Germanic parade of professors for the last few pages. The persona and title of "professor" had reemerged in the Middle Ages, and first had come into popularity in the early Renaissance. But its diffusion as an academic system came by way of the Continental Protestant Reformation. Furthermore, the diffusion of the professorate as a system— in place of medieval masters and fellows as at Oxbridge—seems to have induced the emergence of the lecture catalogue as a regular publication, albeit slowly and fitfully.[15]

### The Calendar, the Curriculum, and the Professorate

The medieval university had neither a professorate nor a calendar in the early modern and modern sense. An official opening date of the academic year did swiftly emerge. And winter and summer vacations existed. But the three term academic year, which Oxford and Cambridge adopted, should tell us that the semester, as a unit of academic labor and time, was not part of the academic state of nature.[16]

Inspection of lists 1 and 2 in appendix 1 may be illuminating. List 1 shows the lectures for the master's degree in arts and philosophy at the University of Leipzig in 1499. A lecture on Aristotle's *Ethics* cost six groschen and would last from six to nine months. The same time-fee equations held for Aristotle's *Metaphysics* and for Euclid's *Elements*. In the middle of the list, a lecture on *De caelo* lasted three to four months and cost four groschen. At the end of the list, a lecture on *Oeconomica* could only last three weeks and only cost one groschen. We see that each lecture had its own calendar and an appropriate set fee.

Ordinary lectures, such as these, could be or should have been taught only during the ordinary days of the academic year, that is, not on holidays, during vacation, or on days reserved for special business or events, such as exams. This fee and time schedule gives us the academic regime before the professorate emerged as the academic system in the Germanies and elsewhere. The lectures for the M.A. in list 1 were given by masters and doctors, who would each collect the fee from each student for each lecture course.

Some endowed or salaried positions did exist. Thus there were what would come to be called "professors." But the medieval (and Oxbridge) academic system did not center on them. Medieval academics typically made their living by collecting fees from lectures and examinations, and from any other duties and privileges to which their degrees bound or entitled them. Many also filled other offices for more money. This medieval regime of masters and doctors displays itself in figure 2.1, although by that time Oxbridge masters and doctors would have been mostly college fellows who obtained an income as a sinecure.

To be a medieval master of arts originally meant to be able to lecture on all of the books taught for degrees. One was master of the Seven Liberal Arts, and eventually of all philosophy, too. The M.A. (and M.Phil. in some places) meant that. During the Middle Ages, arts and philosophy faculties instituted ever more hoops for the mastership. It took longer and longer to be a qualified or "incepted" master. But once one was, one could lecture during ordinary term time on whatever books one wanted—with the obvious bad results.

In 1367 at the University of Prague, a mere twenty years after its foundation, the arts and philosophy faculty faced the "rancor and envy among the Masters, as one competes with the other in lecturing on the same book." Masters battled over enrollments for some books—probably those with the highest fees or best time-fee equation—while other books were not read at all. So the Prague arts faculty resolved to end the masters' right to choose freely. The faculty decided that lectures would be assigned based on choice via seniority. Senior masters, probably by seniority of degree, could choose the most desirable books or classes.[17]

The University of Heidelberg set distribution of lectures by seniority in its oldest statutes circa 1387. The University of Freiburg im Breisgau, founded in 1460, also had distributed lectures by seniority but, to inhibit specialization, eventually set a five-year no repeat rule. When a master chose a given text, he might not choose it again for five years. The University of Vienna had used seniority, but moved in 1391 to distribution by lot. That seemed more egalitarian and guaranteed to check tendencies to specialize. The University of Leipzig also distributed lecture courses by lot. The University of Ingolstadt at first did, too.[18]

However, by the early sixteenth century, Ingolstadt no longer distributed expensive ordinary lectures by lot, but rather by election from the arts faculty council. As academic councils had become oligarchies of senior masters, doctors, and fellows by that time, they prepared the way for the German system of ordinary or full professors as chair holders.[19]

## Chairs and the Ordinary Professors

List 2 in appendix 1 shows typical ordinary professors of the new German system. At Leipzig in 1558, we no longer have a list of magisterial and doctoral lectures as the essential thing. We have instead a list of ordinary or full professors. An ordinary professor or *ordinarius* was one who had an ordinary salary, that is, was funded from the standard or ordinary endowment or budget. In the German system, each of these professors was said to hold a chair, a *Lehrstuhl*. Some or all of the chairs might have had some funds or endowments legally bound to the chair as a foundation at law. The impetus in the German system would be, however, toward salaries paid from an annual budget. Juridical or legal entities such as endowments were medieval. Budgets are modern. They present an important wedge for ministerial leverage over academic labor.

Extraordinary professors would also arise, and we shall meet them in chapters below. These were special professors in a touchy sense. They were professors extra to the ordinary budget or endowment. In that, they resembled modern soft money positions. But, unlike the latter, the early modern German extraordinary professor (*extraordinarius*), depending on the time and place, might have no salary. Such professors still lived, like the lecturers, under the medieval system. They collected fees directly and per head from their students. Being an extraordinary professor, however, gave them the title of a professor, and a foot firmly in the faculty. By the hallowed practice of musical chairs and opting up, they counted on a chair.[20]

Ordinary professors each had a special subject, over which they had monopolistic rights. Professorships had existed since the Middle Ages as canonries for theologians and jurists. The Renaissance brought forth some secular chairs in the arts and philosophy faculty for humanists, usually ad hominem positions. Humanists needed the salaried positions since the new topics they taught—Greek, Hebrew, advanced mathematics, and so on—did not form part of the curriculum for examination at the time. Thus, humanists could not usually survive from the money to be made from student fees and examinations for degrees.

As noted, the professorate as an academic system emerged in the Germanies and generally, excepting at Oxbridge, as a consequence of the Protestant Reformation and Jesuit Counter-Reformation. Basel changed to a salaried professorate in arts and philosophy in 1532/39. The University of Wittenberg, largely there in 1516, completed the process in 1536. The reformation of universities then went on under Wittenberg's auspices, that is, under the guidance of Luther and his right-hand man, Melanchthon, *Praeceptor Germaniae*.[21]

Post-Reformation, new universities had a professorate from the outset. Ordinary professors now taught the ordinary lectures. Masters and doctors without a chair needed the permission of the academic senate or faculty council to lecture. And the ordinary professors now composed the senate and councils. Unlike the medieval-Oxbridge system, professors now ran the university—and later displayed themselves in the parade of the lecture catalogue.

So far, the lecture catalogue shows that a traditional university was a "moral" community, like a cathedral chapter or a craft guild. The catalogue indicates that the hierarchy or parade of persons and their seniority was more important than a system of knowledge, even when German professors had replaced medieval masters and doctors. The order of precedence of the four faculties formed a moral or juridical order, that is, a canonical order, not an epistemic one. Academic musical chairs or opting up shows that position in the hierarchy was a juridical matter. The catalogue presented the professorate not as a work force of supposed specialists, but rather as a Latinate, corporative, collegial, and incestuous body—thus the juridico-ecclesiastical cast or caste of medieval and early modern academia.

We turn now from parades to paperwork, and then to publicity, to see how ministries and markets modernized academic manners and lecture catalogues.

## PAPERWORK

It is ministerial magic and this section examines it: how the professorial parade and academic manners reflected in the original, Latin lecture catalogue became modified by ministerial agendas, how German governments beset the ivory tower and reformed its inhabitants.

The early modern Germanies witnessed the advent of a "police state." We shall begin by considering what that meant for academics. We shall find a new necessity for academics to report about their teaching and schedules to ministries of state, which gradually refined techniques to insure the good policing of academic labor. The publication of such reported schedules of labor will furnish one of the bases of the lecture catalogue. We shall see the reflection of ministerial good policing in the appearance of a disciplinary catalogue.

### The German "Policey-Staat"

The early modern Germanies witnessed the emergence of the *Policey-Staat*, the police state. That was not a terrorist state. Such a notion would be unfair to the police who, unlike terrorists, prove fairly good at keeping records. And paperwork constitutes the essence of police power, as an instrument of the modern bureaucratic state. The early modern German *Policey-Staat* sought to achieve the good policing, *die gute Policey*, of the land by monitoring and regulating the behavior of subjects by paperwork.

The police ordinance, *Policey-Ordnung*, blossomed as a genre in the sixteenth century Germanies. On 19 November 1530, the emperor of the Holy Roman Empire issued an ordinance for the good policing of the empire. By the late sixteenth century, a flood of police ordinances, issued by emperors, kings, and princes circulated through the Germanies. In the early modern era, German sovereigns moved from managing their house and court (*Haus und Hof*) to policing the whole land and people (*Land und Leute*). Attempts to police German subjects slowly pervaded the whole of society, encompassing nobles, officers, soldiers, managers, entrepreneurs, craftsmen, farmers, and even harmless academics. "[T]he realm of policing remained so large up to the close of the eighteenth century that one could take it for the entire domestic politics at the level of administration."[22]

On one side of academia, good policing bureaucratized the ministries above it. On the other side, it industrialized the guilds below it. In the latter case, this reached all the way down to villages. The good policing of guilds sought to transform them from complex traditional groups, which grasped the whole person, into mere occupational groups, or to restrict them altogether. Rituals and other old-fashioned practices had to give way to new, rationalized notions of production. The professionalization of agriculture would await the nineteenth century; but, beginning in the seventeenth century, German governments aimed to break up traditional social structures at the local level, including academic kin groups.

Good policing restricted the occasions when groups could collect and what they did. As Marc Raeff has noted, "Traditionally the accepted behavior patterns of these events were designed to involve the whole community . . . Instead [of this] the state endeavored to privatize the family . . . The everyday pattern of life was to become compartmentalized; public and private events were to be kept distinct." New ministerial policies sought to augment productivity. Such policies effectively extracted the concept of work or labor from the complex moral life of guilds and kindreds, and translated this labor into the public sphere. It created an economy in the modern sense. "The tenor of ordinances indicates that new attitudes were being fostered, attitudes that viewed the activities of guild members in strictly technical and economic terms, rather than as a complex social and cultural behavior."[23]

## Reports and Schedules

"Things are done according to how they are reported" (*Wie man berichtet, so geschehe*), as Conrad Ischinger, a German villager, noted in the nineteenth century. He spoke of the magic of paperwork, its power to fashion reality, or at least humans. Reality is not so much recorded as rather more wrought by the report.[24]

In 1569, the elector of the Palatinate, who was patron of the University of Heidelberg and sovereign over the land, ordered the university to send a report containing the names of the professors, what topic and at which time each professor lectured, and how many students attended each lecture. To this order the university wrote in protest and in error that such a request was completely unheard of. The university implied that the sovereign had no need to try to supervise them, as they had, could, and would continue to take care of their own business. But in fact the elector's ancestors had occasionally demanded similar reports from the university, as early as 1410 and as recently as 1547. So, in 1569, despite their protest about the elector's supposedly unheard of request, Heidelberg professors complied.[25]

Founded in 1502, the University of Wittenberg may lay some claim to the title of the first (early) modern university. It reported—sometimes regularly, sometimes fitfully—as early as 1516. The duke elector of Saxony, the patron and sovereign, demanded monthly reports in 1530 on the lecture topics and hours of professors, an order he had to repeat in 1534. On the whole, the university failed to report monthly. Here and elsewhere we see a pattern of paperwork sent from the ministry to the university, wherein the ministry demanded reciprocity of paperwork. Academics received money. The ministry wanted reports.[26]

Such reports, unheard of among medieval ears, would become a chief tool to re-form modern academics. The spotty academic reporting of the fifteenth century would slowly grow to a deluge of professorial paperwork. As hierarchy and parades prove essential to seeing the original lecture catalogue as an emblem of the ivory tower, so are paperwork and reporting essential for seeing the lecture catalogue as a tool of the early modern police state and its ministries. The bureaucratic rationalization of academic life bared its teeth here.

The Jesuits had big ones. They were masters of paperwork. At the latest by 1546, the provost general in Rome had requested monthly reports from each Jesuit house and college. A decree of 1550 mandated them. Quarterly reports had been coming to Rome since 1548. Circa 1565 there were semiannual reports, supplanted by annual reports after 1565, some of which had already appeared after 1552. By 1571 the Jesuits had carved Europe into their own provinces, which now annually reported to Rome. The monthly and quarterly reports went to provincial governors. The 1577 rules for the provincial governors required them to report to the provost general at the close of each term on the talent and academic progress of each of the brothers. Masters of bureaucratic discipline, Jesuits faithfully filed their reports.[27]

Academic reporting in Protestant lands went hand in hand with the professorate. The ordinary or full professors wrought by the Reformation were also "public" professors. They received salaries (see list 2 in appendix 1) for giving public lectures, that is, lectures free of charge to the academic public. For the public lectures, students were no longer required to pay fees, such as those in list 1. In the Basel catalogues above, the classes taught *publicè* (publicly) usually appear after the name, titles, and chair(s) of each professor. Professorial salaries might or might not have flowed directly from the sovereign's or town's treasury. But since professors now filled a public office, ministers of state and town councils undertook to regulate professorial labor. Even in advance of the Reformation, some new foundations and statutory revisions had instituted times for the ordinary or public lectures.[28]

A statutory revision at Leipzig in 1558 set the exact lecture schedule (list 2). But neither the 1546/1554 statutes of the new University of Königsberg, nor the 1560 statutes of the University of Marburg, nor the 1568 statutes of Jena, nor the 1576 of Helmstedt, nor the 1607 of Gießen set times of day for professorial lectures. Statutes of those new universities mandated that there be a precise schedule, but left determination of it for the rector and/or deans and/or faculties. A clever modernizing ministry allowed academics to set their own schedule. The essential point was that there was one, whatever it was, and that it was kept. That meant paperwork, the essence of modern ministerial power and knowledge.[29]

## Spies, Professorial Slips, and Printed Prospective Reports

One solution to the all too common lackadaisical academic reporting lay in setting up spies. At Vienna a 1556 decree provided for paying two individuals to keep daily notes on lecturers and professors. The two hired hands gave the superintendent a weekly report on professors and their lapses.

The superintendent, moreover, monitored the monitors and set up other avenues of surveillance. The superintendent—an intramural minister or director appointed by the sovereign—was itself a new but typical early modern office. In a like manner, after 1564 in Marburg, the beadle kept a list of lectures missed by professors, and gave it quarterly to the rector to impose fines. Another method of monitoring lay in the practice of ministerial visitations, also an academic novelty in the early modern era and subject of a later chapter.[30]

Compared to their Jesuit colleagues, Protestant academics were resistant to or retarded in the perfection of the bureaucratic discipline of reporting. That is doubtless, in part, what drove the ministries to set up spies. But like the market's magic with financial instruments, modern ministerial magic lies in paper and its circulation.

2.4. *Professorenzettel* of Michael Mästlin, University of Tübginen, 1607.

2.5. *Professorenzettel* of Andreas Osiander, University of Tübginen, 1607.

*Professorenzetteln* became a common technique to reform Protestant academics. They were typically small slips of paper on which professors noted each term what they had taught. Figures 2.4 and 2.5 are examples from 1607 from the University of Tübingen. The professorial slip in figure 2.4 comes from Michael Mästlin, professor of mathematics and astronomy. He gives a rather detailed report of what he taught during the past semester. The professorial slip in figure 2.5 comes from Andreas Osiander, professor of theology. It looks like he does not work much or, more likely, does not take this report so seriously. The dean of the faculty would usually gather the paperwork, meticulously or laxly done, from the professors and give it to the rector of the university. The rector would, then, typically send all of it to the ministry supervising the university.[31]

Professorial slips offered retrospective reporting. The next step seems obvious. Ministers soon also wanted prospective reports—one of the roots of the lecture catalogue. In the sixteenth century, Latin lecture catalogues, of the sort we saw above, began appearing. (List 1 in appendix 2 shows the first known appearances of or first mandates for lecture catalogues.) Given the bureaucratic rebellion or laxness of Protestant academics, a ministerial mandate for a printed catalogue is not ipso facto evidence for the existence of one. However, the fact that a state ministry wanted a report on planned lectures constitutes a significant datum. As a case study, we shall look at universities in Brandenburg-Prussia.[32]

---

Before 1809/10 and the foundation of the University of Berlin, Brandenburg-Prussia had universities in Frankfurt an der Oder (a.d.O.), Duisburg, Königsberg (now Kaliningrad), and Halle (an der Salle). For Frankfurt a.d.O., a reform of 1611 mandated that professors should relate what they will lecture on in the coming year in the annual report, and that this should be published as a lecture catalogue. By the eighteenth century this catalogue had to be sent in advance to the ministry for approval. For Königsberg in 1672, the Prussian ministry commanded that a lecture catalogue appear henceforth. In 1717 the ministry reminded the university the lecture catalogue must contain the times of all classes, so that those who neglected their duty might be better monitored. Reports were tied to all this. In reports sent by the 1720s, Königsberg enclosed its printed lecture catalogue. Of Halle in 1731, the ministry ordered a lecture catalogue and, sensibly, enjoined the professors to discuss with each other the times of their lectures. By decrees of 1748 and 1764, the university was to send the lecture catalogue to the ministry with a report on which lectures had been actually held. For Brandenburg-Prussia in general, a 1753 decree enjoined semester reports tied to the lecture catalogue. After 1781 the textbooks had to be listed in the catalogue, thus giving the ministry de facto the power to veto textbooks by vetoing the proposed catalogue.[33]

---

The Jesuits had mastered the regular, unpublished report by the middle of the sixteenth century. Mastery by the Prussians and, indeed by Protestants generally, took longer and seems to have come by way of a report including a printed lecture catalogue. Publication of lecture catalogues does not appear to have been regular in the sixteenth century. The printed Latin lecture catalogue emerged as a typical and regular Protestant periodical in the seventeenth century, and only became canonical and completely general in the eighteenth.[34]

Austrian Jesuit universities made do throughout much of the eighteenth century without a lecture catalogue. More modernizing German Catholic ministries, however, began imitating Protestants in order to become enlightened, as they put it at the time. They ordered their universities to print lecture catalogues which, as we'll see later, had to do in part with publicity. The enlightened needs of academic policing and publicity—the needs of ministries and markets—dovetailed marvelously in the printed lecture catalogue.

### Göttingen's "Scientific, Systematic" Catalogue

Important changes in the structure of the lecture catalogue came in the eighteenth century. In 1789 a Prussian minister and academic, Friedrich Gedike, visited fourteen universities outside Prussia on commission of the king. In his report, Gedike noted of the University of Göttingen, as though it were noteworthy:

> In Göttingen two lecture catalogues are printed bi-annually.
> 1. A Latin one in which the professors, ordered one after the other in terms of seniority, announce their lectures. In this catalogue only the professors are listed, and not the lecturers (*Privatdocenten*).
> 2. A German one in terms of a scientific, systematic order (*nach einer wissenschaftlichen systematischen Anordnung*). In this one, all the lecturers are also included.[35]

The first of the Göttingen lecture catalogues that Gedike mentions was the garden-variety catalogue like Basel's above. The second of the Göttingen lecture catalogues that he mentions here was a relative innovation, but in 1789 it should have been no rarity.

In 1748 the periodical *Göttingische Zeitungen von gelehrten Sachen* published a German-language catalogue for summer semester. Prefatory remarks claim that it has been given a nontraditional structure so that everyone would be able to see "how complete the scope of the disciplines offered by our instructors is." The prefatory remark notes that the times of the lectures now set the order of the professors in the catalogue rather than their rank. But, except for a few wrinkles, the catalogue still looks largely like the garden variety we saw above. We have here, nonetheless, a relatively new idea: within each faculty, its work and the disciplines taught structure the parade and not the professors' seniority.[36]

The Göttingen lecture catalogue vacillated thereafter between the new and the old styles until winter semester 1755/56. The German-language Göttingen catalogue then suddenly appeared in a new form. It structured each faculty neither by the seniority of the professors nor the times of the lecture plan, but rather by subjects and disciplines.[37]

This German-language catalogue at Göttingen for 1755/56 opens with a part one, "Knowledge [*Wissenschaft*] in General." Here appear notices about the Göttingen Society of Sciences and about the university library. This rubric is followed by a part two, "Particular Disciplines." Under this, we find the following list with the lectures and classes for each discipline under it— for clarity, I have given the disciplines a lettering from *a* to *j*, not in the original: (a) theology, (b) jurisprudence, (c) medicine, (d) philosophy (*Weltweisheit*), (e) mathematics, (f) history, (g) (Classical) philology, criticism, and antiquities, (h) German language and oratory, (i) other living European languages, (j) physical exercises.

The disciplines under *a* to *c* indicate the superior faculties in the traditional order of academic precedence. The disciplines under *d* to *i* make up the arts and philosophy faculty. At the level of the document as paperwork, however, the listing of the disciplines, above all *d* to *i*, subverts the old faculties. The old juridical order of the catalogue is on its way to a new disciplinary ordering. Here not parading but rather labor will be central.

Under each discipline, *a* to *i*, in the 1755/56 Göttingen catalogue, we find ordinary professors, extraordinary professors and lecturers (*Privatdocenten*) listed not in an order of seniority, but rather in an order of disciplines and subdisciplines, that is, in a rationalized order of academic labor. Figures 2.6 and 2.7 below from the University of Berlin in the nineteenth century well represent this new disciplinary order. The order of precedence that once structured the faculty on parade would come to bedevil the disciplines themselves, as questions arose concerning what the rational order of disciplines would be.[38]

Whence the change to an intrafaculty disciplinary ordering in the Göttingen catalogue in 1755/56? The published explanation seems to be a typical Göttingen propaganda and marketing ploy, to which we'll return in the next section. The following explanation is more likely. In an originally anonymous history of universities, Professor Michaelis at Göttingen explained how it came about that the lecturers began appearing in the Göttingen catalogue. That fact does not concern us here; the grounds behind it rather do: "it began simply because the *Curator* [the Hanoverian minister] at the time, the immortal Mr. von Münchhausen, demanded a tabular list of classes, as a means for easing his correspondence, and the person to whom he entrusted this advised him to include the lectures of the *Privatdocenten*—be it tabular [systematic], as in Göttingen, or alphabetic."[39] In other words, the disciplinary ordering emerged at Göttingen to facilitate ministerial paperwork.

## The Disciplinary Catalogue

Some universities appear to have altered the catalogue of their own accord. In *Erfurtische gelehrte Zeitungen*, a German-language lecture catalogue of the University of Erfurt for 1769 appeared as ordered by disciplines and with the comment, "Following the custom of other universities, we provide . . . [a catalogue] according to the order of the various disciplines" (*in der Ordnung der verschiedenen Wissenschaften*). But then for the next semester, the German catalogue reappeared as ordered by professors with the comment that it appears so "in view of the wishes of some readers." The some readers here were perhaps senior professors at Erfurt who wanted the old parade reinstated.[40]

*Erfurtische gelehrte Zeitungen* claimed to be following the custom of other universities in 1769, but I know of only four that published catalogues ordered by the disciplines by that time (see table 2 in appendix 2). Unlike at Erfurt, a number of such catalogues before and after 1769 appeared explicitly by order of state ministries.

The Prussian ministry ordered the University of Halle in 1768 to produce a lecture catalogue structured by the disciplines from then on. Königsberg received a like order in 1770. The duke elector of Saxony enjoined the University of Leipzig to publish a German-language lecture catalogue. It appeared after July 1773 and was in fact ordered by disciplines, not professorial seniority. On 11 May 1775, a Swedish ministerial visitation commission to the University of Greifswald—under the control of Sweden since 1618—ordered that the rector would henceforth give the chancellor a tabular list of the classes taught that year. This tabular list was to be ordered according to disciplines so that the chancellor could "inspect without effort what has been done or what has been lacking." Most such examples involve a ministerial mandate to the effect that a disciplinary catalogue must be produced. In tune with the times, during the late eighteenth century universities such as Erfurt followed suit, but not all. In the nineteenth century, however, such a disciplinary catalogue became standard.[41]

Figures 2.6 to 2.7 exhibit two pages of the German-language lecture catalogue, ordered by disciplines, for summer semester 1822 from the University of Berlin. The two pages concern the philosophy (and arts and sciences) faculty. The first rubric in figure 2.6 is called "philosophical sciences." The courses

Angewandte Naturgeschichte für Thierärzte und Oekonomen Hr. Dr. Lorinser, viermal wöchentlich.

Die Knochenlehre der Hausthiere, Herr Dr. Neckleben zweymal wöchentlich.

Ueber Geschichte der Heilkunde, Herr Dr. Hecker wöchentlich vier Stunden.

Hippokrates Aphorismen, vorzüglich in Beziehung auf ihre noch Statt findende Anwendung bei dem Heilungs-Verfahren wird Herr Prof. Berends Sonnabends von 10 — 11 Uhr öffentlich in lateinischer Sprache erklären.

Zu einem privatissime zu veranstaltenden Repetitorium u. Disputatorium über medizinische und chirurgische Gegenstände erbietet sich Hr. Dr. Bähr.

Ein Disputatorium über medizinische Gegenstände wird Herr Dr. Hecker wöchentlich in 2 Stunden halten.

Unterricht in den Augenoperationen und in einzelnen Gegenständen der Medizin, Chirurgie und Augenheilkunde wird Hr. Dr. Jüngken privatissime ertheilen.

## Philosophische Wissenschaften.

Die Grundlehren der gesammten Philosophie, Herr Dr. Schopenhauer sechsmal wöchentlich.

Logik und Metaphysik, Herr Prof. Hegel fünfmal wöchentlich um 5 Uhr, nach seinem Lehrbuche: Encyklopädie der philosoph. Wissenschaften §. 12 — 191.

Logik, Herr Dr. Ritter fünfmal wöchentlich Morgens um 7 Uhr.

Die Grundzüge der Dialektik, Herr Prof. Schleiermacher fünfmal des Morgens um 6 Uhr.

Anthropologie und Psychologie, Herr Prof. Hegel viermal wöchentlich um 4 Uhr nach seinem Lehrbuche: Encyklopädie der philosophischen Wissensch. §. 299 — 399. Ueber diese wie über die oben angekündigte Vorlesung des Hr. Prof. Hegel wird Herr Dr. v. Henning zweimal in der Woche Repetitionen nebst Conversatorien halten.

Philosophische Anthropologie, lehrt Herr Dr. Fichte fünfmal um 5 Uhr.

Psychologie Herr Dr. Stiedenroth fünf Stunden wöchentlich von 4 — 5 Uhr.

Die Philosophie des Rechts und Politik Herr Dr. v. Henning fünfmal um 8 Uhr Morgens nach Hegels Grundlinien der Philosophie des Rechts.

Die Sittenlehre Hr. Dr. Fichte viermal wöchentlich.

Aesthetik Hr. Dr. v. Keyserling fünfmal um 8 Uhr.

Geschichte der alten Philosophie erzählt Hr. Dr. Ritter viermal um 6 Uhr.

Geschichte der neuern Philosophie seit Kant Hr. Dr. Fichte zweimal um 12 Uhr.

Geschichte der Philosophie trägt fünfmal wöchentlich von 5–6 Uhr vor Hr. Dr. Stiedenroth.

## Pädagogik.

Pädagogik lehrt Hr. Dr. v. Keyserling dreimal um 9 Uhr.

## Mathematische Wissenschaften.

Reine Mathematik lehrt Hr. Prof. Grüson viermal wöchentlich.

Dieselbe mit besonderer Rücksicht auf den metaphysischen Theil der Mathematik Hr. Dr. Ohm fünfmal um 5 Uhr.

Die Elemente der Arithmetik und der Analysis endlicher Größen verbunden mit einem Examinatorium, Hr. Prof. Ideler wöchentlich sechsmal.

Höhere Geometrie trägt Hr. Prof. Dirksen dreimal vor um 4 Uhr.

Sphärische Astronomie derselbe dreimal um 4 Uhr.

Algebra lehrt Hr. Prof. Grüson viermal wöchentlich.

Algebra und Analysis Hr. Dr. Ohm fünfmal um 5 Uhr.

Die Theorie der Auflösung algebraischer Gleichungen behandelt Hr. Prof. Tralles öffentlich.

Die vorzüglichsten Eigenschaften der Linien und Flächen zweiter Ordnung trägt Derselbe privatim vor.

Von den Kegelschnitten handelt Hr. Prof. Grüson viermal wöchentlich.

Differential- und Integralrechnung trägt Derselbe viermal wöchentlich vor.

Von der Anwendbarkeit der Wahrscheinlichkeitsrechnung auf Naturwissenschaften handelt dreimal wöchentlich privatissime Hr. Prof. Dirksen.

Ueber die analytischen Evolutionen handelt Derselbe öffentlich einmal.

Zu anderen mathematischen Privatissimis erbietet sich Hr. Dr. Ohm.

Ein Disputatorium über die synthetische und analytische Auflösung einiger geometrischen Probleme hält Hr. Mag. Lübbe viermal wöchentlich.

## Naturwissenschaften.

Experimentalphysik lehrt Hr. Prof. Turte viermal wöchentlich von 2 – 4 Uhr.

Ueber Licht und Wärme liest Hr. Prof. Erman wöchentlich dreimal.

Meteorologie, Derselbe wöchentlich dreimal.

Ueber Elektricität, Magnetismus und Licht liest Hr. Prof. Fischer in zwei wöchentlichen Doppelstunden.

Allgemeine Chemie, erläutert durch Experimente, trägt Hr. Dr. Wuttig Mont. Mittw. und Freit. um 9 Uhr vor.

Analytische Chemie der organischen und unorganischen Körper Herr Professor Hermbstädt Mont., Dienst., Mittw. und Donnerst. von 9 bis 10 Uhr.

Dieselbe lehrt Hr. Dr. Wuttig Dienstags und Donnerst. von 5–7 Uhr.

Experimentalchemie Hr. Prof. Turte, Mont. Dienst. Donnerst. und Freit. von 5–6½ Uhr.

Den ersten Theil der Experimentalchemie mit erklärenden Versuchen, trägt Hr. Prof. Mitscherlich Mont., Dienst., Donnerst. und Freit. von 9 – 10 Uhr vor, nach Berzelius Lehrbuche, übersetzt von Bloede, Dresden 1820.

Ueber medizinische Chemie wird Hr. Prof. Hermbstädt seine Vorlesungen öffentlich fortsetzen und die animalischen Körper abhandeln.

Pharmacie mit steter Rücksicht auf die Pharmakopöe lehrt Hr. Prof. Turte Mittw. und Sonnab. von 6 – 8 Uhr. Morgens.

Zu Vorlesungen über medizinische, pharmaceutische, technische und ökonomische Waarenkunde erbietet sich Hr. Prof. Hermbstädt Mont. Mittw. Donnerst. und Freit. um 10 Uhr.

Die Farbenlehre erläutert Hr. Dr. v. Henning wöchentlich zweimal um 12 Uhr nach Göthe.

Allgemeine Naturgeschichte verbunden mit Encyklopädie und Methodologie der Naturwissenschaften lehrt Hr. Prof. Link viermal um 10 Uhr.

Allgemeine Zoologie Hr. Prof. Lichtenstein täglich um 1 Uhr.

Naturgeschichte der Thiere Deutschlands erste Hälfte trägt Derselbe Dienst. Mittw. und Freit. um 5 Uhr vor.

Entomologie lehrt zweimal wöchentlich Hr. Prof. Klug und mit besondere Botanik nebst Demonstrationen und Exkursionen Hr. Prof. Link täglich um 7 Uhr.

Allgemeine Botanik verbunden mit Demonstrationen lebender, insbesondere der mehresten Arzneygewächse lehrt Hr. Prof. Hayne wöchentlich sechsmal um 11 Uhr.

Forstbotanik Derselbe wöchentlich viermal um 9 Uhr.

Botanische Exkursionen stellt derselbe wöchentlich einmal mit seinen Zuhörern an.

Den zweiten Theil des mineralogischen Kursus mit Examinationsübungen verbunden trägt Hr. Prof. Weiß fünfmal um 12 Uhr vor.

Geognosie, Derselbe viertägig um 9 Uhr.

2.6. *Vorlesungsverzeichnis,* University of Berlin, Summer Semester 1822, p. 3.

## Kameralwiſſenſchaften.

Die Staatswirthſchaft lehrt Hr. Prof. Hoffmann Mont. Dienſt. Donnerſt. und Freitags um 6 Uhr.

Die Grundſätze der Polizeigeſetzgebung Derſelbe an denſelben Tagen um 4 Uhr.

Politiſche Arithmetik Derſelbe Mittw. und Sonnab. um 12 Uhr.

Dieſelbe Hr. Dr. Ohm fünfmal um 4 Uhr.

Allgemeine Technologie trägt Hr. Prof. Hermbſtädt wöchentlich fünfmal um 8 Uhr nach ſeinem Grundriſſe vor und wird wöchentlich eine technologiſche Exkurſion veranſtalten.

Chemiſche Fabrikenkunde lehrt Hr. Dr. Wattig wöchentlich zweimal.

Vom Waldbau handelt Hr. Prof. Pfeil Mont. Dienſt. Donnerſt. und Freit. um 8 Uhr.

Von der Forſtbenutzung und Forſttechnologie Derſelbe viermal um 9 Uhr an denſelben Tagen.

Vom Forſtſchutze Derſelbe Mittw. und Sonnab. um 9 Uhr.

Die Jagdlehre trägt Derſelbe an denſelben Tagen um 8 Uhr vor.

## Hiſtoriſche Wiſſenſchaften.

Allgemeine Erdkunde lehrt Hr. Prof. Ritter fünfmal um 12 Uhr.

Alte Geſchichte Hr. Prof. v. Raumer viermal um 12 Uhr.

Deutſche Geſchichte Hr. Prof. Wilken nach ſeinem Handbuche der Deutſchen Geſchichte, Heidelberg 1810 fünfmal um 8 Uhr.

Vaterlandskunde lehrt Hr. Prof. Zeune wöchentlich zweimal.

Allgemeine Geſchichte der neuern Zeit Hr. Prof. Wilken viermal um 7 Uhr.

Geſchichte des achtzehnten Jahrhunderts und der Franzöſiſchen Revolution Hr. Prof. v. Raumer viermal um 4 Uhr.

Statiſtik der Europäiſchen Staaten nach Meuſel mit beſonderer Rückſicht auf Verfaſſung und Verwaltung Derſelbe viermal um 11 Uhr.

Statiſtik der Europäiſchen Staaten Hr. Dr. Stein Montags und Donnerſt. von 5—7 Uhr.

Ueber die bei den alten Völkern, den Aegyptern, Babyloniern, Griechen und Römern gebräuchliche Art der Zeiteintheilung Hr. Prof. Ideler fünfmal wöchentlich.

## Kunſtgeſchichte.

Ueber die Geſchichte, die Grundſätze und erhaltenen Denkmäler der antiken bildenden Kunſt lieſt Hr. Prof. Tölken um 12 Uhr.

Hr. Prof. Hirt wird ſeine Vorleſungen zur rechten Zeit am ſchwarzen Brett anzeigen.

## Philologie.

Allgemeine Geſchichte der Sprachen trägt Hr. Prof. Bopp zweimal wöchentlich vor.

Den zweiten Theil der Griechiſchen Grammatik wird Hr. Dr. Wolf, Mitglied d. Akad. d. W., viermal wöchentlich um 2 Uhr vortragen.

Die Metrik lehrt Hr. Prof. Böckh viermal wöchentlich Mont. Dienſt. Donnerſt. und Freit. von 9—10 Uhr.

Ariſtophanes zwei oder drei Komödien wird Hr. Dr. Wolf, Mitglied d. Akad. d. W., viermal wöchentlich in einer Vormittagsſtunde erklären.

Die Republik des Platon erklärt Hr. Prof. Böckh in Verbindung mit einer Einleitung in Platons Schriften und Phi-

loſophie wöchentlich viermal, Mont. Dienſt. Donnerſt. Freit. v. 10—11 Uhr.

Des Apollonius von Alexandria Buch vom Aeonom. Hr. Prof. Bekker nach ſeiner Ausgabe vier Stunden wöchentlich.

Des Terentius Andria und Eunuchus wird Herr Prof. Böckh erklären und zugleich die Silbenmaaße der älteren Römiſchen Dramatiker erläutern, 4mal wöchentlich Montags Mittwochs, Donnerſtags und Sonnabends von 11 — 12 Uhr priuatim.

Das Weſen der bei den alten Dichtern, beſonders den Römiſchen, erwähnten Auf- und Untergänge der Geſtirne wird Hr. Prof. Ideler Mittwochs und Sonnabends von 12—1 öffentlich erklären, und die dahin gehörigen Stellen des Faſti des Ovid erläutern.

Arabiſche Grammatik lehrt Herr Prof. Bopp viermal wöchentlich um 5 Uhr.

Sanskrit-Grammatik, Derſelbe viermal um 6 Uhr.

Die Anfangsgründe der Syriſchen Sprache lehrt Herr Lic. Tholuck zweimal die Woche öffentlich.

Derſelbe erbietet ſich zum Unterricht in der Hebräiſchen, Arabiſchen und Perſiſchen Sprache privatiſſime.

Ueber die Quellen der Gedichte des Hans Sachs lieſet Herr Prof. Schmidt Sonnabends um 11 Uhr.

Calderons Schauſpiel el magico prodigioso erklärt derſelbe Montags, Mittwochs, Donnerſtags und Sonnabends um 12 Uhr (nach der kleinen Zwickauer Ausgabe) und verbindet damit eine Einleitung in die ſämmtlichen Werke des Calderon.

---

Herr Lector Franceſon wird unentgeltlich einige Geſänge des Orlando furioso von Arioſt erklären einmal wöchentlich um 1 Uhr.

Desgleichen Racine's Luſtſpiel les plaideurs einmal wöchentlich um dieſelbe Zeit.

Derſelbe wird höhere Stilübungen in der Franzöſiſche Sprache anſtellen und dabei Schillers Geſchichte des dreißigjährigen Krieges überſetzen laſſen.

Herr Lector Dr. v. Seymour wird Youngs Gedicht zweimal wöchentlich von 4 — 5 Uhr erklären und von der Engliſchen Ausſprache handeln.

Derſelbe erbietet ſich zum Privatunterricht im Engliſchen.

In der Muſik unterrichtet Herr Klein unentgeltlich.

Unterricht im Fechten und Voltigiren giebt der Fechtmeiſter Felmy.

Unterricht im Reiten wird auf der königl. Reitbahn ertheilt.

## Oeffentliche gelehrte Anſtalten.

Die königl. Bibliothek iſt zum Gebrauch der Studirenden täglich offen. Die Sternwarte, der botaniſche Garten, das anatomiſche, zootomiſche und zoologiſche Muſeum, das Mineralienkabinet, die Sammlung chirurgiſcher Inſtrumente und Bandagen, die Sammlung von Gyps Abgüſſen und verſchiedenen kunſtreichen Merkwürdigkeiten werden zum Theil bei den Vorleſungen benutzt und können zum Theil von Studirenden, die ſich gehörigen Orts melden, beſucht werden.

Die exegetiſchen Uebungen des theologiſchen Seminars leitet Herr Prof. Dr. Schleiermacher, die kirchen- und dogmenhiſtoriſchen Uebungen leiten Herr Prof. Dr. Marheinecke und Herr Prof. Dr. Neander.

Im philologiſchen Seminar wird Hr. Prof. Böckh Mittwochs und Sonnabends von 10 — 11 Uhr den Euripides lateiniſch erklären laſſen und die übrigen Uebungen der Mitglieder leiten.

Hr. Dr. Buttmann, Mitglied der Akademie der Wiſſenſchaften, wird die Mitglieder des Seminars in der Auslegung des Horaz Mittwochs und Sonnabends von 9 — 10 Uhr üben.

---

2.7. *Vorlesungsverzeichnis,* University of Berlin, Summer Semester 1822, p. 4.

above this are from the medical faculty. Philosophy per se thus claims pride of first place in the philosophy faculty. Next appears pedagogy, with just one lecture. Then follow mathematics, natural sciences, cameral sciences, historical sciences, art history, and (classical) philology. As in the Basel catalogues above, modern languages, music, and physical exercises appear still last and least.

The lecture catalogue in this form offers a means for the ministry to supervise academic labor. One of its aims and probable effects was to bring academics to conceive of themselves as workers and especially as specialists. As we saw, policies of the German police state served to extract the category of labor from that of academic life. Such policies helped to dissolve the traditional, juridico-ecclesiastical space of academic charisma, embodied in the catalogue of professors, and to replace it with the new rationalized, politico-economic regime displayed in the catalogue of disciplines, a list of labors.

In keeping with such good policing, the enlightened cameralist Johann Justi, in his *Foundations of Police-Science* (*Grundsätze der Policeywissenschaft*), called for ministerial supervision of university lectures, and by implication supervision of the catalogue, too. "Just as all parts of learning must be taught together at a university that would attract students to it, so too must a rational division of lectures be made. To this end, all instructors must report their upcoming lectures on time, so that one [that is, the ministry] can judge whether there is a lack in the presentation of this or that discipline." A disciplinary lecture catalogue allowed the ministrial gaze to discern what topics were being taught and what were not. When enlightened ministries apprehended "a lack in the presentation of this or that discipline," they could intervene. They did, as we shall see.[42]

Whether disciplinary lecture catalogues appeared at the direct behest of state ministries or not, such catalogues reflected ministerial mentalities. The perfection of the police state would only arrive—and make it seem as though that state had disappeared—once its subjects internalized its values and policed themselves. Thus it would have been better if German academics had hit on the idea of the disciplinary catalogue without any ministerial intervention. It would show that policing had achieved its aim to alter academic manners and produce the new sort of rationalized academic persona envisaged by the ministry.

## PUBLICITY

The interests of ministries and markets dovetailed, as noted, in publicity. A published lecture catalogue—a periodical—perfected the catalogue as a politico-economic report.

## Publication

On 20 October 1805, the Austrian *Studienhofkommission,* the ministry for education, enjoined all Austrian universities to produce a lecture catalogue henceforth and to include the textbooks used. On 14 May 1810 the ministry returned to this important matter and explicitly explained the dual purpose of the published catalogue. It functioned as a report to the ministry, so as to insure that universities were adhering to guidelines about lectures, and it also served to make the university known, *bekannt zu machen.*[43]

The Austrian lands had resisted most academic innovations of Protestant Germany far longer than the Catholic parts of what was to become Bismarckian Germany, the Second Reich. But in the first half of the nineteenth century, the Austrians, too, would begin casting their academics in the market—a process only completed after the great turmoil of 1848.

A Jesuitical past informed Austrian resistance. The Jesuits had kept pace with Protestant universities in the sixteenth century (see appendix 2, list 1 and table 1). Contemporary reports indicate that the Jesuits used these early catalogues, in the words then of the dean of the Cologne arts faculty, as advertisements, *Werbung.* As such they formed part of the propaganda of the Counter-Reformation. The very first published lecture catalogue, of which I know, appeared at Wittenberg in 1507, antedating the Reformation by a decade. But Wittenberg's rector clearly intended the 1507 catalogue as a marketing device. As propaganda and panegyric, the rector's preface to the catalogue praised, among other things, the quality of the air and the "humanity" of the burghers in Wittenberg.[44]

A number of German universities published lecture catalogues in the sixteenth century, but only one did so one regularly (see appendix 2). After an initial spate of publication, especially the Jesuits appear to have ceased. Jesuit colleges and universities had been new foundations or reformations of existing ones. Lecture catalogues appeared in part to announce that. Among the Protestants, Marburg and Jena were fairly new foundations and issued their catalogues in the same spirit. The Wittenberg catalogue of 1507 appeared five years after that university opened and served as a vehicle to market the new university. When Leipzig issued a catalogue in 1518, Luther remarked that it had done so in imitation of Wittenberg, that is, to compete with it. When the curriculum settled down again and was fixed in statutes after the Reformation and Counter-Reformation, Protestant academics and Jesuits generally appear not to have set much store in regular publication of the catalogue.[45]

Protestant ministries, however, took an evident interest in the publication of the catalogue, even if they did not keep up constant supervision. From the sixteenth century onward, statutory revisions for universities and subsequent ministerial decrees to universities enjoined that lecture catalogues be published and posted. Some of these statutes and decrees went so far as to stipulate that the published catalogues appear in advance of the annual bookfairs in Frankfurt am Main (a.M.) or Leipzig. In the eighteenth century, as each province or university town acquired its own newsletter or learned journal, ministerial decrees commonly ordered universities to publish their lecture catalogues in such periodicals.[46]

## The Periodical

The Enlightenment was the age of the periodical. It was as well the age when the lecture catalogue became a regular fixture in academia, at least in the Germanies. The great historian of German periodicals, Joachim Kirchner, circumscribed the genre of the early and especially the academic periodical as an odd sort of never-ending book.

A periodical or journal is a work that appears periodically, though not necessarily regularly, and without an end envisaged, thus possibly to appear forever. The contents are public, as opposed to private correspondence or reports, and appear each time with a certain identity and unity of form and content, which are achieved by the editor, even though the content in fact varies from issue to issue, and even though such formal aspects as the title and editor might change. The parts of a periodical form a mere collectivity or aggregate, as opposed to the envisaged integration or organic wholeness of a normal book; and its audience is not identical with the public per se, that is, is not the envisaged universal audience of the newspaper (or, similarly, the police ordinance).[47]

In light of the above, the lecture catalogue was arguably one of the original academic periodicals, if not the original one, albeit with minimalist contents. In the seventeenth century or even earlier, some lecture catalogues had begun appearing on a semiannual or annual basis. To be sure, given the nature of the early periodical, a great hiatus in publication might often appear. In its form as in figures 2.2 and 2.3, the catalogue was most suitable for posting, like a handbill. In the course of the eighteenth century, the catalogue grew to include more and more pages, especially in its disciplinary form. It became a small periodical pamphlet. The regular appearance of the lecture catalogue went hand in hand with the regular change of the curriculum. The latter did not simply lead to the former. The regular catalogue and the changing curriculum served as mutual cause and effect of each other. The periodical press of the eighteenth century necessitated novelty even in academia for its eternal issues.[48]

In 1731 the Prussian ministry wrote to the University of Halle on the semesterly publication of its lecture catalogue. The ministry said that "a catalogue should be brought to everyone's attention by publication." The ministry ordered that professors meet the Mondays before the Leipzig Easter and autumn book fairs to hammer out the catalogue in time for publication and distribution at the fairs. Professors who could not attend the meeting were required to submit their lecture schedule in advance.[49]

The university proved itself, in this case, ahead of its own rationalizing ministry. In 1729 in *Wöchentliche Hallische Anzeige*, the University of Halle published the first (if we neglect a few anomalous cases) German-language lecture catalogue. Thereafter, the university regularly published its lecture catalogue in German in this local academic periodical. Other universities began to follow suit in their own or in relevant newsletters or journals.[50]

In 1748 the University of Göttingen did likewise. It published a German catalogue in *Göttingische Zeitungen von gelehrten Sachen*, as noted above. In its retitled *Göttingische Anzeigen von gelehrten Sachen*, the university organized the German-language catalogue by disciplines in 1755, also as noted above. The stated reason for this step was not the one later revealed by historian Michaelis who wrote that Minister von Münchhausen in Hanover wanted a tabular overview of the lectures. The stated reason was rather that fathers of prospective students had written asking whether the university taught such and such a topic. According to the putative account, the university had resolved to publish a catalogue both in German and organized by disciplines, since such an ordering seemed better in view of prospective students and their fathers' interests.[51]

So the catalogue was ministerial paperwork and academic publicity, an overview of academic labor and a marketing device that put work and wares, not persons, on display.

## False Advertising and the Market

In 1798 an exposé of lecture catalogues appeared. In *Über öffentliche Lehrveranstalten insbesondere über Lektionskataloge auf Universitäten*, the anonymous author explained that the lecture catalogue, as a technique of publicity, often ended up as false advertising. Many courses advertised never took place—often due to a want of students. Such lecture catalogues, he explained, resembled an apothecary shop in which the jars contained false contents or, worse, nothing. As an instrument of publicity, the lecture catalogue had become a domain where false seduction and propaganda reigned.[52]

That caused paperwork problems. It shows why ministries demanded reports about which of the classes advertised actually had been taught to completion, and which not. In the survey report of 1789 cited above, the Prussian minister Gedike noted that the Göttingen disciplinary lecture catalogue included the lecturers, adding that most lecturers appeared there "only for appearance's sake." Seldom did a mere lecturer get enough students to make his advertised class feasible to conduct. In the same vein, a notorious publicist for Göttingen, a certain Boell or Böll, wrote, "Deceitful [lecture] catalogues are like much promising restaurants in which one is either served nothing or but poorly."[53]

Why were so many classes advertised but not offered? Figures 2.2 and 2.3 above show that many Basel professors taught private courses along with their public lectures. Public courses were open to the academic public and free of charge. After the reforms of the sixteenth century, ordinary professors held public lectures in their role as salaried professors.

The public lectures were supposedly held every semester, or every year, or at least regularly. They formed the stable part of the curriculum, and were the descendents of the medieval "ordinary" books or topics required for degrees. The state graced the public lectures with good policing. Professors were fined for canceling such lectures. Private courses remained an entrepreneurial undertaking. For those courses, a student would have to pay the professor a fee, set by the professor. It was a bit like the medieval system, except that now professors themselves set the fees. And a professor could refuse admission to anyone, and could also alter the private or extraordinary courses every semester, or cancel them at will.

The classes taught privately were commodities in the free market of letters. Like a popular play, a trendy private class could catch a tidy or even a handsome fee. Such private classes had to interest the student as a consumer, whose demands they in part created. Such private classes were above all the ones that needed a regular lecture catalogue. But many of the private courses never took place because not enough students attended them. Private classes advertised in lecture catalogues frequently resembled a theatrical production that failed to secure an audience large enough to make it viable for more than one performance.

Ordinary and extraordinary professors taught private classes in order to supplement their salaries, which were seldom sufficient to support intelligent life. Early modern lecturers, the *Privat-Docenten* (which later became *Privatdozenten*), moreover, were academics who aspired to a professorial position, but who had no academic salary per se, and who pursued in the meantime a modern medieval (or vice versa) existence, living from fees obtained by teaching such private classes. The same was often or even typically also true of the extraordinary professors. As we saw above, such professors worked outside the ordinary funding or budget.

When Minister Gedike said that many of the lecturers in the Göttingen disciplinary lecture catalogue appeared there only for appearance's sake, he meant that, due to lack of students, most lecturers had to cancel their offerings each semester. The philosopher Immanuel Kant in Könisgberg, for instance, advertised at times more classes than was believably possible to give, in the words of one historian. Academics overadvertised to see what the market would bear. And such a catalogue made a seductive bit of marketing to send to unwise fathers.[54]

The anonymous author of 1798 above meant this, in part, when he called lecture catalogues a domain of false advertising. But he also meant that many of the public lectures were also not given—a scandal. If ministers relaxed their vigilance, lazy professors tried to shirk their duties by canceling their public lectures and teaching only privately for extra cash.

## The Competition of Academic Entrepreneurs

After the temporary suppression of the Jesuits in 1773, some Catholic, non-Austrian universities began, as they put it, to enlighten themselves. Many took Göttingen as a model. A reform proposal, written circa 1777 and sent to the bishop elector of Mainz, recommended not only producing a regular lecture catalogue, but also having more than one lecture on major topics in each faculty, in order to foster competition. That had been the policy at enlightened, entrepreneurial Göttingen, where everyone was allowed to compete with each other in attracting the student body.[55]

Ordinary and extraordinary Göttingen professors and even lecturers could teach private classes that competed with the public lectures of other ordinary professors. And everyone could offer private courses on whatever they wanted, within reason of course. Proud ordinary professors felt driven to compete to keep rich students (like sausages, a Göttingen specialty) in their own free lectures, and away from the private classes of rival and up-and-coming extraordinary professors and lecturers, who might be awaiting the ordinary professor's demise.[56]

Things became more complex in the nineteenth century. Figures 2.8 and 2.9 show two pages of the philosophy faculty listed in a Latin lecture catalogue from the University of Berlin, summer semester 1821. Figure 2.8 is page 12 of the catalogue and lists the first ordinary professors of the faculty.

# IV. ORDINIS PHILOSOPHICI.

### 1. Professorum ordinariorum.

**G. W. F. HEGEL, Dr. Dec.**

Privatim 1. *Logicam et metaphysicam* duce libro suo (Encyclopaedie'der philosophischen Wissenschaften §. 12 — 191.) quinquies p. hebd. hor. V — VI. 2. *Philosophiam religionis* dieb. Lun. Mart. Iov. et Ven. hor. IV — V. exponet.

**I. BEKKER, Dr.**

*Demosthenis Isocratisve orationem unam et alteram* critice interpretabitur.

**A. BOECKH, Dr.**

Privatim 1. *Historiam litteraturae Graecae* enarrabit ad Passovii librum quinquies p. hebd. d. Lun. Mart. Merc. Iov. Ven. h. XI — XII. 2. *Terentii Andriam* et *Eunuchum* interpretabitur, et *metra, quibus prisci Romanorum poetae scenici usi sunt,* una explicabit, quater p. hebd. d. Lun. Mart. Iov. Ven h. III — IV. 3. *Pindari Pythia, Nemea, Isthmia* ex sua editione minore interpretabitur quater p. hebd. d. Lun. Mart. Iov. Vener. h. X — XI.

**P. ERMAN, Dr.**

Privatim 1. de *magnetismo, electricitate* et *galvanismo* disseret. 2. *Atmosphaerologiam meteorologicam* docebit.

**S. F. HERMBSTAEDT, Dr.**

I. Publice *lectiones chemicas medicas* dieb. Merc. et Sat. hor. XI — XII. persecuturus *corpora metallica* demonstrabit. II. Privatim 1. *Technologiam universam* duce libro suo: Grundrifs der Technologie, sexies p. hebd. hor. mat. VIII — IX. exponet ac semel p. hebd. *excursiones technologicas* instituet. 2. *Chemiam analyticam corporum organicorum et anorganicorum* d. Lun. Mart. Merc. et Iov. hor. IX — X. explicabit et experimentis illustrabit.

**A. HIRT, Dr.**

Lectiones tempestive indicabit.

**M. H. LICHTENSTEIN, Dr.**

Privatim 1. *Zoologiam universam* sexies p. hebd. hor. I — II. 2. *Ichthyologiam* dieb. Lun. Ven. hor. V — VI. tradet.

**F. de RAUMER, Dr.**

1. *Statisticam* duce Meuselio hor. XI — XII. 2. *Historiam antiquam* hor. XII — I. 3. *Historiam saeculi XVIII.* imprimisque turbarum Gallicarum inde ab anno MDCCLXXXIX. hor. IV — V. tradet.

**I. G. TRALLES, Dr.**

I. Publice *doctrinam aequilibrii solidorum et fluidorum* exponet dieb. Lun. et Iov. hor. III — IV.

2.8. *Index lextionum,* University of Berlin, Summer Semester 1821, p. 12.

**H. RITTER, Dr.**

Gratis docebit *Logicen* quater per hebd. horis adhuc definiendis.

**F. G. V. SCHMIDT, Dr.**

I. Gratis *Horatii epistolam de arte poetica* explicabit d. Merc. h. V — VI. II. Privatim *historiam poesis dramaticae, et veteris et recentioris* enarrabit d. Lun. Mart. Iov. Ven. hor. V — VI.

**A. SCHOPENHAUER, Dr. .**

Privatim *philosophiae universae,* sive doctrinae de essentia mundi et mente humana *principia* ac *fundamenta* explicabit, quinquies p. hebd. hora V — VI. et die Saturni hor. XII — I.

**C. G. D. STEIN, Dr.**

Privatim *statisticam civitatum Europae primariarum* exponet secuturus librum suum (Handbuch der Geographie und Statistik) dieb. Lun. et Iov. hor. V — VII.

**E. STIEDENROTH, Dr.**

Privatim tradet 1. *Encyclopaediam philosophicam et logicam* sexies p. hebd. hor. VII — VIII. 2. *Metaphysicam* quinquies p. hebd. hor. XII — I. 3. *Psychologiam* quinquies p. hebd. h. V — VI.

**I. F. C. WUTTIG, Dr.**

1. *Hylognosiam* ternis p. hebd. h. docebit et experimentis illustrabit. 2. *Technologiam chemicam* ex suis schedis ternis p. hebd. h. tradet.

---

## RECENTIORUM LINGUARUM DOCTRINA ARTIUMQUE GYMNASTICARUM EXERCITATIO.

**C. F. FRANCESON, Lector,** gratis horis adhuc indicandis interpretari perget 1. *Dantis Aligherii divinam comoediam* semel in hebd. 2. *Cornelii tragoedias,* quarum interpretationi Voltarii comm..ntarium adiiciet, semel in hebd. Idem litterarum recentiorum studiosis scholas offert privatissimas *Gallicas, Italicas, Hispanicas.*

Linguae *Anglicae scholas* offert C. A. E. DE SEYMOUR, **Dr.** Lector, qui gratis *Popii carmina* bis p. h. horis indicandis interpretabitur, et *de pronunciatione Anglica* disseret.

*Musicam* docebit KLEIN.

*Arma tractandi* et *in equum insiliendi* artem docebit FELMY.

*Equitandi modos* discere cupientibus copiam faciet HIPPODROMUS REGIUS.

---

2.9. *Index lextionum,* University of Berlin, Summer Semester 1821, p. 15.

Figure 2.9 is page 15 and lists the last lecturers of the same faculty. In between them, on pages 13 and 14, not reproduced here, the extraordinary professors appear, as well as the first lecturers. In this nineteenth-century Latin catalogue, academics no longer appear by seniority.

The first person in figure 2.8 is none other than the philosopher Hegel. He comes first because he is the dean (next to his name is "Dr. Dec.")—so mighty still is the charisma of office. After the dean come the ordinary professors. They now appear alphabetically instead of by seniority. The extraordinary professors also march among themselves alphabetically, as do the lecturers. Modern, egalitarian sentiments have come into play here. Excepting the archaic charisma of office vested in the dean, the traditional authority of seniority and academic precedence have given way to the arbitrariness of the alphabet.

Many professors such as Hegel here only teach private classes this term. For example, Hegel is teaching logic and metaphysics privately on weekdays from five to six in the evening. In figure 2.9, the third lecturer from the top is the philosopher Schopenhauer. He is also teaching philosophy privately on weekdays from five to six in the evening. As the story goes, this was one of the semesters when the youthful Schopenhauer purposely and notoriously scheduled his lectures at the same time as Hegel's, to compete with him for the student body. For boldly risking this academic competition, Schopenhauer found, however, no body in his private class, alas.

Figure 2.6 above reproduces the German disciplinary catalogue from Berlin, one year later, summer semester 1822. On the left side, under "Philosophische Wissenschaften," the second class listed is Hegel's on logic and metaphysics, again. He still teaches it weekdays from 5:00 to 6:00 p.m. Hegel's class stands near the top of the list not because of his seniority or his fame, but because his class is a general as opposed to a specific one. The first class listed here is Schopenhauer's class on the foundations of philosophy. This comes first for the same reason that Hegel's stands listed near the top: it is a general or introductory class. In place of an ancient parade, now a systematic, rational order informs the German disciplinary catalogue.

In the disciplinary catalogue, a lowly lecturer might precede an august professor. After Schopenhauer had failed to attract anyone by competing with Hegel the previous year, in this semester Schopenhauer, although offering the same class again, now left the time open. The anecdote is a lesson about academic labor, entrepreneurs, and the new charisma.

## CONCLUSION

The lecture catalogue is a marvelous literary genre. If one had to save one and only one academic genre for alien anthropologists and interplanetary culturologists, one would be best advised—at the loss of university statutes, matriculation registers, and even academic satires—to save the lecture catalogues, the great subconscious of the academic world.

In the modern era, academic charisma would be preserved. It would not fall wholly victim to the disenchantment of the world wrought by bureaucratization and rationalizing processes generally. The ministries of the early modern German police state did work hard, even overtime and nights, to dissolve much of the archaic charisma and traditional authority vested in academic faculties as kindreds, guilds, chapters, and colleges, with their deans and so on. Ministries did try to dissolve the corporate, collegial academic identity evident in the Basel lecture catalogues with which we began. German ministers most certainly sought to exterminate the mentality embodied in Cambridge on parade and its charmed costumes.

But academic charisma reemerged in the market—whence the anecdote of Hegel and Schopenhauer in the German and Latin lecture catalogues of 1821/22 Berlin. We shall have to attend to things like competition, novelty, fame, fashion—as well as being à la mode and a genius.

# 3

## The Lecture
## and the Disputation

The two essential academic activities from medieval Scholasticism up to nineteenth-century Romanticism were the lecture and the disputation. These had been modeled on the sermon and the joust. Other academic activities were modulations of or ancillary to them. Despite innovations in the Enlightenment and Romantic era, the lecture has remained more the same than it has changed since the Scholastics, or even since Aristotle and the Peripatetics.

Disputation has drastically changed since the Middle Ages. Much that we shall consider in the four chapters after this—the examination (chapter 4), the seminar (chapter 5), the dissertation (chapter 6), and the professorial publication (chapter 7)—developed from or around the disputation. Those chapters will trace the advent of the modern academic from the alteration of disputational practices. The matter of writing, the hegemony of the visible and legible over the oral, dominates chapters 4 to 7, as it does chapter 2 (the lecture catalogue) and chapter 8 (the library catalogue), forming sort of bookends for the first part of the book.

The only term comparable to the modern notion of research is "disputation" in its medieval and early modern senses. Disputation was a protean practice. It inhabited the juridico-ecclesiastical sphere of knowledge. Modern research forms part of the politico-economic sphere. It tends to be collaborative. Originality has become central to it. Medieval and early modern knowledge, however, did not seek originality in the modern sense of novelty, but rather in the original sense of stemming-from-the-origin. Traditional academia revolved around orthodoxy. It was homiletic and agonistic. It was oral and dialogical. It concerned the disputation of canonical texts read aloud in the lectures.[1]

We'll begin with the medieval lecture, and then move to the disputation.

In the second part of this chapter, we'll repeat the same movement from lecture to disputation for the early modern era.

## THE MEDIEVAL REGIME

### The Sermon

Here is a paraphrase of a medieval description of an ideal lecture hall.

---

The house to be used as a school should be located where the air is fresh and pure. It should be set off so that women cannot visit it continually. It should be removed from the bustle of the square, from the galloping of horses, the squeaking of coaches, the barking of dogs, and above all from everyday uproars. The lecture hall should be in the top floor. It should be wide and long enough and obtainable by a convenient staircase. It should have enough windows for lighting and airing. The walls should be painted uniformly green. There should be no paintings on the wall, since they might distract attention. The lecture hall should have only one entrance. The lectern (*cathedra*) should be located so that the lecturer can see all who enter. The lecturer must be able to have a view of trees, a garden and a meadow, since viewing nature strengthens memory. All seats for the students should be of the same height, so that all can see the lecturer sitting elevated above them. The better and more famous students should be seated, however, together in the more dignified spots. Excepting the places reserved in view of office, nobility, and merit, everyone should be seated with those of their own province or nation. The order of seating should not vary and no one should be allowed to occupy a different seat. Each should always sit in the assigned seat. I have never seen a hall constructed in this manner, but think one should be.[2]

---

Thus an ideal lecture hall as described in the early thirteenth century. The layout of the lecture hall cleaves it into two perspectives: the lecturer and the audience. The lecturer alone sits elevated and has a view of the only entrance. The lecturer has a view outside, of greenery, which matches the color of the bare walls. The walls direct the students' attention to the lecturer, while the latter's view of nature aids his concentration, or so one thought. Hierarchy and nationality articulate the audience, which is unified in seemingly passive opposition to the lecturer. Individuals of the same locality or nationality sit together, while nobles and other personalities receive the places of greater dignity, not spelled out here. One and all in the hall

3.1. Heinrich the German's lecture hall by Laurentinus de Voltolina.

have assigned seats and must remain in them thereafter, including the immobile lecturer. This scholastic hall reflects the ideals of a hierarchical society.

HEINRICH THE GERMAN'S HALL. Figure 3.1 is a black and white
reproduction of a painting by Laurentinus de Voltolina. It shows a lecture
given by Heinrich the German in Bologna, circa 1380. The hall does not ful-
fill the ideal above. Windows on the wall give auditors a chance to be dis-
tracted. Excepting the floor, not distinguishable here, no greenery is offered
to the lecturer. The walls are various shades of red, but at least are bare. The
elevated chair resembles an episcopal *cathedra,* the place from which the
bishop gave the sermon. The image seems to set the audience at one level,
though a slight inclination upwards from front to rear might be suggested
by the curvature of the pews.

The audience in figure 3.1 consists of twenty-four individuals. As recommended in the ideal lecture hall above, as well as being the actual norm
up through the eighteenth century, nobles and persons of elevated charisma
have the best places. Here it is in terms of front to rear. The bearded gentleman in the front pew might be the tutor of the auditor next to him, as might

be the bearded one facing the audience like the lecturer—that would explain the beards. (But what of the one in last pew?) The headdress also goes
downscale from front to rear. With an aquiline and even feminine visage,
the auditor in the middle of the front pew, for instance, sports a *cappuccio*,
stylish in the Italian Renaissance. Besides seats, beards, and hats, books and
attention differentiate members of the audience by status, class, or wealth.

The lecturer has a book, as the practice of the medieval lecture was to
read aloud. The book is not a printed one; the press had not yet been invented. Whoever could afford it in the audience might purchase the relevant book or manuscript, read by the lecturer or reader. One followed the
text that the lecturer read aloud, digested, and commented on. The possession of such a book or text at the time, even if only for the period of one's
studies, would have indicated wealth, and in this figure, the number of
books drops off from the front to the rear of the hall.

Those in closest proximity to the lecturer seem to be paying the most attention. The third pew, or second from the rear, has particularly interesting
people. The person closest to view is sleeping or retching. The person next
to him has a book and seems to listen. The third and fourth persons are facing each other and not the lecturer. The fifth person exhibits industry, the
inverse of the first person in his pew, and is the only one writing in this hall.
Since attention seems greater in the front two and side pews, the image intimates that those of higher social standing pay most attention—a curious
notion, today at least.

A sole note taker in the entire auditorium, amid a fair number of book-
readers, indicates the provenance of the lecture in the sermon. One does not
typically take notes at a Christian church service. The note taker may be
writing on paper, which had appeared in Europe by way of Islam in the
twelfth century. Note-taking, like book-owning, was neither a necessity nor
a frivolity at the early university. The note taker is perhaps preparing a transcript for the lecturer for future use, or for rental via the *pecia* system,
whereby students rented a manuscript piece by piece to copy it at home. But
on the whole, medieval training focused on memory. And it remained
mostly oral-aural, as we'll see more below.[3]

THE SCHOLASTIC LITURGY. In the High Middle Ages, much of
the curriculum was Aristotelian, while the style of lecturing ceased being
peripatetic. Tradition has it that Aristotle walked back and forth in his
lyceum while lecturing. His pupils imitated him, whence the Greek "peripatetic"—to wander—as an appellation for Aristotelians. The high medieval universities enshrined what had probably been the rule since the
Early Middle Ages at least in the cathedral schools: the master remained

immobile and, eventually, elevated at a *cathedra*, as depicted in Heinrich the German's lecture hall in figure 3.1.[4]

The *cathedra* or chair instantiates, signifies, and conveys charisma in the juridico-ecclesiastical academic regime. As noted in chapter 1, the professorial chair not only resembles but also traces its lineage, by way of the secular canon's chair or *cathedra*, to a bishop's chair, an episcopal chair. Only a bishop could occupy the latter legally. The ability to sit lawfully in this chair entailed the ability to speak with recognized authority on orthodox and canonical doctrines and to instruct the flock.

Heinrich the German had similar ability: to speak with authority on canonical academic texts, apropos his particular degree. A master or doctor of theology could read and interpret canonical theological texts publicly in lecture. A doctor of jurisprudence could read and interpret canonical juridical texts publicly in lecture, as could doctors of medicine and masters of arts with the texts authorized in their faculties. The lecture, like the sermon, had a liturgical cast and aura. One must be authorized to perform the rite, and must do it in an authorized manner. Only then does the chair convey genuine charisma to the lecturer.

In this book, we are mostly concerned with members of the arts and philosophy faculties. From the High Middle Ages into the early modern era, philosophy included most knowledge beyond the arts, as well as sciences such as the physics of the time. The philosophy in the medieval curriculum centered on Aristotle's until the Late Middle Ages.

At first, specific texts set the curriculum. In time, the curriculum became specified lectures using a set text, which by the Late Middle Ages might have been anti-Aristotelian. The medieval lecture thus at first had treated certain texts as canonical; eventually the topics became canonical. The lectures were supposedly uniform, over certain times and places. This canonical curriculum, the scholastic analogue of the liturgy and calendar, cohered with the cast of the lecture halls. Both reflected the juridico-ecclesiastical academic regime.

List 1 in appendix 1 shows the ordinary lectures and exercises for the master's degree at the University of Leipzig in 1499. Some lectures declare an Aristotelian heritage in their names. *Meteorologica, De caelo, Topics, De generatione* are the names of actual Aristotelian texts. Ethics, Metaphysics, and Politics are also Aristotelian titles that became disciplinary appellations. The list exhibits a text-centered curriculum in which original or derivative texts set a canonical script for lecture.

Figure 3.1 exhibits the performance. The lecturer did what the word means: he read. The text behind the class provided the script. Session by session, the lecturer read aloud from the text and commented on it. From the Middle Ages up to the Romantic period, how lecturers read and commented probably varied widely. A chief option lay in whether one went constantly back and forth between reading and commenting, or whether the session fell into two parts, a reading then a commentary. The latter more resembles a typical sermon. A second principal option consisted in the overall balance of reading versus commenting. Finally, the lecturer had to decide how much glossarial or secondary literature to mention.[5]

The solidarity of the medieval system lay in the supposed uniformity of the lectures or the texts behind them. A lecture in Paris should amount to the same as a lecture in Oxford or Bologna or elsewhere on the same topic. The uniformity of scholastic degrees hinged on that. Ideally, a master or doctor cast in Oxford or Bologna should be able to perform in the scholastic theater as well as one cast in Paris since the same texts supposedly lorded over all. In practice, however, a degree from Paris meant more. Like aristocrats or nobles, the texts traced their authority by their descent from antiquity. Medieval scholars existed to serve these texts, but some came in time to topple them. In between the high medieval and the early modern periods, a battle of books ensued, and perhaps is not as well known as it should be.

THE BATTLE OF THE BOOKS. A scandal of the two ways, the *via antiqua versus via moderna*, marked the fifteenth century and forms a hinge between the medieval and early modern worlds. It marks the first great transformation in the bases of the lecture. For a disputation of the canon occurred—a battle of the books read in lecture.

An academic prologue to the Reformation, the late medieval battle of the two ways subverted scholastic ideals of knowledge by dividing the curriculum into two rival academic liturgies and calendars. From the thirteenth to the fourteenth century, more variation than similarity might have afflicted the curriculum as one moved from Rome to Prague to Paris to Oxford and all the universities in between. But in principle, a canonical liturgy with its orthodoxly established texts or readings obtained throughout pre-Reformation Europe.

During the fourteenth century, however, a controversy broke out in Paris about William of Ockham's modern nominalist philosophy, opposed to the ancient realist orientation. The latter stemmed from glosses on Aristotelian philosophy by Albert the Great and Thomas Aquinas. That dispute, which was about logic and metaphysics, lies beyond our scope. But some social aspects of it are important here and will reemerge later.

The battle of books called for replacing the canonical texts or lectures with a new canon. The first sign of the battle appeared in 1425, when the

University of Cologne resisted an attempt by German electors and princes to impose a curriculum based on the *via moderna* or modern way, in place of the *via antiqua* or ancient way. The controversy spread throughout the German lands in the fifteenth century. Some universities, such as Erfurt where Martin Luther would study, adhered fairly strictly to the *via moderna*, while others, such as Cologne, remained piously loyal to the *via antiqua*. Circa 1425, Cologne even refined its burses or colleges according to the two chief subways of its way. The Bursa Montana taught only Thomism thereafter, while the Laurentina and Kuckana burses or colleges were Albertist—Albert having been the teacher of Thomas. Humanists would mock all this.[6]

Nominalist at its foundation in 1386, Heidelberg offers a nice example of the battle. Attempts to introduce the Aristotelian-Thomistic *via antiqua* in 1444 and 1451 transformed the scholastic dispute into a social controversy. The battle moved into a new phase by 1464, as the rival curricular paths had cloven the colleges and burses into one or the other camp. In 1472 the arts faculty enjoined that no one could switch from one way to another—an attempt to keep the camps apart. The late fifteenth and early sixteenth century saw fistfights between students. Indeed, those in the new realist colleges claimed to have heard nominalists say, "We are thirsty for Realists' blood" and "This sword still needs to eat three Realists."[7]

## The Joust

In the Roman law code of the Emperor Justinian, there is an important passage that concerns the privileges of a crowned athlete or athletic hero in imperial Rome. The code defines an athletic hero as one who had withstood at least three trials of courage in competition. The great medieval Bolognese jurist Bartolus and his pupil Baldus found that important passage in the course of ransacking Rome law to justify privileges for scholars.

The jurists argued that a scholar underwent three trials of courage at the university and, thus, by Roman law was a hero. First, during all one's studies one was tested by masters and doctors. Second, in the private examination one was tried and tested by representatives of the faculty. And, third, in the public examination and disputation one was tried under the auspices of the university and academic public generally. Taking the three steps as trials of courage, Bartolus and Baldus argued that Roman law gave scholars the privileges of a crowned athlete. These jurists could easily liken academic training to athletic competition in imperial Rome because medieval disputation resembled a joust.[8]

THE MARTIAL ARTS. "If it should so happen, which thing God may forbid, that the Master be taken by the Saracens." The Hospitallers had such real worries. Despite the battle of books in the fifteenth century, little evidence exists that academics risked kidnap, capture, or torture by their opponents. Nonetheless, a rhetoric and theater of warfare, combat, trial, and joust have been central to scholastic and academic practices since the twelfth century.[9]

In that century, strange military religious orders, such as the Hospitallers and Templars, came into being. Scholasticism and the medieval university took root in same culture and climate. Monasticism had dominated the intellectual life of the Early Middle Ages. Military metaphors did not fail then, but monks usually battled only against their own demons and unbelievers. Monks pursed knowledge more in the spirit of the Roman notion of the contemplative life, the *vita contemplativa*, not the sophistic-scholastic agonistic life.

Peter Abelard spread the new martial arts of the scholastics. His exploits as a canon secular in the first half of the twelfth century—his persecution by monastic orders, his seduction of his female pupil, Héloïse, his castration by her kin, the burning of his writings—became the stuff of legend. He wrote, "You have since heard of these things, how after the return of my Master to the city [of Paris], our scholars held combats in disputation with him and his disciples, and what fortune gave to us and especially to me in these wars."[10]

Before Abelard's exploits made him legendary and infamous, his disputational skills had made him famous. The novelty of Abelard's mode of disputation lay not in the dialectical method itself. It came, rather, from his subjection of the authoritative texts to that method. The monastic and ascetic discipline of learning—*lectio, meditatio, oratio, contemplatio*—had had ties to meditation, tears, and silence. Abelard and his disciples transmuted this into a loud, dry-eyed, agonistic art—*praelectio, quaesitio, disputatio, determinatio*—with ties to the rhetoric of controversy, polemics, and trials. Abelard spread the fashion of forensic cases of yes and no, *sic et non*, a disputative and synoptic questioning of canonical authorities.[11]

Abelard's method portended danger. He paid a price befitting his hubris. But the emergence of the university in the next two generations made him a victor in death. The method that he championed became, alongside the lecture, the essential method of university instruction. The learned jurisprudence of Scholasticism particularly embraced disputation.

The practice of law in medieval Europe had a martial cast, especially at trials. Those embodied trials of wills, character, and power, as much as, if not more than, trials of fact. European academia acquired its agonistic, polemical, disputational bent from such trials. Ecclesiastical elements inform the lecture, while juridical or judicial etiquettes imbue the disputation. Together, the sermon and the joust embody the juridico-ecclesiastical academic order, and represent different aspects of academic charisma: the prophet and the warrior.

DISPUTATIONAL ROLES. The disputation varied over the near millennium in which it structured academic practices. Here we can consider only the most general aspects; we shall return to the matter in a later chapter. Three roles stood out in a disputation: the presider (*praeses*), the respondent (*respondens*), and the opponents (*opponentes*). One usually disputed preset theses, which could be arbitrarily chosen. The exercise concerned form more than contents.

The presider typically set the theses and presided over the disputation. The presider had to be a master or doctor. The respondents and opponents might be anyone, but were usually scholars (a juridical title for matriculated students), bachelors, masters, or doctors. The respondent usually affirmed the theses and responded to the objections of the opponents. From the Middle Ages onward, disputation might be formal or informal, public or private and, depending on the era and the sort, might take place daily, nightly, weekly, monthly, quarterly, semiannually, or annually. Academics might have to dispute additionally as presider or respondent publicly once, twice, or even more times per year in ordinary disputations.

Like modern research, disputation filled a manifold of medieval and early modern academic spaces. Here we are concerned with the final trial in the jurists' list: the formal, public disputation. The next chapters will take up other sorts of disputation and related fora.

Figure 3.2 is emblematic, rather than realistic, with its five panels surrounding the title in the middle of the page. But that makes it all the more interesting. The five panels are labeled "Lectio" on the top left, "Disputatio" on the top right, "Promulgatio" in the middle left, "Executio" in the middle right, and "Remuneratio" on the bottom left to right. The image embeds lecture and disputation within the context of judicial and ecclesiastical promulgation, execution, and remuneration—the juridico-ecclesiastical order of things.

The top right panel of figure 3.2 and figure 3.3 show the typical two-tiered lectern or *cathedra*. (The bottom panel of figure 6.1 in chapter 6 may be the best illustration.) The layout resembles an early modern legal trial. In figure 3.2, the presider (*praeses*) of the disputation stands on the upper tier of the lectern, while the respondent or defendant stands on the lower tier. In figure 3.3, a master or doctor stands at the podium, with no respondent

3.2. Title page of Johann M. Meÿfart, *Christliche und aus trewen Herzen wolgemeinte auch demütige Erinnerung von der Erbawung und Fortsetzung der Academischen Disciplin auff den Evangelischen Hohen Schulen in Deutschland . . .*, Erfurt 1636.

at the moment at the lower one, while the hall slowly fills. At this point, such a scene could depict either a disputation or a lecture, with the latter typically given from the upper podium. If a respondent was scheduled to appear, a disputation would ensue; if not, then a lecture.

Figure 3.3 shows a separated and elevated bench to one side of the podium. Academic officers and nobles sat there, since their juridical personae or charisma demanded that they be set off from the general public.

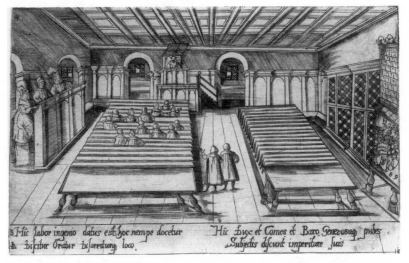

3.3. Lecture and disputation hall at the Collegium Illustre, University of Tübingen, 1626.

The latter occupy the auditorium per se. Members of the general public would usually play the opponents, though the officers and nobles could also play the role. In the original medieval sense, the disputation was public, since all members of the university or academic public might attend and, indeed, play the role of opponent. The use of designated opponent(s) came later and indicates decadence, more about which later.

THE ACT AND ENDS OF DISPUTATION. The event could begin with speeches by the dean or others. Such decanal and other orations would most likely attend the more solemn disputations, such as for reception of an academic degree (*disputatio pro gradu*), or for assumption of a place in the faculty as a fully incepted or "habilitated" master or doctor (*disputatio pro loco*). In the latter case, the habilitated master or doctor might then lawfully ascend to the upper tier of the *cathedra* to preside over disputations and lecture under no one's supervision.

The presider at a disputation would also commonly give an oration. The presider's oration typically praised the candidate(s) and might end in an exemplary disquisition on one of the theses. Then the disputation per se would begin. The presider or respondent might read the theses aloud, or the theses might have been printed and posted in advance on the door of the chapel or disputation-lecture hall, so that an actual reading of theses was unnecessary.[12]

An opponent opened the polemics by repeating the respondent's theses and bringing his first objections to the theses in strict syllogistic form. Then it was the respondent's turn. He began by stating the *status controversiae*, the state of the controversy, that is, the opponent's objections. The respondent first declared whether he accepted the opponent's arguments as contradicting the actual theses. If he did, then he sought to respond, that is, to bring arguments in strict syllogistic form against the opponent's arguments. The respondent ended the first round by demanding the opponent reestablish the cogency of his objections.

In the second round, the (perhaps new) opponent sought to do that. Hereafter precise syllogistic form might be abandoned and, as the early modern era ran its course, was probably abandoned more and more. The opponent could try to reestablish only the points that the respondent demanded be addressed, the *status controversiae*. After the opponent had attempted to reestablish his objections, the respondent ended the second round by repeating the last arguments of the opponent, the state of the controversy, and essaying a refutation.

And so it went in the third and other rounds, with or without new opponents. During the disputation, the opponent(s), the respondent, and especially the presider made sure that the other parties stuck to the *status controversiae*, that is, to articulating and refining the arguments currently at stake. The role of the presider consisted in intervening when someone breached the state of the controversy, or when decorum broke down, or when the respondent stumbled. The latter case most indicates the provenance of the disputation in the medieval joust, where the knight-bachelor or squire jousted under the protection of a knight-master who intervened if an opponent threatened to best his man. In medieval form, the respondent could not be defeated in this agonistic theater of words, although the presider might be.[13]

The disputation was an oral event. It aimed not at the production of new knowledge but rather at the rehearsal of established doctrines. What was produced—oral argument—was consumed on the premises. The disputation did not accumulate and circulate truth. It, rather, disaccumulated or dismantled possible or imagined error. The roles instantiated differential relations of power and knowledge. Protected by a presider, a respondent learnt the dialectical arts needed to fend off erroneous arguments of opponents. One learnt, ultimately, how to defend the canonical as proclaimed in lecture. The repetition of the *status controversiae* was supposed, step by step, to reduce opponents' objections to a formal or doctrinal flaw. The respondent engaged in trials of courage with opponents, and the disputation should always have the same happy ending: the presider and respondent should defeat illogical or unorthodox opponents.

In the course of studies, one passed through various academic statuses. First, one was a mere scholar, then a bachelor (to the extent that degree survived in Continental Protestant Europe), and then, for those who went on, one was a master or doctor. The latter two, after disputing for the degree, might remain at the university and try to become *habilis*, that is, fit for the faculty by engaging in the disputation for a place (*pro loco*) in faculty.

In passing from degree to degree, one occupied the various places of power in the auditorium. One enacted the various personae of opponent and respondent and, for those who wanted to teach, of presider. One proved not that one was different or original, but rather that one could perform heroically, just like everyone else. The disputation aimed at the production of polemical, yet orthodox heroic types. One learnt to stand guard over the truth in the canon and be able to anticipate and combat illogical and unorthodox theses. The practice might concern arbitrary theses, for one never knew whence an attack on the canon might issue.

On 31 October 1517 Martin Luther supposedly posted ninety-five theses for disputation on the Wittenberg court church—no surprise then that the Reformation did not abolish the practice of disputation. The humanists had been on the scene for more than half a century and had launched withering attacks on the practice of disputation. Humanists wanted to replace such "scholastic barbarism" with classical oratory. But the academic reforms under Luther and his right-hand man, Melanchthon, "Praeceptor Germaniae," added oratory, while preserving and even reemphasizing scholastic disputation. Reformed universities throughout the Germanies upheld the practice of disputation. The Counter-Reformation also emphasized disputational arts. And at Oxbridge, the reformations from 1549 to 1553 reinforced disputation which, as we'll see, survived into the nineteenth century, albeit in a moribund state.[14]

## THE EARLY MODERN REGIME

### The Public Lecture

We now turn back to the lecture and consider developments in the early modern era. By the late Baroque and early Enlightenment, a definite decadence had befallen both the lecture and the disputation. Disputation would not be saved. But efforts undertaken by the German police state rehabilitated the lecture and, one might argue, much facilitated its survival.

LECTURE HALLS. Figure 3.3 shows the lecture hall of the Collegium Illustre of the University of Tübingen. Such spaces might have been the norm at Oxbridge colleges, if one counts their chapels as lecture halls. In the Protestant Germanies, however, few colleges of that sort survived the Reformation. Indeed, few had existed anyway. The university per se usually owned the teaching spaces, such as there were. Typically, each of the four early modern faculties had or at least desired some moral claim to a lecture hall of its own.

At the University of Kiel, for example, each faculty had rights to a hall of its own. Public lectures had to be held there, excepting in winter when they could be at the professor's home. That was necessary since public halls were commonly unheated—thanks to miserable academic budgets before the modern era. The order of precedence determined to some extent the nature of the faculties' halls. The theology faculty had best claims to the "auditorium maximum," or *audi-max*, which was at first in fact and later only nominally the university's largest hall.

Theology usually had the largest enrollments and the best claims over a chapel, if one existed. Law faculties also often had rather large enrollments and wealthy students, and so likely possessed a large and exclusive lecture hall. Medical faculties usually had small enrollments, but they eventually needed rather well equipped anatomical theaters of their own. Last and least in the order of precedence, arts and philosophy had in some places low and in some places high enrollments, and made do as opportunity allowed, sometimes with its own hall, sometimes sharing the theologians' hall.[15]

PLAYING TO AN EMPTY THEATER. Attendance at arts and philosophy lectures declined in the early modern era. In the Middle Ages, specific lectures formed part of the requirements to advance to degree. Ordinary lectures and texts (as in appendix 1, list 1) were required for advancement to a degree and given at specific times of day and/or year. Over the course of the early modern era, at least in the Protestant arts and philosophy faculties, the public or ordinary lectures taught by these ordinary professors tended to become empty requirements.

The medieval student had been obliged to swear or even produce testimonies that he had attended all the required ordinary lectures. The early modern Protestant student, however, only had to pass the relevant examinations. Whether or not he had attended any lectures became his own affair. At Oxbridge, by the end of the seventeenth century, the situation here resembled the Germanies. The earlier university-wide lectures by the regent masters had pretty much disappeared, while professorial lectures went unvisited or ungiven or both. The college tutors at Oxbridge had taken control and care of the education of bachelor's candidates. The tutors may or may not have lectured in the old formal sense. More likely they gave tutorials in something like the modern sense. We'll return to this in a later chapter.[16]

In the lower faculties at the Protestant Germanies, lack of listeners constituted a real problem. First was the matter, as mentioned, that a student no longer had to swear, much less prove, attendance at the ordinary lectures. Furthermore, unlike the bachelor's degree in Catholic lands and Protestant England, the B.A. disappeared at most universities in the Protestant Germanies by the seventeenth century. The bachelor's curriculum had been taken over by the new *gymnasium academicum*, a new sort of secondary school that had emerged in the wake of humanism.[17]

By the eighteenth century, most students matriculated directly from the gymnasium into a superior faculty. Auditors of arts and philosophy lectures appeared often out of actual interest. That meant, however, that attendance tended to drop during the term, as students had to devote themselves to studies in one of the superior faculties. A ministerial visitation commission in 1712 asked a professor at Frankfurt a.d.O. how many students he had. They got a very academic response: "Counting Apollo and the nine Muses, eleven."[18]

Despite the persistence of the B.A. in England, professorial lectures did not fare much better. Students had no great incentive to attend the lectures, because they usually lay outside the subjects examined for degrees. As we'll see in a later chapter, the tutors did most of the training for the exams, in view of which professorial lectures could easily seem a distraction. In the famous anecdote on the low attendance at Sir Isaac's lectures, Humphrey Newton said, "So few went to hear Him, & fewer y$^t$ understood him, y$^t$ oftimes he did in a manner, for want of Hearers, read to y$^e$ Walls." Newton often lectured for only a half hour and, when no students had come, he would leave after a quarter of an hour. Some of Newton's biographers try to exculpate his performance by attributing the low attendance to a failure by students to ascend to the heights of his genius. In other words, Newton was a bad lecturer.[19]

That may have made him exceptional, or may not have. The low attendance he enjoyed was, however, a professorial norm for arts and sciences in the early modern era. Newton's predecessor in the Lucasian Chair, Isaac Barrow, had previously been professor of Greek at Cambridge and had complained then of the lack of listeners for his Greek lectures. Newton's successor to the chair, William Whiston, appears to have been a better and more thoughtful lecturer, but his enrollments were probably not much higher, if higher at all.[20]

PROFESSORIAL PERFORMANCES. As early modern arts and philosophy lectures became marginal events for students, academics came to view their role as ordinary professor as only a role. The medieval master had been a master of the Seven Liberal Arts and philosophy, and thus might try to lecture on most any book from the scholastic liturgy. The early modern professor had become officially professor-of-this-or-that. But many felt able to impersonate in lecture, if not every professorial persona in the faculty, then at least a number of them. That is why pluralism and opting up from chair to chair seemed perfectly reasonable in the ivory tower.

Lecturing resembled acting, which, at least for academics, was tied to the public persona associated with the chair. An academic who held a chair was required to enact a persona in a theatrical space, which, given low enrollments, might have meant playing to an empty hall, and all too often did. The system of semesters reinforced the liturgical aspect of lecturing. At least ideally, the same parts of an academic liturgy were repeated at the same time every year as part of the "biannual drama of the lecture" in which the professor played "his role."[21]

Pluralist professors officially had a lot of public lecturing to do. As noted earlier, many professors and especially those in the poorly paid arts and philosophy faculty also offered private lectures and other classes for a fee. A consequence of teaching so many hours, and five or six days a week, was lack of time to prepare a well-thought-out lecture. A 1642 lecture plan for the Jesuit philosophy faculty at Ingolstadt, for example, set an ideal, doubtless often not met at Protestant universities: the first half hour of each lecture was to be for dictation and the second half hour for glosses and exegesis. Many early modern lectures seem to have become chaotic commentaries, or remained readings aloud, dictations page by page of a textbook.[22]

Another strategy relied on a micrology of textual commentary. A notorious example comes from the Tübingen professor of theology, Ulrich Pregizer, who spent more than four years in his public lecture on the book of Daniel. After that he moved on to Isaiah, which took him twenty-five years to complete in lecture. Upon completing that great book, he began on the same day to lecture on Jeremias, a book to which he dedicated his public lecture for over fifteen years, stopped only by his untimely death at the age of eighty. In view of such an endless lecture, old-fashioned dictation with minimal commentary had something to recommend it.[23]

D. A. Winstanley's work on enlightened Cambridge has a long chapter on the professors, which begins, "The Professors of the eighteenth century have incurred the indignant scorn of posterity, and for the most part they deserve it." Despite the wills of most founders of chairs, professors tended to treat the chairs as sinecures. And the university did little to make them think otherwise. Some professors gave their inaugural lectures and then stopped there. Others, like Newton, lectured for some years, then appear to have ceased altogether. Except for one case, the eighteenth-century professors of Hebrew, for example, do not seem to have done much, as "most of them had probably only a smattering of Hebrew. A few of them may have lectured occasionally; but it was certainly only the few and only very occasionally."[24]

The chair for Modern History, founded in 1724 by George I, is a nice example. The first occupant gave an inaugural lecture in 1725, "but never lectured again." Not a word was heard from successive occupants of the chair, until John Symonds, "breaking a silence that had existed from the foundation of the chair, began to lecture in 1773." The explanation of one chair holder serves for them all: "The excuse for this prolonged silence was the impossibility of collecting an audience, and there was sufficient truth in this plea to make it plausible."[25]

POLICING PROFESSORIAL LECTURES. We find similar inclinations and tendencies in the mentalities of academics in early modern England and the Germanies: professorial lectures, especially in the arts and sciences topics, did not seem so very important or interesting. The differences between England and the Germanies sprang from the absence or presence of ministerial interventions. After the Reformation, the colleges at Oxford and Cambridge preserved most of their medieval corporate autonomy and, on the whole, the English crown left Oxbridge alone. The English collegiate university retained more autonomy than the German professorial one.

German princes and their ministers did not leave German professors alone. The lack of richly endowed colleges in the German lands weakened academic resistance to ministerial wills. In the Protestant Germanies, and eventually in the Catholic ones, good policing slowly changed bad habits of professors in their lectures. Jurists argued that professors received public salaries; if a public servant became derelict in duty, then the percentage of the salary, corresponding to the hours missed, might be deducted from the servant's pay. Such fines for neglected lecture hours and other offices spanned the early modern Germanies.[26]

In sixteenth century Basel, for example, if a professor thought he was clever enough to deliver his public lectures so poorly so as to have no students and be rid of his public lecture hours, the Basel Town Council had other news. To keep his salary, the professor must lecture even should but one auditor appear. And, if no one appeared, the professor must still come and wait for the whole hour each lecture in case someone did. At Königsberg too, after 1717, to get his full pay, a professor had to remain for each lecture, even if no students appeared. Professors had to be in their rooms by the time the bell rang and to give the lecture even if only two students came. In 1721 this was relaxed, so that at least three students had to appear since, as Roman law held, *tres faciunt collegium.*[27]

Ministries sought to control the lecture hall and, as we know from chapter 2, to control the calendar too. They enjoined universities to improve lecture plans by discussing course offerings in advance. Decrees commanded no lecturing at home in the case of the public lectures (of course excepting in the dead of winter). For, if professors gave public lectures at home, ministers could not be assured that professors were doing their duty. Decrees also stated that lectures must fill the time and end on time, daily and/or annually or biannually. To stop professors such as Pregizer from spending their entire lecturing lives never getting through the text, ministries ordered that each lecture must come to a proper end at the end of the term, and that the professor must develop the themes of a particular lecture to fit the duration of the term. In a history of Protestant universities, published 1768–76, Michaelis noted that lectures in the Germanies now mostly ended properly with the semester—the fine fruits of good policing.[28]

Ministries went so far as to try to take control of the style of lecturing. As early as 1582, Bavarian ministers had tried to stop dictation in lecture at the University of Ingolstadt. This prohibition had to be renewed in 1746; the eighteenth appears to be the century when dictation was first stopped, even if only erratically at first. Forbidding dictation with the aim of encouraging publication of textbooks, ministries were perhaps, again, striving to emulate Göttingen, whose professors famously wrote the textbooks for their lectures.[29]

In Prussia, a decree of 31 March 1781 forbade dictation but required lecturers to use a textbook—an implicit suggestion to write one. Reforms elsewhere set out how the lectures were to be taught. Survey style lectures should put knowledge in good order and in digestible bits, giving a literary history of the discipline, too. No dictation was allowed and professors had to keep their lectures up to date. It should come as no surprise that the eighteenth century was the classic age of the textbook or, rather, of textbook production.[30]

As noted in chapters above, German cameralists advocated such a visible ministerial hand to reform and maintain professorial lecture habits. The preceding chapter cited Justi to this effect. The citation seems important enough to repeat and extend at greater length here:

[I]nstructors must not only know the disciplines that they are to teach in their complete scope, but must also be lacking in pedantry, able to discern the fundamental and the useful in knowledge, and be masters of a flowing and pleasant lecture style. Just as all parts of learning must be taught together at a university that would attract students to it, so too must a rational division of lectures be made. To this ends, all instructors must report their upcoming lectures on time, so that one can judge whether there is a lack in the presentation of this or that discipline.[31]

Protestant and some Catholic German ministries acted in accord with such sentiments before the cameralists appeared to theorize the matter as police science. In the German lands, a rationalization of labor amplified professorial voices, while many fell silent in England or played to empty halls. Filling halls for arts and sciences topics would remain a problem for many German universities until the nineteenth century. But a work ethic had been forged.

This is not to say that no one worked at Oxbridge. But study there remained for far longer a part of the *vita contemplativa* nourished by liberal leisure. In the Germanies, the rationalization of labor had made such liberality antique and suspect.

LECTURE NOTES. Figure 3.4 comes from the seventeenth century. The details are not wholly clear, but all pastimes recognized in the medieval lecture above appear to be exemplified. The lecturer, probably a professor, sits in the magisterial chair or *cathedra,* significantly above the audience. Though it is difficult to make out in this image, some students sit at the front of the hall, lining the wall on both sides of the *cathedra,* and facing in the same direction as the lecturer. Some of them appear to have books at which they are looking. These students at the front, facing the observer, are likely the well-to-do. As in the medieval scene of figure 3.1, as well as in a theater still, the wealthy and worthies receive the better seats and a program, so to speak.[32]

The rest of the hall is filled with garden-variety students. Some are sitting in the windowsills. The rest sit on benches that have no backrests and no support for their writing pads. This compels them to write on their laps. Some of these students appear to be taking notes. It is hard to see what the broad mass in the middle is doing; but, as most students around them seem to be taking notes, the rhetoric of the figure leads one to presume the same for the mass. Some are looking at and perhaps conversing with a neighbor. Others daydream or sleep. But most seem to be paying attention. The per-

3.4. Seventeenth-century depiction of a lecture and disputation hall
from *Speculum Cornelianum*, 1879.

vasiveness of apparent note-taking, in comparison with figure 3.1 from the
Middle Ages, stands as a striking modern development.

When medieval students took notes, they usually did so at home, slowly
and carefully, using borrowed or lent manuscripts, or other digests. Early
modern students became note takers in lecture, sometimes manically, according to some eighteenth-century reports. The sound coming from lectures—that "clear, dry, tingling sound," like the wind in late fall—arose
from so many taking copious notes in eighteenth-century Wittenberg. "We
knew very many at Wittenberg who spent their three years there attending
five lectures each day and who filled the remaining hours by rewriting their
lecture notes . . . [or] when not rewriting them, then filling the holes in
them by other notes." F. Laukhard, in reminiscences on his academic travels in the mid-eighteenth century, had found the students in Halle to be
even greater note takers than those in Wittenberg—a work ethic at work.[33]

But not everyone took notes. Some had notes taken for them. At
Leipzig, for example, wealthy students—usually law and perhaps medical
students—sent note takers in their stead to lectures. Theology and arts and
philosophy students tended to be poorer. The avid note takers above at Wittenberg and Halle were most likely theology students. Writing about a the-

ology lecture at Leipzig in 1783, C. Rinck noted that the students "have no desk-chairs, so many write in their laps, or on each others backs, and some have to stand."[34]

A rather harsher depiction of such Leipzig theology students stems from another pen:

> It's a great amusement to see them galloping from lecture to lecture . . . This zealousness, in which one tries to outdo the other, is necessary since they mostly sit on benches, which aren't reserved [and have no writing tablets]. Hardly has one pushed his way into the hall and taken possession of his seat, when . . . he breaks out his notebook, pen and inkbottle and awaits the professor. As soon as the latter arrives, note-taking starts, and one can only with difficulty restrain one's laughter over the awful gestures with which they try to get everything neatly on paper that comes out of his mouth.[35]

Measures of German police states, in league with a spirit of the age and the Protestant Ethic, would save the lecture from its threatened descent into decadence. In chapter 11 on professorial voices, we'll return to the revival of the lecturer's charisma.

### The Public Farce

Unlike the lecture, the public disputation was not to be saved. The Baroque's topos of the theater of the world facilitated its understanding of disputation as theater. But a pervasive decadence set in then that, with the Baroque's notion of dissimulation and role-playing, would ill suit the new moral economy of knowledge emerging during the Enlightenment.[36]

Often a good sign of decadence, a history appeared. A certain Leigh's history of 1715 held that disputation did not exist in Paradise. Nor really did it arise with Cain and Abel. Disputation rather emerged first with Greeks, especially with Socrates' new methods. Plato's dialogues and Aristotle's analytics gave disputation its canonical form. The practice also existed among the ancient Jews and was taken up into the early Church. In 1715, however, much abuse exists, Leigh surmised, since one disputes minute, silly, and often fruitless matters.[37]

Other enlightened academics noted the decline, too. In 1755 J. Chladenius remarked that some now said disputation provided no good means to investigate the truth, and that disputation often resolved nothing. Chladenius defended oral disputation over polemical writings. In oral disputation the polemics ceased with the actual event, after which the interlocutors were (supposedly) friends again. He made clear that oral disputation served as theater, a play, where the actors only appeared playing roles. In polemical writings, however, one was not playing the same game, since personal reputation stood more at stake.[38]

In a history of Protestant academia written in the mid-eighteenth century, Michaelis also noted the decline. He, too, defended disputation against the personalized polemics of the journals. Michaelis argued that disputation worked well for sharpening Latin skills, that it brought silent students to speak, and that, although once too scholastic with syllogisms, it was now not scholastic enough. One now sought applause, *Beifall*, from the audience.[39]

Michaelis and others noted a new problem with the role of the presider. On the one hand, some presiders played too much of a role by intervening too often. For his part, Michaelis held that one ought to allow the respondent to defend the theses, and that the presider should only enter when a clear need existed. On the other hand, he noted a tendency to do away with the presider altogether in disputations for an academic degree. Many students now wanted to dispute for their degree *sine praeside,* that is, without a presider.[40]

The decadence of disputation followed above all from the reduction of the play to its rehearsal, that is, from the dissolution of any spontaneity. The practice of designating opponents in advance, coupled with the ability of the respondent at some places to choose the opponents, and further to dispute without a presider, made possible a complete scripting of the play. The declining Latin speaking skills of most led to the practice of rehearsal. And, as the converse, the still superior Latin skills of some led to a sort of perverse theater.

Reflecting on eighteenth-century experiences, K. Bahrdt noted that, thanks to his good Latin, many respondents wanted him as presider and were willing to pay for it, since he could usually defend them against unfriendly opponents. Bahrdt studied at Leipzig. The persistence of medieval manners there allowed opponents to appear unarranged and unannounced in the audience. Bahrdt thus also often played a merciless opponent-from-hell to his adversaries. He aimed for opposition that was "sharp and, where possible, productive of laughter."[41]

At enlightened Oxbridge, too, public disputation fell into great decadence. As in Germany, some bemoaned its decline, and some did not. William Whewell, who attended Cambridge when disputation was "far advanced in the decay which precedes dissolution," noted that "the syllogisms were such as would make Aristotle stare, and the Latin would make every classical hair on your head stand on end." But he still thought the exercise worthwhile and lamentably being lost. By 1830, at least at Cambridge, one performed disputation as rehearsed in advance between the respondent and opponents, until it was finally abolished in 1839. Public disputation would fade, above all at Cambridge, in favor of a new process of oral and then finally of written examination—to which we turn in the next chapter.[42]

As Michaelis noted, the gravest fear in the Enlightenment concerned the dissolution of the disputation to farce, where one sought applause from the audience or, worse, like Bahrdt, laughter. The mock or joke disputation enjoyed an ancient pedigree, but it was supposed to constitute the exception. During the Baroque and the Enlightenment, the disputation seems to have become more and more played as academic farce, an empty ritual.

Late in the eighteenth century, a satire appeared called "On the Learned Theater"—"Der gelehrte Schauspiel, oder *Forma dat esse rei*":

> Come along, you scholarly gentlemen [*Kommt mit, Ihr Herren von Studium*],
> Into the grand auditorium [*Ins große Auditorium*],
> There you'll see agitation [*Da sieht Ihr auch—agiren*].
> One calls it Disputation [*Man nennt es Disputiren*],
> Editing a specimen [*Ein Specimen ediren*],
> Exercising oneself academically [*Sich academisch exerziren*] . . .
> And the roles have been rehearsed [*Auch sind die Rollen einstudiert*],
> In friendship have the opponent [*In Freundschaft hat der Opponent*]
> and repondent [*und Respondent*]
> *Quae succurrebant*, communicated with each other [*Quae succurrebant, sich kommunicirt*].
> They've translated it into Latin [*Sie haben ins Latein vertirt*],
> And, as Mister *** has corrected it [*Und, wie's Herr *** revidirt*],
> So they've been studying for eight days [*So lernen seit acht tage sie*]
> With bitter efforts [*Mit saurer Müh*]
> To practice objection and response [*Einwurf und antwort recitiren*] . . .
> And if despite all the preparation [*Und wird, trotz aller Präperation*],
> In the second and third act the principal person [*In zweiten, dritten Akt die Hauptperson*]
> The author-respondent remains mute till after twelve
> [*Autor Respondens bis nach zwölf stumm*],
> So say the courteous [*So sagt die Höflichkeit*]:
> It is modesty [*Es sei Bescheidenheit*],
> He is responding by silence [*Er respondiere per silentium*].[43]

The next chapters trace disputational developments to break this silence.

## CONCLUSION

The lecture and the disputation formed the central academic activities at the medieval university. Both were oral activities and both were based on a written canon. The lecture and the disputation, as the sermon and the joust, crystallized the juridico-ecclesiastical academic order. During the early modern era, both became endangered species in academia.

At Oxbridge, the persistence of the medieval notion of the endowed professorial chair, whose occupant had tenure for life, put most such occupants beyond discipline. Over the course of the era, fewer and fewer students attended the lectures, since on the whole the lectures did not address subjects for examination. Most professors for their part were content to treat the chairs as real sinecures, which good numbers even dared to hold in absentia.

In the German lands, the waxing police state endeavored to discipline professors. That proved possible since they had been reconstituted as public professors after the Reformation. They were paid salaries from funds increasingly de facto, if not yet de iure merely budgetary and no longer endowed. The budget, in place of the endowment, served as a crucial tool for rationalizing practices. The emergence of the lecture catalogue and its ancillary devices such as the professorial slips, traced in the previous chapter, facilitated the ministerial disciplining of professorial lectures. Ministries normalized terms and enforced lecture hours upon penalty of fines or mulcts. During the Enlightenment, ministers even tried to influence the style of lecturing: dictation was to be stopped and survey lectures given. Students, especially the poorer ones, became devoted or even manic note takers. From the fruits of good policing, the lecture survived and would link the medieval and the modern academic regimes. In chapter 11, we shall return to the professorial voice and its charismatic persistence in the lecture.

The decadence of the disputation, however, would not be remedied. From the medieval trials of courage to certify a hero of knowledge, the disputation had descended into Baroque farce. By the eighteenth century, the disputation had become comic theater in which some or maybe many now played for applause. The latter, as we'll see in later chapters, had become the central notion in the commodifying of academics for both ministries and markets.

Chapters 4 to 7 will trace the development of academic institutions and practices that emerged from the decline of the disputation: the written exam, the seminar paper, the doctoral dissertation, and the professorial ethos of publish or perish. The emergence of note-taking in the lecture may serve here as a harbinger of things to come. Writing would loom ever larger in academia and academic charisma would become ever more vested in it— but not completely.

# 4

## The Examination

Excerpts from a doctoral exam: "What is the goal of higher education?"—To make a person into a machine. "What are the means for that?"—One must learn to be bored . . . "Who is the perfect human?"— The bureaucrat . . .

Friedrich Nietzsche, *Götzen-Dämmerung* (1889)

In the top panel of figure 4.1, the caption on the right reads, "Is the gentleman also a Wolffian?" (*Ist der Herr auch ein Wolffianer?*). The professor placing the question rests his left hand in an open book and raises a right index finger. Five other professors listen, while the candidate, standing on the left, gives an answer to the question on Wolffianism.[1]

Related to the confession, the inquisition, and the sentencing, examination of the sort depicted in the top panel of figure 4.1—the private exam—has a judicial provenance. The scene shows the oral of a doctoral exam, probably in the theology, but possibly the arts and philosophy faculty, at the University of Jena around 1740. The setting resembles a session of an academic body—a senate or faculty council—reading a judicial sentence, as in figure 4.2, which concerns the expulsion of student and is from the same collection as figure 4.1.[2]

Among doctoral or professorial emblems, three were often held to be most essential: the chair, the book, and the hat or *pileus*. In the top panel of figure 4.1, six professors sit in chairs around the table. Next to their hands on the table are their hats. The academic hat, the *pileus*, signified academic freedom. A book lies on the table. This space embodies professorial power and authority. It is a space of professorial academic freedom. There is no empty chair for the candidate; he must stand. Next to the book on the table rests a quill, and above the book an inkwell. Some things are being written: the candidate's answers.[3]

"Is the gentleman also a Wolffian?" The question on Wolffianism concerns Christian Wolff and orthodoxy. Upon the machinations of Joachim

4.1. A doctoral oral and subsequent celebration, University of Jena, circa 1740.

Lange and his Pietist pals, Christian Wolff had been fired in 1723 from the University of Halle and ordered to leave Prussia within forty-eight hours upon pain of death. Wolff had supposedly adhered to unorthodox views in theology and philosophy. The straw that broke the camel's back had been his rectorial speech of 1721 in praise of Chinese culture, which was in fact non-Christian, as enlightened. Upon his banishment, Wolff went to the University of Marburg in Hesse-Cassel where he became a *cause célèbre* of the nascent Enlightenment, but still opposed by conservative elements in the Germanies.

The examiner's question here seems thus more appropriate for a judicial inquest than for an exam. The judicial-confessional aspect of examination is put clearly on the table. (And what does the questioner mean by "*also* a Wolffian"?) The candidate, standing to the far left in the top panel, answers orthodoxly, "Down with Wolff. Long live Lange" (*Pereat Wolff Vivat Lange*).[4]

The tables now turn in the bottom panel of figure 4.1. Here a table again dominates, but a different sort. Instead of a table setting a formal scene of ordeal, the bottom panel has an informal scene of celebration after examination. Down to gratuitous details, the scene reflects an absolute inversion of the above professorial space of examination. The table is now square instead of circular. Seven students sit wearing colorful coats. At least two of the sitting students have an elbow on the table, while two others are standing. The motif of sitting versus standing carries no power relations or implications here. There are not only empty chairs for the two standing students but also an extra one to the far right, perhaps for the observer.

Emblems of student academic freedom—chiefly smoking and drinking—decorate this space. All students have large clay pipes. On the table sit two mugs of beer. The student standing to the far right holds a glass of beer or wine. By the concerted inverted symmetry of the image, this would be the subject of the ordeal from the top scene, the student having been examined and now celebrating. Running from his mouth to the ceiling and unveiling the interested nature of academic examination as confession, the caption now reads unorthodoxly, "Long live Wolff. Down with Lange" (*Vivat Wolff Pereat Lange*).

As we saw in the previous chapter, medieval jurists had glossed passages in Roman law that concerned the three trials of the crowned athlete to apply to academics. Nearly the whole of medieval university education had been interpreted as an agonistic regime of perpetual examination. The pervasiveness and extent of disputation in good part underlay that regime. Most disputation prepared for examination. And most examination was disputational.

This chapter analyzes the performance, registration and evaluation of academic examination up to the Romantic era. There are three central aims: to present the essentially oral, disputational nature of traditional examination; to investigate the emergence of written examination in the early modern era; and to sketch practices of evaluation and the rise of the academic grading system. The focus remains on the Germanies. But crucial reference will be made here to Oxbridge practices. In fact, the emergence of the written examination and modern grading system stands out most clearly, and perhaps surprisingly, at Cambridge.

The written exam and the grading system had great ramifications on the student body. Most especially, they clove it into the two groups now called "undergraduate" and "graduate" (or "postgraduate") students. The undergraduates would be subjected to the full rigor of the new bureaucratic system of written exams and standardized grading. As we'll see here and in the next chapter, the graduate students, however, continued to enjoy more lax medieval practices. Oral exams would remain vital, at least for the doctorate, and writing for graduate students would tend to be different, favoring the research paper over the mere exam.

The table haunts this chapter (as well as the next) and in two guises. Tables are, first, of wood. One sits at them for an oral as well as a written exam. But tables are also of paper. The modern grading system first emerged as a tabular form of reporting and evaluation. This chapter presents a history of the table manners of examination and grading, and illuminates a nice relation between the juridical and the disciplinary—the tables of tribunal and confession versus the tables of policing and bureaucracy. The table, in its two senses, shows the transition from the traditional juridico-ecclesiastical to the modern politico-economic academic order.[5]

This chapter will take a number of sudden twists and odd turns, but the overall structure is simple. The chapter falls into two parts. The first essentially concerns traditional oral exams. The second considers mostly modern written exams and the grading system.

## THE ORAL

### Table Manners

When did exams (and our seminars) first begin to take place at tables? Maybe ancient Greeks and Romans took exams while reclining on pillows, postures perhaps typical at Socratic symposia. One must call into question the seeming self-evidence of European furniture.

Social anthropologists and art and social historians know well of the once parochial nature of the chair, and thus also of our elevated and massive tables. The origins of the chair lie in ancient Egypt and Greece. Thereafter, with the great exception of China, the chair and its attendant high table were till relatively recently restricted mostly to Europe and parts of the world under its cultural or, rather, colonial sway. The oral, as we saw above, involved tables.[6]

We'll begin by considering general etiquettes or table manners of traditional European oral exams. Then we'll look at two examples of academic oral exams for advanced degrees: a master's exam from the Baroque, and a doctoral exam from the Enlightenment.

ETIQUETTES OF EUROPEAN EXAMS  The most famous exams in medieval monasteries were the Lentine. Each Benedictine monk had to read a specific book during Lent and had to pass an exam on it. The exams eventually became formalized, public affairs. All brothers assembled in the chapter house. The bookkeeper read the name of each monk. When called, one by one, each monk placed the book he read on the carpet. The prior or his designate took the book in hand and publicly examined the brother on it. If the brother did not pass, he had to reread the book. The exam was not disputational and did not take place at tables. The table symbolized monastic community but—perhaps for that reason?—did offer not a site of examination.[7]

The scholastics broke with monastic manners. In the previous chapter, we noted the notion of the academic joust. That allowed medieval jurists to turn to the topos of the three trials of the hero or crowned athlete in Roman law and to apply it to academic degrees. Medieval jurists held the three heroic trials to be three steps of scholastic education, seen as perpetual examination or trial. Early modern jurists knew this topos of the three trials.

First, there was the regular probing by one's teachers during study. This consisted not of the sort of regular written exams and quizzes typical at modern American universities. It consisted, rather, of regular, informal oral disputations and exercises, at which we shall look more closely in the next chapter. The second of the jurists' heroic trials was the private exam by the faculty for a degree, which we shall consider here below. Finally, the third and last of the heroic trials or tests was the public disputation, which the previous chapter touched upon and which the chapter after the next will treat in more detail.[8]

Medieval and early modern academic examination had the cast of a trial and an ordeal in theory and in practice. This chapter and the next two aim to show the original centrality of oral disputation, and the gradual emergence of writing to the center stage in the examination of undergraduates, in the training of graduate students, and in the award of the highest academic degrees.

Beyond all metaphors of trial, scholastic exams concerned the juridical persona of the candidate. Not just knowledge but also morals stood under review—originally examined by the university chancellor, a clerical office at base. Among other things, candidates had to swear to legitimacy of birth, as well as not to seek revenge should any part of the exam go badly. To be a student and able at all to advance to candidacy for exams, one needed a specific juridical persona: a candidate had to be legitimately born, Christian, male, the proper age, essentially corporally intact, present, alive, sane, and able to see and speak. Some of these conditions might seem absurd, but only to someone unacquainted with juridical niceties.[9]

Early modern jurists presumed that the private and public examinations were serious events. The jurist Itter held that the candidate should be "examined diligently and rigorously." The jurist Walther explained that the exam usually had a private and a public part. It could move randomly from topic to topic, or could be more rigorous. In the latter case, for example, a candidate might be given time to elaborate on a difficult text. A written part

4.2. A senate or faculty council sentencing a standing student to a three
year suspension, University of Jena, circa 1740.

or *scriptum* might form part of an exam for these jurists, but did not constitute its center.[10]

Walther commented on the proper style of examination. It should be
moderate, humane, and placid. Examiners should not try to incite fear or
uncertainty in the candidate. Questions should not split hairs or involve
wholly useless knowledge. The exam should be free of ire, hate, loathing,
envy, severity, and other such emotions. The time and place of exams were
irrelevant, although they should accord with the reasonable and customary
(so, for example, candidates should not be awakened in the middle of the
night and examined).[11]

Walther's explanation set an ideal from which practice might have
shown very grave departures and perversions. A student manual from the
eighteenth century, for example, agreed that examiners should not vex candidates. But it conceded that such vexing examiners did exist, as "there are
such super-clever ones who imagine they can hear grass growing."[12]

Like figure 4.1, figure 4.3 shows an eighteenth-century scene of the
private exam. As noted above, figure 4.2 shows a session of the academic
senate or the philosophy faculty council, dealing with the expulsion of a stu-

4.3. An oral exam, University of Tübingen, 1770.

dent from the University of Jena. Figure 4.3 shows an exam from the University of Tübingen, circa 1770. Here there are three examiners at the table, while figure 4.1 has six. Figure 4.2 has the senate or faculty council, or at least a quorum. Senate or council sessions had to have a quorum of the faculty but, the notion of representation so pervaded Europe from the Middle Ages onward, exams could be conducted without a quorum. Faculty committees, in other words, did most exams.

The number of examiners at the private exam seems to have been mostly irrelevant in the early modern era, although it most probably could not have been less than three. The examiners formed a collegium and had to vote on the outcome. And, based on Roman law, it takes three to make a collegium, since voting would seem absurd with one or even two, at least in the eyes of Roman law. As with many matters, academics typically wanted it both ways here: to have the right but not the duty to attend every exam in the faculty.[13]

A MASTER'S EXAM AT BAROQUE WITTENBERG. The dean's protocol of a master's exam in the arts and philosophy faculty at the University of Wittenberg in 1639 offers a good example of the second and middle part of the jurists' three heroic trials for a degree. It is the so-called private exam by the faculty, in advance of the public exam. This case may be an extraordinary example of the early modern table manners of examination, but it will prove illuminating.[14]

The protocol of the exam appears to be in the handwriting of the dean.

He thus either served as secretary during the exam, or wrote the final protocol from notes given him by the examiners, concerning their questions and the candidate's responses. According to the protocol, the entire arts and philosophy faculty showed up for the exam, in accord with the custom at Wittenberg ("decanus pro more totum collegium . . . conveniren lassen"). The faculty thus most likely conducted the exam together and sat around a table as in figures above. Indeed, the third professor in the protocol began, "From the discourse of the Dean . . . ," indicating that they were probably together and doubtlessly (or self-evidently?) at the same table.[15]

Seven arts faculty professors and one adjunct examined the candidate, Stellanus Fiedler, a pastor at Zschoppach. The exam began with questions from the dean. Next came questions from the faculty senior. The exam then ran through the other five professors, ending with the adjunct. The order of questioning in this juridico-ecclesiastical ordeal most probably went in the exact order of academic seniority—the most senior faculty would come first, the next senior would follow, and so on. The charisma of office, however, put the dean first, as noted. (In chapter 1, we saw that the deanship was usually a rotating office, and not one reserved for particular academics by dint of their own charisma, as it often is now in the United States, for example.)

The dean's composite protocol spans seven handwritten pages. How much time the exam took is not recorded. In view of the protocol, the exam cannot have taken more than three hours, unless many pauses intervened. The protocol begins by noting that the candidate had failed to submit the written part (*scriptum*), so we know there was a written part to such a master's exam to be done in advance. It probably consisted of the interpretation of a text, with both the text and written part in Latin. The rhetoric of the examination as indicated in the protocol suggests that the first two professors appearing in the exam—the dean and faculty senior—took the most time. That accords with good academic manners. Examination is a forensic and ceremonial event. The most important personae should speak longest and most fully.

The candidate answered most questions by a hallowed academic strategy: with silence. As the least important person in the room, the candidate fulfilled the exam's ceremonial and forensic nature by speaking least. The first two professors responded to the candidate's silence or ignorance at length, in part by giving the answers or trying to elicit them. The rhetoric indicates the exam's link with teaching as a perpetual examination, as well as its nature as professorial theater. The examiners performed as much for each other as they did for the candidate. And although all seem to have sat at the same table, no hint of conversation exists in the protocol. The table at which the examiners sat produced one-on-one exchanges between each examiner and the candidate. Only the one instance—where the third professor began by noting a question the dean had asked—suggests a possibly conversational space of exchange. Examination as table-talk seems rather disciplined, at least as written in the protocol.

To give an example of the less senior academics, I'll translate the questions posed by the fifth professor and the candidate's responses. On each line, the protocol records the question posed and a note on the answer. The "he" in each case means the candidate.

---

Mister M(aster) Sperling, Physics Professor [as Examiner].

What are the classes (*genera*) of animals? He was silent.

What is the human soul called? He responded: mortal!

What are the faculties of the rational soul? He was silent.

Save the intellect and will, would there be other faculties of the rational soul? He was silent.

What is the soul of brutes called? He was silent.

What of the faculties of the sensitive soul? He was silent.

If there are five external senses, what are they? He responded: touch, smell, sight, hearing.

What of the internal senses? He was silent.

If the third class of souls is the vegetative, how would such souls be called? He responded: vegetative.

What would be the faculties of the vegetative soul? He was silent.

Would stones have a soul? He said no. But to the syllogism: "Whatever eats, grows and procreates likes of itself has a vegetative soul; stones eat, grow and procreate their own likes: *ergo* stones have a vegetative soul"—he was silent.

Would stars have a soul? He said no. But to the syllogism: "Whatever moves, moves by a soul; stars move: *ergo* stars have a soul"—he was silent.

---

Alas, most of the candidate's answers resembled those given to Professor Sperling. A conversational moment arose as Sperling tried to break the candidate's silence on occasion by almost giving him the answer. Beyond being blissfully ignorant, the candidate perhaps feared tricks hidden in the questions. And when the candidate valiantly risked an actual "No" to the last two questions, examination became disputation. The professor reduced him to silence by clever syllogisms. In view of all the silences here, this candidate was going to have a hard time in the final, public exam—the disputation as an agonistic theater of scholastic syllogisms.

The dean noted at the head of the protocol that the candidate was "very ill in arts and languages." At the close of the protocol, the dean noted further that, after the exam, the examiners discussed the candidate's performance which, as one could see, was poorly accomplished. Here we see the first real reflection of conversation among the professors: in the evaluation of the examination as a past event. The dean reminded them that, in view of the statutes, they ought to suspend the candidate, since he had failed even the easiest questions and had committed atrocities, such as saying that "the human soul was mortal."

But the examiners decided to pass him. They brought into consideration: (1) his office as pastor; (2) his marriage, which brought the widow of a Catholic back to the "true faith"; (3) his household, which had inhibited his studies; and (4) the examiners' hopes that he would be more diligent in his studies. They voted to take the most lenient option and agreed to admit him to candidacy, if he promised with a handshake to send in a few weeks the written part penned by himself, and to practice himself one more year in arts and philosophy, "so that he finally might fruitfully grasp something and defend his title," namely, the master's degree. The candidate so promised and shook everyone's hand. He paid his fee and was admitted to candidacy for the master's degree in arts and philosophy.

Thus the private part of a master's exam from Baroque Wittenberg, which was doubtless not exactly the norm. But it offers an interesting glimpse of academic theater as a forensic play of prolixity, syllogisms, and silence, where handshakes can work near wonders.

A DOCTORAL EXAM AT ENLIGHTENED GÖTTINGEN. The first known examination in the German lands of a woman for a doctoral degree in arts and philosophy took place in 1787 at the University of Göttingen. Dorothea Schlözer, a professor's daughter, took the exam. The degree of the doctor of philosophy—the Dr. Phil. and the Ph.D.—had a problematic existence at this time in the German lands and in the world generally. Officially, no such degree existed. By statute, only the traditional M.A. or M.Phil. existed. We shall postpone such interesting issues until a later chapter. Here we consider the exam itself and, as above for Baroque Wittenberg, restrict attention to the faculty's private exam. This exam will also prove enlightening.[16]

Given the lack of public spaces in early modern academia, the exam took place at the home of the dean, Professor Michaelis, the author of an anonymous history of Protestant universities, whom and which this book often cites. Present also were, in order of academic seniority of service, Professors Kästner, Gatterer, Kulenkamp, Feder, Heyne, and Meister. We have here a typical examination committee, as opposed to the entire faculty. From Dorothea's own protocol, it seems that candidates by this time, at least in Göttingen, sat at the table, though "at the far end," perhaps separated from the examiners. To put the "fragile" candidate at ease, the dean, however, bade her to sit between Kästner and him at the head of the table!

The dean, per custom, put the first question, about which he fell into a dispute, unresolved, with Professors Gatterer, Kästner, and Meister. Examination is here no longer a mere dialogue, as it had been in 1639. Professors now conversed and disputed with one another. Michaelis put the second question, too, whereafter they broke for tea, so that the candidate might collect herself. After tea, Kästner came as second examiner. In the best performance tradition, he pulled a rock out of his pocket and asked her to classify it. After a couple more questions, he said he was going to ask her one on the binomial theorem but, as he reckoned most of his own colleagues knew nothing of it, he decided to skip it.

So they broke for tea, again. During that time, Feder spoke up. Other than seemingly confessing ignorance and complimenting the candidate's performance, he appeared to have not much to say. After tea, Meister posed some questions on art history. Dorothea quite rightly quipped that she had not put such topics on her curriculum vitae, so could not be examined on them, but answered anyway. We see here that the notion of the implicit major within the arts and philosophy faculty had arisen: one should no longer be examined on everything. Kästner then came back with a question, which she answered better than someone who had gone on to be a lecturer in the faculty, as he noted. Meister then tried to get a question in, but Kulenkamp, who appears not to have made a peep to that point, objected that it was 7:30 and time to quit. So the exam seems to have lasted about two hours or so.

Near the twilight of the *ancien régime,* Dorothea Schlözer's exam exhibits remarkable developments. The medieval juridico-ecclesiastical cast of academic examination had been broken. A woman taking a doctoral exam indicates the decline of the notion that a particular juridical persona informed the candidate—one that had included being male among other things. At least at enlightened Göttingen, candidates also now apparently sat at the table, though "at its far end." The dean and the faculty senior, Michaelis and Kästner, however, put candidate Schlözer between them at the head of the table. Such table turning had the odd effect of emblematizing the nonneutrality of the senior judges of the exam. As a Göttingen professor's daughter and an enlightened experiment, could she, indeed, be allowed to fail?[17]

The forensic nature of examination had altered too. The dean and the faculty senior do seem to have spoken most, if we judge by the caesurae of the exam, the twofold taking of tea. And the least senior professor, Meister, was handled most unceremoniously. Kulenkamp silenced him at 7:30, and none less than the candidate called his questioning improper, but answered nonetheless. The professors in the middle by seniority seem, however, to have hardly spoken. Gatterer's only intervention appears to have been his opening dispute with the other men at the table. His strategy seems clear: he did not deign to talk to her. Nor did Kulenkamp. And if we take Feder's tact precisely, he only spoke with her off the table, as it were, during a tea break. At first, I took such silence as expressing opposition to the candidate's existence; it turns out that at most three professors could officially question a candidate in this private exam.

By the late eighteenth-century examination for an advanced degree appears to be far less the simple ritual that it had been at Baroque Wittenberg. The latter case indicated that in 1639 one could pass the private exam, and thus be admitted to candidacy for the final, public part of the exam, the disputation for a degree, even though one had failed to submit the written part in advance, and even though one had responded to most questions in the oral with the disputational strategy: *respondeo per silentium* (I respond with silence).

We saw in the previous chapter that, from the Baroque into the Enlightenment, the third and final part of the three heroic trials, the disputation for the degree, had become ever more a farce, rehearsed and played for applause. If the second part of the heroic trials, the private exam by the faculty, had been tending to allow a ritualized silence from the candidate (who had also not done the written), then only the first part of the three trials—the supposed testing of the student during the whole time of study—would remain to ensure education.

As noted in the previous chapter, that first heroic trial—the regular probing and testing by one's teachers during one's studies—had itself become hard to enforce in the early modern era. Attendance at lectures had become nonmandatory, and there never had been tests or quizzes in medieval and early modern lectures. The disputational lessons and exercises (to be considered in the next chapter) offered the traditional places of the regular oral examination during one's studies, but had also become optional and less attended than in times past.

In other words, decadence might have graced the entire edifice of examination.

But Dorothea Schlözer's exam from Göttingen in 1787 suggests something else. By that time and place at least, not even a professor's daughter could enact a farce in the private exam by the faculty. As noted, archaic or traditional juridico-ecclesiastical aspects of the ritual had become attenuated and relaxed. The candidate thus could be female. The candidate sat at the table, now more an egalitarian academic space than in the past. Hints of conversation emerged. Some professors performed silently. There were tea breaks and so on.

As traditional rituals relaxed, modern and bureaucratic aspects of the rite entered the scene and became most salient. Thus Dorothea answered difficult questions and could not respond with silence. She was not supposed to be tried ritualistically about the entire Seven Liberal Arts and three branches of philosophy, (the rational, natural, and social). She, rather, had focused her studies in the faculty, and implicitly had major fields in the modern sense. She should be examined only about those fields. But, even when questioned about subjects outside her implicit major, she did not respond with silence. Epistemic aspects of the exam came to center stage, as juridico-ecclesiastical elements withdrew into the shadows.

This new or perhaps recovered rigor of the second heroic trial, the faculty's private exam, would be matched by wholly new demands for the third of the trials, imposed upon candidates aspiring for the newly emerging but long nonstatutory doctorate in philosophy (which we shall consider in chapter 6). Such new rigor was matched or, rather, perhaps driven by early modern projects—most intense in the mid- to late eighteenth century—to examine, rank, and even grade students with numbers for the bachelor's degree.

### Ranking at Medieval Ingolstadt

Judging by their statutes, universities were less concerned with ill-begotten examiners, and more concerned about irked candidates seeking revenge. Unlike actual judicial process, little statutory recourse for appeals of redress of grievances about poorly run or unfairly judged examinations existed (or exists still). And given the nature of the private examination, as noted above, it could be conducted by a small and supposedly representative committee.[18]

Both case studies above—the master's exam from Baroque Wittenberg and the doctoral exam from enlightened Göttingen—concerned exams for degrees beyond the bachelor's. For many reasons, and especially due to the dearth of candidates over the course of the early modern era, exams for the master's and doctor's degrees eventually typically centered on one candidate per exam. That is reflected in figures 4.1 and 4.3, where several professors at a table examine one candidate.

The examination of candidates for the bachelor's degree, as well as the examination of pupils at institutions below the university, usually involved the processing of multiple and sometimes many candidates at once, often in the same room and at the same time. Some of the dilemmas of examination stand out most clearly when such larger numbers appear on stage. The problems of ranking and, later, of grading the candidates were the most challenging of all.

THE TWO WAYS. The dilemmas of academic examination emerged very clearly in the scandal of the two curricular ways, the battle between the rival academic curricula in the fifteenth century, which we touched on in the previous chapter. The battle of the two ways subverted the scholastic system of knowledge by cleaving it into two rival liturgies. Recall that, in the Germanies, the *via antiqua* was a realist curriculum based on Aquinas along with Albert the Great, or correlatively with the near nominalist Scotus. The *via moderna* meant the nominalist orientation based on Ockham, Buridan, and others, perhaps even also Scotus.[19]

Events at the University of Ingolstadt show the problems induced at examinations by this battle of the books. We shall use them as a case study for the ranking of students. Excepting matters of size, a German university such as Ingolstadt, at this time, resembled an English university such as at Cambridge, or any European university—at least north of the Alps. (Italian universities had a somewhat unique development.) Into the early sixteenth century, European universities remained officially Catholic and had large student bodies of collegians studying for a B.A. North of the Alps, such students lived in colleges or dormitories, the "burses." (German collegians would disappear as a result of the Renaissance and Reformation and the rise of the *gymnasium academicum,* a new humanistic high school that supplanted the B.A. curriculum.)

At foundation in 1472, Ingolstadt had two arts and philosophy faculties divided by the two ways. In 1476/77 the university resolved that there should be but one arts and philosophy faculty. The *via antiqua* had fewer faculty and students than the *via moderna.* Since that would lead to problems, the adherents of the *via antiqua* complained. All were well aware that it now became crucial how the examination committee would be chosen: by designation from above, by popular election, by lot, or by co-optation of the previous committee? If committee co-optation or popular election determined the examiners each term, then the instructors from the more numerous *via moderna* could expropriate complete control. This would allow them, should they dare, to fail or give low rank to all students of the *via antiqua.*

RANKING STUDENTS. We shall focus not on the dispute about the examination committee, but rather on ranking. Acts from 1472 to 1476 set the order of the bachelors in the *via moderna* by seniority and place, but did not spell out the latter. The question arose: should place be set by social status, or by academic seniority, or by performance in the exam? If exam performance was used, then the evil feared by the *via antiqua* might be perpetrated. In fact, some time after 1476, performance at examination came to set place. That collided with the system of seniority and was a recipe for disaster. A ducal inquisition appeared in 1488, then a ducal visitation in 1497, in good part about the curricular battle The following is a paraphrase from the Ingolstadt debate on ranking or placing bachelor's and master's candidates in 1497.[20]

The theologian Adorf pleaded for returning to placement or precedence according to simple seniority of time of study. Baumgartner agreed that place or location of Bachelors should be by seniority of matriculation. But nobles, sons of doctors, priests and monks must be set first, and masters also ought to be located by seniority in view of the B.A., again with nobles first. Peisser said it would be nice if precedence or placement could be really set by ability [ascertained by exam], but this did not work, since [while claiming to place by ability] it was done by favor, so he recommended the same as the two above, again with nobles and priests located first. Hainel said that the examiners, who swore an oath to rank by ability and not by favor, were doing so, which he supported, again with nobles located first. But Arnold said he knew of cases where an instructor had said to a student, "Give me five gulden [and I shall pass you]," or said to another instructor, "Friend, if you pass this one for me, I shall pass one for you." He also knew of a master who had been given third place at graduation, became a school master in Rotemburg, but had to leave the post, since he knew nothing. Prentel supported doing away with ranking based on the oaths of the examiners [regarding the ability of the candidates]. Rafaelis agreed that ranking based on oaths [by the examiners] was difficult. Krapf mused that there was no getting around placement, but now all that was needed was favor, so that [true] scholars had to take a low place, while the unlearned were raised up; so from now on seniority should decide [as it does elsewhere]. Hohmaier recommended that, as in other universities, placement be by seniority. Ricker held that ranking was leading to conspiracies for whoever had money was getting to the top, while the others had to take a place lower or even the pig-place [last place], though they often were more able than those at the top [of the ranking]. Widensinn, who had obtained his M.A. two years previously, said that in his six years at Ingolstadt he had gathered that ranking [by examination] has been no good, as it brought great jealousy and hate; [the examiners] set him above scholars who were more able, and set above him others whose school master he might have been. Weiss claimed that ranking has been until now much involved with money, so that instructors have given [high] placement for money.

Thus some of the protocol from 1497 on placement or location or ranking. The duke's commission first dealt with this in a reform of 19 March 1507. About examination, the ministry decreed that placement should be not on the basis of favor, but rather on examined ability, for much irritation had come of the former. In order to put an end to quarrels, the ministry would actually prefer that placement be done by seniority of registration, excepting for nobles and canons and the like for, as they noted, one ought to give way to the higher by dignity, as happens elsewhere. But the ministry left the final decision to the university. A reform from late summer or early fall 1507 on the curriculum returned to the matter and overturned the first decision. The Bavarian ministry now mandated that placement be by examined ability.

MEDIEVAL AND MODERN MENTALITIES. Trusting Hohmaier above, when he claimed that other universities placed students by seniority, one can envisage the practice of ranking in view of supposed performance at examination as a novelty. The dispute of 1497 indicates unfamiliarity with the practice and how to make it work. To most of these very late medieval academics, ranking by examined ability, that is, grading, seemed outlandish. Though some agreed with Hainel above, and recommended ranking by examined ability, which would be a meritocracy, the majority testified against the idea. The dispute shows the working of three criteria in deciding academic placement: social status, academic seniority, and examined ability.

To a modern, meritocratic, and bureaucratic mentality, examined ability seemed more essential in deciding how to rank or place students. To the medieval, hierarchical, and juridical mentality, social status and academic seniority seemed more essential. From the 1497 protocol, the charges of bribery, favoritism, incompetence, and so on indicate the opacity of a modern meritocracy, a system of ranking by examined ability, in the eyes of late medieval academics. Social status and academic seniority could be clearly recognized by all. Who could really claim that about examined ability? In view of a low ranking, those affected, as well as their instructors who did not serve as examiners, had no appeal to solid, clear criteria other than the oaths of the examiners.

The juridical nature of traditional examination epitomizes itself in the centrality of the examiners' oaths here. The emergence of the 1497 dispute during the collapse of consensus into the warring camps of *via moderna versus via antiqua* shows that examination itself, as a condition of its possibility, presupposes a social consensus, ultimately of the very same sort underlying social status and academic seniority. Imposed by the Bavarian ministry against the will of most of the Ingolstadt faculty, ranking then grading would be the means to manage young students in the nascent disciplinary regime. The application of the tool of ranking by examined ability, that is, grading, had implications for the students being ranked, as well as for the academics applying the tool. New table manners would develop for examinations.

## Ranking at Enlightened Cambridge

The above dispute at late medieval Ingolstadt facilitates our grasp, by way of contrast, of events at late enlightened Cambridge. The modern techniques of ranking and grading by examination attained a most articulated form in eighteenth-century Cambridge. We shall thus look at events there in detail. We shall consider the traditional cast of Cambridge undergraduate or collegian exams, then turn to the great eighteenth-century transformations. This will provide a segue to the second part of the chapter on the rise of the written exam and modern grading system.

TRADITIONAL EXAMS AT CAMBRIDGE. At Cambridge as well as at Oxford, significant exams ancillary to the public disputations for academic degrees extend back before 1648. From 1648 to 1848, examination slowly but surely replaced disputation for the award of the B.A., as a candidate's performance in exam set the order and thus ranking of the bachelors.[21]

A Cambridge B.A. candidate in the seventeenth century, after having been examined by his college, went to the "publick Schools," that is, to an intramural but intercollegiate, university-administered forum where he sat for three days. During that time he could be examined ad libitum by "Proctors, Posers and other regents," that is, by any fellow who was a regent master of not more than five years of seniority in the degree. In 1763 a privilege by the senate, reaffirmed in 1779 and 1791, extended this ability to all masters of arts. Since the college tutors had secured effective control of teaching, this right to examine any B.A. candidate constituted one of the few prerogatives remaining for the typical Cambridge college fellow or master of arts who was not an official college tutor.[22]

The B.A. candidates sat in groups, probably by college. The original point of the Cambridge B.A. exam was only to fine-tune the impression given by one or more candidates at the disputations. However, as the candidates came to be ranked in the eighteenth century, this exam grew in importance. What was in origin only a tool for fine-tuning became in time a primary mechanism for ranking candidates.

The results of the seventeenth-century Cambridge university-administered B.A. exam were compiled in a list known as the *Ordo Senioritatis*. From our attention to the incidents at late medieval Ingolstadt, it should cause us no surprise that this list was at first just what it claimed. Like the academic Cambridge parade from chapter 2, it constituted an order of seniority, an exemplar of traditional authority. Winstanley remarked, "This list, which was styled Ordo Senioritatis, was unclassified [that is, lacked ranking] until the eighteenth century and was, as its name indicates, more an order of precedence than an order of merit."[23]

The inability of the modern mind to fathom the traditional one is evidenced by Winstanley's curious phrase here, "more an order of precedence than an order of merit," apparently presuming it should be the latter. He went on, "There is however some reason to think that the names at the top of it were arranged in some order of merit, but not those lower down which were often grouped according to colleges." Whether or not the seventeenth century had already done so, the eighteenth century clearly displaced an order of seniority with a ranking by merit, as well as with a rudimentary grading system, as we'll see. The grading system embodies the eclipse of traditional authority by bureaucratic rationalization.[24]

In 1710/11 the first seventeen names in the *Ordo Senioritatis* were listed as "1st Tripos," the next sixteen as "2nd Tripos," and the rest as grouped by colleges. The odd term *Tripos*, as a designation of the classes or grades, was soon replaced by Latinate terms, from which *optime* came to designate the two divisions or classes of honors as senior and junior optimes. In 1753 the first class became further divided into wranglers and senior optimes. That gave three grades or classes of Cambridge honors degrees: wranglers, senior optimes, and junior optimes. All others were simply passed. One called the latter the "hoi polloí," then the "polly-men," and finally the "Pollmen." Use of "wrangler" for the highest honors indicates the traditional, disputational cast of thinking still held sway, even though the exam was becoming increasingly mathematical and written, as we'll soon see.[25]

THE SENATE HOUSE EXAMINATION AND WATSON'S IN-NOVATION OF 1763. In 1730, construction of the Cambridge Senate House was completed. Thereafter the university held the exam there and the exam became known as the Senate House Examination until the nineteenth century. Beginning in 1747/48, the lists of the candidates and their ranking were printed and publicly posted. In 1763 Richard Watson served as a moderator, one of the official examiners. He made a further change that proved momentous. Instead of examining groups by colleges, he formed groups in terms of a preliminarily determined order of ability or merit.

Whereas the disputations had been the principal exercise for award of the B.A. since the Middle Ages, they now became merely the means by which the preliminary order of ability or merit was set for the exam. Watson's innovation drew on prior practice, since for some time the tutors had been setting their students into three groups—"hard-reading," "reading," and "nonreading men"—in advance of the actual disputations. One expected the hard-reading men to dispute with other hard-reading men, thus to be most pressed in the disputations. The nonreading men could huddle— in effect, they recited rehearsed responses collectively, as in the rehearsed disputations, which we encountered in chapter 3 above.[26]

In 1763, Watson set eight classes or brackets of ability, which were later collected into three groups. One examined those of equal class within each group together. At the Senate House Examination each year, a candidate could contest his prior classification and insist on competing in a higher class. But on the whole, the preliminary classification implicitly set in advance the fuzzy outlines of who would be a wrangler or senior or junior optime. It set out in advance the groups to be graded with first, second, and third class honors, as opposed to the hoi polloi or Pollmen who simply passed or not. The chief point of the exam became, then, to set the final ranking within the three honors classes or grades.

Let's now consider the conduct of the exam. Of his Senate House Examination in 1751, Richard Cumberland remarked years later these now much quoted words,

> It was hardly ever my lot during that examination to enjoy any respite. I seemed an object singled out as every man's mark, and was kept perpetually at the table under the process of question and answer. My constitution just held up to the expiration of the scrutiny, and I immediately hastened to my own home to alarm my parents with my ghastly looks, and soon fell ill of a rheumatic fever, which for the space of six months kept me hovering between life and death.[27]

The motif of sickness unto death by examination would become a modern cliché. If it has a medieval pedigree, I am ignorant of it. The medieval exam was an ordeal, but not deadly.

An account from 1757 explains that each B.A. candidate gave the maid-servant of the master of his college a half crown for a paper of pins, which the candidate took with him to play push-pin in the Senate House, while waiting. It is unclear whether all candidates sat the entire three days in the Senate House, or whether each college only sat for some set hours each day. But the former seems to be the case. From this account, it is, however, clear that each group endured examination only for some specific hours each day. And not everyone had to perform. "Whilst there waiting, they amuse themselves on the benches at push-pin. Some few are examined . . . but scarce one in ten, and these only pointed out as young men who can stand the test."[28]

As noted, up to 1763 the groups were formed by colleges; after 1763, groups were formed by classes of ability at disputation. An account, seemingly from 1763, implies that the group to be examined waited in the Senate House at the foot of stairs leading up to a gallery where the moderators or official examiners were seated. The candidates seem to have gone up the stairs, one by one, to be examined. Of his exam in 1761, John Venn recorded that they sat in the Senate House for three days and were questioned by official examiners, while qualified fellows took some candidates out at liberty, probably to the fellows' rooms for one on one questioning.[29]

Thus, up to this point, not all candidates seem to have been examined. Into the 1760s, it appears that the group to be examined waited on benches and played push-pin, while one or more candidates were examined. A candidate might be examined in one or both of two fora. One might be taken aside by a fellow to corner of the Senate House or to the fellow's rooms or elsewhere for a one on one exam. In addition or instead, one might be examined by the moderators or official examiners. Cumberland's account from 1751 stated that he "was kept perpetually at the table." The account from 1763 described this table as being in an elevated gallery. The examiners seem to have sat at a table, as in figures 4.1 and 4.3, to which candidates came one by one and where they probably stood. In this form, the Senate House Examination remained a typical early modern oral exam, no matter how nuanced it was.

## THE WRITTEN

### Writing, Ranking, and Grading at Enlightened Cambridge

As we saw in a couple places above, a written or *scriptum* could form part of an academic exam before the eighteenth century. The latter century, however, witnessed the first major steps in the rise of the written exam and its dominance over undergraduates. Events at Cambridge are not crystal clear, but still offer an excellent example of the process.

JEBB'S ACCOUNTS AND THE RISE OF THE WRITTEN EXAM, 1772–74. John Jebb's accounts of the exam from 1772/73 and 1774 are much quoted. His accounts merit all the more importance since they record a conduct of the Senate House somewhat different from the above—a change that has apparently gone unnoticed in histories of this matter.[30]

Jebb notes that at 8:00 a.m., the B.A. candidates enter the Senate House. Their names are called one by one. As set by prior classification, they sit in their relevant groups or divisions. They seem still to be sitting on benches. There are two moderators, that is, official examiners, and each takes a table (Jebb 1774a, 285, 291, 294). Two of the divisions of students are called to each of the two tables where a moderator sits. The students "sit with him round a table, with pens, ink, and paper, before them" (1774a, 291).

So we no longer see candidates standing and examined one by one. We have, rather, a group seated at a table with a single examiner. "Seldom more than six are examined together at the moderator's tables [*sic*], which tables stand at a distance from each other, and are intirely [*sic*] withdrawn from public observation" (1774b, 368). And students write now.

In the 1770s, on Jebb's account, the moderator keeps the division of students the whole hour and varies the exam according to the class, that is, the predetermined ability of the students. "If any person fails an answer, the question goes to the next" (1774a, 291). This implies that some perhaps large part of the exam is still oral, despite the pens, ink, and paper. But some amount of writing nonetheless now forms part of the exam. If the examiner finds the students on the whole able to answer, he moves to more difficult topics.

> When the division under question is one of the higher classes [that is, the first or second class, the prospective wranglers], problems are also proposed, with which the student retires to a distant part of the senate-house, and returns, with his solution upon paper, to the moderator, who, at his leisure, compares it with the solutions of other students, to whom the same problem has been given. (1774a, 292–93)

Most candidates, who so "retired to a distant place," did so to a window in the Senate House. By metonymy, this written part of the exam became known as the "window problems."

In Jebb's day, the exam ran from 8:00 to 9:00 a.m., 9:30 to 11:00 a.m., 1:30 to 3:00 p.m., and 3:30 to 5:00 p.m., with breaks filling the missing hours.

The second day mirrored the first. On the third day, candidates were excused at 11:00 a.m. During the exam, each of the classes or divisions, which consisted of six to eight candidates, was examined once by each of the two moderators. As only two moderators conducted the exam (in 1779 there would be four), most students might be in their divisions on benches and unoccupied most of the time.

The unoccupied time, at least of better students, was occupied by "fathers"—fellows of other colleges who tested the "sons" of rival colleges. "The father of a college takes the student of a different college aside, and sometimes for an hour and a half altogether, strictly examines him in every part of mathematics and philosophy which he professes to have read" (1774a, 295). The father or fellow "and the student always retire to a place by themselves" (1774b, 368), either a corner of the Senate House, or perhaps the fellow's rooms.[31]

During the breaks and at dinner, moderators and fellows, who took part in questioning, conferred. By the end of the second day, the moderators produced a tentative list with the top twenty-four candidates, who were further examined, perhaps individually, on the third day by the proctors, probably in their private rooms. From that examination, one divided the twenty-four into the divisions of wranglers and senior optimes, and placed all of them in a rank order of merit. The examiners probably also composed a second list of another twelve, the junior optimes, which were perhaps ranked. In the first list, the names of four students, nobles or the like, might be inserted ad libitum honoris causa or, rather, on account of nobility.

Jebb's account above most likely simply fills out much of what had been the general practice of conducting the Senate House Examination, especially the method of conferring to set the ranking. It does seem, however, that a radical alteration took place unheralded and even unrecorded between 1763 and 1772. As noted, it was the transition from the typical early modern exam, where a single candidate stood before a table of masters or doctors and took an oral exam, to the modern exam, where candidates sit as a group at tables, eventually one-person tables or desks, and are thus able to write an exam.

At this point, however, it seems that candidates still spent most of their time on benches—although Jebb does not mention them—where they probably still played push-pin while waiting to be called as a group to the moderators' tables, or were "taken out by a father." By the 1780s, moreover, only the first and second classes or divisions typically went to the moderators' rooms on the Monday and Tuesday of the exam for evening problems. As one scholar later recollected, the evening problems proved more difficult than the day problems. This all concerned fine-tuning the ranking at the higher end.[32]

CAMBRIDGE MATHEMATICS AND SYSTEMS OF RANKING AND GRADING. By the 1750s, the Cambridge Senate House Examination had begun to emphasize mathematics and to neglect the traditional topics of philosophy, classics, and religion. The hegemony of mathematics, the emergence of the written exam, and the fetish of marking and ranking seem to have formed a synergetic triad at Cambridge. Moreover, by the second half of the century and before 1772, the exam, unlike the disputations, had shifted from Latin to English. Jebb noted that, too.

The change to English and the emphasis on mathematics indicate not a decline but rather an increase in the rigor and importance of the exam. In the same vein, in 1779 the exam was extended to four days, and the number of moderators increased from two to four. From 1769 to 1799, on average, forty-five students out of one-hundred-fourteen Cambridge B.A. candidates studied for honors, that is, submitted to the Senate House Examination. Aristocrats and wealthy students (fellow-commoners) did not have to take the exam. The student placed first, an honor evermore hotly contested, became the senior wrangler. In time, Cambridge and the parts of English culture under its influence vested considerable charisma in that person. The lowest junior optime, the lowest honors student, got the Wooden Spoon.[33]

As the written part of the exam slowly emerged, there appear to have been written problems, other than the window problems. Writing thus began to take place at the tables where the candidates sat together. At first, examiners dictated the questions, that is, posed them orally. When one candidate had finished writing, an examiner dictated a new problem. The swiftest student thus controlled the pace of the exam, as the others had to break their train of thought, copy down the new problem being dictated, and then return to their previous, unfinished problem(s). The window problems remained only for those competing for highest positions in the ranking. After 1791 the window problems were printed in advance—a major milestone in the transition from the premodern oral to the modern written examination.[34]

Watson was the moderator who made the momentous switch in 1763 from examining students by colleges to examining them by predetermined classes of ability. He felt that this method served to obviate partiality. For Cambridge faced its own version of the dilemma of the *via antiqua versus via moderna*, similar to that at late medieval Ingolstadt, only worse. Ingolstadt had had two rival ways that induced adherents toward partiality contra the other's students. Cambridge was possessed of numerous colleges and each wanted its sons ranked high if not first. This policy of ranking seems to have been a Cambridge specialty. Oxford does not appear to have rigorously ranked its B.A. candidates in an order of merit from first to last, as Cambridge began doing for honors students in the eighteenth century.

The pressures at Cambridge exams led to academic rationalizations. A moderator's marking book from 1778, for example, indicates that letter grades were possible as a means of evaluation, at least in the disputation. Grades given there were: A+, A, A– for very good; E+, E, E– for good; a+, a, a– for fair; and e+, e for indifferent. And after 1792, such marks appeared for each question, and not simply for the entire performance.[35]

British historians regard the Cambridge examination as an academic institution sui generis and unparalleled until the nineteenth century. The dynamic of the university versus the colleges played a role, for the exam served as a principal means by which the university per se began its slow recovery of power from the colleges. And, as the college tutorial system had pushed most masters to the margins pedagogically, the exam allowed them a point of leverage against the tutors. Since any regent master, and post-1763 any master, could participate in the exam along with the moderators, it meant that fellows could press the candidates of other colleges and thus exert some influence on what tutors taught. Moreover, it gave fellows an opportunity to serve as private tutors to help students cram for the exam, as such last minute studying was already called. After 1785, it seems that few fellows exercised the right to participate; nonetheless, the exam continued its seemingly irrevocable development.[36]

A proposed parliamentary visitation commission of 1749 had perhaps played a part in the amazing development of the Cambridge written exam. Fears about the envisaged visitation may have reinforced the elaboration of the Senate House Examination into a true test of merit—to show that Cambridge was serious about reforming itself, thus in no need of parliamentary commissions. (But Oxford did not introduce such an exam.) The ever-increasing stress on mathematics after 1750 perhaps formed part of the same historical process, as one thought that mathematics tests measured merit most easily. "As the examination grew more competitive, so the examiners placed increasing emphasis on subjects which naturally lent themselves to a system of marks . . ." The form of the exam, competitive ranking, and its content as useless mathematics, all proved mutually reinforcing and synergetic.[37]

For the mathematics examined, though difficult, remained the increasingly insular Newtonian-Cambridge calculus, which had little relevance to anything except the examination. The mathematics tested in the Senate

House Examination was not current with contemporary Continental analysis. Even if it had been so, it would have been of little use to most candidates in their future careers, that is, as pastors, gentlemen, and civil servants. Examination of useless but difficult materials developed into a mandarin ideology in the nineteenth century. Such exams functioned less as a certification of pragmatic or expert ability, and more as trials to ascertain charismatic leaders—as though Cambridge sought to ascertain a true genius and son of Newton annually. Such exams also served to rank students as an end in itself.[38]

Enlightened Cambridge was the utopia of examination. Jebb wrote the above-cited remarks in 1772 and 1774 on the Senate House Examination in the context of proposing the institution of annual university-administered examinations for all years of students. The colleges on the whole resisted such a mad scheme (as one thought then), since it would have eroded their power vis-à-vis the university even further. In part to counter Jebb's proposal, St John's, one of the two largest Cambridge colleges, instituted its own collegiate exams.

St John's used its exam as a means to provide a preliminary estimate of a student's ability to perform in the Senate House Examination. Tutors could thus work on students' weaknesses. The reputation of the St John's exam, as an aid to preparation for the Senate House Examination, spread rapidly and helped propel it past Trinity in enrollments. That meant war. Trinity countered with its own exam in 1790. Soon Cambridge went examination mad.

## German Tables and the Grading System

Grading arose as a means to discipline not only the subjects of examination. The two cases studied above, Ingolstadt and Cambridge, indicate that crucial aspects in the developmental dynamics of examination emerged as means to control examiners, to discipline those in power.

The investigation turns back now to the Germanies. We shall consider the evolution of the grading system also at schools, that is, at educational sites below the university. As noted above, in the Protestant Germanies the Renaissance and Reformation led to the devolution of the university B.A. curriculum onto a new sort of high school outside the university: the *gymnasium academicum,* later called the *Gymnasium.* The German grading system was born and nurtured at schools such as the gymnasium. Later it spread its empire into academia.

ORDINAL RANKING AND CARDINAL GRADING. It is hard to tell how old the ranking of students is in practice. Published statutes from medieval and early modern universities contain little implying that ranking and grading took place generally before the Enlightenment. If it occurred, and it probably did, it must have been more a matter of practice than statute. Given the role of precedence at the traditional university, bachelors and masters had to march and sit in a way reflecting academic precedence. But should it be by social status, academic seniority, or performance in exam? The case history from Ingolstadt showed the dilemma of the latter.

In chapter 2, we saw that the academic parade marched to the tune of academic degrees and seniority. Modernizing universities, such as late medieval Ingolstadt, toyed with using performance in examination to set precedence among the students. Wittenberg was also a modernizer. The anonymous *Historia* (1587) of Doctor Faust claims that he placed first among sixteen at the master's exam at Wittenberg in the early sixteenth century. Simon Wilde did not fare as well as Faust. Simon wrote home, on 29 April 1542, that he had been given sixth place at the master's exam there. But the generality of such ranking remains unclear in the Renaissance and Baroque. And mere ordinal ranking is not grading, as we'll see.[39]

The movement from ordinal ranking to grading most likely entered academia by way of lower schools and found its first point of academic application on scholarship students, that is, on the poor. A 1587 ministerial visitation to Wittenberg shows that one examined scholarship students quarterly and kept a list about their performance, though it is unclear if one ranked or graded them. Important was however the sheer regularity and frequency of examination, a discipline to which normal students were long not subjected.[40]

A 1592 visitation to Helmstedt contained evaluations of the scholarship students. But the evaluations were simply discursive reports: whence they came, how old they were, what classes they were taking, what disputations they had done, in which disciplines they showed talent, and where they were remiss. From this report and others like it, no ranks or grades seem to have existed in sixteenth-century academia generally, even among the poor.[41]

The statutes of the Jesuit University of Paderborn, circa 1616–30, offer a teasing look at ranking and perhaps even grading The statutes set the following for bachelors candidates. An alphabetical list is made of all candidates. The list bears an implicit table, for running counter to the names are implicit columns: ability, diligence, and pass-fail. *A* is for passed or admitted; *R* for failed or rejected; and *D* for dubious cases. In ability and diligence, each student receives numbers: "per notam numeri 1. 2. 3. etc."

This "etc." is, alas, not spelled out. The numbers might serve as the ordinals: first, second, third. The "etc." here would extend the ordinals up to the number of candidates. Or the numbers might serve as cardinals: one, two, three, and so on. This would refer to an absolute ideal of ability and diligence, against which one measured the candidates and which did not perforce extend the cardinals one-to-one with the candidates. In the last case, it would be possible for more than one student, or for none, to have a 1 or 2 (or an A or B), and so on.[42]

The former case, the numbers as ordinals, embodies a traditional system of ranking. The latter case, the numbers as cardinals, promises a modern system of grading. Could the Jesuits have been so far advanced in the bureaucratization of academic persona? They had taken a step between 1616 and 1630 that most instructors at Ingolstadt in 1497 could not imagine. The Jesuit statutes stipulated that the six highest would be demarcated in a catalogue of students for graduation and, if nobles or clerics wished to appear there without submitting to the exams, their names would appear in an addendum, so that they did not appear ahead of the six best examined. The Jesuits had separated social status and examined ability apart here.

The onset of grading in a systematic way appears to be an event of the eighteenth century, and to take much of its course for perfection. In the section above, the evolution of the Cambridge *Ordo senioritatis* into the Tripos exam embodied just such a change. Cambridge articulated both an ordinal ranking and a cardinal grading of B.A. candidates. The three honors classes—wranglers, senior optimes, junior optimes—were effectively what they are now, the cardinal marks or grades of 1, 2, 3, while the Pollmen just got passed or not. All the members of each of the three honors grades were then, additionally, ordinally ranked.

GRADING AND TABLES. The emergence of grading is tied to the table as a report in the Germanies. This appears also to be an event of the Enlightenment. Before then, a few tables and grades can be found. But those were exceptional instances, unless one looks at schools.[43]

A school in Saxe-Gotha circa 1642–85 subjected its pupils to ordinal tabulation, but probably not grading. After this, one finds grading tables in the County of Waldeck (1704), in the Duchy of Württemberg (1729), in Brunswick-Wolfenbüttel (1753), in the County of Ravenberg (1754), in Brandenburg-Prussia (1763), and in Electoral Saxony (1773).[44]

Consider figure 4.4, the grading table or report schema mandated for the County of Waldeck in 1704. Called a *Censur-Tabell*, it served as an exemplar for instructors. It indicates that this technique, namely grading, had to be explained to them. Horizontally across the page are columns for the names of the pupils, their ages, and grades in general and particular. Vertically down the page are exemplary entries.

| Nomen & Patria. | Aetas & Ingenium. | Profectus Catechetici in verbis. | Profectus Catechetici in sensu. | Profectus in Latinit. inprim. in explic. aut. Class. | Profectus in Graecis. | Profectus in He-braicis. | Profectus in Oratoria. | Mores & Vita. | Absentia cum aut absque venia. |
|---|---|---|---|---|---|---|---|---|---|
| 1. Johannes N. von Corbach. | 18. Ann. Libe-ralis ingenii. | fertig. | gut | fein | gut | ziemlich | gut | fromm | 4 stunden cum venià. |
| 2. Christian N. von Wildun-gen. | 17. Ann. stu-pidus. | nicht viel. | noch schlimmer | schlecht | etwas | nichts | wenig | ungehorsam. | 12 stunden abs-que venià. |
| 3. Georg N. von Menge-ringhausen. | 19. Ann. plus memoriae quam judicii. | lernt fleissig | mediocriter | schreibt ziem-lich explic. aut. noch schlecht. | ziemlich | wenig | nimmt zu | störrisch | 2 stunden c. v. 4. stunden a. v. |
| 4. Caspar N. von Rhoden. | 15. Ann. egre-giae indolis. | fertig | achtsam | hat einen gu-ten anfang. | thut das feine. | bestessiget sich. | macht eine gute Chrie. | gibt gute Hoff-nung. |  |
| 5. Jeremias N. von Landau. | 16. Ann. in-genio tardus. | nicht eine zeit wie die ander. | von wenigem Begriff. | faul. | keine Begierde. | auch nicht | nichts | ungezogen. | 14 stunden abs-que venià. |
| 6. Ludwig N. von Ense. | 14. Ann. pe-netrans. | unfleissig | kan wol fassen | in explic. aut. noch nicht viel. | gut | nichts | methodicus | variable. | 4 stunden c. v. 8 stunden a. v. |
| 7. Henrich N. von Sachsen-hausen. | 16. Ann. in-gen. docilis. | leich irrig | fasset wol | ist zu loben. | von den besten | thuts vielen zu vor | hat keine Lust dazu | läst sich fagen | |
| 8. Johannes N. von Sachsen-berg. | 14. Ann. inge-nio tardus. | ziemlich | von schlechten Begriff. | etwas | auch etwas | nichts | jejunus | gehorsam | 6 st. c. v. |
| 9. Nicolaus N. von Sachsen-berg. | 15. Ann. sim-plex. | unfleissig. | unachtsam | wenig | etwas | schlecht | nichts | widerspen-stig. | 16 st. a. v. |
| 10. Bernhard N. von Twi-ste. | 16. Ann. ver-sutus. | lernt bald. | disputax | Confusus. | nimmt zu | hat gute Pro-gressus | bene | garrulus | 6 st. a. v. 2 st. c. v. |
| 11. Caspar N. von Freyen-hagen. | 17. Ann. spe-culativus. | fleissig. | profundus | egregius | gut | ziemlich | nicht viel. | sittsam | |
| 12. Justus N. von Wildun-gen. | 18. Ann. inge-nium extem-poraneum. | lernt bald und vergißt bald | confundirt sich leicht | egregiè | so hin | thut das feine | wol | mendax | 6 st. a. v. 8 st. a. v. |

4.4. Model grading table for the County of Waldeck, 1704.

Pupil 1 is Johannes N. from Corbach. Column 2 records his age to be eighteen and general ability (*ingenium*) to be ample. Columns 3–4 concern the catechism: his memorization of it is complete and understanding of it is good. Columns 5 to 8 concern Latin, Greek, Hebrew, and Oratory, where his grades are, respectively, fine, good, proper or decent, and good. Column 9 grades his conduct and behavior as pious. Column 10 records he has been absent four times, but with a valid excuse. Johannes N. so begins the table as exemplar of a near model pupil.

Pupil 2, Christian N., from Wildungen, serves as a model good-for-nothing. He is seventeen years old and in ability is "stupid." His memorization of catechism is "not much," and his comprehension of it is "even worse." Here one sees that the grades, even in this exemplary table, have not been fully abstracted: the "even worse" makes internal reference to an earlier grade. Christian's Latin is "bad," Greek is "a bit," Hebrew "nothing," and Oratory "little." In conduct he is disobedient and has been absent twelve hours without valid excuse.

Other pupils in the table exhibit the spectrum. For general ability, possible grades here are more memory than judgment, outstanding in talent, slow in ability, penetrating, quick in ability, simpleminded, wily, speculative, ability to improvise.

| Schul-Tabell, Wie solche jedesmahl bey denen Visitationen aufzuweisen. | | | | | | | | | | |
|---|---|---|---|---|---|---|---|---|---|---|
| Nahme. | Vatter. | Alter. | Gelernig-keit. | Answendig lernen. | Lesen. | Schreiben. | Sitten. | versaumte Stunden. | Mangel. | |
| **I. Class.** | | | | | | | | | | |
| 1. | Joh. Georg. | Joh. Georg Rueff. | 7. | fähig. | guth. | guth. | guth. | fromm. | 12 kranck. | hat keinen |
| 2. | | Wagner. | | fertig. | mittelmäßig. | mittelmäßig. | mittelmäßig. | gehorsam. | | Psalter. |
| 3. | | | 10. | | | | | sittsam. | 6 ohne noth. | |
| 4. | | | | mittelmäßig. | schlecht. | schlecht. | schlecht. | still. | | fehlt das |
| 5. | | | | | | | | | | neue Testa- |
| 6. | | | 12. | langsam. | | | | mittelmäßig. | 3 muth- | ment. |
| 7. | | | | | | | | schlecht. | willig. | |
| 8. | | | Jahr. | schlecht. | | | | muthwillig. | | Kinderlehr. |
| 9. | | | | hart. | | | | widerspenstig. | | |
| 10. | | | | thumm. | | | | gottlos. | | |
| 11. | | | | | | | | | | |
| 12. | | | | | | | | | | |
| 13. | | | | | | | | | | |
| 14. | | | | | | | | | | |
| **II. Cl.** | | | | | | | | | | |
| 1. | | | | | buchstabiren. | | | | | |
| 2. | | | | | | | | | | |
| 3. | | | | | | | | | | |
| 14. | | | | | | | | | | |
| **III. Cl.** | | | | | | | | | | |
| 1. | | | | | | | | | | |
| 2. | | | | | | | | | | |
| 3. | | | | | | | | | | |
| 14. | | | | | | | | | | |

4.5. Model grading table for Württemberg, 1729.

The grades for general ability are in Latin, while the grades for particular disciplines and conduct mix a little Latin with mostly German. There is little systematic about them and, rather than being a modern system of grading, they point back to traditional notions of types or temperaments. The grades or evaluations for columns 3 to 9, Catechism to Oratory, approach the notion of ranking in a cardinal way, thus of grading. Some colorful terms appear, such as "disputer," "lackluster," and "had a good beginning." Albeit here still in untamed profusion, most terms have become the colorless terms of our own grading: "good," "fine," "bad," "adequate," "little," "something," "nothing," "middling," "shows progress," "excellent," and so on.

It remained but to reduce the grades to a colorless few, whose number and order were set. Figure 4.5, from Württemberg in 1729, took that great step. This *Schul-Tabell* was to be shown to the supervisors of the school. It served again as exemplar to teach a new technique to instructors. Column 1 indicates that the class or level should be indicated. Column 2 has the pupil's name, column 3 his father's name, and column 4 the pupil's age. Column 5 sets a general evaluation as ability to learn (*Gelirnigkeit*). Under this column appear "capable," "fit," "middling," "slow," "bad," "hard," and "dumb." When seen in the context of columns 6 to 9, those terms trace seven cardinal points from best to worst. The terms express a closed system of grading. While column 5 on the ability to learn still has echoes of an old typology, columns 6 to 8 have grades in the modern sense, and reduced to only three: good, middling, bad. Column 9 on morals is again more effusive. Column 10 records hours missed, while column 11 serves as the miscellany, the final refuge for earlier discursive notes.

It took a long time before cardinal grades, as they appeared in the tables discussed above, colonized German Protestant universities. But an Austrian decree of 1784 instituted grades for its universities, which had been free of Jesuit influence since the papal suppression of them in 1773. Given the lack of distinction in Austria between the lyceum (or high school), college, and university, grading included at least students in the arts and philosophy faculty. Four grades were set in words and in numbers, the latter called classes. The grades were "bad" as third class, "middling" as second class, "good" as first class, and "very good" as first class with eminence. The Jesuitical past facilitated such bureaucratic rationalization of academic persona in the Habsburg lands.[45]

In 1789 Friedrich Gedike, a Prussian minister of education whom we shall meet often, visited universities outside Prussia to study them. Gedike found tabulation of students noteworthy at Catholic Mainz and Erfurt, as well as at Protestant Erlangen. At Mainz he saw a 1784 reform in effect. Instructors noted absent students at each class and reported them in monthly tables. Professors judged and "classified" their students quarterly, from which a table was made. Erfurt had improved a 1777 plan by 1789. Professors there evaluated students monthly in tabular format, and sent these reports to the ministry in Mainz. At Erlangen professors evaluated their students quarterly in a tabular schema, which they sent to the ministry in Bayreuth. Gedike did not describe such tables, so it's not clear if grading existed.[46]

As the modern regime of examination gradually took hold of the student body during the eighteenth and nineteenth century, some serious rationalizers asked this question: If pupils and students were to be graded, why not grade professors in the same way?

Austrian regulations of 1777/78 and 1781 set up a system mandating annual tabular reports by directors and prefects on lyceum instructors. The table had columns for name, country, age and status, talent, diligence, didactic ability, manner of conduct with pupils, honesty, civility, knowledge of languages and sciences. Vertically, the tables show the to-be-graded as the professors of (Latin) poetry, oratory, and grammar. Use of "professor" for such instructors shows the lack differentiation between the secondary school or lyceum and the university in the Austrian system, a remnant of the Jesuits. But its existence shows the long march of the rationalization of academia in Austria, far outstripping the Prussians.[47]

EXAMINATION AND CORPORAL PUNISHMENT. On 14 October 1775, the ministry in Vienna mandated this for all Austrian schools. In the first year Latin class, there was to be frequent and unrelenting examination by the teacher. Soon this regime of frequent and unrelenting examination would encompass both the university and the school, replacing the rod and corporal punishment with catalogues, report cards, and tables.

A 1780/81 instruction for Austrian school directors enjoined, "All physical punishments are to be abolished at lycea, and only humiliation is to be incurred as a consequence of punishable action." In the same year, 1781, the ministry mandated schools to send quarterly reports in a preset schema. In 1784 the Austrian ministry further commanded that examinations be held regularly during the year to measure progress and diligence. Instructors had to keep a record of the exams and show it to the school's director.

On 4 October 1790, Vienna moved such notions into academia. It decreed that the seats in the lecture halls were to be numbered, one for each student, and its number recorded in a catalogue, so the instructor might more easily note absences. Every semester the seat assignments were to be changed, so as to prevent associations among the students. Moreover, every professor every day had to pick several students, without their knowing in advance and thus not alphabetically, in order to test them. Such were the new no-nonsense post-Jesuitical Austrian methods for policing a population ranging from school to university.[48]

In the Protestant city of Hanover, the capital city of the German state of the same name, pupils were still being beaten in the early 1770s. The Saxon school plan of 1773, however, advocated an end to the rod, an end to corporal discipline at school. The last third of the eighteenth century witnessed the decline of the rod, which was destined to become a pointer in the pedagogue's hand. In place of beating, the Saxon school plan foresaw at the end of a term:

> Hereupon without delay must be reported in the usual way to the Supreme Council about examination. In addition to enclosure of the written specimens, it must be earnestly indicated what the rector and his colleagues [instructors] in every portion of their teaching have done and completed in the last half year, so that one may judge whether they have proceeded according to [the 1773] instruction. To this report is to be appended a tabular list of the pupils, in which about each is indicated his ability in each subject, and his conduct and morals, and in what [subject] each shows outstanding talent.[49]

In 1788 at Berlin's Friedrichwerdesches Gymnasium, headed by our ubiquitous Prussian minister and pedagogue, Friedrich Gedike, they used

corporal punishment only on hardened cases. On the whole, the new methods worked. The teacher had a notebook where he recorded the performance of each pupil after every lesson. There were monthly general exams,
followed by reports with evaluations based on the daily summaries. The report had to be signed by the pupil's parents, and returned the next day. Poor
performance led to segregation in the classroom, and an application of the
above new tortures weekly.[50]

Spaces once pedagogically filled by the rod and corporal discipline were
taken over by unrelenting examination, tabular report cards, and the grading system. These techniques emerged as the authorized means for formation of future civil and academic servants of the German state. The report,
table, and grade internalized the discipline that the rod, like policing, had
tried so clumsily to impose externally. The German *Abitur* formed part of
this process.

THE PRUSSIAN ABITUR OF 1788. On 23 December 1788, the new
Prussian Supreme School Council, of which Gedike was a member, set up
the exam that would become a university entrance examination. The oral
and written exam became called the *Abitur*, from Latin *abitus*, that is, departure from school. The Prussian and later German *Abitur* amounted to a
sort of baccalaureate-equivalent exam, administered outside the university.

The regulation of 1788 concerned itself essentially only with formalities.
The Prussian ministry said it envisaged a canonical form for the *Abitur*, but
for now left its structure for provincial boards to set. The ministry expected
biannual reports, and instructors should conduct the examination only in
the presence of the local school directors and a deputation of the provincial
school board. The provincial deputation and the rector were to set the questions. The exam must enable easy and precise grading, and permit pupils to
write it over a half-day. The provincial deputation was to keep the originals
of the completed exams and a protocol of the exam. Evaluation of exams
proceeded by simple majority vote of the examiners and members of the
deputation.

The Prussian ministry did not set actual grades in 1788; but it held that
the evaluations should be given in few words, without rambling and avoiding indeterminacy and ambiguity. This invited grades such as "excellent,"
"good," "middling," "bad," and the like. The deputation was to send a report
to the provincial school council, giving a tabular overview of the results. The
provincial councils, having received the tabular reports from their schools,
were to make a general table for the province and send this to the Supreme
School Council in Berlin.[51]

Despite the onset of the grading system as seen above, the final grade for the *Abitur* was pass or fail. Finer grading of the *Abitur* would await the nineteenth century. But the injunction above—that the examiners give evaluations of the specific subjects in few words and without rambling, avoiding all indeterminacy and ambiguity—signaled the examiners to avail themselves of the new winds blowing toward the cardinal systems of grading. In the first half generation after 1788, grading of the *Abitur* seems to have been fairly lax, despite the provincial deputation's surveillance and policing. Instructors, rectors and probably the provincial councils did not want to look bad by having immature or failed pupils.

Only in the first decades of the nineteenth century did the *Abitur* achieve its modern perfection as "a sort of torture," bending would-be students in this new rite of passage. Taking the *Abitur* would not be mandatory for entrance to the university until 1834. Until then, only the poor and needy had to submit to the *Abitur*. The regulation of 1788 had only made university scholarships contingent on passing this exam. Recall that the Cambridge Senate House Examination had also been originally a voluntary exam for honors. Before the culture of examination conquered Britain, the hoi polloi and well to do did not partake.[52]

In 1788 the Prussian ministry not only set up the *Abitur*. It also issued edicts commanding proper religious belief and instituting censorship on all domestic publications, academic or otherwise. In 1791 Prussia instituted an examination commission to investigate and approve the allegiance to the state of all applicants for religious and teaching offices.

In light of such measures from 1788 to 1791, here are some of the questions put to pupils, mostly poor or needy, taking the *Abitur*. On 19 August 1791, "Whereby was the [wonderful] transformation of the Roman Republic into a monarchy brought about? What caused the [sad] decline of the latter?" On 5 April 1794, "What advantages does the Christian religion have above all others?" On 24 February 1795, "What are the typical forms of government, and what are their advantages and disadvantages? . . . What advantages does the Prussian state [being a monarchy] enjoy that protect it from every revolution [namely, like the one in France in 1789]?" On 13 March 1802, "How can one explain the apparent decline in morality associated with the [erstwhile and happily no longer] expanding Enlightenment?"[53]

L ittle evidence has appeared to date implying that grading existed in a general way at the university before the eighteenth century. The system of academic grading seems an event of the late eighteenth and early nineteenth centuries. Schools pioneered grading and it took shape in paper tables—to discipline pupils, later students, and to control the discourse and prolixity of examiners. These tables carved a neutral space in which a sort of egalitarian, meritocratic community could be achieved. But, in the spirit of the politico-economic world of modern rational authority, one sought egalitarianism by techniques of standardization and normalization. Reduction of flowery discursive evaluations to a colorless minimum—such as good, middling, and bad, or 1, 2, 3, or A, B, C—effected the transition from open ordinal ranking to closed cardinal grading. The ABCs gave the key to a modern grading system.

From a global perspective, such techniques have been central to bureaucratic systems of registration which, like systems of actual bookkeeping, are "much further removed from speech, being largely composed of lexemes that are lifted from context and of numbers that form so distinct a 'set' of their own . . . ," that written discourse is not needed or useful.[54]

The Prussians, like others, eventually saw that the magic of the modern bureaucratic system lay in the form, not the contents. The modern bureaucratic state could thus be a liberal *Kultur-Staat,* as opposed to a police state. The cultural state could cease propagandizing students in the Jesuitical manner of the *Abitur* questions above. The essence of the modern system is that, irrespective of the contents of education, undergraduates must be ranked or graded. That makes them tested bureaucratic products and subjects. What is taught—once it has been properly depoliticized—is, at base, harmless academic babble.

## Grading in the German Seminar

The Cambridge Senate House Examination and the Prussian *Abitur* exhibit most articulated means of examining and grading undergraduates or their equivalents at the gymnasium. The seminar offers insights into the manners of handling advanced students. The question here was: should advanced students—the graduate students of a later era—also be graded?

In 1787, the year before the Prussian Supreme School Council set up the *Abitur,* two important seminars were founded in Prussia. Gedike, our ubiquitous Prussian minister above, had a hand in both. With Gedike himself as the director, a nonuniversity pedagogical seminar was attached to the Friedrichwerdesches Gymnasium in Berlin at which Gedike served as rector. This seminar had the mission of training or certifying future instructors for college or university preparatory secondary schools, the gymnasia in the modern sense.

In the same year, Gedike negotiated with the philologist and professor at the University of Halle, F. A. Wolf, about the foundation of the first university seminar in Prussia in the arts and philosophy faculty. As we'll see in detail in the next chapter, a seminar at this point meant a budgeted institute—the budget mostly went for scholarships for the seminar's participants. As a case study, we shall look at the means of reporting that Wolf worked out at the University of Halle for his seminar, in the face of Gedike's ministerial agenda. The evaluation and perhaps grading of seminar students became a ministerial concern, for they were not only advanced students but also, as noted, had state monies for scholarships.[55]

WOLF'S REPORTS. Wolf filed his first report on the new seminar to the ministry on 15 October 1787. He enclosed a table of the seminarists, as we'll call them, in four columns: name, native province, school graduated, how long at the university. On 22 January 1788, Gedike wrote Wolf that, besides the table, the ministry wants Wolf's "judgment of the aptitudes, abilities and talents of each and every seminarist" so that the ministry may see "what may be expected of each one." Wolf should also send such a report each semester so that the ministry may be apprised of the progress of the members.

Wolf wrote to the ministry on 5 February 1788 that he did not want to evaluate the students in the manner suggested, fearing such evaluations would alienate them, especially those whom he would have had to evaluate poorly. On 12 February, Gedike responded that the evaluations as desired by the ministry would serve to promote the diligence of the seminarists and to influence future promotion in the good offices of state. And, although the evaluations would play a role in determining the future of each seminarist, the ministry reassured Wolf that it would keep the evaluations confidential. And, should the evaluations leak out, they would serve to spur the seminarists to greater accomplishments anyway.

Wolf found the ministry's position reprehensible. On 10 March 1788, he reported he had found all seminarists diligent and so on. He referred to the seminarists as a whole. He stated further that, if he must give individual evaluations, he would want to characterize only the best few. He did not want to give other students a poor character in the report, since they were at an age when daily improvement was possible. Someone in the ministry has marked this section of his letter in blue pencil. Wolf noted further, "Since judgment of knowledge and ability is something very relative and, thus, if not supported by a sufficient series of data of all sorts, it can make quite different impressions on different readers" of a report. He hoped it would be acceptable if he only individually evaluated the few best, and then the seminar as a corpus. On 18 March 1788, Gedike gave in and approved the style of reporting Wolf suggested. On 22 March, Gedike produced a regulation for the seminar along Wolf's lines.

Under the terms negotiated with Gedike speaking for the ministry, Wolf filed his first report on 11 November 1788. The report is discursive. Wolf mentions each seminarist, some only briefly in a line, and some in a whole paragraph. Contrary to his own expressed concerns, he gives a poor evaluation to one of the graduating members. He knows this will terminate any bright future in Prussia for that student. Wolf's reports of the mid-1790s are on the whole brief, with minimal information on most students.

On 21 July 1795, Gedike revisited the matter of reporting and asked Wolf to enclose a list of seminarists to date. He also indicated that printed specimens should be enclosed henceforth in reports. Gedike noted that in future reports Wolf should give detailed evaluations of seminarists, so that one may "have detailed, authentic reports of their progress in the acts, and thus be acquainted with the students" who have used their time well and thus be "justified in well founded hopes for the future." From 1796 to 1799, however, a gap appears in Wolf's seminar records, so that it is unclear what form his reporting took, if any. The next report is dated 30 April 1799 and contains a list of members theretofore in the manner requested in 1787. In the report of 1799, Wolf tells the ministry "one can be assured of soon having an outstanding elite" of Prussian gymnasium teachers.

On 16 May 1801, the University of Halle's regular report to the ministry touches on the touchy subject of Wolf's seemingly missing reports. Interesting in Wolf's resistance to the bureaucratic regime of reporting is precisely the matter of tables. As early as 1787, Wolf had drawn up exemplars of tables in which to cast his reports, which he seems to have filed fitfully. In 1803 another exemplar for tabular reporting appeared in the acts.

WOLF'S TABLES. Figure 4.6 shows a tabular report filed by Wolf for summer semester in 1805. Columns on the top half, from left to right, specify name, province of origin, age, school attended, time at the university, academic major, time in the seminar, and how much longer estimated to be at the university. Twelve individuals are listed and numbered 1 to 12 in the columns on the top half. Columns on the bottom half graded the individuals above in terms of the number given them from 1 to 12. The columns from left to right measure natural talent, diligence, progress and knowledge, conduct and moral character. These were all to be graded in terms of just three grades: excellent, good, common.

As seen, such a system was not then common in academia. And Wolf had problems sticking to three grades in evaluating morals. Then on 1 April 1806 he submitted the table in figure 4.7. Bureaucratic rationalization achieved perfection here. Wolf reduced the three grades to a, b, c. His adoption of cardinal grading came as a consequence of his capitulation to

4.6. F. A. Wolf's grades for his seminar students, University of Halle, 1805.

4.7. F. A. Wolf's grades for his seminar students, University of Halle, 1806.

tabular evaluation. Like other forms of bureaucratic rationalization of authority, the table's rationality seems in part a technique to effect "intimate distance."[56]

After 1810 the explicit grading of students in the Prussian seminars apparently ceased. The indignities to which Wolf was subjected must have seemed illiberal then, a vestige of the police state. Seminar directors did regularly report, but the *Kultur-Staat* had a relaxed attitude about reporting. The ministry now left much to the idiosyncrasies of professors. So, for instance, the directors of the seminar in Bonn filed long but discursive reports in the 1820s. If professors evaluated seminarists, then they did so in words, without tables or ABCs.[57]

The drawing of a boundary—a boundary one day between undergraduate and graduate students—began to emerge here. The seminar trained advanced students. As we'll see in the next chapter, such students would prove themselves not so much in written exams, but rather more by the originality of their research papers, which were not as amenable to tabular rationalizations. The seminar would cultivate a new sort of academic charisma.

## The Fine English Art

The most interesting part was not the further development at Cambridge.

THE FURTHER DEVELOPMENT AT CAMBRIDGE. Below is a quoted description from 1802 of the Cambridge Senate House Examination. It demonstrates the fine English art of examination.

---

On *Monday* morning, a little before *eight* o'clock, the Students, generally about a *Hundred,* enter the Senate-House, preceded by a Master of Arts, who on this occasion is styled the *Father* of the college to which he belongs. On two pillars at the entrance of the Senate-House are hung the *Classes;* and a Paper denoting the hours of examination of those who are thought most competent to contend for *Honors.*

Immediately after the University clock has struck *eight,* the names are called over, and the Absentees, being marked, are subject to certain fines. The classes to be examined are called out, and proceed to their appointed tables, where they find pens, ink, and paper provided in great abundance. In this manner, with the utmost order and regularity, *two thirds* of the young men are set to work within less than five minutes . . . There are *three* chief tables, at which *six examiners* preside . . . The first two tables are chiefly allotted to the first *six* classes; the third or largest to the *hoi polloí.*

The young men hear the Propositions or Questions delivered by the Examiners; they instantly apply themselves; demonstrate, prove, work out and write down, fairly and legibly (otherwise their labour is of little avail) the answers required. All is silent; nothing heard save the voice of the Examiners; or the gentle request of some one, who may wish a repetition of the enunciation. It requires every person to use the utmost dispatch; for as soon as ever the Examiners perceive any one to have finished his paper and subscribed his name to it [,] another Question is immediately given. A smattering demonstration will weigh little in the scale of merit; everything must be fully, clearly, and scientifically brought to a true conclusion. And though a person may compose his paper amidst hurry and embarrassment, he ought to ever to recollect that his papers are all inspected by the united abilities of *six* examiners with coolness, impartiality and circumspection.

The Examiners are not seated, but keep moving round the tables, both to judge how matters proceed and to deliver their Questions at proper intervals. The examination . . . is varied according to circumstances: no one can anticipate a question, for in the course of five minutes he may be dragged from *Euclid* to *Newton* . . . While this examination is proceeding at the three tables between the hours of *eight* and *nine*, printed Problems . . . are delivered to each person of the *first* and *second* classes; these he takes with him to any window he pleases, where there are pens, ink, and paper prepared for his operations. It is needless to add that every person now uses his utmost exertion, and solves as many Problems as his abilities and time will allow.[58]

---

The first generations subjected to the Prussian *Abitur* described it as torture. Many who underwent the probably more fearsome Cambridge written exams had similar feelings.[59]

The Cambridge Senate House Examination, as described above in 1802, shows an inversion of the oral exam, as depicted in figures 4.1 and 4.3. It is now the candidates who sit as a group, while the examiners, albeit two to a table, stand or, rather, strut about. We no longer have unoccupied students waiting idly on benches and playing push-pin. Every candidate "now uses his utmost exertion" to complete the exam. All the candidates now sit at three separate tables, the third being a rather large one for the hoi polloí.

Except for the window problems, the questions are still given orally. But the entire exam now appears to be a written one. Acceptable answers must be "fully, clearly, and scientifically brought to a true conclusion," as the examiners will mark the papers with "coolness, impartiality and circumspection." The entire examination now runs "with the utmost order and regularity," like a well-oiled machine. "All is silent; nothing heard save the voice of the Examiners," or a meek query of a student. In this Cambridge utopian space of examination, everyone has "appointed tables, where they find pens, ink, and paper provided in great abundance"—a recurring bad dream of mine and of many more I'm sure.

In 1808/09, a fifth day was added to the Senate House Examination. The first three days, from Monday to Wednesday, concerned mathematics, while moral philosophy was Thursday. On the first three days, the exam ran for six hours each day, not counting the private, evening sessions in the moderators' rooms, involving the likely highest wranglers, for whom the daily toll might reach ten hours of examination. On Friday, the examiners fought over the brackets or class boundaries, negotiated the complete classification and rankings of candidates within them and, as the exam developed over time, publicly announced the senior wrangler by midnight. On Saturday the final list of all candidates was published.[60]

THE NEW TRIPOS EXAMS. In 1822, Cambridge instituted the Classical Tripos, using an odd word we met above. The Classical Tripos offered an additional exam in Classics that one might opt to take but, up to 1850, only after having passed with honors the Senate House Examination, soon called the Mathematical Tripos to differentiate it. Although Cambridge, like Oxford, still effectively trained mostly future gentlemen, pastors, and civil servants, the excessive emphasis on mathematics in the examination persisted until 1850. Oxford for its part imparted and tested primarily classics (as did also the Romantic Germanies), which was just as useless as Cambridge "maths" for the real lives that most candidates would pursue.[61]

An interesting account of the Mathematical Tripos Examination in the 1820s comes from J. M. F. Wright. At the time, six divisions or classes for honors were set each year in advance, either by college examination at the modernizing colleges, or by the medieval method of disputation at the traditional ones. The six classes for honors sat at tables, two classes to a table, thus still as in the account from 1802 above. Wright had scored high enough in his college exam so that he would pass the Tripos with certainty. As he had no hopes of high honors, he decided to "gulph it," that is, effectively to do nothing during the exam. When the examiners perceived that he was gulphing it, they sent him off to join the hoi polloí, who had a simple exam, but were supposed to take it. Cheating here remained rather easy and honorable, both by whispers and by ogles, as Wright explains.[62]

CAMBRIDGE COLLEGE EXAMS. Wright's lackadaisical efforts at the Mathematical Tripos Examination stand in stark contrast to his valiant efforts at the college exam at Trinity. All assemble at 9:00 a.m., as he recounts. The Reading (and Hard-Reading) Men wear their anxiety on their faces. For fear of losing time due to faulty implements, some have "a handful of the *very best pens,* although there is an ample supply upon every table." Fear has become a central motif of such examination. "Well, the men of every year being seated at the table with abundance of pens, ink, and paper (in the form of quarters of sheets), a printed paper is presented to each man, with a request that he will *write on only one side of the paper . . ."*[63]

On the first day, from 9:00 a.m. to noon, the freshmen are orally examined, while the junior sophs have a written exam. From noon to 3:00 p.m. the students have a meal and cram further. The afternoon session inverts the two groups on the oral versus written exam and runs from 3:00 p.m. till dusk, with the implication that "men were allowed to continue scribbling as long as they can see." But the hall usually emptied by 9:30 p.m.[64]

The next day at 9:00 a.m., all assemble again. "Pale and death-like as were most of us, from excessive reading before the Examination commenced . . . [p]aler and paler still grew every man as the Examination proceeded." The second day appears to mirror the first in its rhythms. Though Wright professed to be on death's door after the first day, the examination seems to last four days. The lucubration and cramming of the students are matched if not exceeded by the exertions of the examiners to mark the exam and rank the students step by step in pace with the examination. Each question on the exam has a predetermined numerical value—"10, 12, 20 and so forth"—in accord with the estimated difficulty of the question, though extra credit is given on an ad hoc basis for exceptional responses.[65]

A student's sums from all questions answered are totaled to give an absolute total. All students are then ranked numerically. The examiners use that list to set eight to nine classes or divisions, from best to worst. Within each class, the numerical totals are then suppressed and the students are listed alphabetically. The exercise thus serves to establish a series of cardinally graded groups or classes, while suppressing ordinal ranking within the groups. All this is preparation for the Tripos exam, as well as for possible use for future Trinity fellowships.

By 1831, such college examination was, if not everywhere as rigorous, then at least generally standard at Cambridge. As to be expected, generalization of the culture of examination at the colleges led to waxing competition in the Tripos exam. Bureaucratic rationalization prevailed. In 1827 for honors degrees, and then in 1828 for ordinary degrees, printed papers completely replaced dictation. The written exam had emerged, nearly in the form that we now enjoy.

In 1836 all written papers were explicitly marked individually for the first time. Up to then, examiners in the Tripos exams had partly relied on their memories of impressions given by candidates in answering, although we can see from Wright's description above that Trinity at least had already adopted such a system of individual marking. If the original alterations in the eighteenth-century Senate House Examination had not been taken primarily to make the exam a test of merit, the nineteenth-century Tripos clearly envisaged a real meritocracy.[66]

In *Masters of Theory: Cambridge and the Rise of Mathematical Physics*, Andrew Warwick has recently dealt with these matters in detail for Victorian Cambridge. Elaboration begat itself decade by decade. The motifs of sickness, metaphorical death and rebirth went from cliché to archetype. "As the most heroic performances became surrounded by tales of altered states of consciousness or physical or mental collapse from overexertion, a student folklore gradually emerged concerning how best to prepare to withstand these trials."[67]

In 1825 the *Times* of London printed the Cambridge order of merit in the Tripos exam, which eventually became an annual national preoccupation. The battle for the title of senior wrangler took on national proportions, with fitting heroic acclaim to the victor. The Cambridge Tripos exam shows that, at the heart of an academic practice embodying a near apotheosis of bureaucratic rationalization, a myth and cult of the hero, a ritual to recognize and celebrate academic charisma, can nonetheless flourish in the modern world.

OXFORD AND THE NEW ENGLISH ART. In the eighteenth century, Oxford had final university-wide examinations after the disputations. Those were in spirit not unlike the Cambridge Senate House Examination, before the latter commenced its great evolution. At Oxford the exam included a broader range of possible topics in which, happily, failure seldom darkened anyone's big day. Like the farce of enlightened disputation that we saw in chapter 3 above, Oxford examination functioned essentially as a ceremonial rite of passage at this time.[68]

While hardly more than five percent had been given a fail in the Oxford exam around 1800, by 1850 about a quarter of all candidates failed. As the exam became a nonceremonial affair, the time and energy dedicated to it, by both examinees and examiners, would greatly increase. In reforms of 1800, Oxford embraced Cambridge's system of ordinal and cardinal grading for a brief time. After 1807, however, Oxford rejected ordinal ranking and settled instead for setting cardinal classes of merit, in which names appeared alphabetically. A period of experimentation after 1825 led to two classes of honors degrees, a first class and a second class honors, followed by candidates with a simple pass. In 1830 Oxford introduced a third class of honors, and further experimented with other sorts of honors or honorary mention.

4.8. R. W. Buss's "Examination of Candidates for the Degree of Bachelors of Arts."

Attempts by mathematics examiners to introduce Cambridge-style ordinal ranking at the top of the first class—that is, attempts to introduce a senior wrangler and company—went down to defeat at Oxford. One saw them as "presumptuous, unwise and unconstitutional."[69]

Drawn by R. W. Buss in April 1842, figure 4.8 depicts the examination of a B.A. candidate at Oxford in midstream, as it were, between the traditional oral exam and the modern written exam. Oxford table manners here merit attention in detail.[70]

On the ground floor in the (Old) Schools, the space shown in the figure was called the "cockpit" in view of the banks of raised seats. As opposed to the Cambridge Senate House and the Tripos exams, Oxford B.A. exams long preserved their tie to public disputation as real public events. Up to 1849, to be admitted to the exam, one had to attend at least twice as a spectator. The four gowned figures in the left foreground of figure 4.8, as well the two gowned and conversing figures in the middle on the far left side, probably depict students fulfilling that requirement. Along the right side from foreground to background, but excluding the student facing the back wall in the furthest background, some or all of the five figures do not appear to be wearing academic gowns and thus seem to be spectators, which indicates that this is a very public event. The three empty elevated seats in the background, middle, are for the vice-chancellor and proctors, should they decide to attend—which they have not in this case.

At the table, the student standing on the right side is currently being examined. Long after the Cambridge Tripos had become a completely written exam, the Oxford B.A. exam preserved an oral component, which remained for a time the central part and thus true to tradition. The public aspect and oral nature of the exam went hand in hand, and the gradual marginalization of the latter was bound to the same fate for the former.

Examinees as well as examiners now feared embarrassment in public. In the first decades of the nineteenth century, candidates reported being able neither to eat, nor to sleep, nor even to move, in anticipation of the "dreadful day." Candidates fainted on the way to the Old Schools, or broke down during the exam, as did some of the examiners. The medieval moment of publicity, coupled with the modern moment of rigor, made academics sick. Extending over twelve hours during two days and attracting a large audience, William Hamilton's exam in 1810, on the other hand, was an acknowledged theatrical triumph.[71]

Once the number of candidates began increasing, as they rapidly did in the century, such an oral exam became increasingly arduous and then impossible for the examiners to hold. By the statute of 1800, at least four examiners had to be present when an honors degree stood at stake, while a simple pass-fail decision required fewer. A description from 1801, which much accords with the layout as depicted in 1842 in figure 4.8, set the examiners—six "sour Masters" in 1801—on one side of the table, while the candidate(s) held the other side.[72]

After 1807, part of the exam became a written at Oxford, but the oral still remained the central aspect. The written part at first served in part to keep some candidates busy while others were being orally examined. After 1827, however, a written component became itself important, if it had not been so even earlier. Candidates wrote for up to five days and then went to the oral exam as depicted in figure 4.8. More importantly, after 1830 examiners were empowered to examine more than one candidate at the same time and with the same questions. In figure 4.8, the two candidates in the background, with their backs to us, doubtless are writing at this exam, in the spirit of the Cambridge window problems.

That practice permits the possibility that the three writing figures at the table in figure 4.8 are also examinees doing a written exam. Following Cambridge practices, mathematics examiners at Oxford had introduced printed problems in 1828. The humanities followed suit in 1831. The three writing figures at the table in figure 4.8 could thus be writing answers to printed questions that rest on the table in front of them—a difficult task amid the oral.[73]

The future belonged in any case to the written exam and the candidates whom it favored. Figure 4.8 casts us into the time of the transition, when the oral still held its own in the presence of the written exam. Despite attempts to preserve the viva or oral exam, its importance for the B.A. declined slowly but surely at nineteenth-century Oxford. As noted, the sheer number of B.A. candidates, increasing as they did during the century, led to the impracticality of nonceremonial orals for B.A. candidates. Written exams save time, once one may process more than one candidate at a time. As had long since happened at Cambridge, at Oxford, too, the public, theatrical, oral exam with spectators faded, while silent, "objective, noncontroversial examinations in written form, became the predominant mode of examining."[74] At Oxford, too, the exam would become the university's reason for being.

> In their lavish scale and elaborate decoration the palatial new Examination Schools, opened May 1882, symbolized the triumph of the examination idea in Victorian Oxford. John Ruskin, who, on his return to the University in 1870, had found the influence of examinations all pervasive as compared with his undergraduate days, thought it "expressive of the tendencies of this age" that Oxford had spent a vast sum on a highly ornamented building "for the torture and shame of her scholars." The Schools, which were the most expensive capital project undertaken in nineteenth-century Oxford, were planned on a scale sufficient to process over 4,500 candidates a year. Such a weight of numbers prompted "bureaucratic" measures in a university otherwise deficient in central administration.[75]

## Modern German Table Manners

This chapter began with an oral exam at the University of Jena in 1740 for an advanced degree in theology or, possibly, arts and philosophy. As noted several times above, the oral retained some measure of its vitality when advanced degrees stood at stake. We shall reach an ending now with an oral exam about a century later.

Made around 1853, figure 4.9 exhibits modern German table manners at an oral, although perhaps no longer contemporary manners. The figure is reproduced from the exemplar in the university archive at Tübingen. Annotations in the archive's exemplar identify all but one of the professors depicted here. Inspection of the lecture catalogues around 1853 shows that professors identified by the annotations are in the law faculty.

As at medieval bachelor's and master's exams, more than one candidate is being examined here. At this time, the law faculty in Tübingen awarded only a license and a doctorate. Figure 4.9 probably depicts the rigorous ex-

4.9. Oral exam in the law faculty, University of Tübingen, circa 1850.

amination for the license. For those going on to the doctorate, a dissertation and a disputation would follow this examination.[76]

Rather than the top-bottom tension between the examiners and the examinees shown in figure 4.1, figure 4.9 exhibits a right-left tension. It is as
if the top and bottom panels of the older image have become fused and
mixed in one room. The economy of standing versus sitting has changed.
The three candidates sit with three professors at the table, while four other
professors stand. The only two visible empty chairs suggest the impossibility for all professors to sit at once. The configuration of the three professors
to the far left in the image suggests no pretence of partaking of in a communal event. No longer examination versus celebration, the tension is examination versus conversation, off the table.

If one attends to the rather precise geometric and dynamic architecture
of the image, there is a counterpart to the sweating student in figure 4.9,
who is taking the exam, which is apparently not going well. The counterpart to the sweating student is the smiling professor. In this strange scene
of a modern German oral, still a theater of professorial freedom, the figure
labeled "3" is the only person smiling and with his back to the table. I end
here with an academic gesture that "speaks about the pleasures of exercising power."[77]

## CONCLUSION

From the Middle Ages to the modern era, much examination evolved from a disputational to a rather more bureaucratic form. Exams may have had a written component (*scriptum*) before the eighteenth century, but the essence and center lay in the oral. During the eighteenth and nineteenth centuries, the weighting of the oral versus the written became inverted for most students. In the modern era, oral exams persist, but are comparatively infrequent, (still) ritualistic, more difficult to fail than a written exam, and usually only for advanced degrees. In step with the expansion of bureaucratic mentalities, the written exam has spread its empire.

The evolution and articulation of the grading system flourished in this empire, albeit unevenly and with local variation. Elaborate systems of ordinal ranking and cardinal grading came into being over the course of the eighteenth and early nineteenth centuries. The grading system replaced the traditional authority of social status and seniority with modern, rational authority. Numerical or alphabetic ranking now marks most students. This effects at once a normalization and standardization of intelligence or ability. It induces differentiation within the student body, and it fosters competition fundamentally. Perhaps it ought not surprise us that capitalist England saw the most refined development of the early modern grading system.

The grading system has become the principal means to shape the modern student body; it has divided that body into undergraduate versus graduate students. Grading and written examination came to be imposed with different incidence and rigor upon those two groups. Undergraduates would be the ones most informed by the bureaucratic rationality of grading. This new system of evaluation and ranking not only reshaped the student body. It also transformed the academics implementing it. Like many bureaucratic devices investigated in this study, the grading system recast academics' own mentalities, and cast its own academics. It forms a key part of the modern ideology of objective evaluation. The modern meritocracy of academia and much of the professional world seem now impossible without this tool.

The traditional exam had been heroic oral theater, analogized by jurists to the three trials of a crowned athlete in Roman law. That heroic theater, colored by metaphors of blood and ordeal, seems to have hurt few. The modern exam has become a mundane, meritocratic exam associated with sweat and labor, but it can make one nearly "sick to death." In extreme forms, such as at Victorian Cambridge, such exams can recur to motifs of heroism. But the first generations that endured the Prussian *Abitur* and the modern Oxbridge exams described the process as torture. As survivors and administrators of such exams, we should not discount the reality of mental torture in modern practices. Torture acts to break spirits and wills. Following chapters investigate more closely the rehabilitation of some of the tortured.

# 5

## The Research Seminar

In contrast, the [nineteenth-century American] followers of research for its own sake usually emerged from their German sojourn with the "mark" of a basic transformation. It is true that they crossed the Atlantic already in a mood to seek knowledge. Yet, at least in the [eighteen-]eighties, the motive of research was usually so frail in the United States that it required the reinforcement of a specific stimulus abroad. For the devotee of scientific investigation, Germany opened up the vista of a new goal, then dramatized it by a process of initiation. The German laboratory and seminar offered these future American professors a novel mode of life.

Laurence Veysey, *The Emergence of the American University* (1965)

The seminar soon conquered American universities as the basis of graduate education. "After initial experiments conducted separately by Henry Adams [at Harvard] and by Charles Kendall Adams [at the University of Michigan] in the seventies, the seminar a decade later had become one of the most pervasive types of instruction in American graduates schools."[1]

M. Carey Thomas, who participated in two seminars at the University of Leipzig in 1880/81, had the idea of using the institution of the seminar even at a college, particularly the new one just outside Philadelphia where she was to be the founding dean. "In Europe she imagined Bryn Mawr [College] as Leipzig in miniature." By 1892, Professor E. R. A. Seligman at Columbia University could remark that the seminar "is the wheel within the wheel, the real center of the life-giving, the stimulating, the creative forces of the modern university. Without it no university [or good college] instruction is complete."[2]

As Veysey noted in *The Emergence of the American University*, the "novel mode of life" offered to American scholars by the seminar was a Romantic one. The seminar proved to be the central site in which the Romantic ethos of originality took hold of academics. Original academic work, that is, research, came to be demanded of advanced or graduate students in the seminars, and then also in the labs.

This all happened as part of the same historical process that consigned undergraduates to rigors of the grading system.[3]

At an historic conjuncture in 1809/10, the time of the foundation of the University of Berlin, two German theorists of the research seminar—C. D. Beck and F. A. Wolf—traced its origins to the 1738 Göttingen seminar for classical philology. The founders of that seminar had not had an institution for academic research in mind, since that notion had hardly existed as such at the time. But by the end of the century, the notion did exist. During the first three decades of the nineteenth century, the German research seminar achieved its decisive form and definition in the philology seminars.[4]

In the early nineteenth century, other humanists, mathematicians, and natural scientists imitated the philology seminars. Some of the earliest university research laboratories were even at first called seminars—or institutes (*Anstalten*) the more bureaucratic name for the seminars. In the course of nineteenth century Germany, the seminars and institutes offered a new principle of organization for the university, refining the superstructure of the four medieval faculties. This had the greatest effect on the arts and philosophy (and sciences) faculty, which became an accumulation of seminars and institutes. In America, the emergence of the modern academic departments—of history, literature, physics and so on—formed part of the same phenomenon: the rise of the seminar as a budgeted institute.[5]

What the Germans (and Bryn Mawr College) call "seminars" are the American departments of this or that. In tracing the origins of the research seminar here, we have thus a twofold task. On the one hand, we shall be uncovering the first steps in the bureaucratic process of the departmentalization of the arts and sciences faculty. Access to and control of a budget was central to that process. On the other hand, we shall be trying to discern how a specific and novel method of teaching—the seminar-style—developed, and how that style of teaching helped to establish the pursuit of research as an activity demanded of advanced students and, indirectly in the seminar, of professors too. This second task also sheds light on the origins of what became the graduate schools in America—which the next chapter will further illuminate.

The two tasks of the chapter will not fall neatly into two parts but rather form two moments of analysis, complexly interwoven in the sections below. The two underlying phenomena—bureaucracy and research—were and are complexly interwoven. The chapter itself, however, does fall neatly into two parts. The first part treats academic practices and institutions that the seminars later developed from and/or replaced; in the first part, we shall also consider what Oxbridge cultivated instead of seminars—the tutorials.

The second part of the chapter examines the research seminar as a specifically German institution, which achieved a canonical form in the philology seminars during the century from 1738 to 1838.

This chapter, like those before and after it, concerns the transformation of a site of oral disputation. The previous chapter examined the second of the medieval jurists' three trials, the private exam by the faculty, and its history in the early modern era, especially in regard to undergraduates. The next chapter will take up the third of the jurists' three trials, the public exam for an academic degree, especially in regard to the doctorate in the arts and sciences faculty, the doctor of philosophy. This chapter commences with the first of the jurists' three trials, the regular trial or probing of a student during the time of study before advancement to candidacy—a topic that the previous chapter also ended up considering.

## FROM THE COLLEGE TO THE SOCIETY

### Colleges, Tutors, and Convicts

The medieval colleges afforded the intimacy sought for disputational exercises to probe and practice materials from lectures, thus accomplishing the first of the jurists' three heroic trials for a degree. At Oxbridge the college tutors and their tutorials performed this private, intimate teaching and eventually secured hegemony within the university, to the detriment of mere fellows and professors. In the Germanies, the collegiate university did not survive the Reformation. To fill the void left when collegial teaching collapsed, a new sort of institution called, among other things, the *convictorium* appeared for the training of a select group.

DISPUTATION IN THE MEDIEVAL COLLEGES. The medieval colleges and halls or "burses" proved to be the best sites to promote informal disputational lessons as a regular practice. The many names for such disputational collegia—*disputationes domesticae, serotinae, quotidinae, mensales, bursales,* and so on—point to the wide diffusion and variability of the practice.

The informal collegia in disputation were private exercises. As such they formed the large and essential space been the public lectures and the public disputations and formal exams. The informal, private, disputational collegia reviewed and further glossed materials presented in the lectures. These collegia also cultivated the manners appropriate for the public disputations and formal examinations. Such private, informal disputations and exercises took place regularly, even daily or nightly, in the colleges and residence halls.

Made circa 1500, the illuminated statutes of the Collegium Sapientiae at

5.1. Informal disputation at the Collegium Sapientiae,
University of Freiburg im Br., circa 1497.

the University of Freiburg im Br. can spare some words here, although perhaps not a thousand. The founder of the college commissioned and supervised the illuminations with some care. Eleven of the illuminations show scenes of private, collegial disputations. Figures 5.1 and 5.2 depict the two principal motifs or scenes.[6]

Eight illuminations resemble figure 5.1: one or more bachelors or masters stand at one or more podiums and practice with one or more students. The groups are small and the lessons informal, though the lectern interjects a moment of distance drawn from the lecture. The statutes enjoin students of the college to participate faithfully in disputational collegia taught under the auspices of the arts faculty, as shown here.

Three illuminations resemble figure 5.2: the bachelor or master teaches without a lectern. This figure depicts a "domestic disputation," meaning that it took place under the auspices of the college, as opposed to the faculty. The statutes enjoin that at least once a week, every Sunday or Thursday after supper for about one hour, students of the liberal arts must dispute in turns as respondent, in a sequence set by the presider, while the other students play the opponents in so far as the ability or maturity of each allows.

In figure 5.2, each of the three sitting students has a book and each appears to be paying pious attention to the standing instructor. The hourglass

5.2. Domestic disputation at the Collegium Sapientiae,
University of Freiburg im Br., circa 1497.

echoes the statutory requirement that the domestic disputation lasts an hour. As compensation for leading the disputation, the presider receives a fee; as a reward for participating, each of the students gets an apple or seasonal fruit. If the presider leads the lesson well—and the judge of that is not stipulated—then he also gets an extra measure (*Maß*) of wine.[7]

A common means of conducting the private or informal disputation was the so-called circular method. The statutes above on the domestic disputation at the Freiburg Collegium Sapientiae probably intend the circular method. In such a case, the roles of respondent and opponents went through or around the circle of scholars. With a master or bachelor presiding, each student took turns as the respondent, while the other students were opponents. The circle could be gone through in each session or through a series of sessions.

In the latter case, one student would be the respondent for a session, then at the next session another student would be the respondent, and so on through the group or circle of students as set by the presider. The two groups in figure 5.1 seem a bit small for the circular method, while the three in figure 5.2 would be just large enough, as "three makes a collegium." The three books with the three students here make it possible that the instructor is expounding upon materials from lectures, that is, is discussing substantial matters, as well as practicing formal skills of disputation. Such collegia thus offered a broad spectrum of possible activities, from the pure private lecture to the pure private disputation.[8]

THE RENAISSANCE AND REFORMATION AND OXBRIDGE TUTORS. In the fifteenth century, Oxbridge students, like most others, resided in halls and burses; the latter were unendowed but under the auspices of the university. Oxbridge colleges at first had little to do with B.A. candidates. For the colleges supposedly offered refuge to advanced students, by supporting the monastic *vita contemplativa* for bachelors en route to becoming masters and doctors, and then seeking suitable occupations elsewhere. That is why Oxbridge fellows originally had no teaching duties and were not supposed to hold their fellowships in life tenure. The Reformation laid the bases for the collegiate university to change things.[9]

During the sixteenth century, the colleges commenced taking on more and more B.A. candidates. Such students were at first the noble and wealthier sort—fellow-commoners and pensioners. The colleges each had a corps of fellows who, on the whole, were not doing much besides courting the Muses. Fellows thus began serving as tutors to a small group of students, much as depicted in figures 5.1 and 5.2. The college and the fellows received an extra income thereby, and students obtained a better education, or at least so their parents seemed to think. An injunction of 1549 by Edward VI to Clare College, Cambridge, held that all students admitted by the college must henceforth have a tutor. In 1570 the revised statutes for Cambridge mandated all students in all colleges to have a tutor.

In the sixteenth century, the tutorship was a temporary office performed by many or most fellows, supervising a small group of students. The tutor saw to both the social and pedagogical disciplining of his charges. Above all, the tutor made sure that the student paid the proper fees. The course of the early modern era witnessed two major evolutions at Oxbridge: the colleges expropriated the entire student body, and the tutorship fell into the hands of a very few who, with the master of the college, assumed control over the students.

Thereafter, one could not study at Oxford (as early as 1580) or at Cambridge unless one enrolled in one of the colleges. Once in control, the colleges eventually restricted the number of fellows who might be tutors. Trinity College, Cambridge, for example, had allowed the odd fellow to tutor a small group up to 1755, when it abolished the practice and set the number of tutors for the whole college at two, a number not increased to three until the nineteenth century. The senior tutor at Oxbridge colleges is in effect a dean of students.

The rise of the collegiate-tutorial system went hand in hand with the collapse of extracollegial, university instruction at Oxbridge, the last vestige of which were professors like Newton. In an earlier chapter, we saw how little attended such professorial lectures became. The tutors proved best able to train students in the subjects and skills needed to pass the exams, which, along with the degrees to which the exams led, constituted basically all that remained of the university's educational authority. The growing rigor of exams at Oxbridge, traced in the previous chapter, offered the chief means by which the university reacquired some control over the colleges in the eighteenth and nineteenth centuries.

The tutorial system could also meet student demands for new and thus nonexamined materials. The so-called cultural revolution in England, which witnessed the arrival of the "gentleman" as a new social type, called forth students' interest in new topics such as French, geography, and so on. Professorial lectures might have cultivated such new topics but, on the whole, seem not to have. The tutors, however, could mobilize resources to teach new topics, if they so chose. Tutors often set up assistant tutors from the fellows to teach examination topics beyond their own proficiency, or the new topics demanded by the nascent gentlemen. The tutorial also allowed for the intimate training depicted in figures 5.1 and 5.2.[10]

This is not meant to sing the praise of the institution but rather to explain its triumph and longevity. For it is likely that the tutors, once in control of college education, tried to resist much curricular change. Edward Gibbon's reminiscences of Oxford in the eighteenth century disparage the tutors of his time: "The silence of the Oxford professors, which deprives the Youth of public instruction, is imperfectly supplied by the Tutors." Gibbon's first tutor, Dr. Waldegrave, had limited knowledge of the extramural world and the current age. Waldegrave's tutorials appeared "devoid of profit and pleasure" to Gibbon, who ceased attending them and incurred no reprimand from the tutor. Gibbon noted of his next tutor, "except one voluntary visit to his rooms, during the eight months of his titular office, the tutor and the pupil lived together in the same College as strangers to each other."[11]

THE DECLINE OF THE GERMAN COLLEGES AND THE EMERGENCE OF THE CONVICTORIUM. The seminar, as a method of teaching and as a funded institute, emerged in the context of the German Protestant universities, which had set the faculties as the primary principle of organization. Opposed to that, Oxbridge and Jesuit universities set the colleges as primary during the Reformation and Counter-Reformation. In the Protestant Germanies, however, residence in the colleges and halls began to fall off in the early sixteenth century.

The satirical *Epistolae obscurorum virorum* of 1515/17 caught this mood well:

> The Masters at Leipsic [*sic*] bitterly lament the scarcity of scholars. It is the Poets [the Humanists] that do them this hurt. Even when students are sent by their parents to [the Masters'] hostels and colleges, they will not stay there, but are off to the Poets to learn stuff and nonsense . . . [So the Masters cry ["W]e cannot make a living. Students will no longer dwell in hostels under Masters . . . And thus the universities throughout all Germany are minished and brought low . . . ["].[12]

During the fifteenth century, students had been forced to reside under masters in university houses—colleges, halls, hostels or burses—across northern Europe. The Leipzig masters above were lamenting the dissolution of this forced residency, which the humanists had spurred on. Precisely during the sixteenth century, however, Oxbridge and Jesuit colleges established themselves as self-contained disciplinary and pedagogical sites, which reinforced polices of forced residency. As noted in chapters above, the Renaissance and Reformation thus had rather opposite academic effects in the Protestant Germanies and England—the latter, interestingly, more resembling the Jesuits than the Germans.[13]

In the early modern era, the German Protestant lands had few colleges of the grand sort such as those at Oxbridge. One such was Tübingen's Collegium Illustre, opened in 1592, mostly for nobility and high gentry. Figure 5.3 shows the dining hall. Like Oxbridge colleges, this college in Tübingen had a "high table," which could be the table at the top right in the background of figure 5.3. But the four figures to the left front look rather important and seem to be headed for the odd looking table in the left foreground.

In any case, the 1666 rules for the college set seating at high table. The Prince of Württemberg, should he be at college, sat at the high table and first. Next in the hierarchy came counts and dukes, then other nobility. If seats remained at the high table, then others who had shown academic excellence might fill them. The other collegians filled the other tables. One could converse at the tables on "godly, rational, political, amusing, useful" things. These elite tables thus had become a space in which conversation was possible, unlike the rather strict monastic silence that had been enforced at medieval college meals. To insure that the conversation only concerned the allowed things, it would have been wise for the college to seat a bachelor or master at each of the tables. I do not know if that was the practice but, if so, academic topics might also have entered the conversation.[14]

After the Renaissance and Reformation and the decline of most German

5.3. Dining hall, Collegium Illustre, University of Tübingen, circa 1625.

colleges, public monies emerged to support poor students. This support ranged from fee deferments to scholarships with room and board in a new sort of institution, the convictorium, from Latin *convictus*, that is, those who eat together. Each German Protestant university typically had at least one institution called the convictorium, or pedagogicum, or similar names. The convictorium resembled a medieval college. In fact, most convictoria inhabited the quarters of what had been a college before the Reformation. The principal difference between a college and a convictorium lay at a juridical level. Unlike the college, the convictorium typically possessed no endowment legally its own and had no corporate existence at law.[15]

The convictoria, however, preserved the monastic life of the colleges. The scholarship students here were supervised and monitored. They took their meals at a common table at which they sat in silence and heard the inevitable reading. The nocturnal cloistering of the college lived on here. Through this ancient regimen, the "convicts" were to be made obsequious and loyal servants of the state. For many states required students in the convictorium to become princely or public servants, such as existed at the time.

As these students were generally poor, that meant they would become preachers or teachers—theology majors at the university, then pastors after graduation. Complementing the ascetic social life of the convictorium, scholastic intellectual discipline persisted here. Above all, the convictorium upheld and preserved disputation and Latinity, the practice of which was slowly but surely declining in the general student body. Enforcement of attendance at disputation and perfection in Latinity could be achieved in the convictorium since the authorities held a point of leverage over these poor students: their scholarships.[16]

The Jesuits also set up convictoria in their colleges, though they seem to have had a different social role. For, justified or not, the Jesuits acquired the reputation for caring most for the well-to-do and allowing their convictoria to become full of such better off boys whose parents thought them in need of disciplining. Thus, while the convicts in the Protestant convictoria constituted the social antipodes of students such as in the Tübingen Collegium Illustre, the case at Jesuit institutions was probably more complex. As in a number of other ways, Jesuit convictoria perhaps most resembled the Oxbridge colleges.

At Protestant and Jesuit tables in convictoria, readings from scripture and other useful works, including eventually newspapers, kept the convicts from overmuch foolish or evil discourse. For it seems that one allowed some conversation to the convicts, at least by the eighteenth century. A regulation of the Jesuit convictorium in Munich, circa 1580, held that one should enter, be seated and leave in silence. By casuistry one might claim that a space here was already left open for speaking while eating, but the matter is murky. Its importance lies in the question concerning the provenance of academic conversation in more or less formal settings, such as a collegial meal or, for the issue at stake here, a seminar.[17]

## Private Settings

Convictoria and colleges could only serve a minority of students at universities in the early modern Germanies. Academics thus developed a range of other institutions to furnish the sort of intimate, personal teaching that colleges and convictoria offered. Most such institutions counted as private, because they lay outside the domain of the official, public fora at the university, namely, the public lectures and public disputations and exams. The seminars would later draw on a number of the private settings to structure their practices.

THE PROFESSORIAL TABLE. Although the collegiate system collapsed in the sixteenth century Germanies, universities sought to institute a version of the Oxbridge tutors. Authorities tried to compel students to have a private preceptor, effectively their tutor. The generality of this solution bespeaks an origin in the medieval notion that every scholar had his master. But, excepting for the noble or wealthy, who usually had private tutors anyway, most students simply neglected the matter. Authorities eventually gave up. The typical early modern German student then enjoyed academic freedom, though many had other names for it.[18]

An ersatz for the office of private preceptor emerged in the *Professoren-Tisch*, the professorial table. From the sixteenth into the eighteenth century or later, many German professors took in boarders, other than their lodgers, on a semester-subscription basis. And the professor supposedly partook of the table with his lodgers and borders. Typical for such a professorial table seems an apostolic twelve or so students per semester. This informal practice became so important that some universities regulated the numbers at each table.[19]

"I ate for two years with [Professor] Ittig, where I enjoyed real Socratic meals. With such desirable opportunity in the art of conversation and discourse, I could . . . advance in such an uncommonly easy and pleasant manner ," or so we hear from a student about a professorial table in late seventeenth-century Leipzig. While the table-talk could hardly be beat, a professorial table often left much to be desired. A case from 1614 reports about a professor whose "meals are so bad that a sponge got cooked with the meat and was served up on the table, that they have to drink flat beer all the time, and that two students died last fall who had eaten at his table." So, eating at a professorial table might be another academic trial of courage. Still, the conversation was mostly good and, as a student manual noted, "if the professor is morose and no friend of questions," one might be able to learn French from someone.[20]

Contemporary sources suggest that table-talk reigned more profusely at professorial tables than at others, although a student had to beware lest he contradict the professor. These tables formed even, implicitly, part of the road, if less than royal, into the academy. In the "curricula vitae of professors is mostly to be seen that they were once [boarders] at a professorial table." For, "that an occult quality inheres in it, is not to be denied."[21]

THE PRIVATE COLLEGIA. The most direct descendent of the medieval private disputations can be seen in the early modern private circular disputations, later called disputational collegia. These were usually private classes, which had to be paid for by each student attending. The fees went directly from student to instructor. Though potentially very informal, these classes commonly used the traditional circular method of disputation, described above.[22]

Reconsidering the Basel lecture catalogues in figures 2.2 and 2.3, one can see that some professors offer private classes that are descendents of such disputational collegia. In figure 2.2, the fourth professor from the top in the philosophy faculty, J. Wettstein, offers to continue "in Collegiis privatis examinatorio-explicationis & disputatoris." Attention to the sixth professor from the top, J. G. Mangold, shows how such private exercises might move in the direction of modern seminar and lab training. Mangold offers private lessons in explication and disputation in "philosophy," and specifically in experimental philosophy. In a modern sense, he may be offering a lab. The fourth professor, T. Zwinger, perhaps also offers lab training along with theory, as he advertises private classes in philosophy and chemistry ("privatis etiam Collegiis tam Philosophicis quam Chymicis").[23]

These few examples indicate the possible range of such private collegia or classes offered to "studious youths": from more or less pure disputational lessons, where the method of disputation was primary, to more or less pure private lectures, where the content—for example, chemistry—was primary. The broad middle contained mixed exercises, for example, a lab, or a collegium in which one read a text and discussed, that is, disputed it.

German lecture catalogues indicate that disputational collegia persisted at some universities into the nineteenth century, after which the general diffusion of the seminars effectively displaced them. The private disputational collegium long remained one of the few classes in which a normal student had to participate actively, in so far as he elected to take such a class at all. Lecture catalogues further intimate that in disputational collegia a student might not only have been obliged to speak but also to write in Latin. (We'll postpone the analysis of writing until further below.) Disputational collegia or classes eventually undertook the circular disputation of essays written for the class, or the circular disputation of texts chosen for the particular class. Ministers of state clearly valued such collegia or classes, and endeavored to maintain them by injunction or otherwise.[24]

Many private collegia evolved, however, into extraordinary or informal lectures, which might have included some discussion or conversation. As noted, such classes, like most disputational classes, were private as opposed to public, that is, they were taught for a fee that each student had to pay directly to the professor or lecturer offering the class.

During his *Bildungsreise* of 1783/84, a certain Rinck noted of his time in Göttingen that Professor Michaelis, for example, demanded complete payment in advance for private classes. A popular or trendy private collegium could command a fittingly high fee. In the late eighteenth century, the Göttingen philologist C. G. Heyne, whom we'll meet often, regularly taught a private class called "archaeology" on classical antiquities. Heyne demanded a fee that contemporary observers found high—one of them, the Prussian minister Gedike, called it a fashionable class (*Modekollegium*). From the mid- to late eighteenth century, the philosopher Kant lectured privately on what he called "anthropology," a new field, in winter semesters every year for thirty years—doubtless, then, a very popular private collegium.[25]

The private collegium became the site in which curricular innovation largely took place. Like the Oxbridge tutorial, it provided an opening through which the noncanonical could enter academia and, in time, enter the canon. Successful private collegia, such as Heyne's archaeology or Kant's anthropology, carved out subject areas for future chairs and their attendant public lectures. The creation of new disciplines became more mundane over time. But in the eighteenth and most if not all of the nineteenth century discipline-founders achieved heroic status. Foundation myths congealed around them—when they succeeded.

Kant, for example, became a founder not of anthropology, but rather of something seen as more important in his time: a new, "transcendental" philosophy. And Heyne's place in the pantheon of classics suffered from the success of his erstwhile and disloyal student, F. A. Wolf, who achieved heroic status as the founder of *Alterthumswissenschaft*, the science of antiquity. Disciples would recount to their own students how they had learnt the new discipline from the founder's lips. As the potential generator of new chairs and disciplines, the private collegium offered a forum for the exhibition of a charismatic leader and creator.[26]

Circumscribed at first by a juridico-ecclesiastical domain of the orthodox, later a politico-economic sphere of the marketable and famous, the private collegium embodied, responded to, and cultivated the private academic interests of instructors and students. In the early modern era, the heart of education moved from the public lectures into the private collegia, from which the seminars and laboratory lessons would in part emerge. Such classes required a lecture catalogue as a regular periodical. And such classes filled it with its novelty and its potential fraudulence, when they were not given due to wanting students.

THE SCENE OF THE PRIVATE COLLEGIUM. Early modern private collegia usually took place in private or domestic spaces, in spaces not belonging to a university or college. In a chapter above, we saw regulations to the effect that the public lectures could not be held in domestic spaces, but rather had to be held in the public lecture halls. Instructors wanted to hold public lectures in private or domestic spaces for a number of reasons. One of them was the general failure to heat the public halls, making them somewhat unpleasant in winter. That, combined with the general lack of public academic spaces in the Germanies, led most instructors to hold as many of their classes as possible in their homes or similar places.

After gaining a professorship, a new professor typically purchased or at

5.4. Collegium in the home of Julius F. Höpfner a lecturer in the law faculty,
University of Gießen, circa 1764.

least rented a house, if he did not own or rent one already. The professor
would usually set one or more rooms aside for teaching. The professor could
then enjoy heated rooms, and he would not be obliged to go out much and
deal with the external world. To make extra money, professors commonly
rented rooms to students and even held a professorial table, as described
above.

Lesser academics—extraordinary (that is, extrabudgetary) professors
and lecturers—held their private collegia where they could. Many rented
spaces from professors. Others made do with the few university rooms that
existed. To take the philosopher Kant as an example again, after he became
a lecturer, he gave his first lectures in winter semester 1755/56. He lived at the
time in the house of a certain Professor Kÿpke, whom we'll meet in a later
chapter. Kÿpke had rooms for informal lectures and collegia, which Kant
used.[27]

There is no shortage of medieval images of lectures and disputations,
and a fair number of early modern images of lectures and disputations also
exist. But we have few images of early modern private collegia. That makes
figure 5.4 all the more interesting. The image comes from the University of
Gießen. It shows the private collegium or class of Julius Höpfner, a lecturer
or *Repetent* in the law faculty, 1763–65. It merits close scrutiny.[28]

The figure to the furthest right in figure 5.4 is clearly Höpfner, the academic whose domestic space is the setting for the gathering. He gives himself away by his bathrobe. Into the seventeenth century academics continued to don clerical gowns in their studies, and perhaps other domestic academic spaces, even if they were married. Academic spaces long retained traces of the celibate state, whence the clerical attire. By the eighteenth century, however, the bathrobe displaced the clerical gown in images of German academics at home. The academic bathrobe coded the space as domestic but remained neutral, void of any obvious sexual import.[29]

In figure 5.4, Höpfner sits at a round table with only one student, who is ready to take notes. This must be a noble or wealthy student who has paid the largest fee to take the collegium. Beyond the round table, the first three figures, from right to left, all seem to sit in chairs, though the chair legs for the person in the middle are hard to see. Nonetheless, these three seem to have chairs, but do not appear to be allowed to sit at the table.

The student almost in the dead center of the image is standing, with no empty chair behind him. To the front, right and left, one can see chairs or stools not being used. Such pre-modern manners—a standing student among empty chairs—might offend our egalitarian sensibilities. But we still have no problem with them at the opera or theater, which is what early modern academia was. We heard in a chapter above, moreover, that students did on occasion have to stand in lectures, though that might have been for lack of seats. The standing student wears the black garb of theology students, who as a group were typically poor and usually figured that way. In any case, as figure 3.1 exhibits a medieval lecture structured by social class, so, too, does figure 5.4 an early modern private collegium.

That helps but not definitively for the interpretation of the left side of figure 5.4. Does figure 5.4 depict the scene of a single event, a single private collegium, even more complexly socially articulated? Or is it a diptych-style scene, as in figures 4.1 and 4.9? Or is it a scene simply with much going on (as in figure 4.8)? Do the students at the square table on the left side of figure 5.4 embody the normal fee-paying students, who merit a table and chairs, but no proximity to the instructor? Or is the figure at the right head of the square table leading a second and separate private collegium here? Such questions go to the tangled roots of the table manners of this—for modern sensibilities—rather odd academic event.[30]

Figure 5.5 shows a private collegium in Göttingen by Jacob Grimm, drawn on 28 May 1830 by his brother Ludwig Emil. The drawing is labeled "in the house *an der Allee*," now the Goethe Allee, the street leading from the train station into town. Summer semester 1830 was Jacob Grimm's first

5.5. Ludwig E. Grimm's "Vorlesung in der Wohnung an der Allee in Göttingen, 28.5.1830."

semester as a professor in Göttingen. His brother Wilhelm would become a professor the next semester. He and Jacob lived in the house *an der Allee* and both had positions in the library. In summer semester 1830, the lecture catalogue shows that Jacob taught only one class, a private collegium on German legal antiquities. The scene depicted in figure 5.5 must thus be that private collegium.[31]

The layout of the room here indicates that such a private collegium was at base a lecture. Indeed, one commonly called it "reading a collegium" (*Kollegienlesen*). Mindful of figures 5.4 and 5.5, we can see that the seminar, as it arose from such practices, did not offer a conversational space in the modern sense. Figure 5.5 probably indicates a typical, if not general, layout for a private collegium or seminar lesson oriented toward the informal lecture. The complex scene of figure 5.4 may indicate a more informal space where questions or dialogue might occur. But the right half of figure 5.4, though it looks informal, actually most duplicates the sort of lecture depicted in Grimm's collegium. The left half of figure 5.4, where all sit at the same table, promises a more conversational, egalitarian space.

THE PRIVATE SOCIETY. Private societies can be found since the Renaissance. Centered on universities and accepting students, such societies were but private collegia grown permanent and more collegial. In that light, every private collegium constituted a potential private society. In these private settings, we find students not only speaking but also writing.[32]

At Jesuit universities neither the private collegium nor the private society existed, but one Jesuit institution did approximate these groups. It was called an "academy" and was a group of students meeting under the superintendence of a member of the order for the purpose of undertaking special exercises related to their studies. The Jesuit *Ratio studiorum* required their universities and colleges to have such academies. Although student members of the order had to participate, other scholars could choose to do so. These academies possessed a republican structure, as the scholars freely elected the officers to govern the academy. Pedagogically the academy much resembled the medieval, collegiate lessons for review and disputation. But an essential departure lies here:

> The academy members [the students] may themselves occasionally give lectures from the lectern in which they learnedly handle some question resolved by their own labor, or exposit the arguments on both sides of some subtle problem, to which one or two members respond.[33]

At Protestant universities, such extracurricular fora arose less frequently, unless we count the private collegia, which we well might. Thanks to the lack of central authority, Protestant institutions showed more variation. At the University of Leipzig, for example, a number of private societies appeared around 1624. All initially styled themselves as collegia and initially aimed at training in preaching. And all arose under the auspices of professors or university masters or doctors as presidents or presiders, but admitted students in pursuit of one degree or another. By 1680 six collegia existed as societies at Leipzig and met weekly. Beginning with the Collegium Gellanium of 1641 and the Collegium Anthologicum of 1655, which both met every Sunday, private societies more oriented to the humanities had made their appearance. Later, private societies for natural sciences can also to be found at Leipzig.[34]

In the eighteenth century, private societies became more common and specialized. Centered on universities and admitting students, at least three private societies for natural sciences (at Halle, Jena, and Leipzig) and at least six for classical philology (at Altdorf, Erlangen, Halle, Jena, Leipzig, and Wittenberg) existed. Unlike mere private collegia, societies had statutes and several categories of members: ordinary, extraordinary, and honorary.

They usually had a treasury, however empty, a cabinet and/or a library, and sometimes a journal. In entering the society, members accepted certain duties.[35]

For ordinary members, that usually meant writing. Whereas the ubiquitous Jesuit academy envisaged written work as perhaps the exception, the occasional Protestant private society considered it the rule. In Leipzig the members of the Collegium Gellanium and of the Collegium Anthologicum met on Sundays to hear and discuss essays that had been written and presented by members, including students. The Collegium Historiae Litterariae (founded 1715) heard and criticized each week two or three papers presented by members. The Latin Society at Halle (founded 1736), though given a pedagogically and politically conservative constitution, still expected participation from its student members. The Latin Society at Jena (founded 1733), possessed of a more democratic constitution than the society at Halle, also required student members to submit written dissertations exhibiting eloquence and erudition. The Latin Society at Altdorf (founded 1762) had similar requirements.[36]

Writing at the university did not spring solely from the private society. We noted above the emergence of writing in some of the private collegia qua disputational collegia in the Protestant Germanies. Moreover, at Cambridge, for example, in the course of the early modern era, students had begun to write a short Latin paper on one of the three theses they had to dispute in their public disputation for the B.A. But, at least in the Germanies, it was through the private societies that an idea foreign to the medieval and early modern university took shape in and hold of the intellectual elite of the student body: writing came to be thought of as the highest form of academic labor. German seminars would fashion charisma in writing.[37]

## THE SEMINARS

### The Seminars and Their Directors

The seminar became a central part of German universities in the century from 1738 to 1838. It drew on practices and institutions discussed above, and some things to come. The seminar fused a particular style of teaching with a particular method of funding. This fusion lay at the basis of the German pursuit of knowledge as research. In this section, we'll consider the phenomenon mostly from the directors' perspective; in the next, from that of students.

THE EMERGENCE AND SPREAD OF THE GERMAN SEMINARS. As noted, Jesuit student academies did not encourage writing as much as the Protestant private societies did. But the Jesuits did develop the convictorium or, to be precise, the seminary in a new direction. Canon 17 in the *Decreta super reformatione* (1563) of the Council of Trent mandated seminaries for the proper education of the clergy. Tying the institution of the convictorium to the seminary, the Jesuits conceived the pedagogical seminar(y), *seminarium repetentium humaniorum*.[38]

The first such seminar(y) appeared in Würzburg in 1568. Others soon followed. Regulations laid out the curriculum precisely, with the schedule for each day stipulated in detail. These pedagogical institutes, socially structured as convictoria, served for the further training of academically advanced members of the order, especially in the humanistic disciplines. The Jesuits would thereby secure a core of future lyceum and university instructors, the humanistic shock troops of the Counter-Reformation.[39]

The origins of the Protestant pedagogical seminar(y) are a harder to trace. The first pedagogical *seminarium* appears to have arisen in the 1650s and concerned primary school training. The first such institution for higher schools was most likely the *Seminarium praeceptorum* founded at Halle in 1695, and which soon had a branch for training advanced members in the humanities. The seminar in Halle aimed to support poor scholars dedicated to a career in teaching. Thus, like a convictorium, the Halle seminar received funding. It had a budget, mostly for scholarships. Unlike a convictorium (and college), the Halle *Seminarium praeceptorum* does not seem to have required the cloistering of its charges. The formation of the academic persona could then assume a more relaxed, less monastic pose at Halle.[40]

Lists 1, 2, and 3 in appendix 3 show the public philological seminars, the private classics societies, and significant pedagogical seminars, from 1695 to 1850 in the Austro-German lands. Seminar(ie)s had existed since the sixteenth century. The Göttingen philology seminar in list 1 did two new things: it integrated aspects of the private societies and pedagogical seminars, and it translated the notion of the state-funded theological seminar(y) into the arts and philosophy faculty. List 1 shows that for over thirty years the Göttingen seminar was a merely local phenomenon. As lists 2 and 3 indicate, classics societies and pedagogical seminar(ie)s most populated the German academic landscape until the 1770s.[41]

But, beginning in the 1770s, the model of the Göttingen seminar started to spread. As we'll see, that probably had much to do with a virtual reinvention of the seminar after Heyne took control in 1763. The reputations of Heyne, the seminar, and the university itself worked synergetically thereafter. By the first decade of the nineteenth century, a new academic institution existed. Thereafter, pedagogical seminar(ie)s transformed into seminars for classical philology and pedagogy, or persisted in the new academic world instituted by them—they became seminars for the new academic discipline of *Pädagogik*.

Similarly, beginning in the last third of the eighteenth century, private classics societies sought status as public, that is, university philology seminars. After 1806, university classics societies arose only as temporary institutions waiting to be confirmed as seminars, or as counterinstitutions opposed to the public seminar, and founded by disgruntled academics. After the foundation of the seminars in Tübingen in 1838, every extant university, excepting one in the Germanies proper—the later Bismarckian Germany—had such a seminar. Only Würzburg did not have such an institution although, as indicated in appendix 3, list 1, one had been planned. Austria founded its first such seminar in 1850 in Vienna.[42]

THE SEMINAR AS STATE INSTITUTE. As opposed to the professorial table, the private collegia, and private societies, the seminar on the Göttingen model was an official institution of the state. As public institutes, such seminars conducted themselves not as intramural corporate and collegiate bodies, but rather more as ministerial instances or agencies of the modern state.

Like the private societies, the seminars typically had statutes; but, unlike the societies, the seminars' statutes appeared as ministerial edicts or regulations. The professor heading the seminar usually had the title of director, which was not a traditional academic title. Neither the university academic senate nor the arts and philosophy faculty council appointed or supervised the director. An extramural ministerial body or even the sovereign itself, rather, usually appointed directors. As we'll see in the chapter on professorial appointments, such new practices fused bureaucratic rationalization with charismatic aspects of the calling or recognition by other charismatic leaders, namely, the sovereign or high ministers.

Much ministerial supervision assumed a mundane but essential form for bureaucratic rationality: the regular report by the director to the ministry. For the Göttingen seminar, no mandate to report appears in its statutes. Extant documents record spotty reporting under the first director, J. M. Gesner, in charge from 1738 to 1762. Under Michaelis, interim director in 1762–63, then under Heyne, director from 1763 to 1812, reporting became fairly regular, but with its format apparently left to the discretion of the director.

In a report of 26 September 1763, for example, Heyne evaluated members of the seminar discursively. One shows "ability, diligence and zeal" and will be a "capable pedagogue." Another "is a good, diligent, moral person" who has overcome his great poverty with "redoubled zeal." A third has written a specimen of erudition and Heyne has "good hope of educating him further." All things considered, the Göttingen director did not have to report in an onerous manner. The Hanoverian state set the seminar in a bureaucratic superstructure but, significantly, did not try to micromanage the seminar, especially after the 1760s.[43]

Other eighteenth-century seminars—at Erlangen, Kiel, and Helmstedt—also reported regularly to supervising ministries. Indeed, in the previous chapter, we saw the trials and travails of F. A. Wolf at Halle about reporting. In the nineteenth century, a mandate for a regular report constituted a typical clause in seminars' foundation documents. Through such techniques of regular reporting, the bureaucratic mentality, so essential to the transformation of academic labor into research, would take shape in and through the seminar directors.[44]

As institutes of the state, the first seminars possessed little autonomy. Though future seminar directors present at foundation probably helped draft the seminar's statutes, directorial autonomy found small scope in the seminar-constitutions. Like the pedagogical seminar(y), the original eighteenth-century seminars had their curriculum and conduct essentially fixed statutorily. In some cases, textbooks were even stipulated at foundation.

For the seminars at Erlangen and Helmstedt, for example, the admission of students came at first not from the director, but rather from the supervisorial instance above him. At Göttingen and Kiel initially, the directors, when reporting vacancies to the ministry, could nominate new candidates for the seminar, but selection came de iure from a superior agency. Ministerial surveillance, if vigilant and thorough, could even eradicate the seminar director's influence over the work of those in the seminar, given the statutorily set curricula.[45]

Facing a detailed curriculum, and standing under the supervision of ministers, who authorized candidates for admission or chose them outright, the first seminar directors in the eighteenth century could not easily use these new institutions to further their own academic interests and projects, and surely not to cater to the private interests or whims of the students.

All that had changed by the first decade of the nineteenth century. Thereafter, state ministries, on the whole, allowed the directors to conduct the seminars on the model of the private collegium. Ministries left the admission of members and the governance of work to the discretion of the directors. Within the superstructure of public or state interest vested in a now loosened ministerial supervision, an infrastructure of private academic interest, a sanctioned domain of directorial autonomy, would be embedded in the seminars.

THE SEMINAR AS A BUDGETED INSTITUTE. The bureaucratic superstructure had ramifying consequences nonetheless. Like the professorial chairs before them, the philology seminars helped transform corporate and collegial academic entities into bureaucratic agencies. What the professorial chair had wrought in the sixteenth century, the seminar-institute would recapitulate more intensively in the nineteenth century: a fragmentation and reorganization of the faculty. Seminars on the Göttingen model did not resemble endowed professorial chairs or Oxbridge colleges. Most seminars were, rather, budgeted institutes. In this they followed in the path that had been blazed by the Protestant convictoria in the Reformation.

The budget (real or virtual) enabled the convictorium and the seminar to fashion students according to state interests. Like the convictoria, much of a seminar's budget usually went to scholarships for the students. As we'll see more in the section below on students, acceptance of a scholarship came with a clear price. Students who did not pay that price—measured among other things by productivity and loyalty—were, so to say, terminated.

As noted, the university academic senates and arts and philosophy faculty councils usually did not supervise the seminar director; nor did they usually oversee the seminar's budget. For the University of Kiel, for example, the king himself initially supervised the institute's finances. At Helmstedt a specially appointed commission of the prince exercised oversight over the seminar. The deputation of four ministers in Bayreuth, who actively controlled the seminar in Erlangen, paid no heed when the academic senate there complained that this arrangement breached the university's traditional corporate autonomy.[46]

When the idea migrated from Göttingen in the 1770s, such institutes long remained mostly ones for classics and pedagogy. Until the second half of the nineteenth century, the only other similarly budgeted institutes whose existence I can establish were these: the Polish seminar at Königsberg (1813), the natural sciences seminar at Bonn (1825), the Lithuanian seminar at Königsberg (1827), the historical seminar at Halle (1832), the mathematics and the natural sciences seminar at Königsberg (both 1834), the physical sciences institute at Leipzig (1835), and the mathematics and natural sciences seminar at Halle (1837/39).[47]

Given our modern ideologies and prejudices, the dearth of budgeted institutes for the natural sciences is striking. One cannot ignore the nearly ubiquitous anatomical theaters, botanical gardens, chemistry laboratories, and *cabinets de physique* in the eighteenth and early nineteenth centuries, especially those given their own incomes. But there is a profound difference between a mechanism for the accumulation of capital and labor, and a system for the bureaucratization of patronage and office. In the latter case, funding in the form of scholarships, that is, money for persons—and not just for things—provided an important (albeit not universal) element of the German research institute in its technical sense.[48]

Chapters below on professorial appointments and the university library will discuss in detail the sad fact that early modern universities possessed, by modern lights, few rational financial structures. In particular, funds for annual discrete purchases—for example, of library books or scientific instruments—seldom existed. Just like the libraries, natural science collections generally grew not by regular, planned acquisition, based on the rationality of a budget. Collections accumulated, rather, as hostage to the vicissitudes of fate and fortune—one depended on endowments, bequests, inheritances, gifts, and so on. In rare cases, a university might find funds to purchase the complete instrument collection of a deceased academic. When that happened, the next generation or two of natural science professors at the particular university would have to augment the collection privately.[49]

Up to the first third of the nineteenth century, the lack of funding for science students paled by comparison with the irregular funding of natural science collections. Much of the magic worked by the German philology seminars came from monies that directors could give or promise to students. But, as we'll soon see, seminar directors in some cases could offer their students only patronage—help in finding money in the future at university or in life.

In the second half of the nineteenth century, the diffusion of the research seminar on the Göttingen model—as a public institute, that is, a budgeted but nonendowed entity—would fragment the medical and arts and philosophy faculties and reorganize them at German universities. Seminars and chairs would evolve into separate, budgeted bureaus of knowledge or, to give them the American name, academic departments in the making.[50]

THE DIRECTORATE OF THE SEMINAR. As state or public entities, the seminars continued and expanded the development of the professorial chairs. In chapters above, we noted the reorganization of the German faculties into a system of public chairs during the first half of the sixteenth century. Oxford and Cambridge became state supervised institutions under the Tudors; but the colleges managed to maintain their legal status as privately endowed bodies. Oxbridge fellows thus in no way served as princely or public servants. Professorial chairs as they emerged at Oxbridge also maintained the status of private endowments, even if their founders, especially the crown, sought to exercise influence over them at times.

In the Protestant Germanies, as we saw in a previous chapter, jurists construed the salaries paid to professors as public salaries. It would take the whole early modern era for the modern notion of the "public servant" to develop fully. But after the Reformation, German professors served de facto as princely servants, *Fürstendiener*. In the course of the early modern era, professors ceased swearing their oath of office to the faculty or university, and swore it to the sovereign instead. "The oath of allegiance in the seventeenth century effects a bureaucratic obligation (*Beamtenverpflichtung*) toward the sovereign." In the late eighteenth century, seminar directors would come to look the most like civil servants, *Staatsdiener*, which is what all German professors would become by the early nineteenth century.[51]

In the eighteenth century, one professor usually ran the seminar as the director (see appendix 3.) As noted, ministerial control of the seminars seems to have strategically loosened during last decade of that century or the first decade of the next. One demanded reports, but let the directors conduct the seminars more or less as they saw fit. When that happened, the seminar fell more and more into the hands of the director. The seminar embodied his institute, as much as his chair was his chair. This laid a basis for transforming an agency of the state into the cult of a charismatic leader or future discipline founder.

Neglecting Professor Michaelis's one-year interim directorship, from 1738 to 1812 only two individuals ran the Göttingen seminar. The seminars at Wittenberg and Kiel likewise each had but two academics who ran the institutes in successive tenures, from 1768 to 1806 at Wittenberg, and from 1777 to 1808 at Kiel. The Erlangen seminar had the same director from 1764 to 1815, as did the seminar at Helmstedt from 1779 to 1809. A second in charge of the Halle seminar is mentioned in one place; but all other sources, including the lecture catalogues in which seminar lessons were advertised, indicate that only one person, namely, F. A. Wolf ran the seminar from 1787 to 1804.[52]

In the first part of the nineteenth century, the seminars at Erlangen (till 1827), Greifswald (excepting one year), Kiel, Königsberg, Leipzig (till 1834), Marburg (after 1825), Munich (till 1827), and Rostock all preserved the pattern of the single director with life tenure, as did Wittenberg and Helmstedt as long as those universities lasted.

Other places instituted a directorate of the director or *Vorstand*, with one or more subdirectors, apparently under the director, but also collaborators in some sense. This was so at Breslau, Dorpat, Erlangen (after 1827), Freiburg im Br., Gießen, Heidelberg, Jena, Leipzig (after 1834), and Munich (after 1827). Given this arrangement, the possibility of the director as autocrat still remained. Such seminars, possessed of subaltern faculty, could become sites for the modern cult of academic personality—which would, indeed, later be an ideology.

In American terms, it would be as if the same professor remained department head until he or she retired. To preclude the conflation of the institute with the persona of one academic, four of the most prestigious philology seminars in the nineteenth century—those at Berlin, Bonn, Göttingen, and Halle, as well as two of the less famous ones at Marburg and Tübingen—sought to compose the directorate more collegially (see appendix 3).

Marburg tried most heroically to erect the directorate as an impersonal agency. From 1811 to 1815, the directorate there consisted of a collegium of three or four academics. Then a revolving directorate emerged, with one or two academics out of a group of six becoming director(s) each year. Continual conflicts arose and the system collapsed in 1825. Marburg then embraced the principle of the single director with permanent tenure.[53]

Less ambitious than Marburg, the seminars in Göttingen and Tübingen set up a triumvirate of equals, while three Prussian seminars—Berlin, Bonn, and Halle—created a bipartite directorate. The arrangement at Göttingen arose in response to the misfortune begotten as the venerable Heyne waned intellectually but ruled on and alone. Indeed, sick of his seminar, students instigated the foundation of a private society in 1811 as a counterinstitution, which contributed to the great problems in the seminar from 1813 to 1815.

The Prussian institution of a bipartite directorate probably emerged from problems with the original one-man-show at Halle under Wolf. In Berlin the seminar had separate sections for Latin and Greek, with a different director for each. In Bonn the two professors leading the seminar shared power, not only with each other but also with a third academic, and thus created a most collegial atmosphere there. At Halle, as reorganized post-Wolf, decorum seems to have been maintained between the two codirectors. But a third philologist, excluded from the seminar, was not a happy man and reverted to archaic behavior. He founded a private classics society outside the seminar, which led to warring camps of students. We'll return to him and this case in the next chapter.[54]

DIRECTORIAL PERSONALITY. As public institutes, the seminars thus faced the dilemma concerning the nature of the directorate. Should it be a personal or impersonal agency? Should it enable one professor, a director for life-tenure, to realize his academic personality as Führer? Or should the entire staff of professors impersonally and collegially administer the seminar? Different lands and universities sought different solutions. But they all eventually gave the directorate the sort of pedagogical, curricular autonomy typical of the private collegium.

The seminar at Göttingen seems to have been the first one in which practices of the private collegium came to hold sway. In 1765 the Göttingen seminar bore little resemblance to its structure as mandated at foundation. Without official proclamation, the ministry in Hanover had apparently allowed the new director, Heyne, who had arrived in 1763, to modify the seminar's structure to his own liking. Either then, or perhaps somewhat later, the ministry granted him the further power to select the candidates for admission.[55]

In Halle the director's autonomy in the seminar emerged more clearly. In the negotiations during 1787 and 1788 for founding the seminar, the director, Wolf, obtained complete control of the institute, including the right to admit its members and to determine the topics of the seminar. At Kiel in 1789 the director of the institute also seems to have acquired at least the right to determine admissions. Most importantly, as in a private collegium, the directors not only could determine who might or might not attend the lessons, but they might also kick people out. Heyne in Göttingen clearly had this power, since he famously (at the time) exercised it, as did also Wolf less famously in Halle.[56]

In the nineteenth century it became the norm to constitute the public seminar as though it were a directorial private collegium. Foundation documents stipulated the directorate's control over admission to the seminar, as well as its right to boot students out. A required curriculum existed no longer. Statutes simply set out the most general character of the work: oral practice in Latin and disputation, the reading and writing of Greek and Latin, philological critique and interpretation, and some experience in teaching. Apart from methodological provisions, control over seminarial labor resided now with the directorate. The directors could teach and research any philological topics that they wished.[57]

In the grips of Romanticism, ministers of state erected these seminars as public institutes, usually properly budgeted, but enabled the directorate to institutionalize its own academic interests or projects in them—that is, to perform research. Even more powerfully than the private collegia, such seminars set a stage for the charismatic leader to appear. Such a leader needed disciples and, also, had to be able to recognize the charismatic among them.

## The Seminarists and Their Training

The seminar was a pedagogical, a disciplinary, a Romantic site, and one of writing, too.

THE SEMINAR AS A PEDAGOGICAL SITE. The philology seminars served as pedagogical institutes of the state. The Prussian seminars contained mostly future teachers, usually for secondary schools, but the nascent ideology of the research seminar prohibited acknowledgement of that in Prussia after 1809. As pedagogical institutes, all the seminars, including the Prussian ones, descended in spirit if not in fact from the convictoria and seminar(ie)s. They thus gave their members access to the lessons in the seminar as free private collegia, and usually also offered scholarships, which might include room and board in the convictorium, or simply just free meals. Through such means of support outside the theology faculty, the secularization of the teaching profession began, as teaching and preaching had previously been linked.[58]

The Göttingen seminar offered free meals and scholarships of fifty reichsthaler for each of nine students. Erlangen provided free room and board, probably in the convictorium, and scholarships of forty gulden for each seminarist. Kiel had a stipend of two hundred thaler for four students, eventually raised to three hundred thaler and free meals. Halle had scholarships of forty reichsthaler for twelve students. Helmstedt offered room and board in the convictorium and provided some financial support of an un-stipulated amount for at least four ordinary members, and possibly also for the six extraordinary ones. The Wittenberg seminar provided the typical salary for its director, but only promised patronage for the seminarists.

All but one of the eighteenth-century seminars could thus provide scholarships, sometimes including board and even room. The single excep-tion, Wittenberg, proves most enlightening. For all the seminars offered their students two things: free private collegia (the lessons in seminar) and patronage. A scholarship formed the most visible and tangible means of pa-tronage, but not the only and ultimately not the most important one. For the seminar directors could be very helpful in the task of finding a future teaching position.

The essential thing about the scholarship, after its existence, was that it was not perforce tied to need, that is, to poverty. Traditional scholarships in the Germanies and elsewhere had been supposedly tied to financial need in the first instance, and then to ability in the second instance. One had to be poor enough to apply for the scholarship in the first place. As conceived in the eighteenth century, the first seminars had projected poor students as their audience, whence the tie to the convictorium, the place for the poor with a scholarship in Protestant academia. The seminar's pedagogical mis-sion, moreover, pointed its graduates to a career not much populated by nobles or gentlemen or men of means, even modest.

Once the directors assumed control of admissions to the seminars, and after the seminars had become trendy institutions in the Romantic era, abil-ity could displace poverty as the criterion of first instance. That is the modern notion of graduate student scholarships. The undergraduate scholarship retains its medieval pedigree. Financial need forms the first criterion, ability the second. For the graduate scholarship as it emerged from the seminars, one was not obliged to attest one's poverty, an often demeaning act in the modern era.

In this sense, the German seminars recalled the original notion of the Oxbridge colleges, as institutions for the further education of academically advanced and promising students. The difference lay in the monastic cast of the colleges, with their pursuit of the *vita contemplativa* and celibacy. The seminars instilled, instead, modern bureaucratic discipline.

The philology seminars founded during the nineteenth century up to 1850 at Bonn, Dorpat, Freiburg im Br., Königsberg, Marburg, Munich, Rostock, and Vienna had exactly stipulated amounts guaranteed as scholarships to their seminarists. The seminars at Berlin, Breslau, Gießen, Greifswald, Leipzig, and Tübingen did not, and we'll soon see the power that gave the director. Tübingen promised its ten seminarists support on a case-by-case basis. The directors at Greifswald could give prize money to a few, and might petition the ministry for grants up to thirty reichsthaler for each of the five ordinary members. Gießen provided free meals for all eight members, plus undetermined prizes for three, and special consideration in general university scholarships for the rest. The seminars in Berlin, Breslau, and Leipzig could only offer access to undetermined prize monies for some of the seminarists, and special consideration for university scholarships for all. Dorpat also made the crucial moment of patronage explicit by promising help in finding a teaching position.

The fundamentals guaranteed by all seminars amounted then to free private collegia and patronage. The patronage came at present or in the near future: as an actual or possible scholarship of perhaps undetermined amount, or in the remoter future, such as help finding a teaching position. Not only Wittenberg and Dorpat but rather all seminars could discipline their students with the latter sort of promises. The philology seminars fulfilled their pedagogical mission not only by functioning as a system for advanced training in the humanities, but also by transforming the academic patronage system for humanists.

The philology seminars in list 1 of appendix 3 emerged largely in the period 1770–1830, the era during which the control of educational systems in the Germanies passed from theologians to philologists and professional pedagogues. As members of ministerial commissions, philologists such as Heyne in Göttingen and pedagogues such as Gedike in Berlin transformed the old Latin School into the modern humanistic gymnasium.[59]

THE SEMINAR AS A DISCIPLINARY SITE. The secularization of teaching happened slowly, and the notion of the student as philology major must be treated with care. Since the Middle Ages each student had to register with one of the four faculties. At Oxbridge the triumph of the colleges meant that each student had to be at one of the colleges. Like the latter registration, matriculation in a faculty constituted in the first instance not an epistemic act but rather a juridical one. A student was in or, rather, under a faculty at first in a legal sense.

One was a justiciable of the faculty (or college) and thus of the university. Each faculty formed a collegium at law in the original sense, that is, a body with its own head (the dean), the right to assemble (important in early modern Continental society in which no such general right existed), the right to have a treasury and a seal for producing legal documents, such as a diploma for an academic degree. The notion of the major or "cultor" in an epistemic sense did occur as early as the Renaissance, but was an aberration then. Rather, the eighteenth is the century in which the modern epistemic notion of the student as majoring in philology or history or mathematics or chemistry or whatnot established itself.

As noted, an important aspect of the philology seminar lay its existence as a budgeted institute outside the theology faculty, thus able to support students with scholarships or promises of such or similar. That having been said, for a long time many or even most seminarists, as we'll call them, appear to have been theology majors, a wise move for anyone intending to pursue a teaching career. Even by the early nineteenth century, when the notion of the student major had definitely arrived, not all seminarists had become philology majors. The case of the Göttingen seminar, although notorious, proves instructive.

Notorious because in 1776/77 the director, Heyne, tried prevent the young student F. A. Wolf—later founding director of the seminar in Halle—from registering in the philosophy faculty as *philologiae studiosus*. Heyne entreated him instead, in his own best interests, to matriculate in the theology faculty. Wolf, however, thought otherwise. This story has entered the folklore of classical philology as a case of the elder and venerable but behind-the-times Heyne retarding the emergence of the new disciplinary consciousness in heroic founders such as Wolf. The legendary status of the anecdote is the more noteworthy since, for instance, in Erlangen philology majors existed as early as 1749, and at Göttingen, too, even before Wolf's great instauration of the "science of antiquity" and the recognition of his heroic act.[60]

Table 1 in appendix 3 records the numbers of Göttingen seminarists by registered majors, broken into three-year cohorts. At the right of the table are four further columns that record the numbers of philology majors, pure or mixed (columns 1–3), and the total of all enrollments from all faculties during the three-year interval (column 4).

The table begins in 1764, the year after Heyne took over. Columns 1–3 show that, though there were philology majors to draw upon, Heyne did not choose them in any significant numbers until after 1787, which coincidentally was when Wolf's seminar came into existence at Halle. (Recall, too, that Dorothea Schlözer took her doctoral exam in Göttingen in the same year, 1787, and protested when she was examined in fields outside her particular focus or major in arts and philosophy.) Up to the cohort of 1788–90, theology majors formed the absolute majority; in 1788–90 a simple plurality. Theology majors went into a decline thereafter, until 1800 when resurgence occurred, doubtless due to the uncertainties caused by the Napoleonic wars. In 1815 the directorate of the seminar passed into new hands, which quickly reduced the theology majors, falling to zero in 1830–32, as the number of philology majors rose absolutely in the seminar, as column 1 indicates.[61]

Although (or perhaps because) given a pedagogical mission, the seminars soon inculcated disciplinary self-consciousness in the seminarists. Wolf's seminar in Halle announced the change. Explicitly intending a secularization of the teaching profession, Wolf admitted theology majors only with reluctance. During one semester at least—winter semester 1801/02—he managed to fill all twelve positions with pure philology majors. But, by the very next semester, eight of the twelve listed either theology or pedagogy as their joint major with philology. Thus, while not precluding theology majors, the preference for pure philology majors had been announced at least programmatically at Halle by Wolf.[62]

Nearly every nineteenth-century foundation embraced Wolf's program. It became all but canonical in the Prussian seminars: the philology seminars served and cultivated students of philology. In Prussia, this disciplinary consciousness held sway by 1820. The major reorientation in Göttingen took place slightly after 1820. It lagged here perhaps a bit behind the Prussian seminars, but probably kept more or less pace with the general drift then. One came to assimilate the professional consciousness of the seminarists to that of the directorate, as specialists in philology. Such seminarists, who became gymnasium teachers to the largest extent, gave the new humanistic gymnasium of the nineteenth century its teeth.[63]

That is a crucial point. As we'll see in a later chapter, disciplinary specialization had by no means established itself as a goal or value in typical professorial mentalities in the eighteenth century. Most professors still proved willing to play musical chairs and, even better, sit in several at once. The emergence of the modern researcher was tied, however, to a new ethos of disciplinary specialization. And the seminar had a role to pay in that. Around Wolf's name after 1800 as a mythical founder of the science of antiquity, one sees the rise of a disciplinary consciousness in philologists, especially those made directors of seminars, and who thus acquired the means to instill this consciousness in advanced students.

Through the seminars, the new corps of gymnasium teachers became the loyal tools of state interests. As pedagogical institutions, the seminars provided a means to standardize the elite of future humanities teachers. The promise of a scholarship, even if dim, coupled with the threat of its removal, facilitated the recasting of seminarists into the standardized shapes sanctioned by the ministry and directorate. One could discipline these students.

In 1774 J. H. Voß, a poet-to-be and seminarist in Göttingen, got into a dispute with the director, Heyne, on the proper writing, interpretation, and critique of poetry. The foolish student persisted in not deferring to the director. An unclever move, for the recalcitrant Voß and a lazy friend of his, to boot, were both kicked out of the seminar by Heyne.[64]

The case of the iconoclastic student indicates the directorate's power to produce seminarists who work along a sanctioned path. The more telling case of the lazy student bespeaks the seminar's power to produce students who work at all. The inculcation of "industry and diligence" lay at the center of the ministry's agenda. Wolf put it this way:

> the twelve seminarists must distinguish themselves as exemplars of industriousness (*Fleiß*), knowledge and good moral character at the university, and also arouse the emulation of others . . . For the state has little use for the mere humanist . . .
>
> Regarding the lessons of the seminarists, the director . . . must always use methods that inculcate industriousness and perseverance, and that also accustom the students to precise, punctual organization in all their required tasks.[65]

A refrain heard in the seminars: Seminarists must exhibit *Industrie*. Punctuality and output count. Written assignments, paperwork, must be handed in on time. Sloth and defiance constitute grounds for expulsion. And directors desired the power to terminate students.

Other means to insure proper work habits worked less drastically. In the nineteenth century, a few seminars—Kiel, Marburg, Munich, Rostock— gave differential amounts of scholarship based on the seniority of the seminarists. Prizing seniority indicates a traditional academic mentality. But a number of other directorates—Bonn, Freiburg im Br., Halle, Königsberg—hit on the more rationalizing tool of differential awards each term based on competition among the seminarists in "industriousness, progress and proper conduct."[66]

Those seminars, which only offered promises of future favor regarding general scholarships (Berlin, Breslau, Gießen, Greifswald, Leipzig), implicitly incorporated the same competitive structures. For not all seminarists would get awards, and not all awards would be the same. The practice of differential amounts seems in fact to have been pioneered by Wolf in Halle. Punctual output, in constant competition, and evaluated in the annual or biannual director's report to the ministry, now marked the successful seminarist. This person was a harbinger of the new academic order, the bureaucratic world of modern research.[67]

The convictorium and seminary's spirit, best described as orthodoxy and piety, gave way through institutions such as the seminar to our modern industrial and bureaucratic sensibility at the university. Like the undergraduate grading system in its sophisticated form, the seminar need not alter the contents of consciousness of advanced students; the seminar, rather, altered attitudes about labor, competition, and leadership.

THE SEMINAR AS A SCHOLASTIC AND ROMANTIC SITE. Although cast into types by the routines and reports of the seminar as a pedagogical and state institute, the seminars nonetheless condemned their members to a domain of autonomy. The ministry and directorate compelled the seminarist to acquire and exhibit an original personality with a charismatic quality.

The German seminarist fashioned himself as routinely normalized but peculiarly differentiated individual. A visitor to Halle in the early 1790s noted, "Most of the seminarists affect peculiar and atypical mannerisms (*sonderbares und von andern abstechendes Aeußeres*) by which they very noticeably distinguish themselves. You can spot them at a great distance on account of their attire and other small details."[68] The seminarist had to cultivate a distinct and specialized academic persona locked in competition. He had to articulate a sphere of private interest and had to personify it for evaluation in writing. This moment of private society, understood as a realm of original writing, completed the constitution of the philology seminar as the research seminar.

That happened first, at least institutionally, in the Göttingen seminar. In its original form, following practices of the pedagogical seminar(y), the Göttingen seminar statutes under its first director, Gesner, had prescribed a detailed curriculum. And, although called a "philological" institute, the seminar had encompassed a wide survey of materials: religion, pedagogy, history, geography, mathematics, astronomy, natural sciences, and even more.[69]

After Heyne took charge in 1763, the seminar changed significantly. One might regard this as a refoundation. Still envisaged as a source of training for gymnasium teachers, the seminar under Heyne abandoned, however, curricular practices of the pedagogical seminar(y). It embraced, instead, those of the private collegium and society. The labors of the seminarists became nearly exclusively philological. Heyne described the new practice in 1765:

> The seminarists are obliged to attend several hours of collegia in the humanities each day. In addition to this, the Professor of Eloquence [that is, Heyne, the seminar director] will offer without charge a collegium in which they will be practiced and instructed in interpretation, and in writing, speaking and disputing in Latin. To this end, each [seminarist] in turn will explicate, both grammatically and critically, an ancient author, as well as writing and defending an essay, written in good Latin, on a topic dealing with [philological] sciences in the same manner (*eine in diese Art der Wissenschaften einschlagende Materie*).[70]

From 1763 to 1812, Heyne ran the seminar and introduced a good bit of the German seminar-method, although Michaelis's report of 15 January 1763 indicates that he had already moved in this direction during his tenure as temporary director. In general, Heyne stressed, as he stated in a report to the ministry, the need to bring the seminarists to produce "diligent writings." The seminars, seemingly rather formal in tone, also furthered the medieval practice of circular disputation, as opposed perhaps to modern conversation.[71]

The importance of disputation stands clear in a contemporary anonymous work on Göttingen, published in 1791 and most probably penned, with poison, by a certain Wilhelm F. A. Mackensen, who had studied in Helmstedt, Göttingen, Leipzig, and Kiel. This work contains the following partly convoluted remarks on Heyne's conduct of the seminar:

> I almost forgot to tell you something about the seminar that Heyne conducts. It's held three times a week, and every week it alternates between interpretation and disputation. This institute (*Anstalt*) is without doubt good, and has already trained many good men. But, in view of the [supposedly?] closer relation with Heyne effected by the seminar, as well as in regard to the institution itself, chiefly concerning disputation (I don't know

*quoniam facto* that this [disputation] is anywhere in G[öttingen] as it should be), there are a number of things to criticize about this institution. Some years ago it [the seminar] had very talented young people, whom it has now begun to lose.[72]

Did Mackensen mean that disputation at Göttingen, including in the seminar, was not scholastic or formal enough, that it had become too conversational? In any case, the Romantic, Wolfian myth of the philology major was already on the loose in 1791, as Mackensen went on to criticize Heyne for encouraging seminarists to major in theology.

List 1 in appendix 3 shows that the other eighteenth-century seminars at Wittenberg, Erlangen, Kiel, Helmstedt, and Halle arose after the inauguration of the new regime in Göttingen under Heyne. But only the last one, founded in Halle in 1787, assimilated and then furthered the new form. The other seminars, which were officially philology seminars, still functioned curricularly as traditional pedagogical institutes. The Göttingen seminar as reorganized by Heyne, along with the Halle seminar as conceived and conducted by Wolf, became the epitomes of the seminar only in the early nineteenth century.

With few exceptions (Dorpat, Marburg, and Tübingen), and those only to a small extent, the foundation of new seminars, or the reorganization of old ones, or the reconstitution of private societies into seminars, created institutes devoted to classical philology as in Göttingen and Halle. More particularly, nineteenth century seminars statutorily enjoined nothing more than the mastery of methodological techniques, as well as practice in disputation and composition. These institutes became research seminars.[73]

In the seminar, students read only works of ancient Greek or Latin authors, or secondary works on classical philology. Methodological training, practice in grammatical analysis, textual interpretation, and critique proceeded not as abstract theory, but rather from the study of the sources themselves. Most directors no longer sought to provide a survey of the accumulated contents of philology, much less of the humanities in general. Collegia outside the seminar and self-study addressed these latter, encyclopedic concerns of the future scholar or teacher. In seminar, one learnt now to be a philologist, a researcher. And if directors taught surveys and encyclopedic lessons, they taught them to that end.

The passive mastery of a canonically prescribed corpus of philological materials gave way to the active cultivation of philological abilities through participation. Seminarial work thus restricted its scope. It sacrificed breadth, and often, alas, perspective for depth. When Wolf gave his seminar in Halle the collective assignment of searching the entire Ciceronian corpus to establish the shades of meaning of a single word, that must have appeared pedagogically nonsensical had one not comprehended the nature of the new persona under construction.[74]

Such an assignment—an insipid exercise in grammatical minutiae made feasible only by well-organized and collective seminarial labor—offers a parable of the new academic practice that is research. Source-referenced, etymological dictionaries arose in the nineteenth century from such exercises. Good pedagogue that he was, Wolf knew the seminarists would have to learn to collaborate effectively to succeed at this task.

But seminarial labor, the discipline of research, embodies no bureaucratic socialism for antiquity's sake. The convictorium and seminary of the juridico-ecclesiastical regime had sought to produce uniform types, namely, the orthodox and the pious. The research seminar of the modern politico-economic order seeks, however, to fashion the seminarist as a normalized but individualized personality. The research seminar shapes the student in the director's image—a figure with personal academic interests and projects, pursued in collaboration, and also in competition. Indeed, most seminarial labor envisages not the collaborative assimilation of the members or the seminar as collective persona, but rather the multiplication of academic personalities through the seminar, their enforced differentiation and thus also their comparison in terms of merit or charismatic originality.

Exercises centered on textual interpretation and exegesis served well the theatrics of individuation through role-playing and reversals, as each came forward from the chorus to play the lead, while the director remained the director and final critic. In Heyne's seminar, the "presentations of the seminarists took place for practice, . . . [for example] in interpretation, where difficult authors or difficult passages, in either Greek or Latin, would be chosen. The seminarist played the role of the teacher." Such took place as well as in less exalted seminars, such as in Freiburg im Br., where the "members of the advanced seminar (*Ober-Seminar*) have the special obligation . . . to lead the seminar (*den Vortrag zu halten*) in interpretive and exegetical lessons as often as the sequence of turns falls on them."[75]

The descriptions above suggest that conversation was still not at home, if it ever would be, in the Germanic seminar. For the seminarist played the teacher by taking turns leading not a discussion, but rather the lesson. Still, a managed discussion or even some sort of academic conversation might have emerged. At Helmstedt, for example, students did not seem to lead certain lessons by turns, but rather collectively. Even if the seminarists in turn only played the director as informal lecturer, instead of a discussion leader, the practice compelled the seminarist to do just that—to play the director for the day.[76]

In the lecture catalogue in figure 2.7 for summer semester 1822, the co-director of the Berlin philology seminar, Böckh, advertises in the lecture catalogue under "Philology" that he will explain or interpret Plato's *Republic* that term. In the same catalogue, in figure 2.7, under the rubric "Oeffent-liche gelehrte Anstalten," where the lessons in the philology seminar are listed, Böckh writes that in the seminar he will be teaching Euripides, but here he says that he will have or let Euripides be explained or interpreted, *erklären lassen*. The text will be interpreted by the seminarists, and in Latin to boot. Aspects of the private society came more into play in the seminar, as opposed to the traditional private collegium.

Such seminarial techniques cultivated the seminarist as professorial persona, as virtual director-for-a-day, and fused the mechanisms for training with those for evaluation. The seminar presupposed a basic common denominator of knowledge. And formal examination, oral or written, might still be inflicted on the seminarist, especially as a rite of passage into the seminar. But those were exceptional circumstances or rites.[77]

Wolf, for instance, argued not only (at first) against the grading of seminarists, but also against typical practices of examination of scholarship students in the seminar. The seminars should be privileged places. Oral examination should give way to the individually evaluated live performance of each seminarist, for example, in his turn as director-for-a-day. So, too, should written examination give way to the individually evaluated performance of each as author of original writings. Fusing the techniques of formation and evaluation of students, the seminar hereby incorporated and elevated elements of the private society.[78]

In incorporating elements of the private society, did these seminars cross the divide from formal disputation and lecture to something approaching enlightened conversation? Were they egalitarian and effervescent places? Thousands of pages of documents, histories and contemporary reports on the seminars in the Enlightenment and Romantic era have not revealed, to date, whether the director and seminarists sat at a table, as in the left side of figure 5.4. Or whether the seminar's setting resembled more the right side in spirit. Or whether a typical seminar in fact resembled Jacob Grimm's private collegium in figure 5.5.

THE SEMINAR AND THE APOTHEOSIS OF WRITING. The seminar crucially enhanced the oral culture of academia by compelling students to speak. But the essential charismatic exhibition lay elsewhere. If the original prerequisite for admission to the seminar had been passing an exam, it became complemented and sometimes replaced by submission of a written paper.

Dorpat, Gießen, Tübingen, Breslau, and Greifswald only statutorily required an examination for admission. The seminar directors at Göttingen (at least under Heyne), Kiel, Helmstedt, Leipzig, Halle, Berlin, Bonn and Königsberg, however, required submission of written work, alongside passing an exam, for admission to the seminar. The seminars in Freiburg im Br., Rostock, and Vienna only seem to have demanded a specimen of writing, sometimes with proof of having properly graduated from secondary school. But, by the time the seminar arose in Vienna (1850), the standards for admission had become formidable.[79]

The movement toward demanding original writings by no means abolished the medieval technique of formation and evaluation involved in the disputation. It rather embraced the disputation as a fundamental practice. The research seminar hereby incorporated and elevated not only the private society but also the private collegium, and in its original form as disputational collegium. So the 1819 statutes of the Bonn seminar explain:

> Every seminarist will present a paper every eighth week, so that once a week at least one [paper] is presented. Whoever, without a valid excuse, is twice late [with his paper] can be expelled. The director will frequently give his own evaluation of the paper and then give the paper to another seminarist for critique, whereupon practice in disputation can follow. Disputational practice can also be held sometimes concerning theses.

Similarly, the 1822 statutes of the Königsberg seminar set out:

> Oral lessons consist in . . . disputation on papers handed in, which two opponents will have carefully read and judged in form and content. The papers must thus be provided to the opponents at least eight days before the disputation, and the director two days previously for his review.[80]

That was the structure of the medieval circular disputations, minus the written paper. As opposed to the medieval colleges, in the modern seminar the disputation centered not on theses drawn from an instructor's lecture, but rather on passages from a student's paper. Nonetheless, the format follows the circular disputation. Each seminarist appears in turn as respondent or defendant in the disputation, and often faces several officially designated opponents, while the director presides. The conduct of the research seminar as disputational collegium was, moreover, part and parcel of its reorientation away from the pedagogical seminar(y). Circular disputation thus become not less but rather more frequent over time.[81]

At early foundations, such as Kiel (1777) and Wittenberg (1768/77), formal disputation in seminar occurred either irregularly or not at all. At Göttingen, in the seminar's initial guise under Gesner's tenure (1737–61), disputation officially structured only the rite of passage from the seminar. At Erlangen (1777), disputation transpired irregularly on written essays, and also regularly on theses, but then only once every six weeks.[82]

Regular circular disputation on written papers emerged unequivocally in Göttingen as a weekly practice some time after 1763 under Heyne. In Helmstedt disputation occurred weekly at least by 1788. In Halle at foundation in 1787, it was perhaps weekly, or perhaps only every eighth week—sources are at odds, as Wolf seems to have altered the structure of the seminar on occasion. In the nineteenth century, the regular circular disputation of papers written for the seminar became the norm and usually took place weekly or fortnightly.[83]

In a typical case, the paper would be written by the seminarist more than a week before the session in the seminar. The paper would thus be written in time for the one or two opponents to read it and prepare a critique in advance. And if possible, the paper would be circulated as well among the other members. If the director had done his job well in teaching them to perform, and was so disposed, he might speak only in prologue and epilogue.

The longevity of the structure of the disputational collegium ought not be a surprise. It persists in the modern academic conference, and especially in the workshop, with its chair, speaker as author, commentators, and other participants. In the seminar, the circular disputation, like the exegetical-critical lessons, made not the director but rather the students the lead performers. Disputation also functioned as a tool for the academic differentiation and self-fashioning of individual seminarists, as each stepped one-by-one into the spotlight.

The disputational lessons, however, proceeded most radically here. In lessons on textual interpretation, though seminarists often did moderate the sessions, the director usually chose the texts and relevant passages for the seminar. In so doing, he fulfilled his role and prerogatives as director. He guided research. In the disputational lessons, however, the students seem to have chosen the texts or passages about which they would write.[84]

The choice of topics for papers had been a hallmark of the private society, but not of the pedagogical seminar(y), in so far as writing existed there at all. Movement toward the private society had commenced with the Göttingen seminar in its initial incarnation. Though the seminar in Gesner's time does not seem to have incorporated disputation and composition as regular lessons, it did so as the rite of passage out of the seminar. "Before leaving the university, every seminarist is bound to hold a public disputation . . . In this the director may give him some help. But the work is to be done so that it can be seen as a specimen (*Probe*) that he [the seminarist] has delivered." As we'll see in the next chapter, the requirement "to hold a public disputation" meant to write a dissertation. The remark limiting the director's help meant that the seminarist would be the one writing the dissertation. That seems a fairly extraordinary notion in the 1730s.[85]

This exceptional work of writing for the seminar became in time as routine as the circular disputation. Before the close of the eighteenth century, the typical seminarist wrote at least once per semester in his turn as respondent or defendant in the circular disputation. And, though no doubt consulting with the director, the seminarist seems to have written on topics he chose himself. Constrained to a greater or lesser extent by the director's interests, the seminarist fashioned himself as an autonomous agent by his choices. He realized and reified personal academic interests or projects, perforce differentiating himself from his colleagues. The seminarist produced research and fashioned himself. "The condition holding for all written work of the seminarists is that their work be not merely a hastily thrown together collection of notes long familiar to the author [the seminarist]; rather, even if imperfect, the written work is to be the result of their own reflection and research."[86]

Publication of a final, perhaps perfected composition would symbolize the transformation of the seminarist's persona, would seal his passage as original creation into the new world of academic labor. The practice of writing in the seminar attained perfection in the institution of the doctoral dissertation, to which we turn in the next chapter.

> It is presumed that the director seeks to guide the studies of the seminarists to the end that each of them at some time chooses to bring some philological topic to such a learned state so as to be worthy of publication. Mindful of this, the seminarists should be rewarded with the costs of graduation and of publication of such essays, when these specimens of industriousness and learning are delivered, as is the norm, with their graduation from the university [as a doctoral dissertation], and thus with their departure from the institute [the seminar].[87]

## CONCLUSION

Chapters above showed the lecture and the disputation to have been the essential sites and practices of the medieval university. Disputation and examination intermingled, becoming almost the same. The jurists' topos of the three trials for an academic degree envisaged the whole of university education, excepting the lectures themselves, as a space of perpetual examination. Elements of the seminar emerged from a number of those agonistic spaces.

At Oxbridge, the survival of the colleges led to a system centered not on seminars, but rather on tutorials. The seminar system developed slowly in the Protestant Germanies after the dissolution of the collegiate university in the Renaissance and Reformation. The convictoria, the private praeceptors, the professorial tables, the private collegia (especially as disputational spaces), and the private societies all appeared in the course of the early modern era. And they all appeared in good part to fill the vacuum in intimate teaching left by the decline of the collegiate university in the Germanies. The Jesuits developed a number of similar institutions. But, like the English, Jesuit academia remained centered on colleges.

The Protestant research seminar grew in the late Enlightenment from a synthesis of the above sites and practices. It attained a canonical form under Romanticism. Around the same time as the seminars, the grading system emerged in the Germanies and at Cambridge—and perhaps even earlier among the Jesuits. Writing moved to center stage for the grading system and for the seminars. But a vastly different form of writing occupied seminarists.

For undergraduates and those below them, the grading system eventually assumed control of the examination and, as a "final cause," of a good bit of education itself. The grading system went hand in hand with a marginalization or disappearance of the oral exam for undergraduates. For the B.A. and it equivalent, the second of the jurists' heroic trials, the faculty's private exam, turned into a largely written exam, perhaps with some oral part, too.

The seminar (and lab) took over the training of master's and doctor's candidates for the heroic trial of the private exam, and in general. The oral for the master's and doctor's exams, although ritualized (still), would not be suppressed by the grading system. But writing papers, not exams, would blaze the path to those degrees. The seminar claimed pride of place as the best way to train a student to write a dissertation. It would also teach one how to speak, if not in enlightened conversation, then at least to pass doctoral orals and academic muster.

As we'll see in the epilogue, the German research university cast its specter over Europe and North America in the nineteenth century. Different lands fastened on different parts of it as most essential. In England, or at least at Oxbridge, adopting German academic practices led to the rise of the professorate, but did not lead to the demise of the collegiate university and the tutorial system. Natural scientists did establish the university laboratory, both publicly and privately funded, as the center for training students outside the lectures. But the humanities and social sciences at Oxbridge did not accord the seminar the central and lofty status that the lab and the German seminar had acquired.

In the United States, however, the adoption of the German research university would enshrine the seminar, although not in its pure German form. "Three basic types of instruction came into prominence in the new American university: the laboratory, the lecture, and the seminar," as Veysey noted in *The Emergence of the American University*. In a 1904 article in *Science*, I. C. Russell wrote of the new relation between professor and student in the seminar as a sort of "radium of the soul." About this new effervescent or radioactive element, Veysey continued, "What Russell called 'the radium of the soul' is now referred to—perhaps with no greater understanding of it—as charisma. The successful American academic seminar was likely to be charismatic in quality . . ." Such seminars took on, as he noted, cultic aspects.[88]

The German research seminar was an institutionalized technique for the formation of normalized but individualized academic personae. Not courtly conversation cultivated and civilized by a Parisian salon, but rather the marvelous nexus of Germanic paperwork accomplished this feat. Embodied as objectified spirit (à la Hegel) in directorial reports, seminarists nonetheless cultivated a subjectified, charismatic spirit in their papers.

The juridico-ecclesiastical space of the medieval colleges and early modern seminaries gave way in the seminar to the politico-economic world of modern institutes and departments. A conceptual space of personal academic projects, one of personality and originality, was conceded to directors and enforced on seminarists. But public and state interests circumscribed directors and seminarists. It did not so much matter what seminars read or wrote upon, since the center of the state's interest had come to reside in the bureaucratic discipline and the view of academic labor that the seminars (and labs) instilled.

The seminars accomplished in their own way for advanced or graduate students what the grading system accomplished in its way for collegians or undergraduate students. An essential difference lies in the fact that the undergraduate exams did not produce new knowledge or research. The seminar's competitive structure, however, differentiated graduate students far more complexly than grades ever could. And it produced research.

Research depends on budgetary power. The directorate's access to and ability to allocate a budget made the seminar a site of research, while the tutorials in the endowed Oxbridge colleges did not in fact become such sites, regardless of the occasional brilliant scholar they produced. In the German Protestant system, the decisions about scholarships came directly from the seminar directors. They eventually did not make such decisions on the basis of need in the first instance. Academic merit became the first and the crucial test.

And it was merit measured in the directorate's eyes. In the seminar, the directorate played the role that peer review would come to play for academics—setting the standards and framework in terms of which work could be evaluated as valid, proper, and original but not idiosyncratic and isolated. Seminarists could choose their paper topics and wear peculiar attire because they had learnt to play the role of director and handed in their work on time.

This Germanic discipline perfected under the bureaucratic state proved itself addicted to the proliferation of discreet but peculiar personalities. As we'll see in chapters to come, these would be ultimately disembodied ones. Apart from their unusual attire, such Germanic souls would find academic freedom as depoliticized thinking substance, as pure spirit. But their work would have to show a charismatic spark of genius—originality. Reconciling Romanticism with the rationality of the bureaucratic state, the doctor of philosophy and the new doctoral dissertation displayed the great achievements of the new seminar system.

# 6

## The Doctor of Philosophy

The academic degree was originally unknown to Druids and Huns, Romans and Greeks, Israelites and Philistines, Arabs and Zulus, Persians and Chaldeans, Hindus and Chinese, Eskimos and Incas. The academic degree, its bizarre rituals and symbols, could have only been conceived by the same barbarians who put gargoyles on cathedrals. It was the Goths.[1]

Of course, today one recognizes the above way of thinking and speaking as archaic. It embodies, however, the mentality whence the academic degree sprang. To grasp the nature of academic charisma in its origins and evolution, it helps to grasp the nature of the academic degree in its archaic origins and modern evolution. The doctorate in philosophy and related degrees in the arts and sciences emerged comparatively late. They first appeared by statute in the eighteenth and but mostly in the nineteenth century.

In the United States, for example, the doctor of philosophy first appeared in 1861, when Yale University elevated a candidate to that rank. In Britain a doctorate in arts and sciences first entered the University of London as the doctor of science between 1857 and 1860, and as the doctor of literature in 1868. Cambridge University did not award its first D. Phil. or Ph.D. until 1882, and Oxford University did not award one until 1917. (In Latin, "doctor of philosophy" may be written as either *philosophiae doctor* or *doctor philosophiae*, whence Ph.D. and D. Phil., identical in meaning.) The Germans abbreviate the degree Dr. Phil., and in this chapter we move rather conspicuously between various abbreviations, in part because the sources did so as the degree developed over time, and in part to dislodge in the reader's mind any self-evidence of the existence of the degree itself.[2]

The late arrival of the doctor of philosophy—which we shall use as the generic name for doctorates in arts and sciences—is not surprising. Rather, it is surprising that academic degrees persisted at all. As we'll see, processes of rationalization and reformation in the early modern era had called the entire European system of academic degrees into question. Beginning with the humanists in the Renaissance, reformers and enlighteners depicted academic degrees as archaic, medieval, barbaric, and, in sum, Gothic. With the collapse of the political *ancien régime* in France in 1789, many anticipated a similar collapse of the academic *ancien régime*, epitomized in academic degrees and titles.

That did not happen. To the contrary, traditional academic degrees survived and flourished. And a new degree, the doctor of philosophy, spread in the German lands after 1789. From there and then, this figure slowly spread through the rest of Europe, to the Americas, and then the rest of the globe. A figure essentially unknown in the Middle Ages, a figure contested during most of the early modern era, as we'll see, would arrive in the modern era as the Germanic conqueror of the academic world, the new hero of knowledge.

This chapter examines the birth and academic career of the "neo-Gothic" figure known as the doctor of philosophy. The two chief parts concern the two chief phenomena: (i) the degree title itself, the Ph.D. or D.Phil., and (ii) the crucial rite of passage for attaining that title, the *dissertatio doctoralis,* the doctoral dissertation.

At the medieval university, the highest degree in the arts and philosophy faculty was the master of arts, a degree of great dignity and worth. Remember that in figure 2.1 from seventeenth-century Cambridge, excepting the anomalous doctor of music, there were no doctors in the arts and philosophy faculty. In conservative academic cultures, such as those in Cambridge, Leipzig, and Oxford, the master of arts essentially retained its great medieval dignity in the early modern era. However, in other academic cultures, including many German universities, the dignity of the master's degree fell lower and lower after 1500.

The first part of this chapter examines that fall and the attempts by the increasingly lowly masters to become doctors, that is, to introduce the title and degree of the doctor of philosophy. In attempting that, the masters hoped to achieve parity with the older academic doctors, namely, the doctors of theology, jurisprudence (law), and medicine. Much of the chapter concerns the attempts by the older doctors to frustrate the masters' innovation.

This first part of the chapter closes with an analysis of the recognition of the doctor of philosophy in many Germans lands. The recognition came under the dual aegis of the Enlightenment and Romanticism, as part of the process of bureaucratic rationalization with which this book is much concerned. In brief, the argument of the first part is that the recognition of the new degree came about as part of the great transformation of academic charisma.

The second part of the chapter treats of the doctoral dissertation, a theme with which the first part actually ends. This second part analyzes aspects of literary production from the 1670s to the 1830s. It compares and contrasts some genres of academic publication from the 1670s to the 1730s with doctoral dissertations written from the 1770s to the 1830s. Special attention will go to doctoral dissertations of students who had partaken of the new seminars, as studied in the previous chapter. In brief, the argument here is that emergence of the doctoral dissertation as a work of research can be traced to the period of the 1770s to 1830s.

This chapter is the shaggy dog story of the book. It has irony as its motif.

## THE DOCTOR OF PHILOSOPHY AS A WORK OF ART

### The Degradation of the Masters of Arts

The Renaissance and Reformation spelt the beginning of the end for the prestige of masters of arts in many German lands. From about 1450 to 1550, the dignity of the master's degree sank much through the machinations of so-called humanists and reformers. It was a result of the vicious work of poets, the treachery of jurists, and the betrayal of theologians.

THE POETS' VICIOUS WORK. Around 1450, the first German scholars returned as humanists from Italy. Wishing to spread the glad tidings, they began to haunt German universities. The humanists saw the bachelor's and master's curriculum, which just happened to exclude the humanists' subjects, as the embodiment of scholastic barbarism. The humanists condemned the bachelors and masters of arts as "Sophists" and "Goths," barbarians of the "Dark Ages," able neither to appreciate classical literature and poetry, nor even to speak correct Latin. They found it lamentable that fellow humanists had allowed themselves "to be given this ridiculous master's title." To a friend intent on being similarly debased, one might write sardonically, "Nonetheless, I wish that you inflict the master's title upon yourself, so that through that mask (*personatus*) you might frighten youths in the dark. For youths and the age inhabit the darkness, when [classical] Literature is known badly, or not at all."[3]

Daring humanists forsook the master's title. Some claimed weird, novel appellations in the university matriculation register, which was the official legal record kept by the university's magistrate, the rector. When the register documented academic condition, it recorded the juridical status of the individual as scholar, bachelor, licentiate, master, or doctor within the corporation of scholars. Many humanists rejected the legal titles and styled themselves such things as: Poet Laureate, Professed in Literature, Praetor of the Republic of Letters, Citizen of Many Italian Universities, Doctor of Medicine, Philosophy, Things Oriental and Poet Laureate Crowned by the Emperor's Own Hands, and so on.[4]

The humanists must have thought these *noms de plume* would subvert the scholastic masks or personae, the traditional titles. Instead of the Gothic title of master of arts, many in fact wished to be called "Poet," reviving the old Roman notion of the poet laureate. Indeed, on 18 April 1487, Emperor Friedrich III crowned Conrad Celtis as the first poet laureate in the Holy Roman Empire. In 1501 the next emperor founded a College for Poets and Mathematicians in Vienna, which created not masters of arts, but rather poets laureate.[5]

At its most extreme, the poets envisaged the eradication of the bachelors and masters of arts. One would replace them with the neo-Romanesque world conceived by the humanists, the Republic of Letters. Authority there was supposed to arise not by juridical investiture of an academic degree, but rather through republican recognition of literary merit, that is, by the applause of the proper citizens, the humanists. Radical poets took to fomenting insurrection in the student body against the Gothic masters. A fictional master lamented,

> the other day I questioned a student about some transgression—straightaway he turned upon me and thou'd me. Then said I, "I will store that up for degree-day . . ." But he snapped back, "To the jakes with you and your baccalaureate . . ." Then said I, "Thou rascal! Wilt thou belittle the degree of Bachelor, that high dignity?" He answered that he thought but little even of Masters . . . See to what a height these scandals grow! Would that all the Universities might join hands and make an end of all these Poets and humanists who are their bane.[6]

Poets not only bade students beshit the masters, but also belittled them, ". . . would dub them dunces, and aver that one Poet was worth ten Masters, and that Poets should always take precedence of Masters . . . in processions . . . , that the Masters were not Masters of the Seven Liberal Arts, but of the Seven Deadly Sins." Poets ridiculed the masters of arts, most shrewdly in the *Epistolae obscurorum virorum* (1515–17) as above, wherein the most learned and vicious satire made constant and easy sport of the "obscure men."[7]

THE JURISTS' TREACHERY. In their degradation of masters, the poets were abetted by jurists, the doctors of law. The latter had long been elevating the doctor's title, at the expense of the masters. In the Middle Ages, "master" and "doctor" had been used rather promiscuously for a time, so that a certain pragmatic synonymy existed. However, juridical treatises on scholastic privileges slowly laid the bases for obscuring that medieval equivalence.[8]

Scholastic privileges originally applied to matriculated academics in general, but had come to depend instead upon academic status. Since the fourteenth century, jurists had postulated not only superior privileges for degree-holders at the university, but also privileges attached to the degree per se, privileges that did not lapse upon exmatriculation or graduation from the university. Since jurists consistently used the doctor's title for their own, they had read into law many privileges for doctors, usually without mentioning masters.[9]

According to jurists' treatises, academia was privileged as a charitable foundation since study benefited the public welfare. Academics were privileged with the benefits of paupers and of peregrinators since, what was seen as the foundation of academic privilege, the *Authentica habita* of 1158, had concerned exactly such privileges to peregrinating scholars. As we saw in chapters above, graduated academics were also privileged with the benefits of a crowned athlete, since scholars had withstood three trials of courage for their degrees. Academics were further privileged with benefit of clergy since study was a spiritual labor. And some jurists even argued for the privileges of knighthood since study was noble.

Given this grounding of academic privilege, it is no surprise that jurists claimed marvelous legal privileges, for doctors at least. The privileges included

- to be able to silence the players of silly games interrupting their studies;
- to be able to stop buildings that would block the light in their studies;
- to be able to stop buildings that would block the light in their lecture halls;
- in cases of equal merit, to have their sons preferred for academic positions;
- to be able to sit in the presence of magistrates;
- to be able to give a legal deposition at home;
- to be freed from quartering soldiers and performing night-watch;
- to be able, along with their wives, to wear the same clothing as nobles;
- to have rights of social precedence over knights;
- after twenty years of teaching, to be held as the equal of counts;
- to receive the benefit of doubt in any suspicion of crime;
- to be free from being either manacled or detained in prison;
- and, happily, doctors could not be tortured.[10]

In such passages asserting privileges for doctors, the words "or masters" were typically noticeably absent. It might thus become unclear if masters of arts, especially exmatriculated graduates, enjoyed the above privileges. The masters' claims to doctoral privileges hinged on the pragmatic synonymy of "master" and "doctor"—and that became increasingly obscured by the jurists. In 1476, the dean of the arts faculty at Leipzig felt the need to remind people, "The master of arts is the same as the doctor's degree." But the actions of the theologians would soon break the old, pragmatic synonymy altogether.[11]

THE THEOLOGIANS' BETRAYAL. Unlike the other three faculties, medieval German theology faculties had used both "master" and "doctor." But some distinction existed. While "master" and its cognates occurred a lot, "doctor" occurred less. Passages about the award of the degree mostly used "master" or "licentiate." Foundation privileges, curial style, and the matriculation registers show the same. In privileges and letters, one originally addressed the university as "masters, doctors, and other scholars." The order of academic precedence underlay the sequence of words, and theologians must always be addressed first. As members of the university, theologians appeared juridically and officially as masters, a status that they acknowledged in discharging intramural offices. Jurists and physicians, in their turns as rector, styled themselves as doctors in the matriculation register. But, up to the late fifteenth century, theologians did not commonly call themselves "doctor" in the register.[12]

Theologians were epithetically doctors of the Church, but their faculty awarded the master's degree. Things began to change only around 1500 when theologians took to omitting their academic degree in the matriculation register and styling themselves "professor," a term earlier seldom used by anyone. The number of doctors in theology statutes grew. But general doctrification awaited a big event. At universities reformed or founded by Protestants, the doctor of theology became statutory after 1533. With the Counter-Reformation, thanks to the Jesuits, it entered most of the universities remaining Catholic. Theologians transformed an old epithet due them, "doctor," into their juridical title.[13]

During the Renaissance and Reformation, from about 1450 to 1550, masters of arts thus suffered degradation at the hands of poets, jurists, and theologians. The acts of the latter proved most serious. Masters of arts had long been last in academic precedence. In academic processions, as we saw in chapter 2, theologians always came first (or last), then the jurists, then the physicians, and finally the philosophers and "artists," the masters of arts. This final (or first) position in the order of precedence had followed more from the inferiority of the artists' discipline, the liberal arts, rather than from their title, the master's degree, since the theologians, who came first (or last), also originally held the academic title of master.

Now that the theologians had assumed the academic title of doctor, being last or least might come to stigmatize artists in regard to their title, that is, as masters. One had addressed the university as "masters, doctors, and other scholars," but would alter this to "doctors, masters, and other scholars." All that might inspire the novel and absurd idea that the master's was a different degree from, even inferior to the doctor's degree. Misguided jurists did eventually say that. And that might have lead others to believe that masters of arts, like students, could be subjected to torture! Indeed, deceitful jurists eventually said that too.[14]

## The Arrest of the Doctor of Philosophy

The solution was elementary. Masters of arts should become doctors, like the theologians. In the 1490s, at Erfurt and Vienna, two characters in fact claimed to be doctors in arts and philosophy. In the first half of the sixteenth century, more artists claimed the same. The Viennese College of Poets and Mathematicians (1501) perhaps helped spread this conceit, for it may have graduated not only poets laureate, but also doctors of philosophy.[15]

But no university, no faculty, no college had statutory authority to make doctors of arts or philosophy. While theologians officially received the title after 1533, the same statutory revisions did not make artists doctors. The doctorate in arts or philosophy was neither a juridical title, nor an epithet due artists or philosophers by tradition. This was a serious matter, for impersonating a doctor constituted a crime.[16]

THE DOCTORS ATTACKED, THE MASTERS DEFENDED. The story now moves to the University of Ingolstadt, where it occurred to a certain Veit Amerbach, poet and professor of philosophy, to use the same tactics against the doctors that the poets had used against the masters. In 1549, Amerbach published a little book, a poem or oration, which seems to have ridiculed doctors. When the Ingolstadt academic senate, dominated by doctors, got wind of the publication, they found that it "contained many absurdities, not to be tolerated." They summoned Master Amerbach to explain the point of this "libelous little book."

Appearing before the senate on 7 February 1549, Amerbach protested that he had in fact shown the manuscript to the rector, Master of Arts Erasmus Wolf, who had read it "with pleasure." Rector Wolf himself had sent the manuscript to the publisher in Augsburg. The academic senate was not impressed by such facts. They imposed a fine on Amerbach, censured the publication, ordered all copies retrieved from Augsburg at Amerbach's expense, and enjoined that they be destroyed in Ingolstadt. The destruction appears to have been thorough, for this is an extremely rare work and I have never succeeded in finding a copy.[17]

Foiled in this attempt to avenge the masters, Amerbach switched tactics. His *Oratio de doctoratu philosophico* of 1571 appeared many years after the suppression of his libelous little book. He now replaced satire with philology. He argued for the traditional, medieval equality of masters and doctors, and for recognition of the doctor of philosophy as a title. The liberal arts and philosophy, he argued, were worthy disciplines, no less so than theology, jurisprudence, and medicine. "Master" was a title of great dignity. Our Lord was called this, as were theologians at the University of Paris, and jurists by a Roman emperor. "Master" and "doctor" were synonyms, and the former ought to have the same privileges as the latter.

Amerbach argued further that the dean of the arts faculty had no less authority than the other three deans. The same chancellor's license preceded the award of the degree in each faculty. Doctors and masters lectured and disputed from the same place on the academic podium or *cathedra*. In all faculties, the ceremony for investment with the highest degree revolved around the same insignia: ascension of the podium, the open and the closed book, the mortarboard or pileus, the golden ring, the kiss, and the blessing. Since the ceremony invested one juridically, the insignia of the artists' ceremony created the same juridical person as did the other faculties.' Finally, the emperor had allowed the German artists the title "Doctissimi." Therefore, the doctor of arts or philosophy should exist.[18]

Amerbach's *Oratio de doctoratu philosophico* was greeted with silence. I know of no discussion of it then or later. As a mental exercise, let us, however, extract from the jurists a likely response to Amerbach, after which two other important matters are treated briefly.

THE JURISTS' REPLY, THE PALATINE COUNTS, AND THE MASTERS OF PHILOSOPHY. Jurists might note that a proper ceremony and costume are needed to doctrify one, but not every ass with a mortarboard is a doctor. And many women are kissed, sometimes even by doctors, but this contributes naught to making them doctors. Furthermore, must not the conveyor be empowered to convey a title? Artists have neither properly invested doctors among them, nor the statutory authority to make them. Etymologies about "master" and "doctor" confuse philology with jurisprudence. Theologians' past usage is immaterial to the case. Artists' rights to the title "Doctissimi" no more makes them doctors, than the jurists' right to the title "Nobilissimi" makes them nobles—a touchy subject.

In sum, masters ought beware, for impersonating a doctor is a crime and, like students, masters could be tortured.[19]

So much for a possible reply to Amerbach, against whose proliferation of the doctorate other considerations arose. The pope and emperor, it seems, had taken to creating doctors by fiat, the *Doctores bullati.* Worse, they had empowered others to do so. The pope curtailed the practice by mid-sixteenth century, after the Council of Trent. But the emperor showed no signs of desisting. He continued creating palatine counts. This was an odd title and dignity, truly reflecting the decadence of the early modern Empire. Some such palatine counts had obtained imperial authority to fiat doctors, that is, to convey the title by simple proclamation. With the palatine counts fiating doctors, and with the theologians recognized as doctors, how could the older doctors allow the hordes of artists and philosophers the title? Such a surfeit of doctors would debase the title. Seemingly in view of all this, the following happened. The masters of arts were allowed to become masters of philosophy.[20]

What was this, some sort of cruel joke? After 1533, university statutes, with few exceptions, substituted "philosophy" for "arts," but retained "master." This change may have meant something in the Republic of Letters, where philosophy was perhaps seen as superior to arts. But, since the academic problem sprang from the master's title, the change was juridically meaningless for the academic corporation, and the legal and social status issuing from it. While theologians became doctors after the mid-sixteenth century, artists became philosophers, but were kept masters, and for a long time. For most faculties stood then under their sovereign's ministries, and had long lost authority over their own statutes.[21]

## The Advent of the Doctor of Philosophy

From about 1450 to 1550, as a consequence of the actions of poets, jurists, and theologians, and despite Amerbach's efforts, the prestige of the master of arts suffered degradation, and the doctor of philosophy was arrested in development. The juridically meaningless change in the master's title symbolized the continuation of their lowly status, from the medieval arts faculty to the early modern philosophy faculty, as inferior of the professional schools, the faculties of theology, jurisprudence, and medicine. In the order of precedence, masters of philosophy came last, and now also by their title, since they alone were masters.

A QUARTER MILLENNIAL STRUGGLE. After 1550 the situation grew worse. German humanists created a baccalaureate-equivalent curriculum at a new sort of high school, the *gymnasium academicum.* This caused the B.A. to wither away at most German Protestant universities in the seventeenth century. The Protestant masters sank to the academic bottom, for there were now no lower degree holders. Worse, enrollments in their arts and philosophy faculties began to fall and went to zero at some places. Students thus directly entered one of the professional faculties after graduation from the gymnasium. Robbed of a subject population, arts and sciences became only ancillary to the professional schools.[22]

The lowly status of the masters of philosophy was reflected in and exacerbated by money. Previous chapters showed that, during the sixteenth century, German universities transformed the medieval structure of endowed benefices and colleges into salaried positions. Luminous cases aside, professors of arts and sciences typically had measly salaries. To earn a decent living, professorial masters of philosophy had to do odd jobs and pinch pennies.[23]

Recalling ecclesiastical practices, professors in the philosophy faculty pluralistically accumulated multiple chairs. Furthermore, such professors often obtained a doctorate in theology, jurisprudence, or medicine. Some left the university thereafter, or moved into one of the professional schools for a better salary. This pattern endured into the eighteenth century. In the early modern era, a life devoted to the arts and sciences got tough.

The advent of the doctor of philosophy, a sign of the modern era, would symbolize the professionalization of the professors of arts and sciences. Only then, as doctors of philosophy, did professors of arts and sciences attain status and benefits equal to those of the professional faculties. It took a quarter of a millennium, from about 1550 to 1800.

THE MASTERS BECOME DEVIOUS AND THE JURISTS TAKE NOTICE. Denied the doctorate after the Reformation, the masters became devious. They no longer called themselves "masters." They employed, instead, sly ambiguities and insinuating circumlocutions.

By the early seventeenth century, one finds cases in which students were graduated not as *Magistri* (masters), but rather with conceits such as: *summus philosophiae gradus,* or *pro suprema in Philosophia Laurea,* or *ad summos in philosophia honores.* And the clever philosophers do not say what this *summus* or *suprema* in philosophy means. Such evasive circumlocutions became increasingly popular, and eventually the norm. Even before 1650, outright insurrections, proclamations of "masters of arts and doctors of philosophy" arose. The illicit phrase was smuggled into the statutes at Heidelberg (1570), Helmstedt (1576), Basel (1632), and Erfurt (1634), though the degree was still officially the master's.[24]

The matriculation registers exhibit further traces of the masters' strategies. After 1550, philosophers rarely styled themselves "master" when signing the register as rector; instead, they wrote "professor." A more fateful practice lay in obfuscation by those with a doctorate from one of the superior faculties, who still taught in the philosophy faculty. Many of these called themselves "philosophiae & theologiae doctor" and the like when they served as rector. This artifice occurred as early as the late fourteenth century, but became common only in the sixteenth. Such rewordings were nonsense, for the important substantive "magister" had been omitted—the correct phrase was "philosophiae magister & theologiae doctor."[25]

Such elliptical phrases were usually written as above, with the "doctor" postpositive to "theologiae," "juris," or "medicinae." But in a few places, an inverted elliptical order appeared, such as "medicinae & philosophiae doctor." That was a grammatical nightmare, since "medicine & philosophy master doctor" was actually meant. The tactic of cognitive disassociation proceeded here to the brink of criminal impersonation. At the University of Vienna, such impersonations of doctors by philosophers went unchecked after 1550. And after the Jesuits took control in 1622, the Phil. Dr. seems a garden variety there.[26]

Jurists soon sat up and took notice. In 1641, Georg Walther formulated a syllogism:

> The master's is the highest degree in philosophy.
> The doctor's degree is superior to the master's.
> *Ergo,* the doctor of philosophy does not exist.[27]

And impersonating a doctor, he argued, is *lèse majesté,* a capital offense.

The issue became a hot topic. Some followed Walther, and denied the doctor of philosophy existed, or said the philosophers' title was the master's. Others engaged in casuistry and said that only a doctor of the superior faculties might use the title. "Phil. Dr." would be an ellipsis of "philosophiae [magister and juris] doctor" and the like. But, by 1700, most seemed hardpressed to dispute the propriety of the degree on juridical grounds. A jurist who knew most everything about academic degrees, the good Itter, had refuted the arguments against the possibility of the doctor of philosophy. And, worse, the emperor had issued patents to some palatine counts that empowered them to create doctors of philosophy. Since German jurists held that the authority over academic degrees resided with the emperor, even those opposed to the degree had to concede the question in principle on this point.[28]

**THE DOCTOR OF PHILOSOPHY, RECOGNIZED AND RE-SISTED.** After Walther's syllogism of 1641, philosophers continued to impersonate doctors, but the degree's status remained a problem. Even at new foundations, statutes still did not formally integrate the degree. And only a few doctors of philosophy pure and simple appeared in matriculation registers. More than a few rectors, however, boldly used inverted ellipsis, such as "Theol. & Phil. Dr." At a number of places, one further finds graduation proclamations of "M. Art. & Phil. Dr.," especially toward the end of the century. Coupled with the drift of the jurists' debate above, this might lead one to expect recognition of the doctor of philosophy soon after 1700.[29]

But the jurists still held their highest card. They and their ilk controlled the ministry. In 1712, a Prussian minister decreed that a certain Professor Strimesius at Königsberg, "who has crowned himself, quite improperly and without authorization, with the title 'doctor philosophiae,' should be strictly forbidden this ridiculous novelty, which will lead to all sorts of quarrels. According with the custom of all other universities, he should be content with the traditional title of 'magister philosophiae.'"[30]

During the first two thirds of the eighteenth century in Prussia and elsewhere, the same old strategies had to be pursued. Proclamations of "M. Art. & Phil. Dr." continued. But, with few exceptions, philosophers still did not style themselves doctors of philosophy when they served as rector. Even inverted ellipsis arose in no greater numbers. Statutes still spoke of the master's degree or used circumlocutions. Göttingen's statutes of 1736, for example, mention the "proclamation of the doctors of philosophy." But the degree is called the "master's degree" and "the highest degree in philosophy." In 1752, Austrian Empress Maria Theresa even commanded a halt to proclamations of doctors of philosophy, no doubt since the surfeit of doctors was debasing the title. In Prussia, Austria, and elsewhere, the advent of the doctor of philosophy would occur only in the final third of the eighteenth century.[31]

In 1771, Prussian minister Zedlitz gave in and recognized the doctors of philosophy. Reasoning that addition of the nonstatutory "& Phil. Dr." to the statutory "M. Art" made a double degree, Zedlitz demanded a double graduation fee for such a degree. This had the desired effect of checking proliferation of the *philosophiae doctor*. But it also opened the door.[32]

The degree spread. In 1784 the new statutes for Mainz implicitly recognized the degree. In 1786 the Austrians reversed course by abolishing the M. Art. and instituting the Dr. Phil. After 1787 Bamberg awarded the double degree, "M. Art. & Phil. Dr." and in 1797 dropped the "M. Art." After 1794 Leipzig also awarded the double degree, as did Tübingen after 1803. After 1798, Jena awarded only the Dr. Phil.; the Bavarians had recognized it by 1805; it was at Heidelberg by 1817 and at Basel by 1823. But awkwardness still bedeviled the Dr. Phil. Though Göttingen's statutes spoke of proclamation of the doctor of philosophy, the title pages of the dissertations were marred into the 1820s by old conceits, such as "pro summis in philosophia honoribus." In Prussia, these persisted even after the 1820s.[33]

Recognition of the doctor of philosophy would be, then, neither universally, nor uniformly, accomplished before the end of the century. And the polemics would not abate either. In 1801 a certain "Herr Magister" noted that, beginning about fifteen years previously, the addition of the "& Phil. Dr." to the traditional "M. Art." had become commonplace, and now many were deviously trying to drop the "M. Art." But this was absurd, Herr Magister argued, for the master's was the original and correct title. A certain "Herr Doktor" replied:

> It's really silly that some still don't want to recognize the doctors of philosophy as doctors . . . Whoever graduates in the philosophy faculty at Göttingen, for example, is created a doctor of philosophy, and publicly proclaimed that. Why shouldn't it mean "doctor" in German . . . , but rather "master"? Such a prejudice seems to stem from the time when one saw the philosophy faculty as maid and minion of the others, and thus held a doctor of philosophy as less important than a doctor of theology, medicine or law.

Herr Magister, Herr Doktor, and others, carried on the debate in subsequent months. Herr Doktor insinuated that the other faculties were conspiring against the philosophers. And that was precisely the case at the University of Leipzig, the seat of German medievalism.[34]

In 1810 the philosophy faculty at Leipzig petitioned the ministry in Dresden to allow its members to employ the doctor's title officially, since usage of the title was still technically nonstatutory at Leipzig. The ministry solicited the opinion of the university prorector and the deans of theology, law, and medicine. A full year expired before the ministry received this response, "Up till now, only the theology, law and medical faculties have had the right to create REAL DOCTORS." The representatives of the superior faculties expressed their hope that the ministry would not overturn this tradition. And it did not.[35]

Adding insult to injury, in 1841 the ministry in Dresden actually enjoined the professors of arts and sciences in Leipzig to desist using the doctor's title, and to use the master's title instead. The putative doctors of philosophy in Leipzig were stunned. They again petitioned the ministry and submitted a staggering claim for Germans, and especially for Saxons. They would rather have no title, they claimed, than to have to bear the "now derided and abased, medieval . . . and thoroughly inadequate title" of a master of arts.[36]

## The Juridical Sublation of the Doctors

What is remarkable is not that the advent of the doctor of philosophy took so long. What is remarkable is that it occurred at all. For academic degrees seemed on the verge of extinction at the time. Like other medievalisms, it appeared they would perish with the *ancien régime*.

REFORMED SCHOLASTICISM, ENLIGHTENED NEOCLASSICISM, ROMANTIC NEO-GOTHIC. The humanists' critique from about 1450 to 1550 had concerned primarily the B.A. and M.A. The doctorate, which insured the status of lawyers and physicians, does not seem to have been attacked. Indeed, from the perspective of the satirical *Epistolae obscurorum virorum* of 1515-17, the humanists' campaign pitted poets and jurists, as purveyors of classical literature and law, only against the traditional, medieval masters, that is, the theologians and artists.

But by 1550, the situation had changed. The path taken by Luther and his right-hand man, Melanchthon, allowed the medieval system of academic degrees to survive both the Renaissance and the Reformation in the newly Protestant Germanies. And, had academic degrees ever been in danger in the lands remaining Catholic, the Jesuit Counter-Reformation insured their preservation. From about 1550 to 1700, diatribes against academic degrees continued, but were launched mostly by radical and marginal sects, largely Protestant.[37]

During the Enlightenment things changed again. Enlightened polemics attacked degrees per se, or rather the faculties generally. One criticized the medieval, corporate, monopolistic guild-practices of the faculties, in favor of modern, industrial, free-market production, typified by the new scientific academies, societies of letters, technical academies, and authors living in the scholarly state of nature or constituting a Republic of Letters. Critique of the academic guild became most poignant when, in the Revolution's aftermath, the French swept away such medieval academic remnants west of the Rhine after 1789.[38]

After Napoleon vanquished the Prussians in 1806, he closed the principal Prussian university, the University of Halle. Impetus for founding a replacement institution in Berlin then became great in Prussia, or, in what was left of it. From 1807 to 1808, the Prussian ministry received thirteen proposals for founding an institution in Berlin. Some of Prussia's leading ministers and citizens had penned the proposals. None of these proposals called the new institution a university. None favored keeping the traditional faculties or degrees. In the modern era, the medieval guild of academic masters and doctors should vanish.³⁹

But between 1808 and the opening of the new institution in 1809/10, a conservative and reactionary spirit emerged. Francophobia and Romanticism gained the ascendant. Neoclassicism gave way to neo-Gothic. The new institution was called the University of Berlin. Latin became its official language. The philosophy faculty would no longer be the minion of the other faculties. One proclaimed it as the foundation of the university. Prussia preserved academic degrees and the University of Berlin officially instituted the doctor of philosophy.

During the debates between 1808 and 1810, the philosopher and theologian Schleiermacher had spoken in favor of the title "doctor of philosophy," and in only that form, without further specification. Titles such as "doctor of history" or "doctor of physics," or even "doctor of natural sciences," he saw as silly. The proper title expressed the unity of the faculty and of all knowledge. According to the Berlin philosophy faculty's first dean, the philosopher Fichte, academic degrees embodied a symbol of reception into the society of the learned. Like priests, degree-holders had been invested by those before them, and these by those before them, and so on, in an unbroken chain. If the anti-intellectual rabble (*Pöbel*) made fun of these degrees, so let them. This did not concern the initiated, since the rabble was but an object that needed to be dis-rabbled (*entpöbelt*).⁴⁰

Academic degrees had survived the animadversions of modern state and society and, indeed, flourished because they had been absorbed, at least in the Germanies, by the civil service. Through this ministerial reconciliation, the academic degree—and the persona and charisma that it instituted—altered essentially. That is what we must now consider. And, in the light of this bureaucratization we must ask: Who or what is the doctor of philosophy?

THE CANDIDATE'S AND DOCTOR'S JURIDICAL PERSONA. In the Middle Ages, award of degrees presumed and transformed a moral subject or juridical persona beyond the physical person. The degree inhabited a juridico-ecclesiastical charismatic sphere similar to knighthood and holy orders. Statutes delimited the required moral subject or juridical persona.

The candidate must be matriculated and have studied at the university in question. The candidate must be of legitimate birth, without infamy, Christian, male, the proper age, and have all antecedent degrees. The candidate must have spent a stipulated period of time between each degree, must swear a pile of oaths, and swear ultimately to the chancellor, a cleric in holy orders. The candidate must be invested, like a knight, by a promoter who had the degree. The candidate had to be physically present, essentially corporally intact, sane, and able to speak and see. And, on the day of the degree's award, the candidate had to be alive.[41]

Not only did award of the degree presume a certain moral subject or juridical persona in the candidate, each degree also transformed it and enhanced one's charisma. Each degree created duties and privileges. The degree marked one juridically for life, as the graduate of this or that faculty, as *Magister* or *Doctor noster*, so one must promise not to receive the same degree from another faculty. One must lead a life without infamy. Further, one must promise to abide for a time after receiving the degree, and at times ascend the podium to preside over disputations. One was enabled, at times obliged, to wear a certain costume.

The degree presumed and modified a moral subject or juridical person within the candidate, created a distinct academic persona. A degree-holder was differentiated from a nonholder by the degree's insignia and costume, by the jural privileges vested in the status they signified. Masters and doctors were differentiated from bachelors since the former could ascend the top of the podium (*cathedra*) to preside and lecture *ex cathedra*. The faculties were individuated by their degrees, which the order of precedence reflected. A doctor, formerly master, of theology was superior to other doctors. A doctor of law was superior to physicians and philosophers, and so on. It is the familiar order of precedence.[42]

Such principles distinguished each academic from all others. But articulation of the principles proved a problem at the early modern university. Do bachelors of theology precede masters of arts? If Faust, a doctor of theology and medicine, becomes a professor in the medical faculty, does he precede everyone in the faculty? Individuating persons of the same degree within each faculty proved especially troublesome. As we saw in chapter 2, seniority usually functioned as the criterion. And it counted for much if one had graduated from the university where one taught, that is, was *Magister* or *Doctor noster*. In the mid-eighteenth century, a certain Master Bel at the University of Leipzig

> sat in the philosophy faculty behind a certain Master Schulmann, who was supposedly a pill. Bel wanted to sit in front of him and thus went to Jena, had himself proclaimed a Doctor [of Philosophy], came back, and wanted precedence over this Master. "Ho ho, Herr Doktor," said he [Schulmann], "you're not *Doktor noster!*" So Bel stayed in his previous place.[43]

Disputes on precedence epitomize the academic mentality in which juristic notions individuate persons. The creation of the modern researcher, the doctor of philosophy, would require the formation of academics who see themselves neither academically individuated, nor personally and professionally defined in that manner. During the course of the early modern era, the candidate as moral subject or juridical person would all but disappear. Though certain traditional charismatic vestiges of the degree remained (for example, academic costumes), degrees survived only because they largely ceased treating the candidate as juridical person, and thus became suitable to the rational authority of the bureaucratic state. From juristic disquisitions, one can see this happening.

THE JURISTS' ENLIGHTENMENT: THE 1670S TO THE 1730S. From the Late Middle Ages onward, juristic disquisitions considered such questions: Can an infamous person obtain or retain a degree? Can bastards obtain degrees? Can children, women, and Jews obtain degrees? Can one obtain a degree from someone not holding it? Can one obtain a degree *in absentia* or *per saltum*—the latter means not having studied a stipulated time and/or not having attained the antecedent degrees? And most interestingly, can the dead obtain academic degrees?[44]

Though some unusual souls had affirmed such questions earlier, it was only during the late seventeenth and early eighteenth centuries when jurists typically affirmed some, or all of them. Elites are usually aware that the costs of their jealously guarded privileges are borne by the excluded. This change of heart should thus be taken not only as hopeful sign of enlightenment, but also as a hint that something else was taking over the function of marking individuals academically—academic charisma was altering in its essential form.

And, in any case, the change of heart had been forced in part. The palatine counts, that odd, early modern imperial dignity that we met above, played a role. Given to venal practices, some palatine counts sold degrees to unworthy candidates, *honoris causa*, without exclusion or exception. But consider now examples of the new attitude on the academic.

Can an infamous person obtain or a person who has become infamous retain a degree? Most jurists still said no. But some things, once thought infamous, might no longer be so. Selling your soul to Satan would clearly make you infamous, as would serving as an executioner. But engaging in a mechanical art or mercantile trade might be all right, at least for a master. The new open-mindedness about infamy found expression regarding the illegitimate in the academy. By analogy with baptism, the illegitimate could be freed of their infamous birth. Indeed, based upon imperial law, palatine counts could legitimize them—for a fee of course. After 1576, imperial charters gave new universities a palatine count's prerogatives. Older universities attained them by appeal thereafter. Illegitimacy then became re-mediable at will by universities and, as was urged, ought not impede study.[45]

After infamy, the sphere of degeneration and sensory defects opened up. Did the all too frequent cases of graduates who neglected their studies, or succumbed to poverty, senility, or insanity require removal of the degree, that is, de-gradation? Walther favored that for neglect of studies but, be-coming broad-minded, tolerated honestly befallen poverty, the natural state for many masters. Sensory defects, unlike illegitimacy or poverty, remained a serious issue. The enlightened Itter argued for allowing the blind degrees. He also discussed the problem of the deaf-mute. Jurists had held them to be similar to the insane, who still could not receive degrees. But even here, Itter argued the case for deaf-mutes.[46]

The mute qua academic posed a big problem. Academia remained es-sentially an oral culture long after the diffusion of the printing press—whence the juridical dilemmas of mutes as academics and of graduation in absentia, that is, the problem of a candidate's submission by mail of a writ-ten oath. Academic oaths, like others, had had to be sworn aloud and in the presence of the person awarding the degree. And the final heroic trial for a degree, the public exam, was originally also perforce an oral exam. The sub-stitutability here of writing for speaking offers a mark and index of the pro-gress of bureaucratic rationalization.

The matter of the juridically mute—minors—concerned, first, whether and which lower age limits should be set for each degree. Theoretically, age should not serve as a necessary condition. Consider, for example, a reincar-nated Jesus Christ. Could he be denied a doctorate in theology at any age? But so long as offices essential to the public welfare stood open to the de-gree-holder without further ado, some conditions on age seemed sensible.[47]

Next, consider women and Jews: Are they perpetual minors, juridically academically mute forever? Jurists now tended to say no. But, in bad faith, most still saw doctorates in theology and law as beyond their reach. In the case of women, palatine counts played a big role, for some had made women poets laureate even before 1733, the year in which the first German university, Wittenberg, awarded a degree to a woman. She was made a poet laureate. The first German doctorate to a woman was an M.D. awarded in 1754 at Halle. Göttingen awarded an M. Art. and Dr. Phil. in 1787 to Dorothea Schlözer, whose exam we considered in a previous chap-ter. In 1721 Frankfurt a.d.O. became the first German university to give a doctorate, an M.D., to an individual of the Jewish faith. It seems that only medical faculties opened their doors to the Jews in the early modern Ger-manies.[48]

Questions about the presence of a candidate also arose. Can a faculty graduate someone *per saltum,* that is, who hasn't spent the statutorily stipulated time between degrees. Furthermore, can a faculty graduate one who hasn't really studied at the university, or who hasn't even matriculated? For the right fee, of course! (Money is a rationalizer.) But foolish faculties, out to make money, ought not copy palatine counts, who sold degrees *honoris causa* to really stupid people. So the applicant *per saltum* shouldn't expect a *creatio ex nihilo,* and should have spent some time some where at some university.[49]

Beyond the case *per saltum,* can a faculty grant a degree in absentia, and can a member of the faculty, who does not hold the degree, convey it? Jurists now gave a qualified yes. Some juridical acts, such as canonization, demanded neither the corporal presence of the subject, nor conveyance from someone with the same juridical persona bestowed by the act. Other acts, such as ordination or investiture, did. Award of academic degrees had been seen as a charismatic act like investiture and ordination. That was being given up now, and the notion of canonization did not replace it. This change epitomizes a disenchantment of academic charisma—it was no longer something nearly magical, transmitted by and bound up with the laying on of hands, but rather bound up with with something new.[50]

Finally, if graduation in absentia is possible, may the candidate be spiritually elsewhere? Can the dead be doctrified? For the truly enlightened, why not? The issue was relevant since, once graduation in absentia was possible, a faculty might doctrify a corpse unknowingly—of concern since doctoral privileges included doctors' wives and children.[51]

As we'll see below, as well as in other chapters, such new juristic attitudes served as both a manifestation and further ground of a great academic transformation that essentially concerns this book: the disembodiment of the academic. From about 1670 onward, the degree candidate was on the way to a rather complete disembodiment. Academic charisma would no longer require a "normal" body. Nor would it manifest itself in precedence and costumes, except in a vestigial and merely ceremonial manner.

FROM THE PHYSICAL TO THE SPIRITUAL, FROM THE JURIDICAL TO THE AUTHORIAL PERSONA. Such enlightenment about academic degrees even penetrated Bavaria. Glossing the Bavarian legal code, the jurist Kreittmayr said the Peace of Westphalia (1648) made religious orthodoxy irrelevant, though he still proscribed doctorates in theology and law for Jews (and probably for women). Infamy still played a role, but it was difficult for him to specify that concretely. In any case, neither legitimacy nor date of birth nor gender nor ethnicity nor even orthodoxy should bear upon the degree, according to our good Bavarian jurist. Only intellectual competency stood at issue, that is, demonstration of "adequate erudition and knowledge."[52]

During the eighteenth century, the degree became largely detached from the physical person and juridical persona of the candidate. One hears less about duties or privileges. By 1785, graduation oaths had been abolished in Austria. In 1804, the Bavarians abolished most graduation oaths, and academic costume, too. As early as 1675, one jurist had even argued that publication might count more than seniority in deciding academic precedence.[53]

The authorial persona would conquer academia and replace the juridical persona as a principle of academic individuation, as a fountainhead of academic charisma. The doctor of philosophy would be born as a real philosopher, pure thinking substance or spirit.

The nineteenth-century statutes of the new University of Berlin constructed the modern doctoral candidate. In addition to exhibition of sufficient existence as a thinking substance, the candidate kept a fragment of its traditional juridical persona. The candidate must have been matriculated for three years, must have actually attended some class or other, must swear a couple of oaths, and must furnish two documents. First, one must submit a curriculum vitae, a literary genre in which the public persona is rendered into a schematic form. Second, one must submit a *testimonium morum*. Perhaps originally a testimony of morals, it soon became an *Unbescholtenheits-atteste,* a document in which the police certified the candidate's freedom from suspicion and the absence of warrants for arrest.[54]

These requirements, especially the two documents, constructed the doctoral candidate not as a juridical, but rather more as a normalized type. A curriculum vitae and clean police files sealed the candidate's normality. One was thus a bureaucrat *in potentia*. Professors had long been de facto princely then public servants, and became so by the nationalization of education—in 1770 in Austria, 1798 in Prussia, 1802 in Bavaria, and so on, ending, as usual, with Saxony in 1846. The academic degree became a title recognized in the civil service and given under the auspices (*Aufsicht*) of the state. The bureaucratic rationalization of the doctoral candidate achieved its ultimate perfection in Austria. The edict of 3 November 1786, abolished the master of arts, recognized the doctor of philosophy, and made award of the degree contingent only upon an examination—no dissertation was required.[55]

In Austria, always at the forefront of bureaucratic rationalization, the doctor of philosophy had been retyped in the image of the rational, modern bureaucrat, the conception of a civil service examination and clean police files. Things would be otherwise elsewhere.

## The Artistic Elevation of the Doctors

The doctor of philosophy's advent accompanied the juridical sublation (*Aufhebung* à la Hegel) of the doctoral degree. The degree and its charismatic power no longer individuated the doctor as a juridical persona; the degree, rather, certified one's normality as a civil servant *in potentia*. But, along with nice paperwork (a curriculum vitae and clean police files), the Prussians would demand something more than the written examination of the Austrian candidate. The Prussian doctor of philosophy arrived as a work of research. The traditional master of arts had only orally defended theses. The doctor of philosophy would take an oral exam, still disputational in tenor, but also research and write a dissertation.

As we saw in the previous chapter, the private or circular disputation, via the university seminar system after 1738, helped establish the advanced student as an author. Growing out of the ethos of the seminar, the Prussian doctoral dissertation effected an artistic elevation of the doctor's persona. In place of the old juridical persona, it instituted a novel authorial persona with a new charisma. But the doctoral dissertation's roots lie in the old theater of the heroic, the public disputation, the jurists' third trial for an academic degree.

As we draw to a conclusion in this first part of the chapter, we shall now attend to the emergence of the doctoral dissertation in the philosophy faculty, that is, the faculty of arts and sciences. In a previous chapter we looked at the evolution of academic manners in the disputation, an oral combat. We now need to review and extend some of those points. The matter is intricate but important to comprehend the evolution of the written from the oral.

THE DISPUTATION FOR A DEGREE. Public disputation was most regulated. The disputation for a degree (*disputatio pro gradu*) and the disputation for a place (*disputatio pro loco*) in the faculty eventually became the most important. But that was not at first the case. In the Middle Ages and Renaissance, only bachelor's candidates disputed for degrees (the *determinatio*). For a bachelor to advance to candidacy for the master's, he might have to dispute several times as a respondent. A new master, moreover, usually had to abide for two years (his *biennium*), during which he lectured and participated in disputations, usually as presider. Award of the master's degree was attended by a ceremony of speeches and so on. But no disputation for a degree originally took place.

Medieval masters also at first did not have to dispute *pro loco*, that is, for a place in the faculty. Instead, a medieval master did his two years service, his biennium. After he had done the stipulated teaching and disputing during the two years, he was then usually a fully incepted or habilitated member—*magister habilis*—of the faculty. The medieval disputation for a place seems to have arisen in the case of masters who wished to teach at a university other than their alma mater. Such masters, who were not "our masters" (*magister noster*), had to habilitate, that is, prove themselves with a disputation for a place.

During the early modern era, two crucial things happened. First, a disputation for a degree emerged, while the disputation for a place became extended to all masters or doctors who wished to teach. The doctoral dissertation emerged from the disputation for a degree. The disputation for a degree occurred before the award of the insignia, with the candidate as respondent at the lower podium. The successful candidate became *magister noster* and was elevated to the upper podium.

For those who wanted to teach, the disputation for a place occurred sometime—days or months—after the award of the insignia, with the master or doctor now as presider at the upper podium. From the disputations for a degree (*pro gradu*) and for a place (*pro loco*) grew, respectively, the doctoral dissertation of the doctor of philosophy, and the *Habilitationsschrift* of the lecturer or *Privatdozent*. In both cases—in the dissertation of the doctoral candidate and in the habilitation of the lecturer—writing displaced speaking.[56]

FROM HEROIC THEATER TO PROSAIC PUBLICATION. During the sixteenth century, it became customary to print a program for graduation ceremonies, and sometimes for simple public disputations. Such programs typically included the theses to be disputed at the ceremony or disputation. Some of these programs, especially for graduations, grew fancy. By the late sixteenth century, it was possible, then somehow customary, for the professor presiding over the dissertation, and thus presiding over the promotion or graduation, to put his oration on paper and have this printed in advance with the graduation program. Such graduation orations became professorial dissertations. The practice spread to the public disputations, where the presider might have a dissertation printed with the disputation's theses.

The modern academic article traces one of its many roots to this practice. Written by the presider and promoter, that is, by the professor, these dissertations were not orally delivered at the disputation. They were, rather, circulated in advance with the theses, and became part of what the respondent, the student, might have to defend at the disputation.[57]

The typography of the dissertation title pages shows the respective roles, and corresponds with the positions in the auditorium. A look at figures 6.1 and 6.2 helps. The bottom panel of figure 6.1 shows a public disputation scene. As we saw in a previous chapter, the personae of the disputation would be as follows. The *praeses*, that is, the professor presiding over the dis-

6.1. Title page of Johann Stier's *Praecepta metaphysicae*, Erfurt, 1641.

putation is the academic at the top or highest part of the raised podium or
the *cathedra*. In a graduation disputation, this would the promoter. The academic standing at the lower part of the podium is the respondent. In a graduation disputation, this would also be the candidate. In front of the podium
we see the academic public, seated on benches. Behind and to the side of
the podium are separate seats for individuals of enhanced charisma, that is,
nobles and academic officers.

The positions of the presider and respondent on the podium in figure 6.1

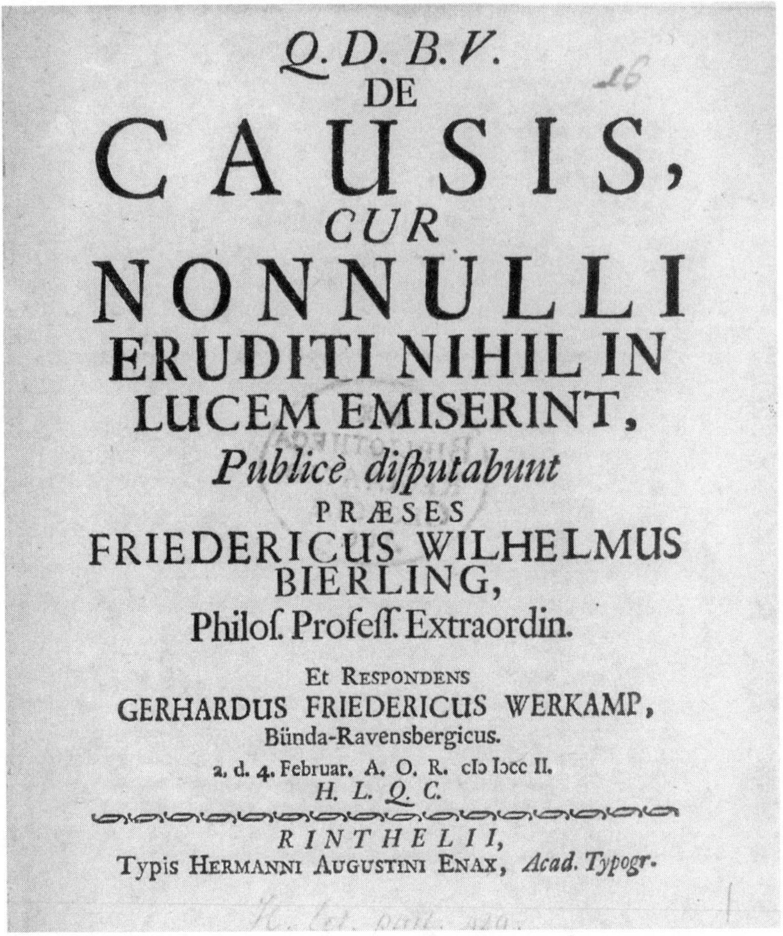

Q. D. B. V.
DE

# CAUSIS,
## CUR
# NONNULLI
## ERUDITI NIHIL IN LUCEM EMISERINT,

*Publicè diſputabunt*

PRÆSES

### FRIEDERICUS WILHELMUS BIERLING,

Philoſ. Profeſſ. Extraordin.

Et RESPONDENS

GERHARDUS FRIEDERICUS WERKAMP,

Bünda-Ravensbergicus.

a. d. 4. Februar. A. O. R. cIↄ Iↄcc II.

H. L. Q. C.

*RINTHELII,*
Typis HERMANNI AUGUSTINI ENAX, *Acad. Typogr.*

6.2. Title page of Friedrich Bierling's (*praeses*), *De causis cur nonulli eruditi nihil in lucem emiserint*, Rinteln, 1702.

match the positions of the presider and respondent on the title page of the dissertation shown in figure 6.2. This title page announces the dissertation *De causis cur nonulli eruditi nihil in lucem emiserint*, that is, "On the Reasons Why Not Few Scholars Bring Nothing to Light."

In the middle of the page, in large type is the name Friedrich Wilhelm Bierling. He is an extraordinary philosophy professor, as the line below his name indicates. The line above his name says he is the *praeses*, that is, presider in the disputation. The next line up tells us this is a public disputation. The line below Bierling's title reads "et respondens," telling us that the name below that, namely Gerhard Friedrich Werkamp, is the respondent at this public disputation, held at the University of Rinteln, on 4 February 1702.

As above and in general, the name of the presider, who stood at the top of the podium, appeared highest on the title page, often in the boldest type. Under the presider's name came the name of the respondent, who stood at the lower level of the podium. And, at least in Prussia after 23 December 1749, the names of three designated opponents, who sat in the audience, appeared at the bottom of the page.

If the disputation was part of a graduation ceremony, then the student—as respondent and candidate—defended the professor's dissertation, written as presider and promoter. Finally, and most interesting of all, the publication costs of such professorial dissertations were often, perhaps usually, borne by the candidate and/or respondent. The student paid for the professorial publication since the program formed part of his advancement to candidacy or graduation ceremony. However unreasonable, this practice was standard.

The practice is in fact clear from the discussion about its demise, as students got sick of paying for professorial publications in this manner. By the eighteenth century, the prestige of the M.A. had sunken so low that few were willing to spend much for so dubious an honor. Professors complained that they could not scare up students to be respondents at disputations. In some places—in Strasbourg, Göttingen, Jena, and Greifswald, for example—that was no small matter, since ministries had begun urging or even commanding professors to publish via public disputation. A Prussian edict of 24 December 1749 enjoined this as a condition for all appointments and advancements, more or less issuing the command to publish or perish, something to which we'll return at length in the next chapter.[58]

The conceit eventually arose among students that payment entailed credit. Students who consented to underwrite such publications wanted more credit for the contents. By the early seventeenth century, some students wanted credit for the disputation's theses. By the end of the century, some students wanted credit for the dissertation! That caused problems.

THE AUTHORSHIP OF THE CANDIDATE AND THE ROLE OF THE DOCTORAL ADVISOR. What was to be the role of the presider? Would the presider write the dissertation, or simply advise the student? And what would that mean? Where does advice or correction end, and collaboration or coauthorship begin? Would the professor's name continue to appear on the title page, and above the respondent's, and in bolder type? At the public disputation, should the student defend the dissertation with the professor at the upper podium? Or should the student dispute with no one symbolically standing over him at the upper podium, thus disputing *sine praeside?* Or should the student now stand at the upper podium?[59]

The question of the author, as well as the relation of authority to writings, became problematic. Until the late eighteenth century, the author seems mostly to have been the presider. But cases exist from early on in which the author might be the respondent, or might be both presider and respondent, or might even be neither of them! It seems that dissertation factories (*Dissertations-Fabriken*) already existed by the mid-eighteenth century. Here the lazy and wealthy vainglorious might buy a ready-made dissertation.[60]

Despite this potential fraud, some universities admitted the student as author. Leipzig, Halle, Tübingen, and others let the student write the dissertation, while Jena, Göttingen, and Bützow required it if the disputation was for graduation. The student as author might dispute without a professor presiding. But, until the end of the eighteenth century, the professor's name usually appeared on the dissertation's title page, and above the candidate's. Such works, penned by the candidate, were often simply eloquent essays, a "specimen of erudition" or perhaps only a specimen of industry. But, with the candidate as author, the center of the trial for the degree would shift, from the heroic theater of the oral disputation, to the prosaic publication of the doctoral dissertation.[61]

Consider figures 6.3 and 6.4 in this regard. Figure 6.3 shows the title page of *De eruditis studiorum intemperie mortem sibi accelerantibus, dissertatio I, eaque historica,* that is, "On Scholars Who Hastened Their Deaths Through Overmuch Study, part 1: Histories." M[aster] Gottfried Boettner is listed as presider in the middle of the page. Below him we find Johann C. Tschanter, who is given as *respondens et auctor,* that is, as respondent and author. So we see that as early as 1704 the respondent could be the author of the dissertation. On 1 December 1703, Taschanter had obtained his B.A. at Leipzig—one of the few universities in the Germanies still granting that degree in the eighteenth century. The disputation announced in figure 6.3 was his graduation disputation for the M.A. degree, which he received on 5 May 1705.

Figures 6.4 gives the title page of *De eruditis studiorum intemperie mortem sibi accelerantibus, dissertatio II, eaque physica,* that is, "On Scholars Who Hastened Their Deaths Through Overmuch Study, part 2: Causes." In the middle of the page, we now find Tschanter himself, declared as *auctor atque praeses,* that is, as author and presider. Tschanter is being a bit overly precise here since, by the custom still at that time, when no author was given, then no one would have presumed Johann C. Wolff, who is listed below as respondent, to have been the author. The disputation announced in figure 6.4 took place on 30 December 1705. If Tschanter had not habilitated before

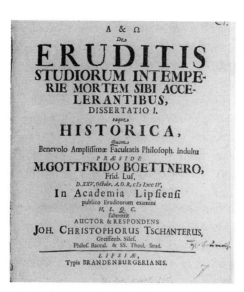

6.3. Title page of Johann C. Tschanter's (*resp. et auct.*), *De eruditis studiorum intemperie mortem sibi accelerantibus, dissertatio I, eaque historica*, Leipzig, 1704.

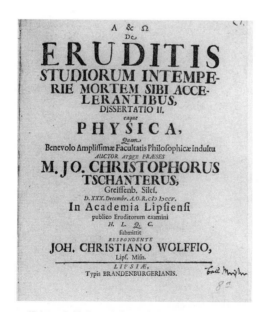

6.4. Title page of Johann C. Tschanter's (*praeses*), *De eruditis studiorum intemperie mortem sibi accelerantibus, dissertatio II, eaque physica*, Leipzig, 1705.

this time, this disputation could have counted as his disputation for a place in the faculty. That would have given him fairly full authority to serve in the faculty as a lecturer, a *Privat-Docent*.

THE TRIUMPH OF THE NEO-GOTHIC AND THE BUREAU-CRATIC WORK OF ART. The story now moves to Berlin in 1810. The decisions made by Dean Johann Fichte and his colleagues between 1807 and 1810 provide a resolution for the first part of this chapter. Fichte and the Romantics, well placed after Prussia's fall to Napoleon in 1806, realized their idea of a university and the academic degree. They helped save the academic degree from perishing altogether.

In "Deduced Plan for an Institution of Higher Learning in Berlin," Fichte not only argued (against the Saxons) that the doctor of philosophy should be instituted, but also premised (against the Austrians) that, in addition to passing an examination, the doctoral candidate should also produce a dissertation. "The masterpiece [of the dissertation] would best consist in a writing specimen ... On the basis of this writing, his own composition, ... [the candidate] will be publicly examined to the satisfaction of his teacher." The Fichtean and Romantic subject would be no mere bureaucratic, disembodied pure spirit or mind. And its dissertation would be no mere prosaic specimen of erudition or industry.[62]

Witness the creation of the doctoral candidate's Romantic persona, the apotheosis of the modern researcher, in the Berlin statutes. They divided the double degree M. Art. and Dr. Phil. into two separate degrees. The statutes set the doctor of philosophy as a degree above the master of arts— a radical innovation at the time. The old master of arts remained an artisanal figure, a uniform type, who only defended theses for the degree's final trial. The modern doctor of philosophy, however, partook of a public disputation—the jurists' third heroic trial—in which not only theses, but also a dissertation was defended. The doctoral candidate defended the dissertation from the lower podium, without a professor presiding.

The statutes did not set the roles of advisor and candidate regarding choice of topic, but the candidate must be the author of the dissertation, from whose title page the professor has withdrawn. Fichte thought the candidate might choose the topic, but that the professor's choice would be better. As we saw in the previous chapter, however, the candidate's choice, with the director's advice, had been the policy of the seminars. That policy seems to have mostly prevailed. One of the few oaths extracted from the candidate consisted in a signed statement in which the candidate's original authorship was sworn. In the past, one would have sworn about legitimate birth. Now one swore about legitimate authorship.[63]

This dissertation put novel demands on the doctor of philosophy. The medieval master of arts had been obliged only to prove himself able to enact an—albeit heroic—disputational role, as good as everyone else, as we saw in a chapter above. But the modern doctor of philosophy must cultivate a modern academic persona, a Romantic authorial persona, exhibited through the masterpiece of the doctoral dissertation in which a spark of charisma or genius, however small, must inhere. "For genius is a general expression, which is used not only of artists, but also of generals and kings, and even of heroes of knowledge."[64]

The doctor of philosophy, as authorial persona, exhibited the qualities of the Romantic artist, "originality" and "personality," aesthetically differentiating itself.

> The master's degree is awarded to whoever can skillfully renew and well order what has been learnt, and thus promises to be a useful link in the transmission of knowledge between generations. The doctor's degree is awarded to whoever shows *Eigenthümlichkeit* [personality, peculiarity, originality] and *Erfindungsvermögen* [creativity] in the treatment of academic knowledge (*Wissenschaft*).[65]

The Prussian doctor of Philosophy embodied an original work of research enframed by a curriculum vitae and good reviews by the police, the reconciliation of bureaucratic and artistic paperwork. The Gothic master of arts, degraded by poets, jurists, and theologians, had refigured itself as the Romantic or neo-Gothic doctor of philosophy—the researcher as modern hero of knowledge, the civil servant as work of art (*der Staats-Beamte als Kunstwerk*). As absolute inversion, it was a work of Germanic irony.[66]

## THE DOCTORAL DISSERTATION AS A WORK OF RESEARCH

The imperial ordinance on the guilds of 1731 had import for academics, even if only symbolically. This ordinance and others like it, issued by individual German states, restricted festivities, ceremonies, excessive gift giving, and work stoppages, including strikes. Guilds fell under increasing supervision by ministerial police powers. Those powers favored notions of manufacture for standardized consumption. The ordinance of 1731 forbade fancy guild masterpieces and, in their place, enjoined useful ones. The mastership should be awarded in view of such specimens. Rationalizing ministries held, as Marc Raeff has put it, that the "masterpiece need be but one of a series, made in order to demonstrate technical competence rather than artistic genius or creativity." In spirit at least, that included academics, too.[67]

The putative artistic genius or originality of the Romantic doctor of philosophy stood at odds with the spirit of the imperial ordinance of 1731 and other regulations of the early modern German police state. Romantic notions of originality were, in fact, more ideological than substantial, when one considers the doctoral dissertations written at the time. Many such dissertations, especially from seminarists, instantiated the Enlightenment's or police state's pragmatic view of the masterpiece: potentially but one of a series, made in order to demonstrate technical competence rather than artistic genius or creativity.[68]

Thus we encounter one of the central contradictions and dilemmas of the modern world of research as it was constructed in the German lands: Romantic ideologies often conflicted with enlightened practices. Ideals about the originality and creativity of research, its artistic and aesthetic aspirations, seem rather delusional in retrospect when one considers the serial and technical works of research, and the artisanal and bureaucratic reality. But, since charisma arises from social relations, the relevant cognoscenti's ascription of originality to a work thus to an author suffices, even if an outside observer takes issue.

In the next chapter we shall consider a Prussian regulation of 1749 that helped institute the modern academic regime of publish or perish, of which the doctoral dissertation became a part and usual first step for an academic. The Prussian ministry had become sensitive to the importance of being "in fashion," and wanted its professors to be in tune with the spirit of the times. This call to be in fashion indicates yet another point of conflict with the later call to be original, that is, to be novel or different. The expectation to publish had much in any case to do with proving diligence—like regulations requiring seminarists to hand in papers, and on time.

The second part of the chapter examines how academic writing practices changed in conjunction with the emergence of the doctor of philosophy and the doctoral dissertation. The analysis is confined to certain academic genres from the 1670s to the 1830s and aims to show that a modern notion of research in fact emerged in German doctoral dissertations for subjects in arts and sciences, and most especially, in doctoral dissertations written by students who had been members of the seminars studied in the previous chapter.

## Specimens of Erudition and Works of Research

Previous chapters have found a sort of high watermark in the decadence of traditional oral academic practices in the late Baroque and early Enlightenment. Professors did not give their lectures, or spoke only to the walls, or engaged in a micrology of textual commentary that one can only call "baroque." The professorial theater of examination tolerated students who maintained blissful silence, or committed atrocities (by saying the human soul was mortal and so on). Students for their part enacted the public disputation as farce and often played for applause. In this section, we shall consider strange and perhaps decadent coeval writings.

BENIGHTED GRAPHORRHEA. Romantic ideologies aside, doctoral dissertations would fill the space between the seminarist's papers and the academic's publications for an appointment. By mid-eighteenth century, everyone—without connections—had to write to get ahead in the Germanies. In the Enlightenment's pragmatic terms, it was about doing useful and, to an extent, fashionable work. Many young scholars wrote much, but against the spirit of the imperial ordinance of 1731. They wrote fancy, or rather, erudite but useless masterpieces or dissertations. Lessing's *Der junge Gelehrte* of 1747 mercilessly satirized them.[69]

Graphorrhea afflicts Damis, Lessing's young scholar (act 2, scene 3; act 3, scene 15). Writing is Damis's illness and essence. It thus grieves him when women enter his study. The sanctity vested in the traditional male celibacy of the study occasions misogynous remarks against learned women littering the play. Damis desires to preserve his celibacy and wishes only to conceive books. The trope of birthing books grounds his bibliophilia. "Each is made eternal in its own way: the woman by children, the man by books" (act 2, scene 11).

So he at first opposes his arranged marriage with Julianne. But he changes his mind by act 2, scene 9, where he proclaims a wish to add his name to the ranks of scholars wedded to "wicked women." He explains here and elsewhere (act 3, scene 4) that to be an academic with the burden of a wicked wife would increase his fame and glory, and surely lead to his inclusion in a future erudite dissertation on the wicked wives of scholars.

Damis in *Der junge Gelehrte* is a fool and fails as an academic. Lessing satirized here old and new topoi: the wicked wives of scholars, academic misogyny, the celibacy of the study, and academic virility as a sizeable list of publications. Birthing books in the study went hand in hand with allegorical male celibacy and virility—at least it did for benighted academics such as Damis. Between the Baroque celebration of (useless) erudition afflicting Damis and the later Romantic apotheosis of (useless?) originality, the Enlightenment marked its time and posed new and potentially conflicting demands concerning usefulness and fashion.

THE AWFULLY ERUDITE DISSERTATIONS ON ACADEMICS, THE 1670s to the 1730s. Thirty years before Damis's celibate graphorrhea, a dissertation had appeared in 1717 entitled *De polyteknia eruditorum ... oder ein Tractat von denen Gelehrten, die von GOTT mit vielen Kindern gesegnet worden.* So it concerned scholars whom God had blessed with many children. It has fascinating anecdotes and tidbits of academic gossip. For example, "Jodocus Badius had written just as much as his wife produced in children. And Tiraquelles carried things so far, he conceived every year a new book and baby."[70]

*De polyteknia eruditorum* of 1717 formed part of a strange fad of dissertations on academics or erudites (such as Damis) in the late Baroque and early Enlightenment. As *micrologia eruditorum*, the genre might be traced broadly back to antiquity. But the period from the 1670s to the 1730s gave birth to dissertations on erudites of a peculiar sort. Such dissertations appeared most intensely in the 1710s and in great numbers around the University of Leipzig, a conservative academic culture, not unlike that in Cambridge and Oxford at the time. I take these dissertations on erudites as being also on academics in the broadest sense. Appendix 4 below lists a good number of such dissertations.

These dissertations on academics provide an interesting contrast with dissertations written from the late Enlightenment onward, especially those that would emanate from the seminars by the 1790s or even earlier. The dissertations on academics from the 1670s to the 1730s embody the academic analogues of the fancy guild masterpieces that the imperial ordinance of 1731 sought to abolish. In a strict sense, they are not research, though one may use them to further it.

Figures 6.2 to 6.4 above come from the same fad of academic masterpieces. Figure 6.2, from 1702, is "On the Reasons Why Not Few Scholars Bring Nothing to Light." And figures 6.3 and 6.4 are "On Scholars Who Hastened Their Deaths Through Overmuch Study, part 1: Histories," and part 2, "Causes." Some such works were academic treatises, not stemming from an academic exercise. But many of these dissertations on academics were disputational dissertations and formed part of the process and act of creating an academic.

In this genre, one finds a dissertation on academics who were farmers. One finds a dissertation on academics who were cobblers, and one on academics who were merchants, as well as one on those who were soldiers. There are dissertations on academics who were precocious, or who were aged, or who were blind. There is a work on academics who perished by water, and one on those who died on their own birthdays. One studies academics who lived to be more than seventy years old. Another treats of academics who were incarcerated. There is one on those with good memories, one on those with bad morals, and one on academics of bad manners. There are dissertations on academics who were bastards, on those who were slovenly, on those who were timid, on those who were idlers, on those who spoke with angels, on those who had familiar spirits, and on those who had made pacts with the devil. There is a dissertation on academics famous abroad but less so at home. Erudite German women and erudite Hebrew women each have a study devoted to them. Several of these dissertations treat the learned woman in general.

Other dissertations in the genre concern academics who could not speak properly, or could not see right, or could not get their books done, or wrote too much, or were maniacs about titles. Academics who bought too many books form the subject of one dissertation, as do those who had no books the subject of another. Short academics of great learning merit a study, as do those with big hearts. More than one dissertation treats of academic recantation (*palinodia*), and love of labor (*philoponia*) is not neglected. A famous dissertation celebrates academics who were charlatans, while a less famous one treats of academic Machiavellians. The religion and the idolatry of academics each have a study, as do the study, the solitude, and the celibacy of academics, too. The health and the diseases of academics merit special works, which of course calls for one on the causes of death most particular to academics. To be sure, there is also a dissertation on the satirical style of academics.

A notorious example of the genre is "On the Wicked Wives of Scholars," *Dissertatio historico-moralis de malis eruditorum uxoribis, (vulgo) von den bösen Weibern der Gelehrten,* published in two parts by Gottlob Matthaeus at Leipzig in 1705. A title page is reproduced in figure 6.5 and lists Matthaeus as author. His position on the page sets him as respondent at the relevant disputation on 19 December. This was, of course, the dissertation that Damis from Lessing's *Der junge Gelehrte* had in mind—Damis reckoning that, if he married Julianne, he would be included in a future new edition of the dissertation.

These dissertations on academics seem, indeed, rather curious. They are typically in Latin, though some have German subtitles for some reason. They were not the most obscure of academic works. A fair number of them enjoyed reprinting one or more times, and at least one of them—Mencke's *De charlataneria eruditorum* of 1715—became famous. Most of them have a respectable scholarly apparatus of one sort or another—notes and sources and so on. Intelligent readers might disagree about the sense of this genre. As one might expect, at least two dissertations—Flachs's *De causis dissensus eruditorum* of 1720, and Kreuschner's *De causis rixarum inter eruditos* of 1719—treat of academic disputes and their grounds. Alas, neither was clever enough to name the genre itself as one of them.[71]

6.5 Title page of Gottlob Matthaeus's (*auct. & resp.*), *Dissertatio historico-moralis de malis eruditorum uxoribis, (vulgo) von den bösen Weibern der Gelehrten*, Leipzig, 1705.

6.6. Title page of Matthaeus G. Schroederus's (*praeses*) *Dissertatio historico-moralis de misogynia eruditorum, von übelgesinnten Gelehrten gegen das weibliche Geschlecht*, Leipzig, 1717.

ACADEMIC ODD BODIES. Roughly coincident with the appearance of this strange genre of dissertations, the juristic consensus, discussed in part one above, emerged from about 1680 to 1730. In that period, jurists discussed the requirements for academic degrees, and whether one might waive them. As we saw, by 1730 enlightened jurists argued that one might obtain an academic degree in absentia and *per saltum,* and even in rigor mortis. The blind and maimed and perhaps even the mute might be masters and doctors. Religious confession, as well as gender and ethnicity, became de jure irrelevant, if not yet de facto. Illegitimacy of birth amounted now but to a trifle. And age meant less than ability—and so on, as we saw.

In the period from the 1680s to the 1730s, the academic became essentially disembodied, at least in juristic views. Most corporal conditions on the academic's body could be waived, as well as most aspects of the traditional juridical persona. Many of the dissertations on academics from the 1670s to the 1730s treated academics with unusual or afflicted bodies. They concerned unusual academics. They treated the materiality of academia and academics, just as they were becoming most dematerialized. Do these dissertations reflect a crisis, perhaps suppressed, about academics and their work? As noted, many of the dissertations appeared as part of a degree exercise creating an academic.

Many of these dissertations on academics seem like satires and ironies. The joke-dissertation has a long history, but little precedent exists for the intensity of the phenomenon from the 1670s to the 1730s which, as we saw in chapter 3, was also the time when the public disputation often became played as farce. Modern research, for its part, does not include farce or satire among its possible genres. And irony is a bit of a problem too. Academic journals have been and, at the moment, remain most reluctant to publish articles known to be satires. And funding agencies look askance at satirical proposals. For the organs of research, satire is a nonacademic genre, and irony had best be incidental or hidden.

Perhaps academic satire made its final flourish in the late Baroque and early Enlightenment. As an example, consider three such specimens. In 1717 Matthaeus Schroeder served as presider at three Leipzig disputations, for which he authored three dissertations. The first of his 1717 dissertations treated misanthropic scholars and was presented in disputation on 17 September. It reads like a serious specimen. In the manner of the genre, it gives historical examples and an account of misanthropic scholars. Figure 6.6 shows Schroeder's second 1717 dissertation. It concerned misogynous scholars and was presented in disputation on 25 September. In view of the aforementioned specimen, one could read this as a yet more refined treatment, concerning academics who did not necessarily dislike all humans, but rather just the female ones.

Schroeder's third 1717 specimen thematized slovenly scholars (*de misocosmia eruditorum*). He presented it in disputation on 2 October. On the surface, this is also serious and concerns historical examples. But, when one sets all three 1717 dissertations by Schroeder side by side, an irony or even a joke emerges. In one year he produced three specimens of erudition; indeed, he must have written all three before he presented the first one. All three concerned a sort of "miso-" ("miso-a" in the first becoming "misa" by vowel reduction): misanthropy, misogyny, and misocosmy. His work on the misogyny of scholars may be, more or less and in part, an ironic instance of its own subject.

ERUDITION VERSUS RESEARCH. The lesson about Schroeder's three dissertations is that they relate and build on one another in a way in which modern works of research usually do not. Works of research do not add up to jokes or ironies. The difference between a traditional specimen of erudition—such as those in appendix 4—and a modern academic dissertation does not lie in the contents of the works. It lies, rather, in the differences between how traditional academic works relate to one another, versus how works of research do.

One could use the erudite dissertations in appendix 4 to produce works of research. One might even use them for a *prosopographia eruditorum,* an encyclopedia or lexicon on the lives, works, and publications of scholars or academics, such as in C. Jöcher's multivolume *Allgemeines Gelehrten Lexikon* of 1750. Jöcher's lexicon—like other such handbooks, encyclopedias, and dictionaries generally—embodies fundamental research. Works of research usually provide a basis for further research and/or relate to other, related works in a complementary and supplementary manner. They add up to something positive.[72]

Most of the erudite dissertations in appendix 4 do not add up to anything beyond themselves. They are specimens of erudition. They resemble displays and exhibitions. They resemble examinations—singular and isolated displays of knowledge or erudition. Oral exams and printed specimens of erudition constitute fragments of knowledge. If fundamental works of research, such as Jöcher's lexicon, do not catalogue and interreference such printed specimens, then they may be as ephemeral as oral exams, and no more useful.

The dissertations on academics in appendix 4 on the whole display much labor and erudition. An author of such a dissertation typically ploughed through many biographies and all other conceivable works to find all the academics reputed to have made a pact with the devil, or who had perished by water, or were unable to finish their books, were known to have been misogynists, and so on. The brilliance of the specimen and display lay in the oddness or outlandishness or difficulty of the topic. It lay in the erudition needed to compose the specimen. That—not the value of the topic for useful research—was the point.

Some erudite specimens on academics did call forth other, related specimens. Here they resembled the later world of research. From appendix 4, one might judge that G. Goetz's 1705 dissertation on academics who were merchants called forth the dissertations on academics who were soldiers by C. Loeber in 1708 and by Wagner in 1715, as well as Goetz's own later dissertation on academics who were cobblers, and the one on gardeners, too. But such an interrelation of the dissertations resembles more the extended joke of Schroeder's three 1717 dissertations on "miso" than it does the interrelation of research.[73]

Of course, there have been handbooks, dictionaries, encyclopedias and all sorts of catalogues since antiquity. The bases for erudition and research are in that sense similar and perhaps even identical. The difference lies in how the fundaments or bases generate specific projects for further works and how those specific works interrelate. And, perhaps more importantly, how researchers themselves interrelate makes a difference.

Before the enlightened and Romantic regimes of research, a typical specimen of academic production in classics, for example, took one of two extreme forms. On the one hand, scholars continually reproduced classical authors, such as Cicero, and their texts for the sake of eloquence, that is, for the sake of the mastery and display of style. Or, on the other hand, one displayed one's own talents by emending and interpreting incredibly knotty, corrupted or obscure passages from some text, famous or obscure. One cultivated the classical or illuminated the obscure. In either case, the point was display, virtuosity the key.[74]

Typical productions of traditional academic mathematicians and natural scientists did not much distinguish themselves. Before (and even after) the research mentality took hold, mathematicians commonly posed the most difficult theorems that they could imagine as challenges for themselves and others. Or they wrote textbooks, or developed mathematics for applications. The interrelation of works, later typical of research, appears most clearly first in applied academic work, for example, in astronomy, which had importance for astrology (thus for medicine), navigation, and the calendar.

In most natural sciences, academics, like natural philosophers or natural historians, acted much like classicists in working on texts. Analogues of the classical or the obscure merited most interest. In natural sciences, the obscure could be a marvel or monstrosity of nature. Difficult problems, such as the orbit of the moon, or the cause of the tides, or of the rainbow, or of gravity, or of magnetism, generated much and perhaps most attention.

The ideology of the classical appeared in natural sciences through theological notions of ultimate, final truth—of attaining results valid or true for all time. The provisional nature of results and the necessity for doing simple, boring things first and thoroughly remained foreign notions for academic production until the modern mentality of research took hold.

If one looks as far back to the Middle Ages from which universities descended, the foreign nature of modern research emerges even more strikingly. As we noted in chapter 3, the space that the modern era fills with research activities were filled by the medievals with disputational activities. Disputation did not aim to validate and accumulate new knowledge. It aimed, rather, to disaccumulate all possible errors. It aimed to secure the orthodoxy of the canon. "Originality" then meant not finding the novel, but rather finding the true and eternal origins, the originals of things. That was the original meaning of "original."

The modern sense of originality, an ironic inversion of the original meaning, appeared in the eighteenth century. Medieval academic knowledge and much early modern knowledge, including Newton's work for example, had originality in the earlier, theological sense. It formed part of the old juridico-theological world we have been articulating throughout.

## Doctoral Dissertations

Research is a practice of the modern politico-economic order. It is one of production and accumulation, one of serial novelty, of "normal science." It is an order that the imperial ordinance of 1731 on the guilds, in part, would have endorsed. Academia has been able to retain many of its archaic rites and ceremonies. And the German police state's restrictions on free association proved antithetical to the liberal bent of research. But industrial and bureaucratic views on production triumphed over traditional ones in the academic world.

A SURVEY OF DISSERTATIONS. Appendix 5 contains schematic results of a survey of doctoral dissertations from selected German universities from the 1770s to the 1830s. As the 1670s to the 1730s constituted the apogee of decadence for traditional academia (or an academic perigee), the 1770s to the 1830s saw the crystallization of the modern academic mentality. Many doctoral dissertations assumed a form recognizable as research in a way that the erudite dissertations were not. As in the case of the seminars, it was the

German classical philologists who first made the doctoral dissertation a site for research generally.

Alas, certain things in the period of the 1770s to 1830s make systematic research on graduations difficult. Above all, the troubles of the Revolutionary and Napoleonic Wars from 1794 to 1818 made academic life itself not only irregular but also impossible at some places for some time. Some data thus have holes. And a sort of reversion to older academic practices arose at some places in the middle of the period for a number of years.

The data and table for Göttingen in appendix 5 exemplify that well. By 1770 and up to 1800, the university had required, with few exceptions, a dissertation for the award of the "highest degree in philosophy," called by many the "Dr. Phil." But, from 1800 to 1822, Göttingen gave its highest degree in arts and philosophy on the basis of printed theses, should the candidate so choose, although such candidates then had no hope of academic careers. Waiving the requirement for a dissertation embodied a reversion to Baroque and earlier practices. Similarly, appendix 5 shows that the University of Gießen in Hesse-Darmstadt, before regularizing the award of the Dr. Phil. in 1802, would offer the degree from 1796 to 1801 optionally with no dissertation.

Gießen was also one of the—perhaps all too common—universities that awarded the Dr. Phil. on the basis of work previously published elsewhere. Gießen in fact did not demand that candidates had attended any classes at Gießen, which made the award of the degree possibly completely *in absentia et per saltum*. Some faculties and universities awarded such degrees not only to honor worthy men, but also to make money in fees. In 1816, for example, the (in)famous *Naturphilosoph* or Romantic natural philosopher, Lorenz Oken, submitted the third book of his textbook, *Lehrbuch der Naturgeschichte*, and received then his Dr. Phil., without apparently ever having been a student in Gießen.

As early as 1803, moreover, a dissertation was accepted in German at Gießen. It would take a generation or more for most German universities to become so liberal. On the whole, one followed Berlin's reassertion in 1810 about the requirement of a dissertation written in Latin, followed by a public defense and disputation also in Latin.

A Hessian regulation of 1821 for the University of Gießen did require that anyone intending to teach, including teaching at a gymnasium, had to write a dissertation and hold a public disputation for the Dr. Phil. Debate then ensued in 1826 at Gießen about whether the faculty should encourage or even push students to write dissertations, thus receive doctorates. The table for Gießen in appendix 5 shows in fact a dramatic upsurge in dissertations from 1823 to 1831.[75]

The Prussians in general pursued stricter policies about awarding doctorates. The University of Halle, nonetheless, continued for a time in old practices. Records are very incomplete at Halle before its refoundation in 1817 after having been closed by Napoleon; but, even thereafter it was apparently possible to receive the highest degree in arts and philosophy without a dissertation, either by submission of previously published work, as at Gießen, or by simple disputation on theses, as at Göttingen up to 1822.[76]

The new Prussian universities at Berlin and Bonn, as well as the refounded university at Breslau (Wroclaw), demanded dissertations—ones written by the candidates and printed at their expense, unless the candidate had a scholarship to that end. Such dissertations typically included a brief biography or vita of the candidate. From these, one can often determine interesting tidbits about the candidate's studies and teachers. At Berlin, the dissertations commonly list three official opponents for the public disputation on the title page. The first listed opponent was typically a Dr. Phil. already, while the other two were usually doctoral candidates. This all suggests the seriousness of the Latin public disputation.

THE MAJOR FIELD IN DISSERTATIONS AND THESES. Prussian dissertations had about four to fifteen theses for public disputation, printed after the dissertation and vita. By the 1820s, theses for the public disputation confined themselves to particular fields. They might be all concerning classics, or all concerning mathematics, or all on mathematics and mathematical physics, or all on physical science. Philosophical theses might more commonly mix with other disciplines, as might also those from the history of science. But, on the whole, doctoral candidates clearly had majors in the modern sense. They wrote dissertations and defended theses in a specialty or major field in arts or sciences.

Göttingen dissertations could be as short as fourteen pages, but common was forty to seventy pages, of course printed. Such dissertations might be followed by five to ten or more printed theses, or have none. By the 1780s, some lists of theses shrank in scope to a narrow field of studies or major. But as late as 1822, Jakob Lehman wrote a dissertation on tails of comets, for which he proposed theses on a wide range of topics, including Copernican astronomy ("It is not necessary to assume the Copernican System to explain the motion of celestial bodies"), and philology ("Aesop's fables are not to be reckoned as poetry"). Such polymath theses harkened back to the degree's name as "doctor of philosophy," instead of doctor of astronomy, or doctor of classics, or doctor of fables, or whatnot.

The tables in appendix 5 indicate a relative poverty of dissertations in natural sciences, as opposed to those in humanities. Many modern disciplines were still nearly nonexistent through the 1830s. Excepting cameralism, social sciences hardly existed. Modern languages also barely existed as doctoral fields. Not even Berlin exhibited a dissertation on German language or literature through the 1830s. Study of Indian philology or Sanskrit, however, appeared by the 1820s. Academic fashion was then, as now, often unpredictable.

As measured by the dissertations, the poverty of natural sciences contrasted with the wealth of classics. Those academic economies match what we found in the previous chapter on the matter of seminars and institutes. By the 1830s, the budgeted philology seminar had become ubiquitous, while funded institutes—beyond mere instrument collections—for natural sciences seemed still rather few and far between. Such differentials in funding most probably played some role in the absolute dominance of dissertations on the ancient world.

The budgeted research laboratory emerged as an institution at German universities by the middle third of the nineteenth century; it became an imposing financial cost by the last third of that century. Until the laboratory became generalized for the education of students in natural sciences, professors often could not easily find suitable topics for dissertations. Like the seminar, the lab is a near self-generator of research topics. Before the ubiquity of the academic lab, many dissertations tended to be theoretical or text-centered, as in classics.[77]

Certain fields more easily lent themselves to dissertations than others. Mathematics, like classics, usually needed no instruments beyond books, paper, and pens or pencils. One finds far more dissertations in mathematics than in physics. Like chemistry, mathematics also had practical applications that could insure a graduate a living. But, unlike chemistry, mathematics was taught at the gymnasium. That was crucial, for the dominance of dissertations on the ancient world came absolutely from the ancient world's dominance at the gymnasium. This was the age of the humanistic gymnasium, and its curriculum was built around Latin and Greek. The gymnasium also formed a primary market of offering teaching positions for the doctor of philosophy.[78]

From appendix 5, we see that the small, new University of Dorpat had, at first, a technical or pragmatic cast, while the University of Bonn, during its first decades at least, produced only three doctorates in natural sciences, and all of those in botany. The extreme dominance of classical philology at Bonn seems exceptional. But the state of nonhumanistic disciplines, for example, at Breslau appears to have been hardly better. Gießen was more balanced between the disciplines, while humanistic fields held a clear edge over mathematics and natural sciences at Göttingen and Berlin. The natural sciences would not improve their academic standing generally until the middle to last third of the nineteenth century. That was of course tied to the boom in scientifically based technologies and industries, which created a new demand for advanced graduates in odd and difficult fields such as physics.

THE ROMANTIC MANDARINS AND ACADEMIC EXCHANGE. The philology dissertations fed off the diffusion of the philology seminars. The number of total doctorates in classics year by year commonly exceeded the number of doctorates in classics by members of seminars (see column 1 in the tables in appendix 5). Thus not just the availability of the seminar scholarships stood behind the large numbers of doctorates in classics. The availability of positions at the gymnasium played a role, as well as the general sentiments of the age.

The seminars and doctorates formed, then, overlapping but distinct spheres. Their combination provided impetus to transforming classics from a discipline to a profession, and set a framework for the routinization of academic labor in classics as research. The combined spheres of the seminar-dissertation also facilitated an exchange mechanism: philologists exchanged doctoral students. This later became important for lab-based modern sciences.

Some students doubtless transferred between universities on their own initiative, or even against the will of previous professors. But philologists endorsed, furthered, and even sometimes micromanaged an exchange of students. After the foundation of the University of Berlin in 1809/10, it soon became an important place to be. August Böckh (a.k.a. Boeckh) codirected the philology seminar and made himself a crucial figure. A biographer of Böckh noted that a practice developed of sending select students from the other Prussian universities—in Bonn, Breslau, Greifswald, Halle, and Königsberg—to Berlin to finish their studies.[79]

A survey of the seminars suggests some truth to the statement—from Berlin's perspective (see appendix 5). The capital city obtained the lion's share of transfers, to be sure. But other Prussian universities had some transfers or returning students, too. Better data on the universities surveyed, and inclusion of the other Prussian universities, would reveal the broader contours of the exchange of students. As with modern lab-based research, one sent students not only to powerful or fashionable places like Berlin, but also to places where certain professors were researching particular things relevant to a specific doctoral student.

And one sometimes sent one's doctoral students to the enemy. In the competitive and collaborative arena of research, professors used doctoral students to spy on certain scholars and build scholarly alliances with others. The circulation of doctoral students in one way simply recapitulates the circulation of journeymen. But, in another way, it also enables exchange of knowledge and ameliorates hostilities between rival groups. In the latter roles, circulation of doctoral students was similar to that of women in traditional societies.[80]

STUDYING WITH THE ENEMY. A rivalry divided classics in the German lands for a generation after 1825, if not from an even earlier date. The rival camps had headquarters at the University of Berlin, in the capital city of Prussia, and at the University of Leipzig, the intellectual capital of Saxony and the most traditional or medieval of the Protestant German universities. In Berlin, Böckh directed the Greek section of the philology seminar. In Leipzig, Gottfried Hermann headed the Greek Society, and after 1834 directed the philology seminar. Perhaps not every classicist had to take sides between the two. But one had to take a position.[81]

In 1825 Hermann gave Böckh's project for an edition of Greek inscriptions a hostile review. Böckh was to head the project, which would be the most important classical project undertaken by the Berlin Academy of Sciences for most of the nineteenth century. Hermann thought the idea a good one, but noted that the academy should have chosen someone to head the project who understood Greek. This occasioned a counterattack from Böckh, who was naturally peeved at the personal attack. Hermann published the polemics, with additional pieces, in 1826. The bad blood between them reached, in fact, as far back as 1809 from a dispute over Pindar's poetry, a central issue to both men. Ill will continued at least through the 1830s.[82]

Beyond their several polemics, a fundamental rift existed between them about how to pursue research in classics. In a nub, Hermann advocated a formalist-philosophical approach, while Böckh favored a hermeneutic-historical approach. Böckh could trace elements and provenances of his approach through F. A. Wolf in Halle, the founder of the seminar there, to Heyne in Göttingen. All three of these men envisaged research in classics as a macroscopic science of antiquity, *Alterthumswissenschaft*. At the risk of gross generalization, one could take the pursuit of *Alterthumswissenschaft* as a Hanoverian-Prussian project. This project would be reflected in the dissertations of numbers of graduate students in those lands.

In the spirit of risky gross generalizations, one could also take Hermann's project as a Saxon one, although parts of the project remained idiosyncratic to him, and other parts true to the general tradition of classical philology. Hermann's "Saxon" project was a conservative or traditional one.

It centered and focused on grammar and critique, on *emendatio,* the editing of texts. Hermann stressed narrow, technical linguistic competence over broad knowledge.[83]

Given the protracted and serious hostilities between Böckh in Berlin and Hermann in Leipzig, the fact that doctoral students in classics transferred between Leipzig and Berlin is noteworthy. Data from the vitae of doctorates done at Berlin between 1815 and 1837 show that seven students who had studied in Leipzig finished in Berlin and received their doctorates there. And this only indicates students who finished in Berlin. Those who spent some time in Berlin but finished in Leipzig have not been ascertained here. The number of transfers between Berlin and Leipzig most likely exceed the seven known (in appendix 5) up to 1837, after which I stopped my survey, and for which I have no knowledge of Leipzig doctorates.[84]

Six of the seven transfers from Leipzig were admitted to the Berlin seminar, of which Böckh directed the Greek section. Six of the seven transfers wrote a dissertation on a Greek topic and/or thanked Böckh in their acknowledgments. Three of the seven had clearly studied with Hermann, then went to study with Böckh, and a fourth likely did. Of the other three, two possibly also had ties to both the philologists whose mutual hostility set the terms of German classical research then. Studying with the enemy strengthens the system.[85]

PREDILECTIONS OF ADVISORS AND CANDIDATES. The issue of the dissertation topic remains touchy. Key to the modern system in its German form from the police state of the Enlightenment to the *Kultur-Staat* of Romanticism was this: circumscription of a realm of autonomy, fashion, and originality, within a broader realm of erstwhile policing, now one of standardization, normalization, and review. For the professor, peer review would manage the circumscribed and the broader realms. For the doctoral candidate, the advisor's views mattered most.

Regarding the general approach to classics, the dissertations from Göttingen, from 1763 to 1800, and above all the dissertations by seminarists, bear a broad similarity to the predilections of Heyne, the seminar director and professor of (classical) eloquence. As noted, Heyne stands as a sort of fountainhead for the macroscopic science of antiquity that Wolf in Halle and Böckh in Berlin would later champion. Up to 1812, when Heyne left the directorship, only two Göttingen dissertations had a strictly critical, grammatical approach (which would later be associated most with Hermann in Leipzig). One was strictly historical, and a few *Geistesgeschichte* or intellectual history dissertations can be found. But most, like Heyne's own works, mixed criticism and interpretation with history. Most centered either on a text or an author or a literary style/genre or its lack, such as Torkill Baden's 1789 dissertation "On the Causes for the Neglect of Tragedy by the Romans."[86]

After Heyne left in 1812, one does see more dissertations that were, to an extent, mere specimens of erudition in the older sense. The grammatical-critical emendation of corrupt passages of an author or text became possible as a topic for a doctoral dissertation. Were such erudite specimens reviewed and referenced—somewhere—as contributions to research, so that future new editions of the relevant texts would profit from them? I do not know. But such dissertations appeared up through the 1830s at places I surveyed, among them Halle and Berlin, where the perhaps opposed ideals of the science of antiquity were taught.

At Berlin one sees, however, Böckh's broad interests in cultural history reflected in many other dissertations. Those included a dissertation on the history of the pentathlon (1827), a history of Roman theater (1828), an attempted reconstruction of folk songs or ditties among the Greeks (1831), and a history of Greek mathematicians (1831). Such topics, fascinating in themselves, grew to more than the sum of their parts, as they became bricks in the foundation of knowledge of antiquity that was in the process of being reconstructed step by step by advisors.

As professors, especially as seminar directors, at various universities began to suggest or urge or even cajole candidates to pursue certain common or related topics, the foundation grew in depth and breadth. A fairly popular dissertation topic became to reconstruct the biography and bibliography of some obscure classical academic. A prosopography of most or even all ancient academics or authors would one day be possible on the bases of such works. Doctoral dissertations achieved a sort of (un)ironic inversion of the erudite specimens here.

Any given specimen on academics, from the 1670s to the 1730s, assembled all academics with some one, odd or obscure common characteristic. But each prosopographical doctoral dissertation, from the 1770s to the 1830s, especially post-1810, usually focused on one obscure but classical academic, for whom it assembled all attestations and traces. Many dissertations did this in a roughly similar way. Isolated, none of the new dissertations seems significant, and surely less fun to read than the earlier erudite specimens on academics. But, taken together as a collective project and invitation for future dissertations to appear, the new dissertations laid the basis for the reconstruction of the academics of antiquity.

Dissertations explored other obscurities as well. One finds dissertations on this or that island (in Berlin in 1817, 1822, and 1826, in Breslau in 1829, and in Halle in 1833, for example). One finds dissertations on this or that forgotten town (for example, in Berlin in 1827, 1832, and 1836, in Halle in 1831, 1835, and in Göttingen in 1837). C. Grotefeld's Göttingen dissertation of 1829 offered an alphabetic catalogue of all attestations of villages in ancient Attica. Like prosopographical dissertations on academics, the collectivity of such works laid an invaluable basis for future politico-geographical works.

A doctoral dissertation might focus on the history of a lost work (Breslau 1835). Another might compare the several editions of a work (Halle 1831). Still another might provide, not an edition of a work, but rather an overview of the codices and critical passages in each, essential for a future edition, for example, of Hesiod's *Theogony* (Halle 1833). One sort of dissertation even mediated between the rival seminars polarizing German classicism.

ROMANTIC CLASSICAL FRAGMENTS. The Berlin Academy's *Corpus inscriptionum Graecarum* appeared between 1828 and 1877 under the editorial supervision of Böckh. The enunciation of this project and Böckh's editorship had occasioned Hermann's review in 1825, which made the hostilities smoldering between them into a controversy affecting all German classicists.

The collection of Greek inscriptions, while not the point here, offers nonetheless an interesting example of low-tech and underfunded modern research. The Berlin academy collected the entire multivolume edition of inscriptions, apparently, without explicitly subsidizing anyone's research in Greece or elsewhere. Böckh and his colleagues collected, when not directly from previously published sources, then from correspondence, and at first from travelers to London, Oxford, Cambridge, Leiden, Paris, Rome, and the rest of Italy. Only later did they request inscriptions from travelers in Greece, without, it seems, paying for the service. I know not if Böckh persuaded any doctoral students to go.[87]

More to the point here, Greek inscriptions were the most incomplete and difficult of classical fragments, occurring here, there, and everywhere in the ambit of the Mediterranean. They were of uncertain authorship and often only fragments of fragments. As such, the collection of Greek inscriptions serves as an emblem and epitome of a sort of project that promised to mediate between the rival paths for classical research advocated by Leipzig and Berlin. What a pity that the Berlin project had met with such abuse at first from Hermann.

In 1817 an anonymous article had appeared by "C.V.O." entitled, "Is It Advisable to Encourage Young Philologists to Collect Fragments?" By the latter, the author meant editions of the fragments of an ancient author whose work was known only because some better-known ancient author had cited it somewhere. Many of the so-called pre-Socratics, for example, are only now known because authors such as Aristotle had cited them. The question was then: Should young philologists, namely doctoral candidates, be given the dissertation topic of searching ancient texts to collect the fragments of this or that obscure author?

The anonymous noted that certain advantages accrued from such work. The student would most likely be obliged to gain acquaintance with a wide range of texts. Editing the fragments would give the student practice at grammatical-critical emendation. There were other good lessons, too. But the danger lay in giving the student a sort of fragmented view of antiquity. The anonymous writer worried that such a project risked producing philologists who lost themselves in textual micrology, who thought good research lay only in small topics.[88]

It eludes me how the anonymous writer hit on asking this question about fragments. I am unaware of any large effort around 1817 to have young philologists collect fragments. Like the ruin, the fragment was, however, a beloved topos of Romanticism. And, regardless of the state of things in 1817, the anonymous writer's question would soon be mooted and answered in the affirmative by doctoral advisors. I know of no further discussion, but numerous editions of fragments were published as doctoral dissertations. As the anonymous noted, it gave the student practice in the sort of skills that Hermann or the Leipzig school would value. Moreover, if the student produced a small biography of the ancient author, it cultivated the sentiments and produced the sort of knowledge that Böckh and the Berlin school would value. And most fragment collectors would have to gain the acquaintance of many texts to assure themselves that they had done the task of collecting every single fragment that was hiding somewhere.

One can sense how sentiments had developed by 1831. At Gießen, C. Marx's *De Mimnero poeta* was essentially a literary critique and brief biography of the poet. But Marx apologized for not giving a collection of the relevant fragments in the dissertation. Some dissertations at other universities focused simply on using or cleaning up prior editions of fragments. But other students pioneered an edition of fragments themselves.[89]

At Dorpat, S. Maltsov's 1836 dissertation implicitly contained the fragments of his subject, though perhaps not all of them. At Halle, E. Munk (1825) and H. Liebalt (1833) produced fragment editions in their dissertations. At Berlin, F. Osann (1816), F. Paul (1821), C. Neue (1822), F. Deycks (1827—a selection), C. Lehmann (1828), H. Duentzer (1835), and E. Koepke (1836) also collected fragments, and each tried to get all of them. At Bonn, fragment editions commonly also attempted a minibiography of the obscure or semiobscure figure, as was done by N. Bach (1825), W. Schorn (1829), A. Capellmann (1829), A. Łozynski (1831), N. Saal (1831), C. Urlichs (1834), and F. Heimsoeth (1836, only a selection). Some students worked in a darkness where even fragments failed, as in F. Wüllner's 1825 dissertation, which tried to reconstruct the themes of the lost poems of an ancient poet.

The importance of such dissertations, above all those on fragments, for the constitution of the doctoral dissertation as research dawned on me one day in the Berlin State Library (then the West Berlin State Library) where I began the research for my doctoral dissertation (on which this chapter is distantly based). I was looking though doctoral dissertations and was working though some of the Bonn dissertations on fragments. To inform myself about who in the world the obscure ancient figures behind the fragments were, I frequently consulted the 1897 edition of *Harper's Dictionary of Classical Literature and Antiquities*. Much to my surprise, in a good number of cases the canonical collection of the work of this or that obscure figure about whom I consulted Harper's 1897 dictionary had been, and was still in 1897, the doctoral dissertation that I held in my hands at that moment.[90]

### The Life and Times and Fragments of Doctoral Candidate Friedrich Ritschl

An interesting case study can put a human, all too human face on the modern heroic drama.

ENFANT TERRIBLE. In lectures on classical philology from 1835 onward, Professor Ritschl defended the collecting of fragments as a particularly appropriate task for German scholars. The professor saw manifold advantages in such a task for beginning professionals. But most of what Ritschl said in lecture simply echoed what the anonymous of 1817 had said, regarding the good things about fragments at least.[91]

Ritschl's academic career spanned the middle two generations of the nineteenth century. He became a lecturer in 1829, then extraordinary professor in 1832 at the Prussian University of Halle, then in 1833 at the Prussian University of Breslau, where he advanced to ordinary professor in 1837. He ended up at Leipzig in 1865. During his career, Ritschl had developed into one of the key philologists who sought to defuse the polemics between Berlin and Leipzig. Figure 6.7, drawn by Adolf Neumann, depicts the young Professor Ritschl.[92]

Ritschl had started off as a polemical *enfant terrible*—or at least a doctoral candidate *terrible*. He had begun his studies in Göttingen in 1824, then moved to Leipzig from 1825 to 1826. He studied with Hermann and was in the Greek Society. Hermann ran the society since he had no hand in run-

*Nil tam difficilest quin quaerendo investigari possiet*

*Friedrich Ritschl*

6.7. Adolf Neumann's drawing of Friedrich Ritschl, from Otto Ribbeck,
*Friedrich Wilhelm Ritschl.*

ning the official seminar until 1834. In 1826 Ritschl transferred to the Prussian University of Halle, where he became infamous.[93]

At Halle, Ritschl studied with Carl Reisig, who had been a student of Hermann's at Leipzig. Reisig had been an extraordinary professor at Halle since 1820. He advanced to ordinary professor in 1824, but did not succeed to codirector of the seminar when the position opened that same year. Instead, a former student of Böckh, Moritz Meier, a Berlin Dr. Phil. from 1818, was brought from Greifswald and made an ordinary professor and codirector of the seminar. Meier effectively functioned as the sole director, since the other codirector was the elderly Christian Schütz, who served only pro forma after 1817.

Reverting to behavior we know from the previous chapter, the insulted Reisig founded a private society as a rival to the seminar in 1824. Soon Reisig felt the insult aggravated. In 1828, Gottfried Bernhardy became an ordinary professor at Halle and codirector of the seminar with Meier (and Schütz pro forma). Like Meier, Bernhardy had been a student of Böckh and a Berlin Dr. Phil. (1822), whose dissertation on fragments we heard of above.

Ritschl studied at Halle mostly with Reisig. Although he was a professor in Prussia at Halle, Reisig had never studied in Prussia. He had studied in Göttingen, Jena, and Leipzig—at the latter, as noted, with Hermann. From 1824 to 1829 at Halle, Reisig found himself locked outside the seminar's directorate, which by 1828 was led by two students of Böckh.

As fate would have it, Reisig died in early 1829 in Venice, before his fortieth birthday. He could thus not partake of Ritschl's doctoral exam later in the same year. Ritschl had been a member of Reisig's society, and a member of the seminar, too, but apparently only attended the Latin section taught by Schütz, as opposed to Meier's Greek section.

In Ritschl's student days at Halle, public disputation enjoyed high esteem anew, especially among the classicists. Nonclassicists trembled when they faced classicists as opponents in disputation, still conducted in Latin. Internecine warfare between the classicists had arisen from the projection of the Hermann-Böckh feud into the camps of Reisig's society versus Meier's Greek section of the Halle seminar. Ritschl had transferred to Halle in 1826, the year after the Hermann-Böckh feud had become bitter. He soon made a name for himself as an opponent at disputation. He sought to annihilate students from the seminar's Greek section—students, that is, of Böckh's student Meier—in disputations.

In 1828, Heinrich Foss, the senior student in the seminar and a devoted disciple of Meier, wrote and tried to defend his doctoral dissertation. Foss himself had previously attacked a student named Wex from Reisig's classics society at Wex's public disputation. Ritschl sought to play the avenger by attempting to destroy Foss at Foss's public disputation in 1828. Foss received his doctorate, but the disputational battle between him and Ritschl supposedly not only split the gown but also the town of Halle in two camps. "Even the ladies" of the town supposedly took sides in this doctoral drama.[94]

A PLAN AND AN EXAM. Ritschl's problems apropos his own dissertation were, however, of his own making. In early 1829, after the death of Reisig, his primary teacher, Ritschl's graduation in the summer appeared endangered. Ritschl had toyed with transferring to Berlin and now thought earnestly about it. But Professor Meier took the high road. Despite Ritschl's neglect of Meier's classes at Halle and, above all, despite Ritschl's infamous attacks on Meier's students in public disputations, Meier invited Ritschl to his home one fine night.

Meier revealed a plan to Ritschl. With Reisig's sudden and unexpected death in Venice, Halle needed someone fast who could teach the sorts of things that Reisig had taught. In Meier's plan, Ritschl not only would receive his doctorate in the summer but would also swiftly habilitate, thus become qualified to be a lecturer (*Privat-Docent*). Then, with Meier's help, Ritschl should become just that in the fall-winter semester of 1829. Meier further promised to intervene with the Prussian ministry to secure a small salary for Ritschl, whom Meier envisaged as collaborating with him in editing the *Hallische Literaturzeitung*.

This was an offer Ritschl could not refuse. The rub lay in the demand that he get his doctorate and habilitate before the fall. Under this sort of pressure, Ritschl continued to do what he had been doing: taking too long to write his dissertation, *De Agathone*. In fact, it looks as if he had not actually finished it in time for the private exam by the faculty on 4 July 1829—the sort of exam we considered in the previous chapter. The dean of the faculty and four other professors, including the philologists Schütz and Meier, examined Ritschl.

In tune with the modern notion of the major, the examiners largely confined their questions to a narrow field: classics. The dean might have questioned him about poetics in general, and another professor did question him about general linguistics. In the protocol of the exam, Schütz, eighty-two years old at the time, noted that Ritschl had attended his Latin seminar lessons and had displayed "industry, talent and linguistic knowledge"—Schütz used notions of the eighteenth century here. Meier noted that he had discussed Ritschl's dissertation, *De Agathone*, with the candidate, but did not say he had seen it.[95]

Meier noted the topics on which he had examined Ritschl, then remarked that the candidate was one of the most worthy whom the faculty could honor with its highest degree. Meier recommended that the words *ingeniosa et docta* appear as citation on Ritschl's diploma. One of the others examiners recommended the predicate *summa cum laude* on the diploma. Meier further suggested *summa cum laude superasse*, which became *summa cum laude superato*, alongside the *docta et ingeniosa*, on the actual diploma. Ritschl, however, had not handed in his proposed dissertation in time to graduate.[96]

A WORK OF THE NIGHT. Ritschl's dissertation had taken too long to write. The proposed work in fact appeared later as his habilitation in 1829 as *Commentationis de Agathonis vita, arte et tragoediarum reliquiis particula*, thus a commentary on Agathon's fragments or "relicts." Halle did not require a dissertation for the public disputation, as noted above, but apparently would not accept one in manuscript alone for the disputation (as Gießen seems to have done).

Ritschl might have given the impression in early July that he had the manuscript of the dissertation on Agathon done, but did not have enough time to have it printed for the disputation. At twenty-three pages, the later habilitation on Agathon was, however, nearly half the length of what became Ritschl's actual dissertation. It appears that Ritschl had not in fact finished writing his dissertation on Agathon. He would have to graduate at the public disputation on the basis only of theses, or reschedule his disputation, thus graduation, thus lose his envisaged position in the fall. But the "learned and ingenious" candidate chose a learned and ingenious alternative. He saved the dissertation for the looming habilitation.

And he produced a new dissertation. Figure 6.8 shows the title page. The iconography is interesting. As noted, doctoral advisors and presiding professors had disappeared from title pages. Three opponents appeared on Ritschl's and had risen to the center of the page—the place previously held by the presiding professor. One of the opponents was already a Dr. Phil., while the other two came from the seminar. Figure 6.8 shows the theses proposed by Ritschl for the public disputation. They all concern classics.

Ritschl saved himself from the shame of graduating only on the basis of the "naked theses" by managing to get the forty-three pages, plus theses, swiftly printed as the dissertation shown in figure 6.8. *Schedae criticae* embodies a dissertation of the old specimen of erudition sort—a grammatical-critical emendation of selected passages. Ritschl probably had the emendations that he turned into a dissertation largely already in hand. Reisig, now deceased, had demanded such *schedae criticae* for admission to his society—a formidable requirement and testament to how far standards had climbed.[97]

Ritschl later wrote that he spent three days, with a total of nine hours sleep, shaping the emendations into a coherent dissertation. He then paid for three typesetters to work through two nights to get the dissertation printed on time—the printer probably had other obligations for the normal day hours. "Thus was the thing composed, set, printed and bound at night—a true work of the night." But it was done. He did the theses (figure 6.9) the night before the disputation. After two hours sleep, he appeared at the public disputation at 10:00 a.m. I do not know if any of Meier's seminar students tried to annihilate Ritschl. But, by 3:00 p.m., 11 July, after five days labor with little sleep, a new doctor of philosophy existed.[98]

Per Meier's plan, Ritschl became a lecturer the same year, habilitating on the basis of his original dissertation topic, *De Agathone*. He went on to a luminous career at Prussian universities in Halle, Breslau, Bonn, and then at

# SCHEDAE CRITICAE

QUAS

LOCO COMMENTATIONIS PROPEDIEM EDENDAE

AUCTORITATE

## AMPLISSIMI PHILOSOPHORUM ORDINIS IN ACADEMIA FRIDERICIA

## SUMMORUM IN PHILOSOPHIA HONORUM

RITE OBTINENDORUM CAUSSA

DIE XI. M. IULII A. cIɔIɔCCCXXIX.

HORA X.

CONTRA ADVERSARIOS

ANTONIUM REINIUM, PHILOSOPHIAE DOCTOREM,
RUDOLPHUM HANOVIUM, SEM. R. PHILOL. SOCIUM,
GUSTAVUM KIESSLINGIUM, SEM. R. PHIL. SOC.

PUBLICE DEFENDET

# FRIDERICUS GUILELMUS RITSCHL

VARGULANUS THURINGORUM

SEMINARII REGII PHILOLOGICI SENIOR
ITEM PAEDAGOGICI ET SOCIETATIS HISTORICAE
SODALIS.

## HALIS SAXONUM

TYPIS EXPRESSUM GEBAUERIIS.

6.8. Title page of Friedrich Ritschl's *Schedae criticae . . .*, Diss. phil.,
Halle, 1829. Reproduced with permission of the Universitätsbibliothek Göttingen.

## SENTENTIAE CONTROVERSAE.

### I.

*Magnesia* et terrae fuit et urbis nomen, ut fallatur Conradus Mannertus Geogr. Graec. et Rom. vol. VII. p. 598.

### II.

M. T. Ciceronis de Senectute capite I. §. 3. *Aristonis Cei* Peripatetici nomen restituendum est ex libro MS. Vinariensi in locum *Aristonis Chii* Stoici.

### III.

*Marsyas* historicus, cuius Harpocratio Μακεδονικά commemorat v. Δητή, non est *Tabenus* sed *Philippensis*.

### IV.

Ex eiusdem Philippensis, non ex *Pellaei* Μακεδονικοῖς hausta sunt, quae apud Harpocrationem leguntur v. Ἀριστίων et v. μαργίτης, et apud Athenaeum lib. XIV. p. 629. D.

### V.

*C. Plinii Secundi* verba Naturali Historia, lib. XXXV. cap. 9. sic sunt reconcinnanda: *Zeuxis Heracleotes......* *a quibusdam falso in* LXXXIX. *Olympiade positus.* *Cum quo fuisse necesse est Demophilum Himeraeum et Neseam Thasium* e. q. s. Lapsus est Iul. Silligius Catalogo Artificum p. 460.

6.9. "Sententiae Controversae" from Friedrich Ritschl's *Schedae criticae . . .,* Halle, 1829.

Leipzig. There he counted, among others, Friedrich Nietzsche as a pupil and doctoral student—a student who would go on to try his advisor's patence with his attacks on the micrology of research and the nearly nihilistic self-destruction of his own academic career. But, about that, in a later chapter.

## CONCLUSION

The doctor of philosophy appeared in good part in response to the decline in prestige of the master's degree, and an unwillingness to forsake academic degrees. In traditional or conservative lands such as England and Saxony, the master's degree had not declined nearly so far as in other lands, thus the impetus to change was far less, and even resisted by some. In lands such as France and Austria, both with a Jesuit past, radical changes came to academic degrees. France abolished the *ancien régime* of academic degrees altogether for a time after 1789, while the Austrians instituted the doctor of philosophy, but viewed it at base as a civil service or bureaucratic title awarded on the basis of a written exam.

The doctor of philosophy, in the form that would one day conquer academia, emerged fitfully in a number of enlightened German lands, such as in Hanover at the University Göttingen, in Saxe-Weimar at the University of Jena, and in Württemberg at the University of Tübingen. But it was the Prussian doctor of philosophy, consecrated at the University of Berlin after 1810, that went forth as the new, Romantic hero of knowledge.

Attempts to introduce the title in the German lands stretched over a quarter millennium, from 1550 to 1800, resisted as they were by jurists and other conservatives. The gradual recognition of the doctor of philosophy began in the last third of the eighteenth century, but had been preceded by a juristic enlightenment that began in the last third of the seventeenth century. The jurists' debate, from about the 1670s to the 1730s, effaced the juridical persona—much of it lodged in physical attributes of the candidate—previously required for academic degrees. By the mid-eighteenth century, a degree candidate had been effectively dematerialized, disembodied, and spiritualized as pure intellectual capacity. That capacity would have to be displayed in oral exams, private and public, and also in writing.

The authorial persona replaced the juridical persona in the degree candidate. In lands following the Prussian model, the title of doctor of philosophy became recognized within the civil service, but required a written dissertation, as opposed to a mere civil service exam, for its award. Romantic notions about originality, as a new sort of academic charisma, would inform expectations about the written specimens—whence the bureaucratization and aesthetization of the candidate, the bureaucrat as work of art.

The academic hegemony of classical philology in the Romantic era signaled the rise of the mandarins in the German lands. As chapter 4 showed, the same era witnessed the apotheosis of classics at Oxford as well, while Cambridge idiosyncratically instilled and examined useless but difficult mathematics as a legacy of Newton's heroic stature. One can read the developments in both England and the Germanies as a rejection of technocratic ideals associated with the French Enlightenment. The conservative aristocratic reaction in England and the Germanies, especially after the advent of the French Revolution, looked askance at the technical and pragmatic training for the ruling class advocated by cameralist and political economists in the Enlightenment. The ruling elite would now not legitimate itself pragmatically by the possession of expert technical (or martial) skills needed to manage a modern society. Elites rather sought to legitimate themselves charismatically, as mandarins, by their mastery of difficult dead languages or useless but heroic mathematical arts.

In the Germanies, the candidate as a Romantic author had emerged from the practice of student subvention of professorial dissertations. By the early eighteenth century, the student or respondent as author had become common, but probably not typical at graduation. The general recognition of the doctor of philosophy, however, roughly paralleled the transfer in authorship of the graduation dissertation from the presiding professor, soon a doctoral advisor, to the graduating student, then a doctoral candidate, by around 1800.

Although Romanticism postulated the charismatic moment of originality in the doctoral candidate as a work of art, the doctoral dissertation as a work of research rather more realized a sort of industrial view of masterpieces formulated by the imperial ordinance on the guilds in 1731 and in other measures by enlightened German police states. The notion of the masterpiece as serial production well instantiated itself in the doctoral dissertations that collected fragments of a single obscure classical academic or author.

Such works of research, in conjunction with the seminars and later the labs, effected one of the greatest academic transformations since the emergence of the universities themselves in the High Middle Ages. Students now wrote a sort of dissertation once written by professors. Seminarists and doctoral candidates—advanced students—now wrote in a professorial manner. The seminars and labs and doctoral dissertations became essential academic bases of the German research university. The matter of academic appointments might then proceed in a way sought by reformers and rationalizers.

# 7

## The Appointment
## of a Professor

To kill the professorial appointment of the notorious Lorenz Oken, the philosophy faculty must have raised the matter of politics, since a Bavarian minister in Munich, Könneritz, made a point of mentioning it in his reply of 18 December 1832. The Saxon ministry in Dresden wanted to hire Oken, a professor and member of the academy of sciences in Munich, but the Saxon University of Leipzig did not. The university saw this as typical ministerial meddling in things that academics knew better.

The faculty's first move to stop the ministry's plan had been to write to Minister Könneritz about Oken. Könneritz answered, "According to the unanimous judgment of impartial and reliable men, Prof. Oken is not to be regarded as dangerous politically." The Leipzig faculty then faced the task of attacking Oken academically, which it did in a letter of 11 January 1833.

There the faculty claimed that he was more known as a literary than an academic author, that his science was peculiar to himself, that he was a bad teacher, and was known "as one of the original founders and defenders of the [student] *Burschenschaft*" movement. The last point, playing a political card, offers a common point of attack in the modern era. But, as every academic knows, one can easily find fault with ideas and academic work. Oken, by the way, was one of those whom we met in the previous chapter who had obtained his doctorate from the University of Gießen *per saltem* by submitting previously published work.[1]

At the Saxon ministry in Dresden, an isolated but nice dossier was put together around the proposed appointment above of Oken. As a means of collecting information about academics, the dossier did not emerge as a general technique or system until well into the modern era. The dossier at the Saxon ministry about this appointment in the 1830s remained a relative rarity, even then, for a time. In this chapter we shall look not only at academic appointments and their rationalization, but also at the ministerial-archival material culture concerning the collecting and keeping of paper-work on academics about such matters.

The chief concern of the chapter is to trace changes in the protocols of academic appointments from the Baroque to the Romantic era. The chapter has two relatively short parts that bookend a long middle part. The first part considers traditional academic practices of professorial appointment, as well as two elements of material culture relevant to the analysis: dossiers and archives. The third part of the chapter looks at the case of Bavaria, where the academic dossier made a comparatively early appearance as a filing system.

The middle and main part of the chapter looks at Brandenburg-Prussia as a case study. In this case, as in the other parts of the chapter, we shall be concerned with the advent of a ministerial-market rationality or capitalistic rationalization imposed by ministries upon academic appointments. From the Baroque into the Romantic era, many German ministers of state sought to expropriate the active role in making appointments, as above in the case of Oken. Ministers sought to impose what they saw as a remedy to the traditional and collegial practices of faculties and universities. State ministries wanted to create a meritocracy based on what the ministry determined was to constitute merit and what not. It would be the sort of meritocracy, in fact, one day grounded in the seminars and dissertations.

The professorial meritocracy overturned practices of appointment at the traditional university and formed a fundamental pillar of the modern research university. But German Protestant ministers instituted an odd sort of professorial meritocracy, one that Jesuits and Austrians (until 1848) could see was bedeviled by irrational traces of academic charisma.

## PROFESSORS AND PAPERWORK

### Traditional and Rationalized Appointments

Drawn by Ludwig Emil Grimm, brother of the Brothers Grimm, and shown in figure 7.1, we see tea and Schlapps on a Wednesday evening circa 1830 at the home of Professor Blumenbach in Göttingen. The artist has humbly made his the only face that we cannot see. To his left is the only other male, Professor Blumenbach himself. On the far right, the maid brings a samovar with tea. The six women at the table are professors' and lecturers' wives or daughters, representing the families Blumenbach, Göschen, and Heine.

Ludwig was not an academic on the make. But consider figure 7.1 as a portrait of part of the protocols and table manners of academic appoint-

7.1. Ludwig E. Grimm's "Thee Schlapps, Mittwoch Abend beim Blumenbach," circa 1830.

ments, an early modern search committee of a sort, in which academic women actually had a bit to say. A polemical and partly satirical work on Göttingen claimed that professors' wives and daughters set the tone in that small academic town, although they seemed unsure of what they wanted.[2]

THE PROFESSOR'S DAUGHTER. In Christian Salzmann's novel *Carl von Carlsberg* (1783–88), a young academic named Ribonius at the fictional University of Grünau learns that an ordinary professorship has become vacant. As senior adjunct or lecturer in the relevant faculty, Ribonius expects that he will be offered the chair. In this light, he meets with members of the faculty, who receive him coolly. They speak of problems, but say no more. The young adjunct is confused and a few days later mentions this to a friend in town. The friend queries whether the naïve adjunct realizes how one actually becomes a professor in Grünau. "Perhaps through bribery," retorts Ribonius, commenting that, if so, he has no chance. The friend disabuses him of such notions. "We have here [in Grünau], indeed, pretty professors' daughters. Marry one! What's it matter? Things will go better."

Enlightened, Ribonius breaks off his current relationship and begins to court the daughter of a certain Professor Biel. "Thus a number of days went by with visits and counter-visits," till at last the happy day arrives when the Biel family could announce Ribonius's engagement to their daughter. The beaming father and professor confides to the expectant adjunct and future son-in-law, "I congratulate you as well now too about the professorship, which is as good as yours," after which all drink to the health of the "new professor."[3]

In a history of Protestant universities (1768–76), the Göttingen professor Michaelis wrote against nepotism, especially concerning sons-in-law. Professors, he held, might raise their own sons to be proper professors, but not so their sons-in-law. Moreover, an academic who married for the sake of his career "must have little confidence in his own merit." Michaelis held it acceptable for already established professors to marry the daughters of other professors, although "marriage should not be a means of preferment at universities." Applications from lecturers who were sons-in-law of professors must thus be looked upon with suspicion. But, as Michaelis conceded, nepotism and intermarriage still flourished.[4]

The subject of late enlightened satire and polemics, the little studied professor's daughter served as a not uncommon path into the early modern faculty. We may take her as emblematic of the traditional Protestant university, excepting Oxbridge. In the Basel lecture catalogues in chapter 2, we had our first occasion to notice the traditional practice of appointment through apparent nepotism as shown in the many duplicated family names. Some good, substantive reasons existed for such now unseemly practices.

Craft guilds particularly favored sons as well as sons-in-law of masters for acceptance into the guild. The similar reason for favoring the husband of a professor's daughter for academic appointment makes sense since early modern universities had almost no budgets for acquisitions of books, instruments, and other capital goods. Such acquisitions of academic capital could come through bequests and dowries. Since professors had to buy many books and instruments they used, the death of a well-endowed professor posed a problem for the faculty and university: one wanted to avoid extramural alienation of academic effects. In many cases, despite Michaelis's view above, a professor's son might not be up to par academically. Thus, besides literal nepotism, the professor's daughter with academic dowry offered a good way to keep the capital goods in the academic family or faculty.[5]

Early modern Protestant universities formed closely-knit kin groups. At the small University of Rinteln, for example, from 1621 to 1809, of the 171 professors, 68 had easily known blood or marital ties. Marburg professors from 1653 to 1806 at least, show the same pattern: one-third of the professorate in 1806 could easily trace its lineage by blood or marriage all the way to 1653. At the University of Heidelberg, a 1767 decree went so far as to rule that a male heir, if qualified, could inherit his father's chair. At Tübingen, a professor's male heirs seem to have held even stronger to claims to the chair.[6]

The family university was not just a German Protestant one. At early modern Edinburgh, the Gregories, Monros and Stewarts all formed professorial dynasties. Likewise at the Swedish University of Uppsala, "a few closely intermarried clans dominated." The great naturalist Linnaeus even received the right to dispose of his chair in 1762 and "he long pondered whether he should save it for a potential son-in-law, or bestow it on his son."[7]

RATIONALIZING APPOINTMENTS. "The most famous and most superb men must be chosen as instructors. Favor and inclination, as well as the claims of patrons, should have no less influence on choices than here." So said the cameralist Justi in his work on police science. The eighteenth constituted the great century for the attack on courtly, corporate, and above all on the familial, kin-based practices of academic appointments. The ministry ultimately envisaged a meritocracy, which upset traditional academic sentiments and habits.[8]

Surveying practices in the German lands in mid-eighteenth century, the Bavarian jurist Kreittmayr said, "On the appointment (*Denominierung*) of professors, it is, to be sure, not uniform everywhere, but it comes mostly from the sovereign himself." By mid-eighteenth century, academic appointment in the Germanies generally lay in the hands of the sovereign and his or her ministers. By very old protocols, the faculty and university would nominate one or more candidates. The sovereign would approve one, or veto them all; but in the original protocol, the sovereign could name no one new. By mid-eighteenth century, most sovereigns had turned a passive, veto power into an active one of initial nomination.[9]

Ministries did not lack power to alter academic practices of appointment. They, rather, often lacked the will to nominate appointees and simply rubber-stamped whomever faculties wanted. But when ministries did not lack the will, useful information and wisdom sometimes failed them.

The chair of Oriental Languages [at Gießen] became vacant when Professor Wolff died. The [Hessian] ministry [in Darmstadt] believed Professor Klotz in Halle [in Brandenburg-Prussia] was learned in this subject and so offered him the position. Klotz thanked them for the honor, and with reason. He understood, as he said in his reply, neither Hebrew nor, indeed, anything Oriental; but, *ceteris paribus*, that should not hinder him from taking the professorship, since within four weeks he thought he could learn as much about these topics as students in Gießen would ever need to know.[10]

State ministries trying to rationalize academic appointments thus could make a mess. Attacking academic nepotism presented a particular dilemma for ministers of state. Insofar as ministers knew of nepotistic nominations, they had to be of two minds. For the vast majority of high ministers of state were aristocrats. And nepotism was their life.

Seniority remained likewise a dilemma. To this day, attempts to establish thoroughgoing meritocratic principles for appointment and especially advancement run into the brute fact of time's merit. To have given one's time in service means to have acquired some merit, and the longer the time, the more the merit. At the early modern university, the chief dilemma about seniority concerned the practice of *Aufrücken* or *jus optandi,* opting up from extraordinary to ordinary professor, or from chair to chair by seniority, as we saw in chapter 2. At the traditional university, opting up offered one of the two chief ways of getting more money and honor. The other was, of course, academic pluralism.

Instead of letting academics play musical chairs or sit in several chairs to earn a salary increase, the solution would be to keep professors in the same chair, while making regular salary increases possible for them, in part through pure seniority, and in part through proven merit. But that solution, especially the second and harder part, had to await the nineteenth, if not the twentieth century, to acquire anything like systematic extent. Traditional academia proved unable to invent a system of regular salary increases based on something like peer review.

Thus most ministers moved mainly to stop opting up. In the 1770s and 1780s the Catholic ministries supervising the universities at Ingolstadt and Mainz, for example, ordered an end to advancement in view of seniority alone. For academic promotion, one should, they said, demonstrate one's learning, one's competency at lecturing, and one's morality in doing one's duty. Consideration, they thought, should also be given to hiring academics "who had secured great public acclaim." To this end, a minister opined that one should acquire charismatic academics by offering a high enough salary so that they would move. Such a solution, namely the commodification of academics, would one day become the rule.[11]

But it was not the most obvious solution to the general question: how to replace candidates chosen by fortune or favor with ones chosen in view of their abilities? A decree from the Saxon ministry in Dresden to the University of Wittenberg in 1732, for example, held that professors nominated by the university to the ministry for appointment must have "expert knowledge" for the chair in question. Alas, the decree did not say how that was to be ascertained. A candidate whom one group or faction of academics believed to have the requisite expert knowledge might be held by another group or faction to lack it.[12]

Others thus tried other solutions. By the early eighteenth century in Basel, for example, desiring to secure some peace among the academic dynasties, the university set up an examination and a trial lecture for those applying for an open position. And, if needed, a lottery was then held among the top three candidates for the position. Here, not fame but rather a strange sort of fortune entered as an impartial judge among applicants.[13]

As we have seen so often above, the Habsburgs, thanks to their Jesuitical past, proved to be the most radical Germanic rationalizers. In the previous chapter we saw that, in the process of formally instituting the doctor of philosophy, the Austrians abolished medieval practices, such as the disputation, for the award of the degree. Unlike the Prussians, they did not then institute the practice of the doctoral dissertation. Instead, as we saw, the Austrians simply set up a sort of modern civil service examination for the degree.

That meritocratic, bureaucratic solution would be adopted as well for appointments. A series of Austrian decrees, beginning in 1777, enjoined that aspiring academics must be examined for positions. This set up what came to be the *Concurs(e)-Normal* or *Concurse*. Probably modeled, as its name suggests, on the French *concours*, the Austrian *Concurse* had become statewide by 1784. In the Austrian exam, applicants had to take a written exam and then give a trial lecture. A further decree of 1798 held that candidates could only take the *Concurse* for a position, if they had already passed exams in the relevant field. The person who performed best in the written and trial lecture of the *Concurse* received the position.[14]

CHARISMATIC APPOINTMENTS. In the case of academic appointments, as in so many others, German Protestant lands did not pursue such radical, Jesuitical policies. Protestant lands would also proclaim merit and ability as the chief criteria for appointment, but one would adjudicate them in a more complex and, arguably, less rational manner than in Austria.

The German Enlightenment and Romantic era in both Protestant and Catholic lands witnessed the rise of powerful ministers of education, or ministers of culture *avant la lettre*. Ministers Zedlitz in Prussia, Münchhausen in Hanover, Goethe in Saxe-Weimar, Superville in Bayreuth, Bentzel in Electoral Mainz, Ickstatt in Bavaria, and Swieten in Austria, among others, took prominent roles in the reformation and rationalization of universities and schools. In Protestant lands, the great ministers tapped and invoked charismatic powers to make academic appointments. While most of the great ministers will not occupy the center of our attention in this chapter, their methods of rational and charismatic appointment will.[15]

In 1609 a ministerial visitation commission to Wittenberg spoke against the practice whereby, in an effort to obviate the collegial will of the university, senior faculty members sent private correspondence to the ministry. During the eighteenth century, that very practice became more and more the rule. During Goethe's tenure as a minister in Weimar, for example, while giving scant heed to recommendations of faculties, he and his associates carried on much private correspondence with select professors for advice on appointments. This had been going on in Prussia at least since the early eighteenth century.[16]

Instead of formal consultation with faculties, ministers began to rationalize appointments by seeking advice privately from confidants. A pay scale for Halle from 1705, when compared with other documents in the archive, indicates that the highest paid Halle professors wrote many of the private letters about appointments there. The hierarchy of professors most valued by the ministry and market pulled the strings behind the scenes. A 1795 article in *Berlinische Monatsschrift,* a journal of German Enlightenment, recommended that sovereigns should not consult universities corporately in formal correspondence; a sovereign should, rather, consult with a few scholars via confidential correspondence.[17]

Meiners, a Göttingen professor and historian, wrong de jure but right de facto, wrote,

> The great [Minister] Münchhausen gave our school of higher learning the right to present or to nominate or to commend [candidates] just as little as [he gave us] a right of free election [of candidates]. For he knew by experience that, although the faculties of learned academies [that is, universities] recognize the men who most merit a vacant position, they are still seldom or never inclined to suggest the most capable they know.[18]

The great Minister Münchhausen, Göttingen's first supervisor or *Curator,* labored on the construction of the founding professorate in the mid 1730s. For the initial appointments, he sought proven specialists or experts. Seeking advice, he corresponded privately with select academics. Once he had assembled the faculties, he continued to correspond confidentially about future appointments, usually using one current Göttingen professor as a favored advisor. But the minister did not usually correspond with a faculty or the university as collegial bodies on such matters. That was crucial, as we shall see more below.

The ministerial policy pursued at Göttingen and elsewhere aimed at breaking up the faculties and universities as collegial and corporate entities. The ministry wanted individual, isolated academic specialists, with whom ministers could speak confidentially. In this way, no one outside the ministry had the complete overview. The ministry's charismatic power grew in the eighteenth century not from spectacular displays of power but rather from concealment of its workings.[19]

The first eight professors hired in the Göttingen philosophy faculty also served in the superior faculties. But by 1788 such practices had long stopped. Göttingen also curtailed promotion within faculties and pluralism between them. The university kept a Protestant religious profile, but singled itself out by appointing individuals from far and wide, regardless of their nationality. Ability and merit overrode notions of traditional academic capital at Göttingen. In some cases, Minister Münchhausen did consider traditional academic capital, such as a scholar's library or instruments, in making appointments.

But Münchhausen transformed publication into the essential modern academic capital. The minister hired Göttingen professors in good part in view of publications or, rather, in view of the fame of their publications. Once appointed, professors should continue to produce, and in the spirit and fashion of the times. They should write not only academic dissertations of the traditional sort, but also articles, reviews, and textbooks—and they should edit journals. Textbooks and journals emerged as a Göttingen eighteenth-century specialty and helped establish its professors as enlightened judges over all European scholarship.[20]

This Hanoverian view of appointments placed the Göttingen professorate at the forefront of academic commodification. But, although enlightened Göttingen had much to do with conceiving the modern system of professorial appointment and advancement, it could not perfect the system. It, too, had a difficult time setting criteria for regular salary increases for professors once hired. The professors proved so modern in another respect, however, that Michaelis bemoaned the intrigues of his Göttingen colleagues, who had learnt to fish for extramural academic offers, so as "to extort more money in the end" from the ministry.[21]

This cameralist-capitalistic, Hanoverian—and ultimately Prussian—charismatic rationality was by no means self-evident, even though it became the modern system. It had emerged as a Protestant practice. Critique of it came from Catholic Habsburg lands. The Berlin author and intellectual, Nicolai, reported hearing in Vienna during a visit in the late eighteenth century, "Catholics have already reproached Protestants that they had turned their universities into annual markets ( *Jahrmärkten* ) where the sciences are set out like wares." It was not just the sciences that the universities set out like wares.[22]

The Austrians weighed publications but, up to 1848, did not allow appointments to be driven by something so irrational as fame in the admittedly poorly policed market or Republic of Letters. True to their Jesuitical heritage and the metaphysics of bureaucracy, the Austrians tested academic applicants for professorial positions, as noted. But an Austrian decree of 30 November 1810 already allowed that "famous men," who had made a big name (and much noise) via publication and so on, might be exempted from taking the *Concurse*.[23]

Two sorts of charismatic power thus invested the putative rationalization of academic appointment in progressive Protestant lands such as Hanover and Prussia: fame attained in the free market of letters, and the recognition of it by a minister and his select circle of supposed cognoscenti. Charisma flowed from the market and the ministry, which transferred it to the chosen one—thus to be appointed neither by the traditional method of collegial voting, nor by the rationalizing method of meritocratic testing.

## Dossiers and Archives

The invention of the dossier—managing the university in terms of isolated academics on file—coheres with Hanoverian-Prussian ministerial-market rationality. Indeed, the systematic use of academic dossiers seems to have first emerged in the Hanoverian-(Welfin) lands. Until 1737 the University of Helmstedt was the only university for all Hanoverian lands. Up to 1712, ministerial acts for that university had the customary character at the primary level of faculty acts: paperwork accumulated in terms of a generalized faculty file or, actually, a faculty pile or bundle in the ministry's archive. In 1712, however, the relevant acts shifted to dossiers for each academic. After the foundation of the Hanoverian University of Göttingen in 1737, the relevant ministerial acts for it also took the form of dossiers.[24]

When I undertook the research for this chapter long ago, I presumed that the sort of rationalization of academic appointments accomplished by the Hanoverians would be accompanied in general by a corresponding rationalization of academic acts in other ministries and archives, doubtless with some time lag. But I did not find that; or, rather, things did not happen as I thought they would. In my supposition, I presumed a sort of technical imperative. The modern dossier seemed to me the right Enlightened-Romantic tool to recast the files of appointments, to mirror how the charismatic rationalizers reformed the appointments themselves. But material and intellectual culture, it seems, may be disjoint.

A SURVEY OF DOSSIERS IN AUSTRO-GERMAN ARCHIVES. Very swiftly, I made a survey on the question of dossiers. The results reported must be taken as a first approximation. The poles of the spectrum are dossiers, that is, acts and files in which the individual forms the primary principle of order and collection, versus what the Germans call "object acts" (*Sachakten*). In the latter acts, an organization, such as a faculty, or an event or a process, such as appointment, provides the primary principle of order and collection. If, for example, the object acts are faculty acts, then any acts relating to a given academic are scattered through the acts, which usually accumulate purely chronologically in piles as the second principle of formation.

In the Schleswig ministry, for the University of Kiel, some dossiers emerged in the nineteenth, but more in the twentieth century. Other acts span a spectrum from quasi dossiers, such as alphabetized volumes with indices of names, to pure object acts. In Canton-Basel, although faculties, later disciplines, gave the primary structure, dossiers served by alphabetical indices appeared by the late eighteenth century. In Baden, for the Universities of Heidelberg, and later for Freiburg im Br., too, ministerial acts show both forms, at least after mid-eighteenth century. There are dossiers for some matters on academics, while complex acts, such as professorial appointments, were kept as object acts—an interesting twist.

Bavaria introduced dossiers systematically in 1806. In some cases, someone reordered acts before that date into dossiers. We'll examine the Bavarian dossiers in the third part below. In Austrian lands until 1848, the ministry filed in terms of object acts set around corporate bodies, such as faculties. After 1848, given a macrodivision of Viennese versus non-Viennese faculty as the primary principle, the Habsburg lands introduced individual academic dossiers systematically—a sign, perhaps, of the reign of charismatic rationality.

In other German-speaking lands surveyed—Hesse-Darmstadt, Hesse-Cassel, Württemberg, Electoral Saxony, Saxe-Weimar, and Electoral Mainz—before the twentieth century at least, no systematic use of academic dossiers can be found. Dossiers might appear now and again for a short period or, as in the case of Lorenz Oken with whom we began the chapter, might collect around an extraordinary individual or appointment. But those came as exceptions to a rule that persisted unexpectedly (to me) long into the modern era.

Brandenburg-Prussia presents the crucial case here, since most of this chapter is devoted to a study of academic appointments there. Up to 1787, Prussian academic acts were object acts, usually collected by faculty, and purely chronologically. A few dossiers or quasi dossiers appeared, such as around Christian Wolff. But those were exceptions. In 1787 the Prussians set up a new ministry, the Supreme School Council, the *Oberschulkollegium* (hereafter OSK). This new ministry supervised all academic appointments in Brandenburg-Prussia. I had expected the OSK would structure its acts as dossiers.

But it did not. After 1787 the Prussian OSK rationalized collection by dissolving the corporate and collegial bodies of provinces and faculties. But, instead of using the academics made into dossiers as a principle of filing, the OSK kept the universities as the primary principle of organization. Under the universities, the OSK collected and piled purely chronologically, again not availing itself of academics cast or isolated into dossiers.

With the foundation of the University of Berlin (1809/10), dossiers did gather around the appointments of a few key academics, such F. A. Wolf, Fichte, and Schleiermacher. Dossiers thereafter also emerged for a few professors, as well as for the filling of a few famous chairs, such as Hegel's. The latter acts became dossiers for the relevant persons. During the 1830s and early 1840s academic dossiers then emerged systematically in Prussia. But in 1843/44, Prussian ministerial acts for some reason went to back to being faculty-centered, the sort of traditional object acts before the foundation of the OSK in 1787.

Dossiers are apparently not crucial to a ministerial rationalization of academic appointments. As we'll see below, the Prussian ministry, like the Hanoverian, imposed a ministerial-market rationality upon academic appointments from the Enlightenment to the Romantic era. But the material form of the acts as a system did not march in step with the contents. In Hanover those two things had gone together, and would also in Bavaria after 1806, and in Austria after 1848. The Prussians marched to a different tune and out of step.

The way a ministry files documents usually becomes the way it archives them. That is its memory. Files remain in the main rooms for a time, then come to a farther room. Acts that I have tried to illuminate here come from such farther rooms called "archives." Perplexities about ministerial filing systems led to interest in the farther rooms themselves. For at the heart of this chapter is an attempt to recount the story of the Prussian rationalization of appointments (of a charismatic chosen one) from acts that materially seemed to belie it.

ARCHIVES AND RECOLLECTION. By 1599 in Brandenburg a gloomy room was set aside for an archive. The 1640s saw attempts to clean up the mess there. Someone introduced small storage boxes and numbers, but did so, apparently, poorly. Some boxes had two or more numbers, while other boxes had titles that accorded as day with night with the papers therein. When boxes got full, someone emptied them and bound the acts together, but also did so poorly.

By the 1650s, memoranda and memorabilia overwhelmed the archive, even though twenty-eight volumes of archival acts had been looted as booty in the Thirty Years War. To seize a princely archive is to seize the princely memory. The duke of Brandenburg was compelled to buy his memory back in 1678 for five hundred gulden. After obtaining the missing acts, and new ones piling up, in 1718 the duke, who was now the king of Prussia, planned for an archive in the new royal castle. But the space was to be under the kitchen.

That was not the only problem. The duke elector of Brandenburg and king of Prussia, despite his fancy titles, refused to fund a full time archivist. Imagine the mess that was growing. In 1747, a minister advised that the post really should be filled. Needed, he said, was a man with perseverance, whose spirit took joy in dust, and whose ambition reached no higher. Perhaps few such were at court. When the position of archivist was finally filled in 1792, it had been vacant in Brandenburg-Prussia for over a hundred years.[25]

Was an archive actually a place to facilitate forgetting instead of remembering? During the seventeenth century in Württemberg, archivists kept acts neatly in hundreds of drawers. Eventually, they stored the acts in boxes which, in time, covered the entire floor of the archive. Someone then hit on the marvelous idea of simply starting over again. A new floor was laid over the first floor, thus covering the boxes, and a new pile was begun.[26]

In Saxe-Weimar, a 1732 report noted that some acts were in twenty drawers. Except for three, the drawers were stuck shut. Most acts, however, lay on the ground in a room where pigeons were breeding. By the late eighteenth century, a third of the acts still covered the ground, which was now thick with an interesting mold, as water had been seeping into the room.[27]

The history of German state archives is apparently the history of ministerial (re)collection lapsing under the weight of object acts, and mold and dust and mice and pigeons and water seeping in from the kitchen, or from the garden on the roof. The lack of perspicuity concerning individual academics in object acts collected purely chronologically by faculties seems to have been compounded, and with a vengeance, by the apparent lack of any working system in the archives. How would a ministry such as the Prussian one sustain the knowledge to enable it to manage academics in the rational ways it now proposed?[28]

I wrote the long study of rationality and charisma in Brandenburg-Prussia most mindful of the following incident as its motto. In 1628 the duke elector of Brandenburg wanted to see a document supposedly stored in the archive, under the care of the registrar of the acts. The duke's ministers returned, however, empty handed and reported about the archive that "everything lay in disorder and many good pieces had been nibbled by mice. Moreover, one could also not ask the registrar about anything, since he is not only nearly completely deaf, but also blind."[29]

## THE PRUSSIAN APPOINTMENTS

This middle and principal part traces changing protocols of academic appointments and advancements at Brandenburg-Prussian universities from the Baroque into the Romantic era. The steps of the analysis reflect the chief persons, entities, and objects in the making of an academic appointment: the applicants, university bodies, referees for applicants, and ministerial bodies. Changes in the late Enlightenment and early Romantic era merit a separate and final treatment. The overall aim is to show the unfolding and imposition of a ministerial-market rationality over academic appointments in the Prussian lands. We begin with further consideration of the material aspects of the relevant acts and their filing.

### The Prussian Piles

Up to 1787, Prussia collected and archived ministerial acts on academics by provinces. The foundation of the OSK in 1787 brought about, as noted, a reorganization of archiving: the provinces disappeared from the ministry's perspective. Acts concerning each university were filed as object acts before and after 1787. Before 1787, the ministerial acts on academics fell into subcollections by the relevant faculty, piled largely chronologically. After 1787, the faculties disappeared along with the provinces as a filing principle. Except for the exceptional periods or persons for which or whom dossiers emerged, the ministry's files and perspective mixed together all academics at each university. (The Prussian acts will be cited in notes according to an abbreviation schema provided in the bibliography. Attention to that schema also reveals some of what happened after 1787.)

Up to 1787, the acts about appointment of this or that academic in Prussia are thus archived in bundles of paper, with each faculty having its own bundles. After 1787, there are just university bundles or piles. The bundles collect acts chronologically on the whole. It is not possible to tell when or how deviations from that order occurred. The appointment or advancement of a given academic went hand in hand with a file or act accumulating the paperwork and authorizing the action. Here and in following sections, the character, size, and alteration in time—the rationalization—of such acts lies at the center of the analysis.

In the time period under consideration, ministerial paper had sufficient substance to serve at once as a writing surface and as a file folder. Ministerial and other memoranda about an appointment thus usually also served as the file folders encompassing the ancillary documentation, such as the candidates' applications, letters of reference, and so on. The complete file or act ended up as a series of nested file folders. Many of the acts for the University of Königsberg are big enough so that a normal center and sequence emerges—the act as a story. I'll describe now an ideal type of such an act as an exemplar.[30]

THE STORY OF THE NESTED FOLDERS. The earliest date concerning an appointment usually lies at dead center of the paperwork. The act grows in both directions from there as a set of nested files or folders. Each folder usually encloses all previous ones—from the faculty's folder at dead center, to the university's, to a provincial ministry's, where one exists. A memorandum by the central ministry, typically in Berlin, encloses and ends the entire act.

The faculty folder at dead center might itself be just a letter accompanying the enclosures, such as letters of application or reference for the persons or issues in question. By old protocols, the faculty was supposed to nominate two or three candidates for a position. The faculty typically listed the candidates in order of preference. The university letter or report, at the next remove from the center, ideally and typically enclosed the faculty file and possibly other enclosures. The university might reorder the faculty's listing of the candidates, but the university was not supposed to add or delete names of applicants.

At the third remove from the center, a letter or file from the provincial Prussian Government in Königsberg enclosed the university file or folder, along with other possible enclosures. The provincial ministers were supposed to comment on the applicants, as well as on the faculty and university preferences. But, by the same traditional protocols of appointment, the provincial ministry should not add or delete names of applicants.

At the fourth and final remove, a ministerial memorandum written in Berlin (or, at times in Coelln, now called Neukölln and part of Berlin) enclosed all previous folders and perhaps other enclosures. The central ministry was supposed to confirm one of the two or three nominated candidates. In the second to worst-case scenario, the central ministry would reject the entire list and tell the faculty to start the process all over again. In the worst-case scenario, the central ministry, violating traditional protocols, would appoint someone who had not been nominated by the faculty and university.

Enough of the Königsberg acts look like this ideal nested folder to suggest that the physical layout of the act embodies the actual temporal sequence or the story. Sufficient disorder exists in the acts to preclude suspicion that archivists later imposed this arrangement. Many of the Königsberg acts exhibit the above fourfold nesting. Some depart from it. And a number show only the ministerial memorandum closing the act.

The fourfold nesting as a type was ideal for appointments, from the faculty's viewpoint, since it meant that the act or (hi)story of the event began with the faculty's letter at dead center. Proper acts by traditional protocols begin with the faculty, and the nesting shows the act moving up the hierarchy for final decision at the ministry in Berlin.

Not ideal from a faculty's and university's viewpoint was a ministerial memorandum gravitating to the center of an act chronologically, or enclosing an otherwise empty act. A memorandum or other ministerial document toward the center of an act exhibits ministerial initiation of an appointment, while a memorandum enclosing an empty act intimates simple imposition. New nominations of candidates by the university, by the provincial ministry, or by the central ministry also violated the traditional protocols of academic appointment.

The nested files from Königsberg offer an image of German academic freedom in the early modern era. The files assumed this nesting, at least for the philosophy faculty, in the 1690s, though the protocol had long existed. The acts persisted in this form for a part of the eighteenth century. But precisely the vision of academic freedom they embodied was what the Prussian ministry worked to rationalize and end. As we'll see, the ministry aimed to liquidate corporate-collegial academic groups as initiators or agents able to express a will. The ministry favored initiating nominations and simply proclaiming a new professor, usually after seeking confidential advice from certain select or chosen academics. In short, rationalization moved the basis of appointment from collegial will to ministerial recognition—from traditional to rationalized charisma.

## Letters of Application and Supplication

Beginning in 1749, the Prussian ministry instituted the policy of publish or perish. As ministries might, the Prussian did not always follow its own policies. The institution of publish or perish emerged in response to a number of things, including the ministry's general bent to rationalize appointments.

But developments within the applications themselves might also have played a role. In the first half of the eighteenth century, the size of some applications had begun to swell as a result of competition for jobs, as we'll soon see. But, first, we shall consider the range of other, earlier aspects of applications.

EXTRAORDINARY PROFESSORS AND THE MISERIES OF SCHOLARS. One of the older applications preserved comes from 1635, the time of the Thirty Years War. An application for the Hebrew chair at Frankfurt a.d.O. (an der Oder), it goes on for three pages, in tiny, anxious handwriting, telling a tale of impoverishment and exile. This candidate seeks to invoke the age-old academic topos of the misery of scholars to win favor. Similar invocations can be found in the first half of the eighteenth century, and even later. One finds candidates who have been recommended in previous applications by the faculty and university, but have been passed over by the ministry. Other applicants tell tales of misery and woe, of mothers and sibling in dire straits. A few applicants worry of conspiracies at the university against them. The worst heroic stories concern being unjustly banished, of which cases existed.[31]

Applicants better expressed their miseries in terms of seniority and service, of diligence and devotion. It personalizes without lowering the supplicant. In 1713, three applicants fought over the same position at Königsberg. One stressed his seniority at the university, and added that he worked from dawn till dusk at his duties. A second applicant noted that he has been teaching at the university for fourteen years without a regular, full-time position. The third applicant had been doing the same, for only nine years, but eight hours a day. He submitted three separate applications here, as if to spread his name diligently throughout the file.[32]

Now we need to recall from chapters above the problem of the extraordinary professor, which is what some of the above applicants were. The extraordinary professor as an institution lies at the base of many of the dilemmas concerning appointments and their rationalization. These professors stood outside the ordinary funding. Depending on the time and place, an extraordinary professor may or may not have had a salary. The latter seems to have been a common case. Extraordinary professors served unsalaried and, like lecturers, lived in the original medieval manner. They collected fees per head and directly from students for each class. They also offered their services for whatever else needed doing, including odd jobs. At best, they might get an ad hominem salary, usually small.

The point of being an extraordinary professor was obvious, at the time. One had, first, the title of professor, even if marred by the cruel adjective "extraordinary." From the previous chapter, we know that the German master's title had sunk greatly in prestige in the Renaissance, and that the doctor's title in arts and philosophy would not be legitimate till the later eighteenth century. Being able to call oneself professor or, more importantly, to be called that by students, counted for much. Second, and here lies the crux concerning jobs, an extraordinary professor had some moral expectance to become an ordinary professor.

When the university and ministry made someone an extraordinary professor, they implicitly encouraged him to remain at the university in good expectation of advancement. In the novel discussed above, Ribonius, senior adjunct or lecturer at the fictional University of Grünau, also had moral expectance of an ordinary position and became puzzled when the faculty turned cool toward him—whence his changed martial plans after being illuminated.

A problem with the institution of the extraordinary professor was this. In many cases, one became generically an extraordinary professor in the arts and philosophy faculty, without reference to a specific discipline. By traditional practices, extraordinary professors would then often apply for nearly any open professorship, regardless of their abilities or druthers. One aimed only to get a foot firmly in the faculty. Given the honored practices of opting up and pluralism (which the ministry wanted to stop), one hoped to move later into a chair for which one might actually have some interest or ability.

Cases of an extraordinary professors appointed in specific fields existed. So one finds extraordinary professors of logic, or of mathematics, and so on. But those caused other problems. Such academics absolutely expected to get the ordinary professorship in the field in question. But, in the run of time, the ministry might have had second thoughts about them or seen someone new. In sum, the extraordinary professor, as a sort of nonmandatory holding position, came in time to crystallize many dilemmas about academic appointments.

Applications for ordinary or full professorships from extraordinary professors usually had sad tales to tell. They recounted that they worked with untiring diligence for the university, but for which they received no salary. Some ruined their health and their eyesight, teaching eight to nine hours per day for fourteen years without a salary. Extraordinary professors at the same university usually had to fight with their peers for an open position. One might cite his seniority. Another could claim competence. Still another would want to succeed his father in the position. And there were—as early as 1757—already academics who knew how to toy with offers from other universities to upset the traditional system.[33]

The last candidate, the one toying with other offers and thus also with the university and ministry, embodied the modern and soon triumphant sentiments of ministerial-market rationality. Other applicants above mentioned their bodies. The body occurred in applications only usually when it had been unheroically bent or broken. Miserable applicants mentioned hours, days, years gone by in service. It personalized them, but negatively. Those who tended to narrative in applications typically legitimated lost time and bad luck. Means to personalize without lowering oneself exist. They lead from narrative, seniority, and the broken body to lists, fame, and good papers. They lead to modern academic capital.

TRADITIONAL ACADEMIC CAPITAL. Moderns tend to think an applicant should show ability for a position. That is, however, a mostly modern and rational prejudice. Conception of the academic as a specialist came as an heroic feat of the Enlightenment. Ministries wanted to impose this mentality on faculties and universities. As noted, academics themselves tended to look on the professorships or chairs—all ordinary German professorships constituted chairs—as being like canonries or, in other words, as sinecures, their actual historical point of origin.

The notion that a meritocracy governed academic appointments and advancements did not originate within academia itself. German ministries imposed the new notion. Since an academic could originally only get a salary increase by moving from a lower paying chair to a higher paying chair, or by accumulating chairs, the entire traditional, nonmeritocratic academic system worked against the notion of professorial expertise being reflected in one's chair. What one published about, if anything, was one thing. What one taught was another. In the traditional system, one's diligent teaching most manifested one's academic merit.

Arts and philosophy professors, being originally masters of arts, meaning masters of the Seven Liberal Arts and the three branches of philosophy (rational, natural, and social), presumed they could teach just about anything. Recall Professor Klotz above at the University of Halle who was willing to accept the chair of Oriental Languages at Gießen, even though he knew "neither Hebrew nor, indeed, anything Oriental."[34]

But cases exist where applicants foregrounded their desire or ability for a specific chair in view of expertise. In an application of 1694 for the chair for poetry, a candidate wrote, "[I] also find not a slight inclination to the poetical profession in myself"—and notice the nice litotes, as we shall attend often to the rhetoric and its transformation in applications. Other applicants might mention that they were practiced in the field in question, in logic or mathematics or whatnot. Extraordinary professors often discussed what they had taught, insofar as relevant, which it often might not be. But some generic extraordinary professors had specialized in this or that in their lectures, and so proclaimed it, truly or not, in applications.[35]

Mentioning academic travel, even if only planned, offered a good way to establish general and specific competency. One of the applicants in 1703 for the librarianship—an important ancillary source of income and often, alas, a sinecure—boasted of his two "completed peregrinations." Another claimed he had been in other lands and seen famous libraries, although he did not list them. Wanting to be extraordinary professor of ancient history and Oriental languages in 1713, a candidate wrote that he planned a journey to universities where biblical philology flourished. He named professors he would visit in Leiden, Utrecht, and Franecker. He would go to France and England and elsewhere. He would confer with famous scholars and acquire the knowledge and books needed.[36]

In 1727 an extraordinary professor of mathematics said he wanted to travel abroad and then receive the first open chair upon his return, although he did not specify that it be in mathematics. He wanted "to confer with learned mathematicians in France and Holland over the most difficult parts of this science" to develop better his "Genie." Applying to be extraordinary professor in physics in 1730, another candidate said that he had studied not only in Königsberg, but also at Halle and other German universities, and in Holland, where he got to know professors and went to lectures in mathematics and physics. Now he was studying "at the world famous Oxford University" but wanted to return to the fatherland.[37]

The supplicants above individuated themselves in relation to a field, in which they made contacts by traveling. They acquired a list of correspondents. Let us call that a sort of academic capital. During the early modern era, academic capital became increasingly impersonalized, less tied to the private person of the academic, more objectified in things, such as in publications. As mentioned above, a traditional, highly personalized form of academic capital, besides a list of correspondents won by traveling, lay in the private instrument and book collection. Academics advertised such things that, like travel, fell into an area between the private and the professional. In addition to an archaic—by modern lights—salary and promotion system, early modern universities did not usually have an annual budget for capital goods. That meant that capital goods, such as books and instruments, were accumulated mostly by private means and acts of academics. It also gave power to a professor's daughter, as noted.[38]

MODERN ACADEMIC CAPITAL. Since antiquity, scholars have been concerned with their fame. Early modern academics set weight on things like connections and seniority in their applications. But they knew that fame, as opposed to infamy, was a very good thing. As time went by, it became not only good but also increasingly necessary, alongside some ability. What counted was the right sort of fame and how to manufacture and circulate it.

Seventeenth and eighteenth century cameralists saw "applause" as creating fame. Locally, one's applause resided in the size and success of one's lectures, the applause generated by students' hands. German ministries desired large and loud enrollments. Academics known to "teach with applause" had recognized charisma. Applicants thus mentioned their large or loud enrollments. Extramural applause also counted, and eventually much more than local hands. Ministers heard invitations to join elite academic societies and scientific academies as extramural applause. Offers from other universities made a most impressive sound. Applicants for appointment or advancement knew that well, too.[39]

Offers from other universities did not become common until the nineteenth century, which celebrated a systematic commodification of academics, an event that occurred on the whole in German academia long before it did elsewhere, even in America. Up to and into the Romantic era, the most common means to manufacture extramural applause lay in publication. This formed at first simply an additional bit of academic capital to set alongside other things in an application. But it became in time the sine qua non of academic capital.

One of the earliest applications mentioning publications of which I know comes from 1689. In 1710, an applicant not only mentioned his dissertation but also underlined the title, as one did in the modern era with a typewriter. Recall from the previous chapter that, when someone said that they had held a public disputation, a publication typically appeared alongside. Who had written the dissertation—the candidate or his dissertation advisor—was another and potentially touchy matter. In any case, apropos publication, applicants might state this euphemistically and possibly fraudulently in terms of how many public disputations they had held. Candidates might stress further that they had, indeed, written the dissertations for the disputations. And, more to the point, candidates might add that their seemly or many publications have made them "known" or brought them "applause from the learned world."[40]

PUBLISH OR PERISH. After 1749, Prussia mandated publication. The regulation of 1749 set a minimum of two disputation-dissertations to be a lecturer. These two dissertations, the first perhaps not written by the candidate but rather by his teacher as *praeses*, traced their descent from the traditional disputations for a degree and for a place, which eventually became the modern dissertation of the doctoral candidate and the *Habilitationsschrift* of the lecturer.

After 1749, to be an extraordinary professor, one needed three more disputation-dissertations or publications. Such works amounted to the size of academic journal articles in the contemporary sense. Finally, to be an ordinary professor by the regulation, one needed three more publications. That made a minimum of seven to eight article-size publications to be an ordinary professor. Publish or perish in 1749 thus did not necessarily mean books. The ministry took its new regulation seriously, somewhat. As read at the time, the regulation enjoyed a nice bit of ambiguity, so one might make a case that, after having received the master's or doctor's degree, one needed only thee more publications to get a chair.[41]

As to be expected, after 1749 applicants mentioned their publications in the light of the new and perhaps ambiguous regulation. Candidates typically mentioned three publications, although for chairs they should seemingly have four or more. Three seems to have been some sort of magic minimum. Counting also led to a notion of competition in terms of mere numbers among applicants for the same position. Some candidates alluded to the fame of their publications. But others took the 1749 regulation as one about diligence, thus similar to being on the job on time. And in part, the ministry had that in mind.[42]

A generation before the 1749 regulation, however, competition over some positions had already led to swollen applications. In 1713 a candidate submitted a list of eleven numbered publications in his application. He claimed that others could not match his numbers. In 1715 another applicant enclosed copies of his dissertation, copies of the lecture catalogue to document his teaching, and other enclosures. In 1735 a candidate noted he had worked "with all loyalty, zeal and diligence" and enclosed a separate sheet: "My few writings published to date," with fifteen titles. An application of 1743 had a list of publications with twenty titles.[43]

Other applications before and after 1749 also swelled with lists, enclosures, publications and letters of references. Some submitted documents that contravened modern notions of confidentiality and authenticity: they enclosed ministerial documents that they seemingly should not have, but submitted them not in original but rather in transcript. It seems that some in government on occasion sent favorites their own transcripts of confidential references on their behalf, which the latter enclosed in a later application.[44]

In any case, despite early incidences of inflated applications, the foregrounding of publications accelerated after the 1749 regulation. Academic capital best realized itself in enclosures, lists, and publications. At this point, publication did not commonly testify to the candidate's competency for the position in question. Such documents, rather, attested the candidate's diligence—and fame, too, real or potential. Some other enclosures point to a sensibility about confidentiality and authenticity at odds with a later one.

## Faculty and University Reports

In the traditional academic protocol of appointment, the faculty and university reports on the candidates were the most important documents. In traditional academia, candidates could apply orally to the faculty and submit no more than their names and degrees. One applied because the faculty wrote a letter reporting that one had applied. The latter report might reduce to the place that a candidate had in the list of nominations submitted to the university.

In the traditional protocol, the faculty and university reports did not in the first instance inform a ministry about the candidates' fame, expert abilities, and so on. The faculty and university letters expressed, rather, collegial will. The faculty and university informed the ministry about the outcome of voting in the faculty council and/or academic senate. The outcomes of such votes embodied only collegial and corporate will—traditional authority.

The course of development from the Baroque through the Enlightenment dissolved the importance of such collegial and corporate will in favor of confidential advice. In short, the value of the documents examined in this section would sink, as the value of the documents in the next section—private and soon confidential letters of reference—would rise in importance. That was part of the ministerial-market rationality imposed on appointments.

In this section, we'll consider the separate cases at the chief three Prussian universities before 1800: Königsberg, Frankfurt a.d.O., and Halle. Before 1787, ministerial agendas took a different tack at each of these universities. Corporate practices and collegial will proved hardest to break at Königsberg, and easier at Frankfurt a.d.O. At Halle, founded in 1694 and seen by some as the first university conceived in the bureaucratic, cameralistic spirit, traditional academic practices would never be countenanced by the ministry.[45]

THE CASE OF KÖNIGSBERG. The University of Königsberg was in Prussia proper, but rather distant from the capital of the combined lands in Berlin, in Brandenburg. Distance, among other things, seems to have allowed the faculty and University of Königsberg to maintain their traditional collegial and corporate prerogatives longer than other Prussian universities.

In the original sense of the protocols, the faculty and university might send letters or reports with minimalist prose to ministries. So in 1691 the faculty or university could nominate candidates described only "as capable subjects." In 1713 one described the candidates together as simply "two skillful subjects." In 1694, growing expansive, the university characterized two candidates for the chair in poetry as both having a reputation "due to their good manner, qualities and poetic knowledge."[46]

In lapidary prose, as minimalist as this, where both candidates might be given only three and the same three characters, nothing distinguished them, other than the order of a list. And the list was the essence. The listing of the candidates indicated collegial will—the order of preference by the faculty, then of the university, whose leeway consisted in withholding or reordering the faculty's list. Personalizing neither themselves nor their candidates, collegial and corporate bodies—faculties and universities—sent short lists of formulaic characters in juridical protocols, which were not at all expert epistemic evaluations.

To secure the candidate of choice, a faculty or university might grow effusive and mention the good qualities of their candidate listed as number one. Such qualities typically included diligence, skillfulness, capacity, and erudition. The professor of eloquence usually gave the ceremonial speeches for the university, so a faculty or university might speak of a candidate's external appearance in this case. As early as 1659, the university used the rhetoric of foreign renown via public disputation, that is, publication, which they also stressed about applicants in 1663, 1689, and 1703. A decree to Königsberg, 28 August 1745, predating the 1749 decree for all Prussia, had in fact enjoined that candidates need "skillfulness proven by various specimens," meaning publications. Ministerial rationalizations of appointment circumscribed collegial will and eventually subverted it.[47]

When faculty and university did not get their way, then their prose waxed. Figure 7.2 from 1670 shows the Königsberg university letter nominating two candidates sent to the provincial ministry. (Before 1690, the protocol seems to have been two instead of three candidates.) The letter is signed as "Rector und Senatus dero Academie." It begins by noting the chair in history has become vacant. It is incumbent upon the university to commend two "capable" subjects for the chair. These are Goldbach(en) and Pfeiffer(n), in that order. The only qualification given both candidates, at once, is that they have lectured and disputed well here and elsewhere and proven themselves useful to academic youth.

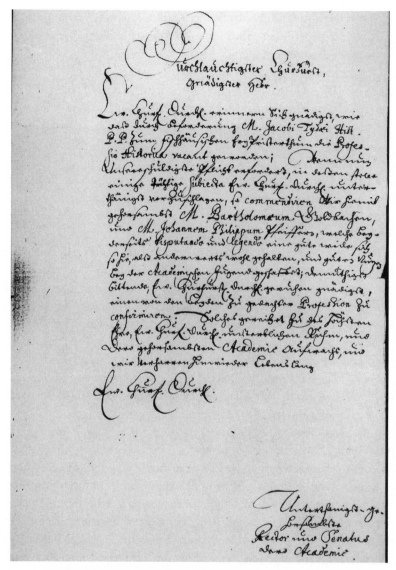

7.2. Letter from the Königsberg Rector and Academic Senate to the ministry, 1670.

But the ministry decided to appoint a certain Sand(ten). When the university heard this, they protested. They sent a letter about a page and half long, so only about twice as long as the one reproduced in figure 7.2. They asserted their right to send the list of candidates from whom the ministry was supposed to choose one. Since Goldbach and Pfeiffer were qualified, they did not see the problem. To qualify the latter two, the university simply reiterated the little it said in the first letter. The university pointed out that Sand had too many duties to be a professor. With this spare prose alone, and without any documentation, the university got its way.[48]

Martin Knutzen has one of Königsberg's best acts. In a case from 1733, the university enclosed a transcript of the faculty letter. The faculty had nominated a certain Ammon and a certain Casseburg, in that order, to be extraordinary professor of logic and metaphysics. The faculty said that they had set Ammon first, since he was the senior master in the faculty and had shown "proven knowledge." They noted, however, that Ammon had been set first "by a plurality of votes." Qualifying the vote as a plurality seems curious and indicates dissension in the faculty. The university letter contains a transcript of the faculty's, praises the candidates for diligence and good conduct, and includes their applications in original.

The university then broke protocol and mentioned the application of Knutzen, whom the faculty had not nominated. Next to Knutzens's name in the university's letter is, moreover, a large ink mark in the margin, in the same ink as the letter—a mark that highlights his name. The university provided a transcript of Knutzen's application and said that he had been praised due to his pious behavior and special capacity in fundamentals of philosophical sciences. With all candidates depicted by faculty and university in an austere manner, the effect of small details was profound. The university violated protocol by slipping in a name, availing itself of the qualified faculty vote and the edge of its pen.[49]

THE CASE OF FRANKFURT A.D.O. Königsberg in Prussia proper was distant from Berlin, while Frankfurt a.d.O. was but a long stone's throw. By the late Baroque period, acts on Frankfurt a.d.O. indicate corporate-collegial consciousness in a process of dissolution by the ministry. Ministerial acts for this university contain fewer memoranda, but more letters and original documents in fair copy—as if formal letters were no longer sent to the university. On the other hand, a surprising number of the university's own internal memoranda are in the ministry's archive—as if an absorption of the university's memory by the ministry's archive were underway. Early on, Frankfurt a.d.O. had shown an active university and faculty, and some acts look like full files. But all that changed quickly in the Baroque.[50]

Frankfurt a.d.O. fell into in a position where it had to convince the ministry to listen, so academic prose tended to some prolixity. Due to the troubles of the Thirty Years War, the ministry had left the logic chair vacant for a time. In 1636, the university and faculty wrote three pages in which they petitioned that the chair be filled. The faculty described the candidate tersely as a man of "singular dexterity" in logic, and of orthodox belief.

The university described him as a man of "singular piety, erudition, modesty and assiduousness in lecturing and disputing" who "due to such lauded qualities . . . has proven himself and is well known to us." In another long letter of four pages the university explained that, due to deaths and opting up, three chairs were now vacant. Yet, this long letter simply described the three candidates collectively as "several well talented, pious and blessed men," and then as "well qualified men," with no comments at all made of them individually.[51]

The late Baroque showed increasing incidence of direct ministerial appointment at Frankfurt a.d.O. This put the university more and more into a passive or reactive position. One finds more and more appointments in the files without any university or faculty letters, while ever more private letters of reference appear (which will be discussed in the next subsection below). In 1651, when an extraordinary professor asked the ministry to turn his position into an ordinary one, the faculty had to write a letter of protest with nine numbered points against this idea. The faculty insisted that it had the right to elect new professors, and that it was not the right of the ministry to grant such things upon private supplications.[52]

In 1688 the university responded to the ministry's query about hiring an applicant for a brand new chair without increasing the budget. That meant everyone would take a cut in pay to finance the new chair. The university was not altogether thrilled by this. One sees by their reaction that they seem not to have the right to refuse. They sent a letter listing ten reasons against the idea. Most of those related to their miserable finances. They also insisted that the faculty could teach the subject of the chair, practical philosophy, so "why should one multiply entities without necessity?" The university then dropped philosophy and attacked the person: he has not studied practical philosophy, they charged, has held no classes in the subject, and can exhibit no relevant publication.[53]

Here we see the university forced into the rhetorical stance of a lowly supplicant. The university now sends not lapidary short lists of candidates without qualities; rather, it sends prolix narratives and lists of miseries, arguments, insinuations, accusations, and defamations. It makes for sad reading. It formed part of the ministry's plot to turn tables.

THE CASE OF HALLE. The ministry did that at Halle from the outset. At the foundation of the university in 1694, the ministry made the initial appointments. Once the faculties assembled, the ministry did not desist from direct ministerial appointment. The Prussian ministry had decided from the outset that Halle would be the flagship university. And it would be a modern university, run cameralistically, without old-fashioned academic etiquettes.

Per the new custom, the ministry had not consulted the university about a ministerial appointment to the chair of poetry in 1695. The university wrote to the ministry, "Now we have not failed to ponder this matter collegially," as if the ministry cared a fig. The university letter praised the appointed person, "a man of good erudition and, as far as we know, of not bad manner, who particularly also exhibited very good specimens in German poetry, not bad for the reputation of the university. So we are altogether satisfied with his person."[54]

The university endeavored here to claim collegial-corporate rights that it had not been given. But the rhetoric, save the "collegially," was inverted. The way the university now spoke was the way that the Baroque ministry used to speak in confirming appointments. Halle showed ability now and again to push its candidates through. But one commonly finds, rather, oppositional reaction to direct ministerial appointments, envisaged or imposed.

The faculties and the university in Halle thus usually had to oppose rather than nominate candidates. They accused some candidates of atheism, lack of orthodoxy, bad morals, and questionable lifestyle. When the candidate was an extramural one, the faculty often complained that they knew nothing or not enough of him. The intramural cases still formed the largest number, as most universities bred the faculty from within. Seniority of position or time meant much to the faculty. One must move up the ladder from lecturer or adjunct, then often to extraordinary professor, and only finally to ordinary or full professor.

The most common type of critique was academic and usually concerned teaching and publishing. One pointed out lack of applause in lecture, as well as an unpleasant lecture style. Of one candidate, the faculty claimed that all students dropped out of his classes. Another applicant was an "Ignorantz." Academic capital might get no credit, as the faculty might be unimpressed by a private library. Publication constituted a big deal early on at Halle, and was bound to and at times equated with fame. Writing might be attacked at basic levels. One applicant had bad grammar. Another had plagiarized. Of one candidate for the chair of poetry, the faculty noted they had only seen German poetry, and not everyone who could rhyme German, as they said, ought to be a professor. Another candidate for the chair in poetry had problems with creditors and also published nothing distinguished—the few poems he published in German recommended him poorly to anyone who had read them.[55]

In a few acts the faculty took the best tack and used ministerial decrees against the ministry. A decree to Halle, 30 August 1723, had ordered that none be made professor who had not already published specimens of erudition. This predated the 1749 decree on publication for all Prussia—Halle was to be the flagship university. Ministerially envisaged appointments might thus be attacked in view of insufficient publication. In 1762, the faculty actually criticized the nature and size of the submitted publications of a particular applicant, claiming that the works were too short and some had appeared in a newsletter. The three publications enclosed were short, but do not seem so different from the typical dissertation then.[56]

THE DILEMMA. That was the problem with publication. The stakes went up around 1750. Given the objective criteria of counting the number or years of service or seniority, the elevated expectations of publication would have been easier to satisfy by counting the number of listed publications. But the notion of extramural fame won through "applause" or "recognized" publication exploded that criterion of evaluation, so that the professorial meritocracy would not resemble the simple grading system slowly being imposed at schools and eventually on undergraduates. The growth in the size of applications with enclosures, traced in the section above, compelled the faculty to attack the enclosures, some of which might be references from faculty members or other worthies.[57]

When Halle sent letters to the ministry, either in the name of the faculty or university, professors frequently cosigned them. That signaled their corporate-collegial weakness. Königsberg usually simply signed such letters as "Dean and Faculty" or "Rector and University," as in figure 7.2 above. That asserted corporate identity and collegial will. If entities ought not be multiplied without necessity (per Ockham's razor), the multiplication of signatures in Halle letters served to emphasize at least collective sentiment. But by their signatures they sealed their lack of authority. Like the simple style "Dean and Faculty" or "Rector and University," the minimalist rhetoric of the list of nominations in earlier letters had expressed collegial, traditional will and its rights. Those now came into jeopardy.

Whatever debates, quarrels, accusations, conspiracies, threats, and even violence took place in a faculty council or academic senate meeting should remain an oral, local, private, collegial matter of the faculty or senate. Such things should not concern a higher body, be it the university over the faculty, or the ministry over the university. Negotiations producing faculty or university lists used to be the secret of the collegial body, whose final resolution appeared before a higher body only as a list of names without qualities, save their order.

This collegial, lapidary, traditional prose succumbed to the prolixity of rationalizing documents. Ministerially driven appointments, based on advice of select academics, made demands for more information and forced faculty and university to personalize themselves and their candidates. One had to turn to and on enclosures. This made collegial will seem perniciously subjective, as a cacophony of documents contradicting one another began to pile up. As faculty and university needed to explain, legitimate, and protest more and more, they had to qualify, differentiate, and oppose individuals, beyond the ritual of the list. Ministerial rationality ironically made the university appear collegially irrational.

## Letters of Reference and Recommendation

This section surveys letters by individuals or a group on behalf of an applicant sent to faculties or universities or ministries. In the course of the early modern era, the weight of ministerial interest shifted from collegial letters written by faculties and universities, treated in the section above, to favor instead the more singular letters of reference by individuals. That shift does not embody simply a new ministerial preference for one sort of traditional authority—private patronage—in place of another—collegial will.

The ministry tended, rather, to see letters by individuals as testimony and, later, as well-informed advice. This rhetoric formed part of the great transition from grace and will in the Baroque era, to the rational authority of knowledge and calculation in the Enlightenment. The collegial will of the faculty looked less and less rational when set beside letters of recommendation from famous or expert academics, who spoke interested in only truth.

Charismatic powers begin to meet here. The charismatic power of great ministers recognizes the charismatic power of special academics. Ministers confidentially consult with the latter chosen ones, who help to recognize new ones. The notion of the academic call or vocation (*Berufung*) is old. In the traditional sense, a collegial vote stood behind the call, even if the sovereign's ministries had made it. In the modern era, the call would lose its traditional sense and acquire a rational cast, as well as a charismatic aura of "recognition."[58]

FROM TESTIMONY TO ADVICE. A letter of reference in the Baroque and early Enlightenment typically meant writing a brief note. It often attested to little else beyond diligence which, as we saw, was how many viewed publication. The little else attested might involve erudition, knowledge, good applause, character, and/or piety. A candidate might be said to have shown merit above others, but no grades or more formal evaluation commonly appeared. Such letters have a distinct air of the juridical and legalistic about them. They seem more like legal testimony under oath than recommendation or evaluation of epistemic merit. Only during the Enlightenment would the letter of reference generally assume the latter, modern form.[59]

Forced to become "modern" very early at the University of Frankfurt a.d.O., a certain Professor Omichius wrote a letter of reference in such a vein in 1627. It concerned the professor of logic, Magirius, who wanted to switch to the chair of eloquence, which probably paid more. Thereupon, the university wanted Lecturer Gustenhofer to get the chair of logic. Omichius pushed the case of Magirius, saying the latter was the best-qualified intramural candidate. Magirius had shown ability in print and had a special desire and interest in this profession. Of Gustenhofer, Omichius wrote that he had spent most of his time studying philosophy, especially logic, and had published a dissertation. Cleverly painting the applicant as someone with fame, Omichius wrote that Gustenhofer could also get a position elsewhere. Probably acting actually on the university's behalf, Omichius spoke the language of devotion to duty and subject, which the ministry apparently already wished to hear, even though a case of traditional intramural musical chairs and opting up was at play here.[60]

By the eighteenth century, good letters of reference mentioned a candidate's academic capital, either traditional or modern. Letters might mention the academic travels of applicants, performed or planned. Recommenders alluded to the books and instruments owned by applicants, or their need for a salary to buy them in the first place. A good letter of reference might point to a candidate's applause, and by so doing itself add to it. As time went on, a letter of reference had best mention the candidate's specimens of erudition, noting that they had been "greeted with applause by the learned world." In view of the rationalizing ministry's bents, a valuable letter of reference mentioned the skill, talent, and knowledge of the candidate, as well as his fame, evinced in his garnered applause.[61]

We noted in the section above that the University of Halle often had to oppose the enclosures in applications. A letter of reference at Halle might then in turn oppose a faculty's opposition. A certain Roloff penned such a piquant letter of reference for a certain Otto. In 1734 Roloff wrote to say the faculty's critique of Otto was prejudiced. Roloff knew Otto, who "has such strong applause that the ordinary professors are jealous." The charge that he taught the Wolffian philosophy was not true. (Wolff was the professor who had been banished in 1723 and had not yet returned triumphant to Prussia.) Roloff's son had attended lectures by Otto and so was himself well informed. Roloff suggested Otto be allowed to prove himself by presiding at a public disputation to unveil the faculty's plot.[62]

WOLFF'S FILES. Figures 7.3 and 7.4 show two letters by the philosopher Leibniz in support of Wolff being made professor at Halle in 1706. The letters exemplify what the enlightened Prussian ministry eventually wanted to see in letters of reference.

Figure 7.3 is a reference from Leibniz to the ministry. It is astutely writ-

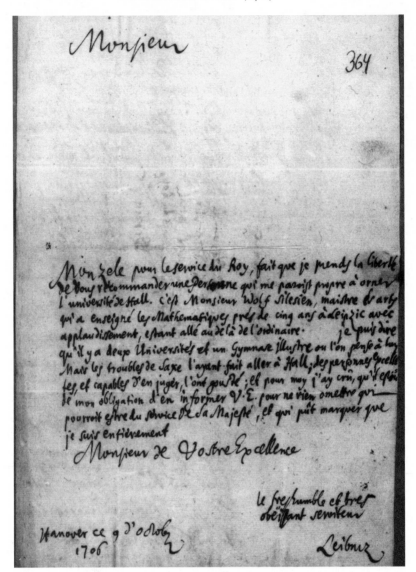

7.3. Letter of reference for Christian Wolff by Leibniz, 1706.

ten and is in French. That gives it more credit at the ministry. Leibniz says
that he wants to take the opportunity to recommend someone who would
adorn the university. It's Monsieur Wolff, a master of arts who has been
teaching mathematics at Leipzig for five years with applause. Two universities and a *gymnasium illustre* are interested in Wolff. But current troubles

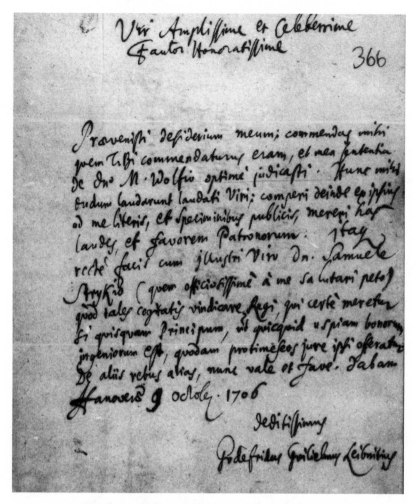

7.4. Letter of reference for Christian Wolff by Leibniz, 1706.

in Saxony lead Wolff to want to come to Prussia and Halle. Excellent persons, capable of judging, favor him. So Leibniz believes it his duty to inform the king about the matter.

In this small space, Leibniz spun a mininarrative—narrative may be interestingly more positive in a letter of reference than in a candidate's own letter of application. Without giving details, Leibniz made Wolff seem most attractive. Leibniz's second letter, figure 7.4, went to Hofmann, Halle's prorector, thus titular chief officer. The letter is in Latin and again astutely penned. Leibniz says that Hofmann has written him about someone, Wolff, whom Leibniz himself wanted to recommend. Respected men have praised Wolff to Leibniz, who himself can vouch for Wolff from letters and publications. So it's good that Hofmann and such an illustrious man as Stryk—to whom he sends his greetings—push Wolff's case.

Hofmann then penned a reference to the ministry. He wrote in German and related that Halle currently had no capable mathematics professor. He stressed the need of teaching this discipline. There was a Master Wolff in Leipzig who had been teaching mathematics for five years and had edited all mathematics passages in the *Acta eruditorum*, a famous journal. But due to the wars, Wolff wanted to leave Leipzig. Hofmann has written to Leibniz, who described Wolff as "the greatest mathematician of the era." Leibniz "not only gave him a laudatory reference for this discipline, but also recommended him in the enclosed reference for Your Excellency." Hofmann went on to write that Wolff has distinguished himself so much that other famous mathematicians, such as Hamberger in Jena and Bernoulli in Basel, have praised him as well.[63]

From the above letters of reference for Wolff, one cannot tell who initiated all this. There is no application at all from Wolff in the extant file. Hofmann implies in his reference that he initiated the appointment. His last remarks above, moreover, indicate that Leibniz's reference to the ministry was sent to him. In any case, Wolff had clever handlers at first. His later problems, leading to his banishment in 1723, followed by his expensive comeback to Prussia, are beyond this book's scope to detail. But let us look briefly and at Wolff's negotiations in 1715 for a salary increase, as it contains fewer puzzles.[64]

As reference he has again a letter in French, with a duplicate, and both unsigned! The reference claims Wolff is recognized, even in foreign lands, since he has published much and in the *Acta eruditorum*. Wolff is able in his profession and, next to a certain Hermann, is without parallel in mathematics in Germany. As mathematics professor, Wolff has but a small salary, from which he must buy expensive instruments. He has done his duty and has contributed to the renown of the university. Mathematics is "the adornment of nobility and necessary for military arts." The reference mentions strategies to turn up extra money for Wolff. Here one might suspect that a confidential advisor at the university or even someone in the ministry has penned this. The reference treats of Wolff's character, and concedes that he has had his problems with colleagues. But "good and sublime mathematicians are so rare, their studies so difficult, and cannot be done by every sort of genius."[65]

To sum up: the letters from Leibniz above have an air of courtly patronage and informed advice. Short as they are, they are more effusive than the Baroque professorial testimonials with which we began above. Leibniz's mininarrative is an effective tack in a reference. The letter of Hofmann, the Halle prorector, about Leibniz's letters moved even more in the direction of evaluation, as opposed to mere testimony. Hofmann reported the extramural specialists in question—famous and foreign mathematicians—who had praised Wolff.[66]

By the middle of the Enlightenment, the rationalizing ministry would want references more like Hofmann's, or at least like Leibniz's. Mere professorial testimony or courtly favor would no longer be enough. Or, rather, they must be cast in the new rhetoric of advice from the expert or famous, best given in absolute confidence to the ministry. Movement in the direction of such advice lay in waxing about extramural applause and renown, especially among the luminous and expert. Hofmann's letter above on behalf of Wolff may serve as an ultimate exemplar of the new era dawning in enlightened Prussia, one in which epistemic evaluation became key and second only to the charisma won by academic commodification.

## Mediating Ministerial Reports

The University of Königsberg stood under the supervision of a provincial ministry, which called itself the Königsberg Preußische Regierung (hereafter KPR). This section treats only of the KPR, which first made itself felt in the acts in the 1690s.

Thanks to the KPR, the Königsberg acts began to collect into the fourfold nesting, traced in a section above. The KPR signed its report with the names of its members. Its reports expressed no collegial will, even if voting had gone on. Indeed, it inverted traditional notions. The essence of faculty and university letters had consisted in the communication of an ordered short list as voted, and in need of no comment. But the KPR obliterated all traces of collegial action or a vote on its part in a report. It communicated an informed ministerial view, expert advice. Its provincial rationality sublimated the irrationality of academics.

PROVINCIAL RATIONALITY. The KPR tended to some prolixity in its prose. It conveyed not its will; it, rather, evaluated and advised. Violating traditional protocols, the KPR's reports sometimes added names not nominated by a faculty or the university. In 1690 for the chair of eloquence, the KPR added three names beyond the two nominated by the university. For the first of its own nominees, Schreiber, the KPR wrote his name in bold characters, using the edge of the pen, so that his name above all others leapt at a glance from the page. The KPR praised his singular talent and laudable specimens. In another letter, the KPR commented that he had good recommendations. The KPR raised the issue of his appearance, which was fine, it noted. But Schreiber had, alas, not graduated. The KPR offered the names of four other cases of nongraduates being made professor—it pulled out all the stops for him.[67]

To the university's mandated two suggestions for a position in 1691, the KPR added five others with a few words on each. The chair here was in po-etry again. Of one of their own nominations, the KPR said that poetry flowed from him very well. To be fair, the provincial ministry noted that one of the university's nominees also wrote nice poetry. So the KPR read at least poetical publications when making its informed judgments, or so it claimed. In some other cases, too, the KPR explicitly let Berlin know that it read candidates' publications.[68]

Despite best intentions, personal considerations for a supplicant often drove the KPR. In 1694 it endorsed the university's candidate and added that he had "already been waiting many years for promotion." Indeed, con-cerning Gütther in 1743, who had been trying to get promises of a chair af-ter years of frustration, the KPR supported him in view, in the first instance, "of the seniority of his many years as [extraordinary] professor . . . not to mention the many well crafted ideas and writings whereby the supplicant has made himself already known and famous with the public and learned world."[69]

In the case of Knutzen, discussed above, the KPR grasped the univer-sity's attempt to subvert the faculty. The faculty had nominated Ammon and Casseburg. The university had broken protocol and added Knutzen to the list. The KPR reported this, restating the faculty's vote for Ammon. The KPR mentioned Knutzen, but remarked that Ammon had taught "al-ready many years as a master" and had "exhibited his skillfulness, so well merits the preference above the others." The KPR subverted the university's subversion of the faculty, and did so again in view of traditional notions, in this case, the seniority of service.[70]

That was the great dilemma of bureaucratic rationality in the provinces. Regarding the individual scholar, academic capital achieved not only its modern form of fame wrought by writing, but also retained traditional traces, such as time served or seniority, a collegial surrogate for merit in evaluation of persons. But the KPR usually tried to think like the central ministry in Berlin, thus more in terms of expertise than of seniority.

SENIORITY VERSUS SPECIALTY. Three applied in 1753 for the chair in Greek: extraordinary professor of Oriental languages Kÿpke, ex-traordinary professor of eloquence Hahn, and master of arts Engelschmidt.

A transcript of the faculty letter sets this order: Kÿpke, Hahn, Engelschmidt. The faculty notes that Kÿpke lectures with approval, has enough publications (by the 1749 regulation), knows Greek well enough and has "made himself known." The last is formulaic and does not imply that his publications are about Greek. The faculty says that Hahn is also worthy, but has not the required number of publications. Finally, the faculty notes that Engelschmidt knows Greek best and, though he does not have the needed publications, soon could. The faculty has, however, put him third. By the way, despite the faculty's remarks above, Kÿpke and Hahn appear to me to have four publications each.

The university letter lists the three in the faculty's preferred order. Of Kÿpke the university remarks that, as extraordinary professor of Oriental languages, he expects the chair, but also has lectured on Greek with laudable effort. Of Hahn the university says that he seems fine, too. Of Engelschmidt they note that he has concentrated on Greek.

The tension between seniority and specialty is now apparent. About the above, the KPR says that Kÿpke is, "to be sure, a skillful man," who has lectured in Königsberg for seven years "with laudable diligence." But he has concentrated on Hebrew and other "Oriental languages." Of Hahn the KPR notes he has the capacity to teach Greek. The KPR then turns to Master Engelschmidt, whom it recommends: he has concentrated on Greek, publishes on it, and was once recommended as extraordinary professor in Greek. The provincial ministry here prefers specialty, the "rational," over seniority, the traditional.[71]

Three years later, the KPR explicitly discussed such issues. In 1756 the faculty and university voted for the following. Hahn, extraordinary professor of eloquence, would become adjunct of logic and metaphysics with expectance of the chair. Gregorov, currently extraordinary professor of logic and metaphysics, would renounce his expectance of that chair. Such musical chairs epitomized traditional ways, where appointment and advancement were essentially intramural, and seniority the primary device to impersonalize such decisions.

Concerning the faculty and university vote, the KPR raised the central issue troubling the rationalizing ministry: promotion via seniority as opposed to expertise in the chair in question. The KPR remarked that extraordinary professors presumed they had a right to an ordinary chair, and thought in terms of seniority. The circle grew vicious since, once an individual acquired an extraordinary professorship, younger scholars ceased concentrating on the subject, because they presumed that the extraordinary professor had blocked that discipline for the near future. What the KPR left out, but was clear at the time, was that the extraordinary professor would try to get the next open ordinary chair, almost regardless of the subject, since academics thought more in terms of seniority than specialty.

The KPR picked up the thread and related that, in view of the above, it could often not find competent (intramural) candidates for positions that suddenly opened. The KPR advised abolishing extraordinary professorships and appointing professors directly out of the pool of lecturers, by implication, in view of specialty. As for this case, the KPR again showed itself a provincial ministry with a traditional face. It did not want to stand in candidate Hahn's way by recommending that he not receive the chair. But Berlin would stand firm here.[72]

So the dilemma of the provincial ministry where one might go native and think like archaic academics. The KPR could be led astray by its proximity, such as in the case when Kÿpke and Hahn had competed in 1755 for the chair in eloquence, which the dying Gütther wanted to pass on to his stepson, Werner. As typical for the eloquence chair, this act has remarks on external appearance. The KPR noted that Hahn was "no orator and has neither the needed exterior nor other requisites," but that Werner, whom the university had listed in fourth place(!), was well developed in body, "vom Leibe gut gewachsen."

Other remarks in its letter suggest that Werner might have been related to a member of the KPR, which praised his Latin and publications, and then moved to semiarchaic academic capital. Werner had the library of his stepfather and the financial ability to purchase more books.[73]

This and other acts show the collision of the two systems for evaluation of academics. One was collegial and traditional. The other was bureaucratic and rationalized, based on objective merit as expertise, above mere publication taken as an exhibition of diligence or fame. Though able to rationalize acts, the KPR as a provincial ministry succumbed from lack of distance to the scent and sight of candidates, who might have served for years awaiting promotion, who might be sons-in-law of professors or nephews of members of the KPR, and who might have collections of private capital, still crucial even to modernizing universities.

## The Central Ministry

For the combined lands of Brandenburg-Prussia, the central ministry was in Berlin, the capital city. The central ministry completed the act of any appointment or advancement. Its file folder, which also served as a writing surface for the memorandum, enclosed all the paperwork from lower instances—faculty, university, provincial ministry—and other paperwork that found its way to the central ministry outside those instances or channels.

At one extreme, a file at the central ministry's archive (*Geheimes Staatsarchiv,* called the *Preußischer Kulturbesitz*) might be completely empty, with only the file folder used as a writing surface. At the other extreme, the file might include hundreds of pages of documents, with central ministerial files inside central ministerial files inside central ministerial files, or any other conceivable combinations and contortions of documents and folders.

In the ideal case described above for Königsberg, there would be a fourfold nesting of files in the acts, running from a faculty file or letter at dead center, through the files of the university and a provincial ministry, and ending with the central ministry's enveloping file folder. The central ministry's memorandum on the decision would be recorded there, as well as the drafts of letters and other documents for the writing of the fair copy letters to be sent confirming or disconfirming the appointment or advancement in question.

BAROQUE MEMORANDA. In the Baroque era, the ministry embodied traditional authority. It based decisions rhetorically on will or mere ministerial authority. In the Enlightenment, the ministry would embody, rather, rational authority, basing its decisions rhetorically more on knowledge. Such is the rhetoric of the acts. It could be that the eighteenth-century ministry acted ultimately in a more authoritarian a manner than the seventeenth-century ministry had. In fact, I believe it did. In the Enlightenment, however, the ministry rationalized its acts.

Baroque ministerial memoranda—that is, what appears on the file folder and, if need be, on added ministerial documents—speak mostly in an austere, ritualistic manner. On appointments, excepting the actual installation into the position, this prose favors passive voice, especially for qualifying the candidate. A nearly canonical phrase is, "To Us . . . has X been lauded (*gerühmt*)." *Rühmen* (to praise or laud) and *Ruhm* (fame) are central notions of early modern German academia and for which no completely adequate translation exists. But the realm of rumor does not lie far away. Someone has been lauded, that is, recommended to the ministry, so that person is being appointed. That is what the central ministry tells itself.

In the traditional protocol, the laudation supposedly came from the faculty and university letters, especially from the ranking of the two or three candidates nominated. The absolutist and authoritarian ministry of the Enlightenment, however, listened to laudations of whomever it chose, including letters of reference from famous men. The austere prose in most ministerial memoranda does not typically allow space for noting who had extolled the virtues of the chosen candidate. When a file is a full one, then one can often surmise that. When the file is thin or empty, then one need look elsewhere or have no idea.

ENLIGHTENED MEMORANDA. The eighteenth century did not lack austere ministerial prose, but the incidence of prolixity rose noticeably. A ministerial memorandum might refer to specific academic capital in rationalizing an appointment. Travel or a *Bildungsreise* might thus be noted. Teaching interested the ministry, so an applicant's applause might also be noted. Extramural *Ruhm* or fame eventually mattered most and meant above all famous publications. In 1734, the central ministry told Otto, whom we met above, to publish more and thus disarm critics in the Halle faculty. The memorandum here referred to the decree of 1723 sent Halle on publication. The ministry told another candidate in 1740 to submit "several specimens" of his work for consideration, since it pursued a policy to appoint only professors "who have already made themselves known in the world by learned writings."[74]

In some acts, ministerial memoranda raised the regulation of 1749, which had set numbers of publications for appointment. In one case in 1755, the ministry put it this way: to be an ordinary professor, one must "either have made oneself famous (*berühmt*) by writings, or at least disputed thrice as *praeses*, and so have shown one's skillfulness" in published dissertations, the latter being the weakened application of the regulation of 1749. So the ministry had turned a candidate down in 1750 since he did not have the stipulated number of publications. And, appointing a candidate as extraordinary professor in 1756, for example, one noted his fulfillment of the 1749 regulation. But regulations could be waived. As we saw above, a certain Werner, the stepson of the dying chair-holder and perhaps related to someone in the KPR, was fast-tracked in 1754/55 with only two publications. He was first made extraordinary professor, then given available extra emoluments, then appointed to his stepfather's chair over Kÿpke, who had more seniority and more publications.[75]

If the ministry considered a candidate without knowing anything of his applause or writings, the ministry might confess ignorance and ask the university. And the ministry might even read the publications. Influenced by the KPR's praise of a candidate's poetry in 1691, Berlin, too, expressed approval. Of another applicant to professor of poetry, Berlin commented in 1741, "The poetry is pretty good." Corrections in one memorandum of 1776 show an alteration toward modernity. The original memorandum appointed the candidate to poetry professor in view of his "good poetic talent." That was then was crossed out; the memorandum now implied not that the professor wrote poetry, as had been traditionally expected, but rather had literary knowledge of poetry, that is, could talk and write about it.[76]

FATTENING UP THE ACTS. Even the Baroque ministry hatched plots. Acts on Frankfurt a.d.O. of 1611 and 1630 indicate how the ministry short-circuited the protocols behind the scenes and acts. Both acts suggest that the ministry had taken the initiative, writing informally to the university to tell them whom they should nominate. Only during the Enlightenment did the ministry simply blatantly expropriate such rights and make direct appointments.[77]

Many ministerial plots involved procuring extramural talent. For the mathematics chair at Frankfurt a.d.O., the university had recommended the eldest son of one of the medical professors in December 1701. A ministerial memorandum of 6 January 1702 discussed the matter and raised the name of an unnominated candidate, L. C. Sturm, who taught outside Prussia. As with most extramural calls, this act grew fat. Correspondence went back and forth between the ministry, university, and others. In the next to last document, 30 January 1704, Sturm submitted, among other things, his moving expenses broken into three categories: (1) books, (2) furniture and instruments, (3) family. It was an interesting ordering.[78]

By the 1730s, memoranda reveal more plotting by the central ministry. It has projects. To make direct ministerial appointments, it needs to look far and wide. Acting on supposed knowledge overtakes simple will. Acts get fatter. The ministry temporizes and grows prolix, but can keep this secret. It corresponds confidentially with cognoscenti, one-on-one. Thus most outside the ministry have no inkling how much more loquacious it has become.

In recruiting a certain Schultze in 1731/32, a protodossier appears in the acts. Memoranda are lost inside memoranda inside memoranda, looking for "skillful" subjects. In searching for a new professor in 1729/30, memoranda get chatty and span an entire year: If we want Gruber for the chair, can we get his release from Hanover, where he's writing the history of the dynasty? If he declines the call, one could find a capable subject at Leipzig, Jena, or elsewhere. It's clear we've got to get an external subject who's made himself known in the world by learned writings and good applause. There is Buder in Jena, who's only an extraordinary professor, so cheaper to get. What do you think if we offer him the chair plus an extraordinary slot in law, with a total salary of five hundred thaler?[79]

The ministry thus weighs and targets subjects for acquisition, as one would call it. The ministry notes Halle's decline in enrollment and takes action in 1730: Chairs must be filled with "solid professors who have not only the needed capacity, but also established renown in the world" to attract students. For two positions in philosophy, a 1733 memorandum lists five candidates to consider targeting for acquisition. Trying to fill a chair in 1765, the ministry may lament to the king, "[A]fter much correspondence and trouble, [I] have found an extramurally famous (*berühmten*) professor . . . whose philosophical writings and teaching have won him a distinguished reputation amongst the learned."[80]

The ministry indicates above, however indirectly, its troubled body or tired hand. Calls by other universities can cause headaches, too. Professor Klotz—whom, as we saw above, the Hesse-Darmstadt ministry wanted to acquire and make professor of Oriental languages, although he knew nothing "Oriental"—has gotten a call to Warsaw in 1756. Halle pays Klotz five hundred thaler, but the wily Poles have offered twelve hundred! Klotz has a "great reputation" and "thorough knowledge of Antiquity and Greek," along with good Latin. But he is not a "distinguished" teacher. Nor is he Prussian. In view of his "character" (and the money), it's going to be hard to keep him. So the ministry recommends letting him go.[81]

ARCHAIC CAPITAL. In regard to traditional aspects of academic capital, a memorandum may be of two minds. In some cases a memorandum admits nepotism in giving a position, as in 1658: "due to the merit of his deceased father as well as his singular genius." But nepotism, if known to the ministry, must eventually fade from a rationalizing memorandum. Thus in 1746 the ministry rebuffed Hahn's attempt to make his son adjunct to his chair, despite university approval. The ministry acted in part because nepotism would violate seniority here. Other more senior academics were already in line for the chair.[82]

It is rather shocking, then, that the ministry confessed in 1770 that the candidate, who had in fact made a reputation through various publications, was also the eldest son of the previous chair-holder. All in all, the central ministry grew wary of appointments driven by nepotism or other traditional academic practices. Berlin wanted a new breed of rationalizing academics.[83]

When the ministry rejected a candidate in 1756, it made an important remark. It said that seniority played no part in promotions, which must be made solely and alone for publication of useful and reasonable writings and disputations, as well as teaching. That was the new policy. But a year later, a certain Weber cited no publications in his quest to foil Eberhard's plot to use a call from Jena to get the next open chair. Weber argued, rather, from pure seniority, and got his way, as the memorandum praised his "applause . . . and merited trust," as well as good service to the university. Even rationalizing Berlin might be so moved.[84]

Personal sympathy could also move Berlin. But it removed such traces from its final memorandum. A certain Thomson wished to come back to Königsberg in 1732. The two earliest memoranda (423r, 426r) reflect the personal motifs. Of the candidate they note "his father's death" and need "to assist his mother and siblings." Should we help Thomson, "who otherwise counts as a skillful man," in view of such a most humble request? It is known "that he studied well" in Königsberg. A memorandum (422) repeats the personal details and says in its first version, "Thomson, who otherwise is supposed to be no unskillful man." The memorandum is amended as, "Thomson, who otherwise counts as a very skillful man."

The litotes and indirect discourse of the initial version become not only positive and more direct, but a "very" also now qualifies his skillfulness, not without eloquence in this austere ministerial prose. The ministry has made a decision to help poor Thomson. The final memorandum (421r) mentions that Thomson is an evangelical preacher, whose "erudition and skillfulness have been most servilely lauded (*gerühmt*) to Us . . . ," with no more note of death and abandonment in the family. This effaces a narrative of personal supplication into enlightened ministerial rationality. Like its growing prolixity and fattened acts, Berlin's lapses into subjectivity and sentimentality apparently now must be kept confidential.[85]

This survey of the central ministry in enlightened Berlin ends now with a look at four interesting cases, parts of which we considered in various sections above. They are those, first, of Knutzen, the teacher of Immanuel Kant, second, of Kÿpke, a one-time landlord of Kant, third, of Kant himself, and finally of Christian Wolff, whose philosophy Kant toppled.

THE CASE OF KNUTZEN. Recall that the university had tried to subvert the faculty by putting a transcript of Knutzen's application into its own letter. The KPR subverted the university's subversion by citing the faculty's choice for Ammon. The KPR noted that it also thought the latter should be set first. The KPR's report is dated 20 November 1733. But a decree from the royal residence in Potsdam, dated 5/8 November, gave Knutzen the position. This royal decree is thus dated before the KPR wrote its report, and is dated but three to five days after the university dated its letter, 3 November, in which Knutzen's name appeared for the first time.

The faculty letter (481r) had noted that its list had been decided by a plurality of votes. Looking at the last few dates above, it appears that the dean of the faculty, who wrote the report mentioning the mere plurality for Ammon, together with the rector, went outside normal channels and sent a secret letter to Potsdam. Other ministerial documents show the workings from 10 to 28 November, the last being the date when Berlin confessed the truth to the KPR: Knutzen had been appointed before 20 November by a royal decree from Potsdam. This act shows the faculty as well as the ministries in both Königsberg and Berlin to have been seemingly outdone by intrigues of individuals writing confidential letters.[86]

THE CASE OF KŸPKE. The 1750s was the crucial decade in Prussia for the liquidation of the traditional system of collegiality. Kÿpke, from whom the young Kant rented rooms for a time, partook of three separate and interesting competitions in the 1750s. Kÿpke, Hahn, and Engelschmidt were last left trying to get the chair for Greek, and having been listed in that order by both faculty and university. The KPR's report of 23 February had, however, favored Engelschmidt, as he had the most expertise in Greek, over Kÿpke, who had been listed first in view of seniority and sufficient publications (four), though not in Greek.

On 9 March Berlin wrote a memorandum giving Kÿpke the job. The next day the king in Potsdam informed Berlin that he had promised the job to his field-preacher, Bock, named by nobody—faculty, university, the KPR, Berlin—in the normal channels. Berlin then tried to kill Kÿkpe's appointment on 11 March, but the letter offering him the job might have gotten into the mail, since a memorandum of 15 April closed this sad act, removing the chair from Kÿpke. This is embarrassing since it shows that, behind Berlin's p(r)ose of ministerial rationality, pure patronage and political authority too often still lurked.[87]

THE CASE OF KANT. Kant also proved embarrassing to Prussia, even before it symbolically ended the Enlightenment by silencing him politically. The young Kant had been, if a blessing in one regard, a problem in another. Kant had been a modern academic, in ministerial views, by putting devotion to his chosen subjects, logic and metaphysics, above money. Thus when Königsberg had offered its Lecturer Kant the chair in eloquence in 1764, he had said no, thereby saying no to the premodern practice of musical chairs and opting up.

In Berlin's new view, Kant embodied the good modern academic, wishing to be wedded for life to one subject, and willing to remain a lecturer till a fitting position opened. Kant had been, however, in another respect no good modern subject. One of Berlin's plots involved moving Kant to Halle, Prussia's flagship university, since none existed then in Berlin. The central ministry went so far as to pen not only a plan, but the appointment, too, without telling Kant. He was appointed ordinary professor of mathematics and philosophy at Halle "due to his thorough learning and his publication of useful writings."[88]

Kant could have legitimated devotion to this chair, but refused now for provincial reasons. He did not want to leave his hometown. In this light, Kant revealed himself antimodern. He stayed in Königsberg pursuing the "lousy existence" of a lecturer. Finally fed up, he was on the verge of answering a call outside Prussia, to Erlangen in 1769/70. To get him a chair in Königsberg, a panicky Berlin tolerated what it now hated: musical chairs.

When the chair of mathematics fell vacant in 1770, Berlin allowed the chair-holder in logic and metaphysics, Buck, to move over to mathematics (perhaps with extra emoluments), so that Kant could get logic and metaphysics. The empty but rare fair copy memorandum, doubtlessly a bit embarrassed, says, "But instead of Buck I can recommend no one as teacher of philosophy who would bring the university more use than M[agister] Kant, famous (*berühmten*) inside and outside Germany by his writings."[89]

THE CASE OF WOLFF. Christian Wolff was the ultramodern academic. Around his recall to Prussia grew one of the fattest files, a proto-dossier in the Prussian ministry, outdoing in size even the act of his earlier banishment. During the long negotiations, whose crucial points lay between 12 August and 21 November 1740 (466–67, 481–85), Wolff extorted a great deal from Berlin. The memorandum of 21 November says that Wolff, "as is known, has made himself famous far and wide by his intelligence (*genie*), skillfulness, thorough erudition and reasonable teaching, as well as his other laudable (*rühmliche*) qualities." The memorandum goes on to say, incredibly, that "he may teach whatever he wants."

Used as one may be by now to the usually austere prose of ministerial memoranda, one can see that Wolff had been recalled not without much ado. The memorandum was in part, by its prolixity, legitimating not only Wolff's freedom to teach without censorship, but also an outrageous sum of money. Wolff negotiated for handsome travel expenses. But his celestial salary and titles—privy councilor, vice-chancellor, ordinary professor of law, and ordinary professor of mathematics—raised him to the academic firmament.[90]

Interesting in that light is a bit of gossip from an undated letter of a certain J. H. Böhmer to the great Hanoverian minister, Münchhausen, who had just set out to acquire the faculty for the soon-to-be-opened university in Göttingen. Münchhausen understood academics who drove hard bargains. Böhmer related, confidentially of course, that while in Berlin he had heard that the King of Prussia was to have said, "He has to get that guy (*Kerl*) [Wolff] back to Halle, cost what it will." Prussian ministerial rationality found perfection in the commodification of academics. Just as the enlightened and Romantic interests of ministries and markets dovetailed in the notion of the "publicity" of the lecture catalogue, so would they also dovetail in the notion of the "celebrity" of the professor.[91]

### From the Supreme School Council to the Ministry of Culture, 1787–1817

That grew more apparent in the crucible of Prussian culture. The creation of the Prussian Supreme School Council, the *Oberschulkollegium* (OSK), in 1787 further rationalized Prussian academic collection. Inspection of the apparatus in the schema of abbreviations—just ahead of the bibliography—shows that up to 1787 the Prussian archive collected paperwork at the primary level around provinces. After 1787, at least for academic matters, the primary level for collection became ministerial (Rep. 76 in the archive), at first under the OSK in 1787, and after 1817 under the new ministry of culture, the *Kultusministerium*.

THE OSK. This ministry still collected at the secondary level around universities. But at the tertiary level the OSK dissolved the faculties. While still seeing universities, the OSK now more clearly managed individual academics, as opposed to collegial bodies. I had expected academic dossiers to emerge at that point—in 1787—in the ministry and archive. But they did not. The tertiary level remained simply chronological, with all faculties bundled together.

The apparatus in the abbreviations shows, however, a regularization in archiving after 1800, and even earlier for Halle. Fascicles or bundles enclose at most three years and usually less. At least for a time, the OSK or archivists appended an index at the front of fascicles. The primary persons in the acts structured the indices. The ministry thus enhanced its ability to recollect academic acts, even if it eventually returned to old ways of filing.

As it cast an ever-greater shadow over the land, becoming all seeing and all knowing in its rhetorical pose, ministerial memory grew tormented by details. Academic acts took longer and longer and longer for Berlin to deliberate. The right person for the job proved harder and harder to recognize. For, if not simple seniority and connections, but rather fame and a cacophony of informed advice hold sway over applications, references, and appointments of academics, who is fully immune to some sort of academic critique?

By 1788 some academics wrote directly to the OSK. To one the OSK gave a gruff reply: Up till now the professor title has been given only to those who have made themselves known by learned writings and lectures. "It is noteworthy that the supplicant, as a young medical doctor, who is completely unknown to the Oberschulkollegium, should apply." The circle turned vicious on the supplicant, who was writing to become known unto the OSK. It seems that, when one was unknown to the OSK, it reflected one's academic status, not the OSK's ignorance. If a supplicant approached with more humility, or if the OSK (renamed the *Oberschul-Department*) felt more kindly, it might greet supplication with "the advice . . . to keep on making yourself known by writings and public lectures."[92]

After the OSK's birth in 1787, the KPR survived in the acts for a time. But an individual "curator" in Königsberg, an office that had existed since 1743, replaced the KPR early in the nineteenth century. The fourfold nesting of Königsberg files continued for a time after 1787, but also soon faded. The central ministry in Berlin and the Königsberg curator soon dominated the Königsberg acts in correspondence with one another or with select academics, whom they used as expert and confidential advisors to target, weigh, defame, or court other academics for acquisition or not. Collegial bodies appeared, especially right after 1787, but soon grew more and more silent, and spoke only when spoken to.

When the Königsberg faculty and university wrote, now it was after having been asked for an opinion of a ministerial plan. The OSK initiated envisaged acts, on which the faculty and university and the KPR, or its altered versions, might be asked for a report, that is, a reaction. Academic initiative ceased being essentially collegial. It became personal instead. For the university to get the jump on the ministry, an academic must unexpectedly die or depart. The OSK also reacted to the initiative of supplicants. In such cases, it usually spoke as to the supplicant above: Put more of yourself onto paper. To one supplicant the OSK wrote that it wanted a list of publications and perhaps enclosures of them. Having six works in three years, the supplicant found favor.

The OSK made itself more distant than earlier ministerial bodies, especially in its rhetoric. It had an easier time rationalizing its acts, to itself and others, than had the earlier version of the central ministry in Berlin.[93]

"WLOCHATIUS MAY DIE OF HUNGER." Thanks to academic pluralism, a certain Mangelsdorff in Königsberg had three chairs. After he passed on in 1802, a large act assembled around his chairs. Sparing most details, consider a certain Wlochatius's part. Faculty and university recommended him for a chair. The KPR noted that "he merits care," as he had taught for thirty-three years without a salary. But he had no publications relevant to any of the chairs. So the KPR recommended someone else. The words "no samples," meaning no publications, are underlined in red pencil. Berlin now did that to passages it saw as key to its decisions. The final decision went with the KPR and came from Potsdam: No to Wlochatius.[94]

When Kant died an even larger act assembled to dispose of his chair and other perks. Consider only Wlochatius's part again. The faculty list put him first, in view of his now thirty-four years of service without pay, but noted it might be best to take time deciding. The university wrote, "Professor Wlochatius is become old and gray in his adherence to the [pre-Kantian] philosophy of Crusius, [and] has not kept in step with the age in the progress of philosophy, so is too little familiar with the genius now holding sway."

Note the sorts of criteria now in play: genius, especially of the age, and progress of knowledge, even in philosophy. The Enlightenment's cameralistic, market oriented view, ready to acknowledge its commodification of academics, had already slipped into the ideology of Romantic genius. Soon academics would have to be original to succeed.

Frustrated that the search was taking so long, Wlochatius wrote to Berlin, which rebuffed him. The ministry said that he should follow channels and not engage in private correspondence with the ministry. As if its archive weren't full of it! A few years later the Königsberg curator wrote to try to get him a salary. Wlochatius has now toiled "with great zeal and the most honest diligence" without a salary "for the long row of thirty-seven years." Students do not attend his lectures much, so "he finds himself robbed of all sources of income and, after a life conducted in honest activity, is in danger of <u>dying of hunger</u>."[95]

Some hand in the ministry underlined good parts of this letter in red pencil. And the last words, "Hungers zu sterben," were underlined twice, as here above. Even the central ministry in Berlin apparently still had some compassion. But it was 1806. Napoleon was on the loose in the land. Prussia now had neither money nor time for such sentimentality.

ACADEMIC WOLFFS AND CHARISMATIC CHAIRS. Kant's passage taxed Berlin. The dealings to fill his chair spilt over into years and fascicles. By metonymy, a chair had become as famous as its most famous occupant. The chair itself might convey great charisma to the next holder. One would say, "He has Kant's chair at Königsberg," or at Cambridge, "He has the chair that Newton held." Successors should thus be, if not as famous, then promising. But even for a seemingly all-knowing ministry, recognition of nascent genius might be hard. Negotiations just to make the call, but not to conclude the deal over Kant's chair, took from February to December 1804, a longer and fatter act than the process leading to Wolff's banishment.

As seen, the faculty put Wlochatius as first on a list that had no chance of going anywhere. The faculty actually advised to wait and look, which is what Berlin did. It wrote interim memoranda. It sighted targets to acquire. It considered their fame and whether one could acquire them, shall we say, cheaply. On 5 December, Berlin offered Kant's chair to extraordinary Professor Krug in Frankfurt a.d.O. He had submitted a list broken down into four sublists of twenty-five publications from 1795 to 1803. This fascicle and the next filled up with negotiations with Krug, who demanded all sorts of nice things from cash-strapped Berlin.[96]

That is what was now happening. A few "Wolffs," rationalizing themselves more and more of the rather humble academic pie, dominate confidential ministerial acts and, given leaks in the confidentiality of such acts, academic gossip, too. When a professor exited the scene, the ministry could sometimes simply order a replacement by fiat. But it might also fatten up an act. The ministry sighted targets. It collected reports. It underlined much in red. It collected not only lists and specimens of publications, but even reviews of the publications, too. Bad reviews were dangerous for young academics—a troubling matter, for who vouched for the rationality and objectivity of the review press, after all an instrument of the market?[97]

OUT OF FASHION IN HALLE. In the matter of publications and their evaluation, things were, as they had long been, uglier at Halle—no doubt the price it paid for thinking so highly of itself. The OSK found itself in a bind in 1790/91 when it appointed a certain Peucker as extraordinary professor there. His work and publications were then trashed by the faculty's evaluation. The university wrote that Peucker needed to write an habilitation first, which he then did.

The faculty then shot back that not only had he passed his master's exam badly, but his habilitation was also awful, with grammatical errors on every page. To lend this more weight, the faculty cited a review in bibliographic form—"*Intelligenzblatt der Allgemeinen Literatur-Zeitung*, Nr. 44, 2 April 1791, S. 364f: III. Vermischte Schriften"—where a lampoon of Peucker's habilitation may be found. The review is admittedly anonymous. But, under the spell of the review press, the ministry confesses to itself that it's in a fine mess now. Berlin ponders how to get rid of Peucker, whose patron is a count, no less.

Peucker writes in self-defense that he's heard that "mean men" are out to get him. He points out that most of the professors in Halle have themselves never officially habilitated, but they put such impositions with impunity on him. Negotiations go on. It's apparent that the ministry wants him to quit. Peucker then says in further defense that the problem with his habilitation's reception is that "it fell out of fashion" (*aus der mode*) at Halle.

That is an interesting remark and is marked in the margin in red pencil by the ministry. Much has been underlined and annotated in red pencil in this case and in others. On the critique of his Latin, Peucker cites a passage from the Halle lecture catalogue, where the Latin is bad, as he points out. To be sure, the ministry also marked this in red pencil in the margin. But all to no avail. Poor Peucker was finally forced to resign his position at Halle.[98]

NO ACADEMIC POLITICS. Not only did academic fame and fortune now lie in Romantic genius and being in fashion and original, the acts show also the new means of academic self-fashioning. One could follow with profit L. W. Gilbert's self-promotion at Halle. Gilbert supplicates for emoluments, for a chair or lectureship and salary, for money for instruments. He pleads his case by citing the better situation at Göttingen and Leipzig, rival universities.

Gilbert's chance comes when the professor of physics, Gren, dies. Gilbert waits but one day to act. He makes his best move by procuring the editorship of Gren's *Annalen der Physik*, "which serves for the extramural glitter (*zum auswärtigen Glanz*) of our academy." So it's Gilbert's duty, he explains to the ministry, to see that the journal does not perish with Gren. Unhappily, the modern system of budgets had still not been institutionalized, so Gilbert must also truck in archaic capital. He writes to the ministry for support in his purchase of the books and instruments from Gren's heirs. Gilbert plays the new game well, but is tried by the ministry's agenda. Berlin sees him as too young. They want someone with fame. And they need a medical doctor for the position, which is actually in the medical faculty.[99]

Applying for a position in 1822, a certain Buhle has nineteen publications in eighteen years. He has had the list of them printed. A good number of publications are books, an especially nice one being *Die Naturgeschichte des Hamsters*. A certain Kaulfuß is also under consideration for a position in 1822 and is requested to send in a list of his publications to Berlin, which he does. The next day he sends an addendum with one he forgot. The ministry is also weighing a certain Meinecke and already has his list. And, it being the modern era, the ministry then consults, in cases like these, with new sorts of experts: the police. The ministry wants to know whether or not the police have any suspicions about candidates, which in the German lands means about politics mostly.[100]

Our last Prussian act comes from the new Ministry of Culture in 1818. For our now refined taste, it is a prolix memorandum, where not only extramural fame, religious orthodoxy, and devotion to one subject, but also politics are decisively (not) in the act.

The chair of philosophy at this university [in Berlin] has been vacant for several years since Professor Fichte's death . . . It is important that a man of decisive reputation (*Ruf*) be called as a teacher who devotes himself exclusively to this science and is responsible for its success alone . . . This chair is highly important not only for the being of the whole university, but is also of decisive influence for its *Ruf* here and abroad. The university's need here has been, to be sure, long recognized; but, the difficulty of finding a man for this chair, who completely meets the demands, has to date frustrated all attempts at resolution. It is very difficult at the current time to find a university instructor for the discipline of philosophy who teaches his science with calmness (*Ruhe*) and level-headedness (*Besonnenheit*), at once distanced from paradoxical, unusual, untenable systems, as well as [distanced] from political or religious prejudice. The only scholar, to whom the teaching of philosophy at the university here [in Berlin] could be entrusted with great confidence in this regard is, in my conviction, Professor Hegel.[101]

## THE BAVARIAN DOSSIERS

I love the smell of archives in the morning. After getting a whiff of a piping hot cup of fresh-brewed coffee and the morning paper (but not a German one), nothing is quite so satisfying as nosing through a big, fat Bavarian dossier. The moment is all the better with a really foul one.

And I wondered once, when stumbling on the strange case of Professor Fischer, why the marvelous technique of the dossier had not allowed the Bavarian ministry to see that Professor Fischer was going slowly, yes, but quite surely mad. The Prussian technique of collecting by faculty acts could have allowed some excuse for this ministerial oversight. But the Bavarian technique of collecting individual dossiers brought the entire sad story together, and so offered a means to better control odd academic subjects, like poor Fischer.

In their new system of organization around 1806, the Bavarians did away with provinces, universities, and faculties, from the ministry's point of view. Under the new Ministry of the Interior, each academic got his own dossier and a separate number. In some cases, such dossiers were formed retrospectively and reached back into the eighteenth century.

Such Bavarian dossiers will be cited here in terms of the apparatus in the abbreviations below, just ahead of the bibliography. I shall omit the "M. Inn." in each case here, and simply cite the relevant dossiers, whose exact number will be given in parentheses in the text. Most of what such dossiers collected was simply the sorts of things we've seen all along above. Though the Bavarians deployed dossiers, they—like the Jesuits and Austrians—were not made mad by publishing, till later. Publication appears in the Bavarian dossiers, but is less prominent than in Prussia. There is, however, much on money.

### Dossiers at Work

The dossier for a certain Merderer (23406) has documents beginning in the late 1770s. A memorandum of 3 August 1780 concerns his reappointment as professor in Ingolstadt. It notes he merits being a professor "by his untiring diligence as well as proven learning in his several excellent publications, well received by the learned world, and his thereby especially acquired merit, particularly with the serene Electoral House" (Nr. 3, 1r).

Dietl (23171) is appointed professor of aesthetics at Landshut in 1800, for he has "the gift of pleasant lecturing, with excellent talent, which he has, moreover, publicly proven through advantageously received literary works ... [and] he would greatly outdistance all natives [Bavarians] who could compete with him, and may be set equal to the capable foreign scholars in this field." But the dossier cites no others names or works.

When they fatten up, dossiers give a different scent to academic acts than do the Prussian piles. Thanks to the nesting in bundles and fragmentation through bundles, the Prussian acts complexly plot the story. But the Bavarian dossiers display the stories usually in strict chronological order. That reduces the complex plot to the linear story.

The well-ordered dossier of Bischoff (23055) clearly shows the story of his progress and struggles. As doctoral candidate he tried to get a fellowship at the academy of sciences in Munich. He had good references in 1812, but, as fellowships go, he had to apply again the next year. In 1816 he wanted to succeed to the chair of his great patron and mentor, the previous professor in Erlangen.

The dossier of Schiegg (23528) shows the ministry began to target him in 1805. Dossiers end when the academic passes, not from the academy, but from the realm, one way or another. Professors are civil servants and pensions must now be paid. The dossier of one individual (23196) constantly hails his "great future," pointing to calls from Jena and rumors that the Prussians are after him.

The dossier of another (23655) allows him to leave Bavaria in 1818, so terminating his dossier, not only since he wants too much money, but also since the review press has accused him of anti-Protestant sentiments, to which Bavaria is now sensitive, given the Fischer affair. The dossier of a third (23604) records a stillborn act, as his attempts to habilitate in 1802 in Landshut are terminated by the faculty's critique of his examination, which is all very interestingly spelt out in the dossier and which I wish I could relate in detail, as the faculty wrote more than the candidate had in his habilitation dissertation.

The dossier of 23372 is nearly as interesting as Fischer's, though no madness haunts this dossier. It reeks rather of attempts over twenty years of self-promotion. We are all now romantically original, and 23372 claims this for his ideas, which "in small and big works brought publicity" (Nr. 28). For comic relief, a report from the police recounts his shenanigans in Munich (Nr. 29: 20 Sept. 1816).

The dossier of 23096 shows the faculty foiling his attempt to perpetuate the practice of pluralism in 1823. The faculty's arguments (57–59) show how the prose of specialty and devotion recast academic mentalities. "Every science needs her man, and a condition of the possibility of lecturing on her in a thorough and educative way is that the instructor embrace her perfectly, have her in his power and dominate her" (*sie vollkommen unfaßt, in seiner Gewalt habe und beherrsche*). The faculty draws toward the dramatic dictum: "Science lives by free love (*lebt in der freÿen Liebe*), and her only right is the truth."

The above dossier tells a strange tale, not only in its rhetoric of disciplinary monogamy and domination, as opposed to musical chairs, but also in its marvelous table. A table in this dossier evaluates 23096, like the table in the dossier of 23195, also made by the Nuremberg Polytechnic and sent in support of the application in 1816/17.

Within the dossier as an Enlightened-Romantic solution for managing academics, rendering the individual's narrative more important than that of the collective body, Bavaria introduces as well a ministerial machination for rationalizing academic persona: a table. Letters from a collegial body, the Nuremberg Polytechnic, have become transcripts of grades, a lapidary figure of rationality, cast by modern bureaucratic authorities to frustrate academic narrative. The dossier versus the table—to narrate or not?

## The Strange Case of Professor Fischer

The dossier is a marvelous ministerial tool to narrate individual academic lives. The first ten documents of Fischer's dossier (23217) give no scent of a conspiracy. Signs of hysteria only emerge after things have gotten out of hand in Würzburg. With the fortunes of war in the Napoleonic era, the Catholic University of Würzburg changes hands and lands. Fischer, a Protestant, had been professor of statistics (*Statistik*) in 1804, but was pushed into early retirement in 1809 by the reorganization of the university. When Bavaria took over, Fischer returned to office, 11 October 1815, as professor of *Statistik und Staatengeschichte.*

For winter semester 1815/16, Fischer announced on the bulletin board that he is offering the lecture in *Universalgeschichte,* the field of Professor Berg, "in accordance with the general wish." Berg finds the wording of this notice insulting. He complains to the local ministry, the *Curatel,* which oversees the university. He requests that Fischer's note be taken down. The Curatel sends the problem to the next ministerial instance, which commands, on 15 November 1815, that Fischer is to remove the note, and that he and all faculty should desist with such insults to one another.

Fischer takes the note down, but writes to the ministry to criticize the report of the Curatel. He says that their transcript of his note was incorrect. He even criticizes their grammar. The ministry grows perplexed. On 20 November, it enjoins Fischer to certify within twenty-four hours whether the Curatel's transcript of his note is correct. Fischer does not answer. The ministry extends the deadline by six hours. Fischer does not answer. The ministry waits. On 24 November it says it presumes the transcript is correct. It reprimands Fischer, saying he sets a bad example and is unworthy of a civil servant.

On 7 December, the second and heavy shoe drops. A note appears by Fischer in the *Allgemeiner Anzeiger der Deutschen* to dispel the rumors that he is being suspended from teaching at Würzburg due to his political and religious views. On 12 December a document appears in his dossier (Nr. 11) in Munich reviewing the matter. The ministry, according to the dossier, views Fischer's notice in the press of 7 December as an "improper use of publicity." The ministry notes in the dossier that it must guard against mixing the borders between "teaching" and "private life." There are to be no "personalities" at the university.

The next document (Nr. 12) is a report from the Munich police, 13 December. This shows that the best way to make the police take notice is to say in the press that there is nothing for them to take notice of. Very suspicious. On 23 December, the ministry in Munich commands Fischer to explain within three days what he meant in his press notice. Since the letter to this effect went by way of the Curatel, the local ministry, and given the Christmas holidays, Fischer first gets notice of this on 29 December. On 31 December, he humbly seeks forgiveness for his strange conduct. And so all would appear to be well that ends well.

But not for long. Like Providence, the ministry sometimes works swiftly and sometimes not. The expansion or contraction time, control of the tempo of events, thus the plot, obscure or inscrutable to those outside, is above all bureaucratic power.

A document of 5 January 1816 (Nr. 14) in Fischer's dossier shows the ministry in Munich internally interested in letting things cool off. The ministry is sensitive to how this is playing in the press, especially abroad. Munich collects notices on the case. On 7 May, the ministry sends a note to Würzburg to close the case. Fischer is to be reprimanded for going outside ministerial channels and into the public press. He is to pay for a retraction of his press notice of 7 December in the same periodical and defuse the political implications. On 14 May, the Curatel thus orders Fischer to appear at 4:00 p.m., 16 May, before the academic senate, so as to convey the above to him and conclude the incident officially.

The nearly half-year ministerial silence seemingly lulled Fischer into a false sense of security. If not, he seems to have become even more unhinged. On the university's account of the matter, on said date at the appointed hour, Fischer asked the beadle to show him where the senate was meeting, but then remarked he had to go and lecture at that hour. After Fischer's lecture, the beadle in commission of the senate informed him that they still awaited him. Fischer replied that he would not appear before them and kept his word.

On 18 May the Curatel tells Fischer to explain this conduct within twenty-four hours. Fischer does not. The Curatel repeats its wish, and now sends a constable instead of a courier. On 20 May Fischer finally pens his answer. He claims that the summons to appear before the senate is illegal in Germany and all of Europe, as it violates traditional academic privileges. On 22 May the Curatel again invites Fischer to appear or to risk suspension from his academic offices. Suddenly Fischer exclaims that he had not realized that the previous invitations had been made in the name of the Bavarian crown!

On 24 May Fischer finally appears before the academic senate and signs a protocol about the incidents, but still protests his ignorance. All documents are sent to Munich, where the ministry ponders this troubling case. The ministry writes its report on 28 May (Nr. 20). It is decided that the professor's misconduct and, above all, his misuse of publicity were egregious. Almost exactly nine months after he had been brought out of his forced early retirement, Fischer is returned to it, 9 July 1816, but given a normal pension.

Fischer's dossier does not end there. Further documents rehash the case (Nr. 26). Fischer wants to emigrate in 1818. His pension is not enough; he needs more money. To defend itself, in 1817 the university publishes,

*Beyträge zur neuesten Geschichte der Königlichen Universität zu Würzburg und zur Berichtigung öffentlicher Nachrichten und Urtheile über dieselbe,* edited by J. C. Goldmayer, Würzburg, with enclosures. This, of course, gets into the dossier (Nr. 33). It is, all in all, a sad and strange story well told by the dossier.

## CONCLUSION

Traditional authority and the old juridico-ecclesiastical regime that we have been articulating are well represented by practices in the Baroque era at Königsberg, vested in the nested acts collected by the KPR. Ideally, the faculty initiated all decisions. The faculty determined the list of nominations, supposedly to bind all higher instances: the university, the KPR, Berlin, and even Potsdam, the royal residence.

The faculty did not need to qualify its nominations with any more than "three well qualified candidates" or the like. The ordered list expressed collegial will, ascertained by voting, a practice to establish traditional authority. The details of the vote—unanimous or a majority or a plurality—did not need to be revealed. While considering things like erudition and ability, the faculty decided mostly in view of collegial matters: need, nepotism, seniority, private academic capital, such as books and instruments, and so on. Typical of traditional groups, the faculty's orientation was local, intramural, familial, personal, and short-range.

Rational authority and the modern politico-economic regime, which we have traced in the chapters above, are well represented in the central ministry in enlightened Berlin. It suppressed collegial will vested in voting, and championed ministerial calculation based on informed advice in confidential correspondence with select academics. When the Berlin OSK got going in 1787, local academic bodies definitively lost the initiative in appointments.

The OSK might solicit the opinion of the faculty as a collegial body on some matter. But in such a case, the faculty served as but one advisor among many. The ministry consulted confidentially with as many advisors as it chose, so nobody else knew who had been consulted. In the Baroque era, the faculty as a local, collegial body could occult itself by concealing the grounds of its decisions. But in the Enlightenment the central ministry occulted itself—a hallmark of modern power-knowledge. The central ministry in Berlin, insofar as it allowed the faculty a voice in appointments, condemned it to garrulity.[102]

Seeking advice, the central ministry looked for the sort of rational authority that it envisaged itself to be. To be sure, Prussian kings remained of two minds about academics: to what extent should academics continue in traditional aristocratic and courtly practices, such as patronage and nepotism, as opposed to the extent to which the modern meritocratic, bureaucratic practices, such as examination and other rationalizing measures of merit, should be imposed.

But all in all, the ministry wanted to ground its decisions about appointments on modern rational criteria: success in exams, proven expertise, diligence, students' and peers' applause, famous publications and, if possible, all numbered and quantified, thus rational and calculable. The later rise of institutes with budgets, on the model of the research seminar, transferred academic capital from private personae to state and public personae: institute directors and their hands. In this and other lights, the ministry wanted specialists, professors with a real profession, a *Beruf*. Like many modern groups, the ministry's orientation was cosmopolitan, extramural, occupational, impersonal, long-range.

The Bavarian dossiers dissolved the faculty's narrative, chaotically told by the Prussian bundles. Dossiers moved the ministry's eye from the collective, collegial story of the faculty to the individual narratives of academics. The dossier gathers the fragments of an academic's life into the ministry's memory in one place. As a system of (re)collection, the dossier entails the paradox of impersonalized collection whose primary index is personal. The number or name of the academic became the primary system of classification—the triumph of the author catalogue in the Romantic era, to which we turn in the next chapter, showed the same development in the constitution of the modern research library.

The archive, armed with dossiers, became a refuge for academic bodies fragmented into isolated bureaucratic souls. Excepting publications, Bavarian dossiers collected documents from a private sphere, be it political or domestic, only when something had gone wrong. So the lesson of Fischer: the ministry, so the dossier, wanted to separate academia from private life. The dossier wished to conceive the academic as a public servant whose paperwork received good reviews by the press, and in no need of notice by the police.

Here we catch a glimpse of the modern production of the academic self, and it seems appropriate to put this in a broader context. One can find further illumination in the transition from the *éloges* of the learned in the eighteenth century to the statistical prosopographies in the nineteenth. Daniel Roche has studied the French *éloges* of the eighteenth century, which we may take as setting the mold. Recapitulating hagiography and religious ascetic ideals, the typical *éloge* framed the scientist or scholar as a modern sort of saint and upheld a traditional, aristocratic mix of public and private lives.[103]

When we reach J. C. Poggendorff's *Biographisch-literarisches Hand-wörterbuch zur Geschichte der exacten Wissenschaften,* whose first volumes appeared in 1863, the normal natural scientist, at least, had acquired the sort of self embodied in the ministerial mentalities above. Poggendorff's prosopography exhibits the typical scientist with a curriculum vitae that encompassed essentially only professional and public activities, unless something had gone wrong or was odd. Thus bodies, for example, do not exist for Poggendorff, unless they had been broken or otherwise beaten. I found the most extreme case there to be that of Ignatz Martinovics, whom Poggendorff reports was beheaded for treason—an unfortunate end. Gustav Fechner presents a less extreme case, as Poggendorff informs us that his career experienced interruption by a severe illness affecting his eyes (and then, as we are not told, by a severe clinical depression). Otherwise, Poggendorff's academics have no private self.[104]

Returning to the summary: the ministry's extramural, cosmopolitan orientation led to the market. The policies pursued by enlightened Hanover and Prussia and Romantic Bavaria mean that ministerial-market rationality drove the academic system. Cameralist policies, as effect and cause, abetted the view that one needed not so much academics who had withstood civil service exams, as in Austria and France, but rather academics who had the charisma of fame. Romanticism would embellish and gloss the charisma of fame as originality and genius.

The ministry ascertained and recognized this charisma, but itself did not manufacture the essential and underlying fame, save insofar as it recognized it. This was crucial, for the appointment of a professor hereby acquired archaic aspects of the recognition of a charismatic religious or military leader. One recognized charismatic academics to some extent by the acclaim given their lectures and disputations (or sermons and jousts), but more by the applause given their "paperwork."

In the next chapter we shall examine the collection and cataloguing of such charismatic works, and the new virtual reality created by them. As we have seen, the Romantic era would complete the process of disembodying the academic, and celebrate the apotheosis of the academic as author. It should not surprise us, then, that the triumph of the author catalogue occurred in the same era, as did a disembodiment of the book as well.

# 8

## The Library Catalogue

Everything is there: the minute history of the future, the autobiographies of the archangels, the faithful catalogue of the Library, thousands and thousands of false catalogues, a demonstration of the fallacy of these catalogues, a demonstration of the fallacy of the true catalogue.

Jorge Luis Borges, "The Library of Babel."

This chapter ends the core analysis of modern academia. The next chapters will examine interesting and perhaps pervasive features of academia. But the principal subjects there—academic babble, ministerial hearing, academic voices—occupy a less central place in the academic economy, compared to the subjects of the chapters up to and including this one.

Chapter 3 concerned lecture and disputation, the two principal academic activities of the medieval university. We saw the preservation and rehabilitation of the lecture through the early modern into the modern era, while the disputation lapsed into decadence. Subsequent chapters traced the development of other academic institutions and practices—the written exam and grading system, the research seminar paper, the doctoral dissertation, publish or perish—in the wake of the decadence of disputation. Those chapters traced the modern academic path from undergraduate evaluation (chapter 4), to graduate training in the seminar (chapter 5), to a new graduate rite of passage in the dissertation (chapter 6). The preceding chapter illuminated the modern path from the doctorate to the professorate.

The process of rationalization reflected in those chapters reveals the eclipse of the oral and the aural by the visible and the legible. Oral elements survived and still flourish in academia. Subsequent chapters will consider charismatic aspects of oral culture. But the importance of writing has overshadowed the oral, at least officially. The written exam, the seminar and lab paper, the doctoral dissertation, and publish or perish evaluated by written peer references for a position or promotion—these constitute much of the core of modern academia. In this chapter we shall look at the place where important academic writings were recorded.

The above chapters also investigated aspects of the material culture that accompanied the triumph of writing in academia. We looked much at wooden tables, still important for academic oral culture. But paper tables proved important, as did the dossier as a place to store—or not store—paperwork. With chapter 2 on the lecture catalogue, this chapter on the library catalogue bookends the intermediate chapters on writing and the core academic institutions. The history of the library catalogue exhibits interesting parallels not only with the lecture catalogue but also with archival registers. For a long time in fact, libraries and archives were not clearly separated, either from each other, or from museums.

The library in the modern sense meant the differentiation and articulation of a space for books and their simulacra, such as catalogues and other virtual registers. This was a feat of the Enlightenment and Romantic era. The transformation in the collection of books went hand in hand with a transformation of the interrelation of books, that is, the system of knowledge. The emergence of the modern research library is correlative with the transformation of the pursuit of academic knowledge from erudition to research.

The Enlightenment took the essential step in the conception of the research library by facilitating a bureaucratization of library practices, especially of acquisition and registration. In the sphere of catalogues, the Enlightenment witnessed the hegemony of the systematic. This rationalized the chaos of catalogues bequeathed by the Baroque era. But the Romantic era offered a stunning defeat to the Enlightenment's rationalization of the catalogue. The Romantic era ushered in the triumph of the author catalogue at the expense of the systematic. This reinforced the Romantic cult of the author. The Enlightenment's systematic catalogue had a cousin in the disciplinary order of the lecture catalogue, while the author catalogue of the Romantic era found a reflection in the system of dossiers in (some) archives.

The chapter has sections on the Baroque, Enlightenment, and Romantic libraries. Amongst those, two sections treat of the *bibliotheca universalis* and *bibliotheca virtualis*.

## THE BAROQUE LIBRARY

Into the Baroque era, colleges and universities did not consistently distinguish between libraries, museums, cabinets, and often not between those and archives and treasuries. In this, academic libraries resembled private collections with their "Wunderkammern." For a good part of the early modern era, spaces that we tend to separate were commonly not. Library catalogues in the Baroque era, when extant, reflected the complexity of the spaces.[1]

## The College Library

Figure 8.1 comes from Johann Puschner's *Amoenitates Altdorfinae,* circa 1715, which depicts a tour of the University of Altdorf. Universities such as Altdorf were at base colleges with three small superior faculties. Through drawn in the Enlightenment, the figure still affords an interesting view of a Baroque college library.[2]

As *Wunderkammer,* the library is a site or sight for visitors. Like everything else, the books in figure 8.1 embody "monstrosities": things on display and to be shown. As monstrosities, the books partake of an economy of the rare. Their materiality, including their covers (from which, as we'll see, they are well judged), has a nature and a history beyond their contents and authors. In the figure, the fossils and the portrait of Johann Christoph Wagenseil hovering above them carve the dynamic center. An isosceles triangle has its vertex at Wagenseil's forehead and points between the feet of the two pairs of observers.

The University of Altdorf acquired Wagenseil's *Wunderkammer* between 1705 and 1708. This included the three fossils: a bear to the left, a stag to the right, a "Croat" on his mount in the middle. Part of the Wagenseil collection, the cabinet to the left of the bear probably contains his and other curiosities or wonders acquired by the university, including a box with Christian holy relics, a Lapp sorcerer's drum, a large dagger with an engraved calendar, objects from a Synagogue, and assorted coins and medals. Here or elsewhere, the library also housed a mineral collection. To the far left rests a valuable armillary sphere.

On the table, right of the sphere, lies *Hortus eychstettensis,* an expensive botanical work, as a token of the really rare. Besides Wagenseil's, portraits of other benefactors or deceased collectors hover like patron saints. To the far right is the portrait of Johann Stöberlein, who bequeathed his private library of medical and philosophical books to the library in 1696. His medical books were shelved with the medical, while his philosophy collection, at first shelved in the philosophy lecture hall, here occupies separate shelves under his portrait. In the figure, a plaque midway down declares these as Stöberlein's testament.

Also shelved intact, Wagenseil's books probably occupy the bookcase under his portrait, facing the observer. Wagenseil had become a full

*Die Bibliothec in dem Collegio zu Altorf.*

8.1. The library, University of Altdorf, from Johann G. Puschner, *Amoenitates Altdorfinae*, circa 1710–20, Nuremberg.

professor at Altdorf in 1667. In 1699 he became librarian too—a typical early modern practice, whereby professors acquired auxiliary offices to supplement salaries. Wagenseil wished his collection to the library, but willed it to his heirs in 1705. They first undertook what inspired fear in colleges and universities: extramural alienation of academic effects. From 1705 to 1706, the heirs tried to sell the library to the University of Leipzig. Ongoing war made Leipzig cash-poor—in the previous chapter we saw that this was just when Wolff was trying to leave Leipzig for the same reasons. Luckily, the heirs resisted dismembering Wagenseil's academic corpus. In 1708, Altdorf raised funds satisfying the heirs, thus bringing "Wagenseil" back to the library.

## The Collectors' Hegemony

Continuing traditional practices, the Baroque academic library grew like that—largely as an aggregated accumulation of the already accumulated. On a visit in 1710 to Trinity College Library, Cambridge, Zacharius von Uffenbach remarked with surprise that the entire collection was not structured, as was common, at least in part by faculties (as in figure 8.1). It was, rather, completely ordered by bequests, "to spur others by such a good example." Every collection had the insignia of its donator above it. At Oxford, for example also, while colleges made some attempts to set up regular funds, on the whole they simply solicited and waited for gifts. When not receiving private libraries en bloc as gifts, early modern academic libraries sought ad hoc funds to purchase the private library of a deceased scholar at auction, as Altdorf did to bring Wagenseil's collection back.[3]

Until the late eighteenth and nineteenth centuries, the instrument of the budget for regular discrete acquisitions—essential for transforming academic knowledge into the pursuit of research—did not exist. At least it did not usually exist in sufficient extent or duration. Composed of monstrous materials, the traditional library grew by extraordinary events. Best were bequests and endowments of books or funds, the latter mostly used to buy collections of deceased collectors who thus lorded over libraries beyond the grave.

For early modern books often came unbound from the publisher. Collectors thus frequently had all their books bound in the same color and style of binding. So you could tell a book by its cover. Not the author but rather the collector gave the key to the Baroque library. The fame or *Ruhm* of a library, an essential part of the reputation of some universities and colleges, rested in good part on the previous fame of private academic or princely collections acquired. Important juridical personae, the biblio-estates or testaments of collectors, such as Wagenseil or Stöberlein, governed whole library shelves, often visible by their bindings.⁴

Though lacking the modern notion of the annual budget, traditional libraries sought some regular acquisitions, but usually made a miserable showing. Typical techniques included channeling student fines or fees to the library. Alas, fees of this sort were low or claimed elsewhere. And fines were hard to collect and usually replaced by incarceration. Many colleges and universities expected the faculty to donate their works, as did many princely or national libraries. But such policies could not be enforced, and made the collection essentially intramural. Beyond such techniques, interest from endowments earmarked for purchases of discrete volumes was all there usually was.⁵

As said, acquisition en bloc of estates formed the chief pillar. One usually displayed such collections intact, as in the case of Wagenseil and Stöberlein, or broke them up and subjected them to the rubric of the disciplines. The sign "Theologia," above the books to the left and rear of figure 8.1, and the sign "Philosophia," to the left of Stöberlein's portrait, show books by disciplines. Collectors' estates and academic disciplines set the primary principles shaping the Baroque library. The tendency of the Enlightenment library would be to shift the center of gravity from collectors to disciplines—to collection via epistemic and ultimately bureaucratic systems, as opposed to the Baroque aggregate of juridical estates and plots.

## The Catalogue as Shelf List

In the physical disposition and cataloguing of books, the Baroque library resisted the hegemony of epistemic system. During the early modern era, save the few monstrously big or small, books typically came in folio, quarto, or octavo format. After the primary division of collectors' estate or academic discipline, the format of the book gave the secondary principle. Shelf-units in figure 8.1 have from seven to nine horizontal shelves. Each shelf-unit has shelves of various heights to accommodate all sizes, from folio at the bottom to octavo at the top. So the book's materiality further refined the collection's articulation. And catalogues furthered that.

For a long time, catalogues, if extant, were usually shelf lists that indicated the physical location of the volume on the shelf. That might seem reasonable. But one of the feats of the Enlightenment and Romantic library was to produce catalogues quite distinct from the shelf list. Until then, the materiality and history of the books, embodied in their format and binding, governed the catalogue, the book of books. Traditional catalogues were usually books, as opposed to cabinets of cards, which came later.

The catalogue sometimes existed only in the librarian's memory. As the transformation of memory and history into epistemic-technical systems was a hallmark of modernity, it is no surprise that the catalogue partook of that development. But at its first manifestation beyond memory, the catalogue at an academic library such as Altdorf's exhibited the history of the collection and collectors. When a college or university acquired a private collection such as Wagenseil's, it typically came with a catalogue, made by the collector or the seller. Like the library, the general library catalogue often existed as an aggregate of books, a virtual catalogue of separate, real catalogues.[6]

And books would be shelved accordingly. Suppose a library had acquired the collection of a Professor X by bequest or purchase. If the collection was large, or if a bequeathed collection so stipulated, the books would be shelved intact, like Stöberlein's in figure 8.1. The accompanying catalogue would remain the catalogue. If the collection was relatively small or if it had been purchased, a librarian might dismember the collection, but usually only in terms of disciplines. If Professor X had been a theology professor, he would tend to have many theology books. One would shelve them intact, divided by format, on the next open shelves in the theology section. One could then use the extant professorial catalogue for the collection with minimal annotations to reflect the new shelf listing.

If Professor X had also bought arts and philosophy books, he usually would have separated them in his catalogue. In so far as the professor had organized his private catalogue by academic disciplines, the arts and philosophy books, for example, could be shelved intact in the relevant section and render that part of his catalogue useable. When collections came without a catalogue, it was still easier to shelf thus catalogue them en bloc, but dismembered by the four traditional faculties. Catalogues were at first usually shelf lists.

Inscribed in the sphere of the *Wunderkammer*, a collection of collections, bequeathed or bought, the Baroque academic library embodied juridical estates in competition with academic disciplines. As a collection of estates or bequests, the library resembled an archive or mausoleum, a juridical plot of private personae, an aggregate of idiosyncratic interests accumulated by extraordinary events. A library of libraries, its catalogue was a collection of books, reflecting the materiality, history, and monstrosity of the collection. Excepting a few odd places such as the Bodleian, in the Baroque catalogue, as shelf list, collectors contested with disciplines for supremacy. Authors had less importance than collectors and disciplines.

## The Bodleian

Oxford's university library fell into dissolution during the sixteenth century. So Thomas Bodley offered to renovate the library in 1597/98. With the university's consent, he did so and in 1602 opened the soon and still famous Bodleian Library. In the Baroque sense, it was also a museum, housing valuable objects as well as books and manuscripts.

Though administered by Bodley as long as he lived, the library belonged to the university. Bodley's private collection founded the library, which grew through his own further purchases and efforts to solicit gifts. Beginning in 1610, all publishers in Britain were supposed to send the Bodleian a copy of every book they published. Measures were taken to compel publishers to send the exemplars. But publishers seem to have done so only fitfully.

On the whole, the Bodleian grew like a typical Baroque academic library. Lacking a meaningful budget, books were acquired essentially by bequests. After 1640, those "shrank to a trickle." The Press Licensing Act of 1652 required submission of three copies of each publication in Britain: one for the Royal Library, one for Oxford (the Bodleian), and one for Cambridge. But publishers did not regularly observe this or other related acts. When Cambridge set up a committee in 1674 to make sure that publishers sent their books, Oxford wrote Cambridge that it had little hope of its sister institution's success.[7]

Apart from its impressive initial bequest and Bodley's further efforts, the library had only one other claim to fame after 1650—its catalogues. In 1605 the Bodleian published its first catalogue, in 1620 its second, in 1674 its third, and in 1738 its fourth. These catalogues, especially the third, lent much to the Bodleian's fame, as well as to Oxford's. The most amazing thing, however, was the mere fact of the publication of the Bodleian's catalogues.

Since the Renaissance, scholars had collected and exchanged inventories of other scholars' libraries. Many reasons existed for the exchange of catalogues, including bibliographic interest, future sale, and vanity. Such virtual exchanges of libraries formed an essential mechanism of manufacturing fame for collectors. By the late sixteenth century, published catalogues for private museums or *Wunderkammer* had become fairly common. But the Bodleian is the first and foremost academic or public library, of which I am aware, that published its catalogues. Publication of the first catalogue in 1605 might be attributed to Bodley's failure to perceive the collection as no longer his own private one. The continued publication of new catalogues, however, cannot be so explained. It was rather peculiar.[8]

## Bodleian Catalogues

When the Bodleian opened in 1602, Thomas James was library-keeper. The catalogue of 1605 was his work and the result of negotiations with Bodley, who favored a disciplinary classification of books. In accord with Bodley's wishes, James ordered the books, first, by the traditional faculties, then, within each, by first initial of the author's surname. The books were all chained, according to custom, to the stalls were they lay. So readers could make do with titles, given first and briefly, followed by the author's name. These were put on tables, a shelf list at the end of each stall. Bodley and James at first planned to publish just the tables, the shelf list. Indeed, the catalogue as published in 1605 was effectively a shelf list, with an author index and an addendum on problem books.

Problem books arose in part from Bodley's practice of binding more and more small works together. Many books on shelves within faculty divisions did not really appear alphabetically. Indeed, the collection was in any case not strictly alphabetical. The arts and philosophy books began, for example, with Aristotle as "A.1, I" in the system, even though the surnames of other authors belonged ahead of his purely alphabetically.

For acquisitions, moreover, Bodley needed more bibliographic information and more uniform entries. From James he thus demanded annual revisions, listing the author's name first, then the title. That, along with the apparent need of an author index, convinced James that the next version of the catalogue should be an author catalogue. This was a remarkable notion for the time.

Nonetheless, James first went to work on a written subject index for internal use. He thought that a subject index would be more useful than the classified or disciplinary ordering of books on shelves. He distinguished the published shelf list from a catalogue or index, be it by author or subject. In 1607, he completed a subject index for theology. The volume consisted of eight hundred folio pages with about ten thousand references. He worked on other subject indices, but brought no other faculties of knowledge to completion.[9]

In 1620 James published the second Bodleian library catalogue. Opposed to Bodley's druthers, it was an alphabetic author catalogue, further arranged alphabetically by titles under each author. James's sentiments would accord with the Romantic era's, but were peculiar in his time, even for published book catalogues. In the seventeenth century, book catalogues for auctions were the most common sort published and, on the whole, they were organized not by authors but rather by disciplines and/or format. Published by

librarian Thomas Hyde in 1674, the third and most famous Bodleian catalogue preserved the alphabetical arrangement by author, subarranged by
genres. Collected works, for example, came first under authors.[10]

## BIBLIOTHECA UNIVERSALIS

A well-constructed library
is *in publicis* a printed Universal Archive.

———————————
Leibniz
———————————

Those are the words of an important but contested librarian, the philosopher Leibniz, who
was deemed an impractical theorist by some, and
whose letters of reference for Wolff we considered in the previous chapter. By the Enlightenment, theorists of library and archival science
would insist on the physical separation of libraries and archives from each
other, as well as from museums and treasuries. At a metaphorical level, however, the library and the archive would continue to be linked. This carried on
the Baroque notion of the museum or *Wunderkammer* as a room reflecting
and representing the whole universe—to the eternal bane of the library.

The paradox and scandal of the Baroque library was then this. Most
Baroque libraries, including the awfully famous Bodleian, metaphorically
much resembled a *Rumpelkammer,* a junk room, while they aspired to embody and represent the universe. The Baroque library intended to be a universal library, a *bibliotheca universalis,* while being actually rather more an
often chaotic aggregate of collectors' idiosyncratic estates or plots. The latter is what the theorists, however impractical their solutions, wished to
remedy.

### Naudé and a Public Library

The French royal librarian, Gabriel Naudé, wrote one of the most influential works on cataloguing for librarians and book dealers: *Advis pour dresser
une bibliothèque* of 1627. The French royal librarian already conceived the
collection to be in spirit not the king's, but rather the people's. Naudé focused on the public use of the collection. In that light, he thought one
should collect all sorts of books. The library should be universal and, in
one's fantasy, it would encompass all books potentially. Useful books, however, were the goal. Only the ignorant, that is, princes, courtiers and vain
collectors, took a book for its cover. A librarian should seek to reduce all expenses for ornate bindings and so on. And on the whole, one should not collect rare books, unless they were indispensable.[11]

Naudé held that one knew the library through the catalogue. The catalogue is the library virtually. Naudé argued that the best arrangement of

both the collection and catalogue for a universal library, that is, a library as-piring to represent the universe, would be by disciplines, subdisciplines, and so on. In the best of all possible worlds, a good library had two catalogues: a systematic disciplinary one to bring all the authors from a faculty or on a subject together, and an alphabetic author catalogue to avoid duplicates and to allow searching for works of a specific author. In the *bibliotheca univer-salis,* the systematic catalogue, however, had logical precedence.[12]

## Dury and a Public Library

In Civil War England, sentiments similar to Naudé's emerged in the Par-liamentary party. After the flight of Charles I, John Dury became deputy to the keeper of the king's medals and library. Dury organized the library and published *The Reformed Librarie-Keeper* in 1650. Perhaps not as influen-tial as Naudé's work, Dury's reflected many of the same notions. He too stressed the "public usefullness" of the library. The king's library should be "not onely an ornament," but also "an useful commoditie by it self to the publick; yet in effecte it is no more then a dead Bodie as novv it is consti-tuted."[13]

And the first thing a good librarian needed, Dury reasoned, was a cata-logue of the "Treasurie committed unto his charge." Such a catalogue should be put "in an order most easie and obvious to bee found, which I think is that of Sciences and Languages; when first all the Books are divided into their *subjectam materiam* whereof they Treat, and then everie kinde of matter subdivided into several Languages." Dury further saw the necessity of keeping the catalogue and the collection up to date. More importantly, he saw the necessity of accommodating new books. He thus made a dis-tinction between a systematic catalogue and the shelf list. So a place "in the Librarie must bee left open for the increas of the number of Books in their proper seats, and in the Printed Catalogue, a Reference is to be made to the place where the Books are to bee found in their Shelves." Dury imagined the differentiation of the systematic catalogue from the actual physical li-brary reflected in the shelf list.[14]

## Systematic Catalogues

The ascendancy of Parliament brought not only the theorist Dury to the royal library but also new men to Oxford. Such men wished the Bodleian to be more "useful." Like Dury, they saw a systematic catalogue as the first and best way to make it so. Recall that after the first Bodleian catalogue of 1605, the librarian James's next version of 1620 renounced a systematic or disciplinary structure for a purely alphabetic author catalogue. At midcentury, members of the Oxford Experimental Club desired a renovation of the original 1605 catalogue and so planned to survey the entire collection.

Gerhard Langbaine, Provost of Queens College, hit on the idea of surveying the Bodleian and thus "to make a perfect Catalogue of all the Books according to their severall subjects in severall kinds." There from, he thought, one would produce a more universal catalogue by incorporating books from private libraries not found in the Bodleian, "so as he that desired to know, may see at one view what wee have upon any subject." Langbaine began the task, as Anthony Wood noted, of making "a universal catalogue in all kind of Learning—but he died [in 1658] before he could go halfway through with it." It would prove a common fate, rivaled only by madness, for the compilers of systematic catalogues.[15]

Members of the Oxford Experimental Club briefly worked on continuing the project but, as the members soon dispersed, the catalogue came to naught. In any case, more pressing became the integration of a large collection—John Selden's estate—that arrived at the Bodleian in 1659. Thereafter, as we saw, Thomas Hyde, the librarian from 1665 to 1700, went to work not on the systematic catalogue, but rather on a new author catalogue.

In the course of the seventeenth century, however, the notion of a systematic or disciplinary catalogue spread. Theorist J. H. Hottinger in his *Bibliothecarius quadripartitus* of 1664, for example, favored a *catalogus realis* over a *catalogus nominalis*. Radicalizing Dury's notion of the systematic or "real" catalogue, Hottinger held that the location of a book had no importance, so long as the catalogues were well kept. The systematic catalogue embodied a sort of universal virtual library, and need not be identical with the real library, as embodied in the shelf list. Thus the physical arrangement of the actual books became ultimately uninteresting to the theorist.[16]

Note that "real" refers to a systematic catalogue here, whereas "nominal" refers to an author catalogue. A *catalogus realis*, in German a *Realcatalog*, as a systematic catalogue, however, is a virtual catalogue in reference to a shelf list, which indicates where the books as physical objects are. The systematic catalogue and the author catalogue locate the books in a virtual space, in terms of related subject matter or alphabetically related authors. In other words, the meaning of "real" in the discussion here is context dependent.

## Leibniz the Librarian

The greatest theorist after Naudé was Leibniz. Some critics have found him wanting as a librarian. Some say that he was good with schemes and so on, but putting things into practice was perhaps not his strong suit. At the libraries in Hanover and Wolfenbüttel, however, he had great influence in practice about the mutual importance of an alphabetic author catalogue and a systematic disciplinary one. The Enlightenment library, at least in the Germanies, arose in his shadow.[17]

The classification of knowledge concerned Leibniz throughout his life. In his *Nouveaux essais,* a late work, Leibniz literally ended the work and much of his life on this note. He distinguished a civil division of knowledge from a philosophical one. The civil division or pragmatic, user-friendly classification usually employed the traditional academic faculties, as found at universities and their libraries, he noted. He went on say that "the civil and received division, according to the four faculties, is not at all to be distained."[18]

The remark would carry weight, at least in the enlightened Germanies. It would give librarians' pragmatic bent the imprimatur of Leibnizean authority. In this late work, in a passage too condensed to be conclusive, Leibniz seemed to hold that a systematic catalogue was the essential one, to which an alphabetic author index would best be appended, in that order. He had previously held that both principal catalogues were necessary. Philosophical emphasis on the rational perhaps had led to such preference for systematic catalogues.

The first of Leibniz's positions as a librarian was a temporary one. In 1667 a diplomat in Mainz hired him to organize a library. To this end, Leibniz studied Naudé, who influenced him as much as others in Germany. This practical experience accorded well with the young Leibniz's interests in the problem of a universal index of knowledge—the contemporary philosophical debate about a universal classification of knowledge. In the course of his life, Leibniz formulated such classification schemas, of which a pragmatic and a philosophical one survive. And, as he would later in the *Nouveaux essais,* he recommended a systematic or classed catalogue for a public library, with the traditional four academic faculties providing the macrostructure for classification.[19]

In 1676 Leibniz became the ducal librarian in Hanover, a position he would hold for the rest of his life. The library had had five separate catalogues for various pieces of the collection. It was a typical princely one and included nonliterary objects. By 1676 a new universal catalogue was begun—perhaps even commenced before Leibniz's arrival—and swiftly finished. This new catalogue used a pragmatic division of knowledge based on the four faculties, with subdivisions for arts and sciences. Letters were used: A-E for theology, F for law, and so on, ending with P for History, and leaving Q-Z astutely open for unforeseen future fields. In a proposal to the duke in 1676, Leibniz noted that one ought to collect useful and basic as opposed to rare books, which, alas, princes mostly tended to collect.

In a letter of January 1677 to the duke, Leibniz explained that he located older books via auction catalogues and other library catalogues. He ascertained contemporary books via book-fair catalogues and correspondence. Like most, he sought to buy libraries en bloc. Perhaps in view of the Bodleian's specter, he held at this point in his life that one ought to create an author catalogue first, though he did not create one in Hanover. The remark cited above from the *Nouveaux essais* perhaps served to justify his own apparent failing in Hanover.[20]

In 1690 Leibniz accepted the additional position of ducal librarian in Wolfenbüttel, where he did create an author catalogue. The library had a shelf list in the form of a classification schema. Leibniz was to keep that schema for the physical ordering of the books. Beyond such a shelf list, he envisaged a newer systematic catalogue, an alphabetical subject index, and an alphabetical author catalogue. He began working on the last first.

Shelf by shelf, he had entries for all books written on sheets of paper, thirty-two books per sheet. The sheets were then cut uniformly into the thirty-two entries, producing slips of paper or *Zetteln* that one alphabetized as the work proceeded. Once every book had acquired its slip or *Zettel*, and once all had been alphabetized, a universal alphabetical author catalogue was to be copied from the slips of paper. Per custom, Leibniz would produce a *Bandkatalog*, a book catalogue—a series of volumes, with empty space for future entries in each volume. In his grand plan, one would then reshuffle the slips of paper in terms of disciplines, and paste them together in a series of volumes, with empty space left for future entries. This would be a *catalogus materiam* or *Realkatalog*, a systematic catalogue.

On paper, it was a fine plan and testimony to Leibniz's practical sense. The author catalogue was in fact completed. But a certain G. Wagner, who was supposed to compile the systematic catalogue from the slips of paper, left Wolfenbüttel before he finished, or perhaps before he started. Although Leibniz continued to stress to the duke the necessity of producing the systematic catalogue, as well as a subject index, they never materialized. About fifteen years after Leibniz's death, a 1731 report recounted the making of the slips of paper for the author catalogue and the envisaged future use of them in a systematic catalogue, but did not say what had happened to the approximately 120,000 slips of paper, which were apparently missing.[21]

## The Order of Books

The aim and dilemma of systematic cataloguing lay in the finite, material representation of the infinite realm of universal knowledge, at once rational and historical: to find a universal order of books to reflect the universal order of things. Leibniz above all appreciated the difference between the shelf list, which catalogued in a linear, mechanical way and was bound to the materiality of objects, versus both alphabetic and systematic catalogues, which might represent polydimensional and organic interrelations and cross-references.[22]

A shelf list showed where a book physically and really existed. Alphabetic and systematic catalogues localized it virtually and ideally. The latter relations recall what Leibniz envisaged in his "monadology": while the physical world resembled a machine, the metaphysical order resembled a well-catalogued library. A catalogue as virtual library lay beyond the physical, while the shelves of material books had the limitations of the physical.

The alphabetic catalogue embodied a historical moment of knowledge; the systematic catalogue embodied the rational. Representing the historical by the author, as opposed to the collector as in the Baroque library, composition of a catalogue became in principle easy and universal for all libraries. Composition of systematic catalogues proved harder, and often maddening. Even insofar as one used a traditional, pragmatic classification as did Leibniz, instead of a philosophical one, the articulation of knowledge in a systematic catalogue still meant refining the disciplines into all necessary subdisciplines, subsubdisciplines, and so on.

Since no universal systematic division of knowledge would come to hold sway, each *bibliotheca universalis,* in view of its systematic catalogue, looked particular, nonuniversal, and idiosyncratic. The Enlightenment library developed in that way. It was a scandal.[23]

## THE ENLIGHTENMENT LIBRARY

Hugo Kunoff, the great historian of the German Enlightenment library, wrote:

> the systematic shelving of books . . . appeared as logical and essential to all who thought that a collection of universal scope ought to mirror the universe of knowledge and the order of the sciences. For such mirroring, the hall libraries of the time, with the collection arranged along the walls of one room, were well suited. One could take in the entire bibliographical universe in a single sweep of the eyes . . . [Thus] there was less need for detailed catalogues.[24]

Figure 8.2 shows such a hall library, the library of the University of Göttingen.

As *Wunderkammer,* the Baroque library aspired to epitomize the uni-

8.2. The library, University of Göttingen, from Georg D. Heumann, *Wahre Abbildung der Köngl. Groß-Britan. u. Churfürstl. Braunschweigisch-Lüneburgische Stadt Göttingen*, Göttingen, 1747.

verse. The Enlightenment took this aspiration earnestly, but it marginalized objects other than books in libraries. Other objects became ornament, interior decorating. Nonetheless, most libraries still adhered to the centrality of the gaze. The *bibliotheca universalis* as hall library remained in the sphere of the visible. Many still collected books to be shown, monstrosities, with gold lettering and ornate bindings. "A characteristic mark of the princely libraries is the outstanding number of French books," the literary equivalent of gold lettering.[25]

> If necessary, the classification sequence was broken to please the eye. The expensive and rare items occupied the most prominent place. To make all books appear the same size, folios were cut, the bindings of quartos extended, and smaller items encased. The visual effect was not to be marred by ugly call numbers.[26]

Despite the continued centrality of the gaze in libraries of the early Enlightenment, cataloguing became a crucial matter, at least in theory, and the more so as time went by. Given the central place of sight and the visual, one called for systematic catalogues that aided the visualization of the collection—something an author catalogue simply could not do.

Professorial publication greatly increased in the eighteenth century, thanks to graphorrhea and publish or perish. Professors could thus no longer purchase all or even most of the books they needed. This made libraries all the more important. University and college libraries had been envisaged as supplemental to private professorial libraries. As we saw in the preceding chapter, professorial appointments had been governed in part by such private capital. But enlightened policies of appointment tended to decrease the importance of professors possessing such private capital as collectors, while at the same time tending to increase the importance of professors as authors. Relatively speaking, academics came to write more but to own fewer books—or at least to own a smaller percentage of the *bibliotheca universalis*. As the eighteenth century ticked on, libraries fell ever more under the curse of the Red Queen: they had to collect more and more just to stay in the same place.[27]

The increase in book production in the eighteenth century made catalogues all the more crucial. In the eighteenth century in the Germanies and probably most everywhere else, save the Bodleian and places under its spell, most librarians did not see an alphabetic catalogue as essential—despite theorists such as Naudé and Leibniz, who called for both principal sorts. The eighteenth century witnessed, moreover, the decline of subject indices (although a new sort would reemerge in the nineteenth and twentieth centuries). In so far as any catalogues existed beyond shelf lists and separate catalogues for separate collections, universal alphabetic catalogues made a decent showing, but the systematic or disciplinary catalogue emerged as the most common sort of general catalogue, even if actually often unfinished by mad or expired librarians who fell into despair about their systems.[28]

## Oxbridge Libraries

On the whole, they got worse. Oxford colleges generally unchained their books in the eighteenth century, something that Cambridge colleges had begun in the seventeenth. In the early eighteenth century, Cambridge structured its university library by disciplines. The catalogue has not survived but seems to have been alphabetical and based on the Bodleian catalogue. Like the latter, Cambridge's library still housed a coin cabinet and other objects. The Copyright Act of 1710 led to a short-term upswing in publishers' deposits of books, but, as usual, such deposits swiftly declined and became erratic. As budgets still did not really exist, the university as well as the college libraries grew mostly by gifts and bequests.[29]

At Oxford, the single great exception to the sad state of college libraries was the new library at All Souls College. In 1710 Christopher Codrington bequeathed his books along with twenty thousand pounds for maintaining and augmenting the collection. Long before the Bodleian did so, All Souls unchained its books. In 1751 the fellows further resolved that the books would be physically arranged by subject and that both systematic or classified and author catalogues would be made. And they actually managed to accomplish all that.[30]

In August and September 1710, Zacharias von Uffenbach made his now well-known visit to Oxford, during which he recorded unfriendly remarks about it, and especially about the Bodleian. In tune with the time, the institution still presented itself as a museum. On the tour, Uffenbach saw not only books but also instruments, coins, and so on. He speculated, perhaps wrongly, that Wolfenbüttel had more books, though he felt the Bodleian had more manuscripts. Of the books, he noted critically that they were shelved by the four faculties, but without any finer subdivisions on the shelves. The catalogue is "according to the alphabet, and one must wonder why none is [systematic here] according to materials."[31]

Despite occasional spectacular purchases, the Bodleian "never had . . . any very consistent buying policy." Bodleian librarians complained that the construction of the Ashmolean Museum in Oxford had siphoned off money. Most resources for the Bodleian, indeed, faded in the second half of seventeenth century. By 1700, the "Bodleian had to some extent lapsed into being little more than a showpiece for visitors, with the contents of the Anatomy School and the Picture Gallery emphasizing its role as a museum of diverse collections." Humfrey Wanley, the assistant, worried much about the books' appearance, reasoning that impressive displays would encourage future benefactions.[32]

From 1700 to 1725, the Bodleian had relatively good funds for purchases, though funds declined after the 1730s. A midcentury increase set operating funds at about seventeen pounds per year, but was inadequate and far behind that of the more affluent colleges. In the first half of the eighteenth century, moreover, no gifts worthy of note arrived, although in the 1750s some did. Till the end of the century, the collection remained subject to the whims of benefactors. The actual day-to-day running of the library consumed most of the funds from the estate. Publishers persevered in not depositing the required exemplars of their books. In 1779/80, the heads of houses finally agreed to set up a realistic budget for the Bodleian, which they pegged at 480 pounds a year. Purchases and accessions improved.

## Princely German Libraries

"It not seldom occurred that the largest libraries of [enlightened] Europe possessed no catalogues that exhibited their actual book collections."[33] Such was the case with German libraries until the nineteenth century. But librarians tried to catalogue.

The two largest collections were princely libraries. Those were not in Berlin and Munich, but rather in Vienna and Dresden. Though Vienna had the largest library in eighteenth-century German-speaking lands, its imperial and royal library functioned more as a symbol of imperial power than as a resource for knowledge. One librarian wanted to produce author and systematic catalogues and a subject index. In 1776 the alphabetical catalogue was begun, and in 1780 a *Zettelkatalog*, probably systematic, too. But enlightened Vienna brought no catalogue to completion.[34]

At 170,000 volumes in 1778, the princely library in Dresden, Saxony, stood second only to Vienna's. In the 1720s, the catalogue still dated from 1595, with some additions and missing volumes. Plans for an update remained frustrated until 1743–46, when over a hundred volumes of a new catalogue were made—seemingly as separate catalogues for each faculty. In 1746–50 librarians worked on a general alphabetic catalogue of disciplines, and then began a general author catalogue in 1750–53, though neither seem to have been completed. Access to the collection long hinged on the book-fetcher's ever more tested memory.

The librarian J. M. Franck reorganized the collection from 1769 to 1771 by disciplines. He chose a pragmatic system, which he called the genetic system. It was geographical-historical. He ordered books by lands, then by chronology, then probably by subject. Francke died in 1775 before he could finish his somewhat idiosyncratic systematic reorganization of the collection. From 1769 into the 1790s, Dresden had no general catalogue. Beginning in 1786, however, a new librarian produced a shelf list, then an alphabetic catalogue that was completed in 1806. He then moved to a systematic catalogue which, par for this cursed genre, remained unfinished. Perhaps he died and found no worthy disciple.[35]

Up to and beyond the mid-eighteenth century, the royal library in Berlin had few regular funds and no European reputation. In 1775 funds were increased and by 1786 the library could boast some 150,000 volumes—a number, however, soon to be exceeded by the university library in tiny Göttingen. As early as 1660, Berlin librarians had set to work on a shelf-list disciplinary catalogue, with a separate catalogue for each discipline.

But such plans had achieved no success by the eighteenth century. The shelf list, disciplinary catalogue still existed as six separate ones, and the author catalogue had not been current for a long time. Under Friedrich the Great after 1740, librarians added new sections to the shelf-list disciplinary catalogue, and pursued the author catalogue more consistently. But as late as 1791, the royal library in Berlin had no up-to-date catalogues. An academic traveler, Laukhard, remarked that he could not find many books he sought there, while others existed in duplicate or even triplicate, probably unbeknownst to the librarians.[36]

The ducal library in Munich had the advantage of being relatively small, until the nineteenth century, so that a bit of money resulted in catalogues finished as planned. From 1746 to 1781 three catalogues emerged: (1) a twenty-five-volume faculty and disciplinary catalogue, divided into seven classes, (2) an alphabetical catalogue, and (3) a subject index. Except for Bavaria, the better-organized German princely collections would be found in smaller principalities, such as Anspach and Weimar. Most of the larger German states, as seen above, had princely, soon to be state libraries, in as bad a shape as their archives, which should occasion no surprise, since such things had not been long separated.[37]

## Professorial Libraries

Many scholars desired a museum-like preservation of their libraries, like Wagenseil at Altdorf. Heirs, however, all too often desired to get cash by selling the library, even if that meant dismembering it. Many professorial libraries did go by inheritance to sons and sons-in-law, but "on the whole, [eighteenth-century] scholarly collections seldom survived the death of their master," at least at Göttingen.[38]

Judging by the library of the University of Göttingen, which was the most modern among the modern, the auction still formed a chief means of book collection for academic libraries, besides bequests. Auctions generally used a printed catalogue of the collection, and pieces were auctioned in parts separately. So one usually printed separate catalogues in terms of the relevant parts of a collection. If the scholar had not kept a catalogue, the heirs would not usually be much interested in producing an auction catalogue that had great bibliographic value, thus great cost. In the Germanies, however, catalogues of professorial libraries typically showed great bibliographic knowledge, so such catalogues were most likely kept by the academics themselves—for scholarly purposes and vanity.[39]

Gerhard Streich's survey of auction catalogues of Göttingen professors' books from 1743 to 1828 found two chief principles of arrangement: systematic versus format. He found none arranged by author. Most catalogues were systematic, and the larger the professorial collection, the more systematic catalogues predominated. In those where format set the superstructure, the finer substructure was typically systematic. "In view of the considerable mass of books [in the larger collections], a systematic arrangement of the collection was indispensable, should the owner and user not lose an overview altogether. Within subject groups and subgroups, however, the arrangement according to formats remained."[40]

## The Göttingen Library

From a report made by Friedrich Gedike in 1789 after he had surveyed many German universities in commission of the King of Prussia, it is safe to say that Gedike found only one library to be worthy of praise. It was not Helmstedt's library. Nor was it Marburg's which, as he noted, was "insignificant," as was Altdorf's, while Gießen's was "highly insignificant." Tübingen's was better than most, but still on the whole of not great merit. Mainz had a good collection of older Catholic works, but few modern ones.[41]

Gedike began his enumeration of Göttingen's institutes in his report of 1789:

> In first place stands the library. Perhaps no public library has ever accomplished as much as the Göttingen [one]. The whole university owes a large part of her celebrity to it . . . Many professors may thank the library for their own literary fame . . .[42]

Opened in 1737, oriented on a pragmatic, rationalizing view of knowledge, the University of Göttingen had become the university of the Protestant German Enlightenment per se. The visible hand behind the foundation, the Hanoverian minister Münchhausen, had not only a plan for the university but also money for the library. Up to the 1780s, he officially budgeted only 250 to 300 thaler annually. Münchhausen, however, transferred huge ministerial surpluses to the library each year. No records were kept. But judging from the growth, the funds must have been immense. In the 1790s a budget was finally set and averaged 3,000 to 4,000 thaler per year. By 1800, at almost 200,000 volumes, Göttingen's library ranked third by size in the Germanies, behind only the princely libraries in Vienna and Dresden, and ahead of those in Berlin and Munich. It was the largest academic library in the Germanies and, far ahead of the Bodleian, probably the largest on earth.[43]

Figure 8.2 above shows the library in 1747 as a hall library. Captions indicate the room as one hundred by forty (German) feet and the collection as based on books bequeathed by Johann Heinrich von Bülow. The next year, expansion began a process whereby the library took over other rooms on this floor then the whole floor in 1764—later the whole building and more.

Figures 8.3 and 8.4 depict the layout in 1765. History, ethnography, and related books occupy the largest and (new) entry hall, wing A. Wing B has

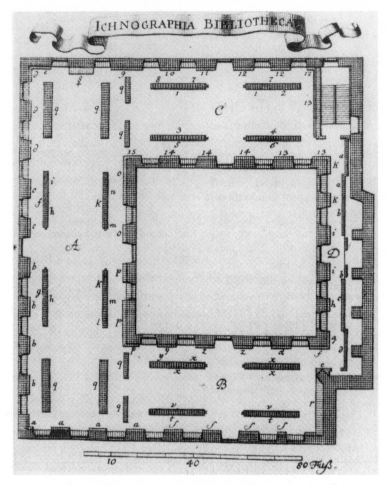

8.3. Floor plan to the library, University of Göttingen.

theology, and wing C houses law. The smallest wing houses medicine, philology, philosophy, mathematics, natural sciences, politics, economics, applied sciences, and arts—all designated miscellaneous. The place given historical and ethnographical works bespeaks Göttingen's—or Minister Münchhausen's—perhaps idiosyncratic but interesting view of enlightenment.

## Göttingen's Catalogues

The size of the collection threatened chaos. Under Münchhausen's aegis, the library responded with three chief catalogues. First came an acquisition

*Erläuterung des Grundrisses von der Bibliothek.*

A. *Der nördliche Saal haupt-*
*sächlich mit Historie besetzt.*
a a a a. Einleitung zur Geschichte, Geographie, nebst den Rei-
sebeschreibungen, Chronolo-
gie, Genealogie, Heraldik,
Diplomatik.
b b b b. allgemeine Weltge-
schichte und Statistik.
c c. Geschichte u. Sammlungen
der Friedens- u. anderer Trac-
tate: c. auch vermischte historische Werke.
d d d. Schriftsteller von alten
Denkmälern und Gebräuchen.
e. Geschichte der alten Reiche
und Staaten.
f. – – – von Italien.
g. – – – von den nördlichen Rei-
chen, Ungarn, Türkey, Asia,
Africa, America.
h h. – – – von Teutschland.
i. – – – von der Schweitz.
k k. – – – von Engelland.
l. – – – von den Niederlanden
m m. – – – von Frankreich.
n. – – – von Portugall und
Spanien.

\* \* \*

o o. die alten Griechischen
Schriftsteller.
p p p. die alten Lateinischen
Schriftsteller.

\* \* \*

q . . . q. Rastelen u. Tische unten
mit Locaten versehen, und mit
volumineusen Sammlungen
besetzt.
♀ Das Bildniß des Curators Erc.

B. *Der westliche Saal, ganz mit*
*Theologie besetzt.*
I. Bibelsammlung, und philolo-
gia und critica sacra.
s s s s. Ausleger der H. Schrift.
t t. Dogmatische Theologie.
v v. Patres und Kirchen-
scribenten.
x x x x. Allgemeine und besondere Kirchengeschichte nebst
den Concilien, und Kirchen-
gebräuchen.
y y. Streittheologie.
z z. Sittenlehre, Casuistik,
Pastoraltheologie.
Homiletik, Ascetik.

C. *Der östliche Saal, enthält auf*
*denen in der Mitte stehenden*
*Repositorien.*
1. 1. Die bürgerliche Rechtsge-
lahrheit.
2. Das Lehnrecht, und Privat-
recht.
3. Das Kirchenrecht.
4. Das Land- und Stadtrecht.
5. Das allgemeine, und Teutsche
Staatsrecht.
6. Die Samlung von Deduc-
tionen.
7. 7 Die juristische Praxin, nebst
Decisionen, Responsis, Consiliis, Obseruation., Disceptat.
etc.
8. Zusammengedruckte Werke
der Juristen.
An der Ostseite.
9. Die Quellen der Arzneygelahr-
heit, nebst der Anatomie und
Physiologie.
10. Die allgemeine Pathologie
Semiotik, Diätetik.
11. Die allgemeine Therapie,
Materia medica, Pharmacie,
Chymie.
12. 12. Die medicinische und
chirurgische Praxin, Medici-
nam forensem, vermischte
Werke.
An der Querwand, und West-
seite.
13. 13. 13. Die Gelehrten-
geschichte.
14. 14. 14. Die Philologie u.
Etitik.
15. Die Werke der neuern Philologen und vermischte Schriften in allerley Sprachen.
D. *oder der schmale Saal enthält*
a a. die Mathematik.
b b. die allgemeine, und besondere Naturlehre.
c. die Philosophischen, alte und
neue, Secten.
d. Logik, Metaphysik, natürliche
Gottesgelahrheit, Recht der
Natur, Moral.
e. Politik. f. Oeconomie.
g. Handlung und Gewerbe.
h. Schreibkunst, Mahlerey, Bild-
hauerey, Musik, Tanz-Fecht-
Kriegskunst.
i i. Dichtkunst.
k k. Redekunst.

§. 117

8.4. Key to the floor plan to the library, University of Göttingen.

catalogue with full bibliographic entries and each book's accession number.
By 1789 an alphabetical catalogue existed, having been revised for the third
time and now—with a page for every author and room for additional
pages—able to encompass new authors far into the future. Finally, finished
in its first revision 1743–55, the third and most famous was the systematic
catalogue, with the following categories: (1) theology, (2) law, (3) medicine,

(4) philosophy, natural sciences, politics, and art, (5) ancient philology, history, and ancillary disciplines, and (6) historia literaria. "The entire [early modern] practice of cataloguing obtains its apogee in the Göttingen system" of these three catalogues, crowned by the latter, systematic one.[44]

G. Matthiae, the earliest principal assistant to the first director, Gesner, had begun the systematic catalogue. J. D. Reuß, later first assistant librarian, and Heyne, philology professor and director of the library, 1763–1812, the latter whom we've met in chapters above, perfected this catalogue and improved the library altogether. Reuß and Heyne composed the greatest staff of librarians in the Enlightenment. Most importantly, they put into practice, radically, what librarians such as Naudé, Dury, and Leibniz had wanted to do.

Reuß and Heyne freed the systematic catalogue from the grasp of the shelf list or physical arrangement of the collection. In fact, they used a book's location in the systematic catalogue to specify its physical location. A major breakthrough came at this mundane level: they specified the book's format—folio, quarto, octavo—as part of the book's signature, a shelf or call number. Reuß and Heyne designated formats of books as 2°, 4°, and 8° in the catalogue. They saw that the systematic catalogue's location of a book, along with the page number in the catalogue, could give each book a unique signature or trace in the system.[45]

In other words, a book's virtual or literary location or signature in the systematic catalogue—in the system of knowledge—dictated its physical location in the actual order of the library. That reversed the traditional relationship of catalogue and books. The catalogue as a virtual library achieved supremacy over the actual library, the physical order of books.

### Acquisition Rationalized

Under Münchhausen's ministry, Heyne rationalized acquisitions as well. Like most, Göttingen sought libraries en bloc—still the best way to get old books. But that no longer gave the envisaged ideal and eventual primary principle of acquisition. The "library's singular strength was the result of programmatic purchasing of new publications," as opposed to being subject to the whims of dead collectors. The bureaucratic instrument of the budget—or better, what Heyne had before he had a budget, namely, almost carte blanche for new acquisitions—changed everything. Before the nineteenth century, Göttingen was really the only academic library that had the means for regular and planned acquisitions.[46]

Administering one of the largest collections on earth, Heyne renounced the fantasy of the universal library. Göttingen's would be no *bibliotheca universalis*. An enlightened librarian confronted finitude, thus made selections. Opposed to typical private collectors, and heeding the advice of theorists such as Naudé and Leibniz, Heyne avoided rare or costly works unless they were deemed essential. In the Enlightenment's spirit, he collected the useful. And there only a book's contents mattered. Göttingen would be a research library, not a museum or *Wunderkammer*. Old and rare books were, indeed, very nice. But essential was, rather, the regular, serial acquisition of the now all too regularly producing academic market.[47]

That notion, along with the systematic catalogue, moved the library's center from the material and monstrous to the formal and rational. It dematerialized books, whose covers became incidental and contents essential. Although Göttingen, too, put some on display, its books were not monsters meant to be looked at, but rather to be read. The library became (and remains) justly famous for its reader-friendly atmosphere as for its catalogues. Indeed the latter were part of the former. In Göttingen dead collectors no longer lorded over the library and its shelves. Future readers were rather served in their research.

The fame of Göttingen's library spread that of the systematic catalogue. An academic traveler named Hirsching noted circa 1790 that the university library in Erlangen consisted of separate, donated collections, and that it had a shelf list and an author catalogue. He went on to say that "there is still neither a scientific register [no systematic catalogue] nor an overview of the parts at hand, [something] that is a most necessary ancillary aid for a large collection, especially for an academic one."[48]

From Uffenbach's visit to Oxford at the beginning of the century, to Hirsching's visit to Erlangen at the end, German academics expected to find systematic catalogues, even at the expense of author catalogues. "For most of the eighteenth-century librarians in Germany, preparation of an author catalogue was clearly less essential than preparation of a *Realcatalog*," that is, a systematic one. Göttingen's library was "the first scientific universal library in the world." It cast the model, albeit eventually revised, for the research library.[49]

Chapter 2 traced the emergence of the disciplinary or systematic lecture catalogue in the eighteenth century. Here we see a preference for systematic library catalogues, over mere shelf lists, which reflect collectors and the history of the collection, as well as over author catalogues, whose arrangement as alphabetic is arbitrary and reflects the provenance of works. The systematic catalogue boded the new and most spiritual *bibliotheca virtualis*.

# BIBLIOTHECA VIRTUALIS

Citing a provocative turn of phrase by Georg Leyh, Heinrich Roloff wrote:

The conviction of the "possibility and the necessity of the dictatorial power of the catalogue over the books" [according to Georg Leyh] found its typical expression in the systematic catalogue (*Realcatalog*), dominating in northern [Protestant] Germany and first developed in Göttingen.[50]

The dictatorship of the catalogue is the hegemony of the virtual over the physical library.

The period from the mid-seventeenth to early ninetieth century witnessed the gradual triumph of the systematic catalogue, first in its disciplinary form, via the four faculties, and then later in its fully systematic, "philosophical" form as at Göttingen. By the end of the eighteenth century, "it was the Göttingen library whose practices enjoyed a canonical status," above all in cataloguing. One saw the systematic catalogue as the crown of library science, the key point of leverage, after a big annual budget, for the rationalization of collection.[51]

In implicit or explicit reference to Göttingen, systematic catalogues were pursued further in the first decades of the nineteenth century—from 1800–06 at Würzburg, 1811–20 at Marburg, and beginning in 1813 in Berlin, but only really pursued from 1845 to 1881, when it was completed. At Kiel an 1832 regulation for the library reads like a verbatim transcript of Göttingen's policies.[52]

But the scandal of the virtual library remained that of the systematic catalogue. For, despite Göttingen's ideological hegemony, its own systematic catalogue had as little success colonizing other libraries as had Leibniz's or anyone else's classifications. If there were to be a universal virtual library, instantiated concretely in the various actual libraries, the virtual library would need to exist somehow in the manner of a literary *bibliotheca universalis*.

## Historia Literaria

Conrad Gesner stands at the origin of modern library cataloguing in that sense. His *Bibliotheca universalis* of 1545 and *Pandectarum . . . [et] Partitionum* of 1548/49 were not only important for the theory and practice of library catalogues before Naudé, but also influential in the genre of *historia literaria*. Gesner's 1545 work was a universal library, a general archive and history of literature, a universal bibliography, which listed books alphabetically by author. The two volumes of *Pandectarum* were structured by twenty-one academic disciplines and subdisciplines. Thus the ideal of both sorts of catalogues.[53]

From the seventeenth to the eighteenth century, such universal libraries were often not ideal. Many split on the historical versus rational classification of books. Some organized by authors, others by disciplines. Organized by disciplines, *historia literaria* held the promise of a universal systematic catalogue, if one author's scheme could triumph. During the eighteenth century, whether organized primarily by authors or by disciplines, works within *historia literaria* became less polymath and descriptive, and more specialized and critical.

So in the 1770s, for example, the physician Albrecht von Haller published critical bibliographies on anatomy, surgery, and applied medicine. He called each a "bibliotheca." At the level of the systematic catalogue, such works replicated the Baroque catalogue as a congeries of separate catalogues, now not of collectors but rather of disciplines or subdisciplines. Assembling all such specialized literary libraries, *historia literaria* as a discipline became a literary library of libraries, a catalogue of the ideal universal library.[54]

*Historia literaria* had envisaged a universal library of the past. Conjoined with the new review journals of the second half of the eighteenth century, the virtual library attained a most potent and imposing form: a virtual library of current works. As Heyne arrived in Göttingen in the early 1760s, book-fair catalogues had already achieved something like their modern, disciplinary form. And that helped for rationalizing library acquisitions.

## ADB and GGA

But the key lay in the appearance of review journals such as Nicolai's *Allgemeine Deutsche Bibliothek* (1765–1806) or *ADB*, as it was known. *ADB* in format resembled the *English Monthly Review*, as did *GGA* (*Göttinger gelehrten Anzeigen*), edited by Heyne. Such review journals allowed for a more rational acquisitions policy than an earlier one, which had been based on book dealers' and auction catalogues. Moreover, a crucial synergy would eventually emerge between review journals and library acquisitions.[55]

In 1765 Nicolai had conceived *ADB* as a virtual German library of the present. He eschewed the subjective choices of previous review journals in favor of "comprehensive coverage" of all academic and literary works in German. Like many review journals in the eighteenth century and for some time into the nineteenth, *ADB* reviews were anonymous, in the interests of a supposedly neutral review. Short reviews followed the order of the disciplines and were to give an objective (*sachlich*) summary of the book's contents.[56]

*ADB* would thus be a systematic catalogue and virtual library of current German works. Possessing it, one might forgo buying many books. It furthered the dematerialization of the book, as the virtual library embodied only a simulacrum of books. But Nicolai soon had to abandon the fantasy of a universal German library. Moreover, the ever more books that appeared meant ever shorter summaries, ever thinner virtual books.

In the Germanies, book production was ten times greater in 1763–1803 than in 1721–63. That made all the more need for virtual libraries such as Nicolai's. Many arose and most called themselves "library" or "archive" or "journal for learned things" or "journal for literature." Alongside *ADB*, *GGA* became important after 1770, and *ALZ* (*Allgemeine Literatur-Zeitung*) became probably the most important after 1785. *GGA* and *ALZ* aimed to review not just German but rather all useful academic and literary works. Heyne edited *GGA* after 1770 and one saw his roles as librarian and as editor as synergetic. All books fit for the library were to be reviewed in the journal, and all books reviewed in the journal were to go into the library. For works published after a certain point, *GGA* became then the virtual double or summary of the real collection, although not in a purely rational space but rather as the trace of its archaeology or history—its yearly growth.[57]

Because the Göttingen faculty was supposedly responsible for deciding what books to buy, and because all new books bought were supposedly reviewed in *GGA* (and vice versa), and because the faculty would supposedly write all reviews in *GGA*, then the library would serve as an archive of what the university as a collective had read. Or, as Heyne saw it, *GGA* should be a sort of diary of what the collective had thought and researched. While collectors, in view of books' covers, had lorded over the Baroque library, the collective, in view of books' contents, came to embody itself in Göttingen's Enlightenment library.

## Serial Acquisition

The acquisition of monstrous materials via extraordinary events gave way to the regulated collection of the serial, normal, and useful. The systematic catalogue, with *historia literaria*, gave an overview for the rational planning of the collection in view of older literature—in other words, one saw what was missing. The review journals indicated new works worthy of acquisition—or, rather, what was already acquired. In 1789 Gedike praised the Göttingen library for its "well-conceived plan" of acquisition. Not the subjective whim of librarians and collectors, but rather the impersonal, objective dictates of research disciplines ascertained through consultation with Göttingen professors determined what would be bought.[58]

As contemporaries saw it, the University of Göttingen—thanks to *GGA*, its collective review journal, as well as its specialized review journals as disciplinary libraries, and not to forget textbooks and works in *historia literaria* produced by the Göttingen faculty—had emerged in the Germanies as a sort of supreme court of the Republic of Letters. Heyne lamented the "lack of policing" (*Policey*) in that republic and hoped through the Göttingen libraries, real and virtual, to instill a "normal-law" (*Normalgesetz*) in the republic for rationality and good taste, and style, too. It was meant as a benign dictatorship.[59]

Göttingen's enlightened serial acquisitions transformed the nature of the library from a juridical and historical plot or mausoleum into a bureaucratic and disciplinary system. Its system of catalogues transposed the order of books from a visual physical space into a rational virtual one. Like a Baroque shelf list, Göttingen's review journal, *GGA*, catalogued the history of the contemporaneous collection and also attested to the collective reading and research of the faculty. Göttingen's enlightened library in its own way also became an archive, a mausoleum of the faculty and its bureaucratic plots or, rather, research interests.

The libraries in Alexandria and Vivarium had epitomized the ancient and medieval worlds. Göttingen's reflected the modern one. Enlightened Göttingen rationalized the *bibliotheca universalis* into a *bibliotheca virtualis*. The virtual library, especially in its mode as a review journal, came to dictate not only the character of the research library, but also the course of professorial appointments. Bad notices in the virtual library could spell death.

## THE ROMANTIC LIBRARY

"More light," said Johann Wolfgang von Goethe on 6 November 1817, and not for the last time in life. After appearing unexpectedly on that day in the university library in Jena, so seriously did this poet and scientist and minister from Weimar take his new position as supreme cosupervisor of the university library, the next day, without consulting the Jena town council, or even anyone for that matter, he had part of the ancient city wall torn down to allow more light into the library. Goethe's ministerial mission, which he discharged in person and with gusto to boot, was to turn the university library into a modern one.

He had the disjoint libraries integrated into one, leaving only the Buder collection, per testament, separate. For the entire collection, he instructed that systematic and alphabetical catalogues were to be begun. Under Goethe's supervision, the library sought a pragmatic division of knowledge, against the overly scientific bent seen as existing—fairly or not—at Göttingen. So the arrangement of the systematic catalogue in Jena did not at all try to articulate a philosophical system of knowledge, but rather only used what were seen, at least since Leibniz, as commonplace thus user-friendly, traditional divisions of knowledge.

Thus Jena did not adopt the Göttingen systematic catalogue per se. But Goethe had the books reorganized so that the shelf list reflected the systematic catalogue, à la Göttingen. So pressing did the task appear, he compelled the librarian to relinquish the editorship of Jena's review journal—the *Jenaische Allgemeine Literatur-Zeitung*, a worthy rival to the *GGA* (and *ALZ*) as a virtual library. Weimar set a good sum for the reorganization of Jena's library, but for a time the annual budget remained small. Jena could thus not really imitate Göttingen's heroic bureaucratization of acquisition.[60]

Goethe's program to follow Göttingen and compile systematic and alphabetic catalogues was typical by and after 1800, but would be slowly abandoned. The Romantic era witnessed the triumph of the historical over the systematic. By mid-nineteenth century, librarians would break with enlightened Göttingen on a crucial point: the dictatorship of the systematic catalogue over the collection. The author catalogue would take hegemony over the systematic one and would not assume the role of a dictator over the collection.

### The British Museum and Oxbridge

The Göttingen model made systematic acquisition essential. The British Museum did not have that into the nineteenth century—note, too, the preservation of the library within a museum. What Heyne was to the Göttingen library in the eighteenth century, Antonio Panizzi was to the British Museum in the nineteenth.

When Panizzi came to the department of printed books in 1831, it possessed about 240,000 volumes. That was less than the princely-cum-national libraries in Copenhagen, Munich, and Berlin, not even to mention Dresden, Vienna, and Paris. In the 1830s there was discussion in and around the British Museum about composing a class catalogue as a systematic one after the example of Göttingen. Panizzi objected, but the project nonetheless was begun in 1831. By 1834 most of the old collection had been done. Only 20,000 volumes of it remained, plus the 120,000 from the king's private library. One estimated ten years to finish, and that was without taking account of the new books piling up. No author catalogue existed.[61]

The library committee then recommended forgetting the systematic or class catalogue in favor of completing an author catalogue instead. The trustees of the library, however, wanted a systematic catalogue and pushed for its completion, at least up to 1837, when Panizzi became the keeper of printed books. Thereafter he got his way. He halted the systematic catalogue in its tracks and had an author catalogue begun.

Alas, a new controversy broke out with the trustees, as they wanted it printed, à la the Bodleian catalogue, which Panizzi also opposed. That notwithstanding, he succeeded in rationalizing acquisitions on the Göttingen model, while actually rejecting its central feature: the dictatorship of the systematic catalogue. Later in the century, one would look back at the earlier controversy of the author versus the systematic catalogue as being now over. A systematic or classified catalogue "may have answered in the library of Alexandria . . ." but modern knowledge was too intricate, had too many departments. Ideally one would have both, but the author catalogue had clear primacy. It now was the essential catalogue.[62]

The Göttingen model of the catalogue interested Cambridge, too. Actually, plans for a systematic catalogue had been homegrown and reached back at least to the mid-eighteenth century, when nothing happened. In 1818 new plans were hatched for a new author catalogue and a class catalogue as well. The new author catalogue was started and finished between 1818 and 1826, but the high cost of the class catalogue had led to its abandonment. Then in 1831, now explicitly drawing on the Göttingen model, plans for a systematic catalogue returned to the table. But in the end, again, they came to naught. What had changed at Cambridge, however, as well as at most other universities in Europe in the nineteenth century, was that a central or university research library had become a self-evident necessity, notwithstanding the continued existence of the old college libraries, and the nascent departmental and institute libraries.[63]

As Oxford would imitate Cambridge in the nineteenth century by instituting rigorous university examinations for degrees, so was Cambridge to some extent imitating Oxford more than Göttingen in getting serious about a university library. As noted, the colleges at Oxford had redeemed the promise of the early Bodleian, as they voted in 1779/80 for significant, regular funding for acquisitions at the Bodleian. The spell of the systematic catalogue would then haunt modern Oxford, too, as the mid-nineteenth century witnessed attempts to reinstall a class catalogue, now that a budget had been secured for acquisitions.

By 1856 Henry Coxe, the sublibrarian, had set out seventy-three subdivisions for it, as well as a new physical arrangement of books by relative location. New accessions were to go into the new system, as one slowly re-classified the old collection. Coxe did not plan to rearrange books physically but only virtually in the new classified catalogue. The systematic catalogue would thus not serve as the shelf list, as it had at Göttingen. Librarians began a revised author catalogue first, and completed it in 1878. Thereafter Coxe hoped to move to the class catalogue. But his project was given up and not pursued thereafter at Oxford.[64]

## Austro-German Academic Libraries

In 1838/39 the provincial Austrian University of Graz complained to the ministry in Vienna. Graz pointed out the Austrian Universities at Lemberg (Lvov), Olmütz (Olmouc) and Innsbruck had, respectively, enrollments of 1,000, 1,000, and 700 students, and library budgets, respectively, of 1,000, 700, and 600 florin, while Graz had more than 1,300 students but only 400 florin per year for the library. Such was the modern rational calculus by which one made points with the ministry. Research required budgets in the eyes of academics, and enrollments dictated the size of budgets in eyes of the ministry.[65]

The University of Freiburg im Br., once part of Anterior Austria, presents an interesting case. Cataloguing went on feverishly and fitfully from 1788 to 1819, resulting in multiple catalogues. These formed not a system as at Göttingen, but rather separate catalogues, as in the Baroque. An author catalogue also existed, but it was by collection, thus not universal. In the 1820s, the assistant librarian, H. Schreiber, began a systematic catalogue for new acquisitions. He framed this catalogue as *standortsfrei*, that is, the systematic catalogue and the shelf list functioned as two separate, unrelated entities.

It was the now familiar distinction between the systematic catalogue as the rational order of knowledge and virtual library, versus the shelf list as representing the physical order of books. Schreiber also envisaged making a universal author catalogue. Sadly, he quarreled with the head librarian Baggeti about which catalogue to pursue first, the systematic or the author. Schreiber advocated the author catalogue, while Baggeti stood for the systematic. A library committee wavered between the two. The matter was decided in 1822, when Schreiber left the library. That spelt the end of the systematic catalogue at Freiburg im Br.[66]

The story elsewhere was mostly the same. Attempts to compose a systematic catalogue like Göttingen's at the university libraries in Breslau, Bonn, Greifswald, Kiel, and other places met with difficulties and failures. An author catalogue was easier and faster to do, and usually done without driving librarians mad or to the grave. Of the state libraries, the Viennese remained for a time the largest, and long beset by catalogue problems. In 1847 a new, universal author catalogue was finally begun, and completed in 1874. At the same time, librarians took to seeing a systematic catalogue as useless, even harmful. Dresden pursued a systematic catalogue, but did not complete it. An author catalogue provided the chief means of access to that collection. Of the major state libraries, only Berlin relentlessly pursued a systematic catalogue in the nineteenth century. It took from 1845 to 1881 to complete.

In Bavaria, as a result of secularizations, the Munich state library experienced huge growth from 1807 to 1811. From 1808 to 1811, J. W. Hamberger, one of the librarians, began a systematic catalogue and produced the first 47 volumes, consisting of 20,000 pages, for the then extant 120,000 volumes in the collection. Hamberger worked feverishly right up to his nervous breakdown. He landed in an asylum, did not return, and found no worthy sane successors. In 1812/13, the library decided to produce an author catalogue instead, which it completed, along with a shelf list, between 1814 and 1818. In 1819 a subject index was begun, and valiantly pursued until 1851, when it, too, was abandoned in Munich.[67]

## German State Archives

Developments at German archives in the late Enlightenment and early Romantic era make the continued attraction of the systematic catalogue at the time clearer. One of the riddles of the previous chapter was the resistance of the Prussian archive to dossiers, while Austria embraced them after 1848, Bavaria in 1806, and the Hanoverian lands long before that. The resistance by Prussia to the dossier seems the obverse of its dogged pursuit of a systematic catalogue. Prussia sought the sort of rational overview produced by the systematic in the state archive as well as in the state library.

From the mid Enlightenment into the Romantic era, German theorists of the archive discussed the question of the systematic versus the alphabetic. German archivists would come to embrace the former, the systematic, as the primary principle for paperwork. This probably reinforced, at least for a time, librarians' inclination to systematic catalogues. Archivists like librarians saw a role for the alphabet and, in the best of all possible worlds, one would have had many mutually interreferencing indices and catalogues—systematic, chronological and alphabetic. The question, as ever, concerned the primary and essential.

Important works from the 1760s to 1780s on the practice of the registry, that is, the accession of paperwork at the ministry and the archive, debated the question of the primary. An alphabetic arrangement of paperwork seemed to be the easiest system on a day-to-day basis. But, as paper piled up merely alphabetically, and was moved from the registry to the archive, finding anything became harder and harder the deeper into the past one looked.

One could keep alphabetic indices to find important persons, corporations, or other entities in the acts. But some argued it would be better for the archive for the system of filing in the registry to mirror the departments of the state, that is, be systematic at the primary level. The secondary ordering principle would best be chronological. The systematic and the chronological allowed one to view matters in the "most natural connections" of things.[68]

The Göttingen systematic catalogue in the library worked in fact exactly that way. It had a primary arrangement by the departments of knowledge, and a secondary one by the chronology or publication date of the work. Göttingen had reversed the roles of the catalogue and the actual collection, but it had still linked them essentially. Instead of making the physical ordering of the library arbitrary, Göttingen used the systematic catalogue to govern the shelf list, that is, the physical disposition of the books. The above discussion by archivists presumed a seemingly self-evident preservation of such a link in the archive, too.

Friedrich Gutscher's very interesting *Die Registratur-Wissenschaft* of 1811 surveyed the discussion theretofore and made a powerful case for a systematic order in the archive. Gutscher wanted to highlight the importance of the registry and archive to the land. The science of these must be able to do all that library science could do, and more. Registering and archiving paperwork posed more complicated problems than did the mere cataloguing books. In the past, a good archivist (like a librarian) lived mostly by memory, as one lacked clear systems to file and find documents. Now one needed such filing systems.[69]

How to file the acts: alphabetically or systematically? Earlier writers on this subject seemed to be in great disagreement, Gutscher noted. Citing authors who advocated an alphabetic order, he agreed that it was the easiest way for the registrar to file documents day to day; but it was not the easiest way to locate them later, especially much later, as Gutscher argued. He also recounted those who spoke against an alphabetic arrangement of acts, including J. Oegg's influential *Ideen einer Theorie der Archivwissenschaft* of 1804.[70]

In Gutscher's review of regulations, Prussia and Bavaria are worthy of note. In Prussia, the regulation of March 1788 held that neither alphabetic nor numeric nor chronological systems were sufficient. Acts must, rather, be filed systematically. "Things are to be ordered *in view of materials,* and the principles of the order are to be taken from the nature of the things themselves," whereafter leeway obtained for subordering. Gutscher noted that the regulation set systematic filing as a norm, without wholly excluding alphabetic filing. For Bavaria an edict of 1799 enjoined that the archives were not to be separately ordered by each department. The archive, rather, "should form a single whole," and be structured in terms of relevant matters systematically, then geographically. The academic dossiers in the Bavarian Ministry of the Interior apparently violated or reversed that sentiment in 1806.[71]

Gutscher himself saw a systematic order as better in general than an alphabetic one. A systematic arrangement allowed acts to be surveyed according to their "true, natural connections." The systematic was the only principle that created unities, *Einheiten.* With the last comments, and in view of the Prussian and Bavarian regulations of 1788 and 1799, we have entered the realm of Romanticism and its notion of organic wholes and unities. Those are sentiments that one would think more conducive to the systematic than to the alphabetic.[72]

## The Research Library and the Author Catalogue

The author catalogue, however, triumphed in the library during the Romantic era. Albrecht Kayser's *Ueber die Manipulation bey der Einrichtung einer Bibliothek und der Verfertigung der Bücherverzeichnisse* of 1790 proved a crucial work in the Germanies. It undermined the dictatorship of the systematic catalogue.

Kayser insists that "the place where a book stands is most unimportant." The idea is simple and, as we've seen, has historical precedents. Its lack of self-evidence is due to the tension between the virtual and the actual library. In the Baroque library, the shelf list—the aggregate of collectors' estates and books by disciplines—had de facto determined the character of a catalogue. In the Enlightenment library à la Göttingen, the systematic catalogue de facto dictated the shelf list, thus the physical order of the books. Despite the theoretical separation of the two orders—the virtual order of catalogues versus the physical order of shelves and books—the primacy of the gaze, the empire of the visual, had bound them closely together. The Romantic library finally cast them asunder.[73]

Kayser's view abandons any visual or rational sense of an overview of the books. A systematic catalogue remains useful, he says, but is not essential. What is, he holds, is a shelf list and an author catalogue. Since the place where a book stands is most unimportant, the physical collection may end up an actual chaos where—eerily reminiscent of the Baroque library—disjoint protocols of ordering might obtain on the shelves. With a shelf list and a signature in the author catalogue, the arbitrary physical location of the book can be ascertained from the list of the authors imposed by the arbitrary nature of the alphabet.[74]

The scandal of the systematic catalogue lay not only in its resistance to completion. It lay as well in its parochial nature. Witness Jena's rejection of Göttingen's classification of knowledge. The author catalogue gave no rational overview of the books, since it was based on the arbitrary arrangement of the alphabet; nonetheless, it served the essential finding function of a catalogue. And in its own way, it possessed universality. It was uniform in principle from place to place.

In the nineteenth century, more and more libraries, including the British Museum and even some North American libraries, would take enlightened Göttingen as a model. A research library meant one like Göttingen's. Budgets eventually increased and allowed a rational collection of current works, reviewed in ever more specialized disciplinary journals. The center of collection moved everywhere from the rare and extraordinary to the regular and serial. Princely libraries became national ones. Acquisition were no longer subject to the whims of the collector-prince but were for the sake of the user-public. Most (German) stacks would eventually become closed, making the catalogue the only means of public access and view.

For a time, the systematic catalogue—the Enlightenment and Göttingen's legacy—remained the librarian's ultimate duty. This led in some places to retardation of the author catalogue, which had become generally seen as the librarian's first and essential duty.[75]

## The Babel of Authors

The essential catalogue thus no longer reflected the Enlightenment's order of things, and not at all the Baroque's lineage of collectors. What then did the author catalogue reflect? Did Romanticism make the author sovereign in the virtual library?

The virtual library of review journals continued to inform acquisitions, although the structure of the central catalogue qua author catalogue no longer mirrored that of the review journals—the latter on the whole still structured by disciplines. General review journals persisted throughout the nineteenth century, while specialized review journals assumed more and more importance during the century. This ever growing decentralization embodied the obverse of the decline of the systematic catalogue in the regime of research. Göttingen's *bibliotheca virtualis* had sought to preserve an aspect of the visible from the *bibliotheca universalis* and *Wunderkammer*. But the pursuit of research occulted an overview.[76]

Authors supplanted an overview in the central library catalogue. The author-function has varied and may be different in different books. It may play one role in literature, another in academia, and still another in the library. The debates we've seen above about systematic versus author catalogues indicate that technical matters, especially the finding-function of a catalogue, played an important role. But if any merely technical matters existed, this was not one of them. In the past, other catalogues with indices have fulfilled the finding-function in libraries. The author catalogue fulfills that function best, if authors take precedence over topics in the realm of knowledge—a medieval and a Romantic view.

In the Middle Ages, certain canonical authors—Moses, Aristotle, Hippocrates, Galen, John, Paul, Pliny, Augustine, Gratian, and others—dominated academia. Lectures, disputations and examinations invoked their names to establish their authority and orthodoxy. "In the seventeenth and eighteenth centuries, a totally new conception was developed when scientific texts were accepted on their own merits and positioned within an anonymous and coherent conceptual system of established truths and methods of verification. Authentification no longer required reference to the individual who had produced them; the role of the author disappeared as an index of truthfulness."[77]

The modern regime of research, illuminated in chapters above, supported this new, anonymous or impersonal framework of knowledge, as did the systematic library catalogue, championed by some theorists after 1650 and put into practice by 1750. But in the rise of the German research university, we have also seen a concomitant emphasis on writing over speaking, culminating in a near apotheosis of the author in the Romantic era. The Romantic author poses not so much as truth-teller, as rather more a creator, a producer of original works, with a charismatic spark of genius. The author's genius or spirit infuses and expresses itself in each of the author's works, which thus constitute not a list but an organic whole.

Romanticism found this organic whole, the author's spirit, in the oeuvre. It became the pivotal unity (*Einheit*) or whole (*Ganze*) in Romantic hermeneutics, mediating between a work and a culture. To understand any given work, say Plato's *Republic,* one must be able to understand each part of the work in terms of the whole work as a unity, and at the same time be able to see the whole in each of the parts. This is the first level of the hermeneutical circle between parts and the whole. But, to understand any given work, such as *The Republic,* one must be able to place this work into the whole of the Platonic oeuvre, which, again, one can only understand by grasping its spirit in each of Plato's individual works. Finally, as the work and the oeuvre mutually inform one another, the culture stands at a third level in the hermeneutical circle. To understand a work by Plato or the Platonic oeuvre, one must understand the culture or *genius populi* that produced it, which genius, however, one cannot grasp unless one knows all its works and authors.[78]

As we saw in chapter 6, philologists sought, by means of their doctoral students, to collect and reconstruct the fragments by obscure classical authors in this period. Ideally, one would assemble the works or fragments of every author into the complete oeuvre, which the author catalogue sets as its ideal of order. The German Romantic ideology of culture, as a *genius populi,* itself undercut the Enlightenment's criterion for collection, that is, the criterion of usefulness. Since every bit of writing is an expression of culture, an expression of the genius of a people, the library would be obliged to collect, in principle, everything by every author.[79]

This nightmare then haunts Romantic fantasies of the library—the need to acquire "the minute history of the future, the autobiographies of the archangels, the faithful catalogue of the Library, thousands and thousands of false catalogues, a demonstration of the fallacy of these catalogues, a demonstration of the fallacy of the true catalogue . . ."

## CONCLUSION

The Baroque sanctified the collector. The Enlightenment adored the system. Romanticism enshrined the author. Those are generalizations and subject to much qualification. But the tensions in the Baroque catalogue had been between the collector and the disciplines. That tension shifted in the Enlightenment and the Romantic eras to a tension between the systematic and the author catalogue. Each era resolved the tensions differently.

In the author catalogue, Romanticism set an alphabet of authors over a Baroque genealogy of collectors and an Enlightenment topology of disciplines. The dynamics of research led to a dialectic of the centralized and collective versus the specialized and individual in the Romantic era. The enlightened reading collective at Göttingen had vested itself in a central library and a general review journal. A congeries of specialized journals and institute libraries arose in and after the Romantic era. This recapitulated the aggregate of the Baroque library, but now as one of research disciplines and not juridical estates.

The triumph of the author catalogue in the Romantic era has interesting parallels and disjunctures with developments seen in previous chapters. Chapter 2 examined the emergence of the disciplinary or systematic lecture catalogue in the late Enlightenment. Such catalogues flourished in the Romantic era. Figures 2.8–2.9 showed that the alphabet came to restructure the old Latin catalogue of academics. The hierarchy of academic ranks—ordinary professor, extraordinary professor, lecturer—remained the primary ordering principle within each faculty, while the alphabet replaced seniority as the secondary principle in those ranks. But that alphabetical order seems not exactly the same as the author-function in the library.

In consideration of developments in the archive above, we saw a preference for the systematic as opposed to the alphabetic in the registry, thus the archive, in the late Enlightenment and early Romanticism. Such a preference for the systematic in the archive should have precluded the advent of dossiers as a filing system. The alphabetic order tied to the use of dossiers mirrors that of the author-function in the library catalogue. The dossier and the oeuvre fashion an academic self at the expense of the collective and the disciplinary.

We have seen here, moreover, a dematerialization of the book, analogous to that of the academic in previous chapters. The book as produced by academic authors became appropriately spiritualized into its intellectual contents. Academics in view of appointments had been reduced essentially to such books and other paperwork. Or had they? Part two pursues the persistence of academic babble and other such noise in the modern era.

# Part 2

## Narrative, Conversation, Reputation

### On the Ineluctability of the Voice and the Oral

# 9

# Academic Babble and Ministerial Machinations

Academic babble was an energy, a force, powerful but ephemeral, was noise, rumor and gossip, something that circulated orally. Ministerial machinations harnessed it, transformed it, made it substantial, and put it to work. The first was grist and the latter the mill—academic babble milled by ministerial machinations objectified noise in a fame machine.

This chapter examines ministerial machinations on academic babble within the broader context of the differentiation of an academic private sphere from a public one, and the insinuation of a market between them. In that, we pick up threads pursued in chapters above, especially in those on the lecture catalogue and on academic appointments. Here we are concerned with the recasting of aspects of academic oral culture by ministerial tools of registration that rendered the oral into the visible and made noise into information.

We thus continue themes of previous chapters but, apropos the division of the book into a first and second part, we shall invert the emphasis henceforth. Antecedent chapters treated the transformation of academic oral culture into a scribal or legible one, where oral elements indeed persisted; but we focused in those chapters on the new centrality of writing. In the next three chapters, we shall continue to trace the hegemony of the visual and legible within academic knowledge. But the emphasis or interest now shifts to the ineluctable oral.

This chapter examines the refabrication of academic identity reflected in certain early modern ministerial practices of inquisition and registration. Expanding on motifs of previous chapters, the chapter attempts to show how ministerial interventions and machinations on academic babble abetted the virtual library of journals—the other great fame machine—in establishing a regime of academic commodification amid the public and private spheres.

We will focus on three tools used in ministerial interventions: the questionnaire, the journal, and the table. Such tools did not so much reflect or record academic reality. Rather, they significantly transformed babble by the way they registered it. In the original sense of Greek geometry, even abstract tools such as lines and figures "cut furrows" in the soil of being. The modern ministry's tools cut furrows in the soil of academia. These furrows were where gossip, rumor, and other noise grew into credit and reputation.

Only one particular point of application of the three specific tools is examined in this chapter—the early modern practice of the ministerial visitation to universities. Such a visitation entailed that one or more ministers and/or their tools came as a commission in name of the sovereign or state to look over, overhear, survey, spy upon, interrogate, record, and transform academic voices or noise into a report on the university. One might best comprehend such early modern visitations in the broad context of European practices growing from the Inquisition. The roots of the early modern and the modern ministerial visitation are, indeed, ecclesiastical and medieval.

The transformation of the visitation from its juridico-ecclesiastical origins into a politico-economic tool in the eighteenth century constitutes the narrative thread here. We shall first consider the institution of the visitation itself. Then we shall look at the visitation of a university in 1597, as a case study of the art of visitation in the juridico-ecclesiastical world. For that visitation, we'll look at how the ministerial commission used a questionnaire to register academic voices. From the case study in 1597, we shall move two centuries later to two case studies of visitations in the 1780s, the twilight of the ancient academic regime. For those visitations, we shall consider the deployment of a ministerial diary or journal and a table. In these later examples, we'll see the politico-economic separation of a public and private sphere, and attend to academic commodification, which the next chapter will pursue further.

## THE EARLY MODERN VISITATION

Visitation forms one of the most ancient rites of the Christian Church. By the episcopal right of visitation ( *jus visitandi* ), the bishop or *ordinarius loci* could send visitors to any body or entity under his jurisdiction. That meant initially only the secular clergy, but in time—under the Carolingians—came to include some monks and other regular clergy. Centers sought to control margins through the ritual and practice of the local visitation.

The bishop or *ordinarius* could inquire about the orthodoxy of preaching, the frequenting of taverns, the consorting with frivolous persons, the presence of blasphemers or heretics, and the quality and content of teaching at the school. In the High Middle Ages, the new sorts of orders—the Cluniacs, Cistercians, Dominicans, Franciscans, and others—placed themselves under papal patronage and received exemption from episcopal authority, including exemption from visitation. In its place, they substituted their own system of regular visitation and general chapters, that is, general meetings.[1]

Documents from Cistercian visitations from 1227 to 1239, for example, have been published and indicate resistance to the visitors. During those twelve years, the paperwork generated by the visitations appears to have been better kept. A list of questions to be put to every institution was sometimes drawn up in advance. By 1233 there seems to have been a visitation protocol, which was preserved and read at the next visitation, to make sure that each foundation had improved since the last visit. Visitation commissions sent to monitor Franciscan foundations from 1232 to 1239 appeared so inquisitorial that the poor friars took the visitors for spies and hated them. The practice had nonetheless proven itself and the Fourth Lateran Council (1215) had taken the logical and final step. It required regular visitations of all other monastic orders and regular clergy, too. The diocese and bishop or *ordinarius* formed the default unit and head. All monks and regular and secular clergy had then become organized in networks of visitation and inquisition, of surveillance and confession by 1215/16.[2]

## The Reformation

Protestant princes assumed episcopal power in their lands. That included the right of visitation. If one presumes that medieval episcopal power had extended over universities, then the Protestant prince could thereby claim the right of visitation over universities in the land. But it does not appear to have happened like that.

On the one hand, papal privileges for universities did not at first exempt them from episcopal jurisdiction. On the other hand, university histories and printed records show little evidence that bishops or their likes conducted formal visitations of medieval universities. Medieval academics seem to have extricated themselves from the ecclesiastical network of visitation, if not at first de iure, then at least de facto. In the case of medieval Oxford and Cambridge, for example, exemption from episcopal authority hinged in good part on the autonomy of the universities in view of electing their chancellors. Oxford achieved further insulation as most of the prelates in its metropolitan and episcopal milieu, as well as a good number of the royal retinue, were soon Oxford men. Bishops played a role in academia as university chancellors; and much correspondence with, as well as some sort of visitation from, bishops took place. But universities were generally not visited in a formal, legal sense.[3]

Wary early modern jurists thus traced the new princely right of ministerial visitation as a right of sovereignty, without tying it to episcopal power. Protestant princes in any case did two things: they took over the clerical apparatus in their lands and, in the matter of the visitation, they subsumed their academics under it. Since Jesuits academics were members of a regular order, they endured visitation as part of the traditional practice.[4]

## England

Prince Philip is the chancellor of the University of Cambridge as I write these words. That the prince is the chancellor is, no doubt, altogether a good thing, although the practice in Britain, as well as on the Continent, has its origins in the nascent absolutism of the Renaissance and Reformation. At that time nonresident chancellors, either nobles or prelates or both, were chosen by the university or, rather, implicitly forced upon it. The prince as chancellor formed the legal ground upon which the visitation was often based.[5]

The English crown had long tried to intervene in Oxbridge affairs. Its interference became endemic after 1520 as an upshot of the Henrician reforms and above all apropos of the divorce. In 1533 the right of visitation was officially vested in the crown. From an academic standpoint, the Reformation began in earnest with the royal visitations of Oxford and Cambridge in 1535. In that year Thomas Cromwell was appointed royal visitor of Oxbridge. He sent a representative, Thomas Leigh, to Cambridge. He visited Oxford himself.

Thereafter injunctions were issued reforming Cambridge and putting its statutes under ministerial supervision. Damian Leader has noted that "the texture of Cambridge life changed after Dr. Leigh's visit in 1535." Writing on Oxford, for which the injunctions of 1535 have not survived, Clare Cross, however, has argued that the Tudor period embodied only an acceleration of late medieval tendencies. In either version, it was a catastrophe for Oxbridge, as visitors commenced meddling in academic, as well as other matters, for better or worse. In 1540 the crown, for example, instructed the bishopric of Westminster to maintain six professorships at each university. That is the origin of the famous regius professorships, doubtless a good thing. An Edwardian injunction of 1549, moreover, codified the role of tutors university-wide, so that all students in all colleges had to have a tutor, whence the origins of the tutorial system as a general one. Royal control accelerated, as visitors or commissions visited one or both institutions in 1548/49, 1554, 1556, 1559, and 1570.[6]

The specter of visitation shrank thereafter, as the individual colleges, each with its own visitor, became the chief locus of visitation. But royal intervention increased again in the seventeenth century, above all under Charles I. His confidant, William Laud, got himself elected chancellor of Oxford in 1630. Laud carried a big stick and supervised university affairs more closely than his predecessors. At the height of his power, Laud and his cronies, which included the king, had been the official visitors of every Oxford college, save one.

The period of the Civil War, the Protectorate and early Restoration found Oxbridge much and, in the 1660s, long visited, as the commission sent to Oxford sat for two years. After the Glorious Revolution of 1688, and more or less as part of the Enlightenment, visitations to Oxbridge essentially ceased. The colleges of course continued to have their visitors, and the crown and others paid ceremonial visits. But parliamentary projects to send visitation commissions to early modern Oxbridge came to nothing, doubtless due to various intrigues, and thanks to Oxbridge's carefully cultivated connections.[7]

## The German Lands

The Renaissance and Reformation more firmly established visitation in the Germanies. The new German Protestant state visitation commissions—1527 in Electoral Saxony, 1535 in Württemberg, 1537 in Hessen, 1540/42 in Brandenburg, and so on—included not only churches and schools but also universities. During the sixteenth and early seventeenth centuries, the Jesuits took control of most Austro-German Catholic universities and colleges, and subjected their academics to visitation. Until about 1800, just about every German university seems to have endured visitations, from once every two or three years, to once or twice per decade, to once every generation, depending on the university and century.[8]

Founded in 1576, the Hanoverian-Welfin University of Helmstedt, for example, was formally visited in its first generation in 1580, 1588, 1592, 1597, 1602, 1603, and 1604. In the second half of the seventeenth century, Helmstedt was further visited in 1652, 1654, 1656, 1661, 1668, 1680, and 1690. In the seventeenth century, the University of Jena in Saxe-Weimar enjoyed ministerial visitations in 1610, 1637, 1644, 1669, 1679, 1681, 1688, and 1696. In the first two decades of the same century, the duke of Württemberg sent visitors to the University of Tübingen every year from 1603 to 1609, then in 1612, 1613, 1618, and 1623. The visitation of churches and schools "became more and more routine in the course of the second half of the seventeenth and in the early eighteenth centuries, as witnessed by the fact that the reports of them became more stereotyped. Eventually, carefully set out and detailed questionnaires were provided for reporting according to formula," as Raeff has noted.[9]

Besides pestering academics, did visitations produce much else? That depended on how often commissions came, what they wanted to achieve, and to what extent they followed up. Very many of the regular small reforms of German universities during the early modern era, if not issued explicitly as visitation decrees, were based on reports filed by visitation commissions. But the interests of this book lie not in the matter of institutional reforms of universities. In this chapter, rather, we are interested specifically in ministerial machinations deployed in visitations, and the relation of such ministerial interventions to academic oral culture, especially as gossip, rumor, and the like. The rest of the chapter concerns practices of visitation only in the Germanies. We shall consider a questionnaire from the 1590s, then move two centuries to the 1780s and consider a journal and a table used in visitations.[10]

## WOLFENBÜTTEL'S QUESTIONNAIRE (1597)

We commence our analysis of ministerial tools for visitation with a questionnaire produced by the ministry in Wolfenbüttel in the Duchy of Brunswick-Lüneburg-Wolfenbüttel to be used at the University of Helmstedt in 1597. The section considers the questionnaire, then some of the protocols, that is, how the visitors recorded responses of professors. In that light, we'll pay special attention to issues of professorial denunciation of colleagues, as well as resistance to the questionnaire. We'll end this section with consideration of the machinations or rationale of the questionnaire, especially concerning the fusion of the public and private.

### The Questionnaire

Early modern visitations were usually made on the basis of a written instruction. This told the commission their mission and legitimated them to the university, insuring the latter's submission to the commission. As part of its instruction, the visitation commission to Helmstedt in 1597 brought a questionnaire of 124 questions for the faculty.[11]

The draft and fair copy of the visitation instruction for the commission were dated on 21 January 1597 in Wolfenbüttel and written in the name of the bishop and duke. The appointed commission consisted of individuals whose titles included: chancellor, treasurer, consistorial and court councilor, abbot, provost, doctor of theology, doctor of law, town councilor. The instruction commands the commission to arrive in Helmstedt toward evening on Sunday, 23 January, and to announce itself to the vice-rector of the university.

The instruction goes on to say that, on the next day at seven o'clock in the morning, all professors must assemble and be shown the instruction for the visitation. The commission was to remind the professors of the last visitation, which took place in 1592, and inform the university that things seem to have gotten not better but rather worse at Helmstedt. Each professor was to be reminded of his oath and then asked to submit to the following questions and "the responses of each are to be diligently protocolled." Then comes the list of the 124 questions in the instruction.

After the questionnaire, the instruction goes on for about two and a half pages to the effect that the visitors might question others in Helmstedt. The visitors should inspect and report about buildings and so on. Professors should be asked why they have not adhered to the mandates set by the last visitation. They should be reminded that the duke does not wish to send commissions in vain. The instruction ends by enjoining the commission to report.

The questionnaire has questions mostly in German and numbered from 1 to 124. The first two ask whether, where, and how long the respondant taught elsewhere, and how he came to be in Helmstedt. Question 3 asks whether one's appointment to Helmstedt was correct and how it came about. It's hard to see what the ministry was thinking here, and the protocol shows that this question, along with the first two, was not asked after the first few professors questioned. Was one being given a chance to confess one shouldn't have received the position? Questions 4–6 ask whether one knows what qualities a professor should have, whether one is lacking any, and how one proposes to remedy this. So the questionnaire has turned into a confession.

Next comes the amazing question 7, which begins, "Whether it is not fitting that a professor be of legitimate descent and of legitimate birth." Next to the second line of the question is a sublist running from A to Z. So question 7 is asking, "Whether it is not fitting that a professor be . . . ," followed by the alphabetical sublist. Question 7 strangely seems to be a response to the questionnaire's own question 4, on what qualities a professor should have and not have. By good luck, there are as many letters of the alphabet as professorial qualities. Either that, or use of an alphabetic list has some-how driven the ministry in Wolfenbüttel to use all letters from A to Z. But not all of the qualities constitute good ones in this odd list.

After legitimacy in A, B-F posit the good professor: (B) God-fearing, (C) modest, (D) genial, (E) moderate in word and deed, (F) zealous in all virtue and true and diligent in his office. G-S suddenly turn and depict the bad pro-fessor: (G) thoughtless, [and] still too friendly with students, (H) drunken or self-indulgent, (I) vainglorious (*Rhumrätig*), (K) ambitious, (L) self-important, haughty and splendorous, (M) scornful, (N) hard to get along with, (O) greedy, (P) envious, (Q) quarrelsome and stuttering [?], (R) lazy, ca-sual and a slacker, (S) inexperienced of communal life. T-Z turn back to good again: (T) of good means and manner, (U) of competent age, (W) of good understanding and judgment, (X) able to speak Latin clearly, (Y) experienced in logic, and (Z)—more or less—whether learned in the discipline one teaches and able publicly to teach and inform youth from fundamentals with-out puerile preparations and cribbing at leisure from glosses [for lectures?].

The next few questions ask whether one and one's colleagues write in good faith to the ministry, above all regarding suggestions for appoint-ments, or whether favor, relation, and similar unseemly affections hold sway, and whether all professors have the above qualities [A to Z], or whether some are lacking and, if so, what their names and failings are. Along with another part of the questionnaire, this part effectively solicits self-confession and denunciation of colleagues which, as we'll soon see, most academics resisted.

Other questions concern the deans, their failings and what to do about them. One question gives a chance to confess failings of friends or foes ex-plicitly in lecturing. A series of questions treats of the four faculties in their proper academic precedence: theology, law, medicine, arts and philosophy, and sciences. The questionnaire turns to other questions: what enrollments are; whether one or one's colleagues cancel lectures or travel without per-mission during term time and where. The questionnaire shifts to a series on students and nears closing with inquiries about changing the composition of the academic senate. Last and perhaps least in 1597, the questionnaire ends with three questions about publications.

## The Protocols

The first person protocolled was the highest university officer, the vice-rector. He began on Monday, 24 January, the commission's first workday. Given the ceremonies that took place first, the vice-rector only got up to question 42. The commission picked up with him on the next day, getting through him and next two professors protocolled. On 26 January, the fourth through seventh professors testified. As time went on, the questioning went faster, as the commission apparently left some questions out. On 29 January 1597, the visitors brought the questionnaire to an end by protocolling the twenty-fourth to twenty-seventh professors. Professors' protocols were numbered in the sequence of questioning, up to the tenth, when the clerk perhaps got bored and lost count. I continued the clerk's count and will thus now refer to professors by their cardinal number, such as Nr. 15 and so on.

Nr. 1, the vice-rector, was protocolled as answering every question, except for question 79, which was a continuation of question 78. A "79" was also written, then crossed out in the margin. Question 2 for Nr. 1 reads "Cessat": it fails. Thereafter all questions, when irrelevant or not put, were protocolled for him as *cessat*, with the appropriate question number. Note that, though questions and most responses were in German, empty answers became Latin. Also going into Latin were a simple yes or no: *affirmat* or *nescit*.

The last two show that responses were protocolled in the third person: "he affirms [it]" or "he knows not." Fuller responses, in German, also went into the third person, so no "I" spoke in the protocols. Voices were third person or impersonal. The chief nuance was a sustained use of the German first subjunctive, which is hard to translate into English. The German first subjunctive established the juridical nicety of rhetorical distanciation in the protocol between the commission and the academic voices. If Nr. 1 said, for example, "I know nothing," then the protocol would read, "He knew nothing (*Er wisse nichts*)." What this subjunctive actually means is: "He said he knows nothing." The protocol registers only professorial allegations.

With professor Nr. 2 the questionnaire fell apart. The protocol collapsed his response to question 10 into another. Question 12 is missing. The protocol jumped from question 14 to 22, though 15 to 17 would have made sense to ask. But, although he was a medical professor, the questions on theology were protocolled as empty, as were those on the law faculty. Indeed, beginning with question 22, he had all questions protocolled up to 124.

Excepting the questions on the law and medical faculties and some on the arts and philosophy faculty, professors Nr. 3–6 also had all numbers protocolled, with question 15 left out once. The nature of the questionnaire as a juridical proceeding perhaps led to the attempt made with these professors to reflect a protocol of a complete testimony of 124 items, even when questions were not posed. The juridical nature of the questionnaire is also clear from the oath. The commission extracted an oath at the outset, and each protocol ended, "Silence was enjoined to him," meaning that what one had confessed would not be revealed.

By Nr. 7 boredom seems to have overcome the commission. Nr. 7's protocol began with question 7, after which many gaps arose, with no *cessat* to fill all absent numbers. And so it went with the professors after Nr. 7. Professors Nr. 1–6 were the important academics to register in testimony. And, as noted, after Nr. 10, the clerk even lost count.

The possible boredom or lack of interest by the visitation commission after the first six professors was countered by the bearing toward the commission of virtually all the professors. At this distance in time, it is hard to put a label or even two on the attitude of the professors toward this questionnaire, a relatively novel tool at the time. Many professorial answers seem ironic or condescending. Or is this projection of a later academic mentality?

### Professorial Denunciation, Resistance, and Submission

After Nr. 7 most protocols began with question 7, the A to Z we saw above. The vice-rector, one of the few protocolled as expounding upon question 7, said that some of the qualities befitted every pious Christian, and others professors per se. His response ended with "affirmat," just to make sure. To question 7 the most common answer was simply: "affirmat." This question seems to be a sort of sermon from A to Z, to impress upon professors their persona as conceived by the ministry. It's hard to believe the commission read the list of A to Z to each professor, only to expect an affirmat, unless we take the questionnaire as an instrument to enforce submission.

To question 4, asking if one knew the qualities needed to be a professor, Nr. 2 said, "He hopes he should know it." To the next question, on his failings, he confessed, "The older, the more failings." To the next, on how he would remedy failings, he said, "With invocation of the Holy Ghost and diligent study." The commission then put question 7, from A to Z, to which he submitted with "affirmat." To question 4, on professorial qualities, Nr. 4 said, "He knew somewhat." To the next questions about his failings and their remedy: "It couldn't be perfect." Is this professorial irony? Or just speaking plain truth?

Questions 10–11 asked the professors whether they and others had the qualities above (A to Z), and if one knew those who didn't, what their names and failings were. These questions were protocolled for all except five professors. They thus seem important. The protocol usually recorded the questions together as 10–11, or as 10. Here was, first, a chance to denounce oneself. In a Christian culture built around confession, it would not be an outlandish notion. But, second, one was also given an invitation here to denounce others.[12]

To these questions, Nr. 27's complete response was, in the subjunctive twist of the questionnaire, "He knew none." Most professors responded in that same terse spirit. Two professors, however, delved into extensive de-nunciations. They were Nr. 2 and Nr. 26.

Nr. 26's response to questions 10–11 occupies a bit more than half a folio page: There were all sorts of failings. He didn't read theological polemics. Among the jurists he knew of no failings. In the medical faculty, Horstius [Nr. 2] was causing problems, as he had published a work against the fac-ulty's wishes. He [Nr. 26] lectured with preparation, but Horstius didn't. He could get along with everyone, but not with Horstius. But he didn't hate or envy him, nor anyone else. Of the other professors he knew not of their imperfections.

Nr. 26 was Parcovius. His foe Horstius, Nr. 2, gave an even longer re-sponse to these questions. Taking question 9 along with 10–11, Nr. 2 offered nearly two pages, the longest list of confessions on colleagues. He ran through a list of the faculty and offered a word or more about each and, where he named names, I'll use letters in my close paraphrase here.

---

He [Nr. 2, Horstius] was against hiring X, who's not a good physician, and was for Y in Wittenberg. A may improve, but did not lecture in the eleventh month, [and] serves better in [private] practice. B was strongly against hir-ing C. He [Nr. 2] didn't concern himself with the law faculty. M was a learned man. B had many failings, [and] to his [Nr. 2's] face was nice but behind his back tried to push things his way in the [academic] senate. Once he [B] had tried to get a law student, whom he'd called a rogue, to be ex-pelled and had got into a fight. He [B] once had a servant who had a whore as a wife. Because of him there were fewer theology students than at other places. C was tight and liked to leech off others, so he could drink for free. L was a little too worldly. Q a good man. S adhered to Ramism. T was a good man. W was like C. E was derisive. N didn't lecture enough, [and] as, he [Nr. 2] has heard, had somewhat of a passion [?]. K was not forthright. J [Nr. 26], as he had admonished [Nr. 2, Horstius] to lecture, he [Nr. 26] was hostile to him [Nr. 2, Horstius], sneered at him, for example [as] happened on 10 January, [and] for example he [Nr. 26] warned others in writing, whereas as *ordinarius* he should not offer reproach but should have patience and let things be. J wouldn't offer his hand at the doctoral [festivities]. Be-cause of V all must suffer. Z is pious. G is pious and diligent. H outstand-ingly learned but too hasty. O doesn't go to the decanal dinners. F conducts himself well. U lacks in nothing. R supposedly has bad pronunciation . . .

---

Other professors saw no need to respond with such denunications and babble. Most responses of other professors were typically more than the mere "affirmat" to question 7. But they were mostly brief, often elliptical, and hardly anyone named names. The denunciations of Horstius and Parcovius above constituted exceptions, suggesting that the failure of others to denounce colleagues came as a resistance to the questionnaire.

Resistance in spirit may be also seen in responses to questions 70–72, regarding enrollments, whether classes were cancelled, and whether and whither one traveled in term time. Question 70, about enrollments, was put as "frequens auditorium." That allowed scope for answers from the precise to the ironic. Nr. 2 said he got around twenty students, but sometimes less, sometimes more, and sometimes a lot more. He confessed to having missed classes, but claimed to have paid the fines. About colleagues, he said he'd already testified. And, finally, he didn't leave town during term time. Nr. 2's adversary, Nr. 26, gave one of the most evasive, original and astute answers on enrollments: "He says he had more students than his likes in Marburg, Leipzig, Wittenberg, [and] Rostock."

To the question on enrollments, Nr. 3 said, "affirmat," taking the "frequens" to mean much. On cancelled classes, he pled illness, and then named colleagues who had been negligent—an actual denunciation here. On traveling out of town in term, he said he did this little. Nr. 4 also took the question on enrollments in a vague way, saying he had seem(ing)ly (*zimlich*) *frequens auditorium*. Nr. 6 to this question said "affirmat." Nr. 19 claimed to get about forty and sometimes more students. About his cancelled class, he said he had to go to a funeral. Nr. 23 had the sort of enrollment curve that the ministry—already in 1597—was much interested in curing: "He says he had at first sixty to seventy, finally fourteen or sixteen or eighteen."

## The Machinations of the Questionnaire

Concocted at the ministry in Wolfenbüttel and conducted in Helmstedt in 1597, this questionnaire produced results bearing no relation to our modern notions of statistical thinking. The protocolled responses above were useless for any such politico-economic knowledge. Even with instruments like this, visitation remained a juridico-ecclesiastical exercise of ministerial power. The ministry seemed to encourage academics to talk about their and colleagues' failings, but sought not so much gossip as rather more confessions. Academics spoke under oath and swore to silence after the act. Nr. 2's response above is informative about the scope sought. He built into his response a list of the faculty, as he ran through what the questionnaire did for the whole university.

Like the questionnaire's own question 7, A to Z, Nr. 2 seemed compelled to confess a list of what he thought of the other professors. He was having problems with B and J, and those got more space. About most of the others, he offered a few words. Like question 7, Nr. 2 didn't distinguish personal or private from professional or public character. He had the whole person in mind and seemed to say the most vivid thing he felt about each.

A modern separation of a public from a private academic sphere existed as little for Nr. 2 as it did for the ministry in Wolfenbüttel. The register of this questionnaire allowed no distinction of public and private spheres. The seeming resistance of most academics to these questions does not imply they adhered to a separation between a public sphere open to the ministry, and a private one closed to it. Rather, most academics simply resisted confession per se.

The instrument of this visitation embodied above all a list. And this list, without statistical sense, existed in some nether world between the medieval inquisition and the modern interview. Inquisitors and interviewers worked and work with some sort of list of questions. But inquisition and interview allowed and allow for the departures and digressions typical of conversation, and thus for revisions of the list during the hearing, in so far as we take a list as laying out a chronicle. As judged by the protocols, the visitors to Helmstedt did not take the questionnaire as an instrument they were allowed to reshape, other than leaving questions out. Apart from the numerals correlating answers with the questionnaire, protocols show no trace of the commission's voice, excepting their use of the German first subjunctive. As noted above, that distances the questionnaire thus the ministry from academic voices and babble.

It is as if the questionnaire were a mechanism that the visitors simply switched on and allowed to produce or not produce nearly standardized, blank confessions to each question without further intervention or specification. Answers seem to have simply been registered as spoken, even if the answers were apparently ironic (from our perspective) or if the questions were not answered at all. Excepting responses by Horstius that ran through the entire faculty, almost all others were brief, even terse. The mechanism worked to control academic and ministerial babble. As was the faculty in its confession, so too was the commission as much regulated and disciplined in its questioning by the list of this mechanical inquisition or truth machine.

The questionnaire translated academic voices into legible traces, but the traditional oral world still reigned here. However mechanical, the process remained forensic rhetoric, with oaths administered, silences enjoined, confessions sought, and dignitaries (Nrs. 1–6) speaking first and most fully. The protocols thus show rank and tempo, moving from higher to lower in academic precedence. This mechanism sought to register oath-bound con-

fessions—to shape subjects to a list from A to Z in a juridico-ecclesiastical
nexus of authority whose questionnaire admitted no separation of a public
from a private persona.

## VACCHIERI'S JOURNAL (1784)

From a questionnaire of the 1590s, we move to a visitor's journal of the
1780s. The transit will bring out the opposition between the two academic
regimes with which we are concerned—the transition from the juridico-
ecclesiastical to the politico-economic. By the 1780s, as we'll see, German
society did separate the public and private, and in a manner close enough
to ours to consider it the same for all practical purposes. My interest lies
in noting how academic voices appear and function in ministerial registers
or records in which the modern bureaucratic separation of home and office,
of public and private selves, exists at least programmatically or ideologically,
if not yet in any sort of perfect practice.

In the section to follow this one, we'll consider how a ministerial visitation processed academic voices at a university in the 1780s, as grist for the
ministerial mill. Before we turn to that great modern feat, it will be useful
to see how ministerial interventions can suppress or "deregister" such things
as gossip altogether. In chapter 7 on appointments, we saw that dossiers in
the Bavarian archive filtered out the private or domestic life of most academics. The dossiers of unproblematic academics contained essentially
materials relevant only to their professional selves. The case of Professor
Fischer in his squabble with Professor Berg, and Fischer's subsequent erratic behavior unbefitting a civil servant, formed the breach through which
things entered the dossier, including stories, that usually would not.

By entering Fischer's dossier, rumor and gossip about his odd behavior,
which he contested, transformed from babble to testimony, which might,
indeed, be only hearsay. That is at least the position I shall argue here, and
have in effect argued in chapters above. Ministerial machinations work on
academic noise or babble by transforming it into something professionally
relevant, or by suppressing it. In this section, we'll consider how a minister
in the 1780s used a journal to suppress a private sphere of academic noise.

Historians often fetishize a scientist's or academic's or politician's journal or diary as the royal road to truth. But a journal is, like all else, bound by
laws of genre. Like every other author, a diary or journal writer assumes a
persona. To bring that out, I shall pursue a strategy of disorientation here.
Though I suspect Vacchieri's journal, which will be analyzed below, lies
much closer to the way we think than does Wolfenbüttel's questionnaire an-

alyzed above, I want to make the journal seem strange. Thus I shall call into question what the journal apparently self-evidently registers and look for what it deregisters and occults.

Subsections below consider, first, the journal as narrative, second, the visitor and his hand, third, the per diem, and, finally, the machinations of disembodiment and domination.

### The Journal as Narrative

I shall read Vacchieri's journal as a narrative. This section of this chapter may be the most difficult and refractory of this book. It has fretted me and manuscript readers of the material the most. But its results are crucial to the chapter and book; moreover, I shall use the framework articulated here for Vacchieri's journal qua narrative in the next and the final chapter as well. Here, we'll engage in a level of microanalysis or petit récit that is a fitting contrast to the macroanalysis or grand narrative of the book. To wit.[13]

The list underlying a questionnaire, in the abstract without reference to time, gives way in the journal or diary to a temporalized list, a chronicle. The lapidary, plotless form of the list may move, however, in the diary or journal or chronicle to the narratival. Consider a famous example. In *Robinson Crusoe*, the "Journal" suddenly appears about one-fifth of the way into the book. Robinson began the journal about a fortnight after having landed on his island and continued it till he ran short of ink, which took about a year.[14]

"September 30, 1659. I, poor miserable Robinson Crusoe, being shipwrecked, during a dreadful storm . . ." He then kept his journal every day until 23 November, when his recording grew lax. The journal's plot revolves around Robinson's toil to maintain himself on the island in his first year and his discovery of religion in so doing. When he was unable to work—his (Protestant) calling on the island—the journal neared the level of mere chronicle.

---

June 19. Very ill, and shivering, as if the weather had been cold.

June 20. Very ill, frighted almost to death with the apprehension of my sad condition, to be sick, and no help: prayed to God for the first time since off of Hull, but scarce knew what I said, or why; my thoughts all confused.

June 22. A little better, but under dreadful apprehension of sickness.

June 23. Very bad again, cold shivering, and then a violent headache.

June 24. Much better.

---

Though a traditional Romance in many ways, *Robinson Crusoe* is one of the first modern novels and helped bear the new genre of bourgeois or formalist realism. Realist genres, like the novel and much historical writing, employ a rhetoric of detail, often gratuitous. The gratuitous detail rhetorically insinuates the prose in the real as opposed to the imaginary. The journal is one device to effect literary Realism, as it dates Robinson's works and days. Indeed, through the journal, Robinson inserts his self into the bourgeois, Christian, European culture that he had at first rejected, which led to his voyage and shipwreck. Robinson's journal is a device for the constitution and maintenance of a bourgeois self.[15]

Hayden White has analyzed the relations between chronicle and narrative history, and I shall apply his theses to the journal below. White looks for the conditions that transform mere chronicle into historical narrative, where continuity becomes most salient. This is achieved neither by filling in empty days or years, nor by setting a linear progression of a story. It is, rather, achieved by emplotment. Let "story" denote the incidents in causal-chronological order (as in a good dossier), while "plot" will mean the way the story is woven and warped in telling or narration, by inverting time orders, dwelling, making digressions, and so on.[16]

White argues that the emergence of historical narrative requires a moral order or social authority—such as God or the state or civil society—in the framework of which the list underlying a mere story—a chronicle or journal—acquires the ideal form that we experience as emplotted narrative. The moral order or social authority authorizes isolation of specific story-elements from the seamless and infinite web of history. It allows the plot to reach an end and have a point, instead of breaking off as a chronicle or journal does. This moral or social authority is often absent in the narrative. It inheres, rather, virtually in it, just as the Christian, bourgeois society lies virtually in or behind Robinson's journal.

On this account, a journal or diary, though forming a chronicle of someone's days, achieves a proper narratival form, beyond the lapidary form of the list, only if there is a plot—only, that is, if some moral authority serves as a formal principle allowing selection of events or story elements to weave them into a temporal sequence with an end or resolution. Isolation of the moral authority or formal principle, in our case below, as a bureaucracy or ministry, will help us see what is registered as much as what is not registered in a journal, that is, what the plot is. Vacchieri's journal from his visitation of 1784 has a plot but does not fall into standard genres of bourgeois realism. Manuals of juristic practice in Vacchieri's era advocate composition of cases and protocols as historical narrative in strict chronological order, but they insist one must omit gratuitous details.[17]

Such bureaucratic prose is not realistic, in the bourgeois sense. Following Northrop Frye's cleavage of literature into the "realistic" versus the "romantic," one could read the prose and plot in Vacchieri's journal as a sort of traditional or naïve Romance, such as epic and folktale, as opposed to modern or sentimental Romance. It is like traditional Romance by its fabrication of an ideal world, here the realm of bureaucratic paperwork. In traditional Romance the notion of "work" tends to be absent and "essentially the whole of human action depicted in the plot is ritualized action." That well captures the bureaucratic mentality.[18]

Vacchieri's journal would be, in that light, a form of traditional Romance, although neither folktale nor epic. His journal reads somewhat biblical in style. It reminded me most of visitations of angels in Hebrew scriptures. Our visitor in 1784 was like an angel who descended from the Kafkaesque ministry down to mortals below, then returned to report.

Let's call this Romance "clerical," as opposed to an epic or folktale. Robinson's journal was a tool for the constitution and preservation of a bourgeois persona. Vacchieri's journal as clerical Romance will be read as a device for the constitution and preservation of a bureaucratic persona. And, much as Wolfenbüttel's questionnaire served as an instrument to discipline the visitors, so too was Vacchieri's journal a technique of self-discipline.[19]

## The Romance of the Cleric and His Hand

The visitation of Ingolstadt in 1784 produced a number of nice documents. The visitor was a Bavarian privy councilor and the university curator, Vacchieri, who had a secretary, Hesenacker, and twenty-five points in his visitation instructions on 17 March 1784. Vacchieri conducted inquiries in Ingolstadt from 22 March to 16 April. The summary to the report was dated 14 April 1784. Thirteen professionally drawn plans for alterations of facilities were also enclosed. On his activities each day, Vacchieri composed and enclosed a "diarium," which made reference to enclosures, mostly protocols on sessions and activities mentioned in the diarium. Since "diary" has connotations in English perhaps misleading, I'll call the diarium a journal. The principal documents—the instruction, journal with enclosures, and summary report—of Vacchieri's visitation to Ingolstadt of 1784 will now be read as a narrative in the sense articulated above.[20]

The first document has the points of instruction composed in Munich and dated 17 March. The instruction is not so much a prologue in heaven, but is rather more like the tasks given the hero of Romance. Dispatched by a paternal figure, ministers descend to discharge their commission. The instructions provide the moral authority for a plot.

Vacchieri is to inspect property such as books and gardens. He is to meet with academics and ascertain if good conduct and concord hold sway. He must see if professors are discharging their duties and determine the "abilities, manner and means of lecturing, and the thoroughness of their teaching" (instruction 8). He must visit lectures, and appear unexpectedly (instruction 9). He should see if semester vacations might be abolished, since they waste time and money (instruction 7). Professors are not to be out of town during term without permission and he is to remind them of this (instruction 20). The visitor may inquire about related matters (instruction 23).

The last two instructions set the per diem of the commission and command a report on return. The instructions thus lay out a story line that the journal emplots and resolves in a final report. The ministry has the context to read the journal as a narrative and expects a plot along such-and-such lines, while so-and-so will be absent, apropos clerical Romance.

Vacchieri's journal is perfectly ordinary and completely strange. He began by writing that it was composed for the commission sent from Munich. And "by dint of this [instruction] the aforesaid commission betook itself to Ingolstadt on 22 March." This betaking itself by the commission transported it as bureaucratic *deus ex machina* from Munich to Ingolstadt with no trace of a journey in the journal. The journey would not constitute part of the plot of the visitation as angelic act in the genre of clerical Romance. Here it resembles some scriptures.

Contrasting the Elohistic-Hebraic style of Romance with the Homeric-Hellenic, and on the story of Abraham sent by God to sacrifice a son, Erich Auerbach has written,

> A journey is made . . . ; but nothing is said of the journey, other than that it lasted three days . . . The lifting of the eyes [by Abraham at his arrival] is the only gesture, indeed, the only thing reported about the journey . . . ; it is as if, during the journey, Abraham up till then had looked neither right nor left, [and] suppressed all signs of life from himself and his companions.[21]

So, too, it seems for early modern academic commissions and missions. Part of their self-discipline lay in looking neither right nor left and suppressing all signs of private life.

After it arrived in Ingolstadt, the commission announced itself to the mayor, rector, prochancellor, deans, and others. The next day, Tuesday, 23 March, the parties paid each other the usual ritual visits and countervisits, "whereupon one began preparations for the upcoming session." This and related devices figure the journal throughout. Vacchieri does not appear as

"I," nor does the commission as "we." Designation as "one"—the abstract, third person singular—instantiates the commission as impersonal, disembodied agency.[22]

For the next day, 24 March, we can infer that Vacchieri went with Hesenacker, his trusty secretary or hand, to the first formal session of the visitation. Moreover, at the first and plenary session, present *ex parte Commissionis* were only Vacchieri and Hesenacker. The few other references to the commission, beyond the impersonal "one," seem to reduce it to only these two: our angelic visitor and his trusty hand.

### Per Diem

Outside the plot lay also the sustenance of the commission. Though they stayed in Ingolstadt for three weeks, little indication emerges that they needed to eat or drink. The issue is relevant since the journal did record a few instances. On 25, 29, and 30 March, and 1 and 4 April, the commission had feasts with faculties and dignitaries. This involved ritual eating and drinking, which we know angels engage in, even though they don't need to eat.

Reading Vacchieri's journal as a narrative, we are cast by its prose into a space where ministers of state seem like beings who transport themselves without effort, looking right nor left, and are able to sustain themselves for weeks with only ritual food or even nothing. The visitor, save for hand and eyes, did not seem to have a body. He is clerical spirit, pure thinking substance, though perhaps needing paper to sustain his hand.

Vacchieri's is a bureaucratically angelic presence. His journal reads as a sort of ministerial book of hours, a register of time spent. "Friday, the 9th, as Good Friday, the commission occupied the time before noon with cultivation of worship, the afternoon however . . . with inspection of the botanical garden, then the anatomy [theater]." The journal glides from one ritual, prayer, to another, inspection. The next few lines record acts of Holy Saturday, 10 April, when a university plenum occurred. Then, near the bottom of the column, "Sunday, the 11th, as Easter Sunday, *Nihil.* Easter Monday, the 12th, likewise *Nihil.*"

Vacchieri's journal abhors a minimal temporal unit without an entry. Like the questionnaire of 1597, this journal of 1784 fills its empty spaces with Latin. The days on which nothing happens are holidays or Sundays, though even these days might embrace by implication a future act. So on Sunday, 28 March, the journal records a *Nihil,* followed by motivation of acts the next day. Vacchieri's instructions enjoined him to monitor the performance of the professors and in particular to visit lectures without announcing it.

The paragraph after the *Nihil* for Sunday the 28th explains then that will be done on Monday. This is a narrative device to overcome mere chronicle by the control of the future.

The feast of 30 March excused the commission from acting that evening, and on 2 April not much seems to have been done in the afternoon, while the business of 6 and 7 April took them past the "usual" evening hour. Virtually every day, when something as opposed to nothing happened, opened with the time when acts began, usually 9:00 or 10:00 a.m. After 3 April, the journal grew vague. Was the commission sleeping in or just getting bored? Even the enclosures cited in the left margin got out of joint from Nr. 23 to 25.

Nonchalance superseded boredom at the close of the journal, which originally ended on 14 April. Neglecting signatures of Hesenacker and Vacchieri at the bottom, seven new lines appear in different ink and relate that a farewell deputation of the university and town magistrate was received. Thereupon "on Friday, 16 April, the return journey was begun." For the first time, a day, 15 April, is missing from the journal! Still more mysterious is the final report on the visitation, dated 14 April, thus written while still in Ingolstadt. What did the commission do the next day and did they dare to claim a per diem?

## Machinations of Disembodiment and Domination

I have presumed no self-evidence of the style of Vacchieri's journal in terms of what he does and does not record. The seemingly self-evident rhetoric of Vacchieri's journal is as much a device to constitute and maintain a specific sort of self as is Robinson's journal. The latter is simply bourgeois, while the former is also bureaucratic, which is why it occults itself so easily into a narrative impersonal "one."

In view of Wolfenbüttel's questionnaire of 1597, a great change is suggested now. Much of what the enlightened middle class regarded as its private life has disappeared from the visitor's eye and register in Vacchieri's journal of 1784. The impersonality and missing "I" encompassing the ministry in the questionnaire of 1597 have grown to encompass the university. This journal registers academics only as public figures. The journal acts here as a sort of filter for academic private selves and their gossip. Vacchieri's journal is a technique to deregister, to occult, and to silence certain traces and voices. That is crucial to its power.

The effacement of the private is tied to the disembodiment of the visitor—a technique of self-discipline and a tactic of domination. Simon

Schaffer and Steven Shapin have written on the literary suppression of experimental labor and "hands" by Boyle and the Royal Society in the late seventeenth century. The authors see this as a tactic of domination in the context not of bureaucracy, but of civil society. Schaffer has pursued such issues into the nineteenth century in regard to self-registering instruments, for which the experimenter's hands and body seem to vanish altogether, to which we'll return later.[23]

David Sabean has studied the early modern "flagging of texts" in ministerial prose: the deletion by euphemism of language having to do with swearing, as well as erasure of animals and human body parts, including the feet. This entailed an impulse by ministers (and their hands) to efface the embodied in their prose. Sabean explicitly argues that this was a tactic of bureaucratic domination. The above all coheres with the thesis of Michel Foucault that, as opposed to premodern sovereignty, modern sovereignty tends to disembody and occult itself.[24]

Chapters of this book have indicated how the bureaucratization of German academics in the early modern era was correlative with the obliteration of the private persona and body, leaving only thinking spirit and its paperwork. We have seen that in the case of candidates for academic degrees and academic appointments, as well as with their books. This facilitated the subjection of academics to ministerial agendas of disembodiment and control.

Reading bureaucratic prose of the clerically disembodied as a sort of Romance, we can apply Frye's dictum: "In every age the ruling social or intellectual class tends to project its ideals in some form of Romance." The ideals of the new enlightened ruling class were not those of the erstwhile horse-riding, sword-wielding, blue-blooded nobility, but rather of the modern meritocratic, paper-pushing, faceless ministry and its hands. "This is the process of . . . kidnapping Romance, the absorbing of it into the ideology of an ascendant class."[25]

Vacchieri's disembodiment, as kidnapped Romance, now clerical, was embodied in such ghostly ploys. After one notes all the corporal absences in his journal, the omnipresence of time and its control, the very form of the journal, becomes most clear. While effacing his own nonritualized embodiment and private "I," Vacchieri's narrative foregrounds time-discipline and control of the future, so essential to modern bureaucratic power. And given the meticulous confession of daily exercises up till the next to last day, the missing day brings this clerical Romance to a marvelous end—nearly an irony about clerical Romance.

## BURGSDORF'S TABLE (1789)

We come now to a tool that transformed academic babble instead of suppressing it. In this section, we'll consider a visitation from 1789, from which the visitor produced a table evaluating the relevant academics. The minister seems to have based his evaluations on a spectrum of academic voices, ranging from reviews in journals to juicy gossip. No technological necessity existed, in view of which a journal must suppress such things and a table transform them. It just so happens that the cases studies in the deployment of these modern tools turned out this way.

The technique of the table, so much a part of our world, is a device that articulates or graphs a nontemporalized horizontal axis onto the vertical flow of the list. The tabular is an amazing visual device to tame the oral—it frustrates babble, conversation, and narrative. As much as narrative serves traditional authority, so too does the table rational authority. No surprise that making tables has become a pervasive modern academic and bureaucratic habit. Like the questionnaire and journal, the visitor's table, which we shall analyze in this section, formed a technique of bureaucratic self-discipline, as well as a technique to shape academics. Its application to the latter, however, did not simply discipline them. It acted rather more like a ministerial machine carving academics and rephrasing their voices.

### The Table of Academics

As part of a visitation report, Minister Burgsdorf, president of the Supreme Consistory of Saxony in Dresden, made an evaluation of professors and instructors at the University of Wittenberg. Burgsdorf put his evaluation, dated 29 December 1789, into a table. The list of academics runs vertically down the page, divided horizontally into four columns. Column *a* has the name and title of each professor or instructor, with a sublist of his publications since 1786. Column *b* notes what classes he is teaching and whether he has "applausum" or a "big auditorium," that is, large enrollments. Column *c* has how much extra monetary benefits he enjoys and whether he needs more. In Column *d* come remarks about him as a scholar and a gentleman. Walter Friedensburg published this document but left out parts and printed it in a form not reflecting the table, now seemingly lost in World War II. Below I'll give a close paraphrase of the evaluations of three professors and cast it as a table which, I hope, might bear some similarity to the lost original.[26]

| a | b | c | d |
|---|---|---|---|
| D. Friedrich Wilhelm Dresde, ordinary Professor of Theology and senior of the theology faculty, and *ephorus* of the electoral scholarship students. As publications are two *Programma*. | has good *applausum;* lecturing on symbolic theology, with a review session for the scholarship students; also lecturing on *Job;* giving private classes in Hebrew on passages in the Psalms which contain prefigurations on Christ, [and?] on Hebrew antiquities; also holds disputational classes. | Has no extra benefits and needs none. | A true theologian and as well a good Orientalist; his speech [in lecture] lacks fineness and grace, but truth and thoroughness recommend him to all studying youth who seek the genuine, so he is one of the most treasured Wittenberg teachers . . . |
| Ernst Florens Friedrich Chladenius doctor juris. Published in quarto a work on the theory of sound. | has few students (*auditores*); lecturing *gratis* on botany and giving private classes on pure mathematics. | Enjoys no [extra] emoluments; but needs support and is of such not unworthy | Doctor Chladenius is, by the witness of those who know him well, a man of genius and accustomed to think philosophically and deeply. However, he is lacking not only knowledge in jurisprudence, but has also given up this field entirely, in order to devote himself more to mathematical and algebraic sciences without disturbance. The "Theory of Sound," listed in col. a, proves what he is able to do in this regard . . . This book has given him extensive fame and is recognized as excellent in its content and presentation. As encouragement, support for him would be much favored, even though he serves the university less in lecturing than he benefits the learned world by discoveries in higher mathematics, [and] also in general extends himself almost too far, as the announced class on botany shows . . . |

Tabular Evaluation of the Wittenberg Faculties, 29 Dec. 1789 (*continued*)

| a | b | c | d |
|---|---|---|---|
| Gottfried August Meerheim, ordinary Professor of Poetry. A *Programm* on political history, and the quarterly poetical *Programma* [required by his professorship] | has no numerous *auditorium* [full of students]; announced an ordinary course on excerpts from Ovid's *Metamorphosen;* privately also one on modern history | Enjoys a 100 Th[aler]. emolument and will have to make do with that for the time being | One accords him learning in philological matters and ability to lecture well. He is even supposed to have been of use once with these gifts. But for a few years now, one reproaches him with complete inactivity and, moreover, with too much dissipation ~~of partly improper sort~~, whereby students in part take part and for the other part supposedly get no good example. He himself, to the contrary, complains about hypochondriac spells and claims they make him incapable of all steady work and make movement and society a necessity . . . |

Thus three examples from Burgsdorf's table. Lack of space compels me to omit the rest of the faculty in Burgsdorf's table above, although I shall cite or allude to many of his other evaluations below. The document of this visitation in 1789 shows the faculty as *dramatis personae.* The visitor will return to Dresden and report what he thinks or has heard about the faculty, with such knowledge based not on official, oath-bound confessions, such as submitted to Wolfenbüttel's questionnaire for Helmstedt of 1597. The juridico-ecclesiastical style of Wolfenbüttel's questionnaire, protocolling who said what about whom under oath, is absent here. This has been replaced, in part, by private exchanges with the visitor. Such exchanges form absent presences behind the table. They have become its passive and impersonal voices. This and other devices give gossip, rumor, and opinion the rational guise of impersonal evaluation. It would soon make such visitations archaic.[27]

Burgsdorf is meticulous about bodies and counting them properly. Each academic gets a number by his place in the faculty. As chapters above showed, academics might be members of more than one faculty. Burgsdorf cross-references such cases, thus evaluating them only once. Vacchieri's journal serves to keep time under control, while Burgsdorf's table disposes over bodies as names and numbers. "This table contains altogether 36 instructors, as 19 ordinary professors, 3 extraordinary professors and 14 lecturers . . ."

The faculties appear in the traditional sequence as theology, law, medicine, and finally arts and philosophy. In each faculty, all names appear in the table in terms of academic precedence. First in the table, Dresde above, is the senior ordinary professor in the theology faculty. He is followed by the next senior ordinary professor and so on. Then come the extraordinary professors in terms of precedence, all ending with the lecturers. Like the old Latin lecture catalogue, the same order repeats for each faculty. And, like Wolfenbüttel's questionnaire, this order is still forensic or juridical. It is the old academic parade.

## The Table's Calculus

One does not read tables. One views them. That is part of their modern magic. Those whose languages are written from left to right tend to view a table from left to right. If the table is an important or interesting one, the viewer slowly abandons the readers' instincts and submits to being overtaken by a table's own figures and gestures and calculus.

Column $a$ of the table above has the person's name, academic positions and titles, and publications since 1786. A complex calculus, the quantity and quality of this list, measures academic virility. The fact that publications get no separate column and that they appear here, as opposed to column $b$ or $d$, suggests a conflation of academics with paperwork—their publications. Confession of a null in this part of the list—Freyberg's "No publications" or Triller's papers "without a publisher" in the table—simulates impotence or dissolution.

Column $b$ concerns the classes announced by the academic, as well as his *applausum* or *auditorium*. This column opens to an entirely different sensory realm from the first. Whereas column $a$ reduces academics to the legible as written or ocular, the language of column $b$ is auricular and, so to say, oscular. An academic announces and lectures or reads aloud (*vor-liest*), so has a mouth or at least a voice. Students are ears, as an *auditorium*, or hands making sounds as *applausum*—as we have seen in chapters above, this was a central concept for early modern German academia and cameralism. Other tables demanded of universities in the eighteenth century wanted to know exact numerical enrollments; moreover, we saw above the "frequens auditorium" in Wolfenbüttel's questionnaire of 1597.

Striking is thus the omission of quantification in column $b$. Burgsdorf might have easily put the enrollments in this column, as the publications are counted in the prior one. But instead, a qualification of *applausum* or *auditorium* or other term occurs in each case, the most common being "good applause," which means one had good or loud enrollments. Use of "auditorium," "auditores," and variants forms a distant second place to "applausum."

The length of the unit also produces qualification, as for Professor Leonhardi, "an outstandingly strong and reverent auditorium." Use of double negatives, as well as the impersonal "one," indirect discourses and other distanciations, appear far less here than in column *d,* as we'll see. Burgsdorf thus heard the *applausum* or saw the strong *auditorium* in the flesh, and the vivid prose conveys it. Temporal qualifications emerge, as with Titius, who "has always had excellent *applausum* and till now known how to keep it"

The last claim must be based either on ministerial memory, or on hearsay heard during the visitation or who knows where. The matter of the aural-oral shows that, although the great transition from an oral academic culture to a written one was long underway, the sounds of and around academics, nonetheless, still possessed and produced noteworthy charisma. One sign of a voice's charisma the lay in strong *applausum.*

Though tables need not be viewed in any set direction, the "*a* to *d*" of the columns lists a preferred direction for a European-language user. If we so view the table, the prose shifts tonality. The paternal, scribal figurations of column *a* set the essence of the modern academic. This column is solid, descriptive, listing names and paperwork, the indisputable facts or "immutable mobiles" that circulate without distortion through space and time. From the solid and cool realm of visibility in column *a,* the table moves in column *b* into a hotter and more fluid realm of orality-aurality, with students' hands heard in *applausum.*[28]

The figures of column *b* indicate more local, acoustical events. *Applausum* in Wittenberg, even if outstandingly strong, cannot be heard outside town. The political economy of these two columns sets two regimes side by side. The modern is column *a,* a print culture where academics circulate paperwork as currency or credit, with publications as academic capital for the free market of letters. By contrast column *b* is premodern, an oral culture where academics produce for a subsistence economy, since sounds as lectures and collegia are produced and consumed on the premises. The rhetoric of the two columns, from left to right, shifts from ocular to acoustical realms, which were then less amenable to registration.[29]

Column *c* concerns money. This column speaks mostly about emoluments, called a *Pension,* and whether or not the person needs more. The extra emoluments constituted an instrument of ministerial leverage. For extraordinary professors and lecturers, not only promotion up the ladder stood at stake, but also often a salary altogether. Lecturers received no salary, and extraordinary professors often did not receive one. They were extra to the ordinary funding, although some might have received an ad hominem salary or some emoluments.

While the questionnaire for the visitation in 1597 exhibited a juridico-ecclesiastical mentality, the table for the visitation in 1789 is politico-economic. That was the great change from 1597 to 1789. Vacchieri's journal in 1784 reflected a disembodied sort of narrative, a clerical Romance. And Burgsdorf investigated the morals of academics. But the key judgment passed by a cameralistic visitor such as Burgsdorf lay now in column $c$ of this table: the other columns gave testimony for column $c$, while it used them as witnesses.

An instrument of rational authority, visitation by the 1780s concerns the politico-economic or cameral management of academia. Vacchieri's journal registers the bureaucratic control of time, while Burgsdorf's table simulates its control of capital and credit, by casting names in a political economy of academia. But we have not passed wholly into a realm of modern credit, currency, and academic capital figured in column $a$. Local voices and applause in lecture as well as patronage via a *Pension* in the academic ancien régime still haunt columns $b$ and $c$. In most cases, columns $a$ and $b$ add up to the judgment of $c$.

When not, column $d$ remains to redeem or damn the soul at stake. Moreover, the hierarchy reflected in the vertical flow of the table is telling. As said, the vertical flow of the table reflects the academic precedence of the individuals. The table moves from the most senior theologian to the most junior member of arts and philosophy. So the table makes both a horizontal and a vertical gesture. The vertical gesture (like column $b$) is premodern and juridico-ecclesiastical. The horizontal (like column $a$) is modern and politico-economic.

Running down the table vertically in each faculty, one sees senior professors with actual publications or positive *applausum*. These add up to favor in column $c$, and vice versa. Most of the top faculty have a *Pension* or extra emoluments, or are doing so well that they have no need. The interesting are the problematic cases. Triller and Chladenius are lecturers in the law faculty, thus have no ordinary salary. Triller has written two works, but found no publisher. He has, moreover, neither great nor happy *applausum*. He receives a *Pension* of a 100 thaler, but wants more, according to column $c$. By the calculus of the table, columns $a$ and $b$ have made more money for him unlikely, unless column $d$ gives good grounds and redeems him.

Chladenius cuts a different figure. As seen above, he has few *auditores* but has published a monograph in the last three years. The calculus of column $a$ holds an implicit quantity-quality equation, where the genre of the work and possibly its worth, discussed in column *d,* may enhance the mere quantity, though the latter is also always good when great. Column *c* for Chladenius says that he has no *Pension,* "but needs support and of such is not unworthy." The double negative or litotes is not vivid, perhaps in view of the few *auditores.* But we are prepared for column *d,* which will push for more support for him.

The *a, b, c* of the table constrains Burgsdorf as much as the 124 questions ruled the visitors from Wolfenbüttel and the calendar governed Vacchieri—just as the *a, b, c* of exams came to govern the grading of students around this time. For the *a, b, c* determines the sorts of things that Burgsdorf can register at all. Within that framework, however, the minister has immense power to shape the faculty by this tool. Indeed, Burgsdorf is clearly laying out a plan for the personnel, to legitimate his own acts or to influence others.

As said, the columns add up. Someone who needs extra emoluments will be noted in column *c* as unworthy or not unworthy or worthy or much worthy and so on, in view of other columns. Column *d* may redeem or condemn unclear cases. The vertical flow mostly puts the questionable cases at a distance from the top. That is the table's twofold gesture.

As we saw in previous chapters, the arts and philosophy (and sciences) faculty was in the early modern era the most poorly paid, reflecting well its final position in the parade. So problem cases may arise there among even the full or ordinary professors. Freyberg is the faculty's third professor by seniority. Columns *a* and *b* confess he has no publications and almost never finishes a term with any students left—not a good thing. Column *c* says he "supposedly" could use more money. No judgment is passed, so his fate awaits column *d.*

Fifth in the faculty, Ebert, needs no extra emolument. But, as the other columns speak so highly of him, column *c* notes he is worth keeping in mind for favor. Meerheim stands seventh in the faculty in seniority and the table's view of him is most blunt: "Enjoys a 100 th[aler] emolument and will have to make do with that for the time being."

## The Unnamed Ones

If the first three columns add up to a positive picture of the academic, column *d* has little to do except to reinforce them. When the echoes of columns *a* to *c* are dissonant, then the final fate falls to column *d.* Furthest from the left, here is where the prose, trying heroically to harmonize reviews with rumors, unfolds as a discourse of indirection and impersonality, of unnamed witnesses, inscribed by the table's final flourish in this column.

Of Dresde, senior theologian and loftiest professor, column *d* confesses his lecturing style isn't the best, but has great praise otherwise for "one of the most treasured Wittenberg teachers." Burgsdorf casts some of column *d* in positive terms, active voices and direct discourse. But much drifts into passive, impersonal, indirect, litotal forms. If we do not presume omniscient ministerial memory, then behind these table-turns are rumors as well as reviews. This tactic, like the disembodiment in Vacchieri's journal, facilitates domination. Burgsdorf never names his sources of information, against whom there is then no appeal.

Consider some souls column *d* wishes to save. We last left Chladenius with one publication, few students, and in need of more money, of which he was "not unworthy." Column *d* pushes his case. It says, "by the witness of those who know him well," but does not say who they are and why we should believe them. "They," however, think he is "a man of genius and accustomed to think philosophically and deeply." His theory of sound, listed in column *a*, shows what they mean. "This book has given him extensive fame (*Ruhm*) and is recognized as excellent." Here appears *Ruhm*, another key term. His *Ruhm* is extensive, but its recognition appears in the passive voice, so again we don't know who "they" are.

Leonhardi, ordinary professor of pathology and surgery, is also someone to whom Burgsdorf, or his table at least, seems to want to give more money. So column *d* stacks up not only positive adjectives bust also adverbs: "thoroughly beloved . . . natural ability . . . outstanding strength . . . untiring diligence . . . treasured, rightly and universally." The table holds his chemical lexicon "is recommended as classical by the toughest expert reviewers" and shows "by assurance of the knowledgeable" how much it exceeds previous editions.

This last evaluation strikes me as particularly strange. The phrase is vivid, even though it is passive and specifies no specific tough expert reviewers. As with Chladenius, the table withholds details, or is based on hearsay. A person like me wants to know who the damn reviewers were and whether we can trust them. But the ministry apparently did not. And that was not in view of omniscience, for then it would already know what was reported.

This style effects a cloud of unknowing over the field of column *d*. As chapter 7 showed, ministerial acts on academics were concerned with their *Ruhm*. An academic was supposed to be *berühmt*, meaning famous or, literally, spoken about much and well. Things about him were *gerühmt* to ministries. The latter is a passive construction whose sense points to the tie of *Ruhm* with *Gerücht*: rumor. The original sense of *rühmen* was intransitive and meant to call loudly, or make loud noise. Its first derived meaning leaned toward "giving loud or great praise." Echoes of the auricular, of *fama*, *Gerücht*, rumor and gossip resonate in the word *Ruhm* and its cognates. An archaic oral culture haunts us here. It is rumor or review that can also come from gossip—not things circulated in journals or called out loudly in public, but rather spoken quietly in confidence. But sources must be concealed in any case.

Consider typical turns of the table in that light or, rather, tone.

About Weber, "One reproaches him with too much passion . . . Nonetheless his good intentions and diligence are undoubted."
About Wiesand, gossip achieves harmony, as "there is only one voice" about his uprightness.
About Hommel, *Ruhm* grows passive, for his diligence and talent is *gerühmt*.
About Wernsdorf, the harmonious unnamed speak, since "according to unanimous witnesses," he is one of the most outstanding in learning and activity.
About Schlockwerder, "one says of him" he is a useful worker.
Mencke is "by reputable witnesses" a talented practitioner.
Of Uhlich, "one accords him" juristic learnedness.
Of Wilisch, "one does not deny him sufficient knowledge of law, but his lectures find no great approval."
Langguth is, "by reliable assurance," a good physician.
Frenzel "is supposed to have proven himself not untalented as a practicing physician . . . And one says of his treatises" that they have useful knowledge.
Freyberg's "knowledge is supposed not to be lacking, but then his speech, by unanimous assurance, is not at all made for the lecture hall."
Anton is seen as a "talented Orientalist by reliable witnesses."
Drasdo's "learning in theology and philosophy are not cast into doubt by those capable to judge him . . . But his speech at the lectern is still so affected and unnatural and thus less useful than it might otherwise be."

Among the litotes, under the impersonals, beside the passives, Burgsdorf never names his sources. His confessional practices reveal him as the best sort of trusted insider. Vacchieri's journal serves to deregister the body and private sphere. Burgsdorf's table conceals the source of information as being this or that actual person. To be fit for the visitor's table, academic voices, no matter what their provenance, must be rephrased as impersonal, authoritative evaluation. That is part of the magic of the table's rationalizing machinations. The point is not that all of the above judgments, as unattributed remarks, are based on gossip or rumor. For some or most of them might be based on expert or peer review, either oral or even written. The point is rather that the prose precludes knowing. In its most cynical statement, it's all just academic babble milled by ministerial tools.

Of Triller we saw he had written two works but had found no publisher. Column *d* opens: "One denies him neither talent nor diligence; one rather says he possesses good knowledge especially in Latin and Greek . . . ; no less does one impugn his moral character." The triple impersonal turns vivid: "But he has a very unpleasant, often incomprehensible speech at the lectern"—a comment reflecting back to column *b.* The table then turns on him: "so much [is] against him in his appearance that, despite sundry requests, it will not succeed him to obtain a professorship or any other position in the faculty." Academics only have a body for Burgsdorf when it is corrupt or decrepit or ugly, and thus damned here.

As Vacchieri had disembodied himself, the bodies of Burgsdorf's academics fall into an unregistered academic private sphere, unless the table finds them displeasing. Aspects of a private self now appear typically only when negatively marked. In the next generation, Fischer's academic dossier at the ministry in Munich would show something similar in regard to erratic or odd behavior. Successful and normal academics registered no private self.

Burgsdorf casts Gottfried August Meerheim as the bad soul. Column *d* begins with an impersonal "one" then moves to, "he is even supposed to have . . . ," then to, "one reproaches him . . ." The table insinuates that he is guilty of "too much dissipation ~~of partly improper sort~~, whereby students in part take part and for the other part supposedly get no good example." The table has charged him with corrupting students, though crossed out the most damning terms. "He himself, to the contrary, complains about hypochondriac spells and claims they make him incapable of all steady work and make movement and society a necessity."

No witnesses or accusers are named as usual. It is also noteworthy that Burgsdorf's table records no real academic dissonance. Chapter 7 on appointments exhibited the problem of collegial cacophony versus ministerial rationality. As the rationalizing ministry began fattening up acts for some appointments, contradictory voices—accusations, insinuations, opposing plots, even character assassinations—began to appear and prolixly dissolve the traditional lapidary prose of academic appointment protocols. The ministerial rationality of Burgsdorf's table countenances no such cacophony. Peer review and private gossip—there is no way to tell which was which—issue from unnamed ones and unanimous witnesses. Burgsdorf's academics have become rhetorically as opaque as Vacchieri's commission.

## The Charisma of the Academic's Name

More than Vacchieri's visitation in 1784 to the Bavarian, ex-Jesuit, Catholic University of Ingolstadt, Burgsdorf's visitation in 1789 to the Saxon, Protestant University of Wittenberg points to the culmination of the ancient arts of visitation: amid the academic babble, whose name would be acclaimed and whose not.

The vertical axis of Burgsdorf's table presents a premodern juridico-ecclesiastical regime of academic seniority and authority, while the horizontal axis casts a modern politico-economic one, a rationalized calculus of academic credit and capital. This suggests a greater articulation of public versus private academic spheres than apparent even in Vacchieri's journal. There was now an official realm of the academic as a public servant or professional, suited for the visitor's table, versus a domestic or personal realm of the private self, unsuited for the table, unless needing negative marking: the office versus the home.

Between home and office, however, the table registered a mediate realm and called forth a new, academic self or being there. The domestic self is typically deregistered, while this new self emerges as a strange private-professional double. It inhabits the sphere of *Ruhm*, of fame and fortune, of gossip and rumor, of capital and credit. It is an essential vehicle of modern academic charisma—the name that circulates outside the office.

In the A to Z of question 7 of the questionnaire of 1597, the letter "I," one of the bad letters for a professor, was *Rhumrätig:* one who seeks and boasts of *Ruhm*. The traditional university abhorred the charismatic individual as a troublemaker for the collective. The negative quality in 1597 has become a nearly essential quality of the academic's private-public "I" or name in 1789. Between the office and the home, the cameralistic table seeks to register— that is, to cast—a simulacrum, a charismatic name, as *Ruhm* or circulating fame.

Like the private sphere or home, this rumor-mill or naming machine lies outside the ministry's control, since it cannot determine who acquires *Ruhm* or credit. But, like the public sphere or bureau, this domain enters the ministry's eyes and ears and registry. It is over this rumor-mill or machinery of the name that Burgsdorf's prose effects deregistration through the table's impersonal, indirect, passive forms, double negatives, litotes, and unnamed ones. Like Vacchieri's disembodiment, that is an effect of its rationalizing power.

## CONCLUSION

The traditional visitation of universities came to an end around 1789. In Prussia, for example, ministerial visitations of the old sort became rare, then ceased. A university sent yearly tables (*Jahrestabellen*) on itself instead. The long night of the early modern police state had disembodied academics and transformed the university into a self-registering machine, no longer in need of visible ministerial hands. In natural science, the Romantic era witnessed something similar, as Schaffer has noted: the emergence of self-registering instruments manned by the disembodied genius, the sort of modern academic whom we have met.[30]

In the ministerial mentalities above, we can also see inklings of our modern academic-scientific prose. Schaffer and Shapin have brought out the earlier production of prolixity in experimental science, as well as the necessity to name witnesses in early modern gentlemanly culture. The use of spare and impersonal forms and passive voices, later so typical of academic-scientific prose, was not typical at this time in science, whose prose remained vivid into the nineteenth century. The bureaucratic style of Burgsdorf's table above predates and perhaps helped produce our modern academic-scientific, bureaucratic prose.[31]

In 1597 most Helmstedt professors refused to name names in the confessional setting of the visitors' questionnaire. Something else seems to underlie Minister Vacchieri's bent in his journal in 1784 to speak of himself and his single hand as the "commission" or "one." This something else also seems to inform Minister Burgsdorf's preference to cite unnamed ones as witnesses. Unlike the late Baroque or early Enlightenment culture illuminated by Schaffer and Shapin, the mid to late Enlightenment in the Germanies sought to suppress the names of witnesses, as reviewers or rumormongers, for ministerial registration. In the chapter above on libraries, we saw the coeval practice of anonymous academic reviews in the journals. Structures of anonymous adjudication (similar to peer review?) seem to have been growing.

From an eighteenth-century perspective, this recalls, as noted, Foucault's thesis that modern sovereignty tends to occult itself. Such structures and practices of self-registration and impersonal review would make the visitation of the early modern police state illiberal. In the same spirit, the modern grading system made the academic rod seem unenlightened.

So, what can we learn from the practice of the visitation in its final flourish in 1789? To put it simply, we have looked at a narrative and a table at the end of the academic ancien régime. As noted here and in chapters above, these serve metonymically as epitomes of traditional and rational authority—or, more literarily, as principal devices used by them.

Vacchieri's journal as a narrative indicates the sort of stories that the nascent bureaucratic mind tells itself, and the sort of master narrator that it conceives. The modern bureaucratic world, as we now know so well thanks to Weber, depends crucially on the production and separation of public or professional and private or domestic selves. Our minister's narrative demonstrated the accomplishment of this production. To appreciate that the bureaucracy must tell itself stories and fashion a narrative voice means to appreciate that rationalization cannot dispense with tools, such as narrative, of traditional societies. The Marxist-positivist dreams of a completely rational social order would seem chimerical.[32]

Burgsdorf's table as *ratio* indicates the importance of such little tools. Ministerial machinations did not simply register but also realized academic persona. Such tables as Burgsdorf's exhibit the modern magic of the bureaucracy, through its reports the "final cause," thus the emplotter of things. Not only the constitution of an impersonal realm of academic evaluation, but also the suppression of the traditional authority of narrative is a strategy for the legitimation of modern rational authority. Early modern confessional and police practices of visitation gave way to modern academic self-registration, as well as to the managerial commodification of academic names, which the next chapter pursues further.

Despite the decline of visitation as a formal ministerial mechanism after 1789, the system of knowledge still could not be run by paperwork alone. Much of the bureaucratic distance imposed by Burgsdorf's prose aimed at obscuring relations between hearsay and reputation. His table nonetheless registered a tension between ocular-scribal versus oral-aural traces of academics (column *a* versus *b*). The charismatic aspect of the academic voice, registered by local *applausum* and circulating chatter, mattered much in ministerial ears. The ministry's procrustean plots foundered on the protean nature of academic babble.

# 10

## Ministerial Hearing and Academic Commodification

The academic newsletters and review press were not only a virtual library in the eighteenth century. They became central banks and stock markets for accumulating and exchanging academic capital, assuming ever more its modern form, like finance capital, as pure paper, credit in circulation. In 1776 Adam Smith saw magic in finance capitalism and its ability to blaze a "wagon-way through the air." Entrepreneurs, especially in a poorly policed market, could manufacture credit, if not from nothing, then out of thin air. The thin air consisted of the rapid circulation of paper transactions, which, if one really looked, had little or no value.[1]

The Adam Smith of police science, Johann Justi, had already written of such modern magic in academia. As a good cameralist, Justi insisted that the Republic of Letters, like every other republic, was ultimately founded on industry and trade, on the mercantile.

> In the Republic of Letters, the academic ware is publicly vended for money. I mean "academic money" there. One needs to know that the Republic of Letters mints a sort of coin called "fame." In the learned tongue, this minting means to cite someone else with much credit (*Einen andern mit vielem Ruhm in seinen Schriften erwähnen*).

That leads to a "trading company," where academics work together minting the coin of the realm—academic credit or reputation—by mutual glowing citation. One did this best in the virtual library, in newsletters and reviews. By good luck, the anonymity of the reviews could facilitate the workings of such a scheme. The virtual library accomplished the sort of magic in manufacturing academic credit that Adam Smith would marvel at in finance capitalism.[2]

But the coin of the realm retained an archaic stamp. There is a strange tradition of the academic importance of making noise, and it has survived the dominion of paperwork. In commenting on the books a library ought to have, the great French royal librarian, Naudé, perhaps harmlessly noted that the noise (*bruit*) and the vogue (*vague*) of the books of one time or place may not be the same in others. Thus, as testimony to the time or place, one should collect some such books. Naudé's use of "noise" seems almost derogatory, but that noise was not unlike what we would see as cultural as opposed to intellectual history.[3]

Leibniz, who knew his Naudé well, noted in a letter of 1677 to Duke Johann Ferdinand what books one should buy for a good library. Leibniz thought that one needed books excellent in respect of others and that "are considerable in view of the noise (*bruit*) that they have made in the world." Leibniz's use of "noise" seems a wholly positive one. And in mid-eighteenth century, J. C. Gottsched wrote favorably concerning the fact that Christian Wolff's oration on China had made the most noise (*das größte Lärmen*) of any work at the time.[4]

The trope of making noise pointed to that of the man with a big name, a trope that spans the early modern era, if not more. The ideological inventors of the Republic of Letters, the humanists, sought to raise a ruckus. The noise they made aimed to inflate their names, individually and collectively, and to capitalize this inflation. As noted in chapters above, the modern system of chairs, although based on medieval notions of canonries, first emerged to accommodate humanists, who could not make an academic living from the traditional medieval means of collecting fees for lectures and exams since their subjects did not form part of the curriculum for examination. It would take centuries (and Protestantism and cameralism) for the idea to prevail systematically that the noise made in the Republic of Letters inflated an academic salary because it inflated a name. I do not know what salary Luther commanded at Wittenberg, but his *An den christlichen Adel deutscher Nation* of 1520 sold 4,000 copies in its first month. This helped further a growing and very big name.[5]

Such early economics as propagated by humanist and reformed views of the academic persona slowly eroded traditional mores. As early as 1611, a certain jurist named Stephanus held that a university ought to accord superior precedence to an academic in view of good publications over mere seniority. Such publications played the noisemakers that inflated the name and made it big. At least one university de facto took up the legal views of Stephanus. The 1640/48 statutes of Frankfurt a.d.O. made an exception concerning precedence, normally set by seniority, for, among other reasons, a man with a big name (*magni alicuius nominis vir*).[6]

By 1810 even the Austrians compromised their meritocratic principles for big names. An Austrian regulation of 1810 waived taking the professorial exam or *Concurse* for "famous men." The regulation depicted this fame as flowing from publications. Such publications had to make not only noise, but also of a certain sort. A Prussian decree of 12 December 1768 to the University of Halle had already specified that to enhance the reputation or *Ruhm* of the university professors must publish "specimens of their learning" and it must be of a certain sort. The ministry urged the professors at Halle, the Prussian flagship university at the time, to publish "more in accord with the taste of the time" (*sich mehr nach dem Geschmack der Zeit zu richten*). That was nothing less than a ministerial call to make fashionable noise.[7]

"'Publicity, publicity' one hears cried out everywhere, and many professors stand among the mass and cry at the top of their lungs," as one anonymous writer of 1798 claimed. Anonymous stressed the need to keep up with new discoveries. But a year earlier, C. M. Wieland had criticized his colleagues' hunt for novelty, *Neuheitsjägerei*. Literature and arts, he held, had become mere wares through the emphasis on being à la mode. He and others could see, however, that the fame machine had taken control. Book reviews in review journals, as the key to fame, now made the best noise. Nicolai's virtual library, *Allgemeine Deutsche Bibliothek* (*ABD*), long a central review journal (1765–1806), had emerged to produce taste and *Öffentlichkeit*, that is, publicity and public-ness. The journals, however, with envisaged serial production forever, drove the hunt for novelty, too.[8]

*ADB* as a review journal meant to substitute for the lack of a central capital city, in the sense of Paris or London, in the Germanies. The journal would remedy the lack of civilized conversation fostered by salons and cafés in Paris and London. *ADB* thus strove to make civilized noise: conversation, discussion, and even critique, but without pedantic polemics. Quite soon German academics desperately wanted to be reviewed in *ABD*. The reviews were, alas, anonymous. And that would trouble ministers and other academics, too.

Our Göttingen historian of universities, Michaelis, noted at the time that the worst way to make an academic appointment was "according to the praise of the learned periodicals." Who was this reviewer after all? "If this Anonymous should be a beginner, an uninformed about the matter, a student, a degenerated master, a friend, an auditor of the author or, indeed, upon removing the critic's mask, the author himself"—what then?

Michaelis confessed that one knew of such cases in the journals. Mere students or masters wrote many reviews, as he noted, and these "are indeed not the worst ones." It portended grave danger, said our historian, when ministers made appointments by relying on reviews in periodicals, as they in fact did. For ministers wanted famous academics. And fame came now more than ever by the noisy circulation of an author's name.[9]

So one had to be reviewed and reviewed well in Nicolai's virtual library, as well as in others. That blazed the path to fame. By the late 1760s, novelty already served as a criterion for positive reviews, as did the relation of a work to others. Reviewers commonly mentioned the current reputation of authors. Peer review was perhaps in the making. But Justi's tricky trading companies, minting mutual academic credit, also doubtless existed, too.[10]

This chapter picks up threads from the previous one. There, as well as in the chapter on academic appointments, we saw what was deregistered as much as what was registered by ministerial paperwork. From Wolfenbüttel's questionnaire of 1597 to Vacchieri's journal of 1784 and Burgsdorf's table of 1789, as well as in the enlightened Prussian piles and the Romantic Bavarian dossiers on academics, we found a juridico-ecclesiastical space displaced by a politico-economic one, as part of the grand narrative being told here. Such paperwork reinforced the distinction between public and private, between office and home. And a mediate realm, the market, emerged, bestowing its own overpowering charisma.

The central section of this chapter will analyze a report made by the Prussian minister Friedrich Gedike (1754–1803) in 1789. With Gedike's report, we have a document like those in the previous chapter since he wrote his report as a minister of state. But unlike Vacchieri and Burgsdorf, Gedike visited universities outside his jurisdiction. Gedike's mission and report assumed the form of a politico-economic or cameralistic travelogue. His interest lay not only in gaining knowledge. Gedike also visited universities to acquire academics, as he put it.

Gedike's report is the most complex of the documents analyzed in this book. It points the way to modern displacements of the early modern practice of visitation. The rite of visitation faded in favor of techniques of academic self-registration and self-promotion, as well as in favor of a political economy of academic acquisition. The central section of the chapter, analyzing Gedike's report, sits between a section pursuing further the themes with which we began above, and a section comparing Gedike's report to a more private sort of travelogue.

## THE UNIVERSITY OF GÖTTINGEN AND
## MANAGERIAL CAPITALISM

Gedike embellished his 1789 report on Göttingen with an unflinching assessment of the university's self-manufactured reputation.

Nowhere did I find among professors so much preference for their university as here. They seem to presume as given that their university is the first and foremost among all in Germany, and thus speak often with a sort of contemptuousness or pity for other universities. Everyone is, so to speak, drunk with the proud sense of their merits, partly real but partly pretended or imagined. Several professors assured me very confidently that the most famous scholars, when they leave Göttingen for another place, lose a significant part not only of their celebrity but even also of their usefulness . . .[;] however, an unknown scholar, if he becomes professor in Göttingen, wins a big name and value simply thereby, since from the glory, which they think constantly embraces the university, a few rays fall upon the head of each and every. One can often, to be sure, hardly keep back a smile when one hears many Göttingen academics speaking in such enthusiastic tones, as though outside the city wall of Göttingen neither light nor erudition is to be found. But this university pride does have here a good effect. It creates a certain *esprit de corps* that I found nowhere else in such extent and kind. Every professor sees not only the honor of the university as his own, but also his honor and that of his colleagues as the honor of the university. So one finds outbreaks of the sort of cabals, envy and the mania for belittlement and insults, that cause so much frustration and bitterness at other universities, far more seldom here or, at least, one notices them less . . . It would be, it seems to me, desirable to have at our Prussian universities this *esprit de corps* that imbues Göttingen professors and makes the honor of their university the focus of all their wishes and aspirations.[11]

But Gedike resisted falling under Göttingen's spell. The final few lines, cited above, give the Hanoverian university its due, as do the rest of Gedike's many pages on Göttingen in the report. At Göttingen Gedike confronted a university and its faculties, which, in good part thanks to their already famous library and review journal, had made such noise in the academic world and cast such an enormous shadow in so short a time—barely over half of a century since its foundation in 1737—as to be nearly beyond belief.

In Göttingen Gedike confronted the avatar of academic managerial capitalism. The Prussians, including Gedike, also saw themselves as adept in this new faith. The fame and name projected by Göttingen's professors, library, and journal testified to the might of virtual reality, the power of the circulation of paper and noise. Those were immense as projected by Göttingen. But when one came to the physical place itself, as Gedike did in 1789, to see, as it were, the machine behind the ghost, that is, to see the academics and institutions behind the specter and noise made by Göttingen, then one was usually shocked or, in Gedike's case, ironically bemused. So much noise, so much projected and circulated spiritual energy, so many big and inflated names from such a tiny town and academic enterprise.[12]

The distant Austrians long resisted Göttingen's spell, too. A university commission rejected a proposal of 13 February 1773 to send Austrian students to study at Göttingen and return as future lecturers and professors. The commission rejected, in fact, the Göttingen academic model. Later, in 1785, an important Austrian, namely Swieten, received a work called *Vorschlag eines Unbekannten über Verbesserung des Universitäts-Wesen* from the emperor, who asked for Swieten's view. Concerning the suggestion again of imitating Göttingen, the minister responded that that university did not work for "national education."

Göttingen, he meant, did not act much like a public corporation for the common good. It rather more resembled a mercantile teaching academy of sciences, a site of research that assembled all branches of knowledge with the aim to attract foreign students. "The entire constitution is one of *financial speculation*, from the standpoint of the instructors and of the government, which seeks to bring in academics with big reputations, since one hopes that increased student enrollments from other states will be wrought by such men."[13]

Michaelis, our often quoted anonymous historian of Protestant universities and himself a professor at Göttingen, on occasion noted such things of his workplace, at times with a sigh. In chapter 7, we encountered Michaelis bemoaning that his Göttingen colleagues had learnt to fish for extramural academic offers, so as "to extort more money in the end" from the ministry. Resigned perhaps to the new commodification of academics, Michaelis laconically noted of his colleagues and their acquisition, "It happens here as at an auction: whoever wants a book that, in view of its rarity, commands a high price, must offer more than the other. No one should want to tell me stories here about love of the Fatherland."[14]

## Academic Cameralism

An anonymous tract of 1782, *Das Universitätswesen in Briefen*, is probably by a certain Friedrich Boell or Böll, whom we'll take as the author. A merciless satire on academic cameralism, the work discusses a University G, doubtless Göttingen. Boell had written a propaganda tract for Göttingen in 1775. The anonymous tract of 1782 consists of a series of letters between a professor emeritus, C.B., and the newly appointed "Curator," V.C., of an unnamed university, probably Helmstedt. C.B. refers on occasion to University G, which is flourishing far better than V.C.'s university. Many are studying at G who, in view of national origins, ought to be studying at V.C.'s university. Historically, that is what happened to nearby Helmstedt soon after Göttingen opened in 1737. C.B.'s letters advise V.C. about how to manage his university properly camerally as its new curator.[15]

C.B. writes to Curator V.C. that a university is but a sort of factory,

> You, Mr. Curator, are the factory-director. The instructors at the academy [university] are the workers (*Gesellen*). The young people studying there and their parents . . . are the customers. The disciplines (*Wissenschaften*) taught there are the wares. Your king is the Lord and owner of his academic factory (*wissenschaftlicher Fabrik*).[16]

In the next letter, C.B. explains that the curator must command the art of visitation. The fame (*Ruhm*) of the university must occupy the center of his interest. At G, several instructors usually teach the same discipline, thus inducing a beneficial competition among themselves, as well as product-choice for customers. And "take a look at how much [more] one works at other universities [than yours]! See academics in the prime of their youth [there] in the cemetery! See the deathly white faces at the lectern! But here [at yours] fat faces and big paunches—on my honor, they're not going to push themselves to death."[17]

A good curator lets the factory's products be seen in good light, but never the inner workings of the machinery. Therein lies the key to the factory's fame. And consider the Prussian army—how 200,000 men can be made to work like a machine. How much easier is that to do with a small army of academics. Indeed, academics are like children. If you pay heed to their screams, they scream all the louder. It is better to give them, so to say, a good whipping. Then they scream no more. In following pages, C.B. touches on the useful effects of envy among faculty members and his scheme to set up a university where no one receives a salary, but where all must live from student fees won by teaching. Since a university is a commercial enterprise, one must also pay attention to ruining the enterprises of others.[18]

The curator must manage the university with a firm hand. Workers at the academic factory tend to think that it exists for their sake and convenience, whereas it exists to serve customers. One must make sure to give each professor "his own chief discipline." But one must also foster competition so that workers don't grow lazy, as a monopolist does. "Well directed freedom is the soul of trade—monopolies are its death." Curator V.C. writes, "You know that police science has long been my favorite study." To which C.B. replies that it is a "divine science." But it's a mistake to let one's own prejudices determine what is taught, that is, what wares would be offered. One best fashions offerings to serve the tastes of the customers. If enough of them want to consume metaphysical junk, as opposed to modern police and cameral sciences, then one ought to offer lectures in metaphysics as well.[19]

Thus the anonymous work of 1782, probably by Boell, and hopefully a satire. It is the most scandalous formulation of academic cameralism as managerial capitalism. The only other work that comes close is "Bemerkungen über Johann Jakob Mosers Rede . . .—aus den Papieren eines verstorbenen Staatsministers und Universitäten Curators." This is an anonymous fragment from the Göttingen milieu and has been ascribed to the founding curator and visible hand behind Göttingen for its first generation, Minister Münchhausen.[20]

### The Last Word on Göttingen and Its Instructors

An anonymous German work of this title appeared in 1791. The author was Wilhelm F. A. Mackensen, who had studied at Göttingen and elsewhere. This student guide to Göttingen and its professors is also a scandalous work.

Like Gedike, Mackensen noted the unusual pride and vanity at Göttingen. Professors behave as if one could not become educated outside the town. They become most perplexed when they learn that you've never heard of them. Mackensen found few really great men there. Most seemed to him "men of the lucky moment," men who possessed the "talent de bien faire" to high degree. The ministry in Hanover intends Göttingen professors to be no pedants or provincials, but rather men of the world. One thus obsesses in Göttingen about reputation won by writings. But, at the same time, one must cultivate a certain manner and what counts most is the art of "minting" oneself with the right "face" on the coin.[21]

This art of minting oneself has manufactured Göttingen's own reputation in large part. "Here it's a big business firm for science" (das große Handelshaus der Wissenschaften). Fashionable superficiality is the modern rule for academic work. Thanks to the library, an academic can easily pillage nine books and fashion a trendy piece out of them. One works, for example, not with the voluminous industry of a deeply learned Benedictine monk bringing the difficult discipline of diplomatics from the darkness. A Göttingen professor, rather, writes a digest or survey of diplomatics. "In short, here you are taught the secret of the scholarly racket." One learns handshakes and business advantages. One sets things in motion and brings forth fashions. One devises tricks to get this or that ware marketed. To keep its place at the top of the heap, Göttingen is willing to try anything, even tarting up academic works as "cream puffs." Thus "all is welcome in Göttingen that makes noise."[22]

## GEDIKE'S HEARING AS NARRATIVE

Gedike's report occupies the center of this chapter on ministerial hearing and academic commodification. Gedike was an important person in his day and age. He seems, moreover, to be a secret (anti)hero of this book. He appears, I think, in more chapters than anyone else. That was an unanticipated result, much as the absence of Prussian dossiers was. But it seems not without rhyme and reason in a book centered on the early modern Germanies, whose analytical end is the late Enlightenment and Romantic era, and for which Brandenburg-Prussia provides some of its most compelling materials.

Gedike became rector of the Friedrichwerdisches gymnasium in Berlin in 1779. It counted as an influential institution since no university existed in Berlin before 1809/10. After 1786 Gedike coedited the *Berliner Monatsschrift*, a central journal of the late Enlightenment. In 1787 he joined the newly created *Oberschulkollegium* (OSK), the Supreme School Council. As we saw in chapter 7, this ministry oversaw among other things all Prussian universities, including the making of academic appointments. As we saw in chapter 4, in 1787 Gedike became director of a new pedagogical institute in Berlin, which would oversee the certifying of teachers for all college preparatory high schools, the gymnasia, in Prussia. And, as we saw in chapters 4 and 5, in his capacity as a minister in the OSK, after 1787 he had a hand in shaping the *Abitur* in Prussia, while also negotiating with F. A. Wolf in Halle on the structure of the first important university seminar in Prussia. More than our two others visitors from the 1780s, Vacchieri in Bavaria and Burgsdorf in Saxony, Gedike in Brandenburg-Prussia embodied a minister with reputation or *Ruhm* outside the realm.

In 1789, from 16 June to 1 August, in the service of the king of Prussia, Gedike visited fourteen universities, non-Prussian and largely Protestant. As part of his mission, during which the French Revolution began, he composed a report of fifty-nine folio pages. A cover letter, dated 17 December

1789, and a list of travel expenses bookended the report. Richard Fester published the report, without the bookends, in 1905. Gedike's report is one of the most important primary sources on early modern German academia. A number of chapters here have cited from it. This central section of the chapter is dedicated to it.[23]

## Time and the Narrator

Gedike opens his report, "I stayed at this university [Helmstedt] two days (the 18th and 19th of June), during which time I had the opportunity of meeting almost all the professors and of hearing most of them." With the city as heading, the first word of the report is "I." Unlike our ministerial visitors from the previous chapter, Gedike not only interjects himself into his report, but also begins it with himself as narrator.

An "I" played a leading part in ethnography and travel literature at the time, and Gedike's was no artifact of composition on the road. Internal evidence—temporal projection and reference to knowledge acquired later—shows that Gedike wrote his report once back in Berlin, even though he put it in a journalistic or chronological form simulating the survey.

"I," the first word of Gedike's report after "Helmstedt," inserts the work between ministerial and ethnographic literary canons. Unlike Vacchieri's journal, which has a narrative voice however angelic in the temporal flow of the book of hours, Gedike's narrative "I," although located in this or that place from 16 June to 1 August, can draw conclusions in the text only possible at the end of the journey. Narrative control over the future enhances the emplotment of this report, while "I" occupies the space between home and office.[24]

Gedike appears not only to have more narrative control over time than Vacchieri. He seems also nonchalant to the point of bureaucratic rebellion about confessing his acts per diem. Not a few of Fester's editorial notes to the report concern trying to figure out which days Gedike spent where. The tables turn at the end for both our visitors though. Recall that Vacchieri gave himself a missing day in the end, as we found a day missing in his journal.

But time caught up with Gedike. His entry for the University of Leipzig, the second to last visit, began, "As I arrived in Leipzig, the time allotted me by His Excellency . . . was already expired. There arose also urgent domestic circumstances." Fester notes that the latter meant the birth of Gedike's son in Berlin on 28 July, who died two days after Gedike's return. Another note by Fester shows that Gedike arrived in Leipzig on the evening of 30 July, left the next day at 11:00 a.m., somehow saw Wittenberg en route to Berlin, and ended his survey on 1 August. These hasty entries show time pressing on our Prussian visitor. Phrases such as Gedike's "domestic circumstances," though euphemistic, are rhetorically impossible in Vacchieri's journal, whose confessions invoke only rituals and professional acts.

### Time, "I," and the Superstructure

Gedike structured the report complexly. The primary structure is chronological, the secondary topographical, and the tertiary thematic or topical. Had the cities given the primary structure, he might have given them any order, such as alphabetic; or he might have laid out the universities in a ranked order, or even woven the report into a thematic form, in the vertical flow of a report like Burgsdorf's table.

Indeed, Gedike might have made a tabular report. But he chose a chronological primary structure, so that the vertical flow of the report simulated his journey as a journal. The next choices of organization moved the report, however, away from chronicle toward locality and thematics. Unlike Vacchieri's journal as book of hours, Gedike's survey, as noted, was offhand about fixing time, until it pressed. In chronological order of visitation, the survey falls into fourteen sections or chapters, one for each university. This set topography as the secondary structure. The effacement of an exact chronicle, that is, the erasure of time, pushed the secondary structure, the list of cities, into the foreground.

As cited above, Gedike began the report with an "I," stating that he stayed two days at Helmstedt. At Göttingen, the next stop, we learn five (printed) pages into the section how many days he spent. It was four and a half days, the most time that he spent anywhere. Of the next stop at Marburg he said, "At this university I spent only a day and a half, since I quickly saw that I could find here only a little stuff for new observations."[25]

Here we see patterns underlying the style. Confession about time, though offhand, defended days spent in each place in view of the "stuff for new observations." Time summoned up Gedike's "I," as it was his time being spent, though at the king's per diem. Marburg shows that a boring or bad university indicated little time spent there, and vice versa. The next town, Gießen, was judged in the first line as one "of the less important." After this, only the fourth town, the report lost track of time. The section on Gießen begins with a footnote from Fester, "Gedike's stay in Gießen probably took place on 30 June."

The secondary structure facilitated Gedike's studied effacement of time in the report. Like Vacchieri angelically transporting himself from Munich to Ingolstadt with no trace of a journey, Gedike in all but one case also simply appeared in his report in each new town, stayed a while, sometimes saying how long, then appeared in the next town, with his days en route not traced. Toward the end of the trip, his dating grew more precise again. In Erfurt he arrived, as he related, on a Saturday, on which day no one lectured. But, as he'd heard so much bad about the university, he decided to move on.

At the third to last stop, Jena, the first paragraph relates, "Indeed, Jena belongs now to those universities that merit most notice and respect. I thus stayed here longer than at most other universities, in that I stayed three days here." He reached his penultimate stop, Leipzig, where his time expired and domestic cares emerged. Bearing in mind that Gedike wrote the report in Berlin and had a diary and notes, his obscuring of time between Marburg and Erfurt did not arise due to lack of information. In view of Fester's valiant editorial attempts to reconstruct the chronology, Gedike did a good job in the deregistration of his time.

## Gedike's "I"

Unlike Wolfenbüttel's questionnaire, Vacchieri's journal and Burgsdorf's table, Gedike's report has one. This "I" visits fourteen universities between 16 June and 1 August 1789. It further concedes to have visited two towns without universities: Nuremberg and Schnepfenthal near Gotha. Only for this last town, the humblest in this report, is the road mentioned: "On the way from Erlangen to Erfurt, I got acquainted with the pedagogical institute in Schnepfenthal, not far from Gotha." The road here served as an excuse.

Gedike's "I" otherwise registers only in towns. Temporal expressions bring "I" to presence, often as confessions about days spent in relation to "stuff" at a university. "I" is temporally well marked near the opening and ending of the survey, but in the middle a cloud of unknowing obscures it. Gedike's schedule appears so unclear in the report, it seems that his modern editor, Fester, fell into miscalculations about where Gedike was when.

"I" has some foreknowledge, but admits to having terminated the survey under the weight of time. "I" is also perspectival and sensitive: "it seemed to me," "it pleased me," "I believe," "I sincerely admit," "it was alienating for me to hear," "so I must admit on the other hand," "I would have gladly heard," "one of the professors whose lecturing pleased and interested me the most," and, of Schiller's lectures Gedike wrote, "I admit, by the way, that it was difficult for me to find the grounds for the overly great applause."

Though on a mission of state, Gedike's narrative persona has emotions, admits lack of insight, expresses wishes, and so on. This is a movement to a sentimental realism of the sort in the eighteenth-century novel. It is a refinement of Vacchieri's clerical Romance. But like the latter's "one," Gedike's "I" comes to presence only as a bureaucratic persona.

We do not find "I" eating or sleeping at all. As angels might, Vacchieri engaged in a few bouts of ritual eating and drinking. But Gedike leaves even such rituals out. "I" doesn't go to anyone's house, is feasted by no one, and receives no one in the report. All those rituals would have helped plot a traditional or clerical Romance like Vacchieri's.

And no one offers "I" coffee or beer or even pretzels. All those gratuitous details would have helped plot a modern sentimental Romance as in a realistic journal, private diary, or novel. Though possessed of a sensibility, Gedike's "I" has less of a body than Vacchieri's "one." Pleased about some things, alienated by others, "I" is neither feasted nor thirsty nor tired. From the report, we don't even know if "I" had a trusty hand in the survey.

## The Tertiary Level

Let's return to Gedike's structuring of the report and look at the tertiary level. The sections on each university revolve not around a schedule or book of hours, but rather topics. A list is implicit: students, money, faculties, institutions, constitution, general, and miscellaneous observations. Behind this lies a virtual table and some topics show a typical clustering and sequence. Students, money, and faculties commonly cluster.

But Gedike also seems to have taken pains to vary the arrangement of canonical topics, so as to make the report read more like a narrative. And in some cases he drops one or more of his canonical topics. The latter reach low tide for the last two universities, Leipzig and Wittenberg. That indicates by absences what a visitor gets by transportation, as Gedike had no real time to see the last two towns. The two sections reduce pretty much to constitutional and institutional notes, which he probably cribbed from books back in Berlin.

The other twelve sections convey a vivid sense of a local site, especially in auricular terms. While Vacchieri's journal lays the plot in strict order of the story or chronicle, Gedike's survey, by playing with the layout of themes, offers a possible subplot for each chapter or university. But each of those chapters has no story line. As noted, it fails thanks to the effacement of Gedike's book of hours. Thus the tertiary level works to block a narrative reading, like Burgsdorf's table, while the primary and secondary levels intimate a story line and plot, like Vacchieri's journal and the Bavarian dossiers.

## Acquisition of Academics

And the overall plot is clear: acquisition in the academic market. Like Burgsdorf's table, Gedike's survey formed part of German cameralism and managerial capitalism. Gedike's six-week mission consisted in scouting out the principal Protestant, non-Prussian universities in the Germanies. The aim was to determine ways to improve Prussian universities, including above all locating professors for acquisition, as Gedike put it.

Visitation had now little to do with orthodoxy. More than in Burgsdorf's table of 1789, academics in Gedike's plot embodied commodities. The marketplace was not the journals so much as the lecture halls. Journals one could see aplenty in Berlin. And by confidential correspondence one might learn a lot of gossip about potential targets of acquisition. But some things, such as voices and applause, could still only be ascertained by hearing the target in person. Visitors might thus now conduct an ethnography of acquisition.

Gedike is interested in the stuff one can best collect on the spot. In all but a few sections, a good part consists in a report on the faculties. Like Wolfenbüttel's questionnaire of 1597 and Burgsdorf's table of 1789, and not to forget the traditional lecture catalogue and the sequence of examiners in an oral exam, Gedike's report usually goes through faculties in the juridical order of academic precedence: theology, law, medicine, and finally arts and philosophy. Gedike typically lists academics in each faculty in accord with their seniority.

That sets a default pattern from which departures arise, especially when he seems bored. The schema emerges for the first university, Helmstedt, where the faculty-report comes after the first paragraph. Of the seven pages here, the faculty-evaluation occupies five. Of five pages on Marburg, the evaluation occupies three. Of eight on Jena, the evaluation has a bit more than half of the pages. Gedike had no chance to see the faculties in Erfurt, Leipzig, and Wittenberg. His failure to see the last university is especially depressing, since his evaluation in summer 1789 would have allowed a nice comparison with Burgsdorf's in winter 1789.

## Hearing

What comes forth most from Gedike's evaluations is not what he saw, though this registers well. What comes forth is rather more what he heard. The unit "I heard" and its grammatical variations occur more than fifty times. Along with the temporal, the auricular brings Gedike's "I" to presence. It does so far more than the ocular, which is usually simply reported without an "I saw." The visible seems more impersonal and transmissible without marking the personal mediator. Though Gedike translates the auricular into the ocular by writing the report, the "I" as witness seems necessary to warrant this.[26]

Gedike mostly marks not gossip or rumor, but rather lectures, talk, speech, academic voice, *Vortrag*, and students' *applausum*. This sort of hearing dominates the sensory report. Gedike, however, almost never reports that "I" spoke with or to anyone. The latter occurs only when he did not go to the person's lecture or collegium. In Helmstedt, about Professor Pfaff, Gedike notes, "I was unable to hear him, since his class on applied mathematics was cancelled due to lack of listeners (*Zuhörern*) [students]. Judging on the basis of oral conversation, I believe nonetheless that his speech (*Vortrag*) may be not unpleasant."

Here I should note the difficulty of translating certain German words. Most of the German terms having to do with academia still had a strong oral-aural aspect. *Vortrag* was not lecture, but rather more a lecturing voice, hence my usual translation as "speech" to capture an emphasis on sound over substance. Similarly, when not metonymically *applausum*, students were mostly *Zuhörer*, listeners. One might translate that as "auditors," were it not for the connotations that has at least in American English. In the above passage, Gedike even qualified his conversation as oral. Evaluation of the *Vortrag* as voice or speech constituted the minimal unit sought about each academic in Gedike's hearing.

Professor Schmid in Gießen "is supposed to have but little applause. From his conversation I concluded that his speech can be hardly very lively or witty." And of Schmid we learnt no more. By Gedike's formulae, the last phrase meant that "I" did not go to Schmid's lectures, since "I" only confessed conversing when auricular surveillance wanted. Moreover, the prospect of poor aural sensations was enough to drive Gedike out of town. "I was just on a Saturday in Erfurt. On that day no one lectures, so I could not hear anyone. And anyway I had already heard too much about the bad condition of the university and of the poor speech of most of the professors to convince me to stay longer."

## Sick Academics

The oral (Burgsdorf's column *b*) embodied the minimal charismatic unit sought. But a famous or attractive academic, thus a potential commodity for acquisition, occasioned a full depiction (Burgsdorf's columns *a, c, d*). When it waxed, evaluation considered age, *Vortrag*, *applausum*, *Ruhm* or reputation, learning, works, salary, power, character; when negative, it considered corporal state. Like Vacchieri's and Burgsdorf's academics, as well as those in the Prussian piles and the Bavarian dossiers on academic appointments, not to mention the new doctor of philosophy, Gedike's academics had no bodies, unless they needed to be negatively marked or damned. As the evaluations of faculties flowed vertically in terms of seniority, ages more or less ran from older to younger with the vertical flow.

The first evaluation of the report is on the Helmstedt theology faculty and reads, "The oldest there, Abbot Carpzov, is already too old and weak to be of any considerable use to the university. But he still holds some lectures, although he is already over 70 years old." With "I" apparently not hearing him, old Carpzov fell from a list of potential Prussian acquisitions. The second to fourth theology professors were much younger. Gedike heard them all and had much to say about the second and third. He noted the high salary of the third.

When Gedike moved to Göttingen, the senior theologian, "who for a few years could do little anyway due to corporal feebleness," had just died, as "I" noted. "The senior of the philosophy faculty is now Privy Councilor Michaelis, Professor of Oriental Languages" (author of the here much cited anonymous history of Protestant universities). "His age has made him already pretty dull and his memory has become markedly weak."

Aged, ugly, odd, frail, sickly bodies, one or both feet in the grave, are so marked. Many academics, like Meiners in Göttingen, are too "timid."

In Gießen, Hezel, besides lecturing too timidly, though not badly, is "in general hypochondriac."

Although of cheery and lively speech, Gatterer in Heidelberg is "somewhat sickly."

In Stuttgart, "Prof. Abel to be sure does not please at first glance by his appearance," but his speech is "thorough, frank and not without liveliness." And Moll, despite great learning, "is in his lifestyle a weirdo (*Sonderling*) and very hypochondriac."

In Altdorf, Jäger and König are also "very hypochondriac."

In Jena, Gruner's "speech is indeed thorough but too little lively. And his appearance is very sinister and misanthropic."

Schreber in Erlangen is not only hypochondriac, but also timid. Loss of power is also are recorded here, as Seiler's "applause has in general decreased, just as has his influence with the ministry."

Gedike possessed many terms to qualify *Vortrag*, and his best concerned Swabian dialects, especially Schiller's. "He read everything word for word, in a pathetically declamatory tone, that very often did not fit the simple historical facts and geographical notes which he had to convey. Altogether the whole lecture was more an oration (*Rede*) than a lecture (*Vortrag*)." Clear from Gedike's evaluations of *Vortrag* is that he did not usually separate sound and substance. Gedike's hearing shows how much the traditional academic oral culture still held sway in 1789, that is, how much charisma academic noise could make.

## The Ocular, the Aural, and the "I"

In 1789 academics still had two essential realms for registration: *Schrift* and *Vortrag*, writing and voice, column *a* and *b* in Burgsdorf's table. *Beifall*, meaning applause and approval, provided a transition. An academic with little aural *Beifall*, as *applausum* given by students to speech in lecture (Burgsdorf's column *b*), would need much ocular *Beifall*, as praise given by reviewers to papers (Burgsdorf's columns *a* and *d*), to be potential prey for Prussian acquisition (like Burgsdorf's column *c*).

Gedike disposed with most of those he overheard, when not by marking them as aged or odd or impotent, then by reducing them to their voice (Burgsdorf's column *b*). Like students' *applausum*, of which they often had little, most academics were a provincial phenomenon, an ephemeral voice, of little interest to the Prussian ministry. The largest number of academics echoed in the report equaled mere *Vortrag*, registered as producers of commodities—academic voices—consumed locally and only by students, instead of circulating as simulacra of academic credit or capital (Burgsdorf's columns *a* and *d*). The political economy of Gedike's hearing resembles and articulates that of Burgsdorf's table.

Here, now, one of Gedike's longest and highest evaluations of an academic:

Court Councilor (*Hofrath*) [and professor in Göttingen] Heyne, as known, is one of the primary and most important pillars of the fame (*Ruhm*) of the university. He has thus enjoyed till now, among all professors, the greatest confidence from the Hanoverian government. One has asked him the most for advice, particularly pondered his suggestions, above all about vacancies [in the faculties], and so on. He was till now, to an extent, the chancellor of the university, without being called such (for since Mosheim's death Göttingen has had no actual chancellor). The bustle and untiring activity with which Heyne works for the honor of the university is universally acknowledged. Humanistic studies have come extraordinarily to the fore in Göttingen thanks to him. At no university are such studies pursued with such enthusiasm as in Göttingen. No university has thus in recent times educated so many learned and tasteful philologists as Göttingen. Even the most refined and richest students attend Heyne's classes. His Archaeology is, so to say, a class in vogue (*Modekollegium*) especially, even though (as quasi-private class) it costs three *Louisdor.* The three higher faculties unanimously acknowledge the great influence that Heyne's lectures have for the more thorough and learned education of their listeners (*Zuhörer*). Most striking is the use to the theologians. And nonetheless is the speech (*Vortrag*) of this splendid man nothing less than brilliant and attractive, as the fruitfulness of his speech and his wealth of new ideas and new applications of old ideas sufficiently well compensate listeners for the lack of the pleasant and likeable.[27]

This is one of the few places where Gedike distinguishes the sound from the substance of speech. The evaluation of Heyne culminates in the last lack in his speech, but in him Gedike sees someone with power in Hanover similar in scope to his own in Prussia. And in this, the longest of Gedike's descriptions of any academic in the report, there is no indication that he spoke with Heyne during his four and a half days in Göttingen! As noted, Gedike's style brings him to confess having had conversation only when auricular surveillance wants.

Though Gedike has an "I" in the manner of a private diary or an ethnography, this ego is even more ethereal than Vacchieri's "one." Gedike seems rather more divine than angelic. What Gedike heard as conversation, gossip, or rumor, goes into indirect discourse or impersonal forms, as in Burgsdorf's table. That is the key absence in Gedike's hearing, or silencing. How Gedike knows what he knows, he, like Burgsdorf, usually conceals. Gedike is also a good gossip. He disguises it as authoritative, impersonal, and objective review.

## A Private Diary and Expense Account

Gedike kept a private diary on his trip. Here he wrote:

> Leipzig, 31 July. Shortly after 8 o'clock we went out to begin the usual course of visits and listening to lectures. But first we went to the post office to see about mail. Two were there. One was from my brother-in-law and had the happy news that last Tuesday (the 28th of July) my dear wife gave birth to a son, though she was not due for another 14 days. My joy and anxiety were indescribable. I had no thought but to be quickly in Berlin.[28]

In this diary Gedike produced a private, domestic, sentimental persona. Perhaps the possibility of writing such a private diary enabled the casting of the ghostly, divine persona we have been learning to love above in the form of a ministerial narrative voice. Here we learn that in fact a "we" made the journey. Gedike's private diary depicts the route and its beauty, as well as the weather. Gedike records here visits to homes of academics, and private amusements and emotions, such as the longing to see his wife and new born son, who in fact died two days after Gedike's return through Zehlendorf to Berlin.

Emotions and a sensibility were the only private parts of Gedike's bureaucratic "I" of the report, whose ascetic style called for omission of lovely roads, nice weather, and so on. But the road does not fail entirely from Gedike's report, if we consider its bookends. Taking Gedike's report as a narrative, like Vacchieri's, we may see the first bookend, the cover letter, as the moral authority enabling the report to have a plot. The other bookend is the expense account, which perhaps offers the moral of modern ministerial ethnographic acquisition.

Here Gedike sums up the miles he traveled as "204½," one more than his diary calculated. The total mileage is broken down into fifteen entries, reflecting the towns and routes from Berlin and back again. Travel and other expenses come to a final sum at the end. The ministry has marked the expense account in red. Annotating or marking in red pencil, though practiced earlier a bit at the ministry in Berlin, seems to have emerged most toward the close of the eighteenth century, as we saw in the chapter on academic appointments.

## Berlin's Red Hand

By its red marks, the ministry shows when its interest is raised in reading. In the first page of Gedike's report, the name of Professor Sextroh, recently acquired from Göttingen, is underlined not once but twice in red. Sextroh is unhappy with Helmstedt, Gedike tells Berlin and gives Sextroh's large salary, 1200 thaler plus student fees, on the report's next page. Gedike registers him as a target for acquisition by Berlin's red hand.

The report is much marked in red from Helmstedt to Göttingen to Marburg. At Gießen, Berlin's red pencil stops underlining and begins marking margins with red here and there. Such marks grow fewer as the report moves on. Erlangen has two lines underlined, but after Erfurt all red fades, till the expense account. This pattern of Berlin's red hand marking matches well the narrative structure of Gedike's report, to which we now return.

## A Descent Narrative

Gedike's hearing was a cameralistic, capitalistic, Protestant, Prussian tale. Coming from Berlin, Gedike expected enlightenment in Göttingen and a few other places. The hearing was otherwise preordained to find less light than in Berlin. Gedike arrived first in Helmstedt, then went to Göttingen, where he seems to have stayed longest.

As we saw, Gedike marked time well in Göttingen. Here and here alone, he also registered the then academically gratuitous details known as women.

> Many students even have mistresses . . . Moreover, coarse excess do not want here either. Even during the few days I was here, a girl (*Mädchen*) was set upon by several drunken students, first on the street, then trailed into her house and maltreated so vulgarly that one feared for her life.

A gang rape must have occurred here. Besides the mistresses, this raped Göttingen girl was the only woman in Gedike's whole six week hearing. In view of how much he successfully repressed, it shows the threshold of repression in his bureaucratic prose and pose.

It shows as well the mark he sets here. After this rape in Göttingen, a descent narrative opens. "The drop (*Abfall*) is very striking when one comes, as I this time, from Göttingen right to Marburg." From Marburg to Gießen, Gedike descends into the lower world of southern Germany. After Gießen he passes to another world altogether.

In Mainz he visits the dark underworld of Catholicism, violating his (angelic) instructions to visit Protestant universities. Between Gießen and Mainz is where and when Gedike's report casts time into a cloud of unknowing and loses track of days. This is where Berlin's red hand would later grow faint. From Mainz, Gedike goes south to Heidelberg, confessionally Protestant and Catholic. Then he passes onto Protestant soil again, but Swabian, which, in view of his apparent dislike of Swabian dialects, proved hard for his hearing.

The University of Stuttgart seems to be a military camp disguised as an educational institution, and so is the epitome of unenlightened modernism for Gedike, who is now writing with his own monarch and ministry in mind. The edicts on censorship and right religion had been issued in Prussia in 1788. From Stuttgart he goes to Tübingen which, since he does not get a chance to see Leipzig, is his antipode to Stuttgart's alarming modernism, that is, a Protestant university that seems still medieval (which Leipzig was in spades).

From Tübingen Gedike transports himself angelically all the way to Altdorf, mentioning no foot put in Bavaria. During that journey, the French Revolution begins. In Altdorf he is still far enough south to strain his ears. He does not like it there, though the next town, Erlangen, gets a good hearing. Moving ever more north, Gedike encounters Erfurt next. Here time becomes precise, on a Saturday when he can't hear anyone. In Jena one has a sense of ascending from a transit through a dark underworld to the overworld of light sights and sounds, as Berlin is not far away. Leipzig and Wittenberg get short shrift as home calls.

### Hard Hearing and Loose Lips

If we read the report as a descent narrative, then our hero sallies forth from enlightened Berlin into southern climes, the realms of Catholicism and Swabian dialects. On such a reading, things begin to get a hard hearing already in Hanoverian Göttingen. Here Gedike not only shook his readers' refined sensibilities by insinuating a rape, but also made his most revealing confessions. He related that Göttingen academics tended only to comment with praise on their university and colleagues, and would not talk about certain things, above all not about their salaries (Burgsdorf's column *c*—the crux of his cameralistic table).

Reluctance to talk about money came from the inability at Göttingen to work out a relation between traditional and modern notions of salary-promotions. Junior professors in Göttingen often made more than the senior professors. Commodification of academics had caused acquisition prices to climb more quickly than most sorts of perks won by seniority. So, failing a suitable offer from outside to leverage, senior professors tended to get frozen at their acquisition price, because modern notions of regular salary-promotions did not exist, not even at enlightened, cameralist Göttingen, at the cutting edge of managerial capitalism.

Combined with Göttingen academics' penchant for self-glorification, this led Gedike to admit that he sought his sources "in sensible and well-informed students, rather than professors." Gedike confessed conversing with students! That was how he probably collected much of what he heard that "I" didn't. It was from gossiping with loose lips.

### A BILDUNGSREISE

In this final section we will consider a private diary as travelogue and contrast it with Gedike's ministerial style. The section then turns to the matters of gossip and coffee.

### Christoph Rinck's Diary

In 1786 a certain Christoph Rinck acquired a parsonage near Pforzheim. He married Sophie Maler, who is mentioned much in the diary of the *Bil-*

*dungsreise* he wrote in 1783/84. Sophie and Christoph named their firstborn after the Margrave of Baden, who had sent Christoph on the *Bildungsreise* to further educate himself and learn how to hold better sermons. Moritz Geyer edited Christoph's diary of the *Bildungsreise* in 1897, and, alas, left more out than he published. But enough appears to make comparisons to Gedike's report. Christoph's diary shows the persona produced in private pages.[29]

The *Bildungsreise* began on 25 August 1783. From 11 December 1783 to 7 January 1784, Christoph was in Berlin, but didn't see Gedike. In his diary Christoph wrote, "Just as well would I have gladly got to know Mr. Gedike . . . but never got around to this pleasure, I know not how." Perhaps Gedike had too much to do to give such a nobody a hearing.

Coming from southern Germany, Christoph did most of his journey in reverse order from the path Gedike would follow in 1789. Near the end of Christoph's journey lay Göttingen, where he stayed (I believe) from 9 February to 5 March. On 3 March, Christoph wrote of a talk with Professor Meiners:

> Our conversation was very trivial. The gentlemen here mostly avoid, almost with great care, allowing themselves to get into a conversation where they might have to give their decided opinion about an important issue. [They] hold everything for a mere state-visit. To me the merely ceremonial is of the least importance. They keep themselves always at a certain distance, [and] no hearty tone holds sway . . . They are too used to the visits of important strangers, so they don't do much for others, and above all for those from whom they don't expect to get anything.

On or about 5 March, Christoph wrote,

> Now it was time to leave Göttingen, my countrymen came to me to spare me running around—Wielandt from Carlsruhe, Hugo and Morstadt accompanied me about a quarter hour by foot, since the weather was so nice . . . I went then about a half an hour alone, musing on why so many Göttingen professors were so aloof toward me. I will ascribe it not to pride or any other bad reason, although I can with perfect right maintain that at no single place during my whole journey was my stay as little blest as here, that all things considered I enjoyed nowhere as little friendship as here. Perhaps I made myself notions too great about Göttingen—the professors are all too busy the whole day . . .

On 17 March Christoph was in Gießen and described a conversation with Professor Schulz.

After his class we visited him. In his messy study, he had only two chairs, which he offered us. That he not stand alone next to us, we also remained standing. [He] has a pretty loose tongue. To win the glory (*Ruhm*) of immortality, he said, was not worth the bother of offering even one day's enjoyment of life. Given the situation in Göttingen, he hopes to get an offer from there and thus to get at least a 50 gulden salary increase. For he won't leave Gießen, where one can loaf about (*faullenzen*) and study when one wants, and when not, forget it. That won't work in Göttingen. Moreover, they have better and cheaper Rhine wine here than there.[30]

Vacchieri was visiting Ingolstadt when Christoph ended his journey on 31 March 1784.

Christoph's private "I" travels on roads with snow. In Basel this "I" stands in the rain outdoors at 4:00 a.m. for about half an hour, so as not to disturb the post-servant's sleep. In Tübingen he nearly sheds tears taking leave of an aged theologian who composed his last book in the midst of a terrible illness. On arriving in Altdorf, Christoph has some fruit, then takes a room in a hostel. He describes the *Vortrag* of scholars he heard. But for him, it's important to make personal contact with these men, and with their wives where appropriate.

He enjoys writing about when an academic takes him into a private study. He often records how long he spent with the person, so as to measure the courtesy shown him. In Jena, Professor Döderlein invites Christoph to a meal, which is "very courteous." Professor Löber offers Christoph coffee when they talk. In Erfurt, a city whose beauty Christoph rightly praises, Professor Froriep offers him coffee, which Christoph terms as "courteous."

I suspect that when someone is called "courteous," it means they offered Christoph, if not a meal, then at least coffee. As might be expected given Christoph's stature, Goethe is not courteous. The time our hero spends with him is measured as about "a half of a quarter hour," so about seven or eight minutes, the smallest temporal measure in a diary meticulous about time. Herder, however, invites Christoph more than once, gives him coffee and lots of time. Christoph meets Herder's wife, and maybe his kids. Such details mark Christoph's diary as modernly realistic. They protocol insertion of his "I" into a private sphere. This constitutes and maintains a private, bourgeois, sentimental persona, like Robinson Crusoe's.

## Gossip and Coffee

Gedike came to Göttingen to hear and perhaps acquire its *Ruhm*, to register in the flesh the Göttingen academic selves circulating in the free market of letters. Yet what he found there and what made his hearing harder was what had made the early modern practice of visitation unnecessary. Founded in 1737, Göttingen was perhaps the first German university never to have enjoyed a visitation of the sort sent to Helmstedt in 1597 or to Ingolstadt in 1784 or to Wittenberg in 1789 or anywhere from 1500 to 1800.

The early modern self had reached a sort of confidential public perfection in Göttingen. Gossip and rumor circulated there only by students and visitors. The professors, good civil servants all, not only filled in their own lists, tables and reports, so being self-registering tools for the ministry, but also otherwise only conversed for credit and capital in the free market. Göttingen much haunted the Republic of Letters with the modern academic double, the big and inflated name, the simulacrum of a public-private self cast in the rumor-mill of the market, an effect of the power of ministerial paperwork and the fame machine.

We see vestiges of the traditional academic self in Gießen. Professor Schulz there was interested in working only as much as he needed to live. Schulz saw more importance in leisure and drinking less costly wine than in acquiring fame. This traditional world was also the one that most Oxbridge fellows and professors still inhabited. Once Oxbridge had been converted by the rationalizers and modernizers in the late nineteenth century, the earlier fellows were "accused of wasting their time and opportunities . . . But the Fellows can be reproached with more than lack of scholarship and industry . . . Indeed the pleasures of the table loomed large in their lives." This traditional academic world of leisure or *otium*, of the *vita contemplativa*, was giving way in the Germanies to the new one heralded by Göttingen, the modern world of *neg-otium*, meaning busi-ness, bent on grinding academics through the fame machine, turning them into modern ghosts, even poor Schulz in Gießen.[31]

Christoph's "I" produced itself best when academics invited him into their homes and offered him coffee. That is what went wrong in Göttingen. He proved unable to privatize himself academically in his diary there. He lost his self. Christoph sensed the new academic distance there. No professor seems to have offered him coffee. Also baffled by its noise, Gedike grew hard of hearing in Göttingen. No professor there would gossip with him either.

## CONCLUSION

In the preceding chapter we looked at length at a narrative and a table from the 1780s—Vacchieri's journal and Burgsdorf's table. In this chapter we have looked at Gedike's report of 1789 as a complex bureaucratic document possessed of narrative elements. Private diaries of Christoph Rinck and of Gedike himself, as well as Vacchieri's ministerial journal, helped shed light on Gedike's narrative voice. The chapter began with attention to works by Justi, Boell, and Mackensen apropos the matter of managerial capitalism and academic commodification, especially concerning Göttingen. Here we heard about academic trading companies fabricating credit by mutual citation, which formed part of the general process of "minting" oneself. This self-production and self-promotion of the academic happened in good part on paper. But, despite the new dominion of writing and the growing "empire of the eye," academic noise persisted. Thus I have endeavored to read Gedike's report as both a narrative and a hearing.

By the 1780s at the latest, visitation had lost its inquisitional focus on orthodoxy and confession. As evident in Burgsdorf's table in the previous chapter, visitation had come to concern, rather, the political economy of academia, its cameral management. In 1789, Gedike's informal visitation of universities outside his land assumed the form of "head-hunting" in modern corporate capitalism. And it was talking heads that he was hunting. If he liked what he heard, he sought to know more than the mere academic voice, so as to determine if the subject might become a target of acquisition by Berlin's red hand. This I took as the plot of Gedike's hearing. But a hearing is also always a silencing. To read for the plot here means to look for the *deus ex machina*, the ghost in the machine of our seemingly self-regulating academic economy.

# 11

## Academic Voices and the Ghost in the Machine

Ladies and Gentlemen. What legitimates making a poet the festive speaker honoring a great researcher? . . . How is it legitimate that a learned society . . . chooses not one of their own, a man of academic knowledge, but rather a poet to celebrate with words the great day of their Master? . . . Does this perhaps come in the belief that a poet as an artist . . . is more suited for celebrating festivals? Is by nature a more festive person than an . . . academic is?

Thomas Mann

Thomas Mann began his speech at Sigmund Freud's eightieth birthday in 1936 with those words. Mann rather quickly uttered the name of Friedrich Nietzsche, an embodiment of the problem of the artist and academic in one. I use "academic" here, as I have generally throughout, as a translation of *Wissenschaftler*, which means more than "scientist."

Nietzsche's early work concerned the theme of art versus academic knowledge. In 1869, at twenty-four years of age, he became a professor at the University of Basel. In early 1872 his first book appeared, *Die Geburt der Tragödie* (*The Birth of Tragedy*). This ruined his reputation as a serious academic and scholar. Artists and friends seem to have liked the book. Franz Liszt quickly read it twice. And Richard and Cosima Wagner loved it. They reported fighting over their only copy. A few of Nietzsche's professional colleagues liked it.

But German academics in general hated it and greeted it at first with silence. Nietzsche's doctoral advisor in Leipzig, Friedrich Ritschl, wrote in his diary that the book was "ingenious vertigo." He said nothing publicly. Apprehensive, Nietzsche wrote him and said that he, Nietzsche, hoped to take control over the younger generation of philologists with the work. About that aspiration, Ritschl wrote in his diary: "megalomania." Nietzsche grew alarmed that nobody was reviewing the book. But by good luck, his friend and colleague, Erwin Rohde, a professor at Kiel, wrote an enthusiastic review that was published in May 1872.[1]

Alas, in the same month, Lecturer Ulrich von Wilamowitz-Möllendorff published an attack. Nietzsche wrote to Rohde that the polemic "reeked of Berlin." Nietzsche hoped for support from other philologists, especially in Leipzig, his alma mater. Under his auspices, Rohde prepared a counter-attack to Wilamowitz-Möllendorff. At the same time, Richard Wagner published an open letter about the affair. Wagner attacked Wilamowitz-Möllendorff and academic philology in general in Germany. The latter attack was not constructive.

By July, Nietzsche wrote that he felt exiled, cast out of the academic guild and sentenced to death. By late October, he had given up hope of finding support even in Leipzig. In November, he wrote to Wagner, "Winter semester has begun and I have no students! . . . I am now so disreputable among my colleagues . . . that our small university [in Basel] is suffering . . . In Bonn a philology professor . . . advised his students that my book is 'pure nonsense' . . . : someone who produces such work is as good as dead." The fame machine can also be a defamation and infamy machine. Academic rumor and gossip can be poison. At twenty-eight years of age, Friedrich Nietzsche, as a professor, had a brilliant future behind him.[2]

Wilamowitz-Möllendorff had opened his polemic by criticizing the tone of *Die Geburt der Tragödie*. He said that Nietzsche did not speak as an academic researcher and his book was rather more "a work of art." Sixteen years later, Nietzsche wrote a self-critique for a new edition. He now said that the book seemed impossible, hardly accessible and strange. It seems he had been trying to pose this question: "The problem of academic knowledge (*Wissenschaft*) itself—academic knowledge for the first time made problematic, made questionable . . ." He had been trying "to see academic knowledge through the optics of the artist." In this book "a *strange* voice . . . concealed itself in the gown of a scholar . . . What a pity that I did not dare to speak as a poet . . . or at least as a philologist."[3]

What did Nietzsche write in this strange book that did not speak in a properly academic voice? *Die Geburt der Tragödie* is Nietzsche's most difficult work and is thoroughly Nietzschean. It is full of contradictions. The book has no footnotes. There are curious factual errors. The book is about the birth of tragedy, but it is also about the birth of the academic voice from the death of the tragic. Nietzsche's thesis is now well known.

Greek art emerged, he argued, from two tendencies, an Apollonian and a Dionysian. The Apollonian embraces the visual, bound with light, consciousness, moderation, control of the self. The Dionysian rules the oral, tied to darkness, instinct, excess, loss of control, loss of the self. Sculpture and architecture embody Apollonian arts, while music and dance define

Dionysian ones. Apollo is the god of truth telling and divination. He is patron of liberal arts and the Muses. Apollo with his lyre was also originally god of music, but Dionysus seized music from Apollo and took it in another direction. Let us turn now to tragedy.[4]

Nietzsche holds that Greek tragedy emerged from the Dionysian chorus. The roots of tragic drama, according to Nietzsche, lie in a Dionysian choral festival of music and dance. The persona of the actor embodies above all a Dionysian figure. The actor is "the instinctive poet, singer, dancer, but as *enacted* Dionysian figure." Tragic drama emerged as a synthesis of Apollonian-Dionysian styles, a synthesis of scene and music, of speaking and singing, of the orator and the actor. The chorus embodies Dionysus. And the core of tragedy, for Nietzsche, was originally the chorus singing and dancing. But the dialogue eventually expropriated the center of tragedy. As tragedy developed from Aeschylus to Euripides, the chorus retreated and the dialogue triumphed. And the dialogue is, according to Nietzsche, Apollonian.[5]

Where is Nietzsche going with all this? He aims to show that the academic, that is, the Platonic dialogue was the ultimate end of this development. He wants to illuminate how Socratic dialectics came out of drama. The original European hero of knowledge, the persona of Socrates and the Socratic voice, emerged from the degeneration of tragic dialogue. In old tragedy, music and dance were central. In new tragedy, dialogue and dialectics became central. Euripides embodies the change from the old to the new tragedy. The Euripidean figure is a Socratic orator in the guise of a comic actor. From here emerged the new comedy. Socrates plays, after all, just such a comic actor, at least as cast in Aristophanes' *The Clouds*.[6]

None less than Aristotle saw Plato's dialogues as comic drama. And, as Nietzsche saw it, Socrates, as cast by Plato, not only took on the Appolonian persona, but also opposed it to the Dionysian. In Plato's dialogues as academic comedies, Socrates embodies truth telling dialogue, moderation, consciousness, and self-control. Socrates, moreover, makes the philosopher or the academic and the artist mutually exclusive. As Nietzsche said, an artistic Socrates is an oxymoron. After Socrates, the artist could only be a Dionysian figure, tied to excess, instinct and loss of self. Socrates gave birth to himself as the first hero of knowledge. He also bore his daimonic Other: the Romantic Artist.[7]

At this point we see that Nietzsche, too, is writing the history of his present. As did Aristophanes and Plato, he casts a persona, a mask, for Socrates. Nietzsche says, "I see the spirit of academia, first brought to light in the person of Socrates, as the belief in the comprehensibility of nature and the universal salvative power of knowledge." Cast in this light, Socrates is a turning point of history: the destroyer of the tragic voice.[8]

This Socrates enacts the disenchanter, the modern academic voice *avant la lettre*. Not only does Socrates take over the role of Apollo. Not only does Socrates demand the artist become solely Dionysian, a Romantic, festive figure. But Socrates also wants to take over the role of Dionysus, a god like Jesus tied to rebirth because he was tied to death. In place of the dying Dionysus, the dying Socrates offered himself as the hero of knowledge.

> Our entire modern world is caught in the web of [a] . . . culture [that] sees its ideal in the theorist, equipped with the highest powers of knowledge and working in the service of academic knowledge. The archetype and grandfather of this is Socrates. All our educational institutions have at base this ideal in mind . . . How incomprehensible to a genuine Greek must appear the . . . modern man of culture, Faust, . . . whom we only need to set next to Socrates to see that the modern individual begins to sense the limits of the Socratic desire for knowledge . . .[9]

Did Socrates haunt Nietzsche? He celebrated his forty-fourth birthday by beginning an absurdist autobiography, *Ecce Homo*. Here he called *Die Geburt der Tragödie* an attempt to assassinate two thousand years of cultural perversity. But the problem with Socrates was that he insisted on being reborn over and over, in ever more grotesque forms, such as Faust and Nietzsche—the eternal return of the same. Nietzsche's view of the Socratic crime changed over time, but he usually cast Socrates as a clown or monster. In *Götzendämmerung*, in a chapter called "The Problem of Socrates," Nietzsche finds Socrates guilty of cultural decadence. Socrates was, in sum, "a great eroticist," thus a most decadent Apollo.[10]

N ietzsche's madness perhaps originated in trying "to see academic knowledge (*Wissenschaft*) through the optics of the artist" or, rather, to hear it in voices of the Other. *The Birth of Tragedy* concerns, as well, the birth of the academic voice in the persona of Socrates and Plato's voice, the dialogue and dialectics deriving from Socratic academic comedies. This book has not explicitly treated of the dialectics of knowledge in relation to motifs of the Apollonian and the Dionysian, but has put part of that at its center: the visual versus the oral.

I had originally structured this chapter in the form of an oral disputation, for which the section above on Nietzsche served as the opening disquisition. I have now recast it into the form of an essay about orality in academia and its relation to academic charisma. But before turning to academic voices and the ghost in the machine, let's look first at the machine.

## THE EMPIRE OF THE EYE / I

If I were speaking, I could achieve the envisaged ambiguity here in English without the artifice of "Eye/I." The course of the early modern era led to the dominion of the visual and legible over the oral and aural, led to the author and reader over the orator and audience, as well as to the triumph of the academic "I" as charismatic individual over the corporate, collegial, collective bodies of academics. Like the rise of the middle class for European historians, the rise of the legible trace forms a commonplace for anthropologists, historians, and sociologists of knowledge, especially those focused on its academic or scientific forms. At issue remains only the chronology of the empire of the eye.

In the next few pages, I shall present some chronological notes on that empire. It is a chronology that cannot lay claims to being a history, although I do not consider it fabulous. My aim here is twofold. First, I want to have a sketch before us that details the central status of visualization and the visual realm in modern academic knowledge before we consider the more marginal but, I argue, still crucial realm of academic orality. Second, I shall use the brief chronology of the rise of the visual as a path to works by Lorraine Daston, Peter Galison, and Simon Schaffer on the emergence of the notion of "objectivity" and the "genius," apropos the modern machine of academic knowledge and the ghost inhabiting it.

To understand "the visual take-off that was to occur with Gutenberg technology," one needs to know that "such a take-off had not been possible in the manuscript ages, for such a culture retains the audible-tactile modes of human sensibility in a degree incompatible with abstract visuality or the translation of all the senses into the language of unified, continuous pictorial space." Marshall McLuhan obsessed about the opposition between the oral and the visual in *The Gutenberg Galaxy* of 1962, an obsession that became displaced in favor of the opposition of hot and cool in *Understanding Media* of 1964.[11]

McLuhan stressed the role of the phonetic alphabet in initializing the (Platonic) bias toward vision as the repository of reality. But he saw the takeoff of visual culture in Europe as inhering in the invention of perspective in drawing and typography in printing. The Gutenberg Galaxy of perspective and typography ushered in, per McLuhan, great changes: the notion of mass production, the bases both of nationalism and of individual-ism, a disassociation of thinking and feeling, a coherent authorial point of view, the reading public, a passion for exact measurement and for the trans-lation of the oral-aural into visual terms. But he held that the new galaxy re-quired centuries to alter mentalities. The first great literary awareness of ty-pographic man arrived in Cervantes's *Don Quixote* (1605 and 1615).

> In short, prose remained oral for centuries after printing. Instead of homo-geneity there was heterogeneity of tone and attitude, so that the author felt able to shift tone in mid-sentence at any time, just as in poetry . . . The "I" of medieval narrative did not provide a point of view so much as immedi-acy of effect . . . It was some time after printing that authors or readers dis-covered "points of view" . . . For the world of visual perspective [where point of view is possible] is one of unified and homogeneous space. Such a world is alien to the resonating diversity of spoken words. So language was the last art to accept the visual logic of Gutenberg technology.[12]

McLuhan relies much on the work of Walter Ong on the French philosopher Petrus Ramus (1515–72), whom Ong sees as the key figure for the programmatic triumph of the eye over the ear and tongue. The Ramist arts sought to free logic and rhetoric from the tyranny of traditional oral culture. Ramus developed all sorts of visual aids—charts, trees, diagrams, and so on—to facilitate thinking or, rather, to replace speaking.

> Ramist dialectic has lost all sense of Socratic dialogue and even most sense of scholastic dispute. The Ramist arts of discourse are monologue arts . . . and tend finally even to lose the sense of monologue in pure diagrammat-ics. This orientation is very profound and of a piece with the orientation of Ramism toward an object world (associated with visual perception) rather than toward a person world (associated with voice and auditory percep-tion).[13]

Schaffer and Shapin have presented the contest between Hobbes and Boyle in the late Baroque and early Enlightenment as a watershed in the constitution of this world of modern science. Boyle and the Royal Society argued that natural philosophy, or natural science, must be based on an ex-perimental philosophy, which necessitates performing real experiments. Seeing is believing, so experiments must be demonstrated in a public set-ting, or at least before reliable witnesses; at that time such witnesses were typically members of the Royal Society. Observation of this sort sets the ba-sis for the more powerful device of virtual witnessing. "The technology of virtual witnessing involves the production in the *reader's* mind of such an image of an experimental scene as obviates the necessity of either direct witness or replication" of the original demonstration experiment. This could multiply witnesses without end, thus "was the most powerful technology for constituting matters of fact."[14]

In following pages, Schaffer and Shapin discuss the prose and iconography of Boyle's reports of his experiments. Here we can see the coexistence of traditional oral forms with the nascent visual culture. Boyle's lab reports take the form of narratives, in which he even recounted failed adventures. Boyle self-consciously couched his narratives in a prolix form, which undercut to an extent the concomitant attack waged by the Royal Society on traditional rhetoric and Baroque oral arts of persuasion. Boyle's wordiness in experimental narrative aimed to simulate the "effet du réel" (Roland Barthes)—it furthered the aim of virtual witnessing to simulate reality, but in traditional oral forms of narrative and rhetoric.[15]

The iconography deployed by Boyle, who supervised his engravers, worked to the same effect, but now as part of the waxing visual empire. Boyle did not want schematic representations or ideal depictions of his instruments and experiments. He wanted depictions of actual instruments, a "detailed naturalistic representation complete with conventions of shadowing." Shapin and Schaffer then note, "By virtue of the density of circumstantial detail that could be conveyed through the engraver's laying of lines, they imitated reality and gave the viewer a vivid impression of the experimental scene. The sort of naturalistic images that Boyle favoured provided a greater density of circumstantial detail than . . . schematic representations" could have. This envisaged circumstantial detail is what Barthes and others identify as the gratuitous detail needed by realism, a technique to simulate the real.[16]

The empire of the eye attained its greatest power as the framework called "objectivity." Daston and Galison have written on the emergence of this notion, which did not assume its familiar form until the middle third of the nineteenth century. To put it baldly, as the criteria of most importance in science, objectivity—now embedded in an extensive realm of the visual and legible—effectively replaced truth, which harkened back to the verbal realm of argument. In the world of modern research, where results remain provisional and ever subject to revision, what came to matter most (except for certain schools of philosophers) was not the verbal-logical notion of the truth of statements, but rather the objective validity of results.

Two senses of objectivity combined around the mid-nineteenth century, according to Daston and Galison. "Mechanical objectivity" sought to remedy errors produced by projections onto nature, induced by particular languages, human judgments, aesthetic prejudices, and so on. The authors call the objectivity sought here "mechanical" because machines or mechanical and related instruments (electrical, chemical, and so on) offered the escape from subjective error. The epitome of mechanical objectivity lay in results produced by photographic cameras and self-registering instruments—generators of images and legible traces.

Daston and Galison deem the other chief sense of objectivity the "communitarian." This sort of objectivity aimed to eliminate errors introduced by observers either individually or in groups. The remedy is communitarian because scientists developed techniques of registering results immune to the errors of and superior to the abilities of single individuals or groups. Standardized tables, charts, maps and so on served here—and furthered the notion that one found objective results in the proper production and interpretation of visual traces.[17]

With different emphasis, Schaffer has discussed the apparent paradox between the modern realm of self-registering instruments and the disembodied genius—homologues or analogues of mechanical and communitarian objectivity. The disembodied genius, taken as the modern academic per se, embodies the sort of objectivity that Daston and Galison see as reflected in the ideal community of observers, where each is wholly replaceable by any other.

> New experimental regimes were designed to distract attention from the person of the experimenter by making instruments into inscription devices and by automating the experimental process . . . These two formations, self-registrative technology and disembodied genius, may seem completely antagonistic. Yet they were produced together. The lesson of the story of self-evidence may be therefore that there is an intimate relationship between the trust placed in the evidence of the self-registering instruments and the moral authority of the scientific intellectual [qua disembodied self or genius].[18]

Taken in the more common sense, the disembodied genius raises the specter of the creative and original agent in science and academia, the subjectivity fabricating objectivity. If objectivity constitutes the modern machine, this latter genius plays a ghost haunting it.[19]

The remainder of this chapter attempts to invoke such ghostly ilk—Socratic daimons and Dionysian, oral manifestations of academic charisma, perhaps marginal, but still active forces in the Apollonian academic world of objectivity and bureaucracy. In the spirit of the oral, the rest of this essay exudes a flattened temporality anathema to most professional history-writing today. Apropos introductory themes above and traditional academic topoi, I shall commence with the Greeks and move forward through canonical epochs, attending to academic voices, oral presences past and present, even when couched in writings. To follow here is thus a sort of counterhistory or counterchronology to the great empire of the eye.

It is surely sophistry to make the case for orality in the face of the modern tyranny of images. But this sophistry dates in spirit at least from the Romantic era. The modern appreciation and recovery of oral culture began with F. A. Wolf's *Prolegomena ad Homerum* and Herder's "Homer, ein Günstling der Zeit" both of 1795. It runs through Nietzsche's *The Birth of Tragedy* of 1872, and Freud's turn to talking, given his ineptness at hypnotism.[20]

## SOPHISTRY

Karl Jaspers noted that one can usually quote Nietzsche on both sides of any issue, as he took apparent care always to contradict himself, sooner or later. An academic penchant to qualify statements to death echoes such sophistry—and indicates the path to relativism, if not nihilism, that sophistry can easily follow. Sophists acquired a bad reputation in antiquity because of their ability to argue both sides of any question. But they saw it as their duty to truth to be able to make a case for the weaker voice. Despite the mechanical consensus essayed by objectivity and bureaucracy, such sentiments still beat in all academic hearts.[21]

The ancient Sophists taught oral arts. They originally gave lessons in poetry and singing, but eventually mostly in rhetoric. Sophistry entails dialectics, if not polemics and agonistics. It presumes a dissonance of voices and amplifies the weaker. In its classical or cliché form, this dissonance became a simple contra to a pro. The scholastic disputation took this as its canonical form, but typically expressed dissonance in order to quash it. The court jester and the *advocatus diaboli* spoke more clearly as voices of the Other. Modern deployments of sophistry sometimes seek to allow such a voice to speak, while a notion of paralogy and heterology, dissonance within dissonance, animates postmodern sophistry.[22]

The rise of the Sophists went hand in hand with the rise of classical democracy, opposed by the Sophists' most famous adversaries, Plato and Aristophanes, who favored an aristocratic social order. Greek *areté* meant the quality giving a man authority among men. Aristocrats claimed this virtue or charisma as theirs. But the Sophists claimed that, by teaching the average citizen to master the power of the spoken word, they could teach the citizen to acquire *areté*, to acquire virtue or even charisma. Two classicists agree that a good circumlocution for "sophistical" in its original sense would be: "with an air of authority . . . almost professorial." Sophistry meant that the virtue manifested as charismatic speech or oral *areté* can be mastered by the people through the professorial exercise of the tongue.[23]

Sophistry faced a dilemma, as writing transmuted the democratic inclination to dissonance. In the academic form of the prose dialogue, especially in the genre of Plato's Socratic comedies and their like, a narrative voice guided the dialogue or discussion. This opened a path to the pure monologue of the lecture, as happened in Plato's final dialogues, which are really treatises. The dialectical impulse of sophistry became displaced into the rhetorical structure of the Aristotelian and, later, the medieval lecture. Commenting on and glossing dissonant voices, one resolved them not by sophistically making the weaker seem stronger but, rather, by authoritatively enunciating the reasonable or orthodox word. The monologue of the lecture echoed dissonant academic voices to harmonize or silence them.[24]

Plato's dialogues aimed to silence sophistry. *The Republic* epitomizes the Platonic bias for the visual as opposed to the oral. The metaphor of the voice or daimon that haunts Socrates in *The Apology* gives way in *The Republic* to the visual allegory of the Cave and Forms. Plato's republic prohibits many oral arts and his academy holds, "Let no one unversed in geometry enter here." So a lengthy study of essentially visual geometric arts precedes and preconditions the study of dialectics in the Platonic academic utopia.[25]

Sophistry, with its admittedly nihilistic bent, subverts such authoritarian regimes. From Plato's eugenic academic republic onward, such regimes seem to favor spectacle over speech. And the progress of rationalization can insulate authorities altogether from the perils of oral arts and make them seem simply silly. "A certain prince, upon being asked why he had no court fool, replied that, when he wanted a laugh, he had a couple professors come to his residence and valiantly dispute with one another," as J. M. von Loen noted in 1742. Another source (I forget which) identified the prince as Friedrich Wilhelm I, king of Brandenburg-Prussia from 1713 to 1740, and the professors as from the University of Frankfurt a.d.O.[26]

## VOX POPULO

The above king's son, Friedrich the Great, said a number of times, "A prince is the first servant of the state," which he occasionally altered to "servant of the people." Like aristocrats, academics may seek to speak for the people, but not as the voice of the people.[27]

This academic voice is "republican" as opposed to the democratic one of sophistry in spirit. The agricultural and martial foundations of the Roman Republic made sophistry as odious a habitus as it was in the Platonic republic. The Latin *sophisticus*, from which our word "sophisticated" stems, had bad connotations for the plain-speaking Roman citizen of the republic. Socrates had likened sophistry to prostitution, since the one vended oral arts for fees, and the other erotic ones. Roman elite society held mercantile occupations in suspicion altogether. But the Romans in fact conceived a sophisticated understanding of fees, as they invented the rather metaphysical notion of public versus private legal agency and acts.

The Romans invented the notion of the "profession" as an occupation done for the *salus publica*, for the public welfare. One might be paid for exercising a profession—such as serving as a priest or lawyer or physician or professor—but that was not to be confused with mercantile occupations—such as being a Sophist—supposedly centered on private profit. By the third century CE, teaching had become a profession in Roman cities as publicly funded positions appeared. In the empire, one called public teachers of the liberal arts "professor." A state funded professorship was called a *cathedra* (chair). The Justinian legal code defined the professorship as a profession, for it held that a professor served and spoke for the good of the people. The law thus gave professors many privileges, while it denied them to freelancing poets and writers, as well as to Sophists, philosophers, and primary school teachers.[28]

As a consequence of the Renaissance and Reformation, law codes on the Continent, although not in England, integrated the Justinian code. Such lands, especially Protestant ones, reinstated the Roman notion of the public welfare—the *res publica* for the *salus publica*—as the basis of the state thus of education. J. F. Gerhard, a Baroque jurist and political theorist, held, "The purpose of academies [which includes universities] is the public good."[29]

On the Continent, as we've seen, the Reformation and Counter-Reformation introduced the professorate and professorial chair as the standard academic system. That did not happen in England, where the use of "professor" is now idiosyncratic and parochial. Early modern jurists said professors lecture "publicly . . . in a faculty." To be a professor demands the "knowledge for the profession and . . . a Master's or Doctor's degree." Professors are "Personae Most Noble and Precious." The professor's office is "to teach diligently, to educate youth in letters as well as in morals." "Professors who teach publicly at universities and *Gymnasia* ought to be paid by a publicly constituted salary."[30]

On the Continent the state expropriated the educational system and reintroduced the notion that education constituted a matter of the public welfare. The professor worked as an educator of higher learning practicing a profession, that is, serving the people. The academic voice as professorial thus spoke with the same public and traditional authority as did the voices of the minister, the magistrate, and the physician. The professorial voice spoke with the charismatic power of a republican institution as a public servant for the people.

But the "public servant" formed a key concept that enabled the modern absolute state or republic. The saying of Louis XIV, "I am the state," finds its better in the saying of Friedrich the Great. Friedrich's greater insight lay in his seeing that the new concept of the king as a public servant—a notion impossible in antiquity where the *servus publicus* really was a slave of the state—allowed the king to speak absolutely in the name of the people.[31]

In *Phänomenologie des Geistes* of 1807, Hegel gave the most famous statement of this paradox in his dialectical analysis of Master and Servant, or Authority and Servitude (*Herrschaft und Knechtschaft*), a thesis that he perhaps took from Fichte, who himself tied half of it to Rousseau. Hegel's world was the *Beamtenstaat,* the bureaucratic state, where supposed public servants had assumed dominion over the public, and where academic civil servants spoke in the name of the people, although perhaps mostly for more ideal interests.[32]


## EX CATHEDRA

In the Middle Ages, the title of "professor" became marginal and, as the distinction between the public and private blurred, the notion of the public welfare faded. The Roman professions became conceived not in terms of the public welfare, as rather more the gift of God, the *donum Dei.* Grace, justice, health, and learning formed essential gifts of God for medievals, so churches, courts, hospitals, and schools ought not make a profit from dispensing them. From the Carolingian period onward, Church councils enjoined that school instruction be cared for by bishops and abbots, ought to include the liberal arts, and should be free to the poor. The medieval conception of professional privilege would find its basis in the disjunction between the sacred and the profane, not between public offices and private gain.[33]

Medieval academic voices of masters and doctors spoke not for the people's good, but rather with the sacral aura of canonical authority. "Canon" has many senses, and I mean them all. While the Romans commenced the metaphysics of legal agency, the medievals perfected that of office. In the High Middle Ages, a Canon Secular held a chair in the chapel and vote in the collegium—this was called *stallum et votum* or *Sitz und Stimme*, a chair and a voice. The academic as professor inherited a chair and a voice from the Canon Secular.[34]

The podium or lectern where the master or doctor lectured and presided over disputations was called, as we know, the cathedra. The medieval academic voice thus spoke *ex cathedra*, although not in the technical episcopal or, later, the papal sense. "Canon" also meant the orthodox and authoritative teachings of the Church proclaimed from the cathedra. Medieval universities formed part of the clerical estate. Medieval masters and doctors thus taught from canonical texts, in the medieval sense of canonical. Early modern academics, befitting them and the era, would teach the canonical texts in an evolving sense: the required, classic, or traditional texts or topics or truths. From the lectern, academic voices upheld the canon.

In the 1790s at the University of Jena, a fountainhead of German Romanticism, Fichte became one of the first German professors who began officially lecturing without a set text. Departure from an actual or even virtual textbook as a basis for lecturing constituted the ultimate break with the sermon. In the traditional Christian form, from which the lecture had arisen, the sermon had combined the reading of excerpts, however brief, from a canonical text, followed by exegesis, commentary and resolution of dissonances, however extensive.

Fichte and other Romantics began lecturing on their own work, without any pretense that they were glossing a text or recapitulating a tradition. Academics had doubtless been presenting their own work in lectures for decades, if not centuries. But the notion of some sort of canon, embodied in identifiable texts, had persisted. The fifteenth century battle of books itself had not assailed the notion of a canon per se, but rather only its contents.

In Romantic Jena and elsewhere, the cathedra became a locus where one created knowledge, became a site of the new, radical stress on spontaneity, creativity and originality. But even Fichte had to concede in time that his auditors often seemed lost at sea in his lectures. It helped but not much that Fichte published many of his lectures, for he usually published them subsequently. It remained for less radical moderns to carve a new relation between the Romantic "I" pontificating from the cathedra and the academic chorus.[35]

## THE ACADEMIC CHORUS

Rather than beginning a speech, I would have preferred to have been enveloped by it . . . At the moment of speaking I would have liked to have felt a voice without name having long preceded me. It would have sufficed . . . had I lodged myself in its folds without anyone noticing me

Michel Foucault,
*L'ordre du discours*

Foucault began his inaugural lecture in 1970 at the Collège de France with those words. He gave this lecture in a "muffled and restrained voice" that apparently shocked the audience, accustomed as they were to his past flamboyance. Foucault spoke here for the academic chorus.[36]

What voice really speaks in a lecture or disputation? To be a public professor of this or that in the early modern era meant to appear in a hall to read and gloss texts, or preside over disputations. Many academics played a persona, or wore a mask. For academia was theater and professors often had no interest in their lectures or disputations. Lack of interest in the lectures came in part, as we know, because extraordinary and junior full professors often had to take whatever chair was empty in order to get a foot in the faculty.

The case of Kant offers a good example. Recall that in 1764 the chair of eloquence and poetry opened at Königsberg. Since the Renaissance, the professor of eloquence and poetry, or a related chair holder, embodied the *os academicum,* the academic mouth. He wore the mask of the festive man at a university. Like a poet laureate, this professor had to write poems and hold speeches for festive occasions, such as the king's or the university's birthday. In 1764, the Prussian ministry offered this chair at Königsberg to the "world-famous" lecturer, Immanuel Kant, because it was the only open chair at the time. Kant might have taken a number of other chairs in the philosophy faculty. We know that as the practice of the time—opting up. But Kant did not see himself as a festive person. He declined this mask.[37]

In 1770 Kant got the chair of logic and metaphysics, his true love in life. But Kant still wore another mask. In his famous essay on enlightenment, he distinguished between what one may say as an author in the Republic of Letters, and what one may say as a member of a public institution, as a civil servant, which Protestant professors essentially were, and would soon officially become. As an author, Kant held he could say whatever he wanted. But as a professor, he had to wear a public servant's mask and sing in the canonical chorus.

Precisely Kant's generation, however, at least in the Germanies, lectured at a time when a new notion of the professor was emerging: the professor as researcher, someone who adds a new note to the chorus. Kant himself still taught from traditional texts that were eventually outdated by his own work.

He used a textbook as a point of departure in lecture. Like the Romantics soon would, Kant began doing philosophy in the lecture hall instead of just talking about it. But whenever he had wandered too far from the text, he would say, "To sum up, gentlemen," and then return to a passage in the text. The professorial voice now had to let itself be heard, while also still singing in tune with a canonical chorus.[38]

In 1970, Foucault ended his inaugural lecture with these words, paying homage to his deceased mentor, Jean Hyppolite, whom he was replacing, "I know well whose voice I would have liked to have preceded me . . . I know what was so awesome about beginning to speak, because I was doing so in the place where I heard him, and where he is no more, to hear me." The professorial speaks from a chair where others have sat. It thus speaks in reverence of the voices that have spoken lest they be forgotten. Foucault said that he wrote in order to have no face. Lecturing, he longed to speak in a choral nimbus, that is, in order to have no voice.[39]

## APPLAUSE AND THE STUDENT BODY

When he gave his first lecture, Kant was surprised to see the auditorium full of students. He got very nervous. He started speaking quieter than normal, a disaster, since he had a weak voice. His power as a lecturer could not come from a booming oratorical manly manner, as one said then. His voice rather had to draw the listener in. In that first lecture, he stopped and sophistically contradicted himself often. In the next lecture, however, he regained his bearings. As a young professor, he was a fine lecturer. But by the time Fichte heard him in 1791, Kant's lectures had become disappointing and sleepy.[40]

Christoph Meiners, a professor at the University of Göttingen, addressed this sort of problem at the time. Meiners described the professorial life as regulated by the biannual "drama of lecturing" in which one plays a "role." Most professors still had to lecture on canonical or required texts. That meant that they had to repeat the same chorus year after year. Meiners conceded that this turned many colleagues into "spiritual automata."

But Meiners defended the drama of lecturing. For a live voice had clarity, even if it got stale. This clarity resulted from lecturing to live students. The student body altered the academic voice. "The irritated twisting of [students'] face muscles, certain movements of the head, hesitation in taking notes, and so on, remind the professor that his auditors do not understand him." Despite the seat of magisterial or professorial authority from which it spoke, the academic voice had to speak to hold attention, if not to garner applause.[41]

Foucault's muffled and restrained voice in his inaugural lecture at the Collège de France shocked the audience because most knew he was one of the best lecturers of the time, "cocky, self-assured and articulate." As a professor at the University of Clermont, "he walked back and forth on the podium [and] talked non-stop . . . in his rapid, staccato rhythm. His voice seemed about to fly off at the ends of sentences, with the melodic lift of a question, only to sink again with the confident inflections of an answer to the problems he had raised." In his last year at Clermont in 1966, the students applauded him at the end of every lecture. It amplified *le bruit* around him, for it had never happened to anyone else before (or after).[42]

## RUMOR (FAMA)

Foucault's *Les mot et les choses* appeared in April 1966. The run of 3,500 copies sold out in a week. In the third week of May, the magazine *Le nouvel observateur* noted that Foucault, along with Giles Deleuze and Michel Tort, was one of "the philosophers people are talking about." A week later in the magazine, an anonymous piece, not signed by the editors, hailed it as "one of the most fascinating books published in a long time." From April to June, three major interviews and some minor ones with Foucault spread the sudden buzz around his name to the general public. *Le monde* published a favorable review on 9 June.[43]

The press printed 5,000 more in June. The second printing sold fast, as 3,000 more were printed in July, another 3,000 in September, and more in subsequent months. In August a bookshop on the Boulevard Saint-Germain had noted that the book was selling like hot cakes and, indeed, it entered nonfiction best-seller lists. An unexpected number of French men and women sat on beaches or in resorts in France and the world in the summer of 1966 with the book in their laps, doubtless many of the copies unread much beyond page 64.[44]

When *Le nouvel observateur* observed that Foucault was one of "the philosophers people are talking about," it was reporting news and rumors—people talking about something. It helped spread the talk. One of the earliest notes on the power of *fama* is in the *Aeneid*. In 1697, John Dryden rendered *fama* as "fame," instead of "rumor" in his free translation:

Fame (*fama*), that great Ill, from small beginnings grows.
Swift from the first; and ev'ry Moment brings
New Vigour to her flights, new Pinions to her wings.
Soon grows the Pygmee to Gygantic size;
Her Feet on earth, her Forehead in the Skies:
Inrag'd against the Gods, revengeful Earth
Produc'd her last of the *Titanien* birth.
Swift is her walk, more swift her winged hast:
A monstrous Fantom, horrible and vast;
As many Plumes as raise her lofty flight,
So many piercing Eyes inlarge her sight;
Millions of opening Mouths to Fame belong;
And ev'ry Mouth is furnished with a Tongue;
And round with listning Ears with flying Plague is hung,
She fills the peaceful Universe with Cries;
No Slumbers ever close her wakeful Eyes.
By Day from lofty Tow'rs her Head she shews;
And spreads through trembling Crowds disastrous News.
With Court Informers haunts, and Royal Spyes,
Things done relates, not done she feigns; and mingles
Truth with Lyes.
Talk is her business; and her chief delight
To tell of Prodigies, and cause affright[45]

Virgil notes the peering eyes at the root of every plume of the monster. These hundreds or thousands of eyes dispose over an equal number of tongues, lips, and ears to spread the *fama*. Despite the role of vision, rumor's primary sense is oral—hearsay. Even if one reads it, one usually spreads it by saying "I heard," or asking, "Did you hear?" Given the authority of the written, to say "I read" is already to make rumor into news. But social psychologists point to the face-to-face, oral transmission of rumor as a source of great power. "Generally, word-of-mouth communication has a strong impact and is convincing."[46]

Dated 26 July 1588 in Prague, "It is rumored here that the Spanish Armada has sailed back to Lisbon because the plague has broken out on board . . . But where this news comes from I cannot find out." Rumor paradoxically gains strength by dint of anonymity. I heard something and tell you, but one spreads it. Hearsay comes from one to another, but its provenance and validity remain open. Otherwise it would be news. Siegfried says to

Arthur, "By the way, what do you think of this new UNESCO chair of literary criticism?" Arthur responds, "News travels fast. It isn't even official yet." So it's really rumor not news.[47]

Rumors spread best about important or interesting things or persons, especially in stressful times, and/or when authoritative media or centers of communication do not exist, fail to function, or conflict with one another. Academia enjoys a lack of a central authority. This makes it prey to academic rumors. "Emory has tons of Coca-Cola money and is trying to buy the Yale English Department." The same mechanisms that Freud isolated in dreamwork, which are also those at work in myth formation, have a hand in the design of rumors. Rumors that persist or experience frequent rebirth become urban folklore in modern society. In traditional ones, they make legends.[48]

*Fama* originally meant "rumor." It later came to designate reputation and fame. Reputation haunts members of traditional societies, and professional groups in modern ones. Circulating academic rumors generate applause and renown, much as reviews and ads do.

## GOSSIP

Aika says to Vlad, "Fulvia is toying with an offer from Yale. They've promised her her own Center." Vlad smiles knowingly, as is his wont, and adds impishly, "Yes, but that's not the best part. I heard that she wants leopard-skin upholstery in the damned Ferrari."

For connoisseurs and those not unused to analytical thinking, Aika above relates a rumor to Vlad, while he risks recounting gossip to her. The difference may be academic, but is worth making. Learned treatises on rumor and gossip (of which not enough exist on the latter) grapple with precise criteria to delimit the one from the other; but demarcation in the end remains a matter of sensibility and context. The crucial distinction, I would propose, is that rumor concerns matters more in a public sphere, while gossip relates more to the private. Alas, the fusion of public and private in the market frustrates resolution of many cases.[49]

If Fulvia above moves to Yale and gets a new Center for Something, this constitutes an event in the public sphere of academia, since careers of young academics, the reputation of a program and university, and even the course of academic knowledge might be altered. But, if we hear she wants leopard-skin upholstery in the Ferrari promised her, this affects only our views of Fulvia's personal tastes. The latter constitutes grist for the mills of gossip.

Context also governs whether statements constitute gossip or not. "She typically wears her hair up on the first day of a conference, then down on the second day, and thereafter no discernable pattern exists." In the context of an anthropological or ethnographic study of self-fashioning at academic conferences, where she is Professor E8$_f$, this is not gossip. But, at night in a bar during a conference, where Trevor relates this to Svetlana about Professor Morgana, it is gossip, malicious or not, depending on Trevor's tone and aims.[50]

Sylvia Schein has written an interesting article on medieval gossip. Here she finds that, typical of a closed and hierarchical social order, medieval society provided fertile grounds for gossip. Authorities disapproved strongly, labeled it uncourtly, mostly blamed women, and trembled at its power to besmirch reputations and undermine authorities. Schein does not give the original words in her sources, which are in many tongues. "Gossip" is an old word, but its associations in English with idle or malicious chatter seem to be postmedieval; its meaning as applied to the talk instead of the talker seems to be a nineteenth-century innovation. Acknowledging the reality in the Middle Ages of the behavior and its problems that Schein finds, I suggest that we not call it "gossip."[51]

As noted above, I suggest that we reserve the word "gossip" for behavior in a society such as our own in which a fundamental distinction exists— even if often breached—between public and private spheres. This modern distinction did not exist in the same sense or with the same force in medieval society. Let us take *rumor* and *fama* as general terms to apply to all societies. And let us acknowledge that some sorts of rumor or infamous or idle talk might particularly affect individuals by revealing their secret fetishes or failings or whatnot, and that most societies look askance at inappropriate chatter about such intimacies or secrets.

But let us take "gossip" as a form of speaking or, derivatively, of writing that violates modern sentiments about public and private spheres. Chapters of this book have striven to show the absence of a separation of public and private spheres, say, around 1500, and its gradual emergence over the next three hundred years, so that by the late eighteenth century a separation that we would recognize had taken hold. The Roman distinction between public and private had essentially juridical force—it embodied a metaphysics of legal agency. The modern distinction effects a more thoroughgoing metaphysics of the person, and underpins our objective-bureaucratic regime, where the office and the home should be kept distinct.

Many chapters in part 1, as well as even parts of the previous two chapters, have discussed the ramifications of the rationalization of academic life and labor in the modern bureaucratic world. We have seen a progressive disembodiment of the academic, ideally, into pure intellectual ability manifested in writings and speaking. We have seen a separation of aspects of public or professional life from those of private or domestic life. In such a world, remarks about academics' private, domestic lives or about their bodies, when present in ministerial documents (and usually negatively marked there), carried immense weight. Such is the potentially heavy weight of gossip, too, in modern academic and professional life.

Like rumor, gossip falls into a category under hearsay. Even if transmitted in writing, gossip bears the oral echo of the "I heard" or "Have your heard?" Those who have thought about gossip, especially in relation and opposition to rumor, tend to stress that gossip must be about one or more persons (although rumor may be, too) and not just about things or events. Gossip typically or essentially concerns some sort of confidential, intimate, private, personal or secret news (otherwise, we have rumor), and the subject(s) of gossip are personally known to the gossipers, or are important or famous persons.

Modern societies attribute many characteristics to gossip that traditional societies attribute to the analogues or siblings of it, such as analyzed by Schein in medieval society. Thus, as opposed to rumor, gossip is supposedly idle, frivolous talk, and depicted by many as typically malicious talk. Idle, frivolous, and malicious sorts of people thus supposedly engage in gossip, the primary purveyors of which are supposedly servants, women, and malcontents. In modern societies, as in traditional ones, most authorities greet this chatter with censure.

Speaking in praise of gossip, one turns such characterizations to its benefits. Gossip affords leverage for the marginalized or disempowered against centers and authorities. It puts a human face on rulers of modern, impersonal bureaucratic offices. Academic gossip thus gives heroes of knowledge human foibles. To be treated as human may or may not demean or defame them. In the eighteenth century, Voltaire used gossip as part of a new sort of sociocultural history, which included academics. Descartes "did not believe it unworthy for a philosopher to give himself to love. With his mistress, he had a daughter who died young and whose loss he mourned much." Newton, on the other hand, "never approached a single woman—this was confirmed to me by the physician and surgeon in whose arms he died."[52]

As essentially narrative in force, gossip opposes the dissolution of narrative wrought by rationalization. If rumor resembles legend in the realm of literary genre, gossip resembles satire and irony, which often traffic in the taboo and aim to bring the lofty lower. It ought occasion no surprise that powers-that-be censure gossiping, and that hierarchical social orders provide most fertile soil for gossipers. Gossip is a transgression of professional, bureaucratic norms, thus bringing the satisfactions of sophistry and sinning. It need not be malicious. To speak of forbidden things, such as the fetishes or body of Professor Morgana, can be pleasurable in itself, even if one speaks in admiration or awe about them.

As a transgression of professional norms, gossiping carries risks. If Vlad misjudges his relationship to Aika, he could find himself the subject of gossip, as Aika recounts his breach of decorum to her confidants, which hopefully do not include Fulvia. Rumors spread through relevant publics (thus academic rumors among academics), while gossip spreads among confidants. Gossip upholds and expands subcollectives or marginal groups within broader ones. Some have likened the gossiping relationship to the joking relationship.[53]

One may joke and gossip with those above in the hierarchy, but with delicacy and as asked. In chapter 7 above, we heard J. H. Böhmer relate to the great Hanoverian minister, Münchhausen, confidentially of course, that while in Berlin he had heard that the king of Prussia was to have said, "He has to get that guy (*Kerl*) [Wolff] back to Halle, cost what it will." Depending on one's sensibility, this is rumor that crosses the line into gossip. Or one insists that the highest circles of the hierarchy do not gossip, for their words are never idle.[54]

Examining the rhetoric of academic appointments in chapter 7, we noted that narrative in a letter of reference seemed to contribute positively to its persuasive powers, while the opposite seemed to be true of (excessive) narration in an application itself, where the lapidary form of the list or catalogue, along with litotes and the like, appeared to work better. One could hazard a guess that the same would be true of rumor and gossip in both cases. We saw further in that chapter that faculties such as those at Halle, which often had to oppose ministerially envisaged appointments, deployed an arsenal of barbs to terminate unwanted candidates—that students dropped one's classes; that another was an "Ignorantz"; while a third had plagiarized works, with bad grammar, and published only in newsletters; and yet another, besides being in trouble with creditors, had only published German poems.

We saw as well that, when the University of Leipzig wanted to kill the ministerially envisaged appointment of Lorenz Oken in 1832, the Leipzig philosophy faculty wrote to a minister in Munich, apparently in the hopes of obtaining dirt about Oken's political activities. Oken had been in fact suspended from his professorship at Jena in 1819 in good part because of his political activities, especially in connection with the student movement of the time.

Recall the story of the ruin of Nietzsche's career, which epitomizes the power of academic rumor and gossip. As we heard above, about nine months after Nietzsche's first book, *The Birth of Tragedy*, had appeared, he bemoaned to Wagner that he had no students and was even disparaged by a professor in Bonn. Less naïve and more practiced academics can conjure a better sort of aura around themselves. In chapter 7 we heard of cases in which apparent hearsay that the Prussians or someone else were after an academic enhanced his value as a rare commodity. Maryann Ayim sees a similar role today for gossip or like exchanges not only in breaking careers.

> Hiring committee at universities (especially for high-ranking jobs) frequently totally disregard formal letter of support for applicants . . . [For] the committees often believe that such a [written] format is not conducive to receiving either substantive or even reliable information about the candidate. In such cases, a committee member is likely to telephone the referee and informally report to the rest of the committee. Such conversations, though they will form an important past of the decision procedure, do not become part of the official record. They remain, like gossip, "off the record," offering the referees a margin of safety conducive to speaking their minds freely and honestly. Most committees will attach more credibility to such an informal chat than to a formal letter. This is not to say that the telephone conversation consisted essentially of gossip, although it may well have. My claim is that it is an informal and unofficial conversation, both features shared with gossip and features that, in this case, render the contents of the conversation more rather than less reliable in the minds of the committee members.[55]

## THE CONVERSATION

"For a century, the course of ideas had been completely directed by the conversation," as Germaine ("Madame") de Staël wrote in the early nineteenth century. The modern conversation, as she saw it, embodied a novel form of speaking best enjoyed in Paris (and best there in a salon or café). The "conversation" offered a new way of interacting in which the form mattered more than the contents. It meant a sort of social talking for its own sake, with a spontaneous, egalitarian give and take, and with no clear point of the activity in sight. Conversation as social speaking produced "a sort of electricity." Moreover, "it is precisely what one calls coquetry. This coquetry does not pertain exclusively to women."[56]

Conversation now constitutes an everyday practice. One uses the word for virtually every informal exchange of words with beings other than animals, infants and computers. When Staël used the word in the early nineteenth century, "conversation" still connoted a rather distinctive sort of exchange, but one, as she points out, that had become crucial to the eighteenth century and, most especially, to the Enlightenment. For Staël, to grasp the intellectual history of the eighteenth century, one must grasp the oral art of conversation.

This is an early modern art. Bernard of Clairvaux, the founder of the Cistercian order, voiced an important criticism in the early twelfth century when he accused Peter Abelard of disputing with boys and conversing with women. The gendering of disputation and conversation here remains intriguing, but *conversari* and its cognates in classical Latin meant "commerce" or "intercourse," in the general sense of having to do with someone. Bernard doubtless intended the range of meanings that "commerce" would entail in English, including verbal and sexual commerce, which Abelard indeed had with Héloïse.[57]

Peter Burke, Elizabeth Goldsmith, and Dena Goodman, among others, have traced the paths by which *conversari* became the conversation that Staël meant. The path begins in sixteenth-century Italy, moves to seventeenth-century France, to eighteenth-century Britain, which feeds back into eighteenth-century France, and the rest of Europe. Like the case of gossip, one might worry about the touchy conflation of different behaviors—stemming from different sociocultural structures of the self or personality—under one rubric. But in the case of conversation, we have members of the several cultures and nations reading, or perhaps misreading, and reacting to the developments in the other cultures and nations.

"While their [sixteenth-century] Italian predecessors had said that conversational skill was the natural foundation of the courtier, [seventeenth-century] French courtesy literature gave it a more transcendent role in determining the worth [or being] of a person in society." This transformation in seventeenth-century France laid the bases for the epoch-making powers with which Staël would invest the eighteenth-century conversation. The crucial event came in the entry of women into the social intercourse of words. This rendered the rather more homosocial—and perhaps latently homoerotic—*conversazione* heterosocial. In time, one called a special site of such heterosocial French oral commerce the "salon."[58]

[In and after the Renaissance,] . . . shedding the Christian ascetic of chivalry, but yet essentially masculine in agonistics . . . , a further increase in the specifically sensational character of the erotic developed in the transition to the increasingly non-militaristic intellectualism of salon culture . . . This rests on a belief in the power of intersexual conversation to create values, for which clear or latent erotic sensation and the agonal display of the cavalier in the face of the lady became an indispensable means of stimulation. With the *Lettres portugaises* [of 1669 presumably by Mariana Alcoforado], the actual problematics of feminine love became a specifically marketed intellectual (*geistiges*) object and the love letters of women became "literature."[59]

The *alcôe* or *ruelle*, later called the "salon," formed the seventeenth-century site in which the nobility fashioned conversation as a form of polite heterosocial oral exchange, with erotic elements latent or not. In the course of that century, the martial mentality of the nobility evolved into the modern mentality of civility and politeness—the nobility or court as the embodiment of civilization and good manners. Unlike Italy in the antecedent century and Britain in the subsequent one, French conversation in the Baroque era revolved around a royal court. Some of the obsessions of seventeenth century society, especially apropos gossip and exclusivity, reflect this new court culture governed by talking and being talked about.[60]

In eighteenth-century Britain, the conversation lost its mooring in salon culture as specifically heterosocial and noble. The coffeehouses came into their own as sites of the conversation, which emerged as bourgeois and more abstractly egalitarian, without reference to a necessary heterosocial aspect, that is to say, without an essential female presence. Such British bourgeois and egalitarian sentiments fed back into French salon culture in its classical or final form in the Enlightenment, such as analyzed, for example, by Goodman. In this context, the conversation became important for academics outside courtly circles.[61]

"Enlightenment salons were working spaces . . . which took play as their model." Under the influence of the aristocratic ethos of leisure, eighteenth-century French salons resisted a bourgeois separation of public and private, or of home and workplace. In so far as the conversation preserved this spirit, it realized a good part of its magic power. Unlike the more homosocial inclinations of British society, French and other Continental salons formed a complex heterosocial sphere from which friendships, affairs and even marriages resulted. Erotic aspects, which Staël characterized as coquetry, could more easily color conversation.[62]

Goodman calls the nexus that arose from conversation and commerce in salons, along with their ancillary apparatus in correspondence and journals, the "Republic of Letters." It

> used the practice of polite conversation invented by the nobility to transform itself from a combative to a collaborative group and assert its autonomy vis-à-vis the state. Whereas the nobility had its chivalric martial tradition, men of letters had the scholastic and Jesuit tradition of disputation to overcome.[63]

As a possible alternative to sophistry, dialogue, and disputation, the conversation facilitated the dissonance of multiple voices, while still maintaining a discursive decorum. Such considerations, as well as Staël's notes above on the electricity of conversation, led me in a chapter above to search unsuccessfully for the advent of this sort of oral exchange in the German seminars—to uncover the transformation of the originally agonistic, combative and, indeed, martial aspects of academic discourse in disputation, into the more collaborative oral arts of academic conversation, which I presumed would characterize the seminar-style of teaching. About the Germans in particular, however, Staël said, "Nothing is more alien to this talent [for the conversation] than the character and the sort of spirit of the Germans—they want a serious result from everything." Unlike dialogue and disputation, as well as jokes and traditional narrative, the conversation aims toward no necessary resolution or punch line.[64]

The notion of academic voices in conversation presents a conundrum, and not only for the Germans. As opposed to dialogue and disputation, can there be any such thing as an academic conversation? Or is it, rather, that modern academia, in which one must profile oneself without destroying the collective discourse, and in which nice gossip and charismatic names circulate so well, has the superstructure of Staël's enlightened electric conversation?

## LETTERS, JOURNALS, NOVELS

Neglecting the more civic culture of Italy and the few residence or capital cities of transalpine Europe, most early modern academics would not have had the opportunity to be civilized in the arts of conversation by a salon. Oxbridge and Jesuit colleges adhered to monastic ideals of celibacy and the separation of the sexes. Most German universities, as well as secular French universities, tended to be in provincial towns. In the German case at least, this had been an explicit policy until it was overturned in the nineteenth century. Authorities wanted academics, especially students, in small towns away from civilization's temptations, which included the company of cavaliers and most women.

By the eighteenth century, the magic of the conversation inhered in its projection into letters and journals, which Goodman traces, as well as the pervasive role of conversation and other oral arts in the most important fictional genre of the time, the novel. In the triad of letter-journal-novel, the letter claims primacy. One of the greatest changes effected by seventeenth-century French culture consisted in shifting epistolary rhetoric from its classical basis to the new one of the conversation embodied in the salons. Manuals for teaching conversation assumed the form of epistolary collections. These helped diffuse the sort of self or persona envisaged by the oral culture of the salon.[65]

The novel did more than that, for it could spread the ideals of polite conversation more effectively, while at the same time confronting such ideals with actual practices. *La Princesse de Clèves* of 1678, published anonymously by Countess Marie-Madelaine ("Madame") de Lafayette, proved influential at least for the French novels of the eighteenth century. Its central theme is not the civilizing power of the conversation, but rather the ineluctable omnipresence of gossip in shaping reputation and lives in polite society.[66]

Like the novel, the journal might offer, on the one hand, a literary site for the ideal space of the conversation, but actually produce, on the other hand, contents largely at odds with such ideals. Of diverse origins and aims, some of which preceding chapters have discussed, the journals doubtless played the greatest part in finalizing the triumph of the legible over the oral, as the modern academic article suppressed its origins in the disputational dissertation and the conversational letter. But if one attends to the discourse of the collectivity of academic journals, at least in the eighteenth century, one could hear Staël's conversation.[67]

As discussed in a previous chapter, Nicolai's *Allgemeine Deutsche Bibliothek* (1765–1806) epitomizes this simulation of periodical conversation. The German lands enjoyed neither the civic culture of Italy nor the metropolitan centering of Britain and France in overpowering capital cities. Mindful of such, Nicolai's *ADB* aimed to remedy German failings and produce polite conversation among the salonless intelligentsia. *ADB* would mute pedantic and polemical academic voices, all too typical of the German professorial culture, with a better tone. This new tone—a key notion by midcentury and onward—could politely criticize public works without polemically insulting persons. Radicalizing the spirit of enlightened conversation as a collective to which all should sublimate the ego, the academic voices in *ADB*, as in so many eighteenth-century reviews, spoke anonymously. Typical of masked affairs, this allowed infelicities ranging from small indiscretions to insults.[68]

Ever since their inception, the review journals and ancillary newsletters had faced the dilemma of the disinterested manufacture of reputation and the all too interested production of infamy, facilitated by anonymity. Martin Gierl has shown that the sale of disputational polemics made good business for publishers. The trade proved most profitable if one could involve famous academics, such as a Thomasius or a Leibniz or a Wolff, in battles. But from the *Acta eruditorum* of 1681 onwards, journals professed an aim to end such polemics. Despite the rhetoric of a republic, the journals and their newsletters dwelt and worked in the marketplace, which liked to leaven polite conversation with professorial polemics.[69]

By the 1820s, in the Berlin milieu at least, one called the practice of anonymity in reviews "the bandit regime (*Banditenwesen*)." Hegel and friends founded a *Societät für wissenschaftliche Kritik* in 1826, to edit and publish the *Jahrbücher für wissenschaftliche Kritik*. Hegel desired to have the society and journal consecrated as an official institution of the state so that the reviews would carry a certain weight. His partners dissuaded him from such plans, arguing that German scholarship had had a republican constitution for three centuries (thus since Luther), so one would have difficulty imposing the state as a manager (*Vorstand*). The society toyed with the idea of having every single review read aloud in its sessions, perhaps to stimulate comment and conversation on it. Moreover, the society and journal decidedly renounced the bandit regime. Such nice sentiments against old-fashioned polemics did stop Hegel from insisting that Schleiermacher not be allowed to partake (the latter, after all, had kept Hegel out of the Prussian Academy of Sciences in Berlin).[70]

## CONFERENCES

Morris explains, "The day of the individual campus has passed . . . Scholars don't have to work at the same institution to interact, nowadays: they call each other up, or they meet at international conferences . . . I work mostly at home or on planes . . . [for, thanks to telephones and travel grants, I'm] plugged into the only university that really matters—the global campus. A young man in a hurry can see the world by conference-hopping."[71]

Admittedly, the oral pleasures of conversation and gossip provide only the second best grounds for going to conferences, while the best grounds are gustatory, which are indeed oral pleasures, but rather more tied to olfaction and digestion than to cognition. As for visual experiences, they are on the whole tolerated rather than edifying or satisfying. Being an historian, my favorite recollection of an academic conference concerns the dead.

The scene was Nuremberg, sometime between 29 September and 3 October 1838. The very first academic conference in history of the Association of German Philologists and Schoolmen (Versammlung deutscher Philologen und Schulmänner) was underway. The association had been formed, in principle, about a year before, in September 1837, at the one-hundredth anniversary of the official opening of the University of Göttingen. Friedrich Thiersch, philology professor at the University of Munich and the Bavarian Academy of Sciences, played a leading role in founding the association. Thiersch had battled Lorenz Oken since the late 1820s on the hegemony of natural sciences versus humanities within the educational system, thus in the contest over the formation of the ruling class. Thiersch and others envisaged the planned annual face-to-face meetings of philologists as a disciplinary move to counter the annual meetings of German natural scientists promoted by Oken.

We met Oken, among other places, above and in chapter 7 in the context of the Saxon ministry's attempt to appoint him to the University of Leipzig. The relevant faculty objected that Oken's science, a curious mix of *Naturphilosophie* and Romanticism, was peculiar to himself. Oken stressed the unity not of only science but also of scientists. To accomplish this, he advocated annual conferences of all German-speaking natural scientists, without perforce excluding other linguistic groups. Under these auspices the first (or perhaps second or third) academic conference in history of the modern sort took place in 1822 in Leipzig—the Association of German Natural Scientists and Physicians, the VdNÄ, later the GdNÄ (Versammlung/Gesellschaft deutscher Naturforscher und Ärzte), arose.

The Swiss had begun such conferences of natural scientists in 1815, so one should doubtless credit them with inaugurating the modern academic art of conferencing. In 1817, Oken attended the Wartburgfest, the first student conference in modern history. Organized in 1815 from the University of Jena, the erstwhile center of German Romanticism and where Oken taught, the Wartburgfest saw about three hundred to five hundred students from Protestant German universities meet at the Wartburg, a hill with a tower near Eisenach in Saxe-Weimar, where Luther had once received asylum. This 1817 student conference had party aims, which, among other things, decidedly included politics, with calls for unity of German students, and Germans altogether, opposing provincialism. One could view the program as liberal or conservative, depending on what one took as the opposition.[72]

Oken was among the few professors who attended the Wartburgfest; indeed, he gave a speech. The conservative reaction in the Austro-German lands to such political party events led to the Karlsbader Beschlüsse of 1819, pan-German proclamations that instituted more censorship and surveillance over academics and others. In the same year, the ministry in Weimar suspended Oken from his professorship in Jena in view of his political activities and other problems. Undeterred, Oken and fellow Romantics and *Naturphilosophen* began proselytizing for such pan-German conferences for natural scientists. Oken edited a journal, *Isis,* which gave him a forum to publicize the idea, despite his academic suspension at Jena.

Amid political and academic suspicions, Oken and his fellow travelers— about 21 or so—met in Leipzig in September 1822 and drew up statutes for the VdNÄ. In basic outline, the association would meet annually in a different city each year, rotating though the various confessional, national, and regional parts of the German cultural space. Anyone could attend and actively participate who had published an article or text, beyond a dissertation, on a topic in natural science or medicine, broadly conceived. In 1823 about 26 showed up to meet in Halle. In 1824, around 37 came to Würzburg, the first Catholic university-town that the association embraced. Signs of success emerged in 1825, as 110 showed up in Frankfurt. In 1826, 115 appeared at Dresden, and 156 in 1827 at Munich. The breakthrough and takeoff occurred the next year.

In 1828 the VdNÄ met in Berlin, where 466 attended. At this meeting, several heavyweights in German natural science—including Alexander von Humboldt and Carl Friedrich Gauss—appeared for the first time and, to be precise, co-opted the association for the mainstream. Charles Babbage also attended. He took the idea back to Britain and helped inaugurate the British Association for the Advancement of Science in 1831, fondly called the "British AAS" and roughly modeled on the German association. The American Association for the Advancement of Science, the "Triple A-S," met for the first time in 1848.

Oken and his likes had conceived the annual face-to-face meetings as a forum to facilitate better communication, to improve the tone of exchanges in periodicals and elsewhere, and, indeed, even to foster friendships among scientists. From 1822 up to 1828, all sessions of the VdNÄ had been plenary, in view of Romantic aims of upholding and furthering the unity of science and scientists. Humboldt coorganized and co-chaired the 1828 meeting in Berlin. He and his colleagues introduced sections for the first time. On this new model, there would be a few plenary sessions for ceremonial and ideological purposes; but most time would go to sections for specific disciplines or topics, at which specialists or fans of this or that could meet and present papers. This model prevailed at future meetings.

The format of a few plenary sessions and numerous specialized sections offered a forum for both central and marginal academic voices, for powers-that-be as well as for up-and-comers. This model prevailed not only at the German VdNÄ but in time throughout the world for the open conference, that is, for those not run as invitation-only, such as the BAAS, the AAAS, the MLA, and so on. In specialized sections, one could meet and hear academics working on specific topics that one found interesting. Opening, closing, and typically, honorific plenary sessions could address disciplinary ideologies and, as the genius of the time and or place allowed, might air extradisciplinary or even sociopolitical issues.

It did not take long for the oral delights to encompass the full range of the pleasure centers. In an effort to ensnare the Austrians in the VdNÄ, it held the 1832 conference in Vienna. Apparently for the first time, a noteworthy number of participants showed up with their wives and even their children. The old imperial capital promised many attractions for Germans, among which those of the palette did not rank low. Social and tourist activities threatened to sap the annual conference of its academic essence. So the association thenceforth took measures to interweave but control the lures of the social and sensual.[73]

The success of the VdNÄ led in 1837 to the resolution in Göttingen that humanists must meet. They had to counter the waxing collective unity of natural scientists feeding off the energy—or Durkheimian "effervescence"—generated by annual oral conferences. As Thiersch had played the leading role instigating the formation of the Association of German Philologists and Schoolmen, one resolved that the first meeting would be in Bavaria, but in the more neutral and central city of Nuremberg, as opposed to Munich. The king of Bavaria expressed reservations about such an association and such a conference, since, as he claimed, "Politics would creep in everywhere and corrupt everything in academic knowledge."

But the conference went forward in 1838. As my favorite such anecdote goes, Thiersch went one evening among the participants. Finding them in heated conversation and, although not so recorded, doubtless also in their cups, and mindful of the king's concerns, thus wary that the conversation turn to politics, Thiersch, searching for a means to turn dangerous academics toward gustatory or nocturnal pleasures, turned out the lights.[74]

## INTERVIEWS

From an interview published in *Le monde* on 6 April 1980:

*Christian Delacampagne:* Allow me first to ask why you have chosen to remain anonymous?

*The Masked Philosopher:* . . . Out of nostalgia for the time when, being completely unknown, what I said had some chance of being heard.

The interview is a strange modern forum. Very little depends on some interviews, while on others an entire career and life might be riding. The popular media offer a dizzying array of books, audio discs, and video discs about how to succeed in interviews—which, I take it, concern the ones on which something depends. I have searched textbooks on classical rhetoric for instruction, but they are one and all silent on this now pervasive oral exchange. Of the thousands and thousands of primary sources (going up to the 1840s generally, and later for some), on which I have laid my eyes, I have never seen an interview among them.

So many traditional and modern fora resemble the interview—the inquisition, the interrogation, the dialogue, the conversation, the conference, and perhaps the confession. The interview draws on most or all of these, but remains something apart. Cognates of the word reach at least back to the sixteenth century, where the notion approximated that of a parley or small but formal conference of potentates. The Oxford English Dictionary indicates that the contemporary sense stems from the second half of the nineteenth century, as journalists published "interviews" with politicians, apparently a practice looked upon somewhat negatively at first by some.

Contemporary usage combines two rather distinct affairs and ends under the one word. In one case, as above in *Le monde,* the end of the interview lies in the publication or broadcast of a sort of conversation. In the second case, an interview concerns an appointment or job, the results of which, to my knowledge, are typically not published or broadcast. The role of the conductor(s) gives the sense of combining both cases under one rubric, although one would perhaps do better to insist on separate words. Unlike an ideal dialogue or ideal conversation, an interview has one or more conductors. It is a directed oral exchange of questions and answers, thus more closely resembles the inquisition and the interrogation. In the case of a job interview, the affair as directed might extend to days and many meetings.

As in most professions, the interview in both cases above has importance in modern academia. For a famous or exotic academic, an interview in a forum like *Le monde* can enhance such charisma even more. The Masked Philosopher's ploy above, however sincere, also adds a tease: Is it Barthes? Deleuze? Derrida? Foucault? Who? For less exotic, more garden-variety academics, interviews in academic journals, local media, or even student newspapers can generate buzz among students and colleagues. Such academic noise matters.

The interview for publication or broadcast often elides from public, professional matters to private ones. The market facilitates and perhaps encourages this elision. The coquetry that Staël saw in the conversation often circulates between interviewer and interviewed, also able to turn gossip into news. "Q: You're in your fifties. You're a reader of *Le gai pied* . . . Is the kind of discourse you find there something positive for you?"[75]

In an interview for an appointment or other position, such a question today would probably be considered out of bounds in its aim and insinuations, and perhaps actionable. One might wonder why. For many academics and other professionals harbor such queries in their hearts during interviews and sometimes signal them to colleagues one way or another. Universities now spend considerable amounts of money, and academics invest considerable amounts of time interviewing candidates for positions. Why does one insist on seeing them all face-to-face? Is it the same desire that sent Gedike on his acquisitive visitation in 1789?

Would it be better if an interviewer—to borrow an example from Gedike's hearing—said to an interviewee, "You look like a weirdo to me," if the interviewer thought so and expressed it after the interview, thus after the interviewee had any chance of response? Is academic repression, mandated by the modern metaphysics of the public versus the private, whereby the body and its likes are taboo, perhaps insidious and invidious?

I dream of an interview in which a smiling interviewer holds up a sheet of paper and says, "This letter of reference notes that you, I quote, 'always dressed nicely and were obedient,' end quote." Still smiling, but waving another letter—borrowing an example from Minister Burgsdorf in 1789—the inquisitor continues, "But it says in this letter of reference that you are guilty of, I quote, 'too much dissipation of partly improper sort,' last four words crossed out, then it goes on, I quote, 'whereby students in part take part and for the other part supposedly get no good example' end quote. Why do think the referee wrote and crossed that part out? Do you engage in improper conduct with students and do you have queer views?"

## ARS EROTICA LINGUAE

The explanation of the dream seemed to me complete. But she brought me an addendum to the dream a day or so later. She said she forgot to say that, when waking up, she always smelled smoke. Smoke . . . indicated that the dream had a special connection to me . . . Against this exclusive reference to me, she objected that Mr. K and her papa were also passionate smokers . . . Since she refused further comment, it remained for me to decide how I wanted to integrate this addendum into the structure of the interpretation of the dream. As clue could help me that the sensation of smoke came as an addendum, thus had to overcome a special effort of repression . . . It could only mean the desire for a kiss, which for a smoker necessarily reeks of smoke . . .
Putting together all the signs that likely constitute a transference to me, in that I am also a smoker, I come to the view that it probably occurred to her one day during the session to wish a kiss from me.

Freud, *Bruchstücke einer Hysterie-Analyse*

Sigmund Freud's patient "Dora" could only respond to this with a philosophical laugh, that is to say, with silence. Freud attempted to seduce her with an entire chorus of academic voices. He spoke to her in theological, juridical, medical, and philosophical voices. He interrogated her in the manner of a pastor, a magistrate, a physician, a philosopher. Freud was a great Sophist. He wanted to help Dora by teaching her to talk— to talk about the important things he said she repressed: bedwetting, masturbation, lesbianism . . .

Steven Marcus has written that Freud's case history of Dora is "a great work of literature." The structure of *Dora* resembles a modern experimental novel. Freud occurs as three personae in *Dora*. First, he partakes of Socratic-Freudian dialogues with Dora. Second, he comments as a narrator on the action and dialogues. Third, in amazing footnotes, he contradicts himself as narrator. Thanks to these dissonant voices, Freud plays the unreliable narrator of modernist fiction. He knew the effect of his sophistical voice. He managed to play not only Socrates but also Apollo, the diviner of dreams. Freud was a great eroticist.[76]

Foucault was, too. But from 1970 to 1984 at the Collège de France, he never got over the nervousness that he displayed in his inaugural lecture. He said he felt isolated, nearly anonymous, cut off from the audience. No one usually dared to interrupt him and ask a question. He said he felt like an actor or an acrobat (*videlicet* Zarathustra) on a stage. The eroticism of the academic voice is bound up with the possibility of dissonance, if not of sophistry, which is why Freud overcame Dora's silent dissonance with other voices.[77]

Socrates wanted to take over the role of Dionysus. Socrates was an actor, like Foucault, who was an acrobat, like Zarathustra. Wilamowitz-Möllendorff did not see this Dionysian streak in Socrates. Nor did Nietzsche at first, even though he saw the dying Socrates as essential. Nietzsche wanted to be a festive man. Wilamowitz-Möllendorff said that he preferred being a Socratic man, but he assimilated that to being a Christian. So, against Nietzsche, he said that researchers learn "the asceticism of self-denying work." Asceticism or the mortification of the flesh is an *ars erotica*, but not of the Dionysian sort.[78]

"Enchantment is the presupposition of all dramatic art," says Nietzsche. Sophists were most interested in training the voice. A deep voice was manly and implied courage. A high voice meant cowardice. The exercise of the tongue was part of the care of the self in Greece and Rome. A Roman medical tract said that vocal exercise helps to cure stomach problems, especially in pregnant women who crave unusual foods. Quintilian quotes Cicero, "Let the orator carry himself with a vigorous and manly posture of the upper body that derives not from actors and the stage but from the army or even the wrestling-grounds."[79]

What changes have been wrought in academic wrestling-grounds by the conversation.

## MODERN GHOSTS

Hans Brittnacher has shown that pre-Romantic ghosts had been very corporal, wearing bloody sheets and carrying noisy chains and messages, too. But, by the Romantic era, ghosts had become our ethereal modern ones—without bodies, "shadowy, disembodied, without tidings and mute." With an arsenal of little tools—questionnaires, journals, tables, dossiers, and reports—modern machinations have recast academics, if not into bloodless Romantic ghosts, then into some other shadowy sorts, fitting inhabitants of the panopticon of modern academia to which angelic visitors need no longer descend per diem.[80]

Jean Baudrillard has argued that modernity lies in the emergence of a culture centered on the circulation and consumption of images, signs, and the play of *différence*. "The mirror of production" gains existence independent of production. The imaginary governs the real, as simulacra and ghostly entities produce their own objects or subjects. Academics become how they are reported and imaged—but also how they are named and rumored. The Masked Philosopher's nightmare: to be haunted by the noise and specter of one's own name.[81]

One motivation for this chapter's musings lay in a mild protest against an obsession with visualization in some studies in recent decades. Such studies have brought out the fundamental role of the visible and legible in modern research. In Foucault's terms, studies of visualization constitute an archaeology of modern knowledge, as they have isolated and exposed the empire of the eye as an essential aspect of the "positive unconsciousness" of modern knowledge, where a nexus of images and legible traces fabricate objectivity.[82]

Much of this book has attempted to add to the recent illumination of the positive unconsciousness of our modern academic order. But many chapters have also striven to indicate that Romantic ghosts of subjectivity and charismatic rationality animate our modern machinery. In the panopticon and amid the mirrors of production, silence does not reign.

# Epilogue

# 12

## The Research University and Beyond

On the morning that I was preparing to pester Naoko Yuge in Tokyo with an email asking her about whether Japan's adoption of Prussian jurisprudence in the nineteenth century in fact went hand in hand with an adoption of the German or Hanoverian-Prussian academic system, I knew that the task envisaged for this epilogue was hopeless.

I originally wanted to trace the nineteenth-century shadow of this German—or Hanoverian-Prussian—colossus in many nations. I found it interesting, and perhaps you would have, too, to discover that the nineteenth-century Russian university system had been explicitly modeled, first, on the University of Göttingen, and then on the University of Berlin. I found it furthermore fascinating that the University of Athens was actually first founded in 1837, and by German liberators or, rather, occupiers. They modeled its constitution explicitly on that of a German university, particularly on Göttingen and Berlin.[1]

But I found dismaying the number of nations that eluded my grasp. Encouraged by friends and colleagues of this or that national or ethnic background, I sought to expand the scope of my survey. From my headquarters in Berlin, the Low Countries seemed easiest to penetrate. From there, both Scandinavia and France would be within reach. Already having a grasp of Russia, and having effectively isolated Britain through my work heretofore, I would move from France into the Iberian Peninsula, and from there into Northern Africa, then the Middle East, from which I could easily target India and blaze a path to Japan.

Resigning myself instead to cultural imperialism, I have focused on Germany, Austria, France, Britain, and the United States. The aim is to outline the consolidation and diffusion of, as well as the resistance to, institutions and practices of research studied in this book. In conclusion, I'll look at

Weber's "Science as a Vocation" and some manifestations of the cult of academic personality in the twentieth century. But I'll begin with the Jesuits.

## THE JESUITS

The Jesuits had resisted the modern bifurcation of the self into private versus public or professional parts. A Jesuit gave himself wholly to the Society of Jesus. He thus had no private life, in the modern bourgeois sense. It's hard to say whether that made Jesuits antimoderns, like aristocrats and peasants who did not usually separate the public from the private persona, or whether it made the Jesuits radical moderns, the ultimate bureaucrats.

Two other characteristics did make the Jesuits into vanguards of modernity: mobility and meritocracy. As we have seen in chapters above, meritocracy, as an oligarchy of talent, certainly did not first emerge within academia. It seems to have emerged in Europe generally through the Jesuits, whence it entered the nascent civil services or bureaucracies of nations with a strong Jesuit presence, especially France and Austria. Given the Jesuits' notion of promotion through proven talent, they seem to have recruited and advanced members in the Society irrespective of social class. Only ability mattered—supposedly.[2]

Along with their meritocracy, the extreme mobility of Jesuits also stands out. Jesuits as academics showed great turnover. At many institutions, a stay of only about five years was typical. A Jesuit might, for example, teach for five years at the University of Bamberg, then be moved by the Society to the University of Würzburg for five years or so, then to other universities. The truly talented might end up at headquarters in Rome, or journey to Japan or even the New World. This mobility served the purpose of breaking any tendencies toward national or provincial or local loyalties. A Jesuit gave loyalty to no particular college, faculty, university or academy. Jesuit academia was cosmopolitan and international in that sense.[3]

But the Jesuits rejected what German state ministries eventually forced on secular academics: disciplinary specialization. Jesuit professors instead usually rotated through the disciplines. In the Jesuit system, a professor often taught the same group of students for a few years. The professor moved with the students from one year or level to the next. The Jesuits thus obviated to a large extent the effects of a division of academic labor. Adam Smith noted,

> The difference of natural talents in different men is, in reality, much less than we are aware of; and the very different genius which appears to distinguish men of different professions . . . is not upon many occasions so

much the cause, as the effect of the division of labour. The difference between the most dissimilar characters, between a philosopher and a common street porter, for example, seems to arise not so much from nature, as from habit, custom, and education . . . By nature a philosopher is not in genius and disposition half so different from a street porter, as a mastiff is from a greyhound[4]

In this Smithian sense, the resistance to a division of academic labor entailed a resistance to the creation of specific personae. The Jesuit was loyal to the Society, and only secondarily or not at all to a discipline or community of academics. But qualifications must be made here.

For a few disciplines, the Jesuits did encourage specialization for some scholars at some institutions. The best Jesuit minds, as noted, often came to Rome to pursue academic work. Indeed, in advance of Protestant systems, the Jesuits set up sabbaticals so that proven scholars could obtain leave, for two to six years, from teaching so as to pursue and publish academic work. But those were all exceptions before the nineteenth century.[5]

In this book, the Jesuits embody masters of bureaucracy, the rationalizers *ne plus ultra*. Jesuitism means the hegemony of ministries without markets. Catholic Austria at first opposed Protestant, Hanoverian-Prussian managerial capitalism. It opposed marketing academics. Austria shared its opposition to academic commodification with the Jesuits, who engaged in propaganda and rumor, but did not cultivate the magic of the market. And modern academic Jesuiticism, as it emerged for example in Communist East Germany from 1946 to 1989, set itself decidedly—or, rather, officially—against the cult of academic personality.

## OLD REGIME, REVOLUTIONARY, AND NAPOLEONIC FRANCE

All academic Gaul was divided into three parts in the ancien régime. On the one hand, there was Paris versus the provinces. Within Paris itself, a further sort of differentiation emerged in the reign of Louis XIV and cemented itself during the eighteenth century. The crucial distinction in Paris set the old academic institutions—colleges, faculties, and universities—against the new ones—academies and technical schools—some of which might even be outside of Paris.

The former, older, institutions were said to be simply for the transmission of knowledge, that is, for teaching. The latter, newer ones were supposed to be for the advancement of knowledge, for research, as it would be called. In his magisterial study of science and polity in the old regime, Charles Gillispie noted that "it is a mistake to suppose that no science at all was taught [or done] at the University" of Paris and all its parts. But French universities and colleges actually play very little role in his story.[6]

This bifurcation of the academic system—against which the German research university would define itself—seems most typical of France. Let's call it "universities versus academies" for short. An older historiography on the scientific revolution, and to a lesser extent on the Enlightenment, generalized that bifurcation across Europe. On that view, modern science emerged essentially outside of and even opposed by the universities. In recent decades a revisionist history, as such things tend to do, has assailed that view and argued the case for the university's importance to the emergence of modern science. That debate, though interesting, relates only tangentially to the concerns of this book. Our concern has not been the emergence of modern science, but rather that of modern research.[7]

We shall look, first, briefly at a few salient points concerning the old system in France. The Jesuitical heritage facilitated an early bureaucratization of academic appointments: a meritocratic system. Secular professorships in colleges and lower faculties of arts and sciences were filled by advertising the position and then testing the applicants via an exam, the *concours*. A faculty board determined the results and voted on the appointment. Save the law faculty, this method pretty much ruled. It is unclear, however, whether de facto castes or dynasties reemerged. Professional faculties—theology, law, and medicine—could pay decent salaries. But salaries in colleges or university arts faculties remained generally too modest to support a lifetime occupation. That produced Jesuitical mobility. A ten-year stint as arts and sciences professor seems about the maximum. Great turnover thus resulted.[8]

Things looked different in the modern French academic system, that is, among the academicians. Alongside the Göttingen professorate, they seem to be the most radical group of modernizers and rationalizers, and very charismatic, too. Parisian academicians, however, apparently did not to need to be entrepreneurs as much as Göttingen professors did.

> A professional bureaucrat [the Parisian academician] could no longer be confused with the cultural polymath . . . His position was conveniently linked to his functional role in the state, rather than the economic fruits of his labor. The existence of an academy of specialists [in Paris] once again reinforced his [the academician's] profoundly elitist values.[9]

By contemporary lights, Parisian academicians constituted *la crème de la crème*. Roger Hahn stressed their nature and role as bureaucrats. Entry to the Parisian Académie des Sciences came by nomination from the Académie itself, then appointment by the king, who at times imposed his will. Social origin supposedly did not matter, but the lowborn and most from manufacturing and mercantile backgrounds found themselves excluded. Musing on the social composition of the other two great academies in Paris—L'Académie Française and L'Académie des Inscriptions—Daniel Roche noted that letters and history remained preserves for the nobility and higher clergy, but that the sciences were becoming bourgeois. But, as he and Hahn observed, academicians of science formed a new academic elite, an oligarchy governed not by blood but rather by meritocracy, expertise and specialization. The latter was what was largely missing from both Jesuitical and traditional academic practices.[10]

Hahn further remarked that academicians, as modern bureaucrats, did not act like traditional groups such as craft guilds or academic faculties. Not only did Parisian academicians seldom intermarry. They also, for example, seldom witnessed each other's weddings. They did not socialize privately with each other, in the way that old-fashioned professors tended to do. Nonetheless, as Hahn argued, we must not see Parisian academicians as modern professional scientists or researchers. "The spirit of research for the furtherance of the rational understanding of nature—which is my definition of [natural] scientific activity—neither coincided completely with the needs of the society of the ancien régime, nor was it encouraged on the scale required to create a professional class of scientists."[11]

In fairly recent decades, much of the Anglo-American discussion of French science and academia—that is, discussion concerning the end of the ancien régime, the Revolution, the Terror, and the Napoleonic era—revolved around the questions of continuity and professionalization. Those two issues might have lost some of their central status in the wake of cultural history in the 1990s. Still, one wanted to know when the modern professional scientist emerged, and if that emergence should be attributed to the ruptures from 1789 to 1815; or rather, whether the essential patterns of the old regime simply continued, albeit intensified and somewhat modified. Maurice Crosland, for instance, has argued that science in fact did emerge as a profession in the modern sense after the Revolution. Dorinda Outram, Colin Russell, and Robert Fox, for example, have called that into question. Such critics or revisionists tend to see continuity from the ancien régime to Revolutionary and Napoleonic France.[12]

Resolution of such matters is, again, not the concern of this book, even though the issues are related. For our purposes, we need only some sense of what happened in France between 1789 and 1815. Egalitarian sentiments waxed for a while after 1789, and directed themselves against elite institutions. Thus the august Parisian Académie des Sciences, the pinnacle of the French system, was closed in August 1793. The next month, the revolutionaries officially abolished the entire old academic system and closed all colleges and universities. That dramatic event and its aftermath in good part underlie the debate concerning rupture or continuity. For quite soon revolutionary and Napoleonic France reincaranted many of the academic institutions of the old regime, to be sure in a modern and secular guise.

In place of the colleges, "central schools" appeared, while many technical academies—some renamed—simply carried on. The Parisian academy reappeared, with some changes, in 1795 as the Institut de France. The old Collège Royal de France omitted the *royal* and lived on—to this day—as the lofty seat for France's most acclaimed and charismatic scholars and scientists. New elite meritocratic institutions, such as the École Normale (1795–1808) and the École Polytechnique (1794) arose, the latter for training the best students in science and engineering. In 1802 the central schools became municipal colleges and lyceums.

Finally, decrees of 17 March 1808 and 16 February 1810 set up Napoleon's Université Impériale de France. This did not mean a university in the traditional sense. It was, rather, an administrative structure to supervise the system of higher learning in France and its conquests. One intended to rationalize the academic career structure. The new system, for example, instituted a doctorate in arts and philosophy. Chair holders were supposed to obtain the new doctorate. But the notion proved stillborn. By 1815 very few such doctors existed. The center of power came to lie with institutions such as the École Polytechnique and its like, which had not even been placed under the Université Impériale.[13]

In sum, post-Napoleonic France ended up with an academic system much like that of the old regime and pre-Napoleonic France. Within the new order, however, the old notion of the university had no place. Institutions of general learning amounted to schools strictly for undergraduates. Advanced training took place at specialized schools or academies. With Napoleon's fall, his Université Impériale de France, in part a tool of his imperial colonial policy, eventually became (between 1824 and 1829) what it really was: a ministry of education.

This French system and its short-lived influence was, as L. W. B. Brockliss has put it, idiosyncratic. "Only in nineteenth-century France was the creation of an alternative higher-educational system permanent (until the reforms of 1892). Elsewhere the collapse of the Napoleonic empire . . . led in turn to the restoration of the traditional university."[14]

# PRUSSIA, THE GERMANIC ACADEMIC SYSTEM, AND ROMANTICISM

In 1773, German book catalogues listed some 3,000 authors. By 1787 that number had doubled. Berlin occupied second place in the ratio of authors to public, as it had 222 published authors for 150,000 inhabitants. First place went to Göttingen with 79 authors for its 8,000 inhabitants. Henri Brunschwig tied the emergence of Romanticism to that bourgeois crisis. Far too many German authors and intellectuals sought to eke out a living. The market could not bear them all. Romanticism's reaction against the Enlightenment would come in part thanks to a generational crisis felt by the over-educated underemployed who returned to mystic and cultic practices. Interestingly, Romantics opposed the Enlightenment's crass commercialization of culture and academia, while their apotheosis of the academic as author would make commodification systematic.[15]

Traditional historiography, concerning 1789 to 1815, tends to see an intellectual and academic crisis, especially in Prussia. I do not intend to take issue with the historiography. But the possibility of a transformation of the German academic system into a French-style one was remote. French influence was felt only temporarily, and only in some places, namely, by French conquest and colonization.[16]

The crucial events in Prussia came in 1787 and 1788, before 1789 and the French Revolution. They were thus not a reaction to it. The Revolution, the Terror, and Napoleon simply accelerated conservative, aristocratic, authoritarian, anti-Enlightenment currents already afoot. Besides decrees on censorship of writings, and proofs of orthodoxy, the years 1787 and 1788 witnessed many of the important academic innovations with which chapters of this book have been concerned. Those two years saw the institution of the new central ministry, the OSK (*Oberschulkollegium*), which supervised the appointment of all school teachers and all university instructors and professors in Prussia. As we saw in chapter 7, the OSK (usually) vigorously followed the ethos of publish or perish in making appointments.

Chapter 4 described how the OSK began the institution of the *Abitur*, the modern university entrance exam. The *Abitur* originally aimed at controlling poor students, most of whom would be future preachers or teachers or even academics. Chapter 5 examined how the pedagogical seminar in Berlin under Gedike and the philology seminar in Halle under Wolf arose in those two years. Both of those seminars had also aimed, in part, to take better control of the formation of secondary school teachers and instructors of higher education.

In 1789 itself, but before the outbreak of the Revolution, Gedike commenced his survey or hearing of non-Prussian universities with a goal of acquiring academics. This we took, in chapter 10, as an epitome of the new ministerial-market rationality that would conquer German academia. Capitalistic visitations or acquisitions of the sort that Gedike undertook in 1789 went hand in hand with the virtual cessation then of visitation of the old juridico-ecclesiastical sort. Tabular self-registration or reporting arose in its stead.

Essential parts of the modern system were thus in place in Prussia and in a few other places, such as Hanover, before 1789. What emerged as a reaction after 14 July 1789 was a Romantic ideology of research and the researcher bound up with a new Ministry of Culture. This Romantic ideology translated the Enlightenment's notion of fame into a new emphasis on the originality of the researcher's work, a new sort of academic charisma. I have perhaps not disentangled these notions sufficiently; but to do so might require another book. In brief, the Enlightenment's notion of fame was shamelessly politico-economic at base. Famous academics meant cash flow and credit for the realm. Romanticism's notion of originality, in my view, mystified the notion of fame by substituting a cultural criterion for the economic one. Academic charisma flowed not from fame, but rather from one's genial originality, the recognition of which generated one's fame (and thus the cash flow and credit and so on).

A traditional historiography—now criticized by others, too—posits an academic crisis, to which the solution would be the foundation of the University of Berlin in 1809/10. A group of prominent Berliners, the Berliner Mittwochsgesellschaft, did indeed criticize academic practices in the 1790s. But the members of that club remained committed to the university tradition, with more or less reform. The club expressed most concern about legal matters, about practice over theory, and about the control of pedantry. Some Germans called for imitation of the new French model, thus called for the institution of specialized schools and academies, in place of the old-fashioned universities, now painted as antiquated guilds and so on. But important defenders of the system existed, such as Kant. Noteworthy is the Göttingen professor and radical racist, Christoph Meiners, whom we met in chapter 11 on the defense of the professorial voice. Meiners polemicized loudly against the destruction of French universities and the institution of special schools and academies in their stead.[17]

## ROMANTIC IDEOLOGIES AND THE
## UNIVERSITY OF BERLIN

The modern academic system was thus under construction, at least in parts of the Germanies, before 1789. Crucial ideologies were forged, nonetheless, only after 1789. Such ideologies emerged especially in response to French military and cultural imperialism. The philosopher Fichte, whom we've met in chapters above, was one of the key architects of the new thinking, especially in his *Deduzierter Plan einer zu Berlin zu errichtenden höhern Lehranstalt . . .* of 1807.[18]

Fichte appeared in chapter 6 on the necessary self-activity, that is, creativity of the doctoral candidate. He stressed the Socratic, dialogical relation of teacher and student, where both conversation and writing played a large part. Academic life was to be one's "home," absorbing the whole person, an end in itself. Fichte set academic life against the utilitarian, commercial demands of civil society and civil service. An instructor must be an autonomous artist, *freier Künstler,* Fichte argued. Here we find the apotheosis and cult of the academic as an academic artist, *wissenschaftlicher Künstler,* the essential oxymoron of modern research. Such notions underlay Fichte's view of the doctorate as a modern masterpiece, a *Meisterstück,* inaugurating a scholar into the veritable priesthood of academia.[19]

F. W. Schleiermacher's *Gelegentliche Gedanken über Universitäten in deutschen Sinn* of 1808 marvelously reflects the Romantic ideology of research. Schleiermacher was a theologian and a philosopher, a professor at Halle then Berlin (and one of the few Prussian professors to have a dossier before 1850). He spoke of the necessary inner unity of the disciplines of learning and thus for the idea of a university. He emphasized the artistic almost to the detriment of the academic or *wissenschaftlich.* Much of the debate revolved around the question concerning how to train the new ruling class. The reaction against France and the Enlightenment became a reaction against the cameralist bureaucrat as technician. The new, elite bureaucrat displayed the charisma of an artist, a Romantic mandarin and a genius.[20]

> As they administer the state, ministers . . . appear to themselves and others more like [Romantic] artists, rather than like those working scientifically. With fortunate foresight, sensing the correct, they unconsciously bring forth and shape with a skillful hand according to an image (*Urbilde*) immanent in them, just like every other artist . . .[21]

Schleiermacher analytically separated the notions of university and academy, then united them in the proper institutions for the pursuit of research. "That is the sense of scientific seminars and practical institutions at the university, all of which have the nature of academies." The essence of the German university—*das Wesen der deutschen Universität*—lay in the unity of sciences and proper education, *Bildung,* even in the specialized disciplines. So Schleiermacher spoke against those "infected by an un-German, corrupting spirit, who recommend to us a reconstruction and dispersal of the universities into special schools."[22]

Schleiermacher argued that ministers should make academic appointments. Academics did usually know whom they should appoint; but, since intrigues and envy ruled academia, academics themselves could not be trusted to make appointments. Schleiermacher advocated the preservation of academic degrees. And the title of the highest degree in arts and sciences should be the doctor of philosophy without further specification of disciplines, for that would well express the unity of the faculty and of knowledge. The higher echelons of the civil service would be restricted to such graduates of the university.[23]

> For the higher civil service, one needs not only an aggregate of well earned knowledge, but also a view of the whole, correct judgment about relations of particular parts, a multifaceted, cultivated ability to synthesize, a wealth of ideas and ancillary methods . . . To pride oneself of this talent, one must have penetrated into the sanctuary of academic knowledge (*in das Heiligtum der Wissenschaft eingedrungen sein*). Thus the state opens it [the sanctuary of knowledge] for its future servants, and will receive them only from it.[24]

Such a modern minister was Wilhelm von Humboldt, made head of the *Sektion für Kultus und Unterricht* in 1808. His was the visible hand behind the constitution of the University of Berlin in 1809/10. Humboldt stayed at his ministerial post less than two years. But his impact on academia, at least ideologically, has been profound. Traditional historiography speaks of an idealistic and Idealist Humboldtian vision, frustrated in practice by Prussian, German, and other academic and politico-economic realities. Again, for our purposes now, it is the Humboldtian ideology itself that is of most interest.

As Napoleon attempted to spread the Université Impériale de France across Europe, Humboldt wrote several position papers for the king and government. In "Antrag auf Errichtung der Universität Berlin" (12 May 1809), he addressed the king's probable ambivalence about founding a university in the old-fashioned form. Humboldt argued that, unlike the new French special schools, the envisaged institution in Berlin must include all the traditional disciplines. Any modern division or omission of the four traditional faculties, he argued, would be harmful for proper academic education, *wissenschaftliche Bildung*. In "Antrag auf Errichtung der Universität Berlin" (24 July 1809), he restated his objection to any division of the faculties into special schools or the like. He stressed the need to bind all relevant academic schools and institutes in Berlin into "an organic whole" via a university, an institution that could grant academic degrees in the traditional sense.[25]

In "Der Königsberger und der Litauische Schulplan" (27 September 1809), a rather unlikely place, Humboldt formulated these now famous phrases on the essence of research.

> The university instructor is no longer the teacher, and the student no longer the taught; the latter rather researches, and the professor guides it . . . Education at the university puts one in a position to grasp the unity of academic knowledge (*Wissenschaft*), and to bring it forth, thus demands creative powers . . . For an insight into academic knowledge as such is a creation, even if a subordinate one . . . To the university is reserved that which one can discover in and through oneself: insight into pure academic knowledge. For this act of self, freedom is necessary, and solitude helpful.[26]

In "Über die innere und äußere Organisation der höheren wissenschaftlichen Anstalten in Berlin" (1809/10), Humboldt explained that a university was essential for uniting academic knowledge with personal formation, *Bildung*.

> It is a further characteristic of advanced institutions of knowledge that they always regard knowledge as a problem not yet solved and thus always remain in [a state of] research . . . The relation between teacher and student thus becomes wholly different from before [at school]. The former is not there for the latter; rather both are there for knowledge . . .[27]

Humboldt argued that one must always treat academic knowledge as something being sought, as a task never perfected. Such knowledge formed no mere collection or aggregate. It was something organic and reaching into the depths. Only pursuit of such knowledge, that is, research, cultivated character. One erred in opposing the university and the academy here. In Germany, professors had developed academic knowledge more than academicians had. And professors usually came to their insights exactly in their role as professor.[28]

Whether or not the University of Berlin, as it became in fact constituted, fulfilled Humboldt's ideals, either at first or ever, is not our concern. Much of the above as expressed by Humboldt certainly had a powerful effect in the realm of ideas and theory, if not in actual practice, and does to this day. Moreover, Humboldt's notion of the relation between a university and an academy of science within it—which, in fact, was the model at Göttingen—became at least de facto the relation between the University of Berlin and the Academy of Sciences there. The members of the Berlin academy formed an elite subset of the university. As at Göttingen, the Berlin academy eventually served essentially as a research and publishing organ for a chosen circle of professors, the cream of the cream of Prussian academia.

René König and Helmut Schelsky have written about Humboldt's notion that solitude and freedom, *Einsamkeit und Freiheit,* were necessary for academic research, and that these entailed an Idealist opposition of state versus society. Idealists saw the state as the general and universal, while civil society embodied the particular and special. Idealists such as Fichte and Humboldt contrasted the pernicious special interests of civil society with the necessary solitude and freedom that should be guaranteed by the state to the university.

On this view, state and university worked together. They opposed the interests of civil society championed by the Enlightenment. But in the end, as Schelsky has argued, the academic politics of both the German Enlightenment and Romanticism—as well as of Idealism and neohumanism—ultimately concerned training civil servants (*Staatsdiener*). They differed only in views on what that meant. And, as König put it, the solution from 1806 to 1810 via Fichte, Schleiermacher, Humboldt, and others was simply to move away from the theory-less enlightened revolutionary to the artistically charismatic Romantic bureaucrat.[29]

The rapid bureaucratization of German academic life in the wake of the so-called Humboldtian reforms would be, then, not a sign of their failure, as the great minister and his epigones may have read them. It would be, rather, a mark of their singular success.[30]

## BEFORE THE REVOLUTION

Up to the 1830s, and perhaps up to 1848 or even later, natural sciences in the German lands had to play on the social-cultural stage erected by philologists and philosophers, by Romantics and Idealists. This meant that the gymnasium and university existed for *Bildung und Kultur.* Proper education (*Bildung*) focused not on pragmatic training (which is *Aus-bildung*), but rather on the sort of spiritual and cultural development articulated above by Idealists and Romantics, such as Fichte, Schleiermacher, and Humboldt.[31]

In the late 1820s and early 1830s, matters about natural science came to a head, as Austria, Bavaria, and Saxony deleted most natural sciences from their gymnasia. They did this for many reasons: to secure more time for Latin, Greek, and other topics relevant to cultural education; to ease the burden on gymnasium pupils, now perceived to be overloaded with too many different subjects; and to combat the waxing dangers of *Industrialismus, Materialismus und Amerikanismus,* which Austria, Bavaria, and Saxony saw as being championed by Prussia, the new enemy, now that France had been tamed.[32]

Lands such as Hanover, Baden, Hessen, and Württemberg shared Prussian ideals, at least in the eyes of Friedrich Thiersch, a philology professor in Munich who spearheaded the attack on industrialism, materialism, and Americanism. The Prussians and their allies, real or imagined, saw Thiersch and his ilk as the party of *Konservatismus, Obscuratismus, und Jesuitismus.* The Prussians advocated the ideology of educational *Universalismus.*

On this view, the gymnasium, like the university, must teach a broad range of fields; but unlike the university, it also must require knowledge of this broad range. (In twentieth-century American universities, the undergraduate breadth requirement recapitulated this view.) Universalism in Prussia and allied lands emerged from a quid pro quo deal between Hegelians and natural scientists, by which philosophy and natural sciences became required parts of the gymnasium curriculum. Prussia's adversaries saw this as overloading.[33]

Thus, pre-1848 natural scientists had to defend their subjects not in the pragmatic, utilitarian terms of the Enlightenment, in which actual or even potential application of knowledge warranted its value. Natural scientists, rather, had to argue for their subjects in view of *Bildung* or Universalism, as opposed to mere training. And they had to battle for a clientele, whence the importance of natural sciences as part of the gymnasium curriculum.

In this context, excepting the medical faculties, the relatively spotty funding of natural sciences continued. At the University of Göttingen, Carl Friedrich Gauss proved an exception to the rule. From 1807 to 1855, as a professor of mathematics with interests in astronomy, geodesy, and electromagnetism, Gauss secured from the ministry in Hanover what he needed for his work, including a new observatory built for him. But Gauss's chief field was mathematics, a field esteemed by neo-Humanists and in which Gauss had been recognized as one of the five greatest mathematicians of all time. It enhanced his value much that the Brothers Humboldt instigated offers for him from Berlin over the course of fifteen years. Gauss got his way without paying much lip service to *Bildung und Kultur*—and despite doing little teaching and allowing his great genius free reign in belittling foes and friends.[34]

Beginning in 1840, Justus Liebig, professor of chemistry at the Hessian University of Gießen, criticized especially Prussia, and argued strongly for state support of university institutes for chemistry. Liebig's polemic had little effect until the 1850s or later. By the early 1840s, Liebig had become internationally famous for his laboratory training of chemists. Liebig had constructed his own chemical institute at the university by tapping an important professional clientele: pharmacists. He pushed further for ties between academic chemistry laboratories and the chemical industry—ties that would in fact first become significant only decades later.[35]

Before midcentury, unless teaching in one of the relatively more well-funded medical schools such as in Berlin, natural scientists typically still had to find private funding for their cabinets and labs, as in the eighteenth century. State-funded university institutes or seminars in natural sciences assumed the form of the seminar for mathematics and mathematical physics at Königsberg (1834) or of the seminar for natural sciences at Bonn (1825).

The seminar at Königsberg constitutes the more exceptional case, since it pursued a more modern research focus, of the sort that Liebig had proven unable to secure for chemistry. Although the Königsberg seminar in fact furthered a substantial amount of pure and applied research in physics, its official mission lay in training mathematics instructors for the entire lands of Brandenburg-Prussia. The directors of this seminar, especially Franz Neumann, took their pedagogical role seriously. As Kathyrn Olesko has described it,

> Neumann's students remembered the seminar thus: Once a week they sat around a table in the university's main building and discussed the mathematical methods of physics. They watched and listened as Neumann, chalk in hand, went back and forth between the table and the blackboard, where he derived the equations he had used in his lectures. At home in the evening, they began the problems he assigned . . . Later in the week, they regrouped in Neumann's teaching laboratory, an extension of the seminar located in his home, where they conducted introductory and advanced measuring exercises, sometimes with instruments of their own design.[36]

After midcentury, the scientific habitus of a Neumann, or a Liebig, or even of a Gauss would become more typical and eventually, as defining a sort of a spectrum, the norm. The seminar for natural sciences at Bonn offered a more common model, in so far as any such seminars or budgeted institutes existed for natural sciences, before the 1850s or 1860s.[37]

In 1825, Prussia funded a seminar for natural sciences in Bonn. In the 1830s, Halle and Königsberg received seminars on the same model, which proved less successful, however, than the original institution in Bonn (the seminar in Königsberg, for example, swiftly falling in the shadow of the seminar for mathematics and mathematical physics). The Bonn seminar embodied one of the last great institutions of *Naturphilosophie* and Romanticism in the sciences. It had five codirectors for its five sections: physics, chemistry, mineralogy, botany, and zoology. The collective directorate and the five sections of the seminar were supposed to represent the unity of nature and natural science. The statutes even enjoined, in addition to one hour per week in each of the five sections, a sixth hour every week attended by all seminarists and all five professors serving as codirectors.[38]

Gert Schubring has studied the Bonn seminar and shown that, despite all odds, the seminar actually enjoyed a golden age from 1855 to 1866. In this period, it trained a good number of the instructors for the new technical schools that blossomed and offered a rival education to the humanistic gymnasium. But after 1866 the seminar fell victim to the division of labor accelerated by the very boom in natural science teaching that had brought the seminar's golden age. After the 1860s, the sort of disciplinary specialization practiced by the likes of Gauss, Liebig, and Neumann set the model for natural science. And the collective directorate enshrined in the Bonn seminar statutes—recalling the collective directorate in many philology seminars that we saw in chapter 5—had become old-fashioned. The typical ordinary professor of a natural science now wanted his own institute to rule alone.[39]

## THE GERMAN COLOSSUS
## AND THE LITTLE BIG MEN

After 1848, and more precisely from the 1860s to the 1910s, the German research university assumed gigantic proportions. As we shall see in sections below, the rest of Europe and North America had to take note and then action.

The historiography of the nineteenth German university system has gone through two phases in fairly recent decades. In the 1960s and 1970s, Joseph Ben-David, Awraham Zloczower, Charles McClelland, and R. Steven Turner, among others, sketched a framework, which this book has called academic "managerial capitalism" and whose roots its has sought to uncover in the early modern era. This phase of research was sociological and generalist in orientation, as framework research generally is. In the 1980s and 1990s a second phase saw historical work by Olesko, Schubring, Turner, David Cahan, Frederic Holmes, Richard Kremer, Timothy Lenoir, Arleen Tuchman, among others, focused on particular individuals and/or more specific, often local, sites, such as a small German land, or a particular field or university, or a particular scientist or laboratory or school of research.[40]

Ben-David was the central figure setting the framework. His work highlighted the role of both ministries and markets in the German system, that is, its managerial capitalism. He also drew attention to the institutional dominance of the ordinary professors, the *Ordinarien-Verfassung*, at German universities, whom, as we'll see, nineteenth-century Oxbridge denounced as the German "professorial oligarchy." In each German faculty a relatively small number of ordinary professors or chair holders controlled the faculty and negotiated its business with the other faculties and the ministry. Ben-David argued that this professorial oligarchy or *Ordinarien-Verfassung* would prove pernicious in the twentieth century, and contribute to the hegemony of the American system that, at least until recently, had fewer oligarchic structures (more about which below). As long as the German system could expand, its professorial constitution remained relatively benign.

> The condition that counteracted the oligarchic tendencies of university senates was the competition among a great number of universities within the large and expanding academic market of the politically decentralized German-speaking areas of Central Europe. Competition among universities checked the development of oppressive academic authority within the individual universities [as long junior academics could sell their services elsewhere].[41]

In other words, as long as German academia enjoyed an expanding market, which lasted from about the 1830s to 1900s, each cohort of young academics could move up and elsewhere in the system (and oppress the next cohort), as long as the seller's market existed. The market forces that early modern Protestant universities had injected into academia contributed the dynamic element, namely the competitive lecturers and junior professors, to the stable structure set by the ministerial bureaucracy and professorial oligarchy.[42]

Ben-David further argued that from about the 1830s to the 1860s, the expanding market grew simply thanks to competition between the individual German universities and states. In the terms of what we have discussed in this book, things like the fashion for certain disciplines, the marketing of certain universities, and the quest for novelty would have driven the expansion. Such internal grounds for the expansion might be more or less ade-quate as an explanation. But the demand for gymnasium instructors also played a role, whence the intensity of the struggle around 1830 about the curriculum. After the 1860s, the tie of laboratory-based university research to medicine and technology clearly drove the expansion, which became massive.[43]

Research in the 1980s and 1990s focused on a fine-grained analysis of all this. Cahan showed that funding for physics remained modest until the 1870s when, beginning with the University of Leipzig in 1872, universities began to establish institutes with their own specially designed buildings. It started with the University of Leipzig in 1872 and ended with the University of Marburg in 1915; such institute-building peaked between 1880 and 1900. Studies by Kremer, Lenoir, Tuchman, Zloczower, and others, on bio-medical sciences, especially physiology, show a similar lack of funding for institutes at universities, with some increase around 1850, followed by a takeoff in and after the 1870s.[44]

From 1870 to 1900, the number of lecturers (*Privatdozenten*) increased by more than 300 percent, and the number of ordinary professors by nearly 100 percent. In 1907, two-thirds of the seminars and labs at German universities had been founded after 1870. In the five year period from 1910 to 1914, Prus-sia, the largest German state, spent 2,000 percent more on science and aca-demia than it had during the ten year period from 1850 to 1859—had it not been for the war, outlays might have approached 5,000 percent more for the 1910s. All of this cost a ("Bégum's") fortune and the management of it con-stituted as complex a task as any in big business. Minister Friedrich Althoff had the portfolio for higher education at the Ministry of Culture in Berlin from 1882 to 1907, and micromanaged this industrialization of German aca-demia in the Second Reich, which Max Weber called the *System Althoff*.[45]

The Little Big Men flourished in the Althoff System. Minister Althoff doubtless did not invent them, but simply followed the genius of the times. To contrast the differences in style and ethos, Lenoir called the system pre-1848 or pre-1860, the "star system." In this regime, a relatively small elite, the stars, such as a Gauss or a Neumann, received the few public funds available for science. Under the Romantic and Humboldtian ideology still holding sway, the stars among natural scientists, like philologists and philosophers, educated and cultivated the elite, the ruling class of bureaucrats. Post-1860, what would become the Althoff System embraced industry over culture, "as science was self-consciously harnessed to the needs of the nascent, indus-trializing, capitalist economy" of the Second Reich. The massive expansion meant that not just the Big Men could get funding for institutes.[46]

To rephrase Lenoir's point, after 1860 everyone could be a star, however dim. The slow dissolution of the Bonn seminar for natural sciences, traced above by Schubring, indicated the triumph of specialization over the unity sought by Romanticism, and pointed to the crystallization of an academic personality system that could not work under the auspices of collective directorates. The Romantic cult of personality not only persisted in the post-1848 brave new world of industrialism, materialism and Americanism, but also grew. A German ordinary professor, who had previously only controlled his chair, now sought to have and hold "his institute." While a chair gave the professor only disposal over some amount of capital, usually small, an institute gave the director control over disciples.[47]

## AUSTRIA AND THE COLOSSUS

England has given the counterpoint to the major motif of Germanic academia in this book, while Austria has provided a counterpoint within the major motif. Close but at once distant—or with "intimate distance" (Peter Becker)—the Austrians have served as the most astute critics of German practices. But they gave in, too.[48]

In Austria the troubles in Europe in 1848 led to a movement to assimilate the German system. A petition of Viennese professors and students in March 1848 demanded "freedom of teaching and learning," *Lehr- und Lernfreiheit,* on what they saw as the German model. By April significant changes, viewed as liberalization by the reformers, were underway.

The Austrians introduced German-style requirements for becoming a lecturer—an *Habilitation* to be a *Privatdozent.* This led to the abolition of the French-style exam for an academic position, the *Konkursprüfung.* Austrian universities remained, like the German, state institutions. But the state now guaranteed freedom in teaching and research, and fostered a research mentality in explicit imitation of the Germans. That included a proliferation of university institutes with budgets: in Vienna, a historical-philological seminar (1850), a physical institute (1850), a mineralogical institute (1850), a meteorological institute (1851), and so on, all in the philosophy faculty at first. Other institutes in other faculties soon followed, but provincial universities did not find much favor until the post-1860 boom.

Conservative resistance to the reforms of 1848/50 made them provisional. Only in 1867 did the envisaged changes come to full fruition. The first significant changes of doctoral graduation requirements in the philosophy faculty since 1786 did not appear until 1872. The new regulations required a German-style dissertation and an exam relevant only to the area of the dissertation, instead of, as previously, to the whole discipline. The 1870s saw the expansion of institutes in Vienna and elsewhere. In 1886 the deconfessionalization of Austrian universities made them wholly secular, state institutions for the first time.

## FROM GEORGIAN TO VICTORIAN ENGLAND

In this book, as noted, English academic practices have served as the major counterpoint to those in Germany. From the perspective of this study, only in the articulation of the grading system did the English or, rather, the Cambridge men prove themselves more radical modernizers than Germans and Jesuits.[49]

Sheldon Rothblatt has argued for the lack of a meritocratic ideal at Oxbridge before the nineteenth century. But John Gascoigne, for example, while acknowledging the probable lack of a meritocratic ideal to account for the origins of the Senate House Examination pre-1750, holds that Rothblatt's view needs some qualification when one considers later developments. One must attend to the use of the Senate House Exam and/or college exams as part of the criteria for awarding fellowships. To be sure, election of fellows varied widely within and between colleges. Some were chosen by founders or their heirs. Some were chosen by quotas set by locales. Some were chosen by electoral colleges of fellows.[50]

And some were chosen by other complex rules. But the eighteenth century did see attempts to make appointments more meritocratic. Trinity College, Cambridge, circa 1700, had set up examinations for scholarships and fellows. The master and seniors fellows met with and reviewed candidates, although the rigor of the process differed from year to year, depending on the committee's composition. Post-1750 other colleges also appear to have moved to choosing at least some fellows via adjudged merit. For example, at St John's from the 1770s onwards, a majority of successful candidates for fellowships had been wranglers or achieved high marks in the Senate House Exam. Larger colleges like St John's could easily use meritocratic criteria since they usually had their own large pool of wranglers from which to choose fellows. Smaller colleges might be compelled and loath to appoint wranglers from other colleges. But, on the whole, by the second half of eighteenth century, performance in the Senate House Exam, later the Tripos, shows a strong and rising correlation with attaining a fellowship. And, from 1753 to 1800, all Senior Wranglers, save one, attained fellowships.

Cambridge "degree courses at the beginning of the nineteenth century were, with one notable exception, much the same as they had been in the

Middle Ages," as Winstanley noted. That meant that professors, at the heart of the German system, continued to have a marginal status at Cambridge. In the first half of the nineteenth century, Cambridge professors did begin to hold their lectures more regularly. But since salaries still stemmed from endowments, sometimes quite old, professorial pay remained typically too meager to support intelligent life. So professors had to make money elsewhere and somehow.[51]

Despite new notions of choosing fellows in view of merit, few real changes emerged in methods to choose professors. Medieval conceptions of appointment—based on protocols and electoral colleges instituted in founders' wills—continued in force. "Therefore, almost inevitably, professorial election, though free from the disfiguring scandals of the eighteenth century, were sometimes determined by considerations which ought not to have been taken into account." A meritocracy did not come easily, especially at traditional Oxbridge.[52]

Oxford had nineteen professors in 1800, and twenty-five by 1854. Its professors were also chosen in various ways, but mostly by various colleges of electors. As at Cambridge, professorial lectures still lay mostly outside the curriculum for examination. Likewise as at Cambridge, the small endowments and salaries of most chairs led most professors to be nonresident by 1800, and thus to lecture little or not at all. By 1800 fellows generally held their position in life tenure, with the proviso of celibacy. At least at Oxford, most fellows did not serve their time as mere idlers. Indeed, the fellows made up most of the dons, the senior academics. At the beginning of the century, however, a don was a clergyman in the first instance, not an academic. The nineteenth century also saw the rise of the coaches, that is, private tutors who prepared students for the ever more demanding exams.[53]

As the nineteenth century wore on, Oxbridge dons and professors came in for more and more abuse. They did not have to face the sort of hands-on abuse meted out by the French as they went about trying to reform Continental academic practices. Abuse in England was largely literary and mostly extramural. In defense of the Protestant German system against the new French system, Meiners, in Hanoverian Göttingen, did not hesitate to point out that it was Oxbridge, not Göttingen, that needed to be fundamentally reformed.

> If one wants that to happen then, from the top down, or in the name of the government, one must carefully look through all freedoms and statutes, and renew the useful freedoms and regulations, and repeal or restrict the harmful. One must especially completely abolish independence, which is illegal

and highly pernicious to schools of higher learning themselves, and with that [repeal as well] the right to make new statutes and arbitrarily interpret old ones . . . , and in place of autonomy, one must introduce a constant Inspection or a powerful *Curatorium*.[54]

More serious than Meiners's critiques from across the channel, beginning in 1802 the *Edinburgh Review* became the locus for attacks on Oxbridge learning disguised as reviews of foreign literature. In England itself, Whigs and radicals deployed praise of German universities—well or poorly understood—as implicit or explicit critique of Oxbridge. Tories on the whole spoke against any German influences. Critiques of Oxbridge, especially those issuing from the *Edinburgh Review,* intensified around 1808 to 1810 and elicited a now famous response in 1810 by Edward Copleston, Fellow of Oriel College, Oxford. Perhaps unbeknownst to himself, Copleston's defense of Oxbridge traditions can be heard as an English variant of the virtually simultaneous defense of the renovation of the university as an institution in Romantic Berlin, especially that by Schleiermacher as cited above.[55]

Copleston defended the tradition of the gentleman, while Schleiermacher and his colleagues in Berlin were trying to reconceive the statesman as artist bureaucrat. Both Copleston in Oxford and the Romantics in Berlin opposed calls for a more pragmatic, utilitarian education. They opposed, that is, the Enlightenment. In defense of the Oxbridge ideal of the gentleman, Copleston famously argued for mental discipline.

The point of true education lay neither in amassing information nor in acquiring technical skills. True education lay in perfecting mental discipline. And for that, something difficult and, above all, useless seemed best—whence Oxford's fetishism of classics, and Cambridge's of useless mathematics. To much the same end, Romantics in Berlin were proposing classics and, instead of useless mathematics, metaphysics. Misunderstanding the new German practice of the seminar, Copleston insisted that Oxbridge's intimate education by tutors was an active one, instead of the passive one of listening to professorial lectures.

The late 1820s and 1830s brought, on the one hand, a soberer view to some about the academic utopia of Germany. It also occasioned, on the other hand, a new fear that foreign universities might be changing for the better, while the English were not. The *Edinburgh Review* got back into the act in 1831 by publishing an attack on Oxbridge by William Hamilton. He argued, perhaps unfairly, that not merit but rather patronage, if not mere accident, governed the choice of fellows. Hamilton called for a royal commission to investigate and to reform the two English universities. Other attacks on the dons pointed to the "ideal of the professorial system as it existed on the Continent and particularly in Germany" as the model to emulate. After 1830, critique began to mount. Some wanted the universities to be pragmatic and useful. Others wanted a truly liberal education. Still others found the Anglican cast of Oxbridge to be the principal problem.[56]

The Tractarian movement at Oxford offered one response to the critique. This movement centered on J. H. Newman, whom Annan called "the charismatic don," as none had "ever captivated Oxford" as he had. The Tractarian movement echoed Copleston's call for preservation of liberal education and had parallels to Fichte's view of a proper university as enunciated in Romantic Berlin. Essentially late Romantic, Newman's agenda amounted to a restoration of what he saw as a truly Anglican or even Catholic tradition. Thus the Tractarians opposed any secularization of the universities and any orientation on utility.[57]

Like Copleston, Tractarians distinguished a mere communication of knowledge from a proper education, which also concerned the heart. Tractarians spoke against turning Oxford into "some Prussian or French academy." Upon the defection of Newman and other Tractarians to Rome, extramural critique mounted. By the 1840s most critics wanted university lecturers and professors strengthened over against college fellows and tutors. Later in life, Newman set the terms of the times as the party of professors versus that of the tutors. The *Edinburgh Review,* a tool of the University of Edinburgh, championed the cause of the professors. The question was "whether a University should be conducted on the system of [German and Scottish] Professors, or on the system of Colleges and College Tutors."[58]

In this climate, the University of London opened as a public institution in 1836. The model of the University of Edinburgh and the German system inspired the foundation in London. It based itself on University College (1826/28) and King's College (1829/31), both private institutions. Outside Oxbridge, private natural science laboratories opened, for instance, at King's College London in 1835 and at Edinburgh in 1840.[59]

After the 1830s, Oxford increased the intensity of examinations in an effort to reform itself. The effect was "to empty the benches at professorial lectures." Such lectures, still not part of the normal exams for degrees, seemed more and more a mere luxury. Much the same happened at Cambridge, where a modernization of parts of the curriculum made them otiose. Holders of science chairs began to take their duties seriously, and laid to plans build research facilities. But such plans bore no fruit. Despite improvements in professorial lectures, in the 1840s fewer and fewer students attended them. "Science lectures held neither the attraction of relevancy [for exams] nor of entertainment, especially when Cambridge professors became concerned with keeping pace with scientific developments."[60]

If the early modern era began in England, academically, with Thomas Cromwell's appointment as royal visitor to Oxford and Cambridge in 1535, one might well say that the modern era began, academically and belatedly, with the appointment of the Graham Commission as royal visitor to Oxford and Cambridge in 1850. The commission sat until 1852, or even later in spirit, if one counts the resistance, especially at Cambridge, to the commission. The vice-chancellor of Cambridge in fact had dubbed the commission "without the form of law, and . . . unconstitutional." He said he would not cooperate and kept his word. The chancellor of Oxford, the duke of Wellington, agreed that the commission was not legal but, as it turned out, Oxford proved far more cooperative than did Cambridge. We'll thus consider the case of Oxford here, and neglect Cambridge, mostly.[61]

The royal commission's report emphasized the need to create a "scholarly profession" at Oxford (and Cambridge too). The commission stressed the importance of the professorate, as opposed to the collegiate organization. It urged the integration of professors into the tutorial system. The visitors recommended suppressing some fellowships so that monies would be available to support university professors and lecturers. The commission envisaged a new hierarchy in which college fellows and tutors would be at the bottom and mostly do what the coaches did. Fellows would be appointed only by merit and would no longer be a rung in the Church hierarchy. Next in precedence would be the university lecturers. At the summit, in truly Germanic spirit, the august university professors would preside over the university. The visitors wanted, further, to set up four professorial boards, effectively four faculties or divisions. These boards would be composed of professors and would have sole control of the examination system and the appointment of lecturers. This proposed Germanic oligarchy of full professors was, not unexpectedly, greeted without much applause. Many Oxbridge academics wanted professors to be better integrated, but not given the power of an oligarchy.[62]

Proposals drawn up by the Oxford Tutors' Association—formed by sixty tutors upon the recommendation of the commission—seemed to offer the best hope for effective reforms. The tutors agreed with the commission about many of the problems, but not about solutions. The tutors favored a professionalization of themselves. Here they pointed with praise to the case of Germany, "where the German teacher is a scholar or philosopher by profession, instead of being compelled, as too often the case at Oxford, to take up scholarship or philosophy as a mere temporary occupation." But the tutors spoke against imposition of a German professorial system and its oligarchic bent. They favored a collegiate system, properly reformed. In the Germanic professorial system, they saw a cult of personality, with "too much importance to the person teaching and too little to the things taught." The tutors spoke for expansion and better integration of the professorate, but against domination by it, which would "'make way for the energetic rule of an official despotism.'"[63]

The official report of the Hebdomadal Board, that is, the Oxford establishment, also opposed "German ideals of professorial dominance." But, not surprisingly, the board at base simply defended existing institutions. Such a proposal implied that the royal visitation had been a waste of time. The compromise reached in the Oxford University Bill of 1854 essentially followed recommendations of the Tutors' Association. The bill left colleges to remodel their own statutes, and put no professorate in charge of the university. The major change consisted in making fellowship appointments more rigorously on the basis of merit.[64]

Further changes came then in fits and starts and usually college by college. By the end of the nineteenth century, fellowships would be linked to teaching, research, and/or administration. But in 1850s fellows had still fought successfully against such an idea. And, in 1872/73 when a large body of reformers at Cambridge insisted that tenured fellowships should be tied to teaching, learning, or science, the Master of Sidney Sussex might still accuse the reformers of drawing their inspiration from German universities. "A Prussian is Prussian and an Englishman an Englishman," he said, "and God forbid it should be otherwise." The master contended that the university's only function was to conduct examinations, and that all teaching, including the support of laboratories, could be managed by the colleges.[65]

Events proved the master wrong. The problems posed to the English tradition by the Germans and the French concerned not only colleges versus faculties or universities, but also the individual versus the state. The stress on individualism and self-help in English academia meant resistance to a notion that the state had a positive role to play. Only after Britain's poor showing at the Great International Exhibition in Paris in 1867 did broad sentiment for more state support of research arise, at least for physical sciences.

The Devonshire Commission, meeting from 1870 to 1876, recommended state support for laboratories and research grants. But the government ignored most of those proposals, choosing instead to direct support through other channels. An address by A. Grant on the educational system of Prussia at the Royal Society of Edinburgh in 1871 had noted that "the problem facing British higher education was how to tap the state's resources without becoming a victim of centralizing bureaucracy" (as in fact happened by the 1990s). Grant nonetheless saw Prussian state support as key and "he ruefully compared the University of Berlin with that of Edinburgh." Laboratories had appeared at some British universities, but cash flowed too feebly to keep them running as impressively as the well-oiled Prussian universities. Thus in "the mid-Victorian period critics of British universities frequently looked to the German universities for inspiration and models."[66]

That meant setting up laboratories as budgeted institutes, at least for the natural sciences. The period after 1866 celebrated the rise of university labs in Britain. William Thomson's private laboratory (1847–55) at the University of Glasgow was the first teaching-research institute at a British university on the German model. Thomson's lab was privately financed in part and actually turned a profit from patents for the director, which he, however, mostly recapitalized in lab equipment. In 1866 Glasgow officially integrated Thomson's lab into the university. New university laboratories arose at University College London and at Oxford in 1866, then in 1868 at Edinburgh and King's College London, and so on. This culminated with the opening of the Cavendish at Cambridge in 1874. In the 1870s specialized teaching on the German model became the rule at university laboratories in Britain. In the 1880s, contemporaries sensed a revolution was taking place. Every university of importance, it was said, must have facilities for science. In 1882 the University of Cambridge required the colleges to give funds for university lectureships and chairs.[67]

If I had to choose one institution as the epitome of the infiltration of the modern, German academic system of research, I would choose that rite that officially creates the researcher: the modern doctor of philosophy, and its cognates, writing an original dissertation. As noted in chapter 6, in Britain the doctor of science entered the University of London between 1857 and 1860, and the doctor of literature in 1868. Cambridge awarded its first D. Phil. in 1882. Oxford held out until 1917. Edinburgh held out even later, as it did not award its first comparable Ph.D. till 1919, though the D.Sc. had emerged in 1895.[68]

## POST-NAPOLEONIC FRANCE AND THE GERMAN PROBLEM

Historians commonly set the decisive event for Britain's awakening at its poor showing at the International Exhibition in Paris in 1867, although some also mention Prussia's defeat of Austria in 1866. France's awakening came from her poor showing in the Franco-Prussian War of 1870/71, the

*Ur-Blitzkrieg.* The Romantic German university had defined itself against the French separation of universities and academies, and the dissolution of universities into specialized schools and academies. Adoption of German practices thus proved especially touchy in France.

Despite post-Napoleonic reforms, the essential academic structures of the Napoleonic period stayed long intact. The first exam or *concours* for the new *agrégation* took place in 1821. Regulations stipulated that chairs in *collèges royaux* were to be filled from the *agréges,* that is, from those who passed the exam. For the faculties above and beyond the colleges, ministers and administrators enforced the requirement of the doctorate in science more slowly. It took till the 1830s to institute the requirements fully. The burdens of examining and teaching in France were not excessive, and became actually less so after 1841. But the increased bureaucratization made professors more and more state functionaries.

The greatest concern for a French professor, especially in the provinces, lay in scaring up an audience. The system gave great impetus to efforts to appeal to a wide public in lectures. Robert Fox notes, "It is clear that the most successful performers, far from resenting their public role, reveled in *haute vulgarisation.*" The need and desire to lecture to a wide public eventually constituted a dilemma for professors who aspired to what they saw as high professional status. At midcentury some protested against a system that seemed to most reward the professorial voice, that is, performance in lecture. The strong oral part of the *agrégation* favored the rhetorically skilled; the "glibness and the mastery of an immense body of received truths were the qualities that brought academic success."[69]

Up to midcentury, the doctorate did not appear to mean much. Doctoral theses or dissertations were usually relatively brief and written with little apparent supervision. Around midcentury, ministerial policies shifted to favor the cultivation of "modest teachers," in place of great and perhaps dangerous orators or Germanic Big Men. Ministerial supervision grew more meticulous after 1851 and a definite politicization of research developed. Ministers held that academic work should be uncontroversial and, if possible, patriotic.

George Weisz has noted that the "basic structure of this system remained intact until the very end of the nineteenth century. Expansion generally followed the logic of functional specialization. Whenever the need for a new kind of specialist was felt, it was met by the establishment of another [specialized] teaching institution." Nonetheless, the 1850s and 1860s saw more and more critique. Reformers endeavored to open France to outside influences, in particular to those of Germany's prosperous and seemingly autonomous universities. Founded in 1858, *Revue germanique* became a vehicle to awaken France to the rising specter of Germany. Such attention to international models went against the grain of state policy in the 1850s and early 1860s. The university system was still dominated by the *agrégation,* which was officially required only for teaching at secondary schools, but in fact required for most university positions as well. Passing the *agrégation* thus continued to dominate educational goals, which meant that students learned rhetorical skills and encyclopedic knowledge.[70]

Ministerial sentiments changed with the appointment of Victor Duruy as minister of public instruction in 1863. Duruy sent French students and academics to universities in Switzerland, Belgium, and Germany. Most returned thinking German academia was better. French doctoral theses or dissertations seem to have increased in size and seriousness, from the 1840s to 1870s, but so did the typical academic's age on completion of the doctorate. "The doctorate often represented a man's lifework, completed relatively late in a career and making advancement possible," as Weisz noted. The French doctorate did not have the aura of the German one as a rite of passage into life as a researcher. Attacks on Duruy led him to resign in 1869. But clamors for reform did not cease. And most in France could soon not ignore, in Fox's words, "the continuing rise of the German universities as centers of research. The standard of the German universities was now the standard to be emulated."[71]

After the Franco-Prussian War of 1870/71, a broad sentiment emerged that French academics had fallen behind the German. Many attributed the French military failure to excessive bureaucracy. Observers as diverse as Louis Pasteur, Ernest Renan, and Emile Zola thought that Prussia had beaten France thanks to the excellence of German science. From 1871 to 1914, "la référence allemande" dominated French academic worries. Numerous articles on the German university system appeared and their number far exceeded that on any other nation. Reformers sought to combine the functions of teaching and research as in Germany.

Serious moves to create *grands universitaires à la Allemagne* only began after 1880 and first saw fruition in the decrees of 1896 setting up the modern French university system. Such universities still performed for a nonacademic audience, although now not a polite one, but rather the industrial-commercial bourgeoisie. French research thus tended to be dominated by concerns of direct utility, as opposed to the ideology of pure research, at least nominally holding sway in Germany. But French or at least Parisian academics had "benefited hugely from the young Republic's determination to outshine the Germans."[72]

In 1915 and 1916, while France waged the Great War against Germany,

Pierre Duhem addressed the specter of German academia in a series of lectures and papers. His musings cast interesting light on the German Colossus as seen from the perspective of a French academic in the provinces, Bordeaux to be exact. Duhem remarks about the German natural sciences that

> in each of these laboratories, as huge as factories, there works a constellation of students with military discipline. Each of them aspires to acquire the envied title of "Doctor" in a reasonable time. Each candidate receives one of the numerous but similar inferences from a theory. The testing of each of these inferences will afford the matter of the students' inaugural dissertations, the slender thesis which their doctorates will crown. The theory is always verified, without complications, without incident, in the allotted time . . . When a theory is accepted by *Herr Professor* and is thus true, they cannot conceive how the consequences which can be rigorously drawn from it could be false.[73]

Duhem criticized this factory and military system as ultimately self-referential, if not circular. The disciples' research, including their doctoral dissertations, will never come into conflict with the framework or theory set out by the director, *Herr Professor*. In another place, in the same lecture series, Duhem likened the German system to a monastery as well. This military-factory, monastic Germanic machine threatened the "civilized" world.

> When, in a dream of the future, Professor Ostwald catches sight of the Europe he desires, Europe organized by a German triumph, he configures it entirely like one of those vast chemistry laboratories on which the universities beyond the Rhine pride themselves. There, each student punctually, scrupulously, carries out the small bit of work which the chief has entrusted to him. He does not discuss the task which he has received . . . He does not feel any desire to put some variety into his work . . . A toothed gear exactly meshed into a precise mechanism, he is happy to turn as the rule says he should turn . . . By virtue of his natural tendencies, he lives in the laboratory . . . in the same fashion as, by virtue of his vows, the Benedictine or the Carthusian lives in his monastery.[74]

## THE ADVENT OF THE RESEARCH UNIVERSITY IN THE UNITED STATES

As Josiah Royce recalled in 1891:

> a generation that dreamt of nothing but the German University. England was passed by. It was then understood not to be scholarly enough. France,

too, was then neglected. German scholarship was our master and our guide
. . . One went to Germany still a doubter . . . ; one returned an idealist, . . .
burning for a chance to help build the American University.[75]

American academics had taken notice of German research and universities
as early as the 1850s. By the 1870s, they dominated American academic dis-
cussions. The symbolic event came in 1876, when Johns Hopkins was
founded on the model of German research university and, as Veysey noted,
"immediately symbolized German research."[76]

Modern graduate training began to take sure shape at Hopkins, as well
as at the University of Chicago, Harvard University, and Columbia University in the 1880s. The 1890s constituted the takeoff decade for the diffusion of the graduate school in America. The peak of student matriculation
at German universities came in 1895/96. Thereafter a more sober view set in
about the German university, as many sensed that American graduate programs had attained near or actual parity. But in "the final quarter of the
nineteenth century, few academic Americans who embraced the ideal of
scientific research failed to acknowledge an intellectual debt to an explicitly
German style of educational experience."[77]

Thus Veysey's chapter on American experiences in and of Germany is
entitled "Research." The turn to the German model of a university and to
research meant the notion of pure knowledge. In the American context,
that appeared to be antidemocratic, elitist, and antipopular. The new
research-oriented professor apparently did not write for the unwashed
masses. As in France, a tension grew between direct utility and pure, perhaps ultimately useless, research. What Americans thought they saw in
Germany did not match what the Germans saw in their universities. The
German rhetoric—that *Wissenschaft* as research was organic, whole, Idealist, and so on—largely eluded most Americans, other than Transcenden-
talists and some Pragmatists.

Most Americans registered only the claim to autonomy and the actual
rigor and micrology of German practitioners. Americans missed the loftier,
rhetorical notions behind the micrology and the rigor. "An insufficiently
differentiated Germany, partly real and partly imaginary, became the symbol for all scientific claims upon American education." Perhaps Americans
actually discerned the new essence of the Althoff System at work in Germany.[78]

The American research university developed its own dynamic. "The
dominant characteristic of the new American universities was their ability
to shelter specialized departments of knowledge," as Veysey put it. Joseph

Ben-David saw that as the crucial difference, as opposed to Germany, where the faculties and institutes still centered on chairs, which restricted new divisions of academic labor. The institution of the budgeted department at American universities preserved collegial or, in modern terms, egalitarian aspects of the traditional university. It also allowed for a rather swift reallocation of resources to drop or add professorial slots by field, in tune with the ways of research or the fashion of the times. The departmental structure in the United States, even with its various ranks of professor, effectively inhibited a Germanic professorial oligarchy of chair holders and institute directors.[79]

## "WISSENSCHAFT ALS BERUF" (1919)

Comparing the American with the German system, Weber notes, "In the United States [as opposed to Germany], the bureaucratic system obtains." Is it not a shock to hear that things in *Amerika* are more bureaucratic than in Germany?[80]

Weber makes the remark while explaining the differing practices of remuneration as regards German lecturers (*Privatdozenten*) and American assistant professors. At that time, German lecturers still received no salary. They lived from student lecture fees and other sources of income. But the German lecturer could not be terminated and, moreover, could see the faculty as morally obliged to look after him, more or less. Despite centuries of rationalization, practices of patronage held and hold sway in paternalistic German academia.

In *Amerika,* the assistant professor gets a salary, but can be terminated until tenured. The notion of tenure forms, indeed, a central part of the academic bureaucracy. But Weber focused his comparison on the salary. He saw that as the bureaucratic moment in *Amerika,* while nonetheless pointing to the very unbureaucratic and rather more capitalistic practice of being able to fire assistant professors. The subsequent *Amerikanization* of academia, even in Germany, has led to a profound penetration of market ideologies and capitalistic values in academia—admittedly hardly as virulent anywhere else in the world as in the United States.

> Now we can see with clarity that here [in Germany] the newest development of the university system is running in the American direction in broad sectors of academia (*Wissenschaft*). Large institutes of the medical or natural science sort are "state capital" undertakings . . . And there appears there the same circumstance as everywhere where capitalistic production

takes hold: the "separation of workers from the means of production." The worker, that is, the assistant relies on tools of labor as supplied by the state. He is thus just as dependent on the institute director as is an employee in a factory—for the institute director conceives, quite credulously, the institute as "his" institute, and sets the rules there in.[81]

But the central theme of "Wissenschaft als Beruf" is not the above proletarianization of lecturers, assistants, and other subaltern academics. It is, rather, *Hasard,* a nice notion not easy to translate. It comes close to meaning "chance," as bound up with games of chance (*Hasardspiele*). "Haphazard" is not so far away in sense. Academia as a vocation would be then characterized by the haphazard, by chance or fortune, as well as by fame—or because of it. Weber treats two aspects of academic chance or fortune, *Hasard:* externally, concerning appointments and promotions, and internally, concerning academic works and their supposed originality.

Concerning appointments, he relates that he knows of no other occupation where accident and fortune play such a role as in academia. That stems in part, he thinks, from the perpetuation of traditional academic manners in the practice of voting on appointments. In a famous comparison, he turns to long-standing practices of the College of Cardinals as papal electors, as well as to (earlier) party practices of electors who selected candidates to stand for election as U.S. president. The sociology of voting on such things uncovers the strange result that, in some putatively objective sense, the "best" candidate is seldom chosen. The second or, more likely, the third "best" commonly wins such a vote in which collegial-committee negotiations play a large role. If such were true in academia, it would at least remove appointments from the realm of the haphazard and give them their own lovely logic.[82]

*Hasard* as chance or luck further holds sway over the academic's ability to play the dual role dictated by the Germanic as opposed to the old French system: the academic researcher must also be a teacher. The Humboldtian ideology canonized that union. Weber notes that academics such as Ranke and Helmholtz—eminent researchers and abysmal teachers—are no rarity. Setting his sentiments on the side of research, he bemoans the importance in a career—haphazard for research—that the professorial voice plays.

> The number of students in a lecture is a quantifiable, graspable index of proving oneself, while the quality of scholarship is imponderable and above all regarding bold innovations often (and quite naturally) contested. Thus everything usually stands under the influence of the inestimable blessing and worth of large student numbers. When one holds a lecturer to be a poor

teacher, it's usually an academic death sentence, even should the scholarship be the best. But the question concerning whether one is a good or poor teacher is answered by the number of students who honor one. And it is a fact that the circumstance that students flock to a teacher is determined to the largest extent by pure externals—temperament, even the tone of voice—to a degree that one should not think possible.[83]

Weber turns then to the internal *Hasard* afflicting academia as a vocation. Success depends on originality, which he designates with cognates of *Einfall,* and which I can only translate as "inspiration." To succeed as an academic, one's work must show some inspiration. "But this inspiration does not allow itself to be compelled . . . Inspiration does not replace work. And work for its part cannot replace or compel inspiration." Weber relates that Helmholtz found his best inspiration by strolls up gently rising streets. If one does not have such a sure recipe, one may often sit at one's desk working and waiting, and in vain. All ultimately depends on whether one is blessed by fate with a gift. Notions of the gifted bring Weber to the modern Germanic cult of academic personality, which he denounces.[84]

## THE HARNACK PRINCIPLE AND THE DIRECTOR'S APOTHEOSIS

During the cold war, François Mauriac exclaimed, "I love Germany so much, I prefer that there's two of them" (*J'aime tellement l'Allemagne que je préfère qu'il y en ait deux*). In 1989 the Berlin Wall fell. By autumn 1990 there were no longer two to love. West and East Germany united—or, rather, the West took over the East. As a result, the academic system in East Germany dissolved.

East Germany had developed a sort of "holier than thou" brand of Marxist-Leninism. East German ideology officially rejected charismatic notions such as the Harnack principle because Communist ideology denounced the cult of personality in academia, while of course pursuing it obsessively politically, and doubtless also behind the scenes academically. Communists stressed the collective over the individual, and this had a ramifying effect at least on the appearance if not on the production of academics and work.

Concomitant with the dissolution of the East German system in the 1990s, academic gossip in West Germany noted a new virulence in the *Ordinarien-Verfassung* of German universities. In other words, the professorial oligarchy grew more imperial. Discussion of the Harnack principle seems to have intensified, too. Indeed, a nearly seven-hundred-page book, including apparatus, about the principle appeared in 1996.[85]

The Harnack principle forms the putative basis setting the role of institute directors in the MPG (Max-Planck-Gesellschaft), the postwar reincarnation of the KWG (Kaiser-Wilhelm-Gesellschaft), the preeminent academic-scientific research body in Germany since 1911. In its barest form, the Harnack principle states: Do not erect academic institutes around a specific field, and then search for a director; rather, recognize academics of extraordinary ability, and erect research institutes around them and what they do. This is the cult of the charismatic academic in its highest modern form: directors matter more than disciplines.[86]

In 1989, Rudolf Vierhaus, codirector of the MPI (Max-Planck-Institute) for History, wrote an article on the myth and reality of the Harnack principle in the KWG-MPG. Vierhaus argued that the practice of the KWG-MPG on the whole belied adherence to the Harnack principle. But he showed the persistence of a rather long-standing ideological embrace of it, as a sort of academic fantasy about KWG-MPG practice. Vierhaus indicated that Adolf von Harnack had never formulated an actual principle about institute directors, let alone named it after himself. This raised the question concerning whether Harnack would have subscribed to the principle bearing his name. I shall not try to resolve that question.[87]

Adolf Harnack had been a professor of theology in Leipzig and Gießen, and had received an offer from Harvard in 1885, before moving to Marburg in 1886 and Berlin in 1888. He might seem an unlikely person to have such a principle named after him. But *Wissenschaft* includes all academic disciplines, and Harnack's power bears witness to the seriousness with which German state and society treated disciplines other than natural sciences at the time. From 1888 until his death in 1930, Harnack enjoyed great power. In 1890 the Prussian Academy of Sciences in Berlin elected him a member. In 1905 he became provisional and in 1906 formal director of the Royal Library in Berlin. In and after 1911 he served as founding and first president of the KWG. Along with these positions, Harnack sat on the sorts of councils and committees that influential academics typically sit on. In 1914 the king ennobled him, so a "von" entered his name.[88]

Harnack's career fell in the time of the emergence of the Second Reich after the defeat of France in 1870/71. This was the time of first modern economic boom in Germany, and the massive funding of German universities, which had already been well funded in comparison with the rest of the world. In 1904, Harnack and Weber, among other German academics, attended a world scientific congress in St. Louis, Missouri. The academic, scientific, and technical development of the United States astonished the German academic visitors and produced conflicting feelings about America. Apropos nationalist sentiments, the visit added fuel to waxing fears of German stasis or even decline. After an all too brief generation or two of political might, economic boom, and academic supremacy, would Germany be eclipsed by America? (In 1989 Dieter Kronzucker and Lothar Emmerich published a book, *Das amerikanische Jahrhundert* [The American Century], whose title hazards an answer.)

For Weber's part, the visit to America provided a vivid picture of what he would characterize in 1917/19 in "Wissenschaft als Beruf" as the Americanization of academia. One could debate whether the Althoff System, which Weber rejected, amounted to the same thing, so that the Weber's construct called "Amerika" represented as much a projection of German fears and fantasies as did the novel *Amerika* that Franz Kafka began in 1911. But in the face of this industrial brave new world, homegrown or not, a good part of the German academic community had fallen into a despair as they faced what Fritz Ringer called the "decline of the German mandarins," a crisis of authority keenly felt from the 1890s onward.[89]

In the grasp of this *fin de siècle* malaise, many German academics felt that German universities had forsaken true Humboldtian ideals of learning and had become fixated on the micrology of research (which was, indeed, what many Americans thought they had found there to emulate) to the neglect of *Bildung und Kultur,* education and culture. If a Nietzschean oeuvre exists, it concerns this crisis and conflict about modernity. Nietzsche did not envisage the Zarathustrian *Übermensch* or superman as a Führer of either Germany or a Kaiser-Wilhelm/Max-Planck Institute. But the notion leads us back to the Harnack principle, and the theology professor's response to the crisis of culture and modernity.

In 1905, a year after the visit to the United States, Harnack published "Vom Großbetrieb der Wissenschaft," a soon and still much cited essay, whose title I would paraphrase as: On Academia as Big Business. The Harnack principle traces one of its roots to this essay. The theology professor opened by mentioning the recently planned exchange of academics between Germany and the United States, as discussed by Minister Althoff and the president of Harvard. Harnack then took the bull by the horns. "Academic knowledge (*Wissenschaft*) is at base and ultimately a matter for the individual (*Sache des Einzelnen*)." But the modern world has compelled us to admit that conventional forms of academic production no longer suffice.

Thus if one speaks today against Academia as Big Business (*den Großbe-trieb der Wissenschaften*)—the word is not pretty, but I find none better—one knows not what one does. And whoever seeks to limit the progressive expansion of this method of mastering the world works to the detriment of the community. We know well the dangers of this business—mechanization of the work, overemphasis on collecting and processing materials as opposed to spiritually penetrating them, and not to mention a sort of stupefaction (*Verblödung*) of the workers—but we are able to preserve ourselves and our co-workers (*Mitarbeiter*) from all these dangers.[90]

Toward the end, the essay returns to the theme of academic exchange and notes that "we" or, actually, a quasi-passive voice—the powers-that-be—have decided that the first exchange will be between Harvard and Berlin, which Harnack terms a humble beginning.[91]

Minister Althoff retired in 1907 and died in 1908. In 1910 the University of Berlin was to celebrate its first centennial. In view of that event, as well as the ongoing discussion about a solution to the crisis of education, culture, and modernity, the Kaiser or his ministers asked Harnack to write a *Denkschrift*, a position paper. Harnack did and his position in the *Denkschrift* of 1909 entailed setting up the sort of society that became the Kaiser-Wilhelm-Gesellschaft, with the sort of institutes that became the Kaiser-Wilhelm Institutes. Harnack never headed a KWI, but he became the president of the KWG and held office until 1930.[92]

In the "Denkschrift" of 1909, Harnack began with a summary of the ideals and practices of the Humboldtian University and why one now needed to supplement them. The Humboldtian ideal, which necessarily bound the researcher to the teacher, might be kept for mere professors, but the modern state needed a corps of truly elite academics freed from the burdens of teaching. For, at the onset of the twentieth century, Germany faced the specter of being surpassed in science and academia by foreign powers, especially by the United States. Harnack advised the creation of research institutes outside the official university system. The institutes would be supported by the German state as well as by captains of industry and capital.

It is very important not to specialize in advance the aims of the institutes to be founded, but rather to give them the widest scope. The institutes should receive their particular line of work (*Arbeitsrichtung*) from the personality of the scholar directing them, as well as from the course of knowledge.[93]

The last sentence set another pillar for the later enunciation of the Harnack principle, although not by the man himself. The theology professor accepted the Romantic-Hegelian notion that every academic had a charismatic spark of genius, "for—even if to a humble extent—every personality has geniality." But the institutes that Harnack envisaged would be directed by individuals of singular geniality, who alone should receive life-tenure at them, and whose "personalities," as he noted, would determine the research of each institute.[94]

In January 1911 the Kaiser-Wilhelm-Gesellschaft came into being with Harnack as its first president. In 1930, in perhaps Harnack's last public report on the KWG, he noted that thirty-four institutes had come into existence since 1911—far more than one institute per year on average. In 1930 he underlined that one of the chief grounds for founding the KWG lay in the inability of the German university system to keep pace with the progress of specialization. In the KWG, one strove to set up institutes to engage in research that the universities, given their essential basis in professorial chairs, could not easily pursue.[95]

The remark has a twofold import. First, it implicitly located the source of the problem, which the KWG supposedly solved, as inhering in the *Ordinarien-Verfassung* of German universities. As noted, American universities had developed the more egalitarian and dynamic structure of departments. This proved able to adapt to and to further progressive specialization better than the German system, in which a rather small number of *Ordinarien* or chair holders ruled over knowledge. Second, it belied any literal truth to the later so-called Harnack principle. For the guiding decision to found KWIs would consist not in recognizing geniuses in need of power, but rather in discerning new fields in neglect at the university, thanks to the professorial oligarchy and its inability to integrate or allow new fields.[96]

Vierhaus has shown that, despite Harnack's remarks in 1930, in 1928 he had come the closest to formulating his eponymous principle: "The Society [KWG] chooses the director and builds an institute around him." In the year of Harnack's death, Friedrich Glum, the general secretary of the KWG, echoed the first president's remark of 1928. Glum said, "The Kaiser-Wilhelm-Gesellschaft should not build institutes and then search for the proper man for them, but rather first find the man and then build an institute around him." Harnack died in 1930 and thus, happily, did not have to experience the alarming institution of the Führer principle as a general maxim in German state and society after 1933.[97]

After 1945 East and West Germany developed in similar and different directions until 1990. The university systems remained more or less in conflict with Humboldtian ideals and modern capitalist and communist realities. The headquarters of the Prussian Academy of Sciences abided in East Berlin, so the East Germans designed their elite institutes around it. In 1989, the Academy of Sciences in East Germany ran seventy-two institutes, with about 23,000 staff members, who mostly divided the little work to do equally. From 1945 to 1948, the KWG arose from the ashes in West Germany, reborn as the MPG, the Max-Planck-Gesellschaft, renamed after the KWG's second president. In 1986, the seventy-fifth anniversary of the society, it possessed sixty-three institutes and 8,500 staff, including academics and engineers.[98]

The MPG upheld the Harnack principle ideologically, now canonized as such, while continuing to pursue more realistic policies in practice. But the power of ideology is reflected in the following anecdote and gossip. In 1968, the MPG resolved to set up an MPI for Researching the Living Conditions of the Scientific-Technical World (*MPI zur Erforschung der Lebensbedingungen der wissenschaftlich-technischen Welt*) in Starnberg, Bavaria, with Carl Friedrich Freiherr von Weizsäcker as founding director. The institute opened in 1970. Jürgen Habermas arrived as codirector in 1971. In 1979 Weizsäcker retired; the section he directed was closed; and the institute was renamed the *MPI für Sozialwissenschaften*. This was completely closed in 1983/84, although Habermas stood ten years before his retirement (in any case, too left-wing for some, he had already moved his work elsewhere after 1981). Gossip had it then and later that Freiherr von Weizsäcker had said in essence, but which I cannot so nicely rhyme in English, "Without me, it's no go *(Ohne mich, geht's nicht)*."[99]

## "I MUST BRING YOU TO MY CENTER"

In 1984, Grant Fjermedal published *Magic Bullets*. It chronicles his quest to find the doctors and directors at work inventing the magic bullets of medicine. The quest, however, led him to the discovery of the waxing monster of the university-biotechnology complex. By chapter 11 of his book, the mask begins to fall from the noble visages Fjermedal had first thought to see. Everywhere he looks, he sees a web of academic-corporate corruption. Biomedical professors and directors of public health institutions in the United States pay lip service to notions of conflict of interest. But, when one looks closely, one finds they are large stockholders or even CEOs of firms that privately capitalize the products of university and publicly funded research, done to great extent by postdocs.

Fjermedal remarked to Robert Day, director of the Fred Hutchinson

Cancer Research Center in Seattle, a nonprofit center with ties to the University of Washington, "If a general owned stock in a defense company, it would be all over the newspaper," if he had an equity position in companies with which he did business. Dr. Day said, "Sure. Sure, sure. Right . . . On the other hand, a policy [for academics] that allows some flexibility and some judgment doesn't seem to me to be necessarily a bad policy. It's how it's carried out that counts."[100]

Flexibility or exceptionalism? On 7 December 2003, the *Los Angeles Times* published an extensive article by David Willman, based on research that the newspaper had begun in 1998. Willman and the *Los Angeles Times* found that many of the directors and top researchers at the U.S. National Institutes of Health (NIH) privately profited from the research that the government paid for—that is, they profited privately from publicly funded research. But it was worse.

> Increasingly, outside payments to NIH scientists are being hidden from public view. Relying in part on a 1998 legal opinion, NIH officials now allow more than 94% of the agency's top-paid employees to keep their consulting incoming confidential. As a result, NIH is one of the most secretive agencies in the federal government when it comes to financial disclosures . . . The trend toward secrecy among NIH scientists goes beyond their failure to report outside income. Many of them routinely sign confidentiality agreements with their corporate employers.[101]

The deputy director of the NIH, Dr. Ruth Kirschstein, remarked, "I think NIH scientists, NIH directors and all staff are highly ethical people with enormous integrity." But Willman found numerous instances of what an outside observer would deem conflict of interest. He found cases of NIH directors and top scientists leading publicly funded clinical trials for drugs to be marketed by certain companies. But, as it turns out, those very same companies either paid the relevant directors and scientists consulting fees, or had given the directors and scientists equity positions. All of this had been kept confidential, that is, secret, until the newspaper's investigative enquiries uncovered and exposed them.[102]

In other words, the directors and scientists had private interests at odds with the possibility that their publicly funded research indicate negative results in clinical trials. By the bureaucratic or professional norms of most groups, such behavior would not be tolerated. The investigative reporting by the newspaper led in subsequent months to congressional scrutiny and regulation of such NIH policies.[103]

At the heart of our modern bureaucratic regime, has the cult of the charismatic Führer not only made academia Big Business, but also created a neofeudalism, a plutocratic order of academic nobility, of directors and Big Men and, now, Big Women who, in view of their superior "ethics," disparage conflict of interest norms mandated for other professions? We have seen that the nobility traditionally has had little grasp of the bureaucratic metaphysics of the home versus the office, and thus cannot distinguish a private from a public, professional self.

In chapter 1, so long ago, it seemed that natural scientists would be most adept at making the modern bureaucratic distinction between public and private, since they work far less at home than professors in the human and social sciences do. Perhaps that was just wishful thinking. In an earlier work, I had in fact presumed that the mentality of traditional Romance—epic and folktale—inhabited scientists, as opposed to the mentality of realism that has governed the novel and middle-class thinking since the Enlightenment. In chapter 9 here, I introduced the notion of clerical Romance to get a grip on the mentality behind Minster Vacchieri's journal. But to explain the mentality and habitus induced by the modern world of the charismatic Führer, perhaps we need a general notion of academic Romance.[104]

In chapter 9, I appealed to Frye's work on traditional Romance: "In every age the ruling social or intellectual class tends to project its ideals in some form of Romance." In traditional Romance, the ruling class is noble. If the ruling class alters, then the conditions constituting nobility need to alter, for instance, from birth to brains. Frye calls this the kidnapping of Romance, the process by which a newly ascendant elite absorbs and adapts the mentality. "Romance usually presents us with a hierarchical social order, and in what we have called kidnapped Romance, this order is rationalized," which is sort of the feat of charismatic rationality that we have been doggedly pursuing in this book.[105]

In Romance the "chief characters live in a kind of atomized society: there is only the most shadowy sense of a community, and their kings and princesses are individuals given the maximum of leisure, privacy and freedom of action . . . The same disintegrated society appears in the cells of hermits, . . . [and] the knights errant who wander far from courts and castles." Perhaps this disintegrated and atomized society, with a shadowy sense of community, rules the small world of charismatic academics who wander from this to that conference, parleying, battling, charming, and enamoring other heroes of knowledge or their bachelors and maidens fair. A Romantic hero is a singular individual, whose communal sense is weak, and the source of whose action lies in him (or her) as charisma or genius, or outside, though this outside is not social, but rather like fate or fortune—or luck in Nordic sagas.[106]

Has an oppressive modern bureaucratic discipline, coupled with the dissolution of academic community in the modern regime of research, created such a neofeudal order of academic plutocrats? Here is an interesting true confession by a famous modern academic:

> Philip Swallow, however, was a rather dim academic . . . He was only a lecturer who hadn't published anything, and he was very diffident in personal relations. So I had to re-jig his character to some extent, or at least explain why, in the intervening ten years, he'd developed. First of all I made him head of department. Then I made him more sexually adventurous . . . I have observed that some men in middle age become, suddenly, more attractive to women. They seem to develop a kind of charisma they never had before. I know at least one person to whom this happened very strikingly, and it happened as a result of going off to conferences, actually.[107]

In the above interview, David Lodge explained that he had written the novel *Small World: An Academic Romance* of 1984 as a modern day Arthurian Romance. Should one see the cunning of history (or something) at work in that decision? Lodge went on to say that he had in fact used Frye's work on traditional Romance as a guide on how to plot the novel—a novel in which department head and Professor Philip Swallow develops marvelous charisma that Lecturer Swallow did not posses in *Changing Places* of 1975.

In *Small World* Morris Zap explains—a decade before the advent of the internet—that top academics now partake of a global university, thanks to airlines, telephones, and Xerox. An elite circle of academics—professors of literary criticism in the novel—meet each other in various parts of the world at conferences, a source then of their power. The most important thing about such conferences, besides the gossip and conversation, is of course the food.

The novel's subplot involves a quest to obtain a UNESCO chair for literary criticism. The 1984 novel now seems dated in this regard, for this grail sought by the top lit crit academics is a mere chair, albeit a "conceptual" one with no duties, no residency obligations anywhere, a secretarial staff in Paris, and $100K salary in tax-free U.S. dollars (a paltry sum by 1989). Two of the contestants for this grail are the nefarious and (as vicious gossip would have it) ex-Nazi, Professor Siegfried von Turpitz, and the enchantress Professor Fulvia Morgana, a wealthy Italian Marxist, of noble lineage, exploiting the contradictions in the system.

The waxing academic proletariat and body of plebs marvel that life imitates art and, in awe of the modern Wolffs rationalizing themselves more of the pie in the twenty-first century, hope a Professor Morgana will perhaps deign to remember their name and, without asking them to kneel or kiss her ring, say sincerely, "I must bring you to my Center."

## THE MASKED PHILOSOPHER

Interviewed by Christian Delacampagne for *Le monde* on 6 April 1980, the Masked Philosopher echoed Weber's lament about the modern cult of personality. Delacampagne's first question concerned, of course, the mask. To this the Masked expressed a longing for a relation with a reader undistorted by the noise of his big name. (Once one has a big name, thanks to the noise, one is no longer really heard.) Proposing a year in which all would be published anonymously, the Masked sighed: No one would publish anything.

"It is too bad I did not have time to combat in you your pernicious Foucaultian reading of Weber's rationalization theories!" One of my teachers wrote that to me, after I had left my alma mater as a freshly baked doctor of philosophy and was teaching at a small liberal arts college where, in 1989, I began the troubled Urtext from which this unforeseen book emerged. My teacher's comment took me by surprise. I had presumed that the sort of work I had undertaken would be read, if not as an *apologia* for academics, then rather as a long-winded diatribe on the ultimate identity of narcissism and nihilism. That goes to show that things are not always what they seem and how wrong you can be.

This book seems to be about how academics became who and what they were and maybe are. It is about authority and autonomy in relation to academic power and knowledge, things about which Max Weber and Michel Foucault cared deeply. I have written this study of a subspecies of *homo sapiens* from the Renaissance to Romanticism—a subspecies from which I am descended—in a Socratic-Freudian belief that self-knowledge is liberating, if not curative. But academic confessional and apologetic works trace a perilous path between the alternation of love and hate, if not of one's friends and enemies, then of one's self.

Nietzsche once said that in seeking knowledge one must be able not only to love one's enemies but also to hate one's friends. Not as bold, and I hope to be not as foolhardy as Nietzsche, I want to have my cake and eat it too. Thus, though this book also calls into question the modern Germanic-Romantic regime of academic knowledge, it was meant as a work of research. It is an academic work about academics and their works, and above all about that subsubspecies that historians of such things, tolerant of very curious origins, have seen as our own progenitor: *homo academicus germanicus protestantus.*

When he was once speaking with Goethe on the nature of tragedy, Napoleon said that the moderns distinguished themselves from the ancients in that we no longer have a fate . . . and, in place of ancient fate, politics has arisen [*La politique est la fatalité*]. This must be used then as the new fate for tragedy, as the irresistible force of circumstances to which individuality must cede.[108]

Instead, Weber resigned himself to the iron cage of bureaucracy. In the Germanic world, bureaucracy—not politics—had replaced the ancients' fate. And the market has become our fortune. Interviewer Delacampagne and the Masked eventually came to discuss the noisy circus of the market and the media. Despite the din, the Masked argued against insulating the mandarins from the market. One must rather "know how to set the differences in play."[109]

# Appendix 1

## List 1. University of Leipzig, 1499

Lectures and Exercises for Master's Degree (in Groschen)

| Fee | Lecture Course | Length of Course |
|-----|----------------|------------------|
| 6 | *Ethics* | 6 to 9 months |
| 6 | *Metaphysics* | " " " " |
| 6 | *The Elements* | " " " " |
| 6 | *Politics* | 5 to 6 months |
| 4 | *Rhetoric* | 3 to 4 months |
| 4 | *De caelo* | " " " " |
| 4 | *Meteorologica* | " " " " |
| 3 | *Perspectiva communis* | 3 months to 14 weeks |
| 3 | *Topics* | " " " " " |
| 3 | *De generatione* | 5 weeks to 2 months |
| 2 | *Theorica planetarum* | 5 to 6 weeks |
| 1 | *Musica Muris* | 3 weeks to 1 month |
| 1 | *Arismetrica communis* | " " " " " |
| 1 | *Oeconomica* | 3 weeks |

Drawn by the author from University of Leipzig 1861, 461.

## List 2. University of Leipzig, 1558

Philosophy Professors and Salary (in Florin)

| Chair | Salary | Lecture Hour |
|-------|--------|--------------|
| Greek, Latin, Ethics, and Politics | 300 | 3:00 p.m. |
| Aristotle (Logic and Metaphysics) | 150 | 4:00 p.m. |
| Mathematics (Astronomy)* | 150 | 9:00 a.m. |
| Physics | 100 | 6:00 a.m. |
| Rhetoric | 100 | 1:00 p.m. |
| Poetics | 100 | 12:00 Noon |
| Mathematics (Elementary) | 60 | 2:00 p.m. |
| Grammar | 60 | 4:00 p.m. |
| Dialectics | 50 | 8:00 a.m. |

* Plus perhaps a supplement.
Drawn by the author from University of Leipzig 1861, 521–22.

# Appendix 2

*Notes:* Publication of lecture catalogues does not seem to have been regular in the sixteenth century (Tholuck 1853–54, 1:96). Until the eighteenth century, university libraries and archives do not generally seem to possess complete runs of the university's own lecture catalogue. Given the current state of research (or of my knowledge of it), we appear to be in a vicious circle here. From Schröder's *Vorläufiges Verzeichnis der in Bibliotheken und Archiven vorhandenen Vorlesungsverzeichnisse*. . . (1964), we do not know how complete the extant collections of lecture catalogue are because we do not know when regular publication began. In list 1, table 1, and table 2 below, dates in many cases represent the earliest exemplars I could find. One could, however, hope to find more catalogues in the ministerial archives that are little or not at all represented in Schröder's survey. Further search of periodicals for *Gelehrte Sachen* and the like in the eighteenth century would doubtless turn up more catalogues and necessitate alteration of some dates below.

## List 1. Universities in German Cultural Space

Printed Lecture Catalogues—First Known by Decree or Appearance

| Latin Pre-Eighteenth Century | German Pre-Nineteenth Century |
|---|---|
| 1507 Wittenberg | 1729 Halle |
| 1518 Leipzig | 1742 Rinteln |
| 1520 Rostock | 1744 Erlangen |
| 1557 Cologne (SJ) | 1745 Helmstedt |
| 1557 Vienna (SJ) | 1748 Göttingen |
| 1557 Tübingen | 1749 Marburg |
| 1560 Marburg | 1748 Freiburg im Br. |
| 1561 Mainz (SJ) | 1750 Duisburg |
| 1561 Trier (SJ) | 1753 Strasbourg |
| 1564 Jena | 1765 Jena |
| 1564 Dillingen (SJ) | 1765 Greifswald |
| 1565 Innsbruck (SJ) | 1766 Rostock |
| 1566 Olmouc (SJ) | 1768 Wittenberg |
| 1567 Würzburg (SJ) | 1769 Erfurt |
| 1568 Ingolstadt (SJ) | 1770 Königsberg ? |
| 1568 Greifswald | 1771 Prague |
| 1576 Altdorf | 1771 Vienna |
| 1576 Helmstedt | 1771 Tyrnau |
| 1611 Duisburg | 1773 Leipzig |
| 1611 Frankfurt a.d.O. | 1776 Olmouc |
| 1629 Gießen | 1784 Ingolstadt |
| 1635 Königsberg | 1785 Würzburg |
| 1655 Heidelberg | 1786 Marburg |
| 1666 Rinteln | 1787 Dillingen |
| 1666 Kiel | 1787 Cologne |
| 1666 Basel | 1792 Frankfurt a.d.O. |
| 1694 Halle | 1792 Salzburg |
| | 1792 Breslau |

## Table 1. Number of Universities in German Cultural Space

Printed Lecture Catalogues—First Known by Decree or Appearance

```
10        J
 9        J                                               g
 8        J                                       g       g
 7        J                                       G       g g
 6        J                                       G       g g g
 5        J                                       G       G G g
 4      P J                                       G       G G g
 3        J P                    P                G       G C G g
 2   P    J P P        P         P                P G G C C g
 1 P P    P P P    P P P    P P       P    P G P P G P C C G
   00 10 20 30 40 50 60 70 80 90 00 10 20 30 40 50 60 70 80 90 00 10 20 30 40 50 60 70 80 90

         16th century              17th century              18th century
```

Key to Chart B:
P = Protestant, Latin language
G = Protestant, German language
J = Jesuit (SJ), Latin language
C = non-Jesuit Catholic, Latin language
g = non-Jesuit Catholic, German language

## Table 2. First Known Lecture Catalogues Ordered in Whole or Part by Disciplines

| Year | Latin<br>All Faculties | Latin<br>Lower Faculty | German<br>All Faculties | German<br>Lower Faculty |
|---|---|---|---|---|
| 1507 | | Wittenberg | | |
| 1564 | | Jena | | |
| 1755 | | | Göttingen | |
| 1765 | | | Jena | |
| 1766 | | | Rostock | |
| 1768/69 | (Halle?) | | (Halle?) | |
| 1769 | | | Erfurt | |
| 1770 | Duisburg<br>Königsberg | | (Königsberg?) | |
| 1771 | Halle | | Prague | Prague |
| 1773 | | | Leipzig | |
| 1775 | | | Greifswald | |
| 1782 | | | Strasbourg | |
| 1783 | | | Erlangen | |
| 1787 | Frankfurt a.d.O. | | Heidelberg | |
| 1790 | | | Kiel | |
| 1792 | | | Breslau | |
| 1798 | | | Marburg | |

*Notes:*
IL: Latin language lecture catalogues (from *Index Lectionum*)
VV: German language catalogues (from *Vorlesungs-Verzeichnis*).
WS: *Wintersemester*
SS: *Sommersemester*
AJ: *auf das Jahr*
UB: *Universitätsbibliothek.*
Unless stated otherwise, the primary principle ordering lecture catalogues is by faculties in the order: theology, jurisprudence, medicine, arts and philosophy. The secondary principle will be referred to as either by professor (the most common method in the IL), or by disciplines (the new method in the VV).

Altdorf: IL 1576 extant (Schröder 1964). No VV found.

Bamberg: Post-Jesuit IL AJ 1776/77 extant (Schröder 1964).

Basel: IL first printed in 1666, and after 1681 regularly (Staehelin 1957, 123f; Bonjour 1960, 273). IL, 1681, extant (Schröder 1964).

Bonn: IL 1783 extant (Schröder 1964).

Breslau (Wroclaw): In *Schlesische Provinzialblätter*, 1792, 15/4:348–53, VV ordered by disciplines.

Bützow: IL extant 1761/62 (Schröder 1964). Hölscher (1885) reprints no lecture catalogue. As the university first opened in 1760, a catalogue was probably printed as advertisement, perhaps with the *Programm* of 20 Oct. 1760, or later in the *Annalen der Rostocker Akademie.*

Cologne: IL, seemingly first 1557, then at least 1558, 1560–63 by the Jesuits (Society of Jesus 1896, 307, 315; 1965– [1974], 108:527ff, 541ff; Hengst 1981, 103, 112f). VV, 1787, 1789–93 at UB Köln (Schröder 1964).

Dillingen: IL, seemingly first 1564, by the Jesuits (Society of Jesus 1965–[1974], 108:556ff). Post-Jesuit IL AJ 1777; VV, 1787, has only the Phil. Fac. VV (Schröder 1964).

Duisburg: IL, 1611, extant (Schröder 1964). In *Berlinische Bibliothek . . .*, 1750, 4/2:282–84, VV is ordered by professors. At BerlSA, I. HA. Rep. 34, Nr. 58a. 1, 1762–82, fol. 13–15 (1764), 17–18 (1764), 21–25 (1764/65), have ILs ordered by professors and written reports as lists of lectures with comments in German; fol. 237–38 and 293–94 have the ILs for SS 1769 and 1770 ordered by professors; fol. 390–91 have the IL for WS 1770 ordered by disciplines; at fol. 380, in a letter of 3 Dec. 1770, the university says that it is responding to a ministerial rescript of 26 May, which I could not locate in this act. At BerlSA, I. HA. Rep. 76. alt. II. Nr. 302, Bd. I, 1787–95, fol. 2–3, the IL for SS 1787 is ordered by disciplines; fol. 103 contains the unfoliated 7 page IL for SS 1793: the public (pp. 4–5) and private (pp. 5–7) courses are separated, with the public lectures ordered by professors, excepting medicine, which is de facto by disciplines, and with the private courses ordered by disciplines.

Erfurt: IL WS 1718/19 extant (Schröder 1964). In *Erfurtische gelehrte Zeitungen*, Nr. 24, 24 March 1769, 187–89, VV ordered by disciplines—"Wir liefern, nach der Gewohnheit anderer Universitäten, einen Auszug desselben, in der Ordnung der verschiedenen Wissenschaften" (187); in ibid., Nr. 74, 15 Sept. 1769, 593–600, VV ordered by professors—"Wir zeigen für diesmahl die hiesige Vorlesungen für das künftige halbe Jahr, nicht nach der Ordnung der Wissenschaften, an; sondern auf Verlangen einiger Leser, nach der Ordnung der akademischen Lehrer" (593).

Erlangen: IL 1742/43 extant (Schröder 1964). In *Erlangische Anzeiger*, Nr. xviii, 30 March 1744, 141–42, VV ordered by professors; in ibid., Nr. xxxvi, 1752, 287–88, VV ordered by professors. In *Erlangische Gelehrte Anmerkungen*, Nr. 44, 29 Oct. 1782, 394–400, VV is ordered by professors; in ibid., Nr. 12, 18 March 1783, 99–107, VV ordered by disciplines; dates before and after those two match that pattern. Lecture catalgoue is under ministerial supervision by 1769 (Engelhardt 1843, 56f).

Frankfurt a.d.O.: Reform of 1611 mandated that Professors in the annual report also relate what they will lecture on in the coming year, and that this should be published as a lecture catalogue (University of Frankurt a.d.O. 1897–1906, 3:92). "Anzeigen einzelner Vorlesungen," 1592–1601, exist in the UB Greifswald (Schröder 1964). These are not recorded here, since they were probably only ads for individual professors. In *Schlesische Provinzialblätter*, 1792, 15/5:[496–99], VV ordered by professors; in ibid., 1794, 19/4:[411–16], ditto; survey of issues in between shows the same. At BerlSA, I. HA. Rep. 76. alt. II. Nr. 197, Bd. I, *Vorlesungen* 1787–96, contains ILs ordered by disciplines, beginning in SS 1787 (fol. 2–5). Freiburg im Br.: 1748 VV extant. UA Freiburg im Br. has "Aufzählungen von Vorlesungen" for Freiburg im Br., 1748, AJ 1752/53, ca. 1769, AJ 1773/74–1777/78, 1785/86, 1795/96 (Schröder 1964).

Fulda: IL extant 1770 (Schröder 1964).

Gießen: IL extant 1629 (Schröder 1964).

Göttingen: IL extant 1736 (Schröder 1964). VV seems to first appear for SS 1748; first actually ordered by discplines in WS 1755/56. See *Göttingische Zeitungen von gelehrten Sachen, 1748, Zugabe zum Märzmonat, Stück* 31, 241–48. *Göttingische Anzeigen von gelehrten Sachen,* 1755, 29 Sept., *Zugabe zum Stück* 117, 1085–98.

Greifswald: A 1568 visitation for Greifswald mandated a catalogue (Pommerania 1765–1802, ser. 1, 2:819f; Kosegarten 1856–57, 2:130). Tholuck (1853–54, 1:96) cites Balthasar (1775, 441) claiming an IL is extant in 1571, but the latter source cites a "seriem lectionum" taken from the annals of the philosophy faculty, which were probably not published at the time: this looks like an internal lecture list. A 1666 visitation ordered that a catalogue would be published and sent with other reports to the ministry; in 1702 the university was ordered to hand out the catalogue in the church (Pommerania 1765–1802, ser. 1, 2:889f, 928). IL, 1685, extant (Schröder 1964). In *Neue Critische Nachrichten,* 1765, Nr. 42, 342–44, VV ordered by professors; in ibid., 1774, Nr, 41, 321–23, ditto; issues in between show the same. On 11 May 1775, a visitation commission to Greifswald ordered that henceforth the rector would give the chancellor each term a tabular list of the classes taught that year, and this was to be ordered according to disciplines so that the chancellor "can inspect without effort what has been done or what has been lacking" (Pommerania 1765–1802, ser. 2, 2:119). UB has VV 1776, 77, 77/78, 1800/01 (Schröder 1964)

Halle: IL, 1694 and 1695 (in Schrader 1894, 2:368–76). In *Wöchentliche Hallische Anzeigen,* Nr. ix, 26 Sept. 1729, 129–24 and 145–51, VV for WS ordered by professors; thereafter by professors, up to Nr. xlii, 16 Oct. 1769, 735–42. Neither IL nor VV found in *(Neue) Hallische Gelehrte Zeitungen,* 1767–70; 1771 et seq. not seen. VV 1772 et seq. in *(Neue) Hallische Gelehrte Zeitungen.* VV, 1803 et seq. in *Allgemeine Literaturzeitung.* UB Halle has *Anzeigen einzelner Vorlesungen* for individual professors (Schröder 1964). Following on a ministerial visitation, the University of Halle was ordered in 1768 to produce a lecture catalogue from then on structured by the disciplines (Brandenburg-Prussia 1754–1822, 4:5049–62, at 5053–54). Halle's lecture catalogue stands under ministerial supervision at least by 1730 (Bornhak 1900, 131f). BerlSA, I. HA, Rep. 52, 159, Nr. 1, 1723–68, has nothing relevant; Nr. 1, 1771–72, has ILs and VVs beginning in 1771/72, with the ILs by discipline, and the VVs traditionally as by person; Nr. 10, 1691–1782, has ILs and VVs from 1779 showing the same. That is the inverse of what was becoming typical.

Heidelberg: Ordered to produce a catalogue in 1655 to attract students; this perhaps went out of practice, as in 1671 the senate moves to publish a catalogue "wie auch früher"; 1773, the elector again enjoins publication, now in time to be appear in the *Mannheimer Zeitungsblatt* (University of Heidelberg 1886, 1:389f; 2:202, 213, 222, 279). IL, 1655, extant; VV, 1777, handwritten; VV 1778/79 *in Frankfurter Gelehrter Anzeigen,* Nr. 82/83, then apparently no longer printed there; 1785– published separately (Schröder 1964). At Göttingen UB, VV SS 1787: ordered by disciplines.

Helmstedt: IL, 1576, extant; VV 1745–1799 in *Braunschweigische Anzeigen* at ehem. UB Helmstedt and StB Braunschweig (Schröder 1964).

Ingolstadt: IL, seemingly first 1561, by the Jesuits (Society of Jesus 1965-[1974], 108:572ff). IL, earliest extant thereafter, 1571 (Schröder 1964). VV AJ 1784/85 at SArch f. Oberbayern, Munich; VV AJ 1789/90 at SB Regensburg; VV AJ 1798-99 at UB Marburg (Schröder 1964).

Innsbruck: IL, seemingly first 1565, by the Jesuits (Society of Jesus 1965-[1974], 108:565f). Later, neither IL nor VV was typical; the first IL after the early Jesuit ones seems to be from 1780 (Luca 1782, 91).

Jena: IL extant as handwritten, 1554; first extant printed, 1564/65 (Schröder 1964). IL, 1564, reprinted in *Neue Beyträge zur Litteratur besonders des sechzehnten Jahrhunderts*, 1793, 4/2:61-74. In this IL of 1564, the superior faculties are ordered by professors and no times of lectures are given; the inferior faculty is ordered by disciplines—Grammar (Latin and Greek), Hebrew, Dialectics and Rhetoric, Geometry, Astronomy, Physics, Philosophy, Ethics, Disputational, and Style Lessons—and no times are given. The 1591 statutes order a catalogue to be printed (University of Jena 1900, 63). In *Jenaischen Zeitungen von gelehrten Sachen*, 1749, no catalogue was found; in ibid., Nr. 26, 4 April 1750, 201-4, VV ordered by professors; Nr. 30, 13 April 1754, 233-37, ditto; issues in between surveyed and show the same. In *Jenaische Zeitungen von gelehrten Sachen*, 1765, Nr. xxxii, 22 April 1765, 274-88, VV for SS ordered by disciplines; in ibid., Nr. lxxxv, 25 Oct. 1765, 747-59, VV for WS ditto.

Kiel: Kiel's statutes of 1666 set up a lecture catalogue to be published semesterly and sent the sovereign (Schleswig-Holstein 1832, 367f, 429f). IL extant 1689 (Schröder 1964). In *Schleswig-Holstein Provinzialbericht*, 1790, 4:182-90, VV ordered by disciplines.

Königsberg: The oldest IL known to Arnoldt (1746-69, I/1, 188f) comes from 1635. On 8 March 1672, the ministry noted a printed lecture catalogue had appeared last term and commanded a lecture catalogue be produced henceforth (Brandenburg-Prussia 1721, 288ff; Arnoldt 1746-69, I/1, 188f, 199ff; I:2, 4087f). In 1770 the *Großkanzler* Fürst ordered a lecture catalogue structured in terms of the disciplines. The IL had this form (Selle 1944, 179f; Universität Königsberg 1999, 1:xlii; 2:307-12). BerlSA, XX HA, EM 139b, Nr. 25, Bd. 4, 1766-70, has ILs in the traditional form; Bd. 5, 1770-72, has ILs by faculty then by disciplines beginning in 1770/71.

Leipzig: Published IL, 1518, noted in a letter to Spalatin by Martin Luther (vol. 1, fol 63b: cited in *Neue Beyträge zur Litteratur besonders des sechzehnten Jahrhunderts*, 1792, 3/2:57). Tholuck (1853-54, 1:96) cites Seidemann (1843, 159) claiming an IL is extant from 1535, but the latter source cites only a report of the university to the elector, wherein it lists the instructors and, in part, what they are teaching. 1641, extant but only for the Phil. Fac.; VV, 1777 et seq. regularly at UB Leipzig (Schröder 1964). In 1773 the Elector of Saxony ordered the university to make sure that the semiannual lecture catalogue appeared at the "proper time," that is, before the beginning of the relevant semester; moreover, the catalogue now began appearing for the first time in German as well as Latin (Schulze 1810, 95). *Neue Zeitungen von gelehrten Sachen* (Leipzig), Nr. lix, 8 July 1773, 425-40, has the first VV and it is ordered by disciplines. The next is in ibid., Nr. lxxxiii, 18 Oct. 1773, 665-80, also ordered by disciplines. Thereafter regularly so in ibid. No VV was found in ibid. for 1770, 1771; nor for randomly checked issues pre-1770.

Mainz: IL, seemingly first in 1561 by the Jesuits (Society of Jesus 1965-[1974], 108:538ff). Post-Jesuit IL 1784/85 (Schröder 1964). According to Schröder 1964: VV, at UArch Mainz, *Kurmainzischen Hof- und Staatskalender*, 1745-98 with VV; at

Göttingen UB, ibid., 1787–92, has only lists of the faculty. VV, 1785 et seq. in *Mainzer Anzeigen von gelehrten Sachen* in UB Mainz (Schröder 1964).

Marburg: 1560 statutes order a catalogue to be printed (University of Marbung 1977, 176f). First extant IL is 1644; VV in UB Marburg and SArch, 1786 (Schröder). In *Marburgische Beyträge zur Gelehrsamkeit nebst den Neuigkeiten der Universitäten Marburg und Rinteln*, 1749, Nr. 2, 376–79, VV ordered by professors; ibid., Nr. 4, 180–83, ditto. At Göttingen UB, VV SS 1798/99: ordered by discipline.

Olmouc: IL, seemingly first 1566, by the Jesuits (Society of Jesus 1965–[1974], 108:566f). VV AJ 1776, 1778–82, 92–99, 1801 et seq. (Schröder 1964).

Prague: VV AJ 1784 et seq. at Statni Knihovna Universitni Knihovna Praha (Schröder 1964). In *Neue Litteratur...*, (August 1771–Feb. 1772), Nr. 16, 23 Nov. 1771, 241–56, VV for WS ordered by disciplines; in *Prager gelehrten Nachrichten*, Nr. 8, 19 Nov. 1771, 126–28, law and medicine are ordered by professors, while theology and arts are by disciplines.

Rinteln: 1671 statutes ordered a lecture catalogue (University of Rinteln 1879–80, 28). IL, 1666, extant; VV at UB Marburg, 1742/43, 1752, 1756 (Schröder 1964). In *Marburgische Beyträge zur Gelehrsamkeit nebst den Neuigkeiten der Universitäten Marburg und Rinteln*, 1749, Nr. 4, 187–91, VV for WS 1749/50 ordered by professors.

Rostock: Tholuck (1853–54, 1:96) claims that an IL appeared in 1520, but I have been unable to check his source. After 1615, IL extant (Schröder 1964). In *Erneute Bericht von Gelehrten Sachen* (Rostock), Nr. 15, 10 April 1766, 145–49, VV ordered by disciplines.

Salzburg: VV, AJ 1792 et seq. (Schröder 1964).

Strasbourg: IL 1747 extant (Schröder 1964). In *Tübingische Berichte von gelehrten Sachen*, Nr.32, 8 Aug. 1755, 435–37, VV are ordered by professors; survey of a few issues before that shows the same. In *Strasburgische gelehrten und Kunstnachrichten*, Nr. 55, 10 July 1782, 442–43, VV are ordered by disciplines; survey of a few issues thereafter shows the same.

Trier: IL, 13 March 1561, by the Jesuits (Hengst 1981, 112f).

Tübingen: Tholuck (1853–54, 1:96) cites Schnurrer (1798, 331) claiming an IL is extant from 1525, but the latter discusses a statutory lecture plan and not a published catalogue or list of lectures. IL extant from 1557; regularly 1658 (Schröder 1964). In *Tübingische Berichte von gelehrten Sachen*, Nr. 16, 21 April 1752, 185–88, VV ordered by professors; in ibid., Nr. 14, 4 April 1760, 177–80, ditto. In *Tübingische gelehrte Anzeigen*, 1783–85, no VV or IL found.

Tyrnau (Nagyszombat): In *Prager gelehrten Nachrichten*, Nr. 11, 10 Dec. 1771, 174–76, VV is ordered by professors.

Vienna: IL, seemingly first 1557, by the Jesuits (Society of Jesus 1965–[1974], 108:532ff). Post-Jesuit IL 1779/80 extant (Schröder 1964). In *Prager gelehrten Nachrichten*, Nr. 9, 26 Nov. 1771, 142–44, VV ordered by professors.

Wittenberg: First printed IL in 1507 (reprinted in *Neue Beyträge zur Litteratur besonders des sechzehnten Jahrhunderts*, 1792, 3/2:55–60; also Grohmann 1801–02, 113f; 2:78ff). IL 1561 (reprinted in ibid., 1790, 1/2:121–36). The IL of 1507 has the superior faculties ordered by professors with no times of lectures given; the inferior faculty in divided into two parts—Philosophy and Humanities—which are both ordered by hours, with the lectures given for each hour; the inferior faculty is further divided into ordinary professors, extraordinary professors, and masters. A prefatory oration to the IL of 1507 by the rector clearly envisages the catalogue as a marketing tool. A VV from 1561 is listed as extant at UB Leipzig by Schröder (1964); but, in a letter to me of 25 April 2001, K. F. Netsch at the UB Leipzig informs me that the library itself only possesses the IL from 1561 cited above; the information given to Schröder must have been erroneous or misunderstood. In 1610 the university re-solved to publish a catalogue regularly (University of Wittenberg 1926–27, 1:728). Wittenberg sends a lecture catalogue to the ministry by 1665 (Saxony 1724, 1:981f). The catalogue is under ministerial supervision by 1740 (Friedensburg 1917, 527). In *Wittenbergisches Wochenblatt . . .* , Nr. 18, 6 May 1768, 153–58, VV ordered by profes-sors; in ibid., Nr. 40, 8 Oct. 1790, 354–58, ditto. Rough survey of issues in between shows the same.

Würzburg: IL, seemingly first 1561, by the Jesuits (Society of Jesus 1965–[1974], 108:567ff). After the earliest Jesuit catalogue(s), the oldest one known to Wegele (1882, 2:225–26) is an IL of 1604; all catalogues are missing, 1729–68 (Wegele 1882, 1:423). VV, 1785/86 et seq. extant (Schröder 1964). *Wirzburger gelehrte Anzeigen,* Nr. xxxii, 22 April 1786, 191–93, has VV for SS ordered by professors; ibid., Nr. lxxxiii, 18 Oct. 1786, 811–15, has VV for WS ditto.

# Appendix 3

*Philology–Pedagogy Academic Seminars,*

*Societies, and Institutes*

| List 1. Public (Classical) Philology Seminars | | List 2. Private Classics Societies | | List 3. Significant Public Pedagogical Seminars | |
|---|---|---|---|---|---|
| Location: | Date Founded: | Location: | Date Founded: | Location: | Date Founded: |
| Göttingen | 1738 | Jena | 1733 | Halle | 1695 |
| Wittenberg | 1771 | Halle | 1736 | Halle | 1765/78 |
| Erlangen | 1777 | Altdorf | 1762 | Berlin | 1787 |
| Kiel | 1777 | Erlangen | 1764 | Dorpat | 1802 |
| Helmstedt | 1779 | Karlsruhe | 1766 | Münster | 1824 |
| Halle | 1787 | Leipzig | 1784 | Tübingen | 1838 |
| Würzburg | 1805* | Leipzig | 1798 | | |
| Heidelberg | 1807 | Landshut | 1805 | | |
| Leipzig | 1809 | Königsberg | 1806 | | |
| Frankfurt a.d.O. | 1810 | Berlin | 1811 | | |
| Marburg | 1811 | Göttingen | 1811 | | |
| Munich | 1811 | Greifswald | 1822 | | |
| Berlin | 1812 | Halle | 1824 | | |
| Gießen | 1812 | | | | |
| Breslau | 1812 | | | | |
| Jena | 1817 | | | | |
| Bonn | 1819 | | | | |
| Dorpat | 1821 | | | | |
| Königsberg | 1822 | | | | |
| Greifswald | 1822 | | | | |
| Rostock | 1829 | | | | |
| Freiburg i.Br. | 1830 | | | | |
| Tübingen | 1838 | | | | |
| Vienna | 1850 | | | | |

*planned

## Table 1. Registered Majors of Göttingen Seminarians, 1764–1835

| | |
|---|---|
| * = Theology | # = Philosophy |
| § = Theology & Philosophy | @ = Liberal Arts |
| + = Theology & Philology | ^ = History |
| x = Philology | % = Law |
| - = Philology & Philosophy | |

Column 1 = New Philology Majors
Column 3 = New Philology and Miscellaneous Majors
Column 2 = New Philology and Theology Majors
Column 4 = Total Enrollments of All Faculties

| | Number of Seminarians by Major | | | | | | | | | | | | | | | | | | | | | Total Majors Columns | | | |
|---|---|---|---|---|---|---|---|---|---|---|---|---|---|---|---|---|---|---|---|---|---|---|---|---|---|
| | 1 | 2 | 3 | 4 | 5 | 6 | 7 | 8 | 9 | 10 | 11 | 12 | 13 | 14 | 15 | 16 | 17 | 18 | 19 | 20 | 21 | 1 | 2 | 3 | 4 |
| 1764–66 | * | * | * | * | * | * | * | * | * | * | * | * | * | * | * | * | # | % | | | | 4 | 0 | 0 | 880 |
| 1767–69 | * | * | * | * | * | * | * | * | * | * | * | * | * | * | * | | | | | | | 2 | 0 | 0 | 837 |
| 1770–72 | * | * | * | * | * | * | * | * | * | * | * | * | * | * | * | | | | | | | 0 | 0 | 0 | 936 |
| 1773–75 | * | * | * | * | * | * | * | * | * | * | * | * | x | @ | % | | | | | | | 5 | 1 | 0 | 1013 |
| 1776–78 | * | * | * | * | * | * | * | * | * | * | * | | | | | | | | | | | 9 | 1 | 0 | 1027 |
| 1779–81 | * | * | * | * | * | * | * | * | * | * | * | x | @ | @ | # | | | | | | | 8 | 0 | 0 | 1187 |
| 1782–84 | * | * | * | * | * | * | * | * | * | * | + | x | x | % | | | | | | | | 8 | 1 | 0 | 1119 |
| 1785–87 | * | * | * | * | * | * | * | * | * | x | x | x | - | % | % | | | | | | | 3 | 2 | 1 | 1043 |
| 1788–90 | * | * | * | * | * | * | * | + | + | x | x | x | x | x | x | % | % | | | | | 16 | 2 | 0 | 1102 |
| 1791–93 | * | * | * | * | * | * | + | x | x | x | @ | @ | # | | | | | | | | | 14 | 3 | 0 | 1028 |
| 1794–96 | * | * | * | * | * | * | * | § | + | + | + | x | x | x | ^ | ^ | | | | | | 14 | 5 | 0 | 967 |
| 1797–99 | * | * | * | * | * | * | x | x | x | x | x | x | - | % | % | % | | | | | | 16 | 2 | 1 | 1031 |
| 1800–02 | * | * | * | * | * | * | * | * | * | * | + | + | + | x | # | # | | | | | | 7 | 5 | 3 | 1020 |
| 1803–05 | * | * | * | * | * | * | * | * | * | * | § | x | x | % | | | | | | | | 7 | 6 | 0 | 1011 |
| 1806–08 | * | * | * | * | * | * | | | | | | | | | | | | | | | | 8 | 2 | 4 | 949 |
| 1809–11 | * | * | * | * | * | * | * | * | * | * | * | * | * | * | * | § | x | x | x | x | | 13 | 4 | 1 | 1087 |
| 1812–14 | * | * | * | * | * | * | * | * | * | * | + | x | x | x | | | | | | | | 19 | 9 | 4 | 1069 |
| 1815–17 | * | * | * | * | * | * | * | * | + | + | + | + | + | x | x | x | | | | | | 14 | 14 | 2 | 1720 |
| 1818–20 | * | * | * | * | * | * | * | + | + | + | + | x | x | x | x | | | | | | | 21 | 13 | 0 | 1708 |
| 1821–23 | * | * | + | x | x | x | x | x | x | | | | | | | | | | | | | 30 | 10 | 3 | 2175 |
| 1824–26 | * | * | + | + | + | x | x | x | x | x | x | x | x | x | x | x | x | x | x | x | x | 38 | 20 | 1 | 2089 |
| 1827–29 | * | * | + | + | + | x | x | x | x | x | x | x | x | x | x | % | % | | | | | 37 | 16 | 2 | 1816 |
| 1830–32 | + | + | + | + | + | + | + | x | x | x | x | x | # | | | | | | | | | 57 | 33 | 1 | 1183 |
| 1833–35 | + | + | + | x | x | x | x | x | x | x | x | # | # | | | | | | | | | 45 | 30 | 1 | 1214 |
| | 1 | 2 | 3 | 4 | 5 | 6 | 7 | 8 | 9 | 10 | 11 | 12 | 13 | 14 | 15 | 16 | 17 | 18 | 19 | 20 | 21 | 1 | 2 | 3 | 4 |

The table contrasts, for any given cohort of three years, the registered majors of students who eventually get into the seminar (Numbers of Seminarians by Major) with the total pool of available philology majors in that cohort (Total Majors, columns 1–3), indicating as well total enrollments (column 4). So, for example, in the first cohort, 1764–66, eighteen individuals who matriculated that year eventually got into the seminar, their majors being: sixteen in theology, one in philosophy, and one in law. Columns 1–3 of "Total majors" indicate that in this same cohort, four individuals had registered as philology majors. Thus, though a pool of philology majors existed to draw on, none of them from this cohort got into the seminar.

Source: This table has been drawn by the author from University of Göttingen 1937; and Pütter et al. 1765–1838, 2:275–78; 3:494–97; 4:169–71.

## List 4. Directors of Classics Societies and Seminars

Neglecting an exception or two, the lists below concern only the period up to 1838—a circumstance of how the data were originally collected. A dash (–) after a date below indicates either that an individual was a director or subdirector at least up to 1838, or that, as far as I know, an institution existed at least up to 1838. Those listed as "director" or "president" seem to have been the head of the relevant institution, though in some cases below there are multiple directors, each then implicitly a codirector. Those listed under "subdirector" seem to have been under the director officially. Institutions listed as "private" may have had some official recognition, but were not officially institutions of the state; the latter are listed as "public," that is, state-sponsored. On the whole, the sources listed below for each institution are sufficient to reconstruct the directors listed; but, for most institutions, I have also consulted the lecture catalogues, which in some cases serve as sole sources of information—I make no further reference below to the lecture catalogues.

## Abbreviations to Directors' Status and Chairs

| | |
|---|---|
| / = simultaneous chairs | H = History |
| , = successive chairs | HL = History of Literature |
| As = Aesthetics | J = Law |
| Ar = Archaeology | L = Latin Literature |
| Aw = *Alterthumwissenschaft* | M = Metaphysics |
| CL = Classical Literature | Ma = Mathematics |
| CP = Classical Philology | o = ordinary Professor |
| Dt = German | O = Oriental Languages |
| e = extraordinary Professor | P = Philosophy |
| E = Eloquence | Pd = Pedagogy |
| EP = Eloquence and Poetry | PD = *Privatdozent* |
| G = Greek Literature | T = Theology |

### ALTDORF
*Societas latina:* 1762–1809 (private)
SOURCES: Will 1801, 151–52; Bursian 1883, 371f; University of Altdorf 1912, 123–26; *ADB* 1875–1912, 13:174; 22:214f; Meusel 1802–16, 10:4ff.
PRESIDENTS:
    1762–88: J. A. M. Nagel (oE/M/O)
    1788–95: W. Jäger (oEP)
    1795–1809: ?

### BERLIN
*Pädagogisches Seminar:* 1787– (public)
SOURCE: Fischer 1888.
PRESIDENTS:
    1787–1803: F. Gedike (*Oberschulkollegium*)
    1803–12: J. J. Bellermann (gymnasium)
    1812–19: K. W. F. Solger (oP)
    1819– : A. Boeckh (oE/CL)

*Philologisches Gesellschaft:* 1811–12 (private)
*Philologisches Seminar:* 1812– (public)
SOURCES: "Reglement . . . 1812" in Brandenburg-Prussia 1839–40, II/2, 560–62; Klausen

1837, 44ff; Hoffmann 1901, 69ff, 471; Hertz 1851, 82ff; Volkmann 1887, 23, 124; *ADB* 1875–
1912, 3:656f; University of Berlin 1955, 14, 18; Eckstein 1966, 74.

DIRECTORS:

GREEK SECTION
1812– : A. Boeckh (oE/CL)

LATIN SECTION
1812–27: P. K. Buttmann (oCP)
1827–29: G. Bernhardy (eCP)
1829– : K. K. Lachmann (oCP/Dt)

## BONN

*Philologisches Seminar:* 1819– (public)

SOURCES: "Reglement . . . 1819" in Brandenburg-Prussia 1839–40, II/2, 621–24; Schrader
1894, 2:29f, 564; Bezold 1920, 232–38; University of Bonn 1968, 112, 207, 331f; Hofmann
1969, 121ff.

DIRECTORS:

1819– : K. F. Heinrich (oCP)
1819– : A. F. Naeke (oE)
1819– : F. G. Welcker (oCP/Ar; unofficially)

## BRESLAU

*Philologisches Seminar:* 1812– (public)

SOURCES: "Reglement . . . 1812" in Brandenburg-Prussia 1839–40, II/2, 679–82; Passow
1839, 29ff; Köchly 1874, 257f; Ribbeck 1879–81, 21ff, 111ff; Bursian 1883, 1:509, 544; 2:753ff;
Schrader 1894, 2:74, 564; Hoffmann 1901, 380f; *ADB* 1875–1912, 10335; 25210–15; 32:125–27,
133f.

DIRECTORS:

1812–13: J. G. Schneider (oE)
1815–32: F. L. Passow (oAw)
1833– : F. W. Ritschl (oE)

SUBDIRECTORS:

1812–13: L. F. Heindorf (oCP)
1818– : K. E. Schneider (oCP)

## DORPAT

*Lehrerinstitut:* 1802–21 (state?)

*Pädagogisches-Philologisches Seminar:* 1821– (public)

SOURCES: University of Dorpat 1822; Eckstein 1966, 166, 399; Schrader 1894, 1:457; 2:563;
Hoffmann 1901, 471; Süß 1928–30, 1:159ff; Engelhardt 1933, 8, 46ff, 55, 147ff, 189; *ADB*
1875–1912, 7:238; 22:231–33.

DIRECTORS:

1802–6: K. S. Morgenstern (oCP/As)
1806–10: ?
1810– : K.S. Morgenstern (oCP/As) :

SUBDIRECTORS:

1821–30: J. V. Francke (oG/Pd)
1831: C. F. Neue (oCP/HL)

## ERLANGEN

*Privatgesellschaft für die lateinische Sprache:* 1764–77

*Seminarium philologicum seu scholasticum:* 1777– (public)

SOURCES: University of Erlangen 1777a; 1777b; 1778; Stählin 1928; Fikenscher 1806,
2:203ff; Engelhardt 1843, 68, 150ff; Eckstein 1966, 301; Bursian 1883, 1:512f; 2:50, 749;
Paulsen 1919–21, 2:46; Kolde 1910, 52, 525, 530; University of Erlangen 1968, 73ff; 1973,
87f; *ABD* 1875–1912, 5:281f; 20:603f; 16:683ff.

DIRECTORS:

1764–1815: G. C. Harles(s) (oEP)
1816–16: J. J. Stulzmann *(Gymnasium)*
1817–26: L. Heller (oCP/P)
1827– : L. Doederlein (oE/CP)

SUBDIRECTOR:

1827– : J. Kopp (eCP)

# FRANKFURT AN DER ODER

*Philol.-Päd. Gesellschaft:* 1810–17 (public)
SOURCE: BerlSA, I. HA Rep. 76 Va. Sekt. 4. Tit. 10. Nr. 2, 1810–17, fol. 1–8.
DIRECTORS:
1810–17?: J. H. Süvern
1810–17: ? Thilo

# FREIBURG IM BREISGAU

*Philologisches Seminar:* 1830– (public)
SOURCES: University of Freiburg im Br. 1830a; 1830b; 1830c; Hoffmann 1837, 63–70; Eckstein 1966, 31f, 156, 632; *ADB* 1875–1912, 6:745–47.

| DIRECTORS: | SUBDIRECTORS: |
|---|---|
| 1830–35: K. Zell (oCP) | 1830–35: A. Baumstark *(Gymnasium)* |
| 1836– : A. Baumstark (oCP) | 1836– : F. A. Feuerbach (oCP/Aw) |

# GIEßEN

*Philologisches Seminar:* 1812– (public)
SOURCES: University of Gießen 1812; 1827; 1907, I, 448ff and "Chronik," 1812 et seq.; Hesse-Darmstadt 1831, 238f; Eckstein 1966, 415; *ABD* 1875–1912, 4:459ff, 28:273; University of Jena 1858, 241f.

| DIRECTORS: | SUBDIRECTORS: |
|---|---|
| 1812–27: J. E. C. Schmidt (oT) | 1812–14: F. G. Welcker (oCP/Ar) |
| 1827– : F. G. Osann (oG/L) | 1812–27: H. F. Pfannkuche (oG/O) |
| | 1812–24: F. K. Rumpf (oEP) |
| | 1816–33: H. C. M. Rettig (PD) |

# GÖTTINGEN

*Seminarium philologicum:* 1738– (public)
SOURCES: University of Göttingen 1737; 1738; Gesner 1743–45, 1:59–76; Pütter et al. 1765–1838, 1:248–50, 2:273–79; 3:494–97; 4:168–71; Gedike in Fester 1905, 30f; Heeren 1813, 250ff; Ecksten 1871, 191, 248f, 377f, 389; Herbst 1872–76, 1:73ff; Kekulé 1880; Hoffmann 1901, 471; Paulsen 1919–21, 2:25ff; *ABD* 1875–1912, 49:311.
DIRECTORS:
1738–61: M. Gesner (oE)
1762–63: J. D. Michaelis (oO)
1763–1812: C. G. Heyne (oE)
1815– : C. W. Mitscherlich (oE)
1815–16: F. K. Wunderlich (eCP)
1815–37: G. L. Dissen (oCP)
1816–19: F. G. Welcker (oAr)
1819– : K. O. Müller (e,oCP)

*Philologische Gesellschaft:* 1811–15 (private)
SOURCE: Hertz 1851, 9–11.
PRESIDENT:
1811–1815: G. L. Dissen (oCP)

# GREIFSWALD

*Gesellschaft für die Philologie:* 1820–22 (private)
*Gesellschaft für die Philologie:* 1822– (public)
SOURCES: "Reglement . . . 1822" in Brandenburg-Prussia 1839–40, II/2, 718–24; Schrader 1894, 2:73ff, 564; Hoffmann 1901, 273; University of Greifswald 1956, 2:121–23; *ADB* 1875–1912, 21:209–11; 32:235–37.

DIRECTORS:
1820–24: M. H. E. Meier (eP)
1824– : G. F. Schömann (oCP/Aw)

SUBDIRECTOR:
1823–24: G. F. Schömann (oCP/Aw)

## HALLE

*Seminarium praeceptorum:* 1695–[1785] (public)
SOURCES: Frick 1883; Fries 1895, 44ff; Eckstein 1966, 86, 170; *ADB* 1875–1912, 4:80f; 7:367–69.
DIRECTORS OF HUMANITIES SECTION:
1702–07: C. Cellarius (oEP)
1707–47: H. Freyer (*Pedagogicum*)

*Societas latina:* 1736–[?] (private)
SOURCE: University of Halle 1736.
PRESIDENT:
1736–?: M. H. Otto (oP)

*Humanistisches Sektion, Theologisches Seminar:* 1765–78 (public)
*Theologisches-Pädagogisches Seminar:* 1804– (public)
SOURCES: University of Halle 1778; Hoffbauer 1805, 96; Eckstein 1966, 503; Fries 1895, 23–26; Paulsen 1896–97, 2:79ff.
DIRECTORS:
1765–69: G. B. Schirach
1769–78: C. G. Schütz
1804– : A. H. Niemeyer

*Erziehungsinstitut:* 1778–83 (public)
SOURCES: University of Halle 1779; 1781; Hoffbauer 1805, 350ff; Körte 1833, 1:143; Schrader 1894, 1:423ff; Paulsen 1896–97, 2:55ff; *ADB* 1875–1912, 38:97f.
DIRECTORS:
1778–83: J. J. Semler
1778–79: C. G. Schütz
1779–83: E. C. Trapp

*Philologisches Seminar:* 1787– (public)
SOURCES: "Reglement . . . 1829" in Brandenburg-Prussia 1839–40, II/2, 775–78; BerlSA, I. HA., Rep. 76. alt II. Nr. 102, 1787–1806; Augustin 1795, 86f; Arnoldt 1861, 1:95f, 102ff, 177ff, 245ff; Körte 1833, 1:144ff, 169ff, 200ff, 215, 243; 2:50ff, 218; Wolf 1835, 308ff; 1935, 1:52f, 55f, 60ff, 70, 75f, 94f, 209ff, 280, 293ff, 313f, 343f, 348f, 388f, 412f; 2:20, 76, 104, 112, 122; Thiersch 1866, 33f; Köchly 1874, 257; Ribbeck 1879–81, 37ff; Bursian 1883, 1:514ff, 519; 2:725; Volkmann 1887, 24ff, 36; Schrader 1894, 2:73ff, 563f; Fries 1895, 24ff; Hoffmann 1901, 273; Paulsen 1919–21, 2:224ff; Süß 1928–30, 1:29, 35ff.
DIRECTORS:
1787–1804: F. A. Wolf (oE)
1806–28: C. G. Schütz (oEP; 1817–, only pro forma director)
1817–24: J. F. A. Seidler (oG)
1824– : M. H. Meier (oG)
1828– : G. Bernhardy (oCP)

*Societas:* 1824–29 (private)
SOURCE: Ribbeck 1879–81, 1:37f.
PRESIDENT:
1824–29: C. Reisig (oCL)

## HEIDELBERG

*Philologisches Seminar:* 1807– (public)

SOURCES: University of Heidelberg 1807; Creuzer 1836–48, V/1, 16ff; Hoffmann 1901, 470; Paulsen 1919–21, 2:230; *ADB* 1875–1912, 1:769–72; 4:593ff.

DIRECTOR:
1807– : G.F. Creuzer (oCP/CL)

SUBDIRECTORS:
1807–22: H. Voß (oG)
1809–10: A. Boeckh (e,oCP)
1823– : J. C. F. Bähr (oCP)

## HELMSTEDT

*Philologisch-pädagogisches Institut:* 1779–1810 (public)

SOURCES: University of Helmstedt 1779; 1780; 1788; 1797; Stahlmann 1899–1900; Eckstein 1966, 616; Gedike in Fester 1905, 10; Hanover 1886–90, 462ff; Koldeway 1895, 153ff; Fries 1895, 25; Stahlmann 1899–1900.

DIRECTOR:
1779–1809: F. F. Wi(e)deburg (eP,oEP)

## JENA

*Societas latina:* 1733/34–1817 (private)
*Philologisches Seminar:* 1817– (public)

SOURCES: University of Jena 1737; 1741–43; 1752–56; 1800b; 1806; 1823; Güldenapfel 1816, 271–82; Eckstein 1966, 134, 137, 200, 223, 225, 307, 415, 605; Köchly 1874, 257; Bursian 1883, 1:531f; Hoffmann 1901, 471; Paulsen 1919–21, 1:556; Goetz 1928, 20ff; *ADB* 1875–1912, 6:742f; 9:487–89.

DIRECTORS:
1734–34: J. H. Kromayer (oP)
1734–50: F. A. Hallbauer (oEP)
1750–51: C. H. Eckhard (oEP)
1752–78: J. E. I. Walch (oEP)
1778–99: K. F. Walch (oJ)
1800– : H. K. A. Eichstädt (oEP)

SUBDIRECTORS:
1818– : F. G. Hand (oG)
1821–25: F. G. Osann (eCL)
1825– : K. W. Göttling (e,oCP)

## KARLSRUHE

*Societas latina:* 1766–[1816] (private)

SOURCES: Karlsruhe, Latin Society 1767–70; Götz 1789, 90; *ABD* 1875–1912, 38:382.

PRESIDENT:
1764– c. 1816: G. A. Tittel (gymnasium)

## KIEL

*Königliches Philologisches Stipendium:* 1777–1810 (public)
*Philologisches Institut:* 1810–20 (public)
*Philologisches Seminarium:* 1820– (public)

SOURCES: University of Kiel 1856; 1956, 3–5, 137,139; 1968, 112; Schleswig-Holstein 1832, 568, 577–82; Ratjan 1870, 89f, 129ff; Eckstein 1966, 404f, 601; Hofmann 1969, 123ff.

DIRECTORS:
1777–88: J. A. Cramer (oT)
1789–1808: S. G. Geyser (oT)
1809–18: K. F. Heinrich (1813–1818 de facto vacant)
1818–20: A. Twesten (eT; provisional director)
1820–25: E. W. G. Wachsmuth (oCP/E)
1825–27: A. Twesten (eT; provisional director)
1827– : G. W. Nietzsch (oCP/E)

## KÖNIGSBERG

[*Philologische Gesellschaft:* 1806/07–1809/10–1832 (private)?]
*Pädagogisches Seminar:* 1809/10–1822 (public?)
*Philologisches Seminar:* 1822– (public)
SOURCES: "Reglement . . . 1822" in Brandenburg-Prussia 1839–40, II/2, 850–55; Eckstein
    1966, 142, 203, 339; Köchly 1874, 254; Prutz 1894, 29, 174, 176; Selle 1944, index; *ABD* 1875–
    1912, 6:195f; 19:29ff.
DIRECTORS:
[1806–1809: J. C. Süvern (oCL)?]
1809–13: K. G. A. Erfurdt (oCL)
1813–14: F. A. Gotthold (gymnasium)
1814– : C. H. Lobeck (oAw/E)

## LANDSHUT

*Philologisches Seminar:* 1805 (private?)
SOURCES: Herrmann 1912, 20, 29; Pauslen 1919–21, 229; this seminar is not in the lecture
    catalogue for 1805.
DIRECTOR:
1805–? : G. A. F. Ast (oCL)

## LEIPZIG

*Philologische Gesellschaft:* 1784–1809 (private)
*Philologisches Seminar:* 1809– (public)
SOURCES: University of Leipzig 1801–4; 1809, 56ff; 1811–13; Schulze 1810, 253ff; *Leipziger
    gelehrtes Tageblatt,* 1794, "Vorrede," iv–viii; University of Leipzig 1810; Eckstein 1966, 34,
    293f; Passow 1839, 30f, 33; Köchly 1874, 82ff, 104, 244ff, 158; Bursian 1883, 1:422f; Lipsius
    1909; Paulsen 1919–21, 2:47; Wolf 1935, 2:104.

| DIRECTORS: | SUBDIRECTOR: |
|---|---|
| 1784–1834: C. D. Beck (oG/L) | 1834– : R. Klotz (eP) |
| 1834– : G. Hermann (oE) | |

*Societas Graeca:* 1798– (private)
SOURCES: University of Leipzig 1836–40; Köchly 1874, 79, 84, 246, 257; Passow 1839, 33;
    Lipsius 1909, 4ff; *ADB* 1875–1912, 197f.
DIRECTOR:
1798– : G. Hermann (oE)

## MARBURG

*Philologisches Seminar:* 1811– (public)
SOURCES: University of Marburg 1811; 1927, 35f, 122, 292f, 33, 335–37, 351–53, 478; Pütter et
    al. 1765–1838, 2:277; 3:495ff; Eckstein 1966, 243, 603; Köchly 1874, 258; Hermelink and
    Kaehler 1927, 695ff; *ABD* 1875–1912, 40:416–18.
DIRECTORS:
1811–12: K. F. C. Wagner (oE), J. F. L. Wachler (oH), A. J. Arnodi (oT)
1812–13: [above 3 plus] G. L. Dissen (eCL)
1813–15: K. F. C. Wagner (oE), J. F. L. Wachler (oH), A. J. Arnodi (oT)
1816–17: K. F. C. Wagner (oE), D. C. Rommel (oL)
1817–18: F. A. H. Börsch (oP)
1818–19: E. Platner (oJ), W. G. Tennemann (oP)
1819–20: D. C. Rommel (oL)
1820–20: C. H. Koch (eG/L)
1821–21: F. A. H. Börsch (oP)
1821–22: F. A. H. Börsch (oP), K. F. C. Wagner (oE)

1822–22: E. Platner (oJ)
1822–24: F. A. H. Börsch (oP), K. F. C. Wagner (oE)
1825–33: K. F. C. Wagner (oE)
1833– : K. F. Hermann (oCP)
While the directorship revolves, the following are teaching in the seminar: Koch (1815–23), Rommel (1816–20), Wagner (1811–33), Platner (1818–25). After 1825, only Hermann and Wagner taught in the seminar.

## MUNICH
*Societas Philologorum Monacensium:* 1811–26 (public, Bavarian Academy)
*Philologisches Seminar:* 1826– (public, University of Munich)
SOURCES: University of Ingolstadt 1812–29, esp. I/2; Spengel 1854a–b; Eckstein 1966, 541; Köchly 1874, 257f; Bursian 1883, 1:734ff; Loewe 1917, 80ff; 1925, 325, 361ff; Bachmann 1966, 122ff, *ABD* 1875–1912, 30:7–17; 35:115f; Weiller 1824, 10ff, 68ff; University of Ingolstadt 1971, 84–91.

| DIRECTOR: | SUBDIRECTOR: |
|---|---|
| 1811– : F. W. Thiersch (oE/CL) | 1827– : L. Spengel *(Lyceum)* |

## MÜNSTER
*Pädagogisches Seminar:* 1824– (public)
SOURCE: University of Münster 1825.
DIRECTOR:
1822–? : ? Nadermann & ? Esser

## ROSTOCK
*Philologisches Seminar:* 1829– (public)
SOURCES: University of Rostock 1829; Eckstein 1966, 173; Köchly 1874, 258.
DIRECTOR:
1829– : F. V. Fritzsche (oEP)

## TÜBINGEN
*Philologisches Seminar:* [1827/1829–] 1838– (public)
*Reallehrer Seminar:* 1838– (public)
SOURCES: University of Tübingen 1838; Württemberg 1843, 717–23; Eckstein 1966, 558, 660; University of Tübingen 1960, 173, 182; *ADB* 1875–1912, 37:342–46; 41:127–29.
DIRECTORS:
1838– : C. L. F. Tafel (oCP), C. Walz (?) and the *Lyceum* Rector

## VIENNA
*Philologisch-Historisches Seminar:* 1850– (public)
SOURCE: University of Vienna 1850.

## WITTENBERG
*Philologisches Seminar:* 1768–71 (private)
*Philologisches Seminar:* 1771– (public)
SOURCES: University of Wittenberg 1768; 1806; Eckstein 1966, 250; Friedensburg 1917, 596, 598; *ABD* 1875–1912, 26:389–92.
DIRECTORS:
1768–91: J. F. Hiller (oE)
1791–1806: J. J. Ebert (oMa)
1806–15: K. H. Pölitz (oH)

## WÜRZBURG

*Philologisches Seminar:* planned 1805

SOURCES: WürzUB, HSA, *Materialien zur Geschichte der Universität Würzburg,* "Projekt eines philologisches Seminar," 411; Ulrichs 1886, 16f; Herbst 1872, II/2, 30ff; Loewe 1925, 168.

DIRECTOR:

1805– : to be J. H. Voß, then G. F. Creuzer

# Appendix 4

## Dissertationes Eruditorum

Note: Titles below are, on the whole, short titles.

Altmann, Christian (*praeses*). 1711. *De senio eruditorum vulgo von denjenigen Haupt-Gelehrten Männern, die in den letzten 3 seculis über 70 bis 80 Jahre alt worden sind,* Christian G. Hoffmann (*resp.*), Leipzig.

Ansorg, Johann G. 1720. *De ignorantia eruditorium obice quae vulgo audit docta,* Jena.

Arnoldi, Gottfried (*praeses*). 1687 *Locutionem angelorum eruditis,* Paul Teutsch (*resp.*), Wittenberg.

Asp, Matthias (*praeses*). 1734. *De retractione eruditorum,* Nicolaus Hackzell (*resp.*), Upsala.

Baumeister, Friederich C. 1735. *Succincta commentatio de eruditis qui sensa animi exprimere nescit, von den Gelehrten, so es nicht können von sich geben. Editio altera et locupletior,* Wittenberg.

———. 1741. *De eruditis qui memoriam quam judicium diligentius colunt: von den Gedächtnis-Gelehrten,* Gorlitz.

Biedermann, Johann G. 1744. *De religione eruditorum,* Numburg.

———. 1750. *De eruditis male habitis,* Freiburg im Br.

———. 1753. *De reliquiis eruditorum,* Freiburg im Br.

Bieberstein, Moritz T. Marschall von (*auct. & resp.*). 1695 *De fatis eruditorum in aula,* Christian Weiss (*praeses*), Leipzig.

Bierling, Friedericus W. (*praeses*). 1702. *De causis, cur nonnulli erudit nihil in lucem emiserint,* Gerhard F. Werkamp (*resp.*), Rinteln.

Bonick, Heinrich. 1693. *De eruditis sine libris,* Leipzig.

Büchner, Georg H. (*praeses*). 1717a. *De stylo eruditorum satyrico,* Sylvester Wettich (*resp.*), Erfurt.

———. 1717b. *De Scylla eruditorum seu lapsu eorundem ab uno extremo ad alterum,* Johann C. Hesse (*resp.*), Erfurt.

Burgmann, Johann C. (*auctor & resp.*). 1718. *De licitia eruditorum invidentia,* Franz A. Aepinus (*praeses*), Rostock.

Ernesti, Johann C. (*praeses*). 1717a. *De eruditorum cunctatione in componendio libris . . . dissertatio prior,* S. G. Schroeter (*resp.*), Wittenberg.

———. 1717b. *De eruditorum cunctatione in componendio libris . . . dissertatio posterior,* August W. Reinhardt (*resp.*), Wittenberg.

Feurlin, Jacob W. (*praeses*). 1716. *De eruditis sine praeceptore,* Georg Buzewinckel (*resp.*), Altdorf.

Flachs, Sigmund A. 1720. *De causis dissensus eruditorum,* Leipzig.

Fricke, Heinrich A. (*praeses*). 1715. *De coecis eruditis,* Georg Wagner (*resp.*), Leipzig.

Fritsch, Ahasver. 1677. *Dissertatio de vitis eruditorum,* Rudolstadt.

Gerlach, Benjamin G. (*auct. & resp.*). 1723. *De patridomania eruditorum,* Johann W. von Berger (*praeses*), Wittenberg.

Goetz, Georg H. 1705. *De mercatoribus eruditis, Vel Gelehrten Kauffleuten,* Lübeck.

———. 1706. *Spicilegium . . . seu additamenta ad diatriben de mercartoribus erudities, vel gelehrten Kauffleuten,* Lübeck.

———. 1708. *De stutoribus eruditoribus, vel gelehrten Schustern, observationes miscellanea . . . ,* Lübeck.

———. 1712. *Museum eruditi variis memorabilibus conspicuum, vel die Denckwürdige Studier-Stube,* Lübeck.

———. 1714. *De coniugo eruditorum,* Lübeck.

———. 1715. *De eruditis, qui vel aquis perierunt, vel divinitus liberati fuerint . . . ,* Lübeck.

———. 1727. *Kepophiloc, seu de eruditis hortorum cultoribus, von gelehrten Gärtnern,* Lübeck.

Greimius, Martin (*praeses*). 1695. *De affectibus eruditorum,* Conrad Curt (*resp.*), Leipzig.

———. 1714. *De sorte eruditorum inter se invicem conspicua seu comparata,* Leipzig.

Gumprecht, Johann P. (*praeses*). 1717. *De polyteknia eruditorum, seu copiosa literatorum sobole, schediasma, oder ein Tractat von denen Gelehrten, die von GOTT mit vielen Kindern gesegnet worden,* Johann G. Fibiger (*resp.*), Leipzig.

Heege, Carol H. (*praeses*). 1723. *De titulomania eruditorum, vulgo Titel-Sucht derer Gelehrten,* Johann G. Stubelius (*resp.*), Leipzig.

Heine, Joahnn F. (*praeses*). 1713. *De misericordia eruditorum Vulgo der Gelehrten Guthertzigkeit,* Johann F. Evers (*resp.*), Helmstedt.

Helwig, Johannes Friedrich (*auctor et resp.*). 1727. *De modestia eruditorum,* Michael Quade (*praeses*), Sedin.

Henke, Martin. 1701. *De Silesiis indigenis eruditis,* Leipzig.

Hilscher, Paul C. (*praeses*). 1693. *De Periergia, seu inani studio eruditorum Apospasmatia,* Christian Cramer (*resp.*), Leipzig.

Hoffmann, Christian G. (*auct. et resp.*). 1711. *De senio eruditorum,* Christian G. Altmann (*praeses*), Leipzig.

Janus, Daniel F. (*praeses*). 1705. *De philoponia eruditorum,* Christian G. Gerber (*resp.*), Leipzig.

———. 1705. *Altera dissertatio . . . de philoponia eruditorum,* Johann C. Barthel (*resp.*), Leipzig.

———. 1720. *De doctoribus umbraticis,* Wittenberg.

Kortholt, Sebestian (*praeses*). 1701. *Opsimathee, sive de studio senili,* Arp Thiling (*resp.*), Kiel.

Kreuschner, Johann H. (*praeses*). 1719. *De causis rixarum inter eruditos,* Johann B. Stein (*resp.*), Königsberg.

Laub, Antonius (*praeses*). 1696. *De peccatis eruditorum,* Wilhelm Schwartz (*resp.*), Helmstedt.

Lilienthal, Michael. 1713. *De Machiavellismo litterario,* Königsberg / Leipzig.

Loeber, Chistoph W. (*praeses*). 1708. *De eruditis militibus prior,* Henricus M. de Broke (*resp.*), Jena.

Mantzel, Joachim. 1709. *Praesagia eruditorum der eruditis*, Dresden.

Matthaeus, Gottlob (*auct. et resp.*). 1705a. *Dissertatio historico-moralis de malis erudito-rum uxoribis, (vulgo) von den bösen Weibern der Gelehrten [Sectio I]*, Gottfried Boet-tnerus (*praeses*), Leipzig.

———. (*auct. et resp.*). 1705b. *Dissertatio historico-moralis de malis eruditorum uxoribis, (vulgo) von den bösen Weibern der Gelehrten [Sectio moralis]*, Gottfried Boettnerus (*praeses*), Leipzig.

Melzner, Joahnn J. (*auct. et resp.*) 1755. *De maiori frequentia apoplexiae in eruditis, quam alius sortis hominibus observanda*, Michael Alberti (*praeses*), Halle.

Mencke(n), Johann B. 1715. *De charlataneria eruditorum declamationes duae*, Leipzig.

Moeschke, Johannes (*praeses*). 1694. *De viris illustribus pacti cum inferis daemonibusque suspectis*, Johannes A. Sartorius (*resp.*), Wittenberg.

Morhof, Daniel G. 1672. *De intemperantia in studiis, et eruditorum qui ex ea oriuntur, morbis*, Kiel.

Mueller, Gottfried (*praeses*). 1720. *De eruditorum in civitatem officiis*, Gottlob Thoma-sius (*resp.*), Leipzig.

Neumann, Georg. 1707. *De eruditis, qui patriam suam nonumquam obscuram nobili-tarunt*, Leipzig.

Neumann, Johann (*praeses*). 1685. *De retractionibus eruditorum*, Peter Hojer (*resp.*), Wittenberg.

Olearius, Johannes C. (*auct et resp.*) 1697. *De palinodia eruditorum*, Johann Schmid (*praeses*), Leipzig.

Omeis, Magnus D. (*praeses*). 1688. *De eruditis Germaniae mulieribus*, Christoph C. Handelius (*resp.*), Altdorf.

Paschius, Johann. 1685. *Gynaeceum doctum; sive . . . vom belehrten Frauenzimmer*, Wit-tenberg.

Pfeiffer, Johann (*praeses*). 1696. *Eruditus thaymaeton in aetate tenera . . . dissertatione priori*, Johann G. Metzner (*resp.*), Leipzig.

Quade, Michael F. (*praeses*). 1706. *De viris statura parvis eruditione magnis*, Johann H. Wübbaer (*resp.*), Greifswald.

Ribovio, Georg H. (*praeses*). 1727. *De controversiis eruditorum*, Joahnn Weise (*resp.*), Helmstedt.

Richter, Georg G. (*praeses*). 1703. *De eruditorum invidia*, Christian E. Ganzland (*resp.*), Leipzig.

Rohde, Johann J. (*praeses*). 1715. *De eruditorum nimio libros coemendi congerendique stu-dio, sive: Von dem unmäßigen Bücher-Kauff der Gelehrten*, Christoph Ast (*resp.*), Königsberg.

Roll, Reinhard. H. 1707. *De eruditis climacterico maximo denatis*, Rostock.

Sauerbrei, Johann (*praeses*). 1671. *De foeminarum eruditione posteriorem*, Jacobus Smal-cius (*resp.*), Leipzig.

Schacher, Polycarp G. (*praeses*). 1719. *De eruditorum morbis*, Johann F. Ortlob (*resp.*), Leipzig.

Schmid, Johannes. 1724. *Foetus eruditorum difficilii partu notabiles*, Rostock.

——— (*praeses*). 1729. *De doctis, qui extra patriam, patriam invenerunt*, Gottlob A. Jenichen (*resp.*), Leizpig.

Schol(t)z(e), Friedrich E. (*praeses*). 1730 [1705]. *De eruditis sine moribus, Von unhöflichen Gelehrten*, Johann G. Krause (*resp.*), Leipzig.

Schrader, Friedrich (*praeses*). 1701. *De eruditorum valetudine*, Franz H. Grübeling (*resp.*), Helmstedt.

Schröder, Christoph J. (*praeses*). 1707. *De rusticis eruditione claris, von gelehrten Bauern*, Joahnn E. Hausmann (*resp.*), Jena.

Schroeder, Matthaeus G. (*praeses*). 1717a. *De misanthropia eruditorum, von mörosen Gelehrten*, Adamus F. Traeiner (*resp.*), Leipzig.

———. 1717b. *De misogynia eruditorum, von übelgesinnten Gelehrten gegen das weibliche Geschlecht*, Gottlieb S. Holtzmüller (*resp.*), Leipzig.

———. 1717c. *De misocosmia eruditorum, vulgo von schmutzigen Gelehrten*, Ehrenfried Ebelt (*resp.*), Leipzig.

Schultetus, David (*auct. et resp.*). 1702. *Accessiones ad Adriani Bailleti librum: Des Enfans devenus celebres par leurs etudes, or par leurs ecrits, de doctis praecocibus*, Heinrich Klausing (*praeses*), Wittenberg.

Schumann, Johann F. (*praeses*). 1720. *De eruditione noxia*, Leopold Fritze (*resp.*), Leipzig.

Schwoll, Caspar P. von (*auct. & resp.*). 1710 *Carcer eruditorum museum*, Johann C. Wolf (*praeses*), Wittenberg.

Seelen, Johann H. van. 1713. *De praecocibus eruditis, qua celeberrimorum viroum Adriani Bailleti, Davidis Schulteti et Ioan Christoph Wolfii huius argumenti scripta supplentur*, Flensburg.

Seiz, Johann F. 1714. *De apoplexia, familiari et fatali eruditorum morbo*, Altdorf.

Silberrad, Elias (*praeses*). 1709. *Peri ton autodidakton*, Johann C. Weiss (*resp.*), Jena.

———. 1712. *De eruditorum invidia*, Johann J. Walther (*resp.*), Strasbourg.

Sommerlattius, Johann F. (*praeses*). 1715. *De eruditis singularis cuiusdam libri amatoribus*, Georg E. Walsch (*resp.*), Leipzig.

———. 1716. *Exercitatio altera . . . de eruditis singularis cuiusdam libri amatoribus*, Johann G. Eyslein (*resp.*), Leipzig.

Starck, Caspar H. 1708. *De doctorum vita privata . . .* , Lübeck.

Stemler, Johann C. 1731. *De idolatria eruditorum*, Numburg.

Steuchius, Mattias (*praeses*). 1680. *De eruditorum peregrinatione*, J. Vallenius (*resp.*), Upsala.

Stübel, Johann F. 1729. *De timiditate eruditorum*, Annaberg.

Tacke, Friedrich P. 1736. *De eruditis, quibus dies natalis fuit fatalis ac ultimus*, Göttingen.

Thomasius, Jacobus (*praeses*). 1671. *De foeminarum eruditione priorem*, Johann Sauerbrei (*resp.*), Leipzig.

Trinckhus, Georg. 1672. *De caecis sapientia ac eruditione claris, mirisque caecorum quorundam actionibus*, Gera.

Tschanter, Johann C. (*auct. et resp.*). 1704. *De eruditis studiorum intemperie mortem sibi accelerantibus, dissertatio I, eaque historica*, Gottfried Boettnerus (*praeses*), Leipzig.

———. (*praeses*). 1705. *De eruditis studiorum intemperie mortem sibi accelerantibus, dissertatio II, eaque physica*, Johann C. Wolff (*resp.*), Leipzig.

Uhse, Erdmann. 1708. *De solitudine eruditorum*, Leipzig.

Wag(e)ner, Gottfried (*praeses*). 1715. *De eruditis militibus*, Johann G. Muehlavius (*resp.*), Wittenberg.

———. 1717. *De eruditis coelibibus*, Wittenberg.

Wagner, Georg C. (*praeses*). 1715. *Eruditi, spirituum familiarium usu suspecti*, Daniel Dost (*resp.*), Leipzig.

Weber, Immanuel (*praeses*). 1707. *De eruditis Hassiae principibus*, J. B. Weisennbruch (*resp.*), Geißen.

Weise, Christoph (*praeses*). 1693. *De spuriis in ecclesia et re litteraria claris, von gelehrten Huren-Kindern,* Johann Vollmarus (*resp.*), Wittenberg.

Werenfels, Samuel. 1702. *De logomachiis eruditorum,* Amsterdam.

Wilde, Johann (*auct. et resp.*). 1679 *De apostasia studiorum,* Heinrich Linck (*praeses*), Altdorf.

Wolf, Johann C. 1708 [1707?]. *De praecocibus eruditis,* Hamburg.

Zeltner, Gustav G. (*prases*). 1708. *De foeminis ex Hebraea gente eruditis,* Johann G. Zeltner (*resp.*), Altdorf.

# Appendix 5

*Doctoral Graduates and Dissertations*
*in Arts and Philosophy Faculties*

Universities surveyed below were chosen because they were either important or representative of medium or small universities, and had a published list of the relevant dissertations.

The horizontal axes in the tables below show numbers of graduates in the highest degree in arts and philosophy—the "Dr. Phil." In the vertical axes, the tables record graduates at two- or three-year intervals, instead of yearly, for the sake of perspicuity. Data were collected from the 1770s, or when the university was founded or refounded, into the 1830s.

The sign code in the tables indicates the field—as classified by me—of the relevant dissertation or previously published work submitted in lieu of a dissertation. Alphabetic symbols have been used for mathematics, natural sciences, and cameralism. Nonalphabetic symbols have been used for all other disciplines or fields—the erstwhile "humanities."

I have looked through most of the dissertations on classics (classical philology, ancient history, and ancient philosophy) and on mathematics and physical sciences (astronomy, physics, chemistry, mineralogy). I have classified the others from the titles.

## UNIVERSITY OF BERLIN
A list of the dissertations is in University of Berlin 1899. By regulation, all Berlin dissertations had to be printed. On the philological dissertations in particular, see Schmack 1975; I have not used his classifications for the table. Most Berlin dissertations are available at the Berlin State Library (Preußischer Kulturbesitz); many missing dissertations can be found at libraries in Munich and Göttingen.

Key to Dissertation Code:
  $ = classical philology
  & = ancient philosophy
  > = ancient history
  : = Indian philology
  * = Middle Eastern Studies
  + = New Testament Greek
  - = philology and linguistics
  @ = history
  % = philosophy
  h = history of mathematical sciences
  m = mathematics

q = meteorology
a = astronomy
r = physics and chemistry
c = chemistry
o = crystallography
p = mathematical and/or experimental physics
n = natural history and biology

Columns
1: Number of known graduates in Philology seminar
2: Number of known "classics" majors transferred from other universities

| Number of Berlin Dissertations by Major by 2 Year Periods | Column | |
|---|---|---|
| Years    1 2 3 4 5 6 7 8 9 10 11 12 13 14 15 16 17 18 19 20 21 22 23 24 25 26 27 28 | **1** | **2** |
| 1815–16   $ $ $ $ & & | 4 | 1 |
| 1817–18   $ > & | 3 | 0 |
| 1819–20   % o | 0 | 0 |
| 1821–22   $ $ $ > > @ c | 3 | 1 |
| 1823–24   $ @ % m r | 0 | 1 |
| 1825–26   $ $ $ $ $ $ > > & : @ @ % % m c o q | 6 | 2 |
| 1827–28   $ $ $ > @ @ % % n | 3 | 4 |
| 1829–30   $ $ $ $ $ $ & : * @ @ @ @ % c c o p p n | 2 | 2 |
| 1831–32   $ $ $ $ $ $ $ & : * * @ @ @ % m c p r n | 2 | 7 |
| 1833–34   $ $ $ $ $ > > > > & * - @ @ m m c c o n n | 4 | 4 |
| 1835–36   $ $ $ $ $ $ $ $ $ > > > * * * @ @ % h m m m m o n n n | 2 | 9 |
| Years    1 2 3 4 5 6 7 8 9 10 11 12 13 14 15 16 17 18 19 20 21 22 23 24 25 26 27 28 | **1** | **2** |
| | Column | |

Detail to column 2 from students' vitae:
In the following years, individuals who transferred from the following universities attained the Dr. Phil. in Berlin in classics. If an individual attended more than one university before graduating in Berlin, the universities are joined with a hyphen; if someone began at Berlin, transferred, then returned, it is listed thus. Thus in 1836, for example, one individual transferred from Leipzig; a second individual, who had begun at Berlin, transferred to Bonn, then back to Berlin; and, a third individual transferred from Breslau. Those three individuals received the Dr. Phil. in Berlin in 1836 with a dissertation in a topics in classics broadly conceived.

| Year | Number | Universities |
|---|---|---|
| 1816 | 1 | Jena |
| 1822 | 1 | Göttingen-Erlangen |
| 1823 | 1 | Heidelberg |
| 1826 | 2 | Leipzig, Göttingen-Leipzig |
| 1827 | 2 | Königsberg, Leipzig-Göttingen |
| 1828 | 2 | Halle, Berlin-Bonn |
| 1829 | 1 | Berlin-Halle |
| 1830 | 1 | Bonn |
| 1831 | 3 | Halle, Berlin-Bonn, Bonn |
| 1832 | 4 | Berlin-Königsberg, Bonn, Halle-Bonn, Bonn |
| 1833 | 1 | Leipzig-Göttingen |
| 1834 | 3 | Breslau, Leipzig, Bonn |
| 1835 | 6 | Breslau-Leipzig, Heidelberg, Bonn, Bonn, Bonn, Bonn |
| 1836 | 3 | Leipzig, Berlin-Bonn, Breslau |

Detail to Leipzig Transfers to Berlin by Year of Doctorate from Students' Vitae:
  1826: E. Ilgen, stud. w/ Hermann in Leipzig, in Berlin Sem., Greek diss. topic
  1826: H. Stieglitz, from Göttingen-Leipzig, in Berlin Sem., Latin diss. topic
  1827: R. Lorentz, from Leipzig-Göttingen, in Berlin Sem., Greek diss. topic
  1833: C. Leps, Leipzig-Göttingen, in Berlin Sem., Greek diss. topic
  1834: F. Kaempf, stud. w/ Hermann in Leipzig, then w/ Boeckh in Berlin Sem.
  1835: J. Sommerbrodt, stud. w/ Hermann in Leipzig, then w/ Boeckh in Berlin Sem.
  1836: F. Glum, stud. w/ Hermann in Leipzig, not in Berlin Sem., Greek diss.

## UNIVERSITY OF BONN

The list of dissertation is in University of Bonn 1897. By regulation, all Bonn dissertations had to be printed. The University of Bonn experienced severe damage in World War II, so many of the dissertations must be sought elsewhere. An edict of 26 May 1819 enjoined that a copy of each Bonn dissertation was to be sent to the state library in Berlin. They may all be there; but, for some reason (which now eludes me), I consulted more than a few of the dissertations at libraries in Göttingen, Munich, and Erlangen.

Key to Dissertation Code:
  $ = classical philology
  & = ancient philosophy
  > = ancient history
  : = Indian philology
  * = Middle Eastern Studies
  < = Indian and Middle Eastern
  n = natural history (botany)
Columns
  1: Number of known graduates in Philology seminar
  2: Number of known "Classics" majors transferred from other universities

| Number of Bonn Dissertations by Major by 2 Year Periods | | | | | | | | | | Column | |
|---|---|---|---|---|---|---|---|---|---|---|---|
| Years | 1 | 2 | 3 | 4 | 5 | 6 | 7 | 8 | 9 | 10 | 1 | 2 |
| 1822–23 | $ | * | * | | | | | | | | 1 | 0 |
| 1824–25 | $ | $ | $ | | | | | | | | 3 | 1 |
| 1826–27 | $ | $ | : | | | | | | | | 2 | 1 |
| 1828–29 | $ | $ | $ | $ | $ | $ | < | n | | | 4 | 2 |
| 1830–31 | $ | $ | $ | * | < | | | | | | 3 | 1 |
| 1832–33 | : | | | | | | | | | | 0 | 0 |
| 1834–35 | $ | $ | n | | | | | | | | 2 | 0 |
| 1836–37 | $ | $ | $ | * | | | | | | | 0 | 1 |
| | 1 | 2 | 3 | 4 | 5 | 6 | 7 | 8 | 9 | 10 | 1 | 2 |
| | | | | | | | | | | | Column | |

Note: Vitae are absent from some of these dissertations, making the column numbers in the table probably lower than in reality.

Detail to Column 2 (see under Berlin above):

| Year | Number | Universities |
|---|---|---|
| 1825 | 1 | Berlin |
| 1827 | 1 | Bonn-Berlin |
| 1829 | 2 | Bonn-Berin, Leipzig (Hermann) |
| 1831 | 1 | Königsberg |
| 1836 | 1 | Bonn-Berlin |

## UNIVERSITY OF BRESLAU (WROCLAW)

The list of dissertations is in University of Breslau 1905. By regulation, all Breslau dissertations (post-1811) had to be printed. I did not travel to Wroclaw (Breslau). The dissertations can be found in libraries in Berlin, Munich, and Göttingen.

Key to Dissertation Code:
$ = classical philology
& = ancient philosophy
> = ancient history
: = Indian philology
* = Middle Eastern Studies
+ = New Testament Greek
- = philology and linguistics
@ = history
% = philosophy
h = history of mathematical sciences
m = mathematics
q = meteorology
a = astronomy
r = physics and chemistry
c = chemistry
o = crystallography
p = mathematical and/or experimental physics
n = natural history and biology

Columns
1: Number of known graduates in Philology seminar
2: Number of known "Classics" majors transferred from other universities

| Number of Breslau Dissertations by Major by 2 Year Periods | | | | | | | | | | | | | | | Column | |
|---|---|---|---|---|---|---|---|---|---|---|---|---|---|---|---|---|
| Years | 1 | 2 | 3 | 4 | 5 | 6 | 7 | 8 | 9 | 10 | 11 | 12 | 13 | 14 | 15 | **1 2** |
| 1814–15 | > | | | | | | | | | | | | | | | 0 0 |
| 1816–17 | $ | $ | | | | | | | | | | | | | | 1 0 |
| 1818–19 | $ | $ | * | | | | | | | | | | | | | 2 0 |
| 1820–21 | p | | | | | | | | | | | | | | | 0 0 |
| 1822–23 | $ | & | | | | | | | | | | | | | | 1 0 |
| 1824–25 | $ | & | & | | | | | | | | | | | | | 1 0 |
| 1826–27 | $ | $ | $ | & | c | p | ? | | | | | | | | | 2 0 |
| 1828–29 | $ | $ | $ | $ | $ | > | m | ? | | | | | | | | 2 0 |
| 1830–31 | $ | $ | $ | $ | & | * | ? | | | | | | | | | 2 2 |
| 1832–33 | > | * | m | | | | | | | | | | | | | 0 0 |
| 1834–35 | $ | $ | $ | > | % | r | | | | | | | | | | 3 0 |
| 1836–37 | $ | $ | $ | $ | $ | $ | $ | $ | $ | * | * | * | * | m | c | 2 1 |
| | 1 | 2 | 3 | 4 | 5 | 6 | 7 | 8 | 9 | 10 | 11 | 12 | 13 | 14 | 15 | **1 2** |
| | | | | | | | | | | | | | | | | Column |

Note: Vitae are absent from some of these dissertations, making the column numbers in the table probably lower than in reality.

Detail to Column 2 (see under Berlin above):

| Year | Number | Universities |
|---|---|---|
| 1830 | 2 | Breslau-Leipzig (Hermann), Breslau-Berlin |
| 1837 | 1 | Halle |

## UNIVERSITY OF DORPAT (TARTU)

A list of the dissertations is in University of Dorpat 1973. I did not travel to Tartu (Dorpat). The dissertations can be found at libraries in Berlin, Munich, and Götting-en.

Key to Dissertation Code:
$ = classical philology
\> = ancient history
@ = history
% = philosophy
m = mathematics
a = astronomy
c = chemistry
b = botany
i = mineralogy
p = mathematical and/or experimental phyics
g = argriculture
k = cameralism and economics
? = topic of dissertation either unclear or of various contents

Number of Dorpat Dissertations by Major by 3 Year Periods

| Years | 1 | 2 | 3 | 4 | 5 | 6 | 7 | 8 | 9 |
|---|---|---|---|---|---|---|---|---|---|
| 1805–07 | @ | k | k | c | c | | | | |
| 1808–10 | @ | ? | | | | | | | |
| 1811–13 | % | k | m | m | p | | | | |
| 1814–16 | @ | k | k | g | c | | | | |
| 1817–19 | | | | | | | | | |
| 1820–22 | | | | | | | | | |
| 1823–25 | k | | | | | | | | |
| 1826–28 | | | | | | | | | |
| 1829–31 | | | | | | | | | |
| 1832–34 | $ | $ | > | > | k | m | a | b | b |
| 1835–37 | $ | $ | c | I | | | | | . |

## UNIVERSITY OF GIEßEN

Lists of the dissertations are in University of Gießen 1971 and 1976. A good number of the dissertations were lost during World War II. Some of the extant are only in manuscript at the University Archive and were perhaps never printed. A fair number of those not in Gießen can be found at the libraries in Marburg, Mainz and Götting-en.

Key to Dissertation Code:
$ = classical philology
\* = Middle Eastern Studies
+ = New Testament Greek
@ = history
# = modern languages
= = pedagogy
% = philosophy
- = philology and linguistics

; = aesthestics
k = cameralism and economics
l = philosophy and mathematics
h = history of mathematical sciences
a = astronomy
m = mathematics
c = chemistry
o = crystals-minerals-metals
p = mathematical and/or experimental physics
n = natural history and biology
? = topic of dissertation either unclear or of various contents

Columns:
A = Graduated with no dissertation or published work
B = Graduated on the submission of previously published work
C = Total graduates

| Number of Published Works and Gießen Dissertations by Major by 3 Year Periods | | Columns | | |
|---|---|---|---|---|
| Years | 1  2  3  4  5  6  7  8  9  10 11 12 13 14 15 16 17 18 19 20 21 22 23 24 25 26 27 | A | B | C |
| 1775–77 | c | 0 | 0 | 1 |
| 1778–80 | * | 0 | 0 | 1 |
| 1781–83 | * | 0 | 0 | 1 |
| 1784–86 | | 0 | 0 | 0 |
| 1787–89 | | 0 | 0 | 0 |
| 1790–92 | n | 0 | 1 | 1 |
| 1793–95 | | 0 | 0 | 0 |
| 1796–98 | | 1 | 0 | 1 |
| 1799–01 | | 3 | 0 | 0 |
| 1802–04 | $  % | 0 | 2 | 2 |
| 1805–07 | @  %  %  n  c | 0 | 3 | 5 |
| 1808–10 | m  k | 0 | 1 | 2 |
| 1811–13 | ;  @  m  k | 0 | 0 | 4 |
| 1814–16 | @  @  n  c | 0 | 2 | 4 |
| 1817–19 | $  $  $  −  %  %  m  ?  ? | 0 | 5 | 9 |
| 1820–22 | $  $  *  *  #  @  ;  %  %  m  p  ? | 0 | 6 | 12 |
| 1823–25 | $  *  *  −  ;  @  @  m  m  m  k  k  k  n  c  ?  ? | 0 | 7 | 17 |
| 1826–28 | $  $  $  $  $  $  *  *  #  @  ;  %  %  %  %  %  %  %  %  k  k  m  c  c  p  ?  ?  ? | 0 | 11 | 27 |
| 1829–31 | $  $  *  @  %  %  %  %  %  n  n  c  p  ?  ?  ?  ?  ? | 0 | 5 | 19 |
| 1832–34 | #  @  ? | 0 | 3 | 3 |
| 1835–37 | @  @  @  #  c  ? | 0 | 4 | 6 |
| | 1  2  3  4  5  6  7  8  9  10 11 12 13 14 15 16 17 18 19 20 21 22 23 24 25 26 27 | A | B | C |
| | | Columns | | |

## UNIVERSITY OF GÖTTINGEN

Göttingen dissertations and pages with only theses for disputation are bound at the university library as *Academica Goettingensia* (Call Nr.: 4° H.L.P. IV, 26/5, [Year]; and 8° H.L.P. IV, 26/5, [Year]). The university archive has a card file year by year of persons graduated, listing the dissertation title, when one had been written. In very few cases, names in the card file could not be matched to dissertations or theses pages. Such "graduates" were not recorded in the totals.

Before 1800, dissertations typically have theses printed after the dissertations. From 1802 to 1822, Göttingen graduated some candidates with its highest degree in the philosophy faculty—a "Dr. Phil."—based only on printed theses (in column 2).

Key to Dissertation Code:
$ = classical philology
* = Middle Eastern Studies
+ = New Testament Greek
@ = history
# = modern languages
= = pedagogy
% = philosophy
- = philology and linguistics
k = cameralism and economics
l = philosophy and mathematics
h = history of mathematical sciences
a = astronomy
m = mathematics
c = chemistry
o = crystals-minerals-metals
p = mathematical and/or experimental physics
n = natural history and biology
Columns:
1 = Number of known graduates in Philology Seminar
2 = No dissertation, only theses submitted
3 = Total doctoral graduations in Arts and Philosophy Faculty

| Number of Göttingen Dissertations by Major by 3 Year Periods | | | | | | | | | | | | | | | | | | | | | | | | | | Column | | |
|---|---|---|---|---|---|---|---|---|---|---|---|---|---|---|---|---|---|---|---|---|---|---|---|---|---|---|---|---|
| Years | 1 | 2 | 3 | 4 | 5 | 6 | 7 | 8 | 9 | 10 | 11 | 12 | 13 | 14 | 15 | 16 | 17 | 18 | 19 | 20 | 21 | 22 | 23 | 24 | 1 | 2 | 3 |
| 1770–72 | $ | * | % | m | | | | | | | | | | | | | | | | | | | | | 1 | 0 | 4 |
| 1773–75 | $ | * | @ | m | | | | | | | | | | | | | | | | | | | | | 1 | 0 | 4 |
| 1776–78 | $ | * | * | % | m | | | | | | | | | | | | | | | | | | | | 1 | 0 | 5 |
| 1779–81 | $ | $ | @ | | | | | | | | | | | | | | | | | | | | | | 0 | 0 | 3 |
| 1782–84 | $ | $ | @ | m | | | | | | | | | | | | | | | | | | | | | 2 | 0 | 4 |
| 1785–87 | $ | @ | | | | | | | | | | | | | | | | | | | | | | | 1 | 0 | 2 |
| 1788–90 | $ | $ | $ | @ | @ | p | | | | | | | | | | | | | | | | | | | 2 | 0 | 6 |
| 1791–93 | $ | a | h | | | | | | | | | | | | | | | | | | | | | | 1 | 0 | 3 |
| 1794–96 | ----------------------------- no data ----------------------------- | | | | | | | | | | | | | | | | | | | | | | | | | | |
| 1797–99 | $ | $ | $ | $ | $ | @ | h | h | | | | | | | | | | | | | | | | | 4 | 0 | 8 |
| 1800–02 | # | = | h | p | n | | | | | | | | | | | | | | | | | | | | 0 | 1 | 5 |
| 1803–05 | $ | | | | | | | | | | | | | | | | | | | | | | | | 0 | 1 | 2 |
| 1806–08 | $ | + | % | % | % | % | k | c | | | | | | | | | | | | | | | | | 1 | 2 | 10 |
| 1809–11 | ----------------------------- poor data ----------------------------- | | | | | | | | | | | | | | | | | | | | | | | | | | |
| 1812–14 | * | m | | | | | | | | | | | | | | | | | | | | | | | 0 | 3 | 5 |
| 1815–17 | $ | $ | % | m | m | | | | | | | | | | | | | | | | | | | | 5 | 7 | 13 |
| 1818–20 | n | | | | | | | | | | | | | | | | | | | | | | | | 1 | 6 | 7 |
| 1821–23 | $ | $ | $ | $ | $ | % | % | o | a | m | m | p | n | n | | | | | | | | | | | 3 | 7 | 21 |
| 1824–26 | $ | * | @ | l | n | c | c | | | | | | | | | | | | | | | | | | 1 | 0 | 7 |
| 1827–29 | $ | $ | $ | $ | $ | $ | + | + | @ | % | % | - | o | m | m | m | c | | | | | | | | 4 | 0 | 17 |
| 1830–32 | $ | $ | $ | $ | $ | $ | $ | $ | $ | $ | $ | $ | * | @ | @ | @ | @ | % | h | n | c | c | c | | 7 | 0 | 23 |
| 1833–35 | $ | $ | $ | $ | $ | $ | $ | $ | * | % | k | m | n | c | c | | | | | | | | | | 3 | 0 | 15 |
| | 1 | 2 | 3 | 4 | 5 | 6 | 7 | 8 | 9 | 10 | 11 | 12 | 13 | 14 | 15 | 16 | 17 | 18 | 19 | 20 | 21 | 22 | 23 | 24 | 1 | 2 | 3 |
| | | | | | | | | | | | | | | | | | | | | | | | | | | | Column |

## UNIVERSITY OF HALLE-WITTENBERG

Dissertations after 1817 are listed in University of Halle 1953. I did other things in Halle (and was spied on by the Stasi), so I did not read dissertations there. Almost all the relevant dissertations can be found in Berlin, Munich, and Göttingen.

Before 1817, there is no way to determine from the Acts of the Philosophy Faculty in the university archive whether the acts relating to graduations are complete or not. In 1817, Halle was given a *Curator* and the University of Wittenberg was folded into Halle. Records are better thereafter. In 1984 Halle archivists told me that circa 1800 the dissertations were supposed to be printed and bound in collections. The volume for 1795–1800 had no dissertations for the arts and philosophy faculty. There was no volume for the period 1800–10. The university had troubles after 1806, and was closed by Napoleon in 1813, then reopened and reorganized in 1817.

At the Berlin State Library (Preußischer Kulturbesitz), there are Halle dissertations from 1770–71 with C. A. Klötz as the presider, but apparently written by the respondents (Call Nr.: Ah 8101-37 to -42). There is also a dissertation from 1777 by A.H. Niemeyer, with J. A. Segner presiding (Ah 8101-43). There are doubtless many others to be found, which one could locate by searching names of professors as presiders.

University of Halle 1953 would allow construction of a post-1817 table such as above, but I decided against it. Like Gießen, Halle awarded the doctorate on the bases of theses and a private exam, should the candidate so choose (University of Halle 1953, 320). It was difficult to classify a fair number of the dissertations from the titles. A significant number of the dissertations were pedagogical in orientation, even where the topic was philological, theological, or mathematical. It is clear from the dissertations that many or most of the graduates would be gymnasium instructors.

Number of Transfers of Classical Philology Students (see under Berlin above):

| Year | Number | Universities |
|------|--------|--------------|
| 1828 | 1 | Berlin-Leipzig |
| 1829 | 1 | Berlin |
| 1833 | 1 | Bonn-Berlin |

Vitae are absent from many of these dissertations, making the numbers here probably lower, perhaps significantly, than in reality.

## UNIVERSITY OF INGOLSTADT / LANDSHUT / MUNICH

The principal state university of Bavaria was founded at Ingolstadt in 1472, moved to Landshut in 1800, then to Munich in 1826. A list of the dissertations and graduates is in University of Ingolstadt/Landshut/Munich 1975–77. The source lists no dissertations for grdaduates until 1801. Some dissertations from Ingolstadt are, however, at the UB Munich (Call Nr.: 4° Phys. 43: 2, 6, 7, 8, 9; and, 4° Phys. 107: 2, 4, 5). Nr. 6 in the first collection was written by the respondent. Nr. 5 in the second collection was edited by the respondent from the presiding professor's lectures. There are, thus, probably more to be found. The 1975–77 source indicate that, even after the move to Munich in 1826, many titles of dissertations cannot be ascertained—which means that they might not have existed. Data did not seem sufficient to attempt a table here or further characterization of the dissertations.

# Appendix 6

## List of Universities in the German Cultural Space

A number of universities about which confusion might occur have been negatively listed as not in the "empire" meaning the Holy Roman Empire (*Reich*). Up to about 1500, German universities acquired a papal privilege as their legal basis as a university; after 1500, they acquired imperial privileges as their legal basis as a university; before and after 1500, some acquired both privileges, especially those remaining Catholic. After about 1806 and the dissolution of the empire, universities only obtained a foundation document from the relevant sovereign government; before 1806, universities not in the empire would not obtain an imperial privilege in any case. Universities were not officially nationalized until the late eighteenth century or later. Universities are thus listed as having a patron, not a state to which they belong. The first date given is the "official" foundation and/or opening date, which may differ from the dates of any or all foundation privileges. If the university was closed, that date follows in the manner of a death date. Changes of patron or religion are given by simple initial dates with no termination or "death" date. The chancellors are given for universities for which the office was held by someone other than the sovereign or its representative at the university. In the Renaissance, most universities acquired an additional appellation as an "academia," a practice that continued through the eighteenth century.

Abbreviations:
ES: Earlier Status; LS: Later Status; PP: Papal Privilege; IP: Imperial Privilege.

*Altdorf: Norimbergensium Universitas* (Academia Altorfina), 1622–1809. ES: Academy: 1578–1622. IP: 1623 (1578 for Academy). Patron: Town Council of Nürnberg, 1622; Bavaria, 1806. Religion: Lutheran.

*Aschaffenburg: Karls-Universität/ Großherzogliche Universität* (Academia Carolina), 1808–18. ES: Lyceum, 1620–1811 + University at Mainz, 1477–1803. LS: Lyceum, 1818. PP: 1476 (based on privilege for Mainz, closed 1803). Patron: Elector/Grand Duke von Dalberg, 1808; Bavaria, 1818. Religion: Catholic.

*Bamberg: Universitas Bambergensis* (Academia Ottonia), 1773–1811. ES: College, 1611–52; Academy: 1653–1773. LS: Lyceum, 1803. IP: 1648 (as Academy); PP: 1648 (as Academy). Patron: Bishop Elector of Bamberg, 1611. Religion: Catholic ( Jesuit institution, 1611–1773).

*Basel: Raurica Universitas/ Studium Basiliense* (Academia Basiliensis), 1460–. PP: 1459. Patron: Town Council of Basel, 1460. Chancellor: Bishop of Basel. Religion: Catholic, 1460; Reformed, 1532.

*Berlin: Universitas litterariae Berolinensis,* 1810. Patron: Brandenburg-Prussia, 1809. Religion: Lutheran. First German university opened with neither PP nor IP.

*Besançon:* In Franch-Comté, thus officially within the empire until 1678, then under French control; university never German language. University: (1485)–1564/65. PP: 1450. Patron: Archbishop of Besançon.

*Bonn: Kurkölnische Universität* (Kurfürstliche Maxische Academie), 1786–98. ES: Lyceum, 1773–83; Academy, 1783–86. LS: Central School, 1798. IP: 1784; first Catholic university without PP. Patron: Archbishop Elector of Cologne, 1784. Religion: Catholic.

*Bonn: Universitas Friderica Guilelmia* (Academia Borussica Rhenana), 1818. Patron: Brandenburg-Prussia, 1818. Religion: Lutheran.

*Breslau (Wroclaw): Universitas Vratislaviensis* (Academia Leoplodina/Viadrina), 1702. ES: College, 1646–60; Lyceum, 1660–1702. LS: combined with Frankfurt a.d.O., 1811. IP: 1702; PP: 1702. Patron: King of Bohemia, 1702; Brandenburg-Prussia, 1742. Religion: Catholic ( Jesuit institution, 1646–1773); Ecumenical, 1811.

*Brünn: Caesareo regia et archiepiscopalis Universitas Brunae,* 1778–82. See Olmütz.

*Budapest:* Never officially within the empire; majority of professors non-German. University: (1389)–96, ante-1465. University of Tyrnau moved to Buda, 1777, then to Pest, 1784. PP: 1389/95. Patron: King of Hungary.

*Bützow: Universität Bützow* (Academia Mecklenburgica), 1758–89. ES: Split from University Rostock, 1758. LS: Recombined with Rostock, 1789. IP: 1758. Patron: Duke of Pommerania. Religion: Lutheran.

*Cassel: Universität Kassel* (Collegium Adelphicum), 1633–53. ES: College, 1605. LS: Corporation combined with Marburg, 1653. IP: 1541; Marburg's IP moved to Kassel, 1633. Patron: Landgrave of Hesse-Kassel, 1633. Religion: Reformed.

*Cologne: Universitas Coloniensis* (Celeberrima Agrippinatum Academia), 1388–1798. LS: Central School, 1798–1804. IP: 1442; PP: (?) 1389. Patron: Archbishop Elector and Town Council of Cologne, 1388. Chancellor: Cathedral Provost of Cologne. Religion: Catholic ( Jesuit College, 1556–1773).

*Cracow:* Not in the empire; university never German language. University: 1364–(1370)–1401– . PP: 1364/97. Patron: King of Poland.

*Dillingen: Universität Dilligen* (Academia Dilingiana), 1553–1804. ES: College, 1549–53. LS: Lyceum, 1804. IP: 1553; PP: 1551. Patron: Prince Bishop of Augsburg, 1553; Bavaria, 1803. Religion: Catholic ( Jesuit institution, 1564–1773).

*Dôle:* In Franch-Comté, thus officially within the empire until 1678, then under French control; university never German language. University: 1422/23. PP: 1422. Patron: Duke of Burgundy. Chancellor: Archbishop of Besançon.

*Dorpat (Tartu): Universitas Dorpato-Persaviensis* (Academia Gustaviana), 1802. Not in the empire, but German language. ES: Swedish/Livlandish University, 1632–1709. LS: Russified in 1890's. Privilege: Czar of Russia. Patron: Estates of Livland, Kurland, Estland, Silten and Czar of Ukas, 1800. Religion: Lutheran.

*Duisburg: Reformierte Universität* (Academia Duisburgensis), 1655–(1806)–1818. ES: Gymnasium illustre, 1636. LS: Courses taught till 1818. IP: 1566 to Jülich, Cleve and Berg. Patron: Margrave Elector of Brandenburg, 1655–1806; Duke of Berg, 1806–15; Brandenburg-Prussia, 1815. Religion: Reformed.

*Erfurt: Universitas Erfurtina* (Academia Ephurdiensis), 1392–1804. LS: Courses till 1816. PP: 1379; 1389. Patron: Erfurt Town Council, 1392; Archbishop Elector of Mainz, 1664; Brandenburg-Prussia, 1803. Religion: Catholic, 1392; Lutheran, 1521; Catholic, 1533 (no Jesuits in Phil. Fac.).

*Erlangen: Universitas Fridericana Erlangensis* (Academia Fridericiana), 1743. ES: *Hochschule* in Bayreuth, 1742. IP: 1743. Patron: Margrave of Bayreuth, 1743; Margrave of Bayreuth-Ansbach, 1769; Brandenburg-Prussia, 1791; Bavaria, 1806. Religion: Lutheran.

*Frankurt a.d.O: Universität Frankfurt a.d.O.* (Viadrum Academia), 1506–1811. LS: Corporation combined with Breslau, 1811. IP: 1500; PP: 1500/06. Patron: Margrave Elector of

Brandenburg, 1506; Chancellor: Bishop of Lebus. Religion: Catholic, 1506; Reformed, 1537/40.

*Frankfurt a.M.: Universitas Carolina,* 1808–14. Landesuniversität des Großherzogtums Frankfurt a.M., composed of Lycea in Aschaffenburg, Fulda and Frankfurt a.M.; Phil., Law, and Theol. Facs. in Aschaffenburg; Law School in Wetzlar; and Med. School in Frankfurt a.M. On "university," see: Aschaffenburg.

*Freiburg im Br.: Vorderösterreichische Universität* (Academia Albertina), 1460. IP: 1456. PP: 1455. Patron: Archduke of Austria, 1456; Baden, 1806. Chancellor: Bishop of Basel, 1456. Religion: Catholic ( Jesuit control of Phil. and Theol. Facs., 1620–1773).

*Fünfkirchen:* Outside of the empire. University: 1367–ante-1465. PP: 1367. Patron: King of Hungary.

*Fulda: Universitas Fuldensium* (Alma Adolphina), 1734–1805. ES: Jesuit College, 1574; Papal Seminar (?). LS: Lyeum / Theol Studium, 1805. IP: 1723/33; PP: 1732/33. Patron: Prince Abbot of Fulda, 1734; Oranien-Nassau, 1803. Religion: Catholic ( Jesuits and Benedictines).

*Gießen: Universität Gießen* (Academia Ludoviciana), 1607–24; 1650. ES: Gymnasium illustre. LS: Corporation moved to Marburg, 1624–50. IP: 1607. Patron: Landgrave of Hesse-Darmstadt, 1607. Religion: Lutheran.

*Göttingen: Georg-August-Universität* (Academia Regia Georgia Augusta), 1734/37. ES: Gymnasium illustre. IP: 1733. Patron: Duke Elector of Hanover and King of England, 1734. Religion: Lutheran.

*Graz: Universitas Graecensis* (Carola-Fransicea), 1585–1782; 1827. ES: Jesuit College, 1573. LS: Lyceum, 1782–1827. IP: 1588; PP: 1588. Patron: Archduke of Austria, 1585. Religion: Catholic ( Jesuit institution, 1585–1773).

*Greifswald: Universität Greifswald* (Academia Gryphiswaldensis), 1456. IP: 1456; PP: 1456. Patron: Town Council and Duke of Pommerania, 1456; King of Sweden, 1618; Brandenburg-Prussia, 1815. Chancellor: Bishop of Kamin, 1456. Religion: Catholic, 1456; Lutheran, 1539.

*Halle: Friedrichs-Universität* (Academia Fridericiana), 1694–(1806)–1813; 1817. ES: Ritterakademie, ante-1680. LS: University of Wittenberg combined with Halle, 1817. IP: 1693. Patron: Margrave Elector of Brandenburg, 1694; King of Westphalia, 1806; Brandenburg-Prussia, 1815. Religion: Lutheran.

*Heidelberg: Universitas studii Heidelbergensis* (Vetustissima Germanorum Academia), 1386–1632; 1652. PP: 1385. Patron: Count Elector of the Palatinate, 1386; Baden, 1803. Chancellor: Cathedral Provost of Worms, 1386. Religion: Catholic, 1386; Reformed, 1544; Lutheran, 1578; Catholic, 1629 ( Jesuit control); Reformed, 1652.

*Helmstedt: Universität Helmstedt* (Academia Julia), 1576–1809. ES: Pädagogium illustre in Gandersheim, 1572. IP: 1575. Patron: Duke of Brunswick-Lüneburg-Wolffenbüttel, 1574; King of Westphalia, 1806. Religion: Lutheran.

*Herborn: Academia Nassauensis,* 1584–1817. IP paid for, but never recognized as a university. Patron: Duke of Nassau, 1584; Duke of Orange, 1743; Nassau, 1806. Religion: Reformed.

*Ingolstadt: Bojorum Universitas Ingolstadiense* (Catholica Ingolstadiensis Academia), 1472. LS: Corporation moved to Landshut, 1800. PP: 1459. Patron: Duke of Bavaria. Chancellor: Bishop of Eichstätt. Religion: Catholic ( Jesuit control of Phil. and Theol. Facs. 1588–1773).

*Innsbruck: Universitas Litteraria Oenipontana* (Academia R. C. Leopoldina), 1669–1782, 1791–1810, 1826. ES: Jesuit Gymnasium, 1562; College, 1606. LS: Lyceum, 1782–91, 1810–26. IP: 1669; PP: 1677. Patron: Holy Roman Emperor, 1669; Bavaria, 1805; Austria, 1815. Religion: Catholic ( Jesuit institution, 1669-1773).

*Jena: Universität Jena* (Academia Johan-Fridericana), 1558. ES: Academy, 1548. IP: 1557. Patron: Duke of Saxony, 1557 (Saxe-Weimar or Ernestine Saxony: Houses of Weimar, Coburg, Meiningen and Gotha). Religion: Lutheran.

*Kaschau.* Never in the empire. Jesuit College: 1633. Raised to University: 1658.

*Kiel: Universitas Chiloniensis* (Academia Cimbrica), 1665. PP: 1652. Patron: Duke of Holstein-Gottorp, 1665; Dukes of Schleswig-Holstein, 1773. Religion: Lutheran.

*Königsberg: Albrechts-Universität* (Academia Albertina), 1544/60. ES: Particular-Schule, 1541. Privilege: King of Poland, 1544. Patron: Duke of Prussia 1544/60; King of Brandenburg-Prussia, 1701. Religion: Lutheran.

*Kulm:* PP: 1386. University not opened.

*Landshut: Universität Landshut:* 1800–26. ES: University at Ingolstadt till 1800. LS: University moved to München in 1826. PP: 1459. Patron: Duke of Bavaria, 1800; King of Bavaria, 1806. Religion: Catholic.

*Leipzig: Universitas Litterarum Lipsiensis* (Academia Lipsiensis), 1409. PP: 1409. Patron: Margrave of Meissen and Landgrave of Thuringia, 1409; Duke Elector of (Albertine) Saxony, 1547. Chancellor: Bishop of Merseburg. Religion: Catholic, 1409; Lutheran, 1539/42.

*Lemberg (Lvov): Johann-Casimir-Univerität:* 1661–1773, 1784–1805, 1817. Not in the empire, but German language, 1784–1871. LS: Closed, 1773–84; Lyceum, 1805–17. Privilege: King of Poland, 1661. Patron: King of Poland, 1661; Holy Roman Emperor (Habsburgs), 1772. Religion: Catholic ( Jesuit institution, 1661–1773).

*Louvain:* In the empire till 1668; university never German language. University: 1425. PP: 1425/31. Patron: Duke of Brabant. Chancellor: Provost of Collegiate Church at Nassau. Religion: Catholic ( Jesuit College, 1547–1773).

*Lüneburg:* IP: 1471. University not opened.

*Mainz: Alma Electoralis Universitas Moguntina* (Academia Moguntina), 1477–1798. LS: Central School, 1798–1803; Lyceum, 1803. PP: 1476. Patron: Prince Bishop Elector of Mainz, 1477. Chancellor: Provost of Liebfraukirche. Religion: Catholic ( Jesuit institution, 1562–1773).

*Marburg: Universitas Marburgensis* (Alma Philippina), 1541. ES: Academy, 1526. LS: Combined with University Cassel, 1653. IP: 1541/1653. Patron: Landgrave of Hesse-Cassel, 1541; Landgrave of Hesse-Darmstadt, 1624; Landgrave of Hesse-Cassel, 1645; King of Westphalia, 1806; Hesse-Cassel, 1815. Religion: Lutheran, 1541; Reformed, 1605; Lutheran, 1624; Reformed, 1653.

*Molsheim: Bishöfliche Universität,* 1617–1701. ES: Jesuit College, 1580. LS: Combined with Strasbourg, 1701. IP: 1617; PP: 1612. Patron: Bishop of Strasbourg, 1618. Religion: Catholic ( Jesuit institution, 1617–1701).

*Munich: Univerität München:* 1826. ES: University in Landshut till 1826. PP: 1459. Patron: Bavaria, 1826. Religion: Catholic.

*Münster: Fürstbishöfliche Universität,* 1780–1818. ES: Academy, 1771. LS: Theological and Philosophical Academy, 1818. IP: 1773; PP: 1773. Patron: Archbishop Elector of Cologne, 1780; King of Brandenburg-Prussia, 1803; Grandduke of Berg, 1808; Brandenburg-Prussia, 1815. Religion: Catholic ( Jesuit institution, 1771–73).

*Nagyszombat (Tyrnau):* Not in the empire; professorate non-German. University: 1635–1777. Moved to Buda 1777. Patron: King of Hungary. Religion: Catholic ( Jesuit institution, 1635–1773).

*Olmütz (Olmouc): Caesaro regia ac episcopalis Universitas,* 1581–1778, 1827. ES: Academy, 1570; 1778–82 in Brünn; Lyceum, 1782. IP: 1576/81; PP: 1573. Patrons: King of Bohemia and Bishop of Olmütz, 1581. Religion: Catholic ( Jesuit institution, 1581–1773).

*Osnabrück: Universität Osnabrück* (Academia Carolina Osnabrugensis), 1632–33. ES: Gymnasium, 1623. IP: 1629; PP: 1630. Patron: Bishop of Osnabrück, 1632. Religion: Catholic ( Jesuit institution, 1632–33).

*Paderborn: Alma ad Paderam Universitas* (Academia Theodoriana Paderbornensis), 1615–1818. ES: Lyceum, 1585. LS: Theology & Philosophy School. IP: 1615; PP: 1615. Patron: Prince Bishop of Paderborn, 1615. Religion: Catholic ( Jesuit institution, 1615–1773)

*Prague: Universitas Carolina Pragensis,* 1348. PP: 1347. Patron: King of Bohemia, 1348.

Chancellor: Archbishop of Prague. Religion: Catholic, 1348 (Hussian interludes); Lutheran, 1609; Catholic, 1622 (Jesuit control of Phil. and Theol. Facs., 1622–38, 1654–1773).

*Pressburg:* Not in the empire. University: 1465/67. PP: 1465. Patron: King of Hungary.

*Regensburg:* University: 1672–? (Jesuit institution). No mention of IP or PP. Probably a lyceum.

*Rinteln: Universität Rinteln* (Academia Schaumbergica), 1621–1809. ES: Gymnasium illustre. IP: 1620. Patron: Count of Holstein-Schaumberg, 1621; Duke of Hesse-Darmstadt, 1647; King of Westphalia, 1806. Religion: Lutheran, 1621.

*Rostock: Universitas Rostochiensis* (Academia Rhodopolitana), 1419. PP: 1419; IP: 1560. Patrons: Town Council and Duke of Mecklenburg, 1419; Town Council, 1760; Town Council and Duke of Mecklenburg, 1789; Mecklenburg, 1827. Chancellor: Bishop of Schwerin. Religion: Catholic, 1419; Lutheran, 1531.

*Salzburg: Juvaviae studiorum Universitas* (Alma Benedictino-Salisburgensis), 1625–1810. ES: Academy, 1618. LS: Lyceum, 1810. IP: 1622/23; PP: 1620. Patron: Archbishop of Salzburg, 1625; Grandduke of Tuscany, 1803; King of Bavaria, 1806; Austria, 1815. Religion: Catholic (Benedictine institution).

*Strasbourg: Treboccorum Universitas* (Academia Argentinensis), 1621–1792. ES: Academy, 1566. LS: Central School, 1795. IP: 1621. Patron: Town Council, Imperial City of Straßburg, 1621 (French control of city, 1681). Religion: Lutheran.

*Stuttgart: Universität Stuttgart* (Academia Carolina), 1781–94. ES: Military Academy, 1770. IP: 1781. Patron: Duke of Württemberg, 1781. Religion: Lutheran.

*Trier: Universitas Treversensis antiquissima:* 1473–1798. LS: Central School, 1800. PP: 1454. Patron: Town Council. Chancellor: Archbishop of Trier. Religion: Catholic (Jesuit control of Phil. and Theol. Facs., 1561–1773).

*Tübingen: Universität Tübingen* (Academia Eberhardina), 1477. IP: 1484; PP: 1476. Patron: Count/Duke of Württemberg, 1477. Religion: Catholic, 1477; Lutheran, 1534.

*Tyrnau:* See Nagyszombat.

*Vienna: Universitas Vindobonensis* (Academia Viennensis), 1365/84. PP: 1365. Patron: Archduke of Austria, 1365. Chancellor: Cathedral Provost of All Saints. Religion: Catholic (Jesuit control of Phil. and Theol. Facs., 1622–1773).

*Wittenberg: Universitas Vitebergensis* (Academia Leucorea), 1502–1817. LS: Combined with Halle. IP: 1502; PP: 1503. Patron: Duke Elector of (Ernestine) Saxony, 1502; Duke Elector of (Albertine) Saxony, 1547; Brandenburg-Prussia, 1815. Patron: Praeceptor of Antonineherrn at Lichtenburg. Religion: Catholic, 1502; Lutheran, 1533/36.

*Wroclaw:* See Breslau.

*Würzburg: Herbipolensium Universitas* (Alma Julia-Maximiliana), 1402/10–13, 1582. IP: 1575; PP: 1402/1575. Patron: Prince Bishop of Würzburg, 1402/1582; King of Bavaria, 1803; Grandduke of Tuscany, 1806; Bavaria, 1815. Religion: Catholic (Jesuit institution, 1582–1773).

*Zürich: Universitas Turicensis:* 1833. ES: Academy, 1559. Patron: Kanton Zürich, 1833. Religion: Reformed.

# Notes

The end notes here make use of a number of conventions. Notes in reference to archival materials use an abbreviation schema under Abbreviations. All other citations refer to the bibliography. Page citations in most notes are made in terms of the now old-fashioned use of *f* for one page following the page number listed, and of *ff* for multiple pages. I have omitted the periods conventionally called for in this citation system. So, for example 40f. becomes 40f and 108ff.becomes 108ff and so on.

CHAPTER ONE

1. Goody 1977; 1986; Foucault 1975; Latour 1987; 1990; Becker and Clark 2001.

2. Foucault 1975, 150.

3. Marx in Marx and Engels 1966, 1:31–60. See also Funkenstein 1986.

4. Weber 1976a, 563 (1956, 571); emphasis of "expert" in the original.

5. See Weber 1976a, 122ff (1956, esp. 122ff).

6. Weber 1976a, 129 (first quotation), 578f (second quotation, emphasis in original omitted), 129 (third quotation, emphasis in original omitted);(1956, 129, 586f, 129).

7. Rosenberg 1958, 73. On Baroque courtiers, see Biagioli 1993.

8. Quotation from Brandenburg-Prussia 1894–1936, 3:577.

9. Haussherr 1953, 13 (quotation); see also 12ff. On the above, see Brandenburg-Prussia 1894–1936, 3:582f; Heinrich 1931, 11f; Bleek 1972, 63ff.

10. On the above, see Heinrich 1931, 13; Dorwart 1953, 189ff; Rosenberg 1958, 160; Bleek 1972, 41, 69; Johnson 1975, 49ff, 218ff; D. Willoweit in Jeserich et al. 1983–88, 1:346ff; Jeserich in ibid., 2:304; Raeff 1983, 158ff; on bureaucracy in general, see Weber 1976a, 551ff (1956, 559ff).

11. Justi 1758, 2:63f (quotation).

12. See Justi 1760–61, 1:3ff; 2:73ff; 1782, 3ff, 10, 15f, 56f, 254ff; Sonnenfels 1771–77, 1:132 (quotation); from Zincke 1742–43, 1:296ff, 319f, 322 (quotation); see also Darjes 1756, 397, 425ff; Dithmar 1755, 154, 172; Förster 1771, 196ff; in general, Small 1909; Brückner 1977, 229ff; Stolleis 1988–92, 1:366ff, esp. 374, 379ff.

13. On the next paragraphs, see Justi 1755, 1:173f, 184, 212ff, 231f, 290ff; 1758, 1:496; 2:56, 63f, 251, 263f; 1760–61, 1:481ff, 505ff, 685f, 698ff; 2:19ff, 37ff; 1782, 34f, 43ff, 59f, 159ff.

14. Justi 1755, 1:xiii–iv, xxiii–iv, 235f.

15. Justi 1755, 1:107; 1758, 2:611 (quotation on giving a gracious audience); 1760–61, 2:47ff, 67f (quotation on freedom of thought), 68ff; 1782, 254ff.

16. On Catholic protests contra commodification, see Nicolai 1783–96, 4:682.

17. On body doubles etc., cf. Kantorowicz 1957; and Boureau 1990, 145ff.

18. See Weber 1976a, esp. 140–48, 654–81 (1956, esp. 140–48, 662–89); 1956, 555–58 (omitted in 1976a); 2001. See also Parsons 1949, 564ff, 661ff; Alexander 1985, 3:84–88, 183–85; Becker 1988; Breuer 1991, esp. 35–67, 215–21; Schluchter 1979, esp. 180ff.

19. See esp. Weber 2001, 122–24, 161, 177–94, 242.

20. Citation from Weber 1976a, 726 (1956, 734). See Schluchter 1979, esp. 184f; at 187ff, he makes a distinction between the routinization (*Veralltäglichung*) and the crystallization (*Versachlichung*) of charisma, seeing the former as relevant to structural aspects, and the latter as relevant to developmental, historical matters. The crystallization of charisma, he notes, does not necessarily entail a depersonalization of it, as routinization typically does; rather, crystallization points to the transmission of charismatic powers from the original figure to "Virtuosi," whose extraordinary powers and abilities represent it.

21. See Weber 1976a [1921], 666ff (1956, 674ff), for passages not about Hitler, but that are able to explain him in advance; 1976a, 725f (1956, 733f), as cited above, indicates that Weber saw the processes leading to "the charismatic transfiguration of reason" (*die charismatische Verklärung der Vernunft*) as also being amenable to bureaucratic and capitalist interests. The Romantic cult of the genius embodies such a charismatic transfiguration of reason precisely because, contra the Enlightenment, it is a form of reason without rules, and that cannot be acquired by rule-governed practice or training or discipline. Genius is a gift.

22. Note that, for Weber, part of the might of modern capitalism is that it avails itself of both bureaucratic and charismatic powers: see Weber 1976a, 658f (1956, 666f). This is what, to echo Marx, makes capitalism's wont to destroy traditional social orders nearly unstoppable. The thesis of the charismatic within the rationalized is derived from Kant's theory of freedom: autonomy exists within the broader sphere of (bureaucratic) duty.

23. On the charismatic aspect of "recognition" and finding the "right one," versus the different mentality of traditional voting, see Weber 1976a, 663 (1956, esp. 671); 1956, 556f (omitted in 1976a, but in 1988a, chap. 9).

24. Lyotard 1979, 7.

25. White 1981, 1; see also the essays in 1987 (containing 1981, too) and 1990. Lyotard 1988, 38f, took back some of the importance of narrative.

26. On irony, cf. Hegel 1970, 13:93–99, for example. Clark 2002 might be read apropos this trope. There is also the interesting role of irony in Friedrich Schelgel's work.

27. "Academic" and its cognates stem from the grove in Athens where Plato taught and where his school, the Academy, resided. The grove had its name from Akademos, a hero whom legend credits with telling the twins Castor and Polydeuces (a.k.a. Pollux)—the Dioscuri, fathered by Zeus—where Theseus, who had killed the Minotaur among other things, had hidden their stepsister, twelve-year-old Helen of Troy. Theseus had abducted her, apparently to wed, and the abduction preceded the later one that provoked the Trojan War.

28. The details are in Houben 1965, 93ff—the official catalogue of 1777 contained itself as an entry, which necessitated not its nonexistence but rather its nonpublication. From 1777 onwards, only a select few could view the catalogue in manuscript.

29. Gibbon 1966, 52. Thanks to Catherine Rice for the reference. I have altered the punctuation slightly.

30. Curtis 1959, 35 (quotation).

31. See Beddard 1997a, 846.

32. Uffenbach 1753-54, 3:84 (quotation), 86 (on Oxford).

33. Winstanley 1935, 256-57.

34. Loyola in Society of Jesus 1919, 1:557 (quotation, translated from the *versio prima*). The Latin constitutions are in Society of Jesus 1934-38, 3: see esp. 137f, 157f, 223ff, 242ff, 254, 262ff, 270ff; in general, see Knowles 1966, 61ff.

35. Fröhlich 1644, 1/3, 289.

36. See Duhr 1907-28; Hengst 1981; Harris 1989; Heilbron 1982, 93-106; and many articles in Ridder-Symoens (ed.) 1996.

37. Weber 1976a, 699 (1956, 707); on literati and ministers in relation to religion, 1988b, 1:esp. 84ff, 395ff; 2:162ff; 3:186ff. Cf. Le Goff 1977, 29ff, 48.

38. Knowles 1966, 62 (quotation).

39. Knowles 1966, 64 (quotation).

40. Marx in Marx and Engels 1970-, I/2, 50f. On Austria, chapters here throughout will recur to this theme; on France, more in the epilogue.

41. On the early modern and modern Germanies, see Holborn 1959 and 1964.

42. On the French versus English universities, see Rashdall 1936, 1:370ff, 497ff; 3:169ff, 293ff; Cobban 1975, 123f, 129, 133ff; Glorieux 1959; Gabriel 1953; 1961, 94f; 1969. One could, of course, suggest France itself as the proper object of study, since the poles grew from its soil; but the later Jesuit influence in France muddies the waters. Developments in Italy form a case sui generis, and of little institutional influence in transalpine Europe.

43. On all of this in more detail, see the epilogue.

44. On European technology and imperialism, see Headrick 1981; McNeill 1984.

CHAPTER TWO

1. On the *Cambridge University Calendar,* see Wordsworth 1877, 364-67. After 1802, the calendar had "a pretty full account of the professors" and the tutors. On the *Oxford University Gazette,* "established in January 1870 to publish the university notices formerly posted in college butteries," see Curthoys 1997, 339.

2. Gockel 1682, 50f (§xxx), tried to legitimate jurists' view of the correct order of uninverted precedence—theology, jurisprudence, medicine, arts and philosophy—by identifying the four faculties, respectively, with the four elements (fire, air, water, earth), and with four grades of being (*esse, vivere, sentire, intelligere*). But why jurisprudence should be identified with life and medicine with sensation is a touchy academic matter, indeed, and eludes my comprehension. A seeming nonjurist linked jurisprudence to Moon, theology to Jupiter, and philosophy to Mars—medicine was not mentioned and the above planets would not seem to give a typical order of precedence: see Schwimmer 1672, Diss. I, Thes. vii,§ lxi. On other justifications of the order of parading and of jurists preceding physicians, see Gastel 1675, 1331; Gisenius 1628, 78f, 93ff; Limnaeus 1629-34, 3:36-43.

3. On the anomalous doctor of music, see Leader 1988, 143f.

4. On the philosophy of clothes, see Rashdall 1936, 3:393; and generally, Hargreaves-Mawdsley 1963.

5. See Dumont 1980 on hierarchical society. On the order of academic precedence, see for instance Bavaria 1756-68, V, 2341; Hausens 1800, 30-33; Gerhard 1655a, Thes. v; Itter 1698, 376ff (*cap. x*); Kundtmann 1644, *mem. sec., art. sec.;* Middendorp 1594, 43; Stephanus 1611, 35ff; Walther 1641, 237ff; Michaelis 1768-76, 2:397ff. At Königsberg in 1678, 1693 and 1706, grave disputes about precedence occurred: see BerlSA, I. HA Rep.

7. Nr. 190, *Med. u. phil. Fak.* 1690–1705, fol. 432–62, 305–60, 255–84; 1706–1713, fol. 521–785.

6. On the origins of the Basel lecture catalogue, the decline of Latin, the notary, and the lack of administrative staff, see Staehelin 1957, 7, 11, 17–19, 35f, 123f. Editing the lecture catalogue was still a duty of the classics or eloquence professor, for example, in the 1838 statutes of the University of Berlin and the 1819 statutes at Bonn: see Brandenburg-Prussia 1839–40, 1:45, 60, 194, 211. On other duties, see Hoffmann 1901, 26–28, 159; Körte 1833, 1:150; Wolf 1935, 1:78; 3:20f; Ribbeck 1879–81, 1:139f; Heeren 1813, 232ff; Köchly 1874, 50f; Süß 1928–30, 1:115, 121, 130f; Creuzer 1836–48, *Abt. 5, Th. 1,* 24.

7. The method of choosing the Basel rector was complex, but the office generally rotated through the faculties: see Staehelin 1957, 11–13. The statutes for the University of Bützow, for example, make rotation through the faculties explicit: see Hölscher 1885, 33, § 31.

8. On the rectorial and academic years at Basel, see Staehelin 1957, 11. The transition to semesters at German universities can be glimpsed in Schröder 1964. Richard Rouse once speculated in conversation that the early division of the academic year into three rather short terms at Oxbridge (currently of eight weeks each) came about as the longest period the masters and doctors could stand to stay in college, that is, away from village mistresses: Oxbridge trimesters constituted the price paid for the maintenance of celibate college life.

9. They may have marched in this order in parades. At the University of Jena, the order of procession of the senate seems to be the uninverted order: see the eighteenth century illustration in Kelter 1908, 44 (Nr. 13, E 1898. 307). See also Puschner 1725a, plate 9.

10. Michaelis 1768–76, 2:403ff, discusses matters of precedence and the contemporary debate about substituting *Dienstalter* absolutely, in place of the faculties for parades and the like, though probably not for the lecture catalogue.

11. Other Basel catalogues shows that 3b was not the universal practice. Biographical data, however, show the order to have been by time of servive (*Dienstalter*). See Staehelin 1957, 68f, on the order of the chairs in the superior faculties; bibliographical data for all Basel instructors, 1632–1818, are in ibid., 543–94. Some eighteenth-century universities tried to entice professors to move by offering them the title of *primarius*— a dangerous practice: see Michaelis 1768–76, 2:397ff.

12. On canonries, see Hinschius 1869–97, 2:55ff, 64, 88ff, 110ff; 615f; Plöchl 1960, 1:427ff; 2:155ff; Schaefer 1965, 109; Feine 1964, 385ff; Schneider 1885, 41ff, 60ff, 70ff, 112ff; Stutz 1972, 320ff; Schieffer 1976, 285; Johag 1977, 34ff; Edwards 1967, 11ff, 251ff. On pluralism, see Roman Catholic Church 1901–27, 22:1018; 1879, *Decret. Greg.*, lib. III, tit. 5, cap. xxviii. The *jus optandi* went into canon law in 1336: see ibid., *Sexti Decret.* lib. I, tit. 4, cap. iv. Cf. statutes of 1247 and 1442 , in Mayer 1791–93, 1:92f; 2:66.

13. On opting up in the philosophy faculty in Basel, see Staehelin 1957, 68ff; on such and other traditional practices for Edinburgh, for example, see Morrell 1997, 2:12ff, 3:160ff; on the same from the standpoint of a discipline, see Meinel 1988. We'll return to opting up and other such practices in many chapters below.

14. On Basel, see Staehelin 1957, 52ff, 405ff. He discusses the nature of paternal, maternal and marital relations through a few exemplary cases, and looks in particular at the web of relations of the faculty listed in the first Basel catalogue (1666/67).

15. On medieval use of "master," "doctor," and "professor," see Weijers 1987, 133–55; Fried 1974, 9–21.

16. On the original Parisian calendar, see Rashdall 1936, 1:489; on the Cambridge trimester, see Leader 1988, 29–30.

17. On lecturing by seniority or lot, see University of Prague 1830–48, 1:68f.

18. University of Heidelberg 1886, 1:33; University of Freiburg im Br. 1964, 118; University of Leipzig 1861, 309; Kink 1854–55, 1:90f; Aschbach 1865–88, 138f; Schreiber 1857–60, II/1, 44. On ordinary and extraordinary books and lectures and so on, see Rashdall 1936, 1:205ff, 433ff; Kaufmann 1888, 2:342ff; Daly 1961, 76ff. For fee schedules, see Lhotsky 1965, 252f; University of Heidelberg 1886, 1:42; Bianco 1850–55, 2:71; University of Leipzig 1861, 312f, 460ff; University of Prague 1830–48, 1:76f; University of Freiburg im Br. 1964, 41, 47; Prantl 1872, 2:75f.

19. Rashdall 1936, 2:283, calls the German system the "oligarchy of permanent and endowed professors," as opposed to the original "popular [democratic] congregations [of masters and doctors], such as still rule our English universities." Rashdall wrote those words in 1895. There seem to have been some changes at English universities in the meantime. The evolution of the arts faculty council into an oligarchy is well illustrated by fifteenth-century Leipzig: see University of Leipzig 1861, 24, 30, 306, 324, 345, 368, 377, 385, 439, 502, 518ff, 525, 527; 1879, 107, 164f, 265. See also University of Ingostadt 1782–1809, 4:77; 142; Liess 1980, 18; Seifert 1972, 170.

20. The dilemma of the extraordinary professors will be treated in chapter 7.

21. See generally Meiners 1802–06, 3:225ff; Bonjour 1960, 117, 121ff; University of Wittenberg 1926–27, 1:14ff, 74ff, 168, 177, 267f. The University of Frankfurt a.d.O. (an der Oder) reformed to a professorate in 1539, the University of Tübingen in 1544, that at Greifswald in 1545, Rostock in 1547, Leipzig and Heidelberg in 1558. The University of Vienna, still Catholic, changed as well, anterior to the Jesuits taking charge. In 1537, the twelve Viennese "collegiati" or college fellows in the arts faculty received disciplinary assignments, the halfway house between college fellows and faculty professors. In 1554, Vienna's new statutes set up twelve salaried professors and one extraordinary professor without a salary. See University of Frankfurt a.d.O. 1897–1906, 6:36ff; University of Heidelberg 1891, 91ff; University of Leipzig 1861, 461f, 518ff; University of Tübingen 1877, 234ff; University of Marburg 1977, 164; Seifert 1971, 109, 163f, 205; Kosegarten 1856–57, 1:193; Pommerania 1765–1802, ser. 1, 2:770ff; Kink 1854–55, I/2, 164ff; 2:352ff, 359ff, 380ff; Arnoldt 1746–69, I/1, 62ff; on Jena in 1568, see DarmSA, Az.: 526C-T4654/89, "Statuta ac Leges Collegii Philosophicis . . . : Prima lex"; see also Paulsen 1919–21, 1:215–48

22. Stolleis 1988–92, 1:370 (quotation)—on the onset of the police ordinance, see 130f, 334ff, 368ff, 378; Wissel 1971–88, 3:35ff; Bornhak 1884–86, 1:181; Raeff 1983, esp. 43ff. Wissel lists only two such ordinances prior to the sixteenth century.

23. Quotations from Raeff 1983, 78, 105—see in general, 78ff, 103ff. On the state to the village level, see Sabean 1990, chaps. 2–3, 5, 8; also Sinemus 1976, 33ff; on the guilds and their reform, Gierke 1868–1913, 1:226ff, 358ff, 384ff, 921ff.

24. Conrad Ischinger is cited and translated in Sabean 1990, 66, 78.

25. Hautz 1862–64, 1:252f, 289, 363f; 2:262, 366ff; University of Heidelberg 1886, 1:147ff, 307ff, 406f; 2:22, 101f, 260f; 1891, 269f.

26. On Wittenberg, see Grohmann 1801–02, 113f; University of Wittenberg 1926–27, 1:74ff, 89f, 162f, 188ff; Saxony 1724, 1:971; Friedensburg 1917, 107, 235. For other cases of reporting, see University of Tübingen 1877, 88; Teufel 1977, 131f; StutSA, A274.17, esp. fol. 94 et seq., 107, 110; Gedike in Fester 1905, 59f.

27. On the Jesuits, see Society of Jesus 1896, xl et seq., 305ff; 1887–94, 1:129; 1934–38, 3:224–26; Knowles 1966, 66f.

28. On the public professor in the Germanies, see Titius 1724, 1250; Lauterbach 1728–29, 3:592ff; Schwimmer 1672, Diss. I, unpag. A schedule of hours for a German university appears in the earliest Latin statutes for the University of Freiburg im Br. (1460). This schedule divides the day into three lecture-periods and sets the books of the arts and philosophy course. In 1476 a like schedule appears at Ingolstadt and regulates the fees, the books, times of day, and more or less lists the lecturers. In the first half of the sixteenth century such regulations of lecture hours, by statute or decree, spread: Wittenberg in 1507/08, Leipzig in 1509/19, Frankfurt a.d.O. by 1511/12, Tübingen in 1535/36, Greifswald in 1545, Vienna in 1554, Heidelberg in 1558. See University of Freiburg im Br. 1964, 54ff, 116f; Prantl 1872, 2:74ff, 88ff, 94f, 109; University of Wittenberg 1926–27, 2:15f, 56f; University of Leipzig 1861, 34ff, 521f; 1879, 371ff; University of Frankfurt a.d.O. 1897–1906, 6:33f; University of Tübingen 1877, 108f, 386f; Pommerania 1765–1802, ser. 1, 2:792, 919f; Kink 1854–55, 2:380ff; University of Heidelberg 1891, 98ff.

29. Brandenburg-Prussia 1839–40, 1:577, 580, 604, 607; DarmSA, 526C-T4654/89, *Jena Statuten, 1568,* "Prima lex"; University of Helmstedt 1963, 123ff, 162–64, 187; University of Marburg 1977, 166, 176; University of Gießen 1881, 17, 20f; also University of Rinteln 1879–80, 18ff, 2; University of Strasbourg 1876, 239ff; 1890–94, 31ff, 142, 144ff, 310ff, 423ff.

30. Kink 1854–55, 2:404; University of Marburg 1848, 88. Visitations will be treated in chapter 9.

31. On reporting and the *Professorenzetteln,* see Tholuck 1853–54, 1:9f; Pommerania 1765–1802, ser. 1. 2:819f, 836, 858f, 889f, 921, 928f, 946ff, 958; ser. 2, 2:119f, 603; Prantl 1872, 2:312, 325ff; Seifert 1971, 346ff; Keck 1965, 113; HanoSA, Cal. Br. 21, Nr. 4132–50, 4159, 4162; University of Jena 1900, 63; University of Frankfurt a.d.O. 1897–1906, 3:92; University of Gießen 1982, tit. 2, § 14; University of Gießen 1907, 1:257; SchlSA, Abt. 47, Nr. 649 (1666–1789); Abt. 47, Nr. 202 (1677–1711); Abt. 47, Nr. 7 (1766 et seq.); Abt. 7, Nr. 2079 (1690 et seq.); Schleswig-Holstein 1832, 367, 429f; also Rodenberg and Volquart 1955, 165ff; Gadendam 1744, "Add. hist.," 23; Wegele 1882, 389ff; Krones 1886, 73f; Stieda 1934, 16; BerlSA, I. HA Rep. 7. 187. Bd. II (1720–27), fol. 1 et seq., 22 et seq.; I. HA Gen. Dir. Ostpreußen. IV. 2488 (1723–57), esp. fol. 86; on Halle in 1731, 1748, 1755 and Prussia generally, see Schrader 1894, 1:346, 382; 2:464; Brandenburg-Prussia 1754–1822, 2:539f; 3:459f; Bornhak 1900, 132–34; BerlSA, I. HA Rep. 34. 58a. 1, (1762–84), fol. 13–15, 17–18, 21–25, 28, 144–15.

32. Here is an excursus on other lands. The statutes of post-Reformation Protestant universities stood under the supervision of the sovereign's ministries: see Stein 1891, 83f; Seifert 1971, esp. 419. Kaufmann 1888–96, 2:110f; but cf. Schindling 1977, 74ff. The 1560 statutes for Marburg enjoined the professors each year to declare publicly, that is to publish, what books they intended to lecture on: see University of Marburg 1977, 176f. Jena's 1591 statutes ordered a lecture catalogue to be published semesterly and sent with a report to the ministry on the current semester; a 1656 ministerial visitation reenjoined it to send a catalogue: see University of Jena 1900, 63; Tholuck 1853–54, 1:33. By order of its sovereign in 1655, Heidelberg was supposed to publish a lecture catalogue; a catalogue appeared that year, although perhaps not regularly thereafter; in 1773 the order had to be restated: see University of Heidelberg 1886, 1:389f; 2:202, 213, 222, 279. By order of a ministrial visitation decree, Wittenberg seems to have been sending its supervising ministry a lecture catalogue by 1665; moreover, since at least 1740, the catalogue had to be submitted for approval in advance of publication: see Saxony 1724, 1:981f; Friedensburg 1917, 527. A 1568 ministerial visitation to Greifswald

mandated a catalogue be sent to the ministry each term, but a 1666 ministerial visitation had to reorder that—in order to see that lectures were in proper order, a catalogue would be published and sent with other reports to the ministry: see Pommerania 1765–1802, ser. 1, 2:819f, 889f, 928; Kosegarten 1856–57, 2:130. Kiel's statutes of 1666 set up a lecture catalogue to be published semesterly and sent the sovereign; a 1778 ministerial decree ordered the catalogue for the coming semester be published five weeks before the end of each semester: see Schleswig-Holstein 1832, 367f, 429f; SchlSA, Abt. 47, Nr. 649, fol. 22. The 1671 statutes for Rinteln ordered a lecture catalogue to be printed regularly and put it under the approval of the chancellor or the sovereign's inspector and visitors: see University of Rinteln 1879–80, 28. In the Austrian lands, in 1751 the professors at Olmouc were ordered to meet regularly each year in order to plan the lectures for the coming year, to print a schema of the lectures and to send this to the ministry—something Prague had been doing since 1747: see d'Elvert 1857, 52. By Erfurt's rector's reform of 1756, professors were to meet each semester a fortnight before publication of the catalogue to decide on upcoming classes, times and texts; a protocol was to be made each time and sent with a report to the Archbishop Elector of Mainz, the sovereign. In 1757 the latter accepted this part of the reform plan, including the protocol and report on the meeting, but ordered the plenary session of the university take place four weeks before publication of the lecture catalogue: see Stieda 1934, 39, 56. At Mainz itself, Bentzel's reform in 1784 also mandated a lecture catalogue be published no less than a fortnight before the beginning of the semester: see Bentzel 1784, 56. At Erlangen by 1769, the lecture catalogue was to be approved by the ministerial deputation in Bayreuth that supervised the university; after 1772, textbooks had to be listed in the catalogue: see Engelhardt 1843, 56f.

33. University of Frankfurt a.d.O. 1897–1906, 3:92; Hausens 1800, 121; Brandenburg-Prussia 1721, 288ff; Arnoldt 1746–69, I/1, 188f, 199ff; I/2, 407f; on Halle, Schrader 1894, 1:344f, 382; 2:465. In 1732, the ministerial acts for Halle have copies of the lecture catalogues of Halle as well as of Duisburg and Frankfurt a.d.O.: BerlSA, I. HA Rep. 52. 159n. 3d, 1725–33, fol. 132–35, 144–47, 153; Brandenburg-Prussia 1754–1822, 1:539–40; 3:459f; Bornhak 1900, 131f. Königsberg's reports, 1719–21, with its catalogue are at BerlSA, I. HA Rep. 7. 187. Bd. II [1720–27], fol. 1 et seq.—at 10–11 they appear to submit the catalogue from 1689 (!) with the report for 27 Jan. 1721; after 1722, the catalogue is absent now and again from the report. Duisburg's reports are at BerlSA, I. HA Rep. 34. 58a. 1, fol. 17 et seq.

34. On the regular appearance of the lecture catalogue, see Tholuck 1853–54, 1:96. This is confirmed by inspection of Schröder 1964.

35. Gedike (1789) in Fester 1905, 26.

36. *Göttingische Zeitungen von gelehrten Sachen*, 1748, "Zugabe zum Märzmonat," Stück 31, 241–48.

37. *Göttingische Anzeigen von gelehrten Sachen*, 1755, 29 Sept., "Zugabe zum Stück 117," 1085–98. I have not been able to see the Helmstedt lecture catalogues of this time period and it is at least conceivable that Helmstedt predated Göttingen here.

38. These two poles—an order of persons versus an order of disciplines—are both evident in what seem to be the earliest catalogues. From Wittenberg in 1507 we have a "Rotulus Doctorum Vittenberge . . ." The "rotulus" stems from the Middle Ages and was a list sent regularly, eventually annually, by the masters and doctors at each university to the pope. In the rotulus, academics petitioned the pope for canonries, prebends, or other monies to be given them in absentia via "papal provision." Such papal practices in fact laid the basis for the "professorial prebend," that is, laid the basis

for the professorship. The order of academics in the rotulus—first theology, then law, then medicine, then arts and philosophy—seems to have been the origins of the traditional order of precedence. The Wittenberg rotulus of 1507 orders the theology, law and medical faculties by individuals; no times are given for their lectures. It divides the lower faculty into arts versus "humanistic letters" as two separate sections. In these sections the next division is by lecture hours; the final ordering is then by individuals. The catalogue for the superior faculties is a "rotulus," while that for the lower faculties is a lecture schedule, and one where work and time set the primary structure. The next extant catalogue, from 1561, has the soon typical order, we saw in figures 2.2 to 2.3. Similarly, the Jena lecture catalogue of 1564 has theology, law and medicine ordered by professors. The arts faculty is ordered, however, by topics taught in this order: Latin and Greek grammar, Hebrew, dialectics and rhetoric, geometry, astronomy, physics, philosophy, ethics, disputation and style lessons. From these examples, it looks like the earliest catalogues might have been at least ordered in terms both of persons and their seniority (the superior faculties) and of disciplines and their times (the inferior faculty). One point of origin for this ordering by disciplines would be the humanists' conceit of academia as not a corporation of persons (*universitas personarum*) but one of letters (*universitas litterarum*), later taken up by jurists, from which emerged the notion of the republic of letters. Be that as it may, during the sixteenth and seventeenth centuries, the cast of the catalogue, that we saw in figures 2.2 to 2.3 from Basel, became typical and the norm: the faculties in their order of traditional precedence within which the faculty usually marched in order of seniority. On the Wittenberg lecture catalogues of 1507 and 1561 and the Jena catalogue of 1564, see appendix 2. On the jurists' formulation of the humanists' *universitas litterarum,* see Stephanus 1611, 2:34; Gisenius 1628, 75f; Mendus 1668, 2.

39. Michaelis 1768–76, 3:9f.

40. *Erfurtische gelehrte Zeitungen,* Nr. 24, 24 March 1769, 187–89, quotation at 187; Nr. 74, 15 Sept. 1769, 593–600, quotation at 593.

41. On Halle 1768, see Brandenburg-Prussia 1754–1822, 4:5049–62, at 5053f. Halle's lecture catalogue stands under ministerial supervision at least by 1730: see Bornhak 1900, 131f. On Königsberg, see Selle 1944, 179f; on Greifswald, Pommerania 1765–1802, ser. 2, 2:119; on Leipzig, see appendix 2. Regarding other universities, in a Prague lecture catalogue in German for 1771, law and medicine were ordered by professors, while theology and arts were by disciplines; in 1771, the German lecture catalogues for Vienna and Tyrnau, two other Habsburg universities, were ordered, however, by professors. At Strasbourg, some time between 1755 and 1782, the lecture catalogue changed to an order by disciplines. At least by 1787, Heidelberg's summer semester catalogue was arranged by disciplines. Erlangen ordered the catalogue by disciplines in 1782. Dusiburg and Frankfurt a.d.O. ordered the Latin catalogue by disciplines by 1787. At least by winter semester 1798/99, Marburg ordered its catalogue by disciplines; Kiel at least by 1790, and Breslau by 1792. Wittenberg's lecture catalgoue was under ministerial supervision by 1740: see Friedensburg 1917 527; Erlangen's by 1769: see Engelhardt 1843, 56f. Unevidenced remarks here are based on appendix 2.

42. Justi 1782, 258. On the ministerial control of lectures and the lecture catalogue in the nineteenth century, see VienSA, St. H.K., 5 Prag A3 [228] (*Vorlesungsordnungen 1835–35*); Brandenburg-Prussia 1839–40, 1:60, 211f; 2:176–80; Mayer 1892–94, 1:28; 2:14; on Rostock, see Mecklenburg 1848–59, 4:257, 260. In 1820, Brandenburg-Prussia issued a blanket decree to the effect that all universities had to publish a German lecture catalogue ordered by disciplines, if they were only publishing a Latin one: see

Brandenburg-Prussia 1855, 1:507; for Halle in particular, 2:178f. For the University of Würzburg, reorganization acts of 3 Nov. and 11 Nov. 1803 did away with faculties and set up sections: a general one, being arts and sciences in four subsections, and a particular one, with four subsections: theology, law, cameral sciences, and medicine. In that sense, the once inferior faculty had become effectively the superior or abstract one. The lecture catalogues of 1803 to 1809 probably thus began with general topics, that is, arts and sciences. The reorganization act of 7 Sept. 1809, § 17, set the lecture catalogue back in terms of four faculties—some academic manners were deep seated: see Wegele 1882, 2:467–82, 507–16.

43. Austria 1840, 1:20.

44. On Jesuit catalogues, see Hengst 1981, 103, 112f; and, Society of Jesus 1896, 307, 315. Schröder 1964 does not record the sixteenth-century Jesuit catalogues; his survey would most probably have caught later ones, had they existed. On the Wittenberg catalogue, see under Wittenberg in appendix 2, which is where more detail on all the above can be found.

45. On Luther, see under Leipzig in the notes in appendix 2.

46. See for example, University of Marburg 1977, 176f; University of Frankfurt a.d.O. 1897–1906, 3:92; University of Heidelberg 1886, 2:202, 279; Schleswig-Holstein 1832, 367f, 429f; SchlSA, Abt. 47, Nr. 649, fol. 22; Becker 1907, 274.

47. Kirchner 1928–31, 2:14ff.

48. On the growing regularity of the catalogues, see the list of extant ones in Schröder 1964—admittedly only prima facie evidence for this point.

49. On Halle, see Schrader 1894, 1:344f; 2:465.

50. On German lecture catalogues, see appendix 2

51. On Göttingen, see *Göttingische Zeitungen von gelehrten Sachen*, 1748, "Zugabe zum Märzmonat," 31 Stück; *Göttinger Gelehrten Anzeigen*, 1755, 29 Sept., 117 Stück, 1085–98, at 1085f. By 1800, the catalogue was so important for marketing that when the University of Würzburg reopened as reoganized in 1805, one feared low attendance due to the delayed publication of the catalogue: see the documents of 5 Oct. 1805 in Wegele 1882, 2:464, 467.

52. Anon 1798, esp. 3.

53. For Gedike, see Fester 1905, 26; for Boell or Böll, see Rössler 1855, 2:479.

54. On Kant's lectures, see Arnoldt 1906–11, V/2, 173–343. In summer semester 1761, for example, Lecturer Kant advertised thirty-four to thirty-six hours of lectures per week, about which Arnoldt 1906–11, V/2, 194, writes, "Dass er alle jene Kollegien wirklich las ist nicht glaublich . . ."

55. On Göttingen as a model for reforming Catholic universities, see Haaß 1952, 14–16, 33, 41, 54–56, 167; Hammerstein 1977, 157. On the proposal for Mainz, see the document in Just and Mathy 1965, 106.

56. See, for example, Lichtenberg 1983–92, 3:219, 299; also Clark 1997, 39f. Heinrich Heine immortalized the fame of *Göttinger Würste*, even eaten with gusto by Kant in far-off Königsberg: about the latter, see Clark 1999b, 464. Personally, I prefer *Thüringer* in Weimar.

### CHAPTER THREE

1. On the agonistic aspect of medieval knowledge, see Kink 1854–55, I/1, 74ff. On the dialogical character of knowledge, see Ong 1983, who however sets the slow onset of our modern "visual" knowledge with Ramus, that is, as pre-Cartesian. On the polemical aspect of early modern knowledge, see Gierl 1997 and 2001.

2. Paraphrase of Bonocompagno 1892 [1220], 279; see Rückbrod 1977, 67, 72f.

3. A discussion of figure 3.1 is in Schwinges 1986, 352f. On the *pecia* system, see Talbot 1958, 67f; and Pollard 1978. On note-taking at medieval Oxford, see Parkes 1992, esp. 463–70, where the existence of the *pecia* system there for the upper faculties, at least, is cast into doubt.

4. The many illustrations in Cardini and Beonio-Brocchieri 1991 show medieval lecturers in the typical immobile position at a *cathedra*, as in figure 3.1.

5. "The extent to which the lecturer dealt with the glossarial literature at the expense of the basic text was a matter of balance and was left to his personal judgement": see Cobban 1988, 163—generally 163–67. Medieval lecture requirements are in University of Vienna 1965, 236, 243; University of Heidelberg 1886, 1:34, 38; University of Leipzig 1861, 310f, 464f, 490; University of Prague 1830–48, 1:48f; University of Freiburg im Br. 1964, 34ff, 40, 46. On the ordinary lectures and so on, see Rashdall 1936, 1:205ff, 433ff; Kaufmann 1888–96, 2:342ff; Daly 1961, chap. 3.

6. On the *Wegstreit* in relation to the universities of the empire, see Ritter 1922. On the more political aspects, see Overfield 1984, 48ff. On Cologne, see Keussen 1934, 296.

7. On Heidelberg, see Hautz 1862–64, 1:304ff, 347ff—quotations at 348; also University of Heidelberg 1886, 1:165, 173f, 193; 2:48, 50. On other universities, see Schreiber 1857–60, II/1, 40ff, 59ff; Mayer 1926, 95ff; Kosegarten 1856–57, 1:132ff; 2:192, 229; University of Frankfurt a.d.O. 1897–1906, 6:36ff; Vischer 1860, 144f, 166f; BaseSA, Univ. Arch., A,1, 1459–1609, *Liber Statutorum:* 1459, 13; R,1, 1492–16. Jh.: *Statuta fac. art.:* 1492, 24; Seifert 1971, 75ff, 407f; Liess 1980, 11ff; Prantl 1872, 2:49f, 72ff, 155f; University of Ingolstadt 1973, 45ff, 67ff; also University of Tübingen 1877, 85, 378.

8. See Roman Empire 1872–95, *Codex,* X, 54 (53); Bartolus 1615, III, 68r–v; VIII/2, 23v–24r; Baldus 1615–16, 8:270v; cf. Solerius 1671, 208f, who sees the trials as exams for degrees from bachelor, to licentiate, to master or doctor.

9. The citation is from Roman Catholic Church 1914, 56. On monasticism and the new religious orders, see Lawrence 1984a, 28; Knowles 1966; von den Steinen 1958/59, 249ff; Southern 1970, 225; Leclercq 1957.

10. Abelard and Héloïse 1962, lines 144–48.

11. On Abelard and the new scholastic methods, see Grabmann 1957; Murray 1967; Luscombe 1969; Evans 1980; Paré et al. 1933, 113ff, 123ff; Ehlers 1974, 64f.

12. These matters will be treated further in chapter 6.

13. On the structure of disputation in the Germanies, see Thomasius 1670, 139; Horn 1893; and Gierl 1997, 124–45; 2000. At early modern Cambridge, despite some different terminology, the *disputatio pro gradu* seems to have been essentially the same: see Winstanley 1935, 41–46; on Oxbridge generally, see Cobban 1988, 167ff.

14. On disputation, see Horn 1893. On Oxbridge, see Simon 1966, 245–67, esp. 253; and Curtis 1959, 88–92. On the Jesuits, see Society of Jesus 1887–94, esp. 2:100ff, 340ff; on the Jesuit University of Innsbruck, for example, see Probst 1869, 166ff. On Luther and Wittenberg, see Wolf 1952; for other universities, see SchlSA, Abt. 47, *Universität Kiel,* Nr. 72, esp. 1709 (3a), 1744 (3b), 1745 (3c), 1764 (3d), 1770 (8b); University of Marburg 1848, 88; 1977, 168ff (1560); University of Gießen 1881, 17 (1607); on Leipzig in 1616 and Wittenberg in 1536 and 1614, see Saxony 1724, 1:917, 955, 963ff; on Frankfurt, see University of Frankfurt a.d.O. 1897–1906, 2:79f (1564); on the decrees to Jena, 1681 to 1696, Schmid 1772, 203; on the eighteenth century, University of Jena 1958b, 1:178; on Königsberg, Selle 1944, 190; on the *pro loco,* University of Marburg 1977, 169; University of Frankfurt a.d.O. 1897–1906, 2:53, 79; Pommerania 1765–1802, ser. 1, 2:926 (1702).

15. On Kiel's unheated lecture halls, see Rodenberg and Volquart 1955, 162. The

halls at Gießen were also clearly unheated: see University of Gießen 1907, 1:140f. Both Kiel and Gießen were universities of average endowment, wealth and size. On anatomical theaters generally, see Richter 1936, esp. 44ff, 76ff.

16. For example, the statutes of Königsberg (1554), Marburg (1560) and Halle (1694) do not stipulate that one must prove attendance at lectures; one must pass exams: see University of Marburg 1977, 162–73; Brandenburg-Prussia 1839–40, 1:525–27, 602–3, 608–11. On Cambridge tutors, see Winstanley 1935, 180f, 268–76; on Oxford, Sutherland 1986a, 479f.

17. On declining enrollments and the fading of the B.A., see Bengeser 1965, 20; Eulenburg 1904, 309–17.

18. Bornhak 1900, 133; see also 131ff.

19. The citation on Newton and a reference to its source are in Westfall 1980, 209.

20. On Barrow, see Feingold 1990, 53–67; on Whiston and Newton, Snoblen 2000, chap 2.3.

21. Meiners 1775–76, 3:118.

22. On Ingolstadt, see Prantl 1872, 1:440f. Taking Kant as a fair example, one can see, as we noted in chapter 2, that he commonly tried to teach more classes than was humanly possible; he clearly did not intend to teach all that he advertised: on Kant's lectures, see Arnoldt 1906–11, V/2, 173–343.

23. See Tholuck 1853–54, 1:88ff; also Bornhak 1900, 134f.

24. Winstanley 1935, chap. 3; the first quotation is from 95, second from 121,

25. Winstanley 1935, chap. 3; the first quotation is from 155, the second from 160, the last from 98. On Oxford, see Sutherland 1986a, 472–75.

26. See Lauterbach 1728–29, 3:596f, 619; also Kreittmayr 1756–68, 5:2336.

27. On lecturing and mulcts, see Thommen 1889, 58; Pommerania 1765–1802, ser. 1, 2:819f, 889f, 918, 928f; Saxony 1724, 1:917f, 967ff; Brandenburg-Prussia 1721, 1:289; Arnoldt 1746–69, I/1, 184f, 188f; I/2, 407–08 (decree of 1717); University of Ingolstadt 1782–1809, 4:194; Siefert 1971, 130, 297, 339f; University of Helmstedt 1963, 184, 189; University of Wittenberg 1926–27, 1:683; University of Strasbourg 1876, 221; 1890, 142f; Württemberg 1843, 236f; University of Rinteln 1879, 36; University of Marburg 1848, 25f, 88; 1977, 166; University of Gießen 1907, 1:142, 274; Keussen 1934, 115f; University of Frankfurt a.d.O. 1897–1906, 2:52, 78; 3:85f; Bornhak 1900, 125, 131ff; Tholuck 1853–54, 1:126f.

28. Michaelis 1768–76, 2:6. On decrees rationalizing lectures and terms, see SchlSA, Abt. 47: *Universität Kiel,* Nr. 649, fol. 22 (29 May 1768); BerlSA, I. HA Rep. 52. 159n. 3d, 1691–1724, fol. 499r (16 May 1696); 1725–33, fol. 217 (12 May 1730); Brandenburg-Prussia 1721, 1:288ff; 1754–1822, 3:459f: Rodenberg and Volquart 1955, 163; Arnoldt 1746–69, I/1, 197ff; I/2, 332; Pommerania 1765–1802 ser. 1, 2:819f, 919f, 928; Saxony 1724, 919; University of Ingolstadt 1782–1809, 4:468; University of Marburg 1848, 48f; 1977, 166, 178; University of Helmstedt 1963, 183ff; Württemberg 1843, 378f, 387, 395, 488f; Rössler 1855, 2:120–21; University of Gießen 1907, 2:274, 276; Tholuck 1853–54, 2:85f; Bornhak 1900, 134f; Brandenburg-Prussia 1737–51, I/2, 37; University of Frankfurt a.d.O. 1897–1906, 2:53; Will 1801, 112. On Vienna, see Austria 1840, 2:55. On other aspects of ministerial control, see d'Elvert 1857, 52; Stieda 1934, 39, 56; Selle 1944, 179f; Paulsen 1919–21, 2:138; Schleswig-Hostein 1832, 430f; Brandenburg-Prussia 1754–1822, 4:5049.

29. On Ingolstadt, see Keck 1965, 114, citing Prantl 1872, 1:290f; on Würzburg, Wegele 1882, 1:434, 439; 2:416; Stosiek 1972, 194; on Göttingen, Streich 1977, 267.

30. On Prussia, Bornhak 1900, 132; on Mainz, Bentzel 1784, 46, 103, 105f. Dicta-

tion must have continued in some places, as Anon 1833, 12, still felt the need to denounce it.

31. Justi 1782, 258. On the ministerial control of lectures and the catalogue in the nineteenth century, see VienSA, St. H.K., 5 Prag A3 [228] (*Vorlesungsordnungen 1835–35*); Brandenburg-Prussia 1839–40, 1:60, 211f; 2:176–80; Mayer 1892–94, 1:28; 2:14; on Rostock, see Mecklenburg 1848–59, 4:257, 260.

32. On hierarchies within lecture halls, see Anon n.d.3, 15, 32; Anon 1778–79, 1:311. The 1591 statutes in University of Jena 1900, 65, indicate that the scholarship students were subjected to an inverted place-discrimation, "das sie In Lectionibus et Disputationibus, diese Bängk unnd stellen einnehmen, So der Cathedra unnd Professori am negsten seint, das sie also denn Professoribus bekanndt, unndt dieselbenn welchergestaldtt von Ihnen die Lectiones Jedesmahls besuchtt, wissenn könnenn . . ."

33. Quotations on Wittenberg from Schalscheleth 1795, 237f. On Halle, see Laukhard 1792–1802, 1:102.

34. Rinck 1897, 91. See also Heun 1792, 1:16ff, a guide for students.

35. Rabiosus 1796, 2:38ff. On note-takers at Leipzig, see Bruchmüller 1909, 82. On having a text, see University of Freiburg im Br. 1964, 40.

36. On the Baroque, see Barner 1970, 86ff, 393ff, 404f. On medieval students' (scripted) views of disputation, see Anon 1476, cap. xii, translated in Seybolt 1921, 79f. On the decline of disputation at Basel as tied to the decline of Latin, see Bonjour 1960, 275f.

37. Leigh 1715.

38. Chladenius 1755.

39. Michaelis 1768–76, 1:238f, 371f; 4:1ff, 11f, 42, 67ff.

40. Michaelis 1768–76, 1:237–39; 4:72f; cf. Walther 1641, 83f. On an example of examination and disputation in the medical faculty, see Kortum 1910, 37ff. In the early nineteenth century, seemingly less well informed than Walther, Hugo 1828, 1:138, held that, in first half of eighteenth century, it was still rare that one disputed *sine praeside*.

41. Bahrdt 1922, 128ff. In Arnim 1857, 16:6–7, one student plans to play the opponent against another and to surprise the respondent by not playing the disputation as rehearsed. On disputation as a joke at Göttingen, see Mackensen 1791, 81f.

42. On Oxbridge generally, see Wordsworth 1877, 22–43; on Oxford, see Mallet 1924–27, 3:162ff; Sutherland 1986a, esp. 475–77, 481–84; on Cambridge, Jebb 1774a, 284ff; Cumberland 1807, 1:99–105; Ball 1889, 163–69, 173–86; Winstanley 1935, 46–49, citation from him and from Whewell at 47; on advance rehearsal at Cambridge and abolition of the disputation in 1839, see Searby 1997, 154–57.

43. Anon 1797. On disputation as rehearsed, Michaelis 1768–76, 3:54f; 4:43ff.

CHAPTER FOUR

1. Figure 4.1 is a *Stammbuchbild*, produced for a student market.

2. A similar image of examination is in Krause 1979, 14 (circa 1751/54).

3. We'll return to academic symbols in chapter 6. See also Walther 1641, 437ff; Itter 1698, 317ff; Solerius 1671 212ff, 221ff.

4. On the Wolff-Affair, see the sources cited in Clark 1999b.

5. On confession and "tables" in the two senses, *la table et le tableau*, see Foucault 1966, 80, 86ff, 229ff; 1975, 150, 187; 1976, 78; 1980, 8 11, 27 [1994 2:345f, 348, 361]. His famous "Two Lectures" of 1976 on juridical versus disciplinary power are in 1980, 78–108; and in Kelly (ed.) 1994, 17–46. On the two models of power, see Kelly 1994, 365–400. Hoskin 1979 is an early example trying to develop Foucaultian themes here.

6. See Rybczynski 1986, 78–82. On the "office," see Friese and Wagner 1993, chap. 3.

7. On exams, see Albers 1900–12, 1:34f, 185; 4:35f; 5:55, 139f; Hallinger 1963–80, 4:26ff, 174; Cluniacs 1853, pt. 1, cap. lii; Schroll 1941, 120ff.

8. On the three trials, see Roman Empire 1872–95, *Codex*, X, 54 (53); Bartolus 1615, III, 68r–v; VIII/2, 23v–24r; Baldus 1615–16, 8:270v. Gisenius 1628, 191ff, gives a slightly different order to the three trials of the exam.

9. These issues are pursued in detail in chapter 6.

10. Itter 1698, 278ff; Walther 1641, 82ff

11. Walther 1641, 82ff.

12. Anon 1726, 152f (quotation), also 147ff; and University of Wittenberg 1926–27, 1:365.

13. On Cambridge, for example, Gascoigne 1984, 554f, explains that, although the bachelor's exam was officially conducted by four "moderators," nonetheless pre-1763 any regent master and post-1763 (until the later reforms) any master could attend and pose a question—the exam was a private one but an affair of the faculty. At Oxford, however, the exam was held to be a public one: see Curthoys 1997, 345f.

14. The final and public exam, the disputation for a degree, is examined in chapter 6.

15. The dean's protocol is reprinted in University of Wittenberg 1926–27, 2:117ff.

16. An account of the exam is in Kern and Kern 1990, 114ff. The problematic nature of the doctorate in philosophy (or arts or sciences) at the time is pursued in chapter 6 below.

17. On Dorothea Schlözer in general, see Kern and Kern 1990.

18. See, for example, the case of Vienna in 1391 in Aschbach 1865–88, 1:115f, 138.

19. See Ritter 1922.

20. The paragraphs below are based on University of Ingolstadt 1973, 45ff, 67ff. On the above, see Prantl 1872, 2:48ff, 72–90, 156.

21. The following discussion of Cambridge is based in general on Jebb 1774a, 291–97; 1774b; Wordsworth 1877, 29–31, 44–58; Ball 1889, 171f, 187–200; Winstanley 1935, 41–57; Curtis 1959, 88ff; Hoskin 1979; Gascoigne 1984; Searby 1997, 154–66; Warwick 2003, chaps. 2, 4, 5. Specific points will be referenced where appropriate below.

22. The tutors' control of education will be pursued in chapter 5.

23. Winstanley 1935, 48

24. Winstanley 1935, 48.

25. On the origins and whimsical evolution of the "Tripos," see Wordsworth 1877, 16–21; and Ball 1889, 217ff.

26. See Watson 1818, 1:29f, 35.

27. Cumberland 1807, 1:105.

28. The account from 1757 is from John Trusler, cited here from Winstanley 1935, 49; I have altered the orthography very slightly.

29. Venn's account from 1761 is in Wordsworth 1877, 30f; the account seemingly from 1763 is in ibid., 47f; the source is unclear to me.

30. The account below is from Jebb 1774a, 291–97; 1774b, 368; 1774a, 306–08, has remarks on Oxford. Citations to Jebb are given in the text.

31. Ball 1889, 190–92, claims that Jebb speaks of three moderators; but, I see no textual support in Jebb 1774a or 1774b for that claim. Wordsworth 1877, 44ff, is worse, since he effectively mixed practices in 1774 with those in 1802. Wordsworth 1877, 30f, claims that John Venn was examined by proctors and moderators, but that was in the time when candidates came one by one to the table at which the examiners sat as a

group. Searby 1997, 160, says that the number of moderators was first increased from two to four in 1779.

32. On the 1780s, see Gunning 1855, 1:80f.

33. Ball 1889, 192ff; Wordsworth 1877, 53; Gascoigne 1984, 551f; Searby 1997, 163; Warwick 2003, esp. chaps 4–5.

34. On the problems, see Searby 1997, 159.

35. See Ball 1889, 171f; Gascoigne 1984, 578, n. 21.

36. One the above and below, see Gascoigne 1984, 560ff, 566ff; also Searby 1997, 160.

37. Quotation from Gascoigne 1984, 568; at 561, he acknowledges that Rothblatt's thesis (Rothblatt 1974, 280ff) on the lack of meritocratic ideal at Oxbridge might hold for the origin of the exam pre-1750, but needs qualification in view of its later development.

38. On the reception of Continental analysis in Cambridge, see Searby 1997, 168ff; Warwick 2003.

39. See Buchwald 1894, 103; Anon 1988 [1587], cap. i.

40. University of Wittenberg 1926–27, 1:529.

41. HanoSA, Cal. Br. 21, Nr. 3878, fol. 105–35. The 1575/83 statutes for Tübingen speak of the *Annotationes* of students: see Württemberg 1843, 181f.

42. The Paderborn statutes are in Freisen 1898, 1:31f.

43. See University of Leipzig 1861, 427; Leube 1921–54, 1:57f.

44. Vormbaum 1860–64, 3:120, 295, 315, 508f, 535f, 543f, 613ff, 690, 700. Those tables are the only ones brought to light from the three volumes above, and the sixty-two volumes of Kehrbach et al. 1886 et seq. A table from a school visitation of 1605 is in Knox 1995, 54f .

45. Austria 1840, 1:71.

46. Gedike (1789) in Fester 1905, 47f, 71, 76; see also Stieda 1934, 115; Bentzel 1784, 45f, 107ff, 131f, 136; Pommerania 1765–1802, ser. 2, 2:119; University of Heidelberg 1886, 2:306f.

47. In Wotke 1905, 319ff, 378ff.

48. On the above, see, for 1775 and 1781, Wotke 1905, 280, 375ff, 380; for, 1784 and 1790, Austria 1840, 2:55, 63; on 1780, Schmid 1859–78, 5:374; see also Probst 1869, 403.

49. On Hanover, see Blättner 1960, 42f; on the Saxon school plan of 1773, Vorbaum 1860–64, 3:637ff, quotation at 637; on the decline of beating, Paulsen 1919–21, 2:155f.

50. On Berlin, see Schwartz 1910–11, 2:389.

51. On the above, see Schwartz 1910–11, 1:122–33.

52. See Schwartz 1910–11, 1:65f, 127, 148; on the poor, Michalsky 1978, 71ff; University of Königsberg 1908–17, 1:cvii.

53. See Schwartz 1910–11, 3:75, 135f, 140, 229.

54. Goody 1986, 94 (citation). See the editors' introduction in Becker and Clark 2001.

55. About all of that, more in detail in the next chapter. On Wolf and the seminar, see BerlSA, I. HA., Rep. 76. alt II. Nr. 102, 1787–1806, fol. 1–2 (plan 4.IX.1787), 4–6 (to the ministry, 6.IX.1787), 17–18 (seminar list, 15.X.1787), 19 (Gedike to Wolf, 22.I.1788), 24–25 (to the ministry, 5.II.1788), 26–27 (Gedike to Wolf, 12.II.1788), 28–31 (to the ministry, 10.III.1788), 32–33 (to the ministry, 9.III.1788), 34 (Gedike to Wolf, 18.III.1788), 35–36 (Gedike's Instruction, 22.III.1788), 37–40 (report, 11.XI.1788), 41–44 (report, 13.VI.1789), 52 (Gedike to Wolf, 21.VII.1795), 62–65 (report , 30.IV.1799); evolution of tabular reporting is at fol. 17–18, 95–97, 121–22, 133–34; Nr. 76 [vol. 4: Catalogus lec-

tionum . . . Halle, 180–02], fol. 32–33, 41–42, 120 (on his missing lists, 16.V.1801), 131–32, 187–88, 253–54. See also Wolf 1835, 308ff, 315ff; 1935, 1:55–57, 63–65, 70–73, 75–76, 94f, 209ff, 280ff; 3:20, 76; Arnoldt 1861, 1:95ff, 102ff, 248, 255; Körte 1833, 1:147ff, 159ff, 169ff, 200ff, 243; and Süss 1929–30, 35, on Wolf's seminar.

56. On the notion of "intimate distance," see Becker 2001.

57. See, for example, BerlSA, I. HA., Rep. 76. Va. Sek. 11. Tit. 10. Nr. 3. Bd. I [1810–24, Königsberg], esp. fol. 5–7, 24–25, 29–30, 34–35, 38, 65, 84–86, 127–29, 136–42; Sekt. 3. Tit. X. Nr. 3. Bd. I [1818–24, Bonn], esp. fol. 9, 25–43, 70, 83–105, 145–56, 175–90; Sekt. 4, Tit. X. Nr. 10. Bd. I [1812–32, Breslau], esp. fol. 34–37, 130–31.

58. University of Cambridge 1796 et seq.: in 1802, xx; cited here from Wordsworth 1877, 45–47 and, in part, from Ball 1889, 198–99. Wordsworth 1877, 53ff, cites more at length from the account of 1802 in the University Calendar.

59. The Austrian *Abitur* or *Maturitätsprüfung* may have been just as severe, but I am ignorant of its conduct and evaluation. In any case, in the next decades the fierce Prussian-style *Abitur* would spread throughout the Germanies generally. On German exam torture, see Schwartz 1910–11, 1:65ff. On the spread of the *Abitur* or *Maturität-sprüfung*, see Schmid 1859–78, 4:638; 5:74; 6:453ff; 7:473; 10:544; Paulsen 1896–97, 2:353ff, 418, 433, 439; Bavaria 1838, IX/1, 567ff; Hanover 1886–90, 1:569, 574f, 577.

60. Ball 1889, 209ff; Wordsworth 1877, 53.

61. On the above, see Searby 1997, 166ff, 176ff; Ball 1889, 211ff. On the origins and sense of the "Tripos," see, as noted above, Wordsworth 1877, 16–21; and Ball 1889, 217ff.

62. Wright 1827, 1:3, note; 2:59–98.

63. Wright 1827, 1:229–323; citations at 229.

64. Wright 1827, 1:229–323; citation at 248.

65. Wright 1827, 1:249 (citation).

66. On the above, see Gascoigne 1984, 557; Ball 1889, 212f; Winstanley 1955, 158–60.

67. On this paragraph and the next, see Warwick 2003, esp. 182–212; citation at 188. I read Warwick's wonderful book too late to integrate it better into this book.

68. The discussion on Oxford here is based on Curthoys 1997; on the eighteenth century, see Sutherland 1986a, esp. 475f.

69. A. P. Saunders, *Obervations on the Different Opinions Held as to the Changes Proposed in the Examination Statute*, 1830, 24, note, cited in Curthoys 1997, 344; see also 366, on the "'strong objections on moral grounds' to the idea of a competitive order of merit," as encouraging pride and envy.

70. A description of the figure is in Brock and Curthoys 1997, xiii, n. 8—probably by Curthoys; see also Curthoys 1997, 345ff. The description in Brock and Curthoys 1997 presumes that there are only three examiners present here, but does not comment about who the others at the table might be. That description holds, however, that "Buss's scenes are, in the main, accurate"—Buss being the artist in question who drew figure 4.8.

71. These incidents are related in Curthoys 1997, 346.

72. The description from 1801 is from *Letters from and to Charles Kirkpatrick Sharpe, Esq.*, ed. A. Allardyce, 2 vols., Edinburgh, 1888, 1:111, cited in Curthoys 1997, 345f.

73. On the printing of the exam, see Curthoys 1997, 346ff; also Rothblatt 1974, 290f.

74. Citation from Rothblatt 1974, 295, and in general, see 280ff, 287, 294.

75. Curthoys 1997, 340; orthography of Ruskin citations altered to American-style. On the spread of such written exams, especially in the Cambridge-spirit, see

Whewell 1845, 209; Forbes, and Latham, all cited in Gascoigne 1984, 548, and 579, n. 30.

76. See Württemberg 1843, 428–30, 533–34, and also cf. 806. The figure is from Anon 1853 at TübiUA.

77. Quotation from Sabean 2001, 90, concerning a different but similar context.

### CHAPTER FIVE

1. Veysey 1965, 154; see also 127, 132f (source of epigraph above).

2. Citation on M. Carey Thomas from Horowitz 1994, 186; on Thomas in Leipzig, see 108–26, esp. 126. Seligman cited in Veysey 1965, 154; the latter's account of the origins of the German seminar at 153–54 is less than accurate; but, given the general state of research on it when he wrote, that is understandable. C. K. Adams was at Cornell in the 1880s, where Moses Coit Tyler, also previously from Michigan, had already introduced the seminar. Thanks to Alix Cooper and Carol Kammen for help on the seminar in the United States.

3. Veysey 1965, 156.

4. See Beck in University of Leipzig 1809, 4; and Wolf's letter of April 1810 in Wolf 1935, 2:104. On the origins of "research" as an ideology and the German seminars in general, see Turner 1971; 1973; 1974; 1980; 1982. The historiography of the seminars began in the eighteenth century with the genre of historical writing on individual German universities. With the appearance in the nineteenth century of biographies of famous philologists, who were usually seminar directors, treatment of the history of the seminars expanded. In a few cases, histories of individual seminars appeared. Most of these will be cited below—and in general, see appendix 3. Numerous but scattered materials on the seminars lie in the nineteenth century histories of philology and philologists, above all in Bursian 1883, Paulsen 1919–21, and Eckstein 1966. The first work on the seminars per se seems to be Erben 1913; Thiele 1938 is about primary school teachers. Fairly recent works in part on the seminars are Grafton 1983, and Leventhal 1986.

5. On America, see Veysey 1965. On Germany, see the references to Turner in the previous note. On the Königsberg physics seminar, as modeled on the philology seminars, see Olesko 1991; on the natural science seminar in Bonn, see Goldfuß 1821; and "Reglement . . . 1825" in Brandenburg-Prussia 1839–40, II/2, 626–31; on Halle, see "Reglement für das Seminar für Mathematik und die gesammten Naturwissenschafen . . . 1839" in Brandenburg-Prussia 1839–40, I/2, 839–41; on Königsberg, see University of Königsberg 1836; 1837; 1838; 1839; and Brandenburg-Prussia 1839–40, II/2, 858–61.

6. See the editor's introduction in University of Freiburg im Br. 1957.

7. See University of Freiburg im Br. 1957, facsimile volume, 39r-v.

8. On the circular and the domestic disputations, see Anon 1476, cap. xii—in Seyboldt 1921, 80f; University of Leipzig 1861, 435f; Horn 1893, 7f; McConica 1986, 24f.

9. On this section in general, see Cobban 1988, 115ff, 133–35, 178f, 206f; Curtis 1959, 36–41, 78–81, 108–14; Simon 1966, 245–67, esp. 251, 333–68. On Cambridge specifically, see Winstanley 1935, 267–78; Leader 1988, 336–39, 347, 349; Gascoigne 1984, esp. 554–57; on Oxford, Mallet 1924–27, 3:56ff; Cross 1986, 117, 127–29, 135–37; McConica 1986, esp. 50, 64–68; Sutherland 1986a, esp.472–75, 479f.

10. Sources for the above paragraphs are given in the previous note. Feingold 1984 shows the extent of specialized training in a specific subject—mathematics—available from fellows as tutors, assistant tutors, and otherwise. On, for example, the scientific revolution and extrastatutory education, see Gascoigne 1985; 1990.

11. Citations from Gibbon 1966, 53, 54, and 57—I have altered the punctuation slightly.

12. Anon 1909 [1516–17], 485f (lib. II, epis. xlvi)—I have altered the orthography slightly. By "hostels" is meant the halls or burses—unlike the colleges, unendowed residences. A contemporaneous letter by the University of Leipzig to Duke Georg of Saxony bewailed the same fact as satirized here: see University of Leipzig 1879, 274 (ca. 1502–1537), also 280ff.

13. On the transformation of Oxbridge colleges into self-contained sites of learning, see Cobban 1988, 115–21. On the emergence of forced residency in Paris and Oxford, and on college discipline, see Rashdall 1936, 1:525f; 3:354ff; Ariès 1962, pt. 2, chap. 2; Gabriel 1961, 103. Imperial universities founded before 1400—Prague, Vienna, Heidelberg, Cologne, Erfurt—did not originally mandate residency in university houses. But the earliest indications of forced residency come from the first founded university: a statute issued in 1385 by the University of Prague seems to mandate residency in colleges or burses: see the University of Prague 1830–48, 3:12f; but cf. Tomek 1849, 21. In Vienna (1365/89) the statutes of 1389 do not mention residency, but those of 1410 require it: see Kink 1854–55, 2:187, 236; Schauf 1904, 13–16. At Heidelberg (1386) the original, undated statutes imply nothing about residency, whereas the 1441 revision requires it: see University of Heidelberg 1886, 1:141f; 186f, implies that in 1469 some scholars might still living outside the burses, but Anon 1909 [1515–17], lib I, epis. xlvi, may be taken to mean that by 1517 scholars must be in burses.

14. The regulation on Tübingen's Collegium Illustre is at StutSA, A202.2599, *Leges et privilegia des collegii illustris*, 1594–1666: see 1666, 10ff.

15. On the lack of juridical personality of the scholarship funds, and perforce of the convictoria, see Sohm 1949, 204, n. 3. On convictoria, *Freitische*, burses and scholarships, see Tholuck 1853–54, 1:207ff; Schmid 1859, 9:261ff; Paulsen 1919–21, 1:224ff, 234, 237ff, 252ff; Kius 1865; HanoSA, Cal. Br. 21, Nr. 3816, esp. § 21; Pommerania 1765–1802, ser. 2, 2:135ff; Brandenburg-Prussia 1721, 1:246ff; Arnoldt 1746–69, I/2, 346ff, 420, 480ff; University of Marburg 1848, 42ff, 63ff; University of Tübingen 1877, 425ff, esp. 445ff; University of Leipzig 1861, 289ff; University of Rinteln 1879–80, 51ff; University of Heidelberg 1891, 136ff, 150ff, 211ff; Beckmann 1707, 44ff; Fröhlich 1644, I/3, 291; Kosegarten 1856–57, 1:209ff; Meyer zu Ermgassen 1977, 206f. On the Jesuits, see Society of Jesus 1887–94, I [II], 424–31; IV [XVI], 249ff; MuniSA, Jesuitica 1761: "Von dem Convict" (ca. 1580).

16. On the social and intellectual order of the convictoria, see Anon 1726, 133ff; Tholuck 1853–54, 1:206ff; in particular, University of Marburg 1848, 45f, 47, 69, 72f; University of Tübingen 1877, 429, 440f, 444, 446; University of Heidelberg 1891, 108f, 136ff, 149ff, 211, 213ff. On social origins of the "convicts" and their relation to state service, see Tholuck 1853–54, 1:206ff, 212, 215; Kius 1865, 103, 115, 152; Kosegarten 1856–57, 1:209; University of Marburg 1848, 15, 40ff, 70.

17. MuniSA, Jesuitica 1761, "Von dem Convict," §10. On Protestant convictoria, see University of Tübingen 1877, 425ff, 445ff; University of Leipzig 1861, 289ff; Hanover 1739–41, 1:733ff; Pommerania 1765–1802, ser. 2, 2:135ff; Brandenburg-Prussia 1721, 1:246ff; Arnoldt 1746–69, 1/2, 346ff, 365ff, 420, 480ff; HanoSA, Cal. Br. 21, Nr. 3816, esp. fol. 21.

18. On private praeceptors, see Horn 1901, 28ff; University of Jena 1858, 97; University of Marburg 1848, 23; 1977, 148ff; University of Leipzig 1861, 72, 90; Keil and Keil 1858, 47; Seifert 1972; Loose 1880, 11, 13.

19. Anon 1726, 31ff; Tholuck 1853–54, 1:80, 215f, 220ff, 228; Fröhlich 1644, 1/3, 281; Horn 1897, 149–53.

20. The first citation is from Tholuck 1853–54, 1:227; see also 80, 215f, 220ff, 228; the second from University of Gießen 1907, 1:130; the third from Anon 1726, 35.

21. The citation is from the satirical Anon n.d.3, 14 and 22.

22. On circular disputation, see Horn 1893; in particular, see Will 1801, 120; Wolf 1952, 335ff; SchlSA, Abt. 47, *Universität Kiel,* Nr. 72, esp. 1709 [3a], 1744 [3b], 1745 [3c], 1764 [3d], 1770 [8b]; Society of Jesus 1887–94, II [V], 341; III [IX], 287, 357, 393.

23. Eighteenth century lecture catalogues commonly listed the disputational collegia. Examples of private collegia as laboratory exercises are in Clark 1992.

24. See Horn 1893, 31ff, 36f, 42ff, 94ff; University of Göttingen 1961, 61; Schrader 1894, 2:491ff, esp. 496f; Brandenburg-Prussia 1855, 2:515–19. The lecture catalogues show, for example, that at Göttingen disputational collegia were already rare by the 1770s. At Halle there were commonly a few each term through the 1770s. At Leipzig, the most traditional of all German universities, many such collegia appeared through the 1780s—for example, thirteen in summer semester 1780—but declined by the turn of the century—for example, six in winter semester 1800—and fell into desuetude between 1810 and 1820. These comments concern the arts and philosophy faculties. In this chapter, I depart from Horn in my assessment of the relation of the private collegium to the seminar: cf. Horn 1893, 41, 94ff; 1897, 17, 19f, 23, 50; 1901, 47; also Paulsen 1919–21, 1:271ff; 2:132ff.

25. On Kant, see Arnoldt 1906–11, V/2, 173–343; Clark 1999, 464–65. On Michaelis, see Rinck 1897, 197, and n. 1, which defends Michaelis. On Heyne, see Mackensen 1791, 51; and Gedike (1789) in Fester 1905, 22.

26. On Kant, see Clark 1999b; Heyne and Wolf appear often in this book, but see in particular Heyne 1772; Wolf 1831; 1833; 1935; Heeren 1813; Bräuning-Oktavio 1971; Menze 1966; Arnoldt 1861.

27. On Kant, see Schultz 1965, 28f.

28. On figure 5.4, see Bernd Bader in Broszinski and Wurzel 1995, 69. The image is from the *Studentenstammbuchbilder*—on this genre, see Lilienthal 1712; Fechner 1981; Keil and Keil 1893; Hofmann 1926; Kohfeldt and Ahrens 1919; Kelter 1908; Kurras 1987.

29. On scholars' garb at home, see Chartier et al. 1989, 225–31, at 230; also Findlen 1994, 49, 101f, 110ff.

30. Cf. the interpretation of Bernd Bader in Broszinski and Wurzel 1995, 69, who sees this figure as a colleague or friend of Höpfner's.

31. The German lecture catalogue is in *Göttingische gelehrte Anzeigen,* 1830, Bd. 1, 44. Stück, 20 März, 425–44. Jacob's class, *Deutsche Rechtsalterthümer,* is listed at 429 under the law faculty. In the published Latin lecture catalogue of 1830, Jacob's class is listed under the philosophy faculty and on page 7 described as, "Jacob Grimm, privatim tradet antiquitates juris Germanici . . . quater per hebdomadem hora V-VI."

32. Götz 1789 records the many extant private societies. On early private societies and "academies" in the Renaissance and Baroque, but not specifically concerned with those admitting students and/or centered on universities, see Buck 1977, 11ff; Ornstein 1928, 73ff; Keller 1895; 1903; 1909; 1912; on the eighteenth century, see McClellan 1985.

33. Society of Jesus 1887–94, II [V], 460ff, 470 (citation).

34. On the Leipzig societies, see Schulze 1810, 177ff.

35. For the natural sciences societies in general, see University of Halle 1779; 1783; 1809; 1879; University of Jena 1767; 1793; 1794; 1800a; University of Leipzig. 1799. On

nonuniversity German natural science societies founded before the nineteenth cenuty, see Berlin, Natural Sciences Society 1791; 1810; 1823; Danzig, Natural Sciences Society 1794; 1843. Sources for the classics societies are in appendix 3.

36. See Schulze 1810, 215ff, 267; University of Halle 1736, 15ff, 25, 28ff; University of Jena 1741-43, vol. 1, "Leges," iii, xxxiii et seq.; Güldenapfel 1816, 271ff; Will 1801, 151ff.

37. On Cambridge, see Winstanley 1935, 44.

38. "Decreta super reformatione" is in Roman Catholic Church 1973, 750-53.

39. On the seminary antecedent to the Council of Trent, see Theiner 1835, esp. 10ff, 28f, 66f, 103f, 106ff. On Jesuit convictoria, see Duhr 1907-28, 1:295ff, 315ff, 531ff; II/2, 552ff, 3278ff; Society of Jesus 1887-94, I [II], 322, 404f, 411ff, 417ff, 441; IV [XVI], 175ff, 187ff, 236ff, 254ff, 261, 265, 268ff, 310ff, 332ff; MuniSA, Jesuitica 1761: "Von dem Convict" (ca. 1580).

40. On Protestant seminar(ie)s, see Thiele 1938, 80ff, 130ff; on Halle, Frick 1883, 1-10.

41. On the seminars, see appendix 3.

42. On transformations and protest institutions, see in appendix 3 the cases of the philology seminars in Berlin, Erlangen, Greifswald, Jena (a bit belated), Königsberg, and Wittenberg, and of the classics societies in Göttingen (1811) and Halle (1824).

43. See GöttUA, 4.V.M.1: Inspection des Seminarii philologici, 1740 . . . , esp. fol. 11r et seq.; 4.V.M.2: 1741-1821 [unfol.], esp. 26 Sept. 1763.

44. On the above, see University of Erlangen 1777b, 620; Schleswig-Holstein 1832, 578ff; Stahlmann 1899-1900, 2:23f. Regular reporting was mandated for the seminars at Leipzig, Berlin, Bonn, Breslau, Greifswald, Königsberg, Freiburg im Br., Munich, and Rostock: see the documents under "sources" in appendix 3. I do not know about Jena, Dorpat, Heidelberg, Marburg, and Tübingen. Regulations for the seminar at Gießen do not explicitly mention reporting but put the institution under ministerial oversight and control.

45. See Hanover 1886-90, 8:467; Stählin 1928, 7, 10; University of Kiel 1856, 37; Pütter et al. 1765-1838, 2:274; further, the sources listed in appendix 3.

46. See University of Kiel 1856, 37; Stählin 1928, 7, 10; Stahlmann 1899-1900.

47. See Brandenburg-Prussia 1839-40, II/2, 621ff, 624ff, 839ff, 846ff, 850ff, 858ff; 1867-68, II/2, 2, 30, 42, 45, 47ff; Eulenburg 1909, 112; Wiener 1909, 24ff, esp. 33ff.

48. On how scholastic the discussion concerning when a physics cabinet became an "institute" for physics can become, see Hermelink and Kaehler 1927, 532, 757ff; Schmitz 1978, 59; cf. Lexis 1893, 2:25ff; 1:619; 174ff lists extant seminar-institutes and budgets.

49. In general on *cabinets de physique*, see Heilbron 1982, 139-44; on anataomical theaters, Richter 1936; on chemistry in the Germanies, Hufbauer 1982, 225-69. On particular German Protestant universities, see Baier 1714, 97f; Will 1801, 90, 187ff, 202; Günther 1881, 9; Bonjour 1960, 333f; Hesse 1879, 90f; Engelhardt 1843, 132ff; University of Gießen 1907, 1:377; Lorey 1940; 1941; Pommerania 1765-1802, ser. 1, 2:1002f; II/ 2, 112; Förster 1794, 100f, 222f; Goetz 1973, 150ff; Schrader 1894, 1:570; Schmidt-Schönbeck 1965, 35ff, 47ff; Wiener 1909, 30ff; Kreußler 1810, 145f; Hackenberg 1972, 107ff; Schmitz et al. 1978, 33, 34ff; Schulze 1927, 757f; University of Rostock 1969, 1:134; Eisenbach 1822, 523ff, 539f. As Heilbron noted, because Jesuit professors had no incomes, regular budgets for natural science collections appeared earlier at Catholic universities. For particular instances, see Weber 1880-82, 338-42; Braubach 1947, 54; Specht 1902, 199f, 530, 576, 595; Wiegand 1967, 160ff; Schreiber 1857-60, II/2, 153; Kangro 1957, 10f; Zeeden 1957, 50ff; Mühl 1961, 36f; Haxel 1953, 75f; Kistner 1937, 113f;

Prantl 1872, 1:529ff, 611f, 676f, 719; Schaff 1912, 165, 194ff, 206ff; Hammermayer 1959, 243; Pölnitz 1942, 78f; MuniSA, GL, Fasz. 1479, Nr. 107:3, 5-7, 108, 114; Steinmaurer 1971, 57ff, 102ff; Probst 1869, 184, 279, 295; Luca 1782, 85f; d'Elvert 1857, 50f, 170, 175, 204, 254; Tomek 1849, 325; Del-Negro 1972, 112ff; Böhm 1952, 62; Haberzettl 1973, 139ff; University of Würzburg 1966, 20ff; O. Volk in University of Würzburg 1982, 758, 782; Wegele 1882, 2:475, 504f.

50. On the departmentalization of American faculties, see Veysey 1965, 153ff, 320ff.

51. Hufen 1955, 160ff, citation at 163. In the last third of the eighteenth century or first decade of the next, lands such as Brandenburg-Prussia, Austria and Bavaria made academics civil servants de jure: see Brandenburg-Prussia 1794, 584; Meister 1963, 25, 29; Doeberl 1916-31, 2:502.

52. In general on directors, see the lists in appendix 3. On Halle, see Körte 1833, 1:206, where an *extrordinarius* as *Inspector* to the seminar is mentioned.

53. The case of Marburg is discussed in Hermelink and Kaehler 1927, 695ff.

54. On the private classics society in Halle, see Ribbeck 1879-81, 1:37-38. The pedagogical seminar at Münster and the philology seminar at Leipzig post-1848 also had a more collegial directorate.

55. On Heyne and the Göttingen seminar, see Herbst 1872-76, 1:76; Pütter et al. 1765-1838, 1:248ff, 274; 4:168; Heeren 1813, 251.

56. On Wolf and Halle, see Wolf 1935, 1:56, 63; Arnoldt 1861, 1:246ff; Körte 1833, 1:202ff, 222. On Kiel, see University of Kiel 1856, 37. At Erlangen the seminar appears to fall under statutory control of the director first in 1827: see Stählin 1928, 14ff.

57. Statutes of the seminars are listed in appendix 3. The statutes of Berlin, Bonn, Breslau, Dorpat, Gießen, Greifswald, Königsberg, Leipzig, and Tübingen clearly give the directorate the power over admission, as also seems to be the case at Marburg. At Rostock the director admitted, with full members of the seminar also seeming to have some say in the matter. At Munich the director had to report to the ministry regarding admissions, though it is unclear if that was only pro forma, as in the case of most other seminars. At Freiburg im Br. admissions came by way of the directorate, of which ministerial officials could conceivably have partaken. I do not know about Heidelberg. The ability to kick students out is also clear in the statutes for Berlin, Bonn, Breslau, Erlangen, Freiburg im Br., Greifswald, Helmstedt, Kiel, Königsberg, and Tübingen. I do not know about Dorpat, Gießen, Heidelberg, Jena, Leipzig, Marburg, Munich, and Rostock on this score, but it is hard to imagine directors would have had to put up with recalcitrants.

58. Schulze 1827, esp. 92ff, asserted the research imperative contra the pedagogical ends of the Prussian seminars. Pedagogical ends are implicit in the statutes, for example, of the Berlin seminar: see Brandenburg-Prussia 1839-40, II/2, 560ff (§ 8, 13). Nonuniversity teaching is what most of the graduates in fact did. On the pedagogical mission of the seminars, see Wolf 1935, 1:53, 55; 2:113, 117; Beck 1809, 56; University of Wittenberg 1806, 243ff; Schleswig-Holstein 1832, 577, 580f; Bavaria 1838, 236; University of Dorpat 1822, 3, 14; University of Freiburg im Br. 1830b, 7, 37f; University of Gießen 1827, 426; Friedländer 1927, 695; University of Rostock 1829, 2; University of Tübingen 1838, 332; University of Vienna 1850, 835f.

59. The proliferation of the philology seminars and the apotheosis of the humanistic gymnasium stood in a mutually reinforcing relation. The so-called cultural battle between humanities and natural sciences over the character of the ruling class eventually emerged from that. See Schwartz 1925; Loewe 1917; 1925; Thiersch 1826-38; 1838; Schulze 1827; Varrentrapp 1889, esp. 415ff; Paulsen 1896-97, 346ff, 359ff; Schöler 1970.

60. On theology majors and philology seminars, see University of Göttingen 1737, 70. On the Heyne-Wolf anecdote, see Körte 1833, I, 40ff, 46ff, 207, 217. On Erlangen, see University of Erlangen 1918, 9.

61. Table 1 was constructed from collating the matriculation register, University of Göttingen 1937, with the list of the seminarists in Pütter et al. 1765–1838, 2:275–78, 3:494–97; 4:169–71. The years in the table are the years of matriculation of the seminarists, not the year of entry into the seminar; most students entered the seminar one or two years after matriculating. For the first cohort, 1764–66, for example, not all of these students would have entered the seminar during those three years, some of them entering only in 1767 or 1768. Eighteen students are listed in Pütter et al. 1765–1838 whom I was unable to find in the matriculation register, and thus could not record in the table.

62. HallUA, Rep. 3, Nr. 260, Acta, iii, fol. 46, has a list of the seminarists from WS 1801/02; see also fol. 168 and 196 for WS 1802/03 and SS 1803. See also Körte 1833, 1:207; Wolf 1935, 1:53, 55f; 2:104; F. Thiersch's visit to Wolf's seminar recorded the same sentiment: see Thiersch 1866, 1:34.

63. The Berlin seminar statutes declare that the seminar is for students of philology: see Brandenburg-Prussia 1839–40, II/2, 560 (§ 2). Later Prussian seminars have statutes to the same effect. Outside Prussia, the case of Erlangen is instructive. The seminar had originally (1777) been for theology majors, while the new statutes (1827) stipulate a preference for philology majors: see Stählin 1928, 9, 15f.

64. On Voß and friend, see Herbst 1872–76, 1:73–76. On seminars as standardizing teachers, see the Göttingen seminar statutes in Vormbaum 1860–64, 3:359f; also University of Freiburg im Br. 1830b, 37.

65. I have combined two separate passages here from Wolf: see his letter of 6 Sept. 1787 in Wolf 1935, 1:55f, and Wolf cited in Arnoldt 1861, 1:255.

66. Königsberg statutes in Brandenburg-Prussia 1839–40, II/2, 853 (quotation). At Freiburg im Br. the bottom two of the twelve got nothing, while the other ten got 25 florin. The top three seminarists at Berlin and Königsberg, for example, got 50 rthlr. each, while the other five got 40 rthlr. At Halle, as reorganized in 1829, the top four got 40 thlr., with the remaining eleven getting 20 thlr. each.

67. On Wolf, see Körte 1833, 1:204, including the note.

68. Augustin 1795, 87.

69. On the ealier structure of the seminar, see Gesner 1743–45, 1:72ff—also as University of Göttingen 1737; see also 1738.

70. Heyne in Pütter et al. 1765–1838, 1:249.

71. As cited above, see GöttUA, 4.V.M.1: Inspection des Seminarii philologici, 1740 . . . , esp. fol. 11r et seq.; 4.V.M.2: 1741–1821 [unfol.], see esp. 26 Sept. 1763.

72. Mackensen 1791, 83.

73. See Arnoldt 1861, 1:102ff, 248ff; Wolf 1935, 1:53ff, 314; University of Erlangen 1777b, 618; Engelhardt 1843, 151ff; Stählin 1928, 9, 15f; University of Wittenberg 1768, 131; 1806, 243ff; Schleswig-Holstein 1832, 578; Hanover 1886–90, II [VIII], 463ff. In all the seminars, including those at Göttingen and Halle, some practical experience with pedagogical matters continued.

74. On a visit to Halle in the early 1790s, Augustin 1795, 86f, reports that Wolf gave his seminar such an assignment. Augustin saw no sense in the exercise.

75. Pütter et al. 1765–1838, 2:273f (first citation); University of Freiburg im Br. 1830a, 3 (§ 16)—second citation.

76. On Helmstedt, see Stahlmann 1899–1900, 1:14. Other examples on the con-

duct of seminars are in Körte 1833, 1:169ff; Arnoldt 1861, 1:103; Thiersch 1866, 1:33f; University of Leipzig 1809, 61; Schulze 1810, 253f; University of Tübingen 1838; Württemberg 1843, 718; University of Vienna 1850, 855f, 859.

77. Thiersch 1866, 1:34, records an example when Wolf gave a seminarist the boot for lack of basic knowledge of Greek, upon hearing of which the director of the seminar in Leipzig, G. Hermann, made the sign of the cross.

78. Contra examination, see Wolf 1935, 2:113. The seminar at Kiel is an exception when it mandates, as was typical for traditional sorts of scholarships, a formal examination after two years, passage of which was needed for the continuation of the scholarship: see Schleswig-Holstein 1832, 578f (§ 9).

79. See University of Dorpat 1822, 4f; University of Gießen 1827, 333; Brandenburg-Prussia 1839-40, II/2, 561, 621f, 680, 719, 851; Heeren 1813, 252; Schleswig-Holstein 1832, 578f; Hanover 1886-90, II [VIII], 465; University of Helmstedt 1780, 618f; University of Leipzig 1809, 60; Arnoldt 1861, 1:246ff; University of Freiburg im Br. 1830a, § 11, 14; University of Rostock 1829, 3f; University of Vienna 1850, 859.

80. Both citations from Brandenburg-Prussia 1839-40, II/2, 623, 853.

81. Leventhal 1986, 257, argues the opposite.

82. On Göttingen, see Hanover 1738, 220; on Erlangen, University of Erlangen 1777b, 618; and Engelhardt 1843, 153. I have found no reference to disputation as a formal exercise in the seminars at Kiel and Wittenberg.

83. On the Göttingen seminar, see Heeren 1813, 252f, which does not say when Heyne began the practice; on later at Göttingen, Pütter et al., 1765-1838, 4:169. On Helmstedt, see University of Helmstedt 1788, 289ff, esp. 295; Hanover 1886-90, II (VIII), 456f, § viii; and, Stahlmann 1899-1900, 1:14. The various accounts of Wolf's practices are in Arnoldt 1861, 1:103f, 248, 255; Körte 1833, 1:169ff, 210, 212, 220; Wolf 1935, 2:53, 55f, 75, 314; 2:104; Süß 1928-30, 1:35. Considering first Prussian universities in the nineeenth century, at Bonn, Greifswald, Halle (as reorganized) and Königsberg, circular disputation occurred every week; at Berlin and Breslau every two weeks: see in general Brandenburg-Prussia 1839-40, II/2, 561, 621ff, 681, 720, 776f, 852f. On Berlin in particular, see also Klausen 1837, 44; and, on Breslau, Ribbeck 1879-81, 1:125. At Leipzig, disputation seemingly took place weekly: see University of Leipzig 1809, 60f, 69f; and, Schulze 1810, 253f. At Freiburg im Br., seemingly weekly to fortnightly: University of Freiburg im Br. 1830a, 1, 3—§ 5 and 16, zu 5, ad 3 and ad 3. At Gießen, weekly: University of Gießen 1827, 428f. At Munich, seemingly weekly: Loewe 1925, 364f. At Rostock, two weeks out of every five: University of Rostock 1829, 5ff. At Tübingen, weekly: University of Tübingen 1838, 332. At Dorpat, probably weekly to fortnightly: Süß 1928-30, 2:162; University of Dorpat 1822, 11. At Vienna, weekly: University of Vienna 1850, 855f, 859. I have no information about Jena, Heidelberg, and Marburg.

84. I know of only one case where the seminarists were allowed to choose the texts for the exegetical-critical lessons—the Leipzig society-seminar under Beck: see University of Leipzig 1809; Schulze 1810, 253f; and, the critique of the practice in Wolf 1935, 2:104f.

85. University of Göttingen 1738, 220 (citation).

86. From the 1822 statutes of the Königsberg seminar in Brandenburg-Prussia 1839-40, II/2, 852. Other sources on the nature and frequency of written work are more or less the same as those for disputation above. The seminars at Helmstedt, Halle, Breslau, Königsberg, Vienna, and Freiburg im Br. mention consultation with the director concerning the paper topic. The seminars at Leipzig, Erlangen, Göttingen, Berlin, Bonn, Geifswald, and Gießen mention only the student's choice, though one

must presume that students consulted with the director. At Tübingen, the director may have assigned topics: see Württemberg 1843, 718.

87. From the 1812 statutes of the Berlin seminar in Brandenburg-Prussia 1839-40, II/2, 562. For provisions regarding publication at the other Prussian universities at Bonn, Breslau, Greifswald, Halle, and Königsberg, see Brandenburg-Prussia 1839-40, II/2, 624, 681f, 721, 778, 853. Publication of essays was also envisaged at Leipzig: see University of Leipzig 1809, 58; as well as at Geißen: see University of Gießen 1827, 429f; at Munich it is implicit: see University of Ingolstadt / Munich 1812-29, IV/1, "Praefatio," v. As cited above, the notion of publication of an essay as rite of passage out of the seminar was instituted by Gesner: see University of Göttingen 1738, 220. In the eighteenth century, the seminars at Halle, Helmstedt, and Erlangen also antici- pated publication of the seminarists' work, the implication being as graduation dis- sertation: see Wolf 1935, 1:56, 75, 211; Engelhardt 1843, 153; Stahlmann 1899-1900, 1:14; University of Helmstedt 1788, 289ff.

88. Veysey 1965, 50, 142ff, 157, 176f; first citation at 153, and Russell's at 156, taken from Russell, "Research in State Universities," *Science*, 19 (1904), 853.

### CHAPTER SIX

1. Michaelis 1768-76, 4:98, saw academic degrees as vestiges of warlike nations for whom honor meant much. On the nations and tribes lacking the academic degree, see Itter 1698, 68-84; on the Goths, see Schubart 1678, 299-300. Due to the slow pace of research in this underfunded field, it is unclear if the Visigoths and Ostrogoths share equal responsibility.

2. On the Ph.D. in the United States, see Veysey 1965, 50; on Britain, see Simpson 1983, 34-36, 48-50, 61-63, 135-37; on Edinburgh in particular, see Morrell 1997, [X] 369.

3. The first citation is from Schmidt 1867, 63-64, citing Mosellanus. The second is from Rufus 1885, 147 (early June 1509). On the arrival of the humanists, see Paulsen 1919, 1:12, 78-89, 97-104, 108-10; and, Kaufmann 1888-96, 2:500-62.

4. Matriculation registers are in the bibliography under "University of." New stu- dents and new teachers inscribed their name and title when appropriate. This initial inscription was necessary in order to enjoy the juridical privileges granted the aca- demic corporation.

5. On the Poets Laureate and the Viennese college, see Kink 1854-55, 1:199-201; 2:305-07; Aschbach 1865-88, 2:66; Paulsen 1919, 1:133.

6. Anon 1909 [1515-17], 509-10 (lib. II, epis. lviii).

7. Anon 1909 [1515-17], 322 (lib. I, epis. xvii).

8. On the evolution of "magister" and "doctor," see Weijers 1987, 133-55; Fried 1974, 9-21; Bornhak 1912, 71.

9. See Rebuffus 1585; Lutius 1582; and, more recently, Kibre 1962.

10. On the above two paragraphs, see Roman Empire 1872-95, *Codex*, X, 54 (53); Bartolus 1615, 3:3v-4r, 68r-v, 142r; 6:219v; 7:122; VIII/2, 23v-24r, 45v-48v; Baldus 1615- 16, 1:3r-5v; 6:25v-28v; 8:269r-270v; Rubenow 1867, 141-45; Rebuffus 1585, 632f; Lutius 1582, esp. 279-92, 340ff; Lenauderius 1583, 2:7r-9r; Halbritterus 1616; Stephanus 1617, 285ff; Walther 1641, esp. 262ff; Feltmann 1691, 522ff; Itter 1698, esp. 340ff, 462f. On the clothing privileges of degree holders, see Holy Roman Empire 1737, 2:31, 48, 78f; on the *Authentica habita*, Ullmann 1954, 130ff; Kibre 1962.

11. University of Leipzig 1861, 417.

12. I neglect uses in reference to canon law. The Viennese theology statutes use "doctor" frequently, while those of Heidelberg, Cologne, Erfurt, Ingolstadt, Tübin-

gen, and Wittenberg show few uses. The case with the Leipzig statutes, 1419–1500, is complex. Examples of curial style are in University of Heidelberg 1886, 1:46; and, Bianco 1850–55, 2:2. Up to the sixteenth century, neglecting canon lawyers, I found only two rectors as "dr. theol." at Cologne; one at Erfurt; zero at Leipzig; one at Greifswald; one at Basel; three at Rostock; seven at Vienna. At later foundations, four from 1476–1506 at Ingolstadt, and six from 1461–1518 at Freiburg im Br. The Leipzig promotion register uses terms like "insignia doctoratus."

13. On medieval use of "master," "doctor" and "professor," see Weijers 1987, 133–55; Fried 1974, 9–21. See also Anon 1909 [1515–17], 292 (lib. I, epis. i); and, University of Tübingen 1877, 262; University of Leipzig 1861, 566–67. On the Jesuits, see Society of Jesus 1887–94, 1:59–61; 2:110–12. At Cologne, theologians did not generally style themselves doctors, when rector, until mid-seventeenth century. On the Protestants, see Melanchthon 1843. The Theol. Dr. entered Wittenberg in Melanchthon's revision of 1533; then in those for Tübingen (1538), Basel (1539), Leipzig (1543), Greifswald (1545) Heidelberg (1558); at the new foundations, at Königsberg (1544), Jena (1558), and Helmstedt (1576). Melanchthon never styled himself "doctor" in the matriculation register when he was rector. At Leipzig, I found no Theol. Dr. as rector, until 1542; at Königsberg, first in 1549; at Marburg in 1551 (or 1544); at Frankfurt a.d.O., in 1551. The title became common after midcentury.

14. On torture, see Gastel 1675, 1342; Sagittarius 1615, unpag. Itter 1698, 545. On the order of precedence, see Middendorp 1594, 43; Limnaeus 1616, Th. vii; Gastel 1675, 1331–34; University of Heidelberg 1886, 1:17–18; University of Tübingen 1877, 61–62.

15. On the above, see the matriculation registers for Erfurt, 1494 and Vienna, 1496; 1500–1550, mostly as rector, one finds the "dr. phil. et art.": at Erfurt 5, Vienna 4, Frankfurt a.d.O. 2, Marburg 1. The statutes of the Viennese College of Poets did not mention doctors, but it the graduates perhaps styled themselves "Phil. Dr." The statutes are in Kink 1854–55, 2:305–7. On the putative Dr. Phil., see Aschbach 1865–88, 2:66; Paulsen 1919, 2:133. At VienUA, I turned up nothing on this.

16. On impersonating a doctor, see Bartolus 1615, VIII/2, 23v; 10:124v; Halbritterus 1616, 7; Walther 1641, 544–45.

17. On this incident, see MuniUA, D, 3:7, 176v–77r. Chris Baswell helped me make sense here of a difficult hand here. The incident is mentioned in Prantl 1872, 1:213. If the work was a poem, it was not included in Amerbach 1550.

18. Amerbach 1571, 352–55, 356, 358–60, 363–64; also Musserlus 1533, "Doctor," unpag. On academic costume, see Itter 1698, 318; Hargreaves-Mawdsley 1963, 150–52. At early modern Oxbridge, the earliest practices are perhaps best preserved. While practically everyone else wears a *pileus quadratus*, the doctors of law and medicine wear birrettas—a vestige of their early attempts to demarcate themselves? See figure 2.1. On the meaning of the symbols, see Rubenow 1867, 146–49; Bartolus 1615, 10:182r–v; Erythraeus 1574, 23–33; Lenauderius 1583, 4v; Middendorp 1594, appendix, 38; Walther 1641, 437–39; Itter 1698, 317–24; Brandenburg-Prussia 1839–40, 1:603, 611–12, 624–26, 646, 671. The cathedra was a sign of magisterial authority; the open book a reminder not to neglect further studies, and the closed book that not all knowledge is in books; the mortarboard and pileus a sign of academic freedom; the ring a sign of marriage to knowledge; the kiss a sign of the fraternity of knowledge; the blessing a sign of the paternal relation of teacher and pupil.

19. See Gastel 1675, 1334 (*Doctor bullatus* as "mitratum asinum"); the misogynous remark on the kiss is in Feltmann 1667, 18 (citing Bartolus); and, in Lauterbach 1728–29, 4:1744 (citing Baldus); Itter 1698, 462–63. Jurists tried to become noble, but an im-

perial noblesse de robe did not emerge: see Bartolus 1615, VIII/2, 50r. Jurists knew theologians were once called "masters," and used to precede doctors in forms of address: see Gisenius 1628, 102; Lansius 1666, 74. On conveyance, see Gastel 1675, 1340–42.

20. On the *Comites palatini* and *Doctores bullati*, see Meyerhoff 1670; Gastel 1675, 744–45; Schubart 1678, 85–366, esp. 227–34; Pütter 1770, 211–12. On the ills of the proliferation of doctors, due especially to the Palatine Counts, see Gastel 1675, 1334–42.

21. On statutes, see Baldus 1615–16, IV/2, 3r–4r; generally, Gierke 1868–1913, 3:456–60; Meiners 1802–06, 2:155; 3:43; Kaufmann 1888–96, 2:110–25. On the decline in value of the master's, see Gastel 1675, 1342. Though nonstatutory, the M. Phil. had appeared by the fifteenth century.

22. On the above, see Bengeser 1965, 20; Eulenburg 1904, 309–17. In the Catholic lands the B.A. lost meaning since so many Jesuit colleges and lyceums could award it.

23. Examples of pay scales are in University of Wittenberg 1926–27, 1:77–78, 162–63; and University of Heidelberg 1891, 62–64, 81–82, 104–06.

24. For circumlocutions to the M.A., see BaseSA, Univ. Arch., AA 9, 1608–1699: see the "Theses" of 1608; University of Leipzig 1909a, 1:lxxiv. By the eighteenth century, such phrases were the norm. Outright nonstatutory proclamations are in BaseSA, Univ. Arch., 11:4, 1C, 1609–1815: see the first *Promotionsrede*, 6; and a *Promotionesrede* (1609), 7. Also Erythraeus 1574, 119, 132; Casel 1602; Sagittarius 1615; University of Leipzig 1909a, lxxiv. For examples of smuggling the Dr. Phil. into statutes that still only award the M.Phil; see University of Erfurt 1881, 2:166; University of Heidelberg 1886, 2:134; University of Helmstedt 1963, 116. Also see BaseSA, Univ. Arch., R, 2, 1632–18.Jh., 1632 statutes, pg. 14.

25. On "professor," see Weijers 1987, 133–55.

26. In Vienna, the first "philosophiae et *xxxx* doctor," was in 1396, whereafter it became common; after 1400, incidences appear at Cologne, Greifswald, Erfurt, Rostock, Basel; after 1500, the conceit is common at these, incidences at other, older universities appear, and commonly at new ones. Instances of the inverted order, "et philosophiae [magister] doctor," are in the matriculation registers at Leipzig (1510), Erfurt (1544 and 1563), Cologne (1566), and Frankfurt a.d.O. (1576). In Vienna's matriculation register, 1550–1650, there are at least eighteen incidences of rectors styled Dr. Phil.; and, Meister 1985, 33, says the degree was "slowly" established in the sixteenth century. One might fix more definite, but later dates. VienUA has Johann J. Locher's *Speculum Academicum Viennense* (Vienna, 1773), 3 vols. (B 141), with vols. 2 and 3 in manuscript as *Speculi Academia Viennsis*, (B 141: 2–3): see 1:139–67; 2: "post-1614" (95 et seq.), and 3: "post-1622" (35 et seq.). The period 1585 to 1622 seems when the Dr. Phil. became established. Earlier use of "D." meant "dominus"; but, by 1585, the "D." must mean "Doctor." The Dr. Phil. was not generalized among the Jesuits. The acts of the Ingolstadt philosophy faculty use "magister" from 1546 to 1676: see MuniUA, OI6: *Akten d. phil. Fak.,* 1546–1773.

27. Walther 1641, 430 (citation); see also 16–17, 229–31, 544–45.

28. Rebuffus 1585, 733–34, held philosophers inferior to Doctors; Gisenius 1628, 172, said the master's was for philosophers. See also Bartolus 1615, VIII/2, 23v; Baldus 1615–16, 8:270v. After Walther, see Kundtmann 1644, "Mem. Tert., Art. Prim.," § 3, 8, 14; Lansius 1666, 69, 71; Feltmann 1667, 15; Fregisßmont 1673, 40; Gastel 1675, 1341; Feltmann 1691, 204–6; and, Besold 1697, 1:612. Middendorp 1594, 43, is implicitly for the degree of Dr. Phil. or Dr. Art., as seem to be also Stephanus 1617, 292; and Dietericus 1730, 13–14. Limnaeus 1629–34, 3:110, seems more circumspect, as also Gerhard 1655b, Th. iix–ix; and Gockel 1682, 98–100. Cellarius 1663, 264f, ridicules Walther's syl-

logism and holds one might show no doctors at all existed on such reasoning. Itter 1698, 20, of course rejects Walther's syllogism. Glud 1695, 50–65, argues for the degree. See also Oelrichs 1758, viii–xi, and n. 15. For causistry here, see Titius 1701, 708; 1724, 1257. Heine 1704, § 21, seems to be contra Titius; and cf. § 24. Lauterbach 1728–29, 4:1712, 1742–44, concedes the term, but not equality. For the Dr. Phil. in general, see Itter 1698, 12–39. On the Palatine Counts and the emperor's authority over degrees, see Fritsch 1667–70, 1:618–20; Schubart 1678, 293–95; Itter 1698, 12–13; Gockel 1682, 97–100; Titius 1701, 712; Feltmann 1691, 566.

29. On the increasing proclamations of the Dr. Phil., see Gockel 1682, 103; D. G. Morhofius, "Descriptio . . . ," and "Oratio IV," in Torquatus 1666, appendices, 10–13, 47–50; Brahl 1691, § xlii; E. Mauritius, "Academia Giessensis de promotionibus . . ." (n.d.) in Itter 1698, appendix, 24; University of Leipzig 1909a, 2:xxxxii; University of Jena 1944–86, 2:xlix; University of Frankfurt a.d.O. 1897–1906, 3:18; MuniUA, OI6, *Akten d. phil. Fak.:* 1546–1773: see the document of 28 März 1676. Doctors of Philosophy appeared in matriculation registers, for example, at Kiel in 1669, Strasbourg in 1694, and Jena in 1702. Graduation proclamations of "m. art. et phil. dr." appeared at Kiel, Jena, Wittenberg, Leipzig, Vienna, Ingolstadt, and Gießen in noteworthy numbers.

30. BerlSA, K3, 1712 131r–v; also cited in Bornhak 1900, 89.

31. Proclamations are in MuniUA, OI6, *Akten d. phil. Fak.:* 1546–1773: see 7. Jan. 1741; also Beckmann 1707, pt. 4, 177; and "Additamenta historiam . . . ," pp. 47–48, 105, sep. in Gadendam 1744; see also Weber 1880–82, 2:658; University of Leipzig 1909a, 2:xxxxii; University of Jena 1944–86, 2:xlix; also Horn 1893, 114–15; University of Göttingen 1961, 184, 188, 190. On Maria Theresa's order, see d'Elvert 1857, 51.

32. On Zedlitz, see Bornhak 1900, 90.

33. On the Austrian actions, see VienSA, St.H.K. (1791), K.2, 323 ex 1786. On Mainz, see Bentzel 1784, 119–20. On Tübingen, see TübiUA, 132, 1: an 1803 diploma awards the Dr. Phil., while the rest award the double degree. On Bamberg, see Weber 1880–82, 218. On Jena, see Fischer 1831, 3–4; University of Jena 1829, 130–31; 1944–86, xlix. On Leipzig, University of Leipzig 1909a, 3:xx. At Kiel, Rostock, and Bützow, in the matriculation registers, rectors styled themselves Dr. Phil. since the 1760s. On Bavaria, see Bavaria 1838, pt. 1, 183; MuniUA, OI6, *Akten d. phil. Fak.,* 1773–1812. Title pages of Munich dissertations exist, e.g., in 1783 from C. Steiglehner and V. Schlögel, reading "pro suprema Doctoratus Philosophici Laurea." Also see University of Heidelberg 1961, 279; BaseSA, Univ. Arch., R6, 1823–65: Diplomae 1823 et seq. Göttingen title pages are at GöttUB: see *Academia Goettingensia,* 4° H.lit.p. IV 26/5, 1770 et seq. C. H. Froemichen's *disp. pro loco,* 1770, has "Dr. Phil." on the title page, as does a *disp. pro gradu* of M. Hissmann, 1776; then, none until the 1820s. Before 1800, the diplomas perhaps contained "Dr. Phil": see *Allgemeiner Literarischer Anzeiger,* 1801, Sp. 1684. See also Kirsten 1785.

34. *Herr Magister, Herr Doktor* and others on the above are in *Allgemeiner Literarischer Anzeiger,* 1801, Sp. 990–92, 1192, 1261–62, 1684–87.

35. DresSA, Loc. *1778, Acta den Antrag der phil. Fac. zu Leipzig . . . 1810,* 9r.

36. Wuttke 1842/43, 120–23.

37. On the radicals, see Walther 1641, 479–81; Aepinus 1702, cap. ii, § 1 et seq.; Schmid 1734, 7.

38. On the above, see Kant 1798, 4–5; Salzmann 1783–84, 1:318–19; 3:77–83; Anon 1790; and Stözel 1889.

39. See Köpke 1860, 31, 44–45, 152, 160.

40. "Rede . . . 16. April 1811," in Fichte 1845–46, 8:216–19; Schleiermacher 1808, 170ff, esp 175. See also Köpke 1860, 162, 166, 176, 221–22. On the post-1806 ideology, see Fichte et al. in Weischedel 1960; also in Anrich 1956. In the nineteenth century, the philosophy faculty recovered its own student body: see Eulenburg 1904, 255, 313.

41. Some of these are only implicit, but later made explicit by jurists. On the above and below, see University of Leipzig 1861, 307–8, 313, 331–336; University of Heidelberg 1886, 1:33–36, 41, 141; University of Tübingen 1877, 352; Lhotsky 1965, 234–35, 238–41, 247f; University of Freiburg im Br. 1964, 43–45; Bianco 1850–55, 2:14, 64–66, 69–70, 76.

42. On the above, see Rubenow 1867, 146.

43. Jugler 1909, 48f (citation); on seniority by *Promotionsalter*, see Bartolus 1615, 4:171r; 9:16r; Itter 1698, cap. x; Gastel 1675, 1333.

44. Such question were negated in whole or part by Bartolus 1615, 3:41r; VIII/2, 46r; Rubenow 1867, 138; Middendorp 1594, 42; Limnaeus 1616, Th. xii; Limnaeus 1629–34, 3:118–20; Gisenius 1628, 197f; Walther 1641, 57–59, 67, 72–75, 80–83, 89–91, 98f, 445, 538–555; Gastel 1675, 1340; Besold 1697, 1:194f; Ziegnerus 1671, Sec. iii:3, § 4; Lenauderius 1583, 5r–v; on the dead, 6r: "Quaero an mortuus possit doctorari?"

45. On changing notions of infamy, see Itter 1698, 592–609; on bastards, Stephanus 1617, 294–95; Limnaeus 1629–34, 3:122; Itter 1698, 233–37; also Müller 1715, 20–21. On Palatine Counts and universities, see Schubart 1678, esp. 244; also Gockel 1682, 96ff.

46. See Walther 1641, 80–81, 553–55; Itter 1698, 214–16, 231–33.

47. On minors, see Itter 1698, 214, 267–72; Titius 1724, 1259.

48. On women, see Itter 1698, 217–22; Aepinus 1702, cap. i, v; Müller 1715, 23; Titius 1724, 1259–60. On the Jews, see Itter 1698, 224–29; Müller 1715, 21–22; in general, Richarz 1974, 28–29; Clark 2003.

49. On the degree *per saltum,* see Itter 1698, 273–78; and, Jacob Bornius, "Programma de promotione per saltum," appendix, Müller 1715, 55–60.

50. On investiture, see Walther 1641, 445; Itter 1698, 316; Müller 1715, 29; Zoepfl 1860–61, 1:365. On award in absentia, Feltmann 1667; Gockel 1682, 83; Itter 1698, 330–40. On conveyance from a nonholder, Limnaeus 1629–34, 3:109–10; Itter 1698, 183–89; Titius 1724, 1724.

51. Müller 1715, 24–25, affirms doctorates for the dead. On privileges including doctors' wives and children, see the imperial decrees of 1498 and 1500 in Holy Roman Empire 1737, 2:48, 78–79.

52. Kreittmayr in Bavaria 1756–68, 4:2333–42.

53. On writting over seniority, see Gastel 1675, 1334. Bartolus 1615, 9:10r, already privileged merit.

54. Brandenburg-Prussia 1839–40, 1:60–61; also Rosenberg 1930/31, 23.

55. On the ministry's *Aufsicht* over degrees, see Rosenberg 1930/31, 3, 19–37; Bornhak 1912, 74–77. On Austria, VienSA, St.H.K. (–1791), K.2, 323 ex 1786. On public servants, see Brandenburg-Prussia 1794, 584; Meister 1963, 25, 29; Doeberl 1916–31, 2:502.

56. Many sources cited here are a recapitulation of a previous note, but on all of this, see Horn 1893, 13–21; Kaufmann 1888–96, 2:311–13; Hölscher 1885, 68f; Brandenburg-Prussia 1839–40, 1:526f, 602f, 611f; University of Frankfurt a.d.O. 1897–1906, 3:26f; University of Tübingen 1877, 362f; University of Erfurt 1881, 2:166; University of Leipzig 1897–1902, 2:lxi; University of Gießen 1907, 1:267ff; University of Göttingen 1961, 188f; Jugler 1909, 49; Schulze 1810, 43f; Will 1801, 77; Michaelis 1768–76, 3:55; Bengeser 1965, 21. On early requirements for disputing, see Bianco 1850–55, 2:64f;

Lhotsky 1965, 236f, 243, 247–49; University of Prague 1830–48, 1:42–44, 51–53, 59; University of Heidelberg 1886, 1:33f, 41; University of Leipzig 1861, 308, 311–13, 317, 331, 336, 390; University of Freiburg im Br. 1964, 34–37, 42, 45, 67.

57. Erythraeus 1574, Casel 1602, and Sagittarius 1615, are examples of promoters' graduation orations.

58. The edict is in Brandenburg-Prussia 1737–51, 4:199–202. On this method of professorial publication, and its collapse, see Michaelis 1768–76, 2:237–39, 372; 3:21; 4:1–98; Thomasius 1724, 229–40; Horn 1893, 35f, 50–88. On the disputation's decline, Chladenius 1755, 2.

59. On students writing the theses, see Meÿfart 1636, 124f, 143f; University of Strasbourg 1876, 222. On the problems of the student as author, see Michaelis 1768–76, 2:238f; 3:54–56; 4:1–98, esp. 12–17, 60; in general, Horn 1893, 51–72.

60. On dissertation factories, see Michaelis 1768–76, 2:238f; 4:16f, 77–83.

61. On requirements about writing a dissertation, see Will 1801, 97, 120f; Hölscher 1885, 68f; Schmid 1772, 204; Staehelin 1957, 2:136, 153f, 162–64; Brandenburg-Prussia 1839–40, 1:526; University of Göttingen 1961, 187–89; on *sine praeside*, Walther 1641, 83–84; Michaelis 1768–76, 2:238; 3:55; 4:60, 82; Hugo 1828, 138; Horn 1893, 46–51.

62. Fichte 1845–46, 8:161.

63. See Fichte 1845–46, 8:161. The Berlin statutes are in Brandenburg-Prussia 1839–40, 1:60–62, 160–65.

64. Hegel 1970, 13:363 (quotation).

65. Berlin statutes in Brandenburg-Prussia 1839–40, 1:160.

66. See Hegel 1970, 13:93–99, on "irony" in relation to Fichte's "Ich." The traditional master of arts, produced by public disputation, had been typed as an heroic role player, perforce embodied (male, corporally intact, and so on). The degree ceremony individuated the master through reconstitution of the candidate's juridical persona. The modern Prussian doctor of philosophy, made by the degree ceremony, was typed as a disembodied bureaucratic spirit (*reiner Geist*). The dissertation individuated the doctor through constitution of an artistic subject. This inverted the role—typing and individuating—of degree and disputation. The arrest and advent of the doctor of philosophy worked through the dialectic of the juridical sublation and artistic elevation of the academic persona.

67. Raeff 1983, 104 (quotation). Imperial and state guild ordinances are in Wissel 1971–88, 3:33ff, 145ff, the imperial ordinance of 1731 being at 109ff.

68. Universities for which dissertations were analyzed are listed in appendix 5.

69. See Lessing 1979.

70. Gumprecht 1717, § xxxii.

71. On the genre, see Forster 1987; and Gössmann 1987. The interpretation below is a different one. On early modern academic *Streitkultur*, see Gierl 1997; 2001.

72. On prosopography, see Clark 2003.

73. Works in appendix 4 such Henke's 1701 *De Silesiis indigenis eruditis* and Weber's 1707 *De eruditis Hassiae principibus* may be exceptional in this regard. Not all of the works in the appendix might belong there, or belong in the same sense. There is neither time nor space to pursue the contours of the genre of these *dissertationes eruditorum*.

74. On such issues, see for example Grafton and Jardine 1986, esp. 17, 61. But, on the whole, the claims are simply based on my assessment of what philologists did up to circa 1800.

75. On the 1820s debate, see University of Gießen 1971, 10–15.

76. See University of Halle 1953, 320.

77. On the rise of insitutes for the natural sciences, see chapters 5 and 12; see also Lexis 1893; Holmes 1989; Olesko 1991; Turner 1982; and the articles in Schubring 1991.

78. On the plight of physics, see Clark 1997, 339–45.

79. Hoffmann 1901, 69.

80. On the exchange of women, as an archaic "ideal type," see Lévi-Strauss 1969.

81. On the Böckh-Hermann dispute, see Bursian 1883, 2:665ff; Hoffmann 1901, 48ff, 171f; Vogt 1979. Vogt rephrases the dispute as a philosophical one about language.

82. Hermann 1826 collects the polemics about Greek inscriptions. Some of Böckh's other critiques of Hermann—some of them only implicit—on additional topics are in Böckh 1858–74, 5:248–396; 7:255–61, 264–328, 404–77.

83. On Hermann, see Köchly 1874. Saxony embodied the academically traditional land. It was the Saxons who most strenuously opposed recognition of the doctor of philosophy; and, it was in Saxony in general and around Leipzig in particular that the erudite dissertations on academics of the 1670s to 1730s centered. Saxony was one of the last German lands to institute an *Abitur* (1829), and to make professors civil servants (1846). The university maintained an essentially medieval constitution into the 1830s. I was once told—by whom I forget—that one spoke Greek in seminars there into the 1870s.

84. Known transfers are shown in the detail to the detail of column 2 to the table for Berlin in appendix 5. Data were only recorded up to 1837. From the details of students' vitae, the only of the seven transfers from Leipzig in appendix 5 who cannot be clearly tied to Böckh in Berlin was Stieglitz in 1826. Three cannot be clearly tied to Hermann in Leipzig: Steglitz in 1826, Lorentz in 1827, and Leps in 1833.

85. Three sure cases are E. Ilgen in 1826, F. Kaempf in 1834, and J. Sommerbrodt in 1835, and likely is F. Glum 1836.

86. On Heyne, see Heeren 1813; Mettler 1955; Menze 1966; Bräuning-Oktavio 1971.

87. See Hoffmann 1901, 35–36, 191–92; Müller 1843, v; Ross 1855–61, 1:5.

88. Anon 1817.

89. Dissertations in 1822 by G. Bernhardy (later a famous philologist), in 1826 by H. Stieglitz, in 1834 by C. Geppert and B. Lhardy, and in 1835 by C. Kiesel, furnish examples of fragment users and/or emenders.

90. *Harper's Dictionary* is listed under Peck 1897.

91. In Ribbeck 1879–81, 1:335–36.

92. See Vogt 1979.

93. On Ritschl, see Ribbeck 1879–81;

94. On this in particular, see Ribbeck 1879–81, 1:45–47.

95. Ribbeck 1879–81, 1:52–57.

96. The protocol and the citation to the diploma are in Ribbeck 1879–81, 1:279–81.

97. On this in particular, see Ribbeck 1879–81, 1:37–38.

98. Ritschl cited in Ribbeck 1879–81, 1:54–56, quotation at 55.

### CHAPTER SEVEN

1. On Oken's case, see DresSA, Min. f. Volksb., Nr. 10211.

2. See Mackensen 1791, 23

3. Salzmann 1783–88, 3:138–47.

4. Michaelis 1768–76, 2:420—in general, contra nepotism, 418ff

5. On nepotism in guilds, see Wissel 1971–88, 1:34–36; 2:34–35, 139–41, 339–42,

382-85. There are two family trees in Decker-Hauff et al. 1977, 3:138-39, 168-69, where nearly all the Tübingen professors' daughters are married to professors. On the professor's daughter and nepotism, see also Euler 1970, esp. 186f.

6. On academic nepotism, see Gisenius 1628, 27-28. Koller 1977, 22f, holds that at Vienna and Cologne, for example, professorial dynasties did not arise until the Late Middle Ages, post-1450. On Rinteln, see Schormann 1982, 198ff; on Marbug, Niebuhr 1983; Euler 1970 treats of the social history of the Basel, Marburg, and Gießen professorates. On Heidelberg and Tübingen, see Cobb 1980, 100, 136. On other matters such as citizenship, confessionalism, nepotism, and so on, see Tholuck 1853-54 1:58ff; Bornhak 1900, 36ff, 58ff, 98ff, 108ff, 115; Eulenburg 1909, 101; Friedensburg 1917, 366ff; Keussen 1934, 109; Keck 1965 107; Turner 1973, 56ff.

7. On Sweden and Linnaeus, see Koerner 1999, 20f (citations). On Scottish academics and in general, see Vandermeersch 1996, 227-29; Chitnis 1976 124, 132-35, 153-54; Morrell 1997 [II] 12ff, [III] 160-64; Jones 1983, 91, 99, 111, 116-17; Shapin 1974; Clark 2003.

8. Justi 1782, 258; see also 1755, 1:107; 1760-61, 2:47ff, 68ff; 1782, 254ff.

9. See Kreittmayr 1756-68, 5:2335. We shall see more on this below.

10. Laukhard 1792-1802, 1:89.

11. Just and Mathy 1965, 45, 83-117, esp. 95f; University of Ingolstadt 1782-1809, 5:506—in general, 25; Keck 1965, 105—citing Prantl 1872, 1:625.

12. On Wittenberg, see Friedensburg 1917, 525f.

13. On Basel, see Staehelin 1957, 2:59ff; see also Tholuck 1853-54, 1:41. By 1791 at Erlangen, for instance, academic disciplines had supposedly been specialized with respect to the relevant professorial ability: see Engelhardt 1843, 71f.

14. On the Austrian exam, see VienSA, II C2 [124], 581/48, 2 Jan. 1798; also Austria 1840 1:168ff; on the Concurse in Freiburg im Br., for example, see Zeeden 1957, 91; on Innsbruck, see Steinmaurer 1971, 65f. On the French exam, see chapter 12 below.

15. On the great ministers, as well as on the general theme of university Kuratoren, see Kluge 1958, 53ff; Rethwisch 1886; Buff 1937; Flach 1952; Sehling 1893; Jung 1966; Müller 1883; Prantl 1872, 1:550ff; Keck 1965, 77ff; Hammerstein 1977, 74ff, 177ff; Meister 1963, 20ff; Kink 1854-55, I/1, 442ff, 479f; Hartung 1923, 142ff.

16. See Gisenius 1628, 26ff, 31ff; University of Wittenberg 1926-27, 1:719; Tholuck 1853-54, 1:40f; Stieda 1934, 153ff; Bentzel 1784, 190; Hartung 1923, 146f; Bornhak 1900, 100ff, 185f.

17. Berlinische Monatsschrift, 1795, 24:364-72, at 368; BerlSA, H1, fol. 395v-96r; in general, Kluge 1958.

18. Meiners 1802-06, 1:280; see also 2:202; on criteria, see Michaelis 1768-76, 2:410ff. The Hanoverian minister Brandes claimed that Göttingen, like other universities, had a statutory right to nominate candidates for positions: see Brandes 1802, 186; cf. University of Götingen 1961, 179. Münchhausen's first appointments are in Rössler 1855, 2:33ff; on the lack of Mitbestimmungsrecht, see Buff 1937, 46ff.

19. See Foucualt 1975.

20. Rössler 1855, 2:478f. On the construction of the Göttingen professorate, see Rössler 1855, 2:33ff, 163ff, 223ff; Heyne's 1770 éloge on Münchhausen is in Ebel 1978, 93ff; see also Pütter et al. 1765-1838, 2:266; Bödeker 1990b, 52; Buff 1937, 46ff; on scholars' libraries as capital, see Streich 1977, 252; on publications, see Rössler 1855, 2:471, 473, 478f; Streich 1977, 263f, 267; on physics textbooks, for example, see Clark 1997.

21. Michaelis 1768-76, 2:355.

22. Nicolai 1783–96, 4:682; see also Anon 1782, 15, 43ff.

23. The decree is in Austria 1840, 1:170f; on Saxony, see Anon 1833, 19.

24. Information on Helmstedt is based on correspondence with the archive.

25. On the above, see Cosmar 1993, 15, 19ff, 25, 34, 39, 45, 59.

26. On Württemberg, see Schneider 1891, 61–64, 70, 73f.

27. On Saxe-Weimar, Burkhardt 1878, 91–94.

28. On the history of the archive in Austria, see Wolf 1871, 3f, 7–10, 15f; on Baden, Krebs 1949, 252; on Bavaria, Neudegger 1881, 118, 151. On memory and space, see Bolzoni 1994, 134–40; also Yates 1966, 231–42; on material systems of archival storage, see Pütter 1765, 1:285–86; Spieß 1777, 73–76; Burkhardt 1878, 93–94; on archival science, see Meisner 1969.

29. Cosmar 1993, 18.

30. See K2, 1690, 708v. The abbreviation K2 and others like it refers to the schema ahead of the bibliography.

31. The application for the Hebrew chair at Frankfurt a.d.O. from 1635 is in F1, Haebraisch, 3 May 1635: 1 May. Others are in K3, 1713, 107r–112v; K5, 1732, 424r; H3, 30 May 1739; K5, 1728, 32–93; 1732–33, 577–728.

32. See K3, 1713, 105–6, 107–12, 114r. Other examples are K4, 1715, 815–16; H2, 1731, 172r; K3, 1713, 3–4; H2, 1726, 413v; K5, 1730, 97v.

33. H3, 26 May 1734: 22 May; 17 Nov. 1750: 21 Oct.; K6, 1735, 712; 1738, 599–608; 1743, 522–23; K7, 1755, 523–69; 1752, 313; H4, 1757, 353–54; 1758, 330.

34. Laukhard 1792–1802, 1:89.

35. K2, 1694, 662r; 1703, 502r; K5, 1726, 157; 1727, 16.

36. K2, 1703, 505, 515; K3, 1713, 3–4.

37. K5, 1727, 16; 1730, 97.

38. H2, 1726, 414v; H3, 26 May 1734: 18 May 1734; 18 Oct. 1740: 7 Oct.; H4, 1754, 509v; K2, 1703, 505v; K3, 1713, 3–4; K5, 1726, 157r; 1727, 16v; 1730, 157r; 1731, 399–400, 409–10; K7, 1752, 313.

39. On intramural applause, see H3, 17 Nov.1750: 21 Oct.; H4, 1754, 509v, K7, 1755, 545v. On extramural, see K3, 1713, 107–12; K6, 1743, 522–23; H1, 1715, 166–86; H3, 17 Aug. 1747: 1 Aug.; 17 Nov. 1750: 21 Oct.; H4, 1733–54, 399–487, esp. 466r; 1754, 512–14; H4, 1757, 353.

40. K1, 1689, 134–35; K3, 1713, 114r; H1, 1706, 378–79; H2, 1726, 413v–14r; 1731, 172r; H3, 17 Aug. 1747: 1 Aug.

41. The regulation of 1749 is reprinted in Brandenburg-Prussia 1737–51, 4:199–212; also at BerlSA, I. HA Rep. 52, Nr. 159, Halle, N. 10, 1691–1782, 460–61 [1749].

42. K5, 1752, 313; K7, 1753, 384–432; K7, 1755, 545–47; 1755, 618r; K7, 1755, 528–36; H4, 1754, 509v.

43. K3, 1713, 107–12; K4, 1715, 829–55; H3, 3 Feb. 1736: 6 Aug. 1735; 3 April 1743: 3 March.

44. H2, 1733, 101–8; H3, 17 Nov. 1750: 21 Oct.; K3, 1713, 107–12; K5, 1730, 96–106; K7, 1755, 528–36; 1755, 619–20; 1750, 603–13; 1753, 384–432.

45. On Halle on this point, see Bornhak 1900, 54; in general, Schrader 1894.

46. K2, 1691, 697; 1694, 660; K3, 1713, 107.

47. K1, 1659, 371; 1663, 307–9; 1688, 18–19; 1689, 129–30; K2, 1694, 660; 1703, 507, 521–26; K5, 1730, 387–90; K7, 1752, 312; 1753, 433–34; 1755, 549, 560; 1756, 599–601; 1776, 511–15.

48. K1, 1670, 284–94. See also K1, 1624, 530, 537–40.

49. On Knutzen, see K5, 1733, 480–82; the marginal ink mark is at 480v.

50. See F3, 23 June 1588. Acts for Frankfurt a.d.O. are a bit disorganized and a collation of them lies beyond the scope of this book. There are duplications, so that F3 and F1–2 in the apparatus contain some or perhaps many of the same acts.

51. See F3, 29 March 1636: 21 and 24 March; 8 April 1653: 29 March.

52. F4, 18 Aug. 1651.

53. F1, Mathematik, 29 March 1688; see also F1, Griechisch, 15 April 1664; F2, Mathematik, 26 Nov. 1666; F3, 26 Nov. 1666.

54. H1, 1695, 561.

55. On the above two paragraphs, see H1, 1706, 350–53, 373–74; 1717, 118–49; H2, 1725, 465–66, 471–74; 1726, 15–16, fol. sep.; 1733, 18; 1735, 177; H3, 18/19 Oct. 1734: 14 Dec.; 31 May 1735: 19 July; 8 April 1737: 1 June; 9 Feb. 1741: 27 June [5 July]; H4, 1754, 517–18; 1762, 270–84.

56. H4, 1762, 267–84.

57. See for example H3, 31 May 1735: 19 July.

58. On the charismatic aspect of recognition, see chapter 1 above.

59. K1, 1624, 542; K3, 1713, 110; K5, 1726, 158r; K5, 1730, 99–103; H1, 1706, 380; H3, 31 May 1735.

60. F2, Logik, 27/17 March 1627; F3, 17 March 1627.

61. K3, 1713, 5–6; H1, 1705, 408–17; H3, 10 March 1749: 4–5 May; 3 April 1743: 21 Feb. 1743; 6 July 1741; 26 May 1734: 1 June; H4, 1755, 524–25; 1756, 356.

62. Otto, H3, 19 Oct. 1734: 21 Dec.

63. Leibniz's letters are at H1, 1706, 364r, 366r; Hofmann's is at 368–69.

64. Wolff 1841 gives more illumination on Wolff's initial appointment; on his early troubles, see H1, 1706, 315–48; on later troubles, H1, 1723, 1–52.

65. On Wolf's supplication for more money, see H1, 1715, 173–84.

66. On the early modern regime of testimony, see Shapiro 1983; Daston 1988, esp. chap. 6.3; Shapin and Schaffer 1989; and Shapin 1994.

67. K2, 1690, 708–11, 719.

68. K2, 1691, 696. See also K2, 1694, 659, 664; 1703, 501, 527; K3, 1708, 373–80; 1713, 109–110 (1709), 103, 123; K5, 1726, 202, 207; 1730, 386, 391; K7, 1754, 444; 1756, 615, 617; 1776, 482, 516.

69. K2, 1694, 659; K6, 1743, 521, 524.

70. K5, 1733, 475, 483.

71. K7, 1753, 376–435.

72. K7, 1756, 595–602.

73. K7, 1755, 523–69, esp. 548.

74. F4, 29 Aug. 1674; K1, 1666, 314r; K3, 1713, 2; K5, 1726, 133–40; 1727, 14–15, 18; 1730, 95r; H3, 2 Oct. 1737; 18/19 Oct. 1734: 20 Oct.; 18 Oct. 1740.

75. K7, 1756, 614; 1755, 477r, 523–69; 1754, 443–44, 449–52; 1750, 603–13; H3, 19 Feb. 1752; H4, 1753, 534r.

76. H4, 1761, 306r; K2, 1691, 695–96; also H3, 9 Feb. 1741: 7 Feb. See as well H2, 1731, 164r. An altered memorandum of 1776 is in K7, 1776, 518r.

77. F1, Hebraeisch, 1 Nov. 1611; F3, 8 July 1630.

78. F3, 14 Feb. 1704.

79. H2, 1731–32, 1–86, fol. sep.; 1729–30, 216–24, esp. 224: 30 Dec. 1729, 222: 16 Oct. 1730, 223: 25 Nov. 1730.

80. H2, 1730, 217r; also H2, 1733, 24, 72–75; H3, 18 Oct. 1740; H4, 1754, 392, 394; 1765, 147–94, esp. 162r, 176r.

81. H4, 1756, 145r. See also H1, 1699, 434–40.

82. F1, Eloquentia, 30 July 1658; K2, 1704, 149; 1746, 65–79; K4, 1716, 793–801; 1725, 103–13; K6, 1743, 518, 520, 521–31.

83. D1, 1770, 345r.

84. K7, 1756, 595, "keines wegens auf die Anciennet, . . . , sondern eintzig und allein darauf setzen werden, wer sich vor andern, in Herausgebung nützlicher und vernünfftiger Schriften und Disputationen, wie nicht weniger Dociren, wird hervorgethan haben." See also H4, 1757, 357–58.

85. K5, 1732, 412–26. Personalizing the ministry as well, for one privy to looking behind the curtain, are the ministerial errors, which it naturally tries to hush and touch up: see H1, 1695, 535–42; on the act of 1726, H2, 1726, 1–19, fol. sep.

86. K5, 1732, 430–69. See also K8, 1779, 202–15.

87. K7, 1753, 376–435, esp. 377r, 378r, 379r.

88. H4, 1763, 208–11; citation at 210r.

89. K7, 1770, 20.

90. H4, 1733–54, 399–487.

91. The gossip on Wolff from Berlin is cited in Rössler 1855, 2:253, note. On 13 December 1733, Münchhausen had written to Wolff about acquiring him for the planned university in Göttingen: see Gottsched 1755, "Beylagen zum dritten Abschnitt," 50.

92. A1, 1791, 63r; A2, 19r.

93. K10, 1794, 30–39; K10, 1799–1800, 135–37, 154–56; K11, 1801, 15–18.

94. K11, 1802, 106–47. Underlining in red pencil by the ministry seems to become a common practice first in the later eighteenth century. Some cases exist earlier. Wolff's supplication—H1, 1715, 166–86—for more pay, given his call to Wittenberg, has underlining in red pencil, as does an earlier act on someone else: H1, 1695, 561.

95. K12, 1804, 82–83, 91, 113; K14, 1806, 41, 46.

96. K12, 1804, 68–128, 141–43, 153–57, and so on, into K13.

97. K13, 1805, 11 et seq.; K15, 1808, 2 et seq.

98. H6, 1790/91, 68–73, 81–86, 101; H7, 1791, 1–11, 30–34, 41–42; *aus der mode* is at H7, 1791, 34r.

99. H9, 1795, 1–6, 44–46, 154–55; H10, 1798, 173–74; H11, 1798, 20–21, 36–37, 56, 97, 127–33, 142–43; H12, 1799, 3–4, 115–16; H13, 1800, 156–57; 1801, 192–95; etc. See also the case of Morgenstern, H8, 1795, 203–05; H9, 1796–97, 117, 127–28, 134–39.

100. H14, 1822, 8–28; H14, 1822, 43–44; H14, 1822, 44–46; H14, 1823, 76. See also G1, 1826, 100–102; C1, 1820, 137–41, 160, 190, 194. On the police, H14, 1822, 48r (quotation), 58r, 65, 68v;

101. B5, 1818, 17. For other acts dealing with filling Fichte's chair, see B2, 1814, 235–36; B3, 1816, 216–17, 220–23; B4, 1816, 6–12, 54–57; 1817, 245–46. A memorandum of 1 April 1816 had put the list of candidates to consider in this order with comments on each: 1. Hegel; 2. Schelling; 3. Schubert; 4. Fries.

102. On the occulting of and by the sovereign, see Foucault 1975.

103. Roche, 1978, 1:166ff; Clark 2003, 235ff.

104. See Clark 1997, 295ff.

CHAPTER EIGHT

1. On the lack of differentiation of libraries, archives, museums and cabinets, see Schlosser 1908, and the articles in Raabe 1977, esp. Fechner 1977. On the Bodleian, for example, see Noel-Tod 1980, 8f.

2. On Altdorf and its collections, see Baier 1714, 91–95; Will 1801, 162ff; Werner and Schmidt-Herrling 1937, 6–22, 38–58.

3. Uffenbach 1753–54, 34; in general, Buzas 1976, 35f; Kunoff 1982, 98; Newman 1966, 10; on particular libraries, see Will 1801, 162ff; Bulling 1932, 1ff; Zedler 1896, 44; Handwerker 1904, 13f; 1932, 18ff; Hirsching 1786–91, 1:141; II/1, 294; Hausens 1800, 125ff; Ebert 1822, 56; Pauntel 1965, 93; Oates 1958; Ker 1985, 309, 388, 418; 1986, 447.

4. See Sturm 1704, 10f, on the fame or *Ruhm* of cabinets at Leiden, Oxford and of private collectors in general.

5. For examples of techniques used at one library, see Zedler 1896, 18, 37ff, 43ff.

6. On Italy, private museums generally, and the apparent origins of such catalogues, see Findlen 1994, 36ff, 48ff; on private library catalogues, see Raabe 1988, 108. He holds that, although most such catalogues no longer exist, private libraries acquired by early modern public or academic libraries usually came with a catalogue of their contents.

7. On the above, see Philip 1983, 28ff, 42 (quotation), 52f. Willison 1977, 40, claims that the Bodleian had an "effective agreement whereby the Stationers Company deposited books," and the library had "an effective annual purchase grant" since the beginning of the seventeenth century. On Cambridge, see Oates 1986, esp. 113ff.

8. On Renaissance catalogues, see Taylor 1986, 3ff; on the printing of catalogues, Findlen 1994, 36ff, 48ff; on published auction catalogues, Wendt 1937.

9. On the above paragraphs, see James 1605; Macray 1890, 34f; Fox 1976, 249f, 261; Philip 1983, 10ff.

10. On the Bodleian and its catalogues, see James 1620; Hyde 1674; Macray 1890, 57f, 139–41, 212–14; Philip 1983, 31f; on auction catalogues, Wendt 1937, esp. 9, 12f.

11. Naudé 1644, 31, 103f, 111f; 1661, 19, 61, 66. On Naudé, see Samurin 1977, 146ff, 154ff, 201f; on cataloguing, 102ff.

12. Naudé 1644, 23, 127ff, 157f; 1661, 14, 74ff, 90f.

13. Dury 1983 [1650], 17 (quotation).

14. Dury 1983, 18–19 (quotations).

15. On the above, see Philip 1983, 44ff, esp. 45 (quotation of Langbaine), 45f (quotation of Wood); also Philip and Morgan 1997, 662f.

16. On the above, see Samurin 1977, 143ff, 184ff.

17. On Leibniz's influence, see Leyh 1957, 123; on critique, Ohnsorge 1962, 33; in general, Kunoff 1982, 175, n. 12. Hartmann and Füchsel 1937, 9, give Leibniz credit for directly influencing the development of the systematic catalogue in Göttingen, when none is likely to be found: see Fabian 1980, 110. Reuter 1966, esp. 356, even tries to give Leibniz credit for the conception of the building built for the library in Wolfenbüttel, 1705–13.

18. In Leibniz 1996, vol. 5, book iv, "De la connaisance," chap. xxi, "De la division des sciences"—the last chapter of the whole work—see esp. 507f.

19. See Samurin 1977, 142; Newman 1966, 10, 13, 29; Feller 1718, 128–36.

20. See Leibniz 1923–, 1st ser., 2:15–18; Lackmann 1966, 324ff; Newman 1966, 17ff; Scheel 1973, 74ff; Ohnsorge 1962, 17ff.

21. On the above two paragraphs, see Leibniz 1923–, 1st ser., 6:55–58, Leibniz to J. T. Reinerding, early July 1691, "und nach die dabey machende Zeddel hernach ferner zu einer sehr leichten Verfertigung des Indices materiam dienen können" (57)—he doubtless means a systematic catalogue, as a subject index would need more than one card per work; also see Uffenbach 1753–54, 1:304–25, 349–89; Bodemann 1888, 119–27; Heinemann 1969, 114f, 327ff; Newman 1966, 23ff, 41ff; Scheel 1973, 74ff.

22. Schulte-Albert 1971, 143f, see also Blumberg 1983, chap 10.

23. On this, see, for example, Kunoff 1982, 120ff.

24. Kunoff 1982, 122. On the universal library, see also Chartier 1994, chap. 3.

25. On professors altering the books in their private libraries for cosmetic reasons, see Streich 1977, 261; on princely libraries, Arnold 1988, 41f, 50, 53 (quotation).

26. Kunoff 1982, 127.

27. See Buzas 1976, 35f.

28. On the above generally, see Leyh 1957, 123ff; on the increase in book production and catalogues, Samurin 1977, 139f; on subject indices, Taylor 1966, 199.

29. On Cambridge, see Oates 1958, 224; 1986, 480ff; McKitterick 1986 27ff, 154f.

30. On Oxford, see Myres 1958, 236f; Noel-Tod 1980, 13-17.

31. Uffenbach 1753-54, 3:86-184, esp. 98ff on his tour; quotation at 91.

32. On this and the next paragraph, see Philip 1983, 55 (first quotation), 59-61, 66f, 74ff, 93ff, 103ff; Noel-Tod 1980, 4, 7, 13 (second quoation).

33. Samurin 1977, 253.

34. On Vienna, see Leyh 1957, 35f; Samurin 1977, 201.

35. On Dresden, see Ebert 1822, 60ff; Leyh 1957, 43-45; Samurin 1977, 204ff.

36. On Berlin, see Pauntel 1965, 12f, 85, 95; Leyh 1957, 41ff; Samurin 1977, 253.

37. On Munich, see Leyh 1957, 36ff. On Anspach and Weimar, see Hirsching 1786-91, 1:6-8, 202-4, 212, 21; on Hanover, see Ohnsorge 1962, esp. 59f.

38. Streich 1977, 243 (quotation).

39. See Streich 1977, esp. 241ff, 264f. On German auction and bookseller catalogues, their bibliographic worth, and on the separate English tradition, see Wendt 1937, esp. 16f, 25.

40. On the above, see Streich 1977, esp. 260ff; quotation at 260.

41. Gedike in Fester 1905, 12, 38, 42, 45, 67, 69.

42. Gedike in Fester 1905, 26.

43. See Fabian 1980, 115ff; at 119, he has more than 200,000 volumes by 1800; Leyh 1957, 116ff, esp. 120, has 120,000 volumes by 1786, only 150,000 by 1800, and 200,000 by 1812; see also Heeren 1813, 262; Kunoff 1982, 109, has Göttingen circa 1800 as second only to Vienna and Dresden. On funding, see Hartmann and Füchsel 1937, 83.

44. See Leyh 1957, 116ff, 123, 127 (quotation); Kunoff 1982, 136ff.

45. See Leyh 1957, 116ff, 121ff, 127; Kunoff 1982, esp. 138ff; Fabian 1980, 120f.

46. Kunoff 1982, chap. 6, quotation at 111; Buzas 1976, 130.

47. See Heyne's report of 1810 in Hartmann 1937, 14-18; also see Heeren 1813, 292-99; on Göttingen's international network of contacts with bookdealers, see Eck 1997.

48. Hirsching 1786-91, 2:298f (quotation). Other examples are these which, in some cases, produced author catalogues before systematic ones—on Greifswald, see Pommerania. 1765-1802, ser. 1, 2:1003ff; on Würzburg, Handwerker 1904, 69ff, 87, 105; 1932, 107ff; on Freiburg im. Br., Mittler 1971, 119, 123-25; on Marburg, Zedler 1896, 59f; on Gießen and Erlangen, Hirsching 1786-91, 1:141; 2:294, 298f; Englehardt 1843, 156ff; Kolde 1910, 39f; on Halle, see Schrader 1894, 1:384; on Olmouc and other Austrian libraries, see d'Elvert 1857, 175, 200ff, 252.

49. On cataloguing generally, Kunoff 1982, 115ff, 125 (first quotation); Fabian 1977, 219; 1980, 110 (second quotation). On the Göttingen library generally, see Heeren 1813, 292-305; Seidel 1953; Schwedt 1983; Hartmann 1937; Hartmann and Füchsel 1937.

50. Roloff 1961, 250.

51. Quotation from Leyh 1957, 281; on the systematic catalogue as the crown, see Buzas 1978, 135f; also Samurin 1977, 140f.

52. See Handwerker 1932, 114; Zedler 1896, 82f; Leyh 1957, 190-96; Schleswig-Holstein 1832, 4:479ff, 485f.

53. On Gesner's works of 1545 and 1548–49, see Taylor 1966, 40ff; Samurin 1977, 115ff; on earlier, monastic libraries, Samurin 1977, 105. On the matter of subject indices generally after Gesner, see Taylor 1966, 58ff, 86, 89ff.

54. On the above, see Gierl 1992, 53–80; Kunoff 1982, 76; Chartier 1994, chap. 3.

55. See Fabian 1980, 118f, 122f.

56. On German periodicals in general, see Kirchner 1928–31; 1958–62, esp. 1:20, on anonymity. On *ADB*, see Schneider 1995, 76, 96, 270–72; Rowland 1995, 17; Van der Laan 1995, esp. 105. On *Das Deutsches Museum* and *Neues Deutsche Museum,* see Hofstaetter 1908; on the *Der Teutsche Merkur,* see McCarthy 1995; and the articles in Heinz 2003. On English review journals, including anonymity of reviews, see Donoghue 1996.

57. On *GGA,* see Heeren 1813, 259–62; Oppermann 1844, 13, 24, 30; on *ALZ,* see Kirchner 1958–62, 1:119ff, esp. 123; Schönfuß 1914. On book production, see Plachta 1994, 187f.

58. Gedike in Fester 1905, 27; on the above in general, see Leyh 1957, 116ff.

59. Oppermann 1844, 27–28; Roethe 1901, 623; also the document in Rössler 1855, 2:478f, perhaps by Münchhausen, perhaps not.

60. Bulling 1932; University of Jena 1958a, 390–433; Kunoff 1982, 133–35.

61. Miller 1967, 81ff; Harris 1998, esp. chaps 3–4.

62. Miller 1967, 108f, 11, 116ff, 103; Garnett 1899, 43f (citation).

63. McKitterick 1986 19, 20, 190ff, 387f—as the scandal of scandals, the Cambridge University Library was actually apparently better off than the pre-Panizzi BM.

64. Craster 1952, 54ff.

65. On Graz and the Austrian universities, see Krones 1886, 528.

66. Mittler 1971, 120f.

67. On this paragraph and the above two, see Leyh 1957, 172ff, 190ff, 281.

68. On archiving, as well as on storage, see Fladt 1764, 57–59; Pütter 1765, I, § 471, 489 et seq., § 500–04; Claproth 1769, 138ff; Spieß 1777, 15f, 73ff; Günther 1783, "Vorerinnerung," i–iii, 13ff (§ 17–20, 22).

69. Gutscher 1811, 26f, 31f.

70. Gutscher 1811, 51ff. Oegg 1804, 43–59, actually holds, however, that the ordering by chronology is the easiest and is always in play at some level.

71. Gutscher 1811, 57–61.

72. Gutscher 1811, 62, 96ff. Interesting tidbits are also in Kiefhaber 1827, esp. 11f. On the above and more, see Wolf 1871, 15f, 139; Bavaria 1838, 116ff; Neudegger 1904, 153, 167–69; Koser 1904, 3ff, 17ff; Schneider 1891, 75; Brenneke 1953, 52–60.

73. Kayser 1790, 5 (quotation). On Kayser's importance, along with Reuß's, for the triumph of the author catalogue, see Buzas 1976, 146f; Taylor 1986, 14ff.

74. Kayser 1790, 9ff, 52.

75. Buzas 1978, 16f, 31, 107, 135–36; Fabian 1977, 209.

76. On the journals in general, including the rise of specialized ones, see Kirchner 1958–62; Carlsson 1969; on *ALZ,* see Schönfuß; on the *Heidelbergische Jahrbücher,* see Kloß 1916; on the *Jahrbücher für wissenschaftliche Kritik,* see Gans 1836.

77. See Foucault 1977, 113–38 ("What Is an Author?"); citation at 126; also Chartier 1994, chap. 2.

78. Three of the most radical formulators of this Romantic hermeneutics were Friedrich Ast, Friedrich Schlegel, and Friedrich Schleiermacher, to which one might add Friedrich A. Wolf, taking off from Friedrich Schelling's notion of organic wholes:

see Dilthey 1970, II/2 [14/2], 658f. Schlegel had mooted the radical notion in 1796 that, in order to understand any given literary work, one must understand the author's oeuvre: see Michel 1982, esp. 141f, 154. Beginning in 1799, Schlegel and Schleiermacher corresponded about a collaborative edition-translation of Plato's collected works, part of the difficulty of which consisted in deleting inauthentic works, and ordering the authentic ones chronologically; Schleiermacher ended up producing the edition alone, beginning in 1804, and the work on Plato proved crucial for his writings in hermeneutics, above all the notion that an editor (or critic) must be able to distinguish authentic from inauthentic works as well as the proper order of works on purely internal grounds—the author's spirit or style—without appeal to external historical authorities or information: see Dilthey 1970, I/2 [13/2], 35–75; II/2 [14/2], 657–89. Ast 1808a, 178, expresses this emerging Romantic hermeneutics thusly: "The principle of all understanding and knowledge is to find the spirit of the whole from the parts, and to grasp the parts through the whole," which must be done simultaneously, thus the dilemma of getting into the hermeneutical circle; at 203f, without explicitly citing Schleiermacher's Plato edition, then underway, Ast uses the example of a Platonic dialogue and the Platonic oeuvre to make the point that one cannot understand a work without grasping the oeuvre. Flashar 1979, 22, writes, "New with Wolf and Ast is that the subject of understanding [hermeneutics] is not longer an entity (*Sache*) but rather an author"—and one probably should include Schlegel and Schleiermacher in this Romantic elevation of the author over topics. Ast (1808a,b) and Wolf (1831 and 1833) frame the goal of classical philology as the threefold task of grasping works, authors, and classical antiquity as spiritual wholes, the last one as a culture.

79. On Romantic "culture," see Elias 1977.

CHAPTER NINE

1. On visitation, see Roman Catholic Church 1879, *Decret.* II, causa x, qu. 1, cap. 9–12, esp. cap. 12; causa. xviii, qu. ii, cap. 28–29; *Decret. Greg.*, lib. I, tit 23, cap. i; 1935–65, 5:648ff; 7:1512–1619; also Ziegler 1679, § i, iv, xx, xxii; Zindel 1791, 82f. On visitation of monasteries in general, see McLaughlin 1935, 45-48, 129–71; Clercq 1936–58, 1:18f, 96; Mahn 1951, 121ff; on orders and the laity, Mörsdorf 1964–67, 1:488ff, 552ff; 2:93ff, 299ff; Plöchl 1953–60, 1:63ff, 176.

2. On Cluny, see Sackur 1892–94, 1:70; 2:439ff; Berlière 1912, 160, 169, 184ff; Galbraith 1925, 9ff; Mahn 1951, 126. On Premonstratensians and Cistercians, see Mahn 1951, 54f, 66f, 75ff, 93, 97f, 120, 131ff, 148ff, 173ff, 218ff, 245ff; on visitation, Cistercians 1878, 259f; cf.1945, 21, also 110f (*Carta Caritatis*); Berlière 1912, 233ff. The 1232–39 visitations are in Cistercians 1946–52, esp. 1:23ff, 98ff; 2:181ff. On Domincans, see Vicaire 1957, 2:210ff, 261; Mandonnet 1938, 1:29f; on Franciscans, Moorman 1968, 28ff, 62, 67ff, 83, 97ff, 106, 147ff, 162ff; on visitations, Bonaventura 1882–1902, 8:458ff. On the Fourth Lateran Council, see Roman Catholic Church 1901–27, 22:999–1002.

3. On early medieval Oxford, see Lawrence 1984b, esp. 125; on late medieval Oxford, Storey 1992. On Cambridge's eventual exemption from visitation, see Leader 1988, 219–21. On Oxbridge generally, see Cobban 1988, 274–99, where he relates the attempt in 1281 by the Bishop of Lincoln to visit Oxford and the university's resistance thereto. Curtis 1959, 20 (citing Rashdall 1936, 3:122–28, 228), claims that Oxbridge achieved ecclesiastical exemption first by appealing to the Archbishop of Canterbury for exemption from their local bishops, then by appealing cleverly to the pope against the archbishop.

4. See Gockel 1682, 64; Lauterbach 1728–29, 4:171ff, 1736f. Stephanus 1611, 13, 18,

115, foregrounds the bishops's and chancellor's power; Ziegler 1679, § xxxix, claims that in Protestant lands the prince inherited the episcopal power to authorize visitations; cf. Zindel 1791, 82f. On the medieval discussion, see Baldus 1615-16, 6:27r-28r. On episcopal jurisdiction over universities and the prince's expropriation, see Stein 1891, 58ff, 96. On the Jesuits, see Knowles 1966; Society of Jesus 1934-38. On the above, see also Maack 1956, 38.

5. On the emergence of nonresident chancellors, see Curtis 1959, 23; Winstanley 1935, 6-9. In the Germanies the practice of nonresident chancellors began in the Late Middle Ages. The chancellorship evolved there slightly differently than in England. The formal head of a German university qua corporate body was the rector, while the chancellor served as head of the *studium generale,* which amounted only to having some oversight of the award of academic degrees, although some chancellors did try to extend their authority. On the Germanies and on Europe generally, see Hammerstein 1996a,b; Ridder-Symoens 1996.

6. In general, see Curtis 1959, 23f, 28; Simon 1966, 197-214, 245-67. On Cambridge, see Leader 1988, 324-25, 331-33, 336-39, 347, 349; on Oxford, Cross 1986, 117, 127-29, 135-37. Cf. Twigg 1990, 4, who plays down the sixteenth-century visitations.

7. See Williams 1986, 403-5; Fincham 1997, 181-82, 198-210; Roy and Reinhart 1997, 723-31; Worden 1997, esp. 748; Twigg 1990, esp. chaps. 2 and 5; Beddard 1997a, 816-17; finally, Gascoigne 1989b, on visitation and reform in particular, and 1989a in general.

8. On aspects of early modern visitations in the Germanies, see Tholuck 1853-54, 1:23-26; Hufen 1955; Schmid 1859-78, 9:705.

9. Raeff 1983, 63 (quotation); see also Strauss 1978, 256-61. Dates on the visitations of Helmstedt, Jena, and Tübingen are based on archival and other sources.

10. Pommerania 1765-1802, ser. 1. vol. 1 and 2 and ser. 2, vol. 2, have many visitation reports and decrees for the University of Greifswald. Saxony 1724, vol. 1, has a number of reports and decrees for university visitations in Electoral Saxony, as does University of Wittenberg 1926-27, mostly for Wittenberg. Visitation reports for Tübingen are at StutSA as A274.16.

11. The visitation documents are at HanoSA, Cal. Br. 21, Nr. 3878, 1597: see fol. 209r-21r (draft of instruction and questionnaire), 225r-36v (fair copy of instruction and questionnaire), 244v-93r (protocols of twenty-seven faculty responses). Another early modern questionnaire for a university visitation was made in Munich for the University of Ingolstadt in 1642: see MuniSA, GL, Fasz. 1479, Nr. 75, 1642, esp. fol. 117r-71r. At the University of Wittenberg, a questionnaire schema was mandated for all future visitations in 1609: see University of Wittenberg 1926-27, 1:717-25.

12. On confession, see Foucault 1976 and 1980.

13. A number of articles in Schönert 1991 deal with the poetics and narrative structures of bureaucratic writing, as do Sabean 2001 and Becker 2001. Relevant literature on narrative theory will be cited below. On European journals, see Hocke 1978—in general illuminating but not very useful for the analysis below.

14. Defoe 1985, 87-117.

15. On Robinson's journal, see Marx 1981, vol. 1, § 4. On the above and similar, see Watt 1987, chaps. 1 and 3; Ray 1990, chap. 3; Barthes 1984, 179-87; Todorov 1978, 9-19.

16. On the above, see White 1981; also 1987, 1-25; Auerbach 1988, chap. 4; Tomashevsky 1965, 66ff; Scholes and Kellogg 1966, chap. 6; Brooks 1984, chap. 1.

17. See Claproth 1789, 11-12, 14-17; Sonnenfels 1785, chap. 4-5, 11; Justi 1775, 273, 313. These do not treat of ministerial journals, but the genres there treated are relevant.

18. Frye 1976, 56 (quotation); on the absence of work, for example, in the Grimms's world, see Bottigheimer 1987, esp. chap. 12; in general, Clark 1995.

19. On the above about Romance, see Frye 1976, esp. 55–57, 161, 177; 1957, 151, 186; Scholes 1974; and, Propp 1968. On bureaucratic ritualism in general, see Herzfeld 1992. Sabean 1984, chap. 2, conveys a similar sort of visitational mediation from on high, where the distant ministry seems not unlike Kafka's castle.

20. Records of the visitation of Ingolstadt in 1784 are at MuniSA, GL, Fasz. 1479, Nr. 93, 107–21, 123–30, esp. Nr. 107:1–2 (visitation instruction), 107:3 (*diarium*), 107:4–12, 108–19 (enclosures and notes), 119:26 (visitation report). These are unfoliated and not in good order in the archive.

21. Auerbach 1988, 11–12.

22. The "historical" third person is advocated for *Relationen* by Claproth 1789, 19.

23. Shapin and Schaffer 1989; Schaffer 1992.

24. Sabean 1996; Foucault 1975.

25. Frye 1957, 186 (first quotation); 1976, 57 (second). See also Elias 1977.

26. The documents are in University of Wittenberg 1926–27, 2:476–95. In a letter to me of 25 May 1994, an archivist at DresSA said the originals (HStA., Loc. 2136) were destroyed in World War II. Friedensburg did not draw the table; moreover, he did not give the actual sublist of publications in column *a*, but rather summarized it in a note.

27. This section of this chapter was originally planned for a conference Simon Schaffer was rumored to be holding on academic gossip long ago.

28. On immutable mobiles, see Latour 1990.

29. On the paper circulation and credit, see Latour and Woolgar 1986.

30. On the genius and self-registering instruments in the Romantic era, see Schaffer 1990 and 1992. On *Jahrestabellen* for Halle and Königsberg by 1786, Duisburg by 1788, and Frankfurt a.d.O. by 1795, see BerlSA, I. HA. Rep. 76. alt. II, Halle, Nr. 42–43; Königsberg, Nr. 238–39; Duisburg, Nr. 285–86; and Frankfurt a.d.O., Nr. 157–58. See also Pommerania 1765–1802, ser. 1, 2:993.

31. See Markus 1987, esp. 13–17; Shapin and Schaffer 1989; Gross 1990, esp. 71–74; Locke 1992, esp. 89–93; Daston 2001; Becker and Clark 2001.

32. That is the conclusion of Parsons 1949 in analysis of the trajectories of Durkheim and Weber, although Parsons focuses more, in Weberian terms, on the charismatic aspects of traditional authority. It is also the critique of Lyotard 1979 of Habermas 1987 [1962].

CHAPTER TEN

1. See Smith 1976, 1:341. Academic newsletters will be discussed in the next chapter.

2. Justi 1760, 2:341–74, esp. 350–51 (citation).

3. Naudé 1644, 63f; 1661, 38.

4. Leibniz 1923–, 1$^{st}$ ser., 2:16; Gottsched 1755, 57.

5. On Luther's sales, see Lindemann 1969, 45ff; in general, see Strauss 1978. Grafton and Jardine 1986, esp. 83ff, 97, discuss the high salaries generated by high profiles in the Renaissance. The appearance of German humanists and institution of salaries and chairs for them has been traced extensively by Paulsen 1919, esp. 1:12, 78–89, 97–104, 108–10; see also Kaufmann 1888, 2:330ff, 500–62; and Overfield 1984, 112f. On particular universities, see Univerity of Tübingen 1877, 71; University of Heidelberg 1886 2:44, 70; Scheiber 1857–60, II/1, 68ff, 88ff; Hautz 1862–64, 1:368ff; Vischer

1860, 180ff; Kink 1854–55, I/1, 199ff; Prantl 1872, 1:137, 145f, 209f; Hradil 1980, 2:37ff, 48f. See also Rufus 1885; on Luder, Wattenbach 1864; on Mosellanus, Schmidt 1867. German humanists made the perhaps loudest noise in *Epistolae obscurorum virorum* of 1516–17: see Anon 1909.

6. On the man "nominis celebritate" (1554), see Kink 1854–55, 2:375; Stephanus 1611, 22ff, 29f; University of Frankfurt a.d.O. 1897–1906, 3:28.

7. Austria 1840, 1:170f; Brandenburg-Prussia 1754–1822, 4:5049. On Edinburgh and the renown of professors via publication, see Morrell 1997, [II] 12.

8. See Anon 1798, 6; on Wieland, see Bürger 1980, 162f, 167; on journals, more in the next chapter.

9. Michaelis 1768–76, 2:428–30.

10. On book reviews and fame, see Donoghue 1996, chap. 2; on *ADB*, Schneider 1995, 78ff, 96, 160f, 204ff, 298ff.

11. Quotation from Gedike (1789) in Fester 1905, 13f. The original is at BerlSA, I. HA. Rep. 76. alt II, (*Generalia*), 1787–94, fol. 16.

12. On intellectual life at Göttingen, see Marino 1995; on Göttingen in general, see Brandes 1802; Buff 1937; Rössler 1855; Ebel 1978; Rupke 2002; Fabian 1977; 1980; Hartmann 1937; Hartmann and Füchsel 1937; Heeren 1813; Schwedt 1983; Selle 1953.

13. On 1785, see Kink 1854–55, I/1, 553f, note (citation, italics in the original); on 1773, Hammerstein 1977, 192f.

14. Michaelis 1768–76, 2:352 (quotation), 355; see also 397ff.

15. Boell 1782, 9. The copy of Boell 1782 at the Göttingen UB (8° HLP II, 160) has "F.P.K. Böll" written on the title page. The library catalogue also ascribes the work to him. His propaganda tract is Boell 1775.

16. Boell 1782, 4.

17. Boell 1782, 8, 12f.

18. Boell 1782, 17–19, 31.

19. Boell 1782, 51–56, 59, 69f, 83f.

20. The anonymous tract is in Rössler 1855, 2:468–86, see 473, 476–77, 481–82. Having entitled it "Bemerkungen über Johann Jakob Mosers Rede . . . aus den Papieren eines verstorbenen Staatsministers und Universitäten Curators," Rössler implies the pages were by Münchhausen, without explicitly saying so. Gierl MS argues that the pages were probably written by Boell, whose anonymous tract of 1782 bears striking similarities to them.

21. Mackensen 1791, 8, 18–19, 32f, 57.

22. Mackensen 1791, 19–20, 31–32.

23. Fester 1905. The report is at BerlSA, I. HA. Rep. 76. alt. II. 1 (*Generalia*), 1787–94, fol. 7 (cover letter), 8–66 (report), 67 (expense account).

24. On the ethnographic "I," see Feuerhahn 2001.

25. Gedike in Fester 1905, 17, writes, "Da ich mich in Göttingen fünfthalb Tage aufgehalten . . ." My photocopy of Fester's *Gedike* was made from that at the Göttingen University Library, where a previous reader took it as five and a half. This reader wrote as marginalia, "S. 17 '5 1/2'," crossing out a footnote by Fester 1905, 13, "Rechnet man zwei Reisetage für die 16 Meilen von Helmstädt nach Göttingen, so wird sich Gedike etwa vom 22. bis 25. in G[öttingen] aufgehalten haben." Fester has Gedike in Göttingen for four days. The Grimms's *Deutsches Wörterbuch* has "fünfthalb" as a shortening of "fünftehalb," which means four and a half.

26. On "immutable mobiles," see Latour 1990.

27. See also the contemporary judgment in Rinck 1897, 203.

28. In Horn 1808, 185. In 1905 Fester could no longer find the diary, though Gedike's biographer had seen it: see Horn 1808, 171–86.

29. See Rinck 1897.

30. I have modernized some of the orthography in the above citations.

31. Quotations on Cambridge fellows in Winstanley 1935, 256–57.

CHAPTER ELEVEN

1. See Hayman 1982, 146f. Letter to Ritschl, 30 Jan 1872, in Nietzsche 1986, 3:281f.

2. Letters to Rohde, 8 June, 7 July, 25 Oct., Nov. 1872, to Ritschl, 26 June 1872, to R. Wagner, 7/8 Nov. 1872, in Nietzsche 1986, 4:7f, 17–21, 70–73, 85–87, 89. The polemical works are all reprinted in Gründer 1969.

3. Nietzsche 1999, 1:13–15. Wilamowitz-Möllendorff in Gründer 1969, 29, 55.

4. Nietzsche 1999, 125–28, 33, 40f, 103, also 581, 583.

5. Nietzsche 1999, 1:52, 55, 59–60, 62, 64f, 73f, 82, 596—"als *gespielten* dionysischen Mensch."

6. Nietzsche 1999, 1:84, 95, 545–47.

7. Nietzsche 1999, 1:63, 83, 94, 96, 545, 544, 621, 634. On Aristotle, see Cooper 1922, 98–116

8. On the above, see Nietzsche 1999, 1:21f, 87–91, 99–101, 111, 115f, 123–29, 144f, 626, 636, 638. Nietzsche's critique of Italian opera in the book indicates that he was aware he was writing the history of his present.

9. Nietzsche 1999, 1:116.

10. Nietzsche 1999, 6:67–73—citation at 71; see also 310f; on *Die Geburt der Tragödie* and cultural perversity, 313. On Nietzsche's Socrates, see Schmit 1969, esp. 5, 162, 196, 317–44

11. McLuhan 1969 [1962], 138 (quotation).

12. McLuhan 1969, 166f (citation—I have put two different paragraphs together)—on *Don Quixote,* see 256ff.

13. See Ong 1983 [1958], 8f, 82f, 181, 194f, 212f, 279ff, 287 (parenthetical remarks in the original), 314ff. On memory and visualization, see Yates 1966.

14. Shapin and Schaffer 1989, 60 (citations). On the hegemony of visual culture in the Baroque, see Maravall 1986, 251–63, an appendix just to this point.

15. Barthes 1984, 179–87. See Becker and Clark 2001 on the Royal Society and rhetoric.

16. Shapin and Schaffer 1989, 61 (first citation), 62 (second). See Myers 1990, 234–49, on the role of gratuitous detail in science. On the Enlightenment and the matter of the visual, see, for example, Stafford 1994, esp. xxiv–vi, 38–46, 218, 282.

17. See Daston 1991; 1992; 1995; 2001; Galison 1997; Daston and Galison 1992; and a forthcoming book by the two authors on this topic. See also Crary 1990, in which Crary argues that the separation and privileging of vision from a kinesthetic realm and, above all, from a tactile component, occurred about the time that Daston and Galison set for the rise of "objectivity."

18. See Schaffer 1992, 362 (citation); 1988; 1999.

19. Schaffer 1990.

20. On Wolf and the Homer Question, see Volkmann 1874, and notes and commentary in the translations: German and English translations are in Wolf 1908 and 1985. See Ong 2003 and Fabian 1983 for fairly recent considerations of orality and visualization.

21. Jaspers cited in Ijsseling 1976, 104. On the Sophists, see Guthrie 1971, esp. 179.

22. Contemporary deployments of sophistry occur, for example, in Feyerabend 1978; Lyotard 1979, esp. chap. 14; Latour 1999, esp. chap 7; and Ballif 2001. Crome 2004 treats sophistry in Lyotard's work in relation to Kant, Hegel, and Heidegger. Christian tradition associates the fool with the devil, seeing a literal meaning in Psalm 53 that the fool says in his (or her) heart that there is no God. Church authorities thus opposed the institution of the court fool or jester, whose representatives often, indeed, served as a sort of devil's advocate. See Brant 1964 on fools, and esp. 430ff (cap 110b); on court jesters, see Amelunxen 1991, 25ff; Ebeling 1888, 117; Mezger 1981; and the papers in Mezger et al. 1984. I know of no scholarly treatise on the devil's advocate, although a number of literary treatments exist. In late medieval hands, such as Oresme's, disputation became more or less "postmodern."

23. Guthrie 1971, 31, agrees with the circumlocution of sophistical as "professorial" by Michael Joyce translating Xenophon; on areté and democracy, see esp. 19f, 25,

24. On Socrates, Plato, and the dialogue, see Kahn 1996.

25. On Plato, sophistry, and rhetoric, see Ijsseling 1976 and Marback 1999. Tradition has it that the entrance to the Academy bore the inscription above it, "Let no one unversed in geometry enter here." Unlike modern geometry, in its Hilbertian construal, Greek geometry depended centrally on the actual images. Plato might exhibit some iconoclastic sentiments; but I would argue for a visual bias in the oeuvre: see for example Ong 2003, 78ff. Plato's Academy endured for nearly a millennium as a school, so "academics" or "academicians" had sufficient time to become unorthodox Platonists.

26. Loen 1742, 557 (citation); I think the other source is Bornhak 1900, but cannot find my notes on it. "To move the psyche, which we have seen to be what the baroque strove for, the most effective means are visual," as noted Maravall 1986, 253—apropos Baroque culture, which he sees as fundamentally authoritarian and absolutist, see also 75, 77f, 239.

27. See Friedrich the Great 1986, 50—there are six records or versions of this saying.

28. See Bonner 1977, 48, 57, 156–61. Relevant passages from Roman Empire 1872–95 are: *Codex*, 10, 52 [53].1–10, "de professoribus et medicis"; and in the *Digesta*, 50, 13, 1. §4, "An et philosophi [i.e., sophisti] professorum numero sint? Et non putem, non quia non oportet religiosa res est, sed quia hoc primum profiteri eos oportet[,] mercennariam operam spernere." See also *Codex*, 10,39.5, 10,42.6 42.8, 10,47.1–.2, 10,48.12, 10,50.1–.3, 10,53–54; 12,15.1, 12,30.8, 12,49 et seq.; *Digesta*, 50,4.18, 50,5.8, 50,6.7, 50,13.1–.4. On privileges, see Kibre 1962, 1–3.

29. On academies as public institutions, see Gerhard 1655a, Th. iii; a view shared by his colleague, Kundtmann 1644, Mem. Prim., Art. Sec., citing his colleague Lansius. On the rise of *ius publicum* in the sixteenth century, Stolleis 1988–92, 1:47f, 66, 76. On political theory, see Gierke 1868–1913, vol. 3, esp. 201f, 501–03.

30. The quotations on the professor are from Titius 1724, 1250; Lauterbach 1728–29, 3:592ff; Schwimmer 1672, Diss. I, unpag. See also Kreittmayr 1758, 5:2336.

31. On the Roman *servus publicus*, esp. as *actor publicus*, see Eder 1980, 79f, 170f. The notion of the "public servant," a slave of the public, seems to disappear in the Roman Empire, and is wholly out of place in the Middle Ages. The comparison of Louis and Friedrich comes from Mayer 1924, 1:38.

32. Hegel 1970, 3:145–55 [§ IV:A], esp. 152; Fichte 1834–46, 6:309.

33. On medieval use of "master," "doctor" and "professor," see Weijers 1987, 133–55; Fried 1974, 9–21. On political theory, see Gierke 1868–1913, vol. 3, esp. 201f, 501ff. On

early medieval conciliar regulations concerning education, fees, and the problem of simony, see Holy Roman Empire 1886–, sect. 3, II/2, 581; Roman Catholic Church 1901–27, 14:1014; 20:509; 22:227f, 455, 999, 1015–18; 1879, *Decret. Greg.*, lib. III, tit. 4, cap. iv; lib. III, tit. 5, cap. v–vi, xxii, xxvii; lib. V, tit. 5. See also Benson 1968, 209ff; Schneider 1885, 114ff; Hinschius 1869–97, 2:74f, 614; Plöchl 1953–60, 2:202; Baldwin 1970, 1:117ff.

34. The canon had "stallum in choro et votum in capitulo." On all this, see Hinschius 1869–97, 2:passim, esp. 55–112; 615f; Plöchl 1953–60, 1:427–30; 2:155–57. On the various senses of "canon," see Schaefer 1965, 87ff; Schieffer 1976, 101ff, 123ff. Chapters above have discussed the institutional origins of the professorial chair in the secular canonry.

35. On Fichte, see Jacobs 1998, esp. 47, 119. Fichte seems to have gradually lost popularity as a lecturer and, as some of his students had problems following his lectures failing a textbook, he was driven to print his lectures, especially the *Wissenschaftslehre*, "dann wird man etwas Festes vor sich haben, worauf man fußen kann, und nicht mehr bloß verhallende Worte": see Ehrlich 1977, 12–22, 27–29, 52–54; citation at 17. On the changing nature of textbooks at the time, see, for example, Clark 1997.

36. On the inaugural lecture in 1970, see Eribon 1991, 219.

37. On Kant, see Schultz 1965, passim, esp. 20–22, 28–33.

38. On Kant, see Schultz 1965, 29. Kant's "Beantwortung der Frage: Was ist Aufklärung?" (1784) is in Kant 1968–77, 8:33–42. I pass over in silence his strange use of "public" and "private."

39. Foucault 1971, 82 (quotation); 1969, 28.

40. Schultz 1965, 28–29.

41. On the above, see "Schutzschrift für den Stand und die Lebensart der Professoren" in Meiners 1775–76, 3:115f—see 118, 136–40, 143, 145f. Meiners's colleague at Göttingen, Michaelis, often cited above, held a good lecturing style was necessary in the philosophy faculty. In the superior faculties, most students were studying in view of a pragmatic career, thus the professor was interesting, not so much in view of what he said, but rather whom he knew. In the inferior faculty, however, where knowledge was mostly useless, the professor's voice had to attract the attention of students: see Michaelis 1768–76, 2:167f.

42. On Foucault's lecturing style as cocky, see Marc Beigbeder, "En suivant le cours de Foucault," *Esprit*, June 1967, 1066f, cited in Macey 1995, 189, 507; see also 183ff, 209. On Foucault at Clermont, see Eribon 1991, 130, 139–41 (quotation at 140), 219.

43. Macey 1995, 160 (citation of *Le Nouvel Observateur*), 169–75.

44. Publication number from Eribon 1991, 156.

45. Virgil 1997, 95f (citation).

46. Koenig 1985, 105 (citation).

47. First citation from *Fugger-Zeitungen* cited in Matthews 1959, 149.

48. See Allport and Postman 1947, esp. 162–66, on legends, and chap. 8 on rumor formation and development. Rosnow and Fine 1976 presents a more biological metaphor. See also Koenig 1985.

49. See Rosnow and Fine 1976, chap. 6; Spacks 1985; Arnaud 2001; and the papers in Goodman and Ben-Ze'ev 1994.

50. On gossip and so on at conferences, see Friese 2001.

51. Schein 1994. The original, medieval meaning of "gossip" was a godfather or godmother: "god-sib." It later meant a chum or friend, especially among women. The

nuances of a news- or rumor-monger seem to be all postmedieval. Even should this not be so, I would argue for the suggested meaning on general, analytical principles.

52. Voltaire 1964 [1734], 91 (first citation), 93 (second).

53. On gossip and joking, see Ben-Ze'ev 1994, 14; Morreall 1994, 56f; Spacks 1984, esp. 49f.

54. In Rössler 1855, 2:253, note.

55. Ayim 1994, 97f (citation).

56. Staël 1968, 1:101–10—citations at 102 and 103.

57. Bernard of Clairvaux 1879, 1:537.

58. Goldsmith 1988, 6 (citation); Burke 1993, 98–102 112f.

59. Weber 1988b, 1:559f (citation).

60. See Burke 1993, 102–8; Goldsmith 1988, esp. 6–13; and Elias 1977 and 1983. On gossip per se, see Arnaud 2001.

61. See Burke 1993, 108–12; Goodman 1994, esp. 125ff.

62. Goodman 1994, 73–89 (citation at 74); Schiebinger 1989, 30–32, 37–65, 153; on a German example, see Hertz 1988.

63. Goodman 1994, 119 (citation).

64. Staël 1968, 1:102. A German literature on the model of or in imitation of the Anglo-French literature on conversation of course exists: see, for example, Rohr 1730, 278ff.

65. See Goldsmith 1988, esp. 29ff; and Goodman 1994, chap. 4, esp. 139f. See also the papers in Van Houdt et al. 2002, which I came upon too late to integrate into my study.

66. See Arnaud 2001, chap. 2; Ray 1992, chap. 2. Goldmsith 1988, esp. chap. 2, shows the positive interrelation between a novelist and the art of conversation in seventeenth-century France. Ray 1990 has pursued the production and "authority" of the self through a number of "canonical" English and French eighteenth century novels. Had I more time and ability, I would try to show the relevance to this book of his work, as it traces the shifting powers of the public and the private spheres, as well as the trajectories of oral arts of conversation and gossip as fame machines in the eighteenth century, which were then eclipsed by more impersonal, abstract, "objective" structures determining selfhood in the nineteenth.

67. See Goodman 1994.

68. See Schneider 1995, esp. 76ff, 160f; Carlsson 1969, 56; Van der Laan 1994; Kirchner 1958–62, 1:20.

69. See Gierl 1997, 369ff, 377, 399ff. Donoghue 1996 shows that, despite practices of anonymity in English review journals, a near antithesis of simulated polite conversation resulted. On the *Acta Eruditorum*, see Kirchner 1928, esp. 81; on the *Intelligenzblätter* as instruments of the market, see Kempf 1991, 92ff; on the origins of the academic newsletters, journals and reviews generally, see Kirchner 1958–62, 1: esp. 20ff, 76ff, 119ff; and Prutz 1845, esp. 418; on individual journals, see Schönfuß 1914, esp. 14f; Hofstaetter 1908; Kloß 1916; Heinz 2003; Oppermann 1844. In general, see Rowland and Fink 1995.

70. See Gans 1836, esp. 12f, 16, 26ff.

71. Lodge 1995, 43f (citation, with several paragraphs woven toegther).

72. On the Wartburgfest, see Frommann 1818, esp. 7f, 11, 20f, 74.

73. Sources on the Association of German Natural Scientists and Physicians are many. See esp. Versammlung [Gesellschaft] deutscher Naturforscher und Ärzte 1828–; Sudhoff 1922; Pfannenstiel 1958; Lampe et al. 1972; Lampe 1975; Schipperges 1976.

There is also much in Oken's *Isis* from 1822 onwards. On Oken, see the papers in Engelhardt 2002. On the BAAS, see Morell and Thackray 1981.

74. Thiersch 1866, 2:503 (citation of the king and the anecdote on turning on the lights). On the association, see Versammlung deutscher Philologen und Schulmänner 1838, esp. 3; on Thiersch versus Oken, more but briefly in the epilogue here below.

75. This interview with Foucault appeared in *La gai pied* in April 1981, translated in Foucault 1989, 203 (citation).

76. On Freud and Dora, see Marcus 1985, esp. 57, 64–66.

77. Eribon 1991, 222f; Macey 1995, 241–47.

78. Wilamowitz-Möllendorff in Gründer 1969, 30, 55 (quotation).

79. Nietzsche 1999, 1:61 (first citation).Quintilian, *Institutio oratoria*, 1.11.18, citing Cicero, *De oratore*, 3–59.220—citation of this from Gleason 1995, 117; for other points here, see ibid., esp. 82–84, 88–89, 106f, 117; cf. Foucault 1984b.

80. Brittnacher 1994, 28, 75, 81–83. On the panopticon, see Foucault 1975.

81. Baudrillard 1968, 275–83; 1972, 8–13, 39–40, 43, 59–94; 1985, 129, 144–45.

82. Foucault 1973, in the preface to the English edition of id. 1966, makes the notion of the "positive unconsciousness" concise and clear; I have failed to check if this important English preface has appeared in the original French in id. 1994. Id. 1969 pursues at length the importance of the visible and legible as "l'énoncé." The work of Baudrillard and Foucault, for example, obsesses not on the oral but rather only, I believe, on the visual—e.g., the mirrors of production and the panopticon—which is central to the tragic spirit. Frye 1957, 223, notes of Aeschylus's *Prometheus Unbound* that "for the crucified Prometheus the humiliation of exposure, the horror of being watched, is a greater misery than the pain. *Derkou theama* (behold the spectacle; get your staring over) is his bitterest cry."

### CHAPTER TWELVE

1. On Russia, see Flynn 1988; Brockliss 1997, 100f. On the University of Athens, see Ross 1863, 40f, 101–8; Seidl 1981, 232f, 238, 368; Bisoukides 1928, esp. 13ff; Demosthenopoulou 1970, 67ff; Russack 1942, 101ff; Zormbala 1991, esp. 271f; in general, Armansperg 1967. On Uppsala, see Lindroth 1976.

2. On Jesuit meritocracy, see Knowles 1966, 64.

3. On Jesuit mobility, see Brockliss 1987, 46f; Heilbron 1982, 96f, and, for example, University of Mainz 1977b, 259–350.

4. Smith 1976, 1:19f.

5. For examples of rotation through chairs, see University of Bamberg 1971; University of Molsheim in University of Strasbourg 1892; University of Mainz 1977b; University of Würzburg 1970, esp. 9; 1972; 1973; in general, Heilbron 1982, 93ff, esp. 97f.

6. Gillispie 1980, 142.

7. Crosland 1975, 139, argues, for example, that at least since the eighteenth century the universities were not at the center of French science. For the revisionist view on the scientific revolution, see, for example, Frank 1973; Feingold 1984; Gascoigne 1985; 1990; and esp. Porter 1996; on the Enlightenment, see Hammerstein 1996b. Sources for the earlier view can be found in the above works.

8. See Brockliss 1987, esp. 39ff.

9. Hahn 1971, 51f.

10. See Hahn 1971, 51f, 69–71, 80f, 108; 1975b, 501ff, esp. 504f; also Roche 1978, 1:285–90; Sturdy 1995, 376–78, 399–401, 414.

11. See Hahn 1975b, 512 (quotation), 504ff; 1975a, 130; also Sturdy 1995, 413f.

12. See Crosland 1975, 140f; Outram 1980; Russell 1983, 114ff; Fox 1984, 73f.

13. On the above on France, see Russell 1983, chap. 7; Ben-David 1984, chap. 6 (an account not without problems); Outram 1980; 1983; Fox 1984, esp. 73f; Gratten-Guinness 1988, 197ff; Schubring 1991, 284ff; Brockliss 1997, 89ff.

14. Brockliss 1997, 101.

15. Brunschwig 1947, 166ff.

16. Some of the classic and/or fairly recent works on this period in the Germanies include König 1935; Schelsky 1971; Turner 1973; 1974; 1991; McClelland 1980, chaps. 2–4; Ben-David 1984, chap. 7; Gregory 1989; Schubring 1991.

17. On the critique of academia by the *Berliner Mittwochsgesellschaft*, see Stözel 1889. Jacob 1798, for example, is for a "total reform" of universities, but doesn't seem all that radical in the end. On critique of the French model, see Meiners 1802–06, 1:323, 338; 4:271ff, 309ff, 330f. Other authors pro and contra are in Weischedel 1960. The "crisis" is formulated, for example, in König 1935, esp. 20ff, 49ff; and Schelsky 1971, esp. 21ff, 32ff, 38, 70. On these issues, cf. Turner 1991; and Schubring 1991. On Kant, Schelling, and Romantic science, see Gregory 1989, esp. 25ff.

18. Fichte 1807 is reprinted in Weischedel 1960, 30–105.

19. Fichte 1807 in Weischedel 1960, 36–37, 41–46, 84ff (§§ 7–11, 44).

20. Schleiermacher 1808 is reprinted in Weischedel 1960, 106–92.

21. Schleiermacher 1808 in Weischedel 1960, 114–15 (citation).

22. Schleiermacher 1808 in Weischedel 1960, 126 (first citation), 134–35 (second).

23. Schleiermacher 1808 in Weischedel 1960, 152–53, 170–75, 177.

24. Schleiermacher 1808 in Weischedel 1960, 176–77.

25. Humboldt 1960–81, 4:29–37, esp. 31, 113–20, esp. 114f.

26. Humboldt 1960–81, 4:168–97 (quotations merged from 170 and 191).

27. Humboldt 1960–81, 4:255–66; quotation in 4:256 (also 1993, 256).

28. On Humboldt's view of knowledge, see "Ueber die Bedingungen, unter denen Wissenschaft und Kunst in einem Volke gedeihen, mit besondrer Rücksicht auf Deutschland und die gegenwärtige Zeit" (1814) in Humboldt 1960–81, 1:553–61, esp. 555, 557; "Geschichte des Verfalls und Unterganges der griechischen Freistatten" (1807) in Humboldt 1960–81, 2:73–124, esp. 74–75, 87; see also 4:257–58, 261–63, 163–64.

29. Schelsky 1971, 70, 102ff; König 1935, 75, 157ff.

30. Cobb 1980, 29ff, speaks of the failure of the Humboldtian vision thanks to the rapid bureaucratization of academia, supposedly contra the ideal of *Bildung*. But he has also traced cotemporal reforms undertaken outside the influence and control of Humboldt and Prussia, revealing some of the substance behind the new ideology: the academic system that had come to fruition pre-1789 at work, as traced in this book— on Marburg, Heidelberg, and Tübingen, see Cobb 1980, esp. 57ff, 70ff, 76, 109ff, 113, 115ff.

31. The best single overview of German natural science in the nineteenth century, albeit from the perspective of physics, is Jungnickel and McCormmach 1986, which surveys the institutional history from 1800 onward.

32. In general, see Schöler 1970; Paulsen 1896–97, 2:426ff.

33. See Schöler 1970, 15ff, 83ff, 101ff; Paulsen 1896–97, 2:346ff, 359ff; Varrentrapp 1889, 390ff, 432ff, 461ff; F. Thiersch 1826, 3:611; III/1, Beilage; 1838, 1:6ff, 116, 225ff, 258ff, 282ff, 379f; H. Thiersch 1866, 2:466ff; Bavaria 1838, IX/2, 567ff, 581ffff, 633ff; Brandenburg-Prussia 1864–73, 1:23; Oken in *Isis* (1829) 1225–31

34. Bühler 1981, esp. 69, 111–13. On medicine, see Hagner 2003.

35. Turner 1982; Holmes 1989.

36. Olesko 1991, 4 (citation). The statutes of the seminar are in Brandenburg-Prussia 1839-40, II/2: 858-61; on Neumann and the seminar, see, beyond Olesko, Wangerin 1907, 148ff; Jungnickel and McCormmach 1986, I, chap. 4.

37. On the seminars, see Jungnickel and McCormmach 1986, esp. I, chap. 4.

38. See Brandenburg-Prussia 1839, II/2, 624-31 (Bonn), 838-41 (Halle); University of Köngisberg 1836-39; Olesko 1991, chap. 1.

39. Schubring 1989.

40. Ben-David 1984 [1971]; Zloczower 1981 [1966]; McClelland 1980; Turner 1971; 1973; 1974; 1980; 1982; Olesko 1988; 1991; Schubring 1989; 1991; Cahan 1985; 1989; 2003; Holmes 1988; 1989; Kremer 1991; 1992; Lenoir 1988; 1992a,b; 1997; Tuchman 1988; 1991. For the early modern era, see Kluge 1958.

41. Ben-David 1984, 123 (quotation); see, in general, chaps. 7-8.

42. In the nineteenth century, German faculties generally recovered some or much say in the nomination of candidates for professorial appointments. I will not pursue that matter here since.

43. Ben-David 1984, 125-33.

44. Cahan 1985; Kremer 1991; 1992; Lenoir 1988; 1992; Tuchman 1988; 1991; Zloczower 1981. Jungnickel and McCormmach 1986 details the expansion of theoretical physics. Johnson 1989 incidentally traces the rise of institutes for chemistry. On medicine in general, see Hagner 2003.

45. Brocke 1990, esp. 17-26; 1996, esp. 6; Laitko 1991, 77; Spinner 1991; McClelland 1980, chap. 7; on Althoff generally, see the collected papers in Brocke (ed.) 1991. Lexis 1893 and 1904 have the statistics on German universities and related institutions in meticulous detail. For detailed statistics, also see Pfetsch 1974, esp. 52. See Verne 1986 [1879], for a related but different view of German (and American) science at the time.

46. Lenoir 1992, 15f (quotation at 16).

47. Brocke 1996, 20, relates an interesting anecdote concerning Hermann Holmholtz's demands for complete control of the institute to be built for him on his call to Berlin in 1871. Zloczower 1981 has a number of interesting accounts of director-assistant relations at institutes. See also Weber 1988a, 582-613, to which we return below.

48. On this section, see Engelbrecht 1982-88, 4:221-31; also Höflechner 1991.

49. For want of space, I'll have to pass over the case of Scotland here. Suffice it to say that, though much like the German system throughout the early modern era, nineteenth-century developments took their own course, at least for the first half or more of the century. As the Scottish Universities Commission of 1826 was set up, the Edinburgh Town Council were still patrons of about two-thirds of chairs there. Morrell holds that the academic structure of Edinburgh was "pre-bureaucratic," as connections and whims still governed appointments. Entrepreneurial activities played a role, but of an early modern nature: professors, paid as they were still by direct fees for lectures, had to compete for the student body within the university. See Morrell 1997, esp. [II] 11ff, [III] 160ff, [VII], 40ff, [X] 360ff; also Chitnis 1976; and Jones 1983.

50. On this paragraph and the next, see Wordsworth 1877, 34ff; Rothblatt 1974, 280ff; Gascoigne 1984, 560ff, 574f; Searby 1997, 95-98, 103f.

51. Winstanley 1955, 149 (quotation).

52. Winstanley 1955, 176ff, 182, 183 (quotation); also Leader 1988, 242-54.

53. On Oxford, see Engel 1974, 305ff; also Duncan 1986. On the coaches at Cambridge, see Warwick 2003, chap. 5; on the dons, see Rothblatt 1981; Annan 1999. In general, see Vandermeersch 1996, 211-14.

54. Meiners 1802-06, 1:280.

55. Winstanley 1955, 148; Engel 1974, 311ff; Briggs 1997, 134ff; Slee 1988, 63ff.

56. Briggs 1997, 138ff; Searby 1997, 430ff; Engel 1974, 313ff, quotation at 315.

57. On Newman specifically, see Annan 1999, chap. 3 (citation at 41).

58. Briggs 1997, 138ff; Nockles 1991, 137ff, 146, 150ff, 154 (first Newman quotation) 159ff; Engel 1974, 317ff, 324f; Searby 1997, 434, 440, 441 (second).

59. Sviedrys 1976, esp. 407f.

60. Briggs 1997, 138ff; Slee 1988, 68 (first quotation); Searby 1997, 430ff; Becher 1980; 1986, esp. 80ff (second quotation at 81).

61. In general, see Searby 1997, 507ff, 520ff, quotation at 523; Ward 1997, 306ff; on Cambridge, Winstanley 1955, chap. 11 (234ff); Searby 1997, 524ff.

62. Ward 1997, 317ff; Engel 1974, 328ff.

63. Ward 1997, 326ff; Engel 1974, 335ff (tutors quoted at 337f).

64. Engel 1974, 341ff; quotation at 343.

65. Winstanley 1947, 263ff; Master of Sidney Sussex quoted at 269.

66. Morrell 1997, [X] 354ff (quotations at 378 and 386); see also [XI] 183ff.

67. Smith and Wise 1989, chaps. 5 and 19; Sviedrys 1970, 129, 133, 138ff; 1976, 409ff, 427ff; Gooday 1990, 27ff.

68. Simpson 1983, 34–36, 48–50, 61–63, 135–37; Morrell 1997, [X] 369.

69. See Fox 1984, 71ff; first quotation at 78, second at 83. See also Werner 1991.

70. Weisz 1983, 20 (quotation).

71. Fox 1984, 94ff, quotation at 102; Weisz 1983, 55f, 60ff, 201 (quotation), 212ff.

72. Fox 1984, 105ff, quotation at 120; Weisz 1983, 6f, 10, 76ff, 134ff, 154ff, Karady 1986, 325f.

73. Duhem 1991, 37; I've combined two paragraphs.

74. Duhem 1991, 122.

75. Josiah Royce, "The Present Ideals of American Life," *Scribner's Magazine,* 10 (1891) at pp. 382f, cited in Veysey 1965, 130.

76. Veysey 1965, 129 (quotation).

77. Veysey 1965, 128ff, 158ff, 171ff (quotation at 126). On the "age of the college," before that of the university after 1876, see Herbst 1988, 38ff.

78. Veysey 1965, chap. 3, 121–79, esp. 122–28; quotation at 128.

79. Veysey 1965, 142 (quotation). See Ben-David 1984, chap. 8, on the difference between the U.S. and the German universities.

80. "Wissenschaft als Beruf" in Weber 1988a, 582–613 (quotation at 583).

81. Weber 1988a, 584.

82. Weber 1988a, 585f.

83. Weber 1988a, 587.

84. Weber 1988a, 589–91.

85. See Brocke and Laitko 1996 on the Harnack principle.

86. See the articles in Vierhaus and Brocke 1990; and Brocke and Laitko 1996. Weber 1956, 690–95, sets an essential opposition between charisma and discipline, the latter taken in the primary sense, but with implications for the secondary sense of an academic field.

87. Vierhaus 1996 [1989]; cf. Grau 1996 and Laitko 1996, in the same volume.

88. See Vierhaus 1990; 1996 [1989]; 2001; Moeller 2001.

89. See Ringer 1969, esp. chap. 5.

90. The essay is in Harnack 1911, 1:10–20 (citations at 10 and 13); and 2001, 3–9 (citations at 3 and 5). In academia, *Mitarbeiter* means "colleague," while it means "em-

ployee" in the business world, the rhetoric of which informs this passage. On the essay, see Vierhaus 2001.

91. On the first exchange, see Brocke 1990, 98, which involved not Berlin but Leipzig.

92. "Denkschrift, Sr. Majestät dem deutschen Kaiser unterbreitet" (1909) in Harnack 2001, 10–25; also 1911, 1:41–64. On Harnack and the KWG-MPG, see the papers in Brocke and Laitko 1996; and in Vierhaus and Brocke 1990; esp. Brocke 1990.

93. Harnack 1911, 1:55; also 2001, 19

94. Harnack 1911, 1:7.

95. Harnack 2001, 75, 80. On the history of the KWG, see the articles in Vierhaus and Brocke 1990.

96. As noted above, see Ben-David 1984, chap. 8; and Veysey 1965, 142.

97. Harnack and Glum cited in Vierhaus 1996, 129 (Harnack), 130 (Glum). On the KWG in the Third Reich, see Albrecht and Hermann 1990. Before Einstein left Germany, the institute founded for him in Berlin embodied one of the purest in conception *à la* the Harnack principle, but probably the humblest in actual practice: see Kant 1996; and Stern 1990. In "Wissenschaft als Beruf," Weber (1988a, 605ff) interestingly denounces the contemporaneous sentiment that a professor should be not only a teacher but also a "Führer"—the sense might be slightly different here than with Harnack; but, for Weber, a charismatic figure is a Führer.

98. See Brocke 1996, esp. 17, for the statistics.

99. On the MPG and the Harnack Principle, see Vierhaus 1996; and Laitko 1996. The history of the closing of the MPI in Starnberg remains to be written.

100. Fjermedal 1984, esp. chaps. 11–12 (citation at 218); for another such scandal, see Brody 1995, esp. 69, 125–31. Vaughan 2000, 107, quotes a clinician to the effect that the change came in the biomedical field in the late 1960s, and at 178 cites Robert Gallo, then at the National Institutes of Health and notorious in the AIDS story (and dramatized in the film *And the Band Played On*), "Science is a grab-and-take business. There are few original thoughts. If someone comes along and sees something and thinks he knows how to use it, how to move it along faster and better, why bitch? Mankind is waiting, after all. And if you can patent it, and it's allowed, then why not?" On the university-biotechnology complex generally, see Kenney 1986. Biotech may have initiated this academic "feudalism," but is surely no longer alone. On Big Science, see the papers in Galison and Hevly 1992.

101. David Willman, "Stealth Merger: Drug Companies and Government Medical Research," *Los Angeles Times* (OC), 7 December 2003, A1, 32–35 (quotation at A32), with ancillary pieces as case studies. I have omitted paragraph breaks in the quotation.

102. Willman, *Los Angeles Times* (OC), 7 December 2003, A32 (quotation of Kirschstein).

103. Further articles by Willman in *Los Angeles Times* (OC), 9 December 2003, A11; 17 January 2004, A11; 2 March 2004, A16. On 1 February 2005, A1, the paper announced a happy ending to the story.

104. See Clark 1995.

105. Frye 1957, 186 (first quotation); 1976, 55, 177 (second); I have capitalized "Romance" in the quotations to be consonant with the capitalization in my text.

106. Frye 1957, 62, 151; 1976, 67, 139–40, 172 (quotation).

107. *Taliesin's Successor: Interviews with Authors of Modern Arthurian Literature* by

Raymond Thompson: interview with David Lodge, 1989, online at www.lib.rochester
.edu/camelot/intrvws/lodge.htm.

108. Hegel 1970, 7:339. Herzfeld 1992 shows, among other things, that in the modern era a discourse about bureaucracy replaced a traditional discourse about fate among the people—in modern Greece in the case of his study. But that, too, is what Kafka's trial and castle are all about for the German lands in general in the modern era.

109. "The Masked Philosopher" is in Foucault 1989, 193–202, citation at 199; in the original, 1994, 4:104–10, citation at 109.

# Abbreviations

| | |
|---|---|
| BaseSA | Basel, *Staatsarchiv (Kantonarchiv)* |
| BerlSA | Berlin, *Geheimes Staatsarchiv, Preußischer Kulturbesitz,* GStA |
| DarmSA | Darmstadt, *Hessisches Staatsarchiv* |
| DresSA | Dresden, *Sächsisches Hauptstaatsarchiv* |
| GöttUA | Göttingen, *Universitätsarchiv* |
| GöttUB | Göttingen, *Universitätsbibliothek* |
| HallUA | Halle, *Universitätsarchiv* |
| HanoSA | Hanover, *Niedersächsisches Hauptstaatsarchiv* |
| MuniSA | Munich, *Bayerisches Hauptstaatsarchiv* |
| MuniUA | Munich, *Universitätsarchiv* |
| SchlSA | Schleswig, *Schleswig-Holsteinisches Landesarchiv* |
| StutSA | Stuttgart, *Baden-Württembergisches Hauptstaatsarchiv* |
| TübiUA | Tübingen, *Universitätsarchiv* |
| TübiUB | Tübingen, *Universitätsbibliothek* |
| VienSA | Vienna, *Oesterreiches Staatsarchiv, Allgemeines Verwaltungsarchiv* |
| VienUA | Vienna, *Universitätsarchiv* |
| WürzIH | Würzburg, *Institut für Hochschulkunde, Universität Würzburg* |
| WürzUB | Würzburg, *Universitätsbibliothek* |

Abbreviations to *Geheimes Staatsarchiv, Preußischer Kulturbesitz,* Berlin, GStA

| | |
|---|---|
| A1 | I. HA Rep. 76, alt II, Nr. 12, Generalia, 1788-1803 |
| A2 | I. HA Rep. 76, alt II, Nr. 13, Generalia, 1803-06 |
| B1 | I. HA Rep. 76, Va, Sekt. 2, Berlin, Tit. IV, Nr. 5, Bd. I, 1810-12 |
| B2 | I. HA Rep. 76, Va, Sekt. 2, Berlin, Tit. IV, Nr. 5, Bd. II, 1812-14 |
| B3 | I. HA Rep. 76, Va, Sekt. 2, Berlin, Tit. IV, Nr. 5, Bd. III, 1815-16 |
| B4 | I. HA Rep. 76, Va, Sekt. 2, Berlin, Tit. IV, Nr. 5, Bd. IV, 1816-17 |
| B5 | I. HA Rep. 76, Va, Sekt. 2, Berlin, Tit. IV, Nr. 5, Bd. V, 1818-19 |
| C1 | I. HA Rep. 76, Va, Sekt. 3, Bonn, Tit. IV, Nr. 1, Bd. VII, 1819-20. |
| D1 | I. HA Rep. 34, 58a, 1, Duisburg, 1762-84 |
| D2 | I. HA Rep. 34, 58a, 12, Duisburg [missing since 1923] |
| F1 | I. HA Rep. 51, 9a, Frankfurt a.d.O., 1539- [Vol. I: in folders by chair] |
| F2 | I. HA HA Rep. 51, 9a, Frankfurt a.d.O., 1539- [Vol. II: in folders by chair] |
| F3 | I. HA Rep. 51, 92, Frankfurt a.d.O., 1560-1732 |
| F4 | I. HA Rep. 51, 93, Frankfurt a.d.O., a.o. Prof. |
| F5 | I. HA Rep. 76, alt II, Nr. 174, Frankfurt a.d.O., Bd. I, 1787-90 |
| F6 | I. HA Rep. 76, alt II, Nr. 175, Frankfurt a.d.O., Bd. II, 1790-92 |

F7    I. HA Rep. 76, alt II, Nr. 176, Frankfurt a.d.O., Bd. III, 1792–97
F8    I. HA Rep. 76, alt II, Nr. 177, Frankfurt a.d.O., Bd. IV, 1797–1802
F9    I. HA Rep. 76, alt II, Nr. 178, Frankfurt a.d.O., Bd. V, 1802–05
F10   I. HA Rep. 76, alt II, Nr. 179, Frankfurt a.d.O., Bd. VI, 1805–08
F11   I. HA Rep. 76, alt II, Nr. 180, Frankfurt a.d.O., Bd. VII, 1808
G1    I. HA Rep. 76, Va, Greifswald, Tit. 4, Nr. 1, Bd. VI, 1824–26
H1    I. HA Rep. 52, Nr. 159n, Halle, 3d, 1691–1724
H2    I. HA Rep. 52, Nr. 159n, Halle, 3d, 1725–33
H3    I. HA Rep. 52, Nr. 159n, Halle, 3d, 1734–52
H4    I. HA Rep. 52, Nr. 159n, Halle, 3d, 1753–1803
H5    I. HA Rep. 76, alt II, Nr. 53, Halle, Bd. I, 1787–89
H6    I. HA Rep. 76, alt II, Nr. 54, Halle, Bd. II, 1789–91
H7    I. HA Rep. 76, alt II, Nr. 55, Halle, Bd. III, 1791–92
H8    I. HA Rep. 76, alt II, Nr. 56, Halle, Bd. IV, 1792–95
H9    I. HA Rep. 76, alt II, Nr. 57, Halle, Bd. V, 1795–97
H10   I. HA Rep. 76, alt II, Nr. 58, Halle, Bd. VI, 1797–98
H11   I. HA Rep. 76, alt II, Nr. 59, Halle, Bd. VII, 1798–99
H12   I. HA Rep. 76, alt II, Nr. 60, Halle, Bd. VIII, 1799–1800
H13   I. HA Rep. 76, alt II, Nr. 67, Halle. Bd. XV, 1805–07
H14   I. HA Rep. 76, Va, Sekt. 8, Halle, Tit. 4, Nr.1, Bd. VII, 1822–23
K1    I. HA Rep. 7, Nr. 190, Königsberg, 1566–1689
K2    I. HA Rep. 7, Nr. 190, Königsberg, 1690–1705
K3    I. HA Rep. 7, Nr. 190, Königsberg, 1706–13
K4    I. HA Rep. 7, Nr. 190, Königsberg, 1714–23
K5    I. HA Rep. 7, Nr. 190, Königsberg, 1726–34
K6    I. HA Rep. 7, Nr. 190, Königsberg, 1735–46
K7    I. HA Rep. 7, Nr. 190, Königsberg, 1747–76
K8    I. HA Rep. 7, Nr. 190, Königsberg, 1776–1808
K9    I. HA Rep. 76, alt II, Nr. 246, Königsberg, Bd. I, 1787–92 [Nicht im Bestand]
K10   I. HA Rep. 76, alt II, Nr. 247, Königsberg, Bd. II, 1792–1800
K11   I. HA Rep. 76, alt II, Nr. 248, Königsberg, Bd. III, 1800–02
K12   I. HA Rep. 76, alt II, Nr. 249, Königsberg, Bd. IV, 1803–05
K13   I. HA Rep. 76, alt II, Nr. 250, Königsberg, Bd. V, 1805–06
K14   I. HA Rep. 76, alt II, Nr. 251, Königsberg, Bd. VI, 1806–08
K15   I. HA Rep. 76, alt II, Nr. 252, Königsberg, Bd. VII, 1808–09


Bayerisches Hauptstaatsarchiv, Munich:
M. Inn.,
23044, 23055, 23064, 23071, 23073, 23096, 23097, 23104, 23110, 23126, 23148, 23163, 23171, 23195,
23196, 23201, 23209, 23217, 23290, 23332, 23372, 23406, 23528, 23556, 23563, 23604, 23655.

# Bibliography

Abelard, Peter and Héloïse. 1962. *Historia calamitatum.* Edited by J. Monfrin. 2nd ed. Paris: Vrin.

*ADB.* 1875–1912. *Allgemeine Deutsche Biographie.* 56 vols. Repr. Berlin: Duncker & Humblot, 1967–71.

Aepinus, Franz (*praeses*). 1702. *Moralitas Graduum Academicarum . . . contra Fanaticos praesertim, asserta . . . .* Johann Carlquist (*resp.*). Rostock.

Albers, Bruno, ed. 1900–12. *Consuetudines Monasticae.* 5 vols. Monte Cassino: Soc. Ed. Castri Casini.

Albrecht, Helmuth and Armin Hermann. 1990. "Die Kaiser Wilhelm-Gesellschaft im Dritten Reich (1933–1945)." In Vierhaus and Brocke 1990, 356–406.

Alexander, Jeffrey. 1985 [1982–83]. *Theoretical Logic in Sociology.* 4 vols. Berkeley: University of California Press.

Allport, Gordon and Leo Postman. 1947. *The Psychology of Rumor.* New York: Holt.

Amelunxen, Clemens. 1991. *Zur Rechtsgeschichte der Hofnarren.* Schriftenreihe der juristischen Gesellschaft zu Berlin, 124. Berlin: de Gruyter.

Amerbach, Vitus. 1550. *Variorum carminum.* Basel.

———. 1571. "Oratio de doctoratu philosophico (ante-1557)," fol. 351v–70r in *Tomus primus orationum Ingolstadiensium.* Edited by Valentin Rotmar. Ingolstadt.

Annan, Noel. 1999. *The Dons: Mentors, Eccentrics and Geniuses.* Chicago: University of Chicago Press.

Anon. n.d.1 *Themata medica de beanorum. . . .* n.l., n.d. [Munich UB: 8° H.lit. 1913: 50].

Anon. n.d.2 *Theses inaugurales. . . .* n.l., n.d. [Göttingen UB: 8° Sat. I, 7265].

Anon. n.d.3 *Curiöse Inaugural-Disputation von . . . Professoren-Burschen. . . .* n.l., n.d. [Göttingen UB: 8° H.i.p. II, 1:2/15; 8° H.i.p. II, 10810].

Anon. 1476 [ca. 1476–81]. *Manuale scholarium.* Heidelberg (?). Repr. in Zarncke 1857, 2–48.

Anon. 1726. *Vernünftiges Studenten-Leben.* Jena.

Anon. 1778–79. *Briefwechsel dreyer akademischer Freunde.* 2 vols. 2nd ed. Ulm.

Anon. 1782. *Abhandlung was die Universitäten in den kaiserlichen, königlichen Erblanden sind, und was sie seyn könnten.* Prague / Vienna.

Anon. 1790. "Gedanken eines akademischen Bürgers über Öffentliche akademische Disputation . . . ," by J. B. In *Journal von und für Deutschland* 7/11:480–89

Anon. 1797. "Das gelehrte Schauspiel, oder forma dat esse rei." In *Allgemeiner Literarischer Anzeiger,* 1279–80.

Anon. 1798. *Über öffentliche Lehrveranstaltungen, insbesondere über Lektionskataloge auf Universitäten.* "Germanien."

Anon. 1817. "Ist es rathsam, junge Philologen zur Fragmentensammlungen anzuhalten?" By "C.V.O." *Athenäum* 1/2: 240–42.

Anon. 1833. *Ueber einige Gebrechenden der deutschen Universitäten.* By "D.E.A." Leipzig.

Anon. 1853 [?]. *Illustrationen zum Burschenleben.* Eßlingen a. N.

Anon. 1909 [1515–17]. *Epistolae obscurorum virorum, the Latin Text (1516/17) with an English Rendering.* Edited and translated by Francis Stokes. New Haven/London: Chatto & Windus.

Anon. 1988 [1587]. *Historia von D. Johann Fausten.* Critical edition by S. Füssel and H. J. Kreutzer. Stuttgart: Reclam.

Anrich, Ernst, ed. 1956. *Die Idee der deutschen Universität.* Darmstadt: Wissenschaftliche Buchgesellschaft.

Ariès, Philippe. 1962. *L'Enfant et la vie familiale sous l'ancien régime.* Paris: Plon.

Armansperg, Gräfin Roswitha. 1967. *Joseph Ludwig Graf Armansperg. Ein Beitrag zur Regierungsgeschichte Ludwigs I. von Bayern.* Miscellanea Bavarica Monacensia, 67. Munich: Kommissionsbuchhandlung R. Wölfle.

Arnaud, Vanessa. 2001. *Gossip as a Social Force in Seventeenth-Century France.* Dissertation, University of California at Los Angeles.

Arnim, Ludwig Achim von. 1857. *Sämmtliche Werke.* 22 vols. Berlin.

Arnold, Werner. 1988. "Der Fürstliche Büchersammler. Die Hofbibliotheken in der Zeit der Aufklärung." In Arnold and Vodosek 1988, 41–59.

Arnold, Werner and Peter Vodosek, eds. 1988 *Bibliothek und Aufklärung.* Wolfenbütteler Schriften zur Geschichte des Buchwesens, 14. Wiesbaden: Harrassowitz.

Arnoldt, David H. 1746–69. *Ausführliche und mit Urkunden versehene Historie der Königsbergischen Universität.* 5 pts. in 3 vols. Königsberg.

Arnoldt, Emil. 1906–11. *Gesammelte Schriften.* 16 vols. Edited by Otto Schöndorffer. Berlin: Cassirer.

Arnoldt, J. F. D. 1861. *Friedrich August Wolf in seinem Verhältnisse zum Schulmann.* 2 vols. Brunswick.

Aschbach, Joseph. 1865–88. *Geschichte der Wiener Universität.* 3 vols. Vienna.

Ast, Friedrich. 1808a. *Grundlinien der Grammatik, Hermeneutik und Kritik.* Landshut.

———. 1808b. *Grundriß der Philologie.* Landshut.

Aston, T. H., ed. 1984–. *The History of the University of Oxford* (see Brock 2000; Brock and Curthoys 1997; Catto 1984, Catto and Evans 1992; Harrison 1994; McConica 1986; Sutherland and Mitchell 1986; Tyacke 1997). 8 vols. Oxford: Clarendon Press.

Auerbach, Erich. 1988 [1946]. *Mimesis. Dargestellte Wirklichkeit in der Abendländischen Literatur.* Bern: Francke.

Augustin, Christian F. 1795. *Bemerkungen eines Akademikers über Halle und dessen Bewohner, in Briefen.* "Germanien."

Austria. 1840. *Systematische Darstellung der Gesetze über höhere Studien in den gesammten deutsch-italienischen Provinzen der österreichischen Monarchie.* Edited by Wilhelm Unger. 2 vols. in 1. Vienna.

Ayim, Maryann. 1994. "Knowledge Through the Grapvine: Gossip as Enquiry." In Goodman and Ben-Ze'ev 1994, 85–99.

Bachmann, Wolf. 1966. *Die Attribute der Bayerischen Akademie der Wissenschaften, 1807–1827.* Münchener historische Studien: Geschichte, 8, Kallmünz: Lassleben.

Bahrdt, Karl F. 1922 [1790–91]. *Geschichte seines Lebens, seines Meinungen und Schicksale,* 4 vols. as 1. Berlin: Dom.

Baier, Johann J. 1714. *Wahrhaffte und gründliche Beschreibung der Nürnbergischen Universität-Stadt Altdorf.* Altdorf.

Baldus de Ubaldis. 1615–16. *Commentaria.* 9 vols. Venice.

Baldwin, John W. 1970. *Masters, Princes and Merchants: The Social Views of Peter the Chanter and his Circle.* 2 vols. Princeton: Princeton University Press.

Ball, W. W. Rouse. 1889. *A History of the Study of Mathematics at Cambridge.* Cambridge.

Ballif, Michelle. 2001. *Seduction, Sophistry, and the Woman with the Rhetorical Figure.* Carbondale: Southern Illinois University Press.

Balthasar, Jacob H. 1775. *Andere Sammlung einiger zur Pommerischen Kirchen-Historie gehörigen Schriften. . . .* Greifswald.

Barner, Wilfried. 1970. *Barockrhetorik: Untersuchungen zu ihren geschichtlichen Grundlagen.* Tübingen: Niemeyer.

Barthes, Roland. 1984. *Le bruissement de la langue.* Paris: Seuil.

Bartolus de Saxoferrato. 1615. *Omnia quae extant opera.* 11 vols. Venice.

Baudrillard, Jean. 1968. *Le système des objets.* Paris: Gallimard.

———. 1970. *La société de consommation, ses mythes, ses structures.* Paris: Denoël.

———. 1972. *Pour une critique de l'économie politique du signe.* Paris: Gallimard.

———. 1985. *Le miroir de la production ou l'illusion critique du matérialisme historique.* Paris: Galilée.

Bauer, Clemens and Ernst Zeeden and Hans Zmarzlik, eds. 1957. *Beiträge zur Geschichte der Freiburger philosophischen Fakultät.* Beiträge zur Freiburger Wissenschafts- und Universitätsgeschichte, 17. Freiburg im Br.: Albert.

Bavaria. 1756–68. *Codex Maximilianeus Bavaricus civilis.* Comm. by Wigulaeus X. A. Freiherr von Kreittmayr. 4 vols. Munich.

———. 1838. *Sammlung der im Gebiete der innern Staats-Verwaltung des Königreiches Bayerns bestehenden Verordnungen: Bd. IX.* Edited by Georg Döllinger. 3 pts. Munich.

Becher, Harvey W. 1980. "William Whewell and Cambridge Mathematics." *Historical Studies in the Physical Sciences* 11/1:1–48.

———. 1986. "Voluntary Science in Nineteenth Century Cambridge University to the 1850's." *British Journal for the History of Science* 19:57–87.

Beck, Christian. 1809. *De consiliis et rationibus seminarii philologici. . . .* Leipzig.

Becker, Kurt. 1988. *"Der römische Cäsar mit Christi Seele." Max Webers Charisma-Konzept. Eine systematisch kritische Analyse unter Beziehung biographischer Fakten.* Europäische Hochschulschriften, Reihe XXII, Soziologie, 144. Frankfurt: Lang.

Becker, Peter. 2001. "Objective Distance and Intimate Knowledge: Concerning the Structure of Criminalistic Observation and Description." In Becker and Clark 2001, 197–236.

Becker, Peter and William Clark, eds. 2001 *Little Tools of Knowledge: Historical Essays in Academic and Bureaucratic Practices.* Ann Arbor: University of Michigan Press.

Becker, W. M. 1907. "Das erste Jahrhundert." In University of Gießen 1907. 1:1–364.

Beckmann, J. C. 1707. *Notitia Universitatis Francofurtae.* 5 pts. Frankfurt a.d.O.

Beddard, R. A. 1997a. "Restoration Oxford. . . ." In Tyacke 1997, 803–62.

———. 1977b. "Tory Oxford." In Tyacke 1997, 862–905.

Beier, A. L. and D. Cannadine and J. M. Rosenheim, eds. 1989. *The First Modern Society.* Cambridge: Cambridge University Press.

Ben-David, Joseph. 1984 [1971]. *The Scientist's Role in Society.* Chicago: University of Chicago Press.

Bender, Thomas, ed. 1988. *The University and the City: From Medieval Origins to the Present.* Oxford: Oxford University Press.

Bengeser, Gerhard. 1965. *Promotion in Deutschland.* Bonn: Raabe.

Benson, Robert. 1968. *The Bishop Elect: A Study in Medieval Ecclesiastical Office.* Princeton: Princeton University Press.

Bentzel, Franz Freiherr Anselm von. 1784. *Neue Verfassung der verbesserten hohen Schulen zu Mainz.* Mainz.

Ben-Ze'ev, Aaron. 1994. "The Vindication of Gossip." In Goodman and Ben-Ze'ev 1994, 11–24.

Berlière, Ursmer. 1912. *L'Ordre monastique, des origines aux XII$^e$ siècle.* Abbaye de Maredsous: Abbaye de Maredsous.

———. 1927. *L'Ascèse bénédictine des origines à la fin du XII$^e$ siècle.* Bruges: Desclée de Brouwer.

Berlin, Natural Sciences Society. 1791. *Plan und Gestalt der Gesellschaft naturforschender Freunde. . . .* Berlin.

———. 1810. *Gesetze der Gesellschaft naturforschender Freunde zu Berlin.* Berlin.

———. 1823. *Zur fünfzigjähriger Stiftungsfeier der Gesellschaft naturforschender Freunde zu Berlin.* Berlin.

Bernard of Clairvaux. 1879. *Opera omnia.* 4 vols. Patrologiae cursus completus: Series latina, 182–85. Paris.

Bernhard, Ludwig. 1930. *Akademische Selbstverwaltung in Frankreich und Deutschland.* Berlin: Springer.

Bernheimer, Charles and Clare Kahane, eds. 1985 [1974]. *In Dora's Case: Freud-Hysteria-Feminism.* New York: Columbia University Press.

Besold, C. L. 1697. *Thesaurus practicus.* 2 vols. Nuremberg.

Bezold, F. von. 1920. *Geschichte der Rheinischen Friedrich-Wilhelms-Universität von der Gründung bis zum Jahr 1870.* Bonn: Marcus & Webers.

Biagioli, Mario. 1993. *Galileo Courtier: The Practice of Science in the Culture of Absolutism.* Chicago: University of Chicago Press.

Bianco, Franz J. 1850–55. *Die ehemalige Universität und Gymnasiums zu Köln.* 2 vols. Cologne.

Bircher, Martin and Ferdinand von Ingen, eds. 1978. *Sprachgesellschaften, Sozietäten, Dichtergruppen. Arbeitsgespräch in der Herzog August Bibliothek Wolfenbüttel, 28. bis 30. Juni 1977. Vorträge und Berichte.* Wolfenbütteler Arbeiten und Barockforschung, 7. Hamburg: Hauswedell & Co.

Bisoukides, Perikles C. 1928. *Griechische Stätten höherer Bildung und Forschung. Universitäten, Hochschulen, Institute, gelehrte Gesellschaften.* Berlin: Prager.

Blättner, Fritz. 1960. *Das Gymnasium.* Heidelberg: Quelle & Meyer.

Bleek, Wilhelm. 1972. *Von der Kameralausbildung zum Juristenprivileg. Studium, Prüfung und Ausbildung der höheren Beamten des allgemeinen Verwaltungsdienstes in Deutschland im 18. und 19. Jahrhundert.* Historische und Pädagogische Studien, 3. Berlin: Colloquium.

Blumberg, Hans. 1983. *Die Lesbarkeit der Welt.* 2nd ed. Frankfurt a.M.: Surhkamp.

Bocerius, Henricus. 1616. *De bello et duello tractatus.* 3rd ed. Tübingen.

Böckh, August. 1858–74. *Gesammelte kleine Schriften.* 7 vols. Edited by F. Anderson. Leipzig.

Böckh, August et al., eds. 1828–77. *Corpus inscriptionum Graecarum.* 4 vols. Leipzig.

Bödeker, Hans E. 1990a. "System und Entwicklung der Staatswissenschaften im 18. Jahrhundert." In Mocek 1990, 88–103.

————. 1990b. "Von der 'Magd der Theologie' zur 'Leitwissenschaft.' Vorüberlegungen zu einer Geschichte der Philosophie des 18. Jahrhunderts." In *Deutsche Gesellschaft für die Erforschung des achtzehnten Jahrhunderts* 14/1:19–57.

Bödeker, H. E. and P. Reill and J. Schlumbohm, eds. 1999. *Wissenschaft als kuturelle Praxis.* Göttingen: Vandenhoeck & Ruprecht.

Bodemann, Eduard, ed. 1888. "Leibnizens Briefwechsel mit dem Herzog Anton Ulrich von Braunschweig-Wolfenbüttel." *Zeitschrift des historischen Vereins für Niedersachsen,* 73–244.

Boehm, Laetitia and Joahnnes Spörl, eds. 1972–80. *Die Ludwig-Maximilians-Universität in ihren Fakultäten.* 2 vols. Berlin: Duncker & Humblot.

Boell [Böll], Friedrich P. Carl. 1775. *Sendschreiben über die Anfrage in was für einen Zustand sich die Rechtsgelehrsamkeit auf der blühenden Georg Augusta befinde. . . .* Colmar.

————(appeared anonymously). 1782. *Das Universitätswesen in Briefen,* n.l. [Göttingen UB: 8° HLP II, 160].

Böhm, Walter, ed. 1952. *Universitas Vindobonensis. Die Universität Wien.* Vienna: Regina.

Bolzoni, Lina. 1994. "Das Sammeln und die ars memoriae." In Grote 1994, 129–68.

Bömer, Aloys et al., eds. 1952–61. *Geschichte der Bibliotheken.* 2 vols. Handbuch der Bibliothekswissenschaft, III/1–2. Edited by F. Milkau and G. Leyh. 2nd ed. Wiesbaden: Harrassowitz.

Bonaventura. 1882–1902. *Opera omnia.* 11 vols. Quaracchi: Collegii S. Bonaventurae.

Bonjour, Edgar. 1960. *Die Universität Basel . . . 1460–1960.* Basel: Helbing und Lichtenhahn.

Bonner, Stanley. 1977. *Education in Ancient Rome: From the Elder Cato to the Younger Pliny.* London: Methuen.

Bonocompagno (Buonocompagno). 1892 [ca. 1220]. *Rhetorica novissima.* Edited by A. Gaudentio. In *Bibliotheca juridica medii aevi* 2:249–97.

Borges, Jorge Luis. 1962. *Ficciones.* Edited and translated by Anthony Kerrigan. New York: Grove.

Bornhak, Conrad. 1884–86. *Geschichte des preussischen Verwaltungsrechtes.* 3 vols. Berlin.

————. 1900. *Geschichte der preussischen Universitätsverwaltung bis 1800.* Berlin: Reimer.

————. 1912. "Das monarchische Titelverleihungsrecht und die akademischen Grade." *Verwaltungsarchiv* 21:63–81.

Bottigheimer, Ruth B. 1987. *Grimm's Bad Girls and Bold Boys: The Moral and Social Vision of the Tales.* New Haven: Yale University Press.

Bourdieu, Pierre. 1972. *Esquisse d'une théorie de la practique.* Geneva: Droz.

————. 1984. *Homo academicus.* Paris: Éditions de Minuit.

Bourdieu, Pierre and Jean-Claude Passeron. 1970. *La reproduction: éléments pour une théorie du système d'enseignement.* Paris: Éditions de Minuit.

Boureau, Alain. 1990. *Histoires d'un historien. Kantorowicz.* Paris: Gallimard.

Brahl, Samuel (*auct. et resp.*). 1691. *Dissertatio politica de jure majestatis circa rem literaria,* Christian Rohrenseen (*praeses*). Wittenberg.

Brandenburg-Prussia. 1721. *Corpus constitutionum Prutenicarum.* Edited by G. Grube. 2 vols. Königsberg.

————. 1737–51. *Corpus constitutionum Marchium. Continuatio.* 4 vols. Edited by Christian Otto Mylius. Berlin/Halle.

————. 1754–1822. *Novum corpus constitutionum Prussico-Brandenburgensium . . . 1755–1810.* 12 vols. Berlin.

———. 1769–85. *Codex diplomaticus Brandenburgensis.* 8 vols. Edited by P. W. Gercken. Salzwedel.

———. 1794. *Allgemeines Landrecht für die Preußischen Staaten.* 2nd ed. Edited by H. Hattenhauer and G. Bernert. Neuwied: Luchterhand, 1994.

———. 1831–33. *Codex diplomaticus Brandenburgensis continuatus.* 2 vols. Edited by G. W. von Raumer. Berlin.

———. 1838–63. *Codex novus diplomaticus Brandenburgensis.* 25 vols. Edited by A. F. Riedel. Berlin.

———. 1839–40. *Die preussischen Universitäten. Eine Sammlung der Verordnungen.* 2 vols. in 3 pts. Edited by Johann F. W. Koch. Berlin.

———. 1855. *Das Unterrichtswesen des preussischen Staates. Eine Sammlung aller gesetzlichen Bestimmungen.* 2 vols. Edited by Ludwig M. P. von Rönne. Berlin.

———. 1864–73. *Das höhere Schulwesen in Preußen. Historisch-Statistische Darstellung.* 3 vols. Edited by Ludwig Wiese. Berlin.

———. 1867–68. *Verordnungen und Gesetze für die höheren Schulen in Preußen.* Edited by Ludwig Wiese. Berlin.

———. 1889–1919. *Protokolle und Relationen des Brandenbergischen Geheimen Rathes aus der Zeit des Kurfürsten Friedrich Wilhelm [1643–1666].* 7 vols. Edited by O. Meinardus. Publicationen aus der K. Preußischen Staatsarchiven, 41, 54, 55, 66, 80, 89, 91. Leipzig.

———. 1894–1936. *Die Behördenorganisation und die allgemeine Staatsverwaltung Preußens im 18. Jahrhundert.* 15 vols. Edited by G. Schmollert, O. Krauske, O. Hintze, and E. Posner. Acta Borussica. Denkmäler der Preußischen Staatsverwaltung im 18. Jahrhundert. Berlin.

Brandes, Ernst. 1802. *Über den gegenwärtigen Zustand der Universität Göttingen.* Göttingen.

Brant, Sebastian. 1964 [1494]. *Narrenschiff.* Translated into modern German by H. A. Junghans. Edited by Hans-Joachim Mähl. Stuttgart: Reclam.

Braubach, Max. 1947. *Die erste Bonner Universität und ihre Professoren.* Bonn: Universitäts-Verlag.

Bräuning-Oktavio, Hermann. 1971. *Christian Gottlob Heynes Vorlesungen über die Kunste der Antike.* Darmstadt: Justus-von-Liebig-Verlag.

Brenneke, Adolf. 1953. *Archivkunde. Ein Beitrag zur Theorie und Geschichte des europäisches Archivwesens.* Leipzig: Koehler & Amelang.

Breuer, Stefan. 1991. *Max Webers Herrschaftssoziologie.* Frankfurt: Campus.

Brewer, John and Roy Porter, eds. 1993 *Consumption and the World of Goods.* London: Routledge.

Briggs, Asa. 1997. "Oxford and Its Critics, 1800–1835." In Brock and Curthoys 1997, 134–45.

Brittnacher, Hans R. 1994. *Ästhetik des Horrors. Gespenster, Vampire, Monster, Teufel und künstliche Menschen in der phantastischen Literatur.* Frankfurt a.M.: Suhrkamp.

Brock, M. G., ed. 2000. *Nineteenth Century Oxford, Pt. 2* (vol. 7 in Aston 1984–). Oxford: Clarendon Press.

Brock, M. G. and M. C. Curthoys, eds. 1997. *Nineteenth Century Oxford, Pt. 1* (vol. 6 in Aston 1984–). Oxford: Clarendon Press.

Brocke, Bernhard vom. 1990. "Die Kaiser-Wilhelm Gesellschaft im Kaiser Reich. Vorgeschichte, Gründung und Entwicklung bis zum Ausbruch des Ersten Weltkriegs." In Vierhaus and Brocke 1990, 17–162.

———. 1991. "Friedrich Althoff-Forschungsstand und Quellenlage; Bemühungen um eine Biographie." In Brocke, ed. 1991, 15-44.

———. 1996. "Die Kaiser-Wilhelm-/Max-Planck-Gesellschaft und ihre Institute zwischen Universität und Akademie. Strukturprobleme und Historiographie." In Brocke and Laitko 1996, 1-32.

Brocke, Bernhard vom, ed. 1991. *Wissenschaftsgeschichte und Wissenschaftspolitik im Industriezeitlater. Das "System Althoff" in historischer Perspektive.* Veröffentlichungen der Forschungsstelle für Universitäts- und Wissenschaftsgeschichte der Philipps-Universität Marburg. Hildesheim: Lax.

Brocke, Bernhard vom and Hubert Laitko, eds. 1996. *Die Kaiser-Wilhelm-/Max-Planck-Gesellschaft und ihre Institute. Studien zu ihrer Geschichte: Das Harnack-Prinzip.* Berlin: de Gruyter.

Brockliss, L. W. B. 1987. *French Higher Education in the Seventeenth and Eighteenth Centuries: A Cultural History.* Oxford: Oxford Univerity Press.

———. 1997. "The European University in the Age of Revolution, 1789-1850." In Brock and Curthoys 1997, 77-133.

Brody, Baruch. 1995. *Ethical Issues in Drug Testing, Approval, and Pricing: The Clot-Dissolving Drugs.* New York: Oxford University Press.

Brooke, Christopher. 1993. *A History of the University of Cambridge, Vol. 4: 1870-1990* (in Brooke 1988-2004). Cambridge: Cambridge University Press.

Brooke, Christopher, ed. 1988-2004. *A History of the University of Cambridge.* 4 vols. (vol. 1 by Leader 1988, vol. 2 by Morgan 2004, vol. 3 by Searby 1997, vol. 4 by Brooke 1993). Cambridge: Cambridge University Press.

Brooks, Peter. 1984. *Reading for the Plot: Design and Intention in Narrative.* New York: Knopf.

Broszinski, Hartmut and Thomas Wurzel, eds. 1995. *Ein Schatz, wird er mit Augen gesehn?: Kostbare Handschriften und Drucke in hessischen Bibliotheken.* Frankfurt a.M.: Sparkassen-Kulturstiftung Hessen-Thüringen.

Bruchmüller, Wilhelm. 1909. *Der Leipziger Student, 1409-1909.* Aus Natur und Geisteswelt, 273. Leipzig: Teubner.

Brückner, Jutta. 1977. *Staatswissenschaften, Kameralismus und Naturrecht. Ein Beitrag zur Geschichte der Politischen Wissenschaften im Deutschland des späten 17. und frühen 18. Jahrhunderts.* Münchener Studien zur Politik, 27. Munich: Beck.

Bruford, W. H. 1965. *Germany in the Eighteenth-Century: The Social Background of the Literary Revival.* Cambridge: Cambridge University Press.

Brunschwig, Henri. 1947. *La crise de l'état prussien à la fin du XVIII$^e$ siècle et la genèse de la mentalité romantique.* Paris: Presses Universitaires.

Buchwald, Georg, ed. 1894. "Simon Wilde aus Zwickau. Ein Wittenberger Studentenleben zur Zeit der Reformation." *Mittheilungen der deutschen Gesellschaft zu Leipzig* 9:61-111.

Buck, August. 1977. "Die humanistischen Akademien in Italien." In Hartmann and Vierhaus 1977, 11-25.

Buff, Walter. 1937. *Gerlach Adolph Freiherr von Münchhausen als Gründer der Universität Göttingen.* Göttingen: Dietrich.

Bühler, W.K. 1981. *Gauss: A Biographical Study.* Berlin: Springer.

Bulling, Karl. 1932. *Goethe als Erneuer und Benutzer der jenaischen Bibliothek.* Claves Jenensis, 2. Jena: Frommann.

Bürger, Christa. 1980. "Literarischer Markt und Öffentlichkeit am Ausgang des 18. Jahrhunderts in Deutschland." In Bürger et al. 1980, 162-212.

Bürger, Christa and Peter Bürger and Jochen Schulte-Sasse, eds. 1980 *Aufklärung und literarische Öffentlichkeit*. Frankfurt a.M.: Suhrkamp.

Burke, Peter. 1993. *The Art of Conversation*. Ithaca: Cornell University Press.

Burkhardt, ?. 1878. "Abriß der Geschichte des S. Ernestinischen Gesammt-Archivs in Weimar." *Archivalische Zeitschrift* 3:80–109.

Bursian, Konrad. 1883. *Geschichte der classischen Philologie in Deutschland von den Anfängen bis zur Gegenwart*. 2 vols. Munich/Leipzig.

Buzas, Ladislaus. 1976. *Deutsche Bibliotheksgeschichte der Neuzeit (1500–1800)*. Elemente des Buch- und Bibliothekswesens, 2. Wiesbaden: Reichert.

———. 1978. *Deutsche Bibliotheksgeschichte der neuesten Zeit (1800–1945)*. Elemente des Buch- und Bibliothekswesens, 3.Wiesbaden: Reichert.

———. 1986. *German Library History, 800–1945*. Translated by W. D. Boyd and I. H. Wolfe. Jefferson: McFarland.

Cahan, David. 1985. "The Institutional Revolution in German Physics, 1865–1914." *Historical Studies in the Physical Sciences* 15/2: 1–65.

———. 1989. *An Institute for an Empire: The Physikalisch-Technische Reichsanstalt*. New York: Cambridge University Press.

———. 2003. "Institutions and Communities." In Cahan, ed. 2003, 291–328.

Cahan, David, ed. 1993. *Hermann von Helmholtz and the Foundations of Nineteenth-Century Science*. Berkeley: University of California Press.

———. 2003. *From Natural History to the Sciences*. Chicago: University of Chicago Press.

Cardini, Franco and M. T. Fumagalli Beonio-Brocchieri. 1991. *Universitäten im Mittelalter. Die europäischen Stätten des Wissens*. Translated by A. Seling. Munich: Suedwest.

Carlsson, Anni. 1969 [1963]. *Die deutsche Buchkritik von der Reformation bis zur Gegenwart*. Bern: Francke.

Casel, Johann. 1602. *Diagraphe Magistrii philosophici*. Helmstedt.

Catto, J. I., ed. 1984. *The Early Oxford Schools* (vol. 1 in Aston 1984–). Oxford: Clarendon.

Catto, J. I. and Ralph Evans, eds. 1992 *Late Medieval Oxford* (vol. 2 in Aston 1984–). Oxford: Clarendon.

Cellarius, Balthassar. 1663. *Politica*. 6th ed. Jena.

Chartier, Roger. 1994. *The Order of Books*. Translated by Lydia Cochrane. Cambridge: Polity Press.

Chartier, Roger et al., eds. 1989. *Passions of the Renaissance, Vol. 3: A History of Private Life*. Translated by Arthur Goldhammer. Cambridge, MA: Harvard University Press.

Chitnis, A. 1976. *The Scottish Enlightenment: A Social History*. London: Croom Helm.

Chladenius, Johann M. 1755. "Untersuchung ob die Erkenntnis der Wahrheit durch die akademische Disputation befördert werde?" (*Göttingische) Philosophische Bibliothek* 1/8:1–17.

Christie, John R. R. 1974. "The Origins and Development of the Scottish Scientific Community, 1680–1760." *History of Science* 12:122–41.

Cistercians. 1878. *Les monuments primitifs de la règle Cistercienne*. Edited by P. Guignard. Analecta Divionensia, 10. Dijon.

———. 1946–52. "Registrum epistolarum Stephani de Lexinton [1227–1239]." Edited by B. Greisser. In *Analecta Sacri Ordinis Cisterciensis*, 1946, 2:1–118; 1952, 8:181–379.

———. 1948. "Cistercii statuta antiquissima." Edited by J. Turk. In *Analecta Sacri Ordinis Cisterciensis* 4:1–159.

Claproth, Justus. 1769 [1756]. *Grundsätze I. Von Verfertigung und Abnahme der Rech-*

*nungen . . . ; IV. Von Einrichtung und Erhaltung derer Gerichts- und anderer Registraturen.* 2nd ed. Göttingen.

———. 1789 [1756]. *Grundsäze von Verfertigungen der Relationen aus Gerichtsacten.* 4th ed. Göttingen.

Clark, John W. 1909. *The Care of Books, an Essay on the Development of Libraries from the Earliest Times.* 2nd ed. Cambridge: Cambridge University Press.

Clark, William. 1992. "The Scientific Revolution in the German Nations." In Porter and Teich 1992, 90–114.

———. 1995. "Narratology and the History of Science." *Studies in the History and Philosophy of Science* 26/1:1–71.

———. 1997. "German Physics Textbooks in the *Goethezeit*." *History of Science* 35/2:219–39; 35/3:295–363.

———. 1999a. "Der Untergang der Astrologie in der deutschen Barockzeit." In Lehmann and Trepp 1999, 433–72.

———. 1999b. "The Death of Metaphysics in Enlightened Prussia." In Clark, Golinski, and Schaffer 1999, 423–73.

———. 2002. "From Enlightenment to Romanticism: Lichtenberg and Göttingen Physics." In Rupke 2002, 72–85.

———. 2003 "The Pursuit of the Prosopography of Science." In Porter 2003, 211–37.

———. 2005. "Einsteins Haar." Translated by Michael Adrian. In Hagner 2005, forthcoming.

Clark, William, Jan Golinski, and Simon Schaffer, eds. 1999. *The Sciences in Enlightened Europe.* Chicago: Chicago University Press.

Clercq, Carlo de. 1936–58. *La législation religieuse franque de Clovis à Charlemagne.* 2 vols. Louvain/Paris.

Cluniacs. 1853. *Antiquiores Consuetudines Cluniacensis Monasterii collectore Udalrico Monacho Benedictino.* Patrologiae cursus completus: Series latina 149: 633–738. Paris.

Cobb, James D. 1980. *The Forgotten Reforms: Non-Prussian Universities 1797–1817.* Dissertation, University of Wisconsin, Madison.

Cobban, Alan. 1975. *The Medieval Universities: Their Development and Organization.* London: Methuen.

———. 1988. *The Medieval English Universities: Oxford and Cambridge to c. 1500.* Cambridge: Scholar's Press.

———. 1992. "Colleges and Halls." In Catto and Evans 1992, 581–633.

Coleman, William and Frederic Holmes, eds. 1988. *The Investigative Enterprise: Experimental Physiology in Nineteenth-Century Medicine.* Berkeley: University of California Press.

Collins, Louise. 1994. "Gossip: A Feminist Defense." In Goodman and Ben-Ze'ev 1994, 106–14.

Conze, Werner et al., eds. 1985–92. *Bildungsbürgertum im 19. Jahrhundert.* 4 vols. Industrielle Welt, 38, 41, 47, 48. Stuttgart: Klett-Cotta.

Cooper, Lane. 1922. *An Aristotelian Theory of Comedy with . . . a Translation of the 'Tractatus Coislinianus.'* New York: Harcourt.

Cosmar, Carl W. 1993. *Geschichte des Königlich-Preußischen Geheimen Staats- und Kabinettsarchiv bis 1806.* Edited by Meta Kohnke. Veröffentlichungen aus den Archiven Preußischer Kulturbesitz, 32. Cologne: Böhlau.

Crary, Jonathan. 1990. *Techniques of the Observer: On Vision and Modernity in the Nineteenth Century.* Cambridge, MA: MIT Press.

Craster, Sir Edmund. 1952. *History of the Bodleian Library 1845–1945.* Oxford: Clarendon.

Creuzer, Georg F. 1836–48. *Deutsche Schriften.* 5 vols. Leipzig.

Crome, Keith. 2004. *Lyotard and Greek Thought: Sophistry.* New York: Palgrave.

Crosland, Maurice. 1975. "The Development of a Professional Career in Science in France." In Crosland, ed. 1975, 139–59.

Crosland, Maurice, ed. 1975. *The Emergence of Science in Western Europe.* London: MacMillan.

Cross, Clare. 1986. "Oxford and the Tudor State 1509–1558." In McConica 1986, 117–49.

Cumberland, Richard. 1807. *Memoirs.* 2 vols. London.

Cunningham, Andrew and Nicholas Jardine, eds. 1990. *Romanticism and the Sciences.* Cambridge: Cambridge University Press.

Cunningham, Andrew and Perry Williams, eds. 1992. *The Laboratory Revolution in Medicine.* Cambridge: Cambridge University Press.

Curthoys, M. C. 1997. "The Examination System." In Brock and Curthoys 1997, 339–74.

Curtis, Mark. 1959. *Oxford and Cambridge in Transition.* Oxford: Clarendon Press.

Daly, Lowrie J. 1961. *The Medieval University.* New York: Sheed and Ward.

Danzig, Natural Sciences Society. 1794. *Rede zur Feier des funfzigjähigen Stiftungs-gedächtnisstages der Naturforschenden Gesellschaft zu Danzig . . . 2. Jan. 1793.* By Abraham Skusa. Danzig.

———. 1843. *Rede zur Feier der ersten Säcular-Feier der naturforschenden Gesellschaft zu Danzig am 2. Jan. 1843.* By August Wilhelm Skusa. Danzig.

Darjes, Joachim G. 1756. *Erste Gründe der Cameral-Wissenschaften.* Jena.

Daston, Lorraine. 1988. *Classical Probability in the Enlightenment.* Princeton: Princeton University Press.

———. 1991. "The Ideal and the Reality of the Republic of Letters in the Enlightenment." *Science in Context* 4/2, 367–86.

———. 1992. "Objectivity and the Escape from Perspectivity." *Social Studies of Science* 22:597–618.

———. 1995. "The Moral Economy of Science." *OSIRIS* 10: 3–24.

———. 2001. "Scientific Objectivity with and without Words." In Becker and Clark 2001, 259–84.

Daston, Lorraine and Peter Galison. 1992. "The Image of Objectivity." *Representations* 40:81–128.

Daston, Lorraine and Katharine Park. 1998. *Wonders and the Order of Nature 1150–1750.* New York: Zone Books.

Debré, Patrice. 1994. *Louis Pasteur.* Baltimore: Johns Hopkins University Press.

Decker-Hauff, H. et al., eds. 1977 *500 Jahre Eberhard-Karls-Universität Tübingen. Beiträge zur Geschichte der Universität Tübingen.* 3 vols. Tübingen: ATTEMPTO.

Defoe, Daniel. 1985 [1719]. *The Life and Adventures of Robinson Crusoe.* London/New York: Penguin.

d'Elvert, Christian. 1857. *Geschichte der Studien-, Schul-, und Erziehungs-Anstalten in Möhren und . . . Schlesien.* Brünn.

Del-Negro, Walter. 1972. "Die Pflege der Naturwissenschaften an der alten Universität." In University of Salzburg 1972, 109–19.

Demosthenopoulou, Elpiniki. 1970. *Öffentliche Bauten unter König Otto in Athen.*

*Begegnung mit Griechenland. Auffassungen und Auseinandersetzungen.* Diss. Phil., Munich.

Dietericus, Johann (*praeses*). 1730. *De non adaequata eruditione in quator facultate divisione,* Johann Siepius (*resp.*). Wittenberg.

Dilthey, Wilehlm. 1961–2000 [1914– ]. *Gesammelte Schriften.* 23 vols. Stuttgart/Berlin/ Göttingen: Teubner/de Gruyter/Vandenhoek & Ruprecht.

———. 1970 [1870]. *Leben Schleiermachers.* Edited by Martin Redeker, 3rd ed. 2 vols. in 4 pts. Vols. 13/1–2 and 14/1–2 in Dilthey 1961–2000.

Dithmar, Justus Christoph. 1731. *Einleitung in die Oeconomische-, Policey- und Cameral-Wissenschaft.* Frankfurt a.d.O.

———. 1755. *Einleitung in die Oeconomische-, Policey- und Cameral-Wissenschaft.* 5th ed. Frankfurt a.d.O.

Doeberl, Michael. 1916–31. *Entwicklungsgeschichte Bayerns.* 3 vols. Munich: Oldenbourg.

Doeberl, Michael, ed. 1930–31. *Das akademische Deutschland.* 4 vols. Berlin: Weller.

Donoghue, Frank. 1996. *The Fame Machine: Book Reviewing and Eighteenth-Century Literary Careers.* Stanford: Stanford University Press.

Dorwart, Reinhold A. 1953. *The Administrative Reforms of Friederick Wilhelm I of Prussia.* Cambridge, MA: Harvard University Press.

Duhem, Pierre. 1991 [1915/16]. *German Science.* Translated by John Lyon. La Salle: Open Court.

Duhr, Bernhard. 1907–28. *Geschichte der Jesuiten in den Ländern deutscher Zunge.* 4 vols. Freiburg im Br.: Herder.

Dumont, Louis. 1980. *Homo Hierachicus: A Study of the Caste System in India and Its Implications.* Translated by M. Sainsbury, L. Dumont and B. Gulati. Rev. ed. Chicago: University of Chicago Press.

———. 1977. *From Mandeville to Marx: The Genesis and Triumph of Economic Ideology.* Chicago: University of Chicago Press.

Duncan, G. D. 1986. "Public Lectures and Professorial Chairs." In McConica 1986, 335–61.

Durkheim, Emile. 1964 [1933; 1893]. *The Division of Labor in Society.* Translated by George Simpson. New York: Free Press.

———. 1965 [1915; 1912]. *The Elementary Forms of the Religious Life.* Translated by Joseph Swain. New York: Free Press.

Dury, John. 1983 [1650]. *The Reformed Librarie-Keeper.* The Augustan Reprint Society, 220. William Andrews Clark Library: Los Angeles.

Ebel, Wilhelm, ed. 1978. *Göttinger Universitätsreden aus zwei Jahrhunderten (1737–1943).* Göttingen: Vandenhoeck & Ruprecht.

Ebeling, Friedrich. 1888 [1862]. *Floergerls Geschichte des Grotesk-Komischen.* Leipzig.

Ebert, Friedrich A. 1822. *Geschichte und Beschreibung der königlichen öffentlichen Bibliothek zu Dresden.* Leipzig.

Eck, Reimer. 1997. "Entstehung und Umfang der spanischen Büchersammlung der Universitätsbibliothek Göttingen im 18. Jahrhundert." *Spanische Forschungen der Görresgesellschaft.* 2nd ser., 33:87–132.

Eckstein, Friedrich A. 1966 [1871]. *Nomenclatur philologorum.* Hildesheim.

Eder, Walter. 1980. *Servitus publica. Untersuchungen zur Entstehung, Entwicklung und Funktion der öffentlichen Sklaverei in Rom.* Forschungen zur antiken Sklaverei, 13. Wiesbaden.

Edwards, Kathleen. 1967 [1949]. *The English Secular Cathedrals in the Middle Ages. A Constitutional Study with Special Reference to the Fourteenth Century.* Manchester: Manchester University Press.

Ehlers, Joachim. 1974. "Monastische Theologie, historischer Sinn, und Dialektik. Tradition und Neuerung in der Wissenschaft des 12. Jahrhunderts." In Zimmermann 1974, 58–79.

Ehrlich, Adelheid. 1977. *Fichte als Redner.* tuduv-Studien, Reihe Sprach- und Literaturwissenschaften, 10. Munich: tuduv.

Eisenbach, Heinrich F. 1822. *Beschreibung und Geschichte der Universität und Stadt Tübingen.* Tübingen.

Elias, Norbert. 1977 [1969; 1939]. *Über den Prozeß der Zivilisation.* 2 vols. Frankfurt a.M.: Suhrkamp.

———. 1983. *Die höfische Gesellschaft. Untersuchungen zur Soziologie des Königtums und der höfischen Aristokratie.* Frankfurt a.M.: Suhrkamp.

———. 1994 [1989]. *Studien über die Deutschen. Machtkämpfe und Habitusentwicklung im 19. und 20. Jahrhundert.* Frankfurt a.M.: Suhrkamp.

Engel, Arthur. 1974. "The Emerging Concept of the Academic Profession at Oxford, 1800–1854." In Stone 1974, 1:305–51.

Engelbrecht, Helmut. 1982–88. *Geschichte des österreichischen Bildungswesens. Erziehung und Unterricht auf dem Boden Österreichs.* 5 vols. Vienna: Österreichischer Bundesverlag.

Engelhardt, Dietrich von, ed. 2002. *Von Freiheit und Verantwortung in der Forschung: Symposium zum 150. Todestag von Lorenz von Oken (1779–1851).* Schriftenreihe zur Geschichte der Versammlung deutscher Naturforscher und Ärtze, 9. Stuttgart: Wiss.-Verl.-Ges.

Engelhardt, Johann Georg Veit. 1843. *Die Universität Erlangen von 1743–1843.* Erlangen.

Engelhardt, Roderich von. 1933. *Die Deutsche Universität Dorpat in ihrer geistesgeschichtlichen Bedeutung.* Reval: Reinhardt.

Erben, Wilhelm. 1913. "Die Entstehung der Universitäts-Seminare." *Internationale Monatsschrift für Wissenschaft, Kunst und Technik* 7:1247–64, 1335–48.

Eribon, Didier. 1991. *Michel Foucault.* Translated by Betsy Wing. Cambridge, MA: Harvard University Press.

Erythraeus, Valentin. 1574. *Oratio de honoribus academicis et eorum Gradibus. . . .* Strasbourg.

Eulenburg, Franz. 1904. *Die Frequenz der deutschen Universitäten.* Königl. Sächsische Gesellschaft der Wissenschaften, Philol.-hist. Kl., Abhandlungen, 24. Leipzig.

———. 1909. *Die Entwicklung der Universität Leipzig in den letzten hundert Jahren.* Leipzig: Hirzel.

Euler, Friedrich W. 1970. "Entstehung und Entwicklung deutscher Gelehrtengeschlechter." In Rössler and Franz 1970, 183–232.

Evans, G. R. 1980. *The Old Arts and New Theology: The Beginnings of Theology as an Academic Discipline.* Oxford: Clarendon Press.

Fabian, Bernhard. 1977. "Göttingen als Forschungsbibliothek im achtzehnten Jahrhundert. Plädoyer für eine neue Bibliotheksgeschichte." In Raabe 1977, 209–39.

———. 1980 "Die Göttinger Universitätsbibliothek im achzehnten Jahrhundert." *Göttinger Jahrbuch* 28:109–24.

Fabian, Johannes. 1983. *Time and the Other: How Anthropology Makes Its Object.* New York: Columbia University Press.

Fauvel, John and Raymond Flood, Michael Shortland, and Robin Wilson, eds. 1988. *Let Newton Be!* Oxford: Oxford University Press.

Fechner, Jörg-Ulrich. 1977. "Die Einheit von Bibliothek und Kunstkammer im 17. und 18. Jahrhundert." In Raabe 1977, 11–32.

Fechner, Jörg-Ulrich, ed. 1981. *Stammbücher als kulturhistorische Quellen.* Wolfenbütteler Forschungen, 11. Munich: Kraus.

Feine, Hans E. 1964. *Kirchliche Rechtsgeschichte. Vol. 1: Die katholische Kirche.* 4th ed. Cologne: Böhlau.

Feingold, Mordechai. 1984. *The Mathematician's Apprenticeship: Science, Universities and Society in England 1560–1640.* Cambridge: Cambridge University Press.

———. 1990. "Isaac Barrow: Divine, Scholar, Mathematician." In Feingold, ed. 1990, 1–104.

Feingold, Mordechai, ed. 1990. *Before Newton: The Life and Times of Isaac Barrow.* Cambridge: Cambridge University Press.

Feller, Joachim, ed. 1718. *Otium Hannoveranum, sive Miscellanea . . . Leibnitii. . . .* Leipzig.

Feltmann, Gerhard. 1667. *Dissertatio de promotione absentia.* Duisburg.

———. 1691. *De titulis honorum.* Bremen.

Fester, Richard, ed. 1905. *'Der Universitäts-Bereiser' Friedrich Gedike und sein [1789] Bericht an Friedrich Wilhelm II.* Archiv für Kulturgeschichte, supp. 1. Berlin: Duncker.

Feuerhahn, Wolf. 2001. "A Theologian's List & an Anthropologist's Prose: Michaelis, Niebuhr & the Expedition to *Felix Arabia.*" In Becker and Clark 2001, 141–68.

Feyerabend, Paul. 1978 [1975]. *Against Method: Outline of an Anarchistic Theory of Knowledge.* London: Verso.

Fichte, Johann G. 1807. "Deduzierter Plan einer zu Berlin errichtenden höhern Lehranstalt, die in gehöriger Verbindung mit einer Akademie der Wissenschaften stehe." In Weischedel 1960, 30–105.

———. 1834–46. *Werke.* 11 vols. Berlin.

———. 1845–46. *Sämmtliche Werke.* 8 vols. Edited by J. H. Fichte. Berlin.

Fikenscher, Georg W. A. 1806. *Vollständige akademische Geschichte der kgl. preussischen Friedrichs-Alexander Universität zu Erlangen.* 3 vols. Nuremberg.

Fincham, Kenneth. 1997. "Oxford and Early Stuart Policy." In Tyacke 1997, 179–210.

Findlen, Paula. 1994. *Possessing Nature: Museums, Collecting, and Scientific Culture in Early Modern Italy.* Berkeley: University of California Press.

Fischer, Gustav (*resp.*). 1831. *De dignitati magistrii,* Heinricus Eichstadius (*praeses*). Jena.

Fischer, Heinz-Dietrich, ed. 1972. *Deutsche Zeitungen des 17. bis 20. Jahrhunderts.* Publizistik-historische Beiträge, 2. Pullach bei Munich: Verlag Dokumentation.

Fischer, L. H. 1888. "Das königliche pädagogische Seminar in Berlin 1787–1887." *Zeitschrift für Gymnasial-Wesen* 42. N.s. 22:1–43.

Fjermedal, Grant. 1984. *Magic Bullets.* New York: MacMillan.

Flach, Willy. 1952. *Goetheforschung und Verwaltungsgeschichte. Goethe im Geheimen Consilium 1776–1786.* Thüringische Archivstudien, 3. Weimar.

Fladt, Philipp W. L. 1764. *Anleitung zur Registratur-Wissenschaft und von Registratoribus deren Amt und Pflichten. . . .* Frankfurt/Leipzig.

Flashar, Hellmut. 1979. "Die methodisch-hermeneutische Ansätze von Friedrich August Wolf und Friedrich Ast-Traditionelle und neue Begründungen." In Flashar et al. 1979, 21–31.

Flashar, Hellmut and Karlfried Gründer and Axel Horstmann, eds. 1979. *Philologie und Hermeneutik im 19. Jahrhundert. Zur Geschichte und Methodologie der Geisteswissenschaften.* Göttingen: Vandenhoeck & Ruprecht.

Flynn, James. 1988. "Russia's 'University Question': Origins to Great Reforms, 1802–1863." *History of Universities* 7:1–35.

Förster, Johann Christian. 1771. *Versuch einer Einleitung in die Cameral-, Policey- und Finanzwissenschaften.* Halle.

———. 1794. *Uebersicht der Universität zu Halle in ihrem ersten Jahrhundert.* Halle.

Forster, Leonard. 1987. "'Charlataneria eruditorum' zwischen Barock und Aufklärung in Deutschland. . . ." In Neumeister and Wiedemann 1987, 1:203–20.

Foucault, Michel. 1966. *Les mots et les choses: Une archéologie des sciences humaines.* Paris: Gallimard.

———. 1969. *L'archéologie du savoir.* Paris: Gallimard.

———. 1971. *L'ordre du discours.* Paris: Gallimard.

———. 1973 [1970]. *The Order of Things: An Archaeology of the Human Sciences.* New York: Vintage.

———. 1975. *Surveiller et punir: Naissance de la prison.* Paris: Gallimard.

———. 1976. *Histoire de la sexualité 1. La volonté de savoir.* Paris: Gallimard.

———. 1977. *Language, Counter-Memory, Practice: Selected Essays and Interviews.* Edited by Donald Bouchard. Ithaca: Cornell University Press.

———. 1980. *Power/Knowledge: Selected Interviews and Other Writings, 1972–1977.* Edited and translated by C. Gordon et al. New York: Pantheon.

———. 1984a. *Histoire de la sexualité 2. L'usage des plaisirs.* Paris: Gallimard.

———. 1984b. *Histoire de la sexualité 3. Le souci de soi.* Paris: Gallimard.

———. 1989. *Foucault Live (Interviews, 1961–84).* Translated by John Johnston. Edited by Sylvère Lotringer. New York: Semiotext(e).

———. 1994. *Dits et écrits 1954–1988.* 4 vols. Edited by Daniel Defert, François Ewald, and Jacques Lagrange. Paris: Gallimard.

Fox, Carolyn. 1976. "The Bodleian Catalogs of 1674 and 1738: An Examination in the Light of Modern Cataloging Theory." *Library Quarterly* 46/3:248–70.

Fox, Robert. 1984. "Science, the University, and the State in Nineteenth Century France." In Geison 1984, 66–145.

Frank, Robert. 1973. "Science, Medicine and the Universities of Early Modern England." *History of Science* 11:194–216, 239–69.

Frasca-Spada, Marina and Nick Jardine, eds. 2000. *Books and the Sciences in History.* Cambridge: Cambridge University Press.

Fregißmont, Johann. 1673. *Discursus Historico-Politico-Juridicus de doctoratum dignitate. . . .* Salzburg.

Freisen, Joseph. 1898. *Die Universität Paderborn.* 2 vols. Paderborn.

Freud, Sigmund. 1981 [1905]. *Bruchstücke einer Hysterie-Analyse. Krankengeschichte der 'Dora.'* Frankfurt a.M.: Fischer.

Frick, Otto. 1883. *Das Seminarium praeceptorum.* Halle.

Fried, Johann. 1974. *Die Entstehung des Juristenstandes im 12. Jahrhundert.* Forschungen zur neuern Privatrechtsgeschichte, 21. Cologne: Boehlau.

Friedensburg, Walter. 1917. *Geschichte der Universität Wittenberg.* Halle.

Friedländer, Paul. 1927. "Zur Geschichte des altphilologischen Seminars." In Hermelink et al. 1927, 2:695–700.

Friedrich the Great, King Elector of Brandenburg-Prussia. 1986. *Friedrich der Große. Texte und Dokumente.* Edited by Bernhard Taureck. Stuttgart: Reclam.

Fries, Wilhelm. 1895. *Die Vorbildung der Lehrer für das Lehramt.* Handbuch der Erziehung und Unterrichtslehre für höhere Schulen, 2/1. Münster.

Friese, Heidrun. 2001. "Thresholds in the Ambit of Discourse: The Establishment of Authority at Academic Conferences." In Becker and Clark 2001, 285–312.

Friese, Heidrun and Peter Wagner. 1993. *Der Raum des Gelehrten. Eine Topographie akademischer Praxis.* Berlin: Edition Sigma.

Fritsch, Ahasver. 1667–70. *Exercitationes variae juris publici.* 3 vols. Nuremberg.

Fröhlich, David. 1644. *Bibliotheca, seu cynosura peregrinatium.* 2 vols. Ulm.

Frommann, Friedrich J. 1818. *Das Burschenfest auf der Wartburg am 18ten und 19ten October 1817.* Jena.

Frye, Northrop. 1957. *Anatomy of Criticism: Four Essays.* Princeton: Princeton University Press.

———. 1976. *The Secular Scripture: A Study of the Structure of Romance.* Cambridge, MA: Harvard University Press.

Funkenstein, Amos. 1986. *Theology and the Scientific Imagination from the Middle Ages to the Seventeenth Century.* Princeton: Princeton University Press.

Gabriel, Astrik. 1953. "Robert de Sorbonne." *Revue de l'Université d'Ottawa* 24/4:473–514.

———. 1961. "The College System in the Fourteenth-Century Universities." In Utley 1961, 79–124.

———. 1964. "Motivation of the Founders of Medieval Colleges." In Wilpert 1964, 61–72.

———. 1969. *Garlandia. Studies in the History of the Medieval University.* Notre Dame/Frankfurt a.M.: Knecht.

Gadendam, Johann W., ed. 1744. *Historia Academiae Fridericianae Erlangensis.* Erlangen.

Galbraith, G. R. 1925. *The Constitution of the Dominican Order 1216 to 1360.* Manchester: Manchester University Press.

Galison, Peter. 1997. *Image and Logic: A Material Cultural of Microphysics.* Chicago: Chicago University Press.

Galison, Peter and Bruce Hevly, eds. 1992. *Big Science: The Growth of Large-Scale Research.* Stanford: Stanford University Press.

Gans, Eduard. 1836. *Die Stiftung der Jahrbücher für wissenschaftliche Kritik.* Berlin.

Garnett, Richard. 1899. *Essays in Libarianship and Bibliography.* The Library Series, 5. London: Allen.

Gascoigne, John. 1984. "Mathematics and Meritocracy: The Emergence of the Cambridge Mathematical Tripos." *Social Studies of Science* 14:547–84.

———. 1985. "The Universities and the Scientific Revolution: The Case of Newton and Restoration Cambridge." *History of Science* 23:391–434.

———. 1989a. *Cambridge in the Age of Enlightenment.* Cambridge: Cambridge University Press.

———. 1989b. "Church and State Allied: The Failure of Parliamentary Reform of the Universities, 1688–1800." In Beier et al. 1989, 401–29.

———. 1990. "A Reappraisal of the Role of the Universities in the Scientific Revolution." In Lindberg and Westman 1990, 207–60.

Gasser, Simon Peter. 1729. *Einleitung zu den Oeconomischen, Politischen und Cameral-Wissenschaften.* Halle.

Gastel, Christian. 1675. *De statu publico Europae novissimo tractatus. . . .* Nuremberg.

Geiling, F. W., ed. 1865. *Bilder aus dem Studentenleben.* Jena.

Geison, Gerald. 1995. *The Private Science of Louis Pasteur.* Princeton: Princeton University Press.

Geison, Gerald, ed. 1984. *Professions and the French State, 1700–1900.* Princeton: Princeton University Press.

Gerhard, Johann F. and Samuel T. Seifert (*auct. & resp.*). 1655a. *Disputatio historico-politica de academia, Prior,* Otto W. Königsmark (*rect. mag. & praeses*). Jena.

————. 1655b. *Disputatio historico-politica de academia, Post.* Otto W. Königsmark (*rect. mag. & praeses*). Jena.

Gesner, Johann Matthias. 1743–45. *Opuscula minora varii argumenti.* 8 vols. Breslau.

Gibbon, Edward. 1966. *Memoirs of My Life.* Edited by Georges Bonnard. New York: Funk & Wagnalls.

Gierke, Otto von. 1868–1913. *Rechtsgeschichte der deutschen Genossenschaften [Das deutsche Genossenschaftsrecht].* 4 vols. Berlin: Weidmann.

Gierl, Martin. MS. "Vom gelehrten Streiter in der 'Trutzberg der Wahrheit' zum höflichen Konkurrenten der 'Aufklärungsfabrik'. . . ."

————. 1992. "Bestandsaufnahme im gelehrten Bereich: Zur Entwicklung der 'Historia literaria' im 18. Jahrhundert." In Gierl et al. 1992, 53–80.

————. 1997. *Pietismus und Aufklärung: Theologische Polemik und die Kommunikationsreform der Wissenschaft am Ende des 17. Jahrhunderts.* Göttingen: Vandenhoeck & Ruprecht.

————. 2001. "'The Triumph of Truth and Innocence': The Rules & Practice of Theological Polemics." In Becker and Clark 2001, 35–66.

Gierl, Martin et al., eds. 1992 *Denkhorizonte und Handlungsspielräume. Historische Studien für Rudolf Vierhaus zum 70. Geburtstag.* Göttingen: Wallstein.

Gillispie, Charles. 1980. *Science and Polity in France at the End of the Old Regime.* Princeton: Princeton University Press.

Gisenius, Johann. 1628. *Vita academicae.* Rinteln.

Gleason, Maud. 1995. *Making Men: Sophists and Self-Presentation in Ancient Rome.* Princeton: Princeton University Press.

Glorieux, Palemon. 1959. *Les origines du Collège de Sorbonne.* Texts and Studies in the History of Mediaeval Education, 8. Notre Dame: Medieval Institute.

Glud, Severina (*praeses*). 1695. *Dissertatio de gradu Magistrii philosophici,* Johann Styling (*resp.*). Hafniae.

Gockel, Ernst. 1682. *Deliciae Academicae.* Vienna (?).

Goetz, Dorothea. 1973. *Das naturwissenschaftliche Aspekt der deutschen Aufklärung an der Universitäten im 18. Jahrhundert.* Diss. Päd., Potsdam.

Goetz, Georg. 1928. *Geschichte der klassichen Studien an der Universität Jena.* Beiträge zur Geschichte der Universität Jena, pt. 1/1. Zeitschrift des Vereins für Thüringische Geschichte u. Altertumskunde, n.s. 12. Jena.

Goldfuß, Georg A. 1821. *Ein Wort über die Bedeutung naturwissenschaftlicher Institute und über ihren Einfluß auf humane Bildung.* Bonn.

Goldmann, Karlheinz. 1967. *Verzeichnis der Hochschulen.* Neustadt a.d. Aisch: Degener.

Goldsmith, Elizabeth. 1988. *Exclusive Conversations: The Art of Interaction in Seventeenth-Century France.* Philadelphia: University of Pennsylvania Press.

Gönner, Nicolaus T. 1808. *Der Staatsdienst aus dem Gesichtspunkt des Rechts und der Nationalökonomie beleuchtet. . . .* Landshut.

Gooday, Graeme. 1990. "Precision Measurement and the Genesis of Physics Teaching Laboratories in Victorian Britain." *British Journal for the History of Science* 23:25–51.

Goodman, Dena. 1994. *The Republic of Letters: A Cultural History of the French Enlightenment.* Ithaca: Cornell University Press.

Goodman, Robert and Aaron Ben-Ze'ev, ed. 1994. *Good Gossip.* Lawrence: University of Kansas.

Goody, Jack. 1977. *The Domestication of the Savage Mind.* Cambridge: Cambridge University Press.

———. 1986. *The Logic of Writing and the Organization of Society.* Cambridge: University of Cambridge Press.

Gössmann, Elisabeth. 1987. "Rezeptionszusammenhänge und Rezeptionsweisen deutscher Schriften zur Frauengelehrsamkeit." In Neumeister and Weidemann 1987, 2:589–601.

Götten, G. Wilhelm, ed. 1735–41. *Das Jetztlebende Gelehrte Europa.* 3 vols. Zelle.

Gottsched, Johann Christoph, ed. (appeared anonymously). 1755 *Historische Lobschrift des weiland hoch- und wohlgebornen Herrn Christians . . . von Wolff.* Halle.

Götz, Immanuel Gottfried. 1789. *Geographica academica.* Nuremberg.

Grabmann, Martin. 1957. *Die Geschichte der scholastischen Methode.* 2 vols. Berlin: Akademische Druck- und Verlagsanstalt.

Grafton, Anthony. 1983. "Polyhistor into Philolog: Notes on the Transformation of German Classical Scholarship." *History of Universities* 3:159–92.

Grafton, Anthony and Lisa Jardine. 1986. *From Humanism to Humanities: Education and the Liberal Arts in Fifteenth- and Sixteenth-Century Europe.* London: Duckworth.

Gratten-Guinness, I. 1988. "*Grande Écoles, Petite Université:* Some Puzzled Remarks on Higher Education in Mathematics in France, 1795–1840." *History of Universities* 7:197–225.

Grau, Conrad. 1991. "Genie und Kärrner—zu den geistesgeschichtlichten Wurzeln des Harnack-Prinzip in der Berliner Akademietradition." In Brocke and Laitko 1996, 139–44.

Gregory, Frederick. 1989. "Kant, Schelling, and the Administration of Science in the Romantic Era." In Olesko 1989, 17–35.

Grohmann, Johann C.A. 1801–02. *Annalen der Universität zu Wittenberg.* 2 vols. Meissen.

Gross, Alan. 1990. *The Rhetoric of Science.* Cambridge, MA: Harvard University Press.

Grote, Andreas, ed. 1994. *Macrocosmos in microcosmo: Die Welt in der Stube; zur Geschichte des Sammelns 1450 bis 1800.* Opladen: Leske & Budrich.

Gründer, Karlfried, ed. 1969. *Der Streit um Nietzsches 'Geburt der Tragödie.' Die Schriften von E. Rohde, R. Wagner, U. v. Wilamowitz-Möllendorff.* Olms: Hildesheim.

Güldenapfel, Georg Gottlieb, ed. 1816. *Literarisches Museum für die Grossherzoglich Herzoglich Sächsischen Lande.* Jenaischer Universitäts-Almanach f.d.J. 1816, 1. Jena.

Gumprecht, Johann P. (*praeses*). 1717. *De polyteknia eruditorum . . . oder ein Tractat von denen Gelehrten, die von GOTT mit vielen Kindern gesegnet worden,* J. G. Fibiger (*resp.*). Leipzig.

Gunning, Henry. 1855. *Reminiscences of the University, Town, and Country of Cambridge from the Year 1780.* 2 vols. 2nd ed. London.

Günther, Karl G. 1783. *Ueber die Einrichtung der Hauptatchive, besonders in teutschen Reischslanden.* Altenburg.

Günther, Siegmund. 1881. "Die mathematischen und Naturwissenschaften an der Nürnbergischen Universität Altdorf." *Mitteilungen der Gesellschaft für die Geschichte der Stadt Nürnberg* 3:1–36.

Guthrie, W. K. C. 1971. *The Sophists.* Cambridge: Cambridge University Press.

Gutscher, Friedrich. 1811. *Die Registratur-Wissenschaft nach ihren Haupt-Gesichtspunkten, Grundsätze, Zeitgebrechen.* . . . Stuttgart.

Haaß, Robert. 1952. *Die geistige Haltung der katholischen Universitäten Deutschlands im 18. Jahrhundert. Ein Beitrag zur Geschichte der Aufklärung.* Freiburg im Br.: Herder.

Habermas, Jürgen. 1968. *Erkenntnis und Interesse.* Frankfurt: Suhrkamp.

———. 1987 [1962]. *Sturkturwandel der Öffentlichkeit. Untersuchungen zur einer Kategorie der bürgerlichen Gesellschaft.* Dramstadt: Luchterhand.

Haberzettl, Hermann. 1973. *Die Stellung der Exjesuiten in Politik und Kulturleben Österreichs bis zu Ende des 18. Jahrhunderts.* Diss. Phil., Vienna.

Hackenberg, Roslind. 1972. *Die Entwicklung der Naturwissenschaften an der Universität Marburg von 1750 bis zur Westfälischen Zeit.* Diss. Med., Marburg.

Hagner, Michael. 2003. "Scientific Medicine." In Cahan 2003, 49–87.

Hagner, Michael, ed. 2005. *Einstein on the Beach. Ein Physiker als Phaenomen.* Frankfurt: Fischer.

Hahn, Roger. 1971. *The Anatomy of a Scientific Institution: The Paris Academy of Sciences, 1666–1803.* Berkeley: University of California Press.

———. 1975a. "Scientific Careers in Eighteenth-Century France." In Crosland 1975, 127–38.

———. 1975b. "Scientific Research as an Occupation in Eighteenth-Century Paris." *Minerva* 13:501–13.

Halbritterus, Johann (*praeses*). 1616. "Oratio de privilegiis Doctorum . . . 1604." Sebastianus Willingius (*resp.*), sep. pag. appendix in Bocerius 1616.

Hallinger, Kassio, ed. 1963–80. *Corpus Consuetudinum Monasticarum.* 12 vols. Siegburg: Schmitt.

Hammermayer, Ludwig. 1959. *Gründungs- und Frühgeschichte der Bayerischen Akademie der Wissenschaften.* Münchener historische Studien: Bayerische Geschichte, 4. Kallmünz über Regensburg.

———. 1972. "Die Beziehungen zwischen der Universität Ingolstadt und der Bayerischen Akademie der Wissenschaft (1759-1800)." *Sammelblatt des Historischen Vereins Ingolstadt* 81:58–139.

Hammerstein, Notker. 1970. "Zur Geschichte der deutschen Universität im Zeitalter der Aufklärung." In Rössler and Franz 1970, 145–82.

———. 1977. *Aufklärung und katholisches Reich. Untersuchungen zur Universitätsreform und Politik katholischer Universitäten des Heiligen Römisches Reichs deutscher Nation im 18. Jahrhundert.* Historische Forschungen, 12. Berlin: Duncker.

———. 1983. "Die deutschen Universitäten im Zeitalter der Aufklärung." *Zeitschrift für historische Forschung* 10:73–89.

———. 1985. "Zur Geschichte und Bedeutung der Universitäten im Heiligen Römischen Reich Deutscher Nation." *Historische Zeitschrift* 241:287–328.

———. 1996a. "Relations with Authority." In Ridder Symoens 1996, 113–53.

———. 1996b. "Epilogue: The Enlightenment." In Ridder-Symoens 1996, 621–40.

Handwerker, Otto. 1904. *Geschichte der Würzburger Universitäts-Bibliothek bis zur Säkularisation.* Diss. Phil., Würzburg.

———. 1932. *Dreihundert Jahre Würzburg Universitätsbibliothek 1619–1919.* Berlin: Springer.

Hanover/Brunswick/Lüneburg. 1738. *Schulordnung vor die Churfürstliche Braunschweig-Lüneburgische Lande.* Göttingen.

———. 1739–41. *Chur-Braunschweig Lüneburgische Landes Ordnungen und Gesetze.* Göttingen.

———. 1814–32. *Verordnungs-Sammlung für die Herzoglichen Braunschweigischen Lande.* 19 vols. Brunswick.

———. 1886–90. *Braunschweigische Schulordnungen von den ältesten Zeiten bis zum Jahre 1828,* Monumenta Germaniae paedagogica, 1 and 8. Edited by Friedrich Koldeway. Berlin.

Hargreaves-Mawdsley, W. N. 1963. *A History of Academical Dress in Europe until the End of the Eighteenth Century.* Oxford: Oxford University Press.

Harnack, Adolf von. 1911. *Aus Wissenschaft und Leben.* 2 vols. Gießen: Töpelmann.

———. 2001. *Wissenschaftspolitische Reden und Aufsätze.* Edited by Bernhard Fabian. Hildesheim: Olms-Weidmann.

Harris, Philip Rowland. 1998. *A History of the British Museum Library.* London: British Library.

Harris, Steven. 1989. "Transposing the Merton Thesis: Apostolic Spirituality and the Establishment of the Jesuit Scientific Tradition." *Science in Context* 3/1:29–65.

Harrison, Brian, ed. 1994. *The Twentieth Century* (vol. 8 in Aston 1984–). Oxford: Clarendon Press.

Hartmann, F. and R. Vierhaus, eds. 1977. *Der Akademiegedanke im 17. und 18. Jahrhundert.* Wolfenbütteler Forschungen, 3. Bremen/Wolfenbüttel: Jacobi.

Hartmann, Karl J., ed. 1937. *Vier Dokumente zur Geschichte der Universitätsbibliothek Göttingen.* Göttingen: Haentzschel.

Hartmann Karl J. and Hans Füchsel, eds. 1937. *Geschichte der Göttinger Universitäts-Bibliothek.* Göttingen: Vandenhoeck & Ruprecht.

Hartung, Fritz. 1923. *Das Grossherzogtum Sachsen unter der Regierung Carl Augusts 1775–1828.* Pt. 2 of *Carl August. Darstellungen und Briefe zur Geschichte des Weimarischen Fürstenhauses und Landes.* Edited by Erich Marcks. Weimar: Böhlau.

Hattenhauer, Hans. 1993 [1980]. *Geschichte des deutschen Beamtentums.* Handbuch des öffentlichen Rechts, 1. Cologne: Heymanns.

Hausens, Carl R. 1800. *Geschichte der Universität und Stadt Frankfurt a.d.O.* Frankfurt a.d.O.

Haussherr, Hans. 1953. *Verwaltungseinheit und Ressortrennung vom Ende des 17. bis zum Beginn des 19. Jahrhunderts.* Berlin: Akademie.

Hautz, Johann F. 1862–64. *Geschichte der Universität Heidelberg.* 2 vols. Mannheim.

Haxel, Otto. 1953. "Zur Geschichte der Physik an der Universität Heidelberg." *Ruperto-Carola* 9/10. Heidelberg.

Hayman, Ronald. 1982. *Nietzsche: A Critical Life.* Harmondsworth: Penguin.

Headrick, Daniel. 1981. *The Tools of Empire: Technology and European Imperialism in the Nineteenth Century.* New York: Oxford University Press.

Heeren, Arnold H. L. 1813. *Christian Gottlob Heyne, biographisch dargestellt.* Göttingen.

Heesen, Anke te. 1997. *Der Weltkasten. Die Geschichte einer Bildenzyklopädie aus dem 18. Jahrhundert.* Göttingen: Wallstein.

Hegel, G. W. F. 1970. *Werke.* 20 vols. Frankfurt: Surkamp.

Heilbron, John. 1982. *Elements of Early Modern Physics.* Berkeley: University of California Press.

Heine, Samuel (*auct. et resp.*). 1704. *Dissertatio Academica de magni aestimandis Academiis,* Erdmann Uhseus (*praeses*). Leipzig.

Heinemann, Otto von. 1969 [1894]. *Die Herzogliche Bibliothek zu Wolfenbüttel 1550–1893.* 2nd ed. Amsterdam: Von Heusden.

Heinemeyer, Walter, ed. 1977. *Studium und Stipendium. Untersuchungen zur Geschichte des hessischen Stipendiatenwesens.* Veröffentlichungen der Historischen Kommission für Hessen, 37. Marburg: Elwert.

Heinrich, Ernst H. 1931. *Das Rang der Beamten.* Diss. Jur., Leipzig.

Heinz, Andrea, ed. 2003. *"Der Teutsche Merkur": Die erste deutsche Kulturzeitscrift.* Ereignis Weimar-Jena Kultur um 1800, Ästhetische Forschungen, 2. Heidelberg: Universitätsverlag Winter.

Hengst, Karl. 1981. *Jesuiten an Universitäten und Jesuitenuniversitäten.* Quellen und Forschungen aus dem Gebiet der Geschichte, n.s. 2. Paderborn: Schöningh.

Henne, Helmut and Georg Objartel, eds. 1984. *Bibliothek zur historischen deutschen Studenten- und Schülersprache.* 6 vols. Berlin: de Gruyter.

Herbst, Jurgen. 1988. "American Higher Education in the Age of the College." *History of Universities* 7:37–59.

Herbst, Wilhelm. 1872–76. *Johann Heinrich Voss.* 2 vols. in 3 pts. Leipzig.

Hermelink, Heinrich and S. Kaehler, eds. 1927. *Die Philipps-Universität zu Marburg, 1527–1927.* 2 vols. Marburg: Elwert.

Hermann, Gottfried, ed. 1826. *Über Herrn Professor Böckhs Behandlung der griechischen Inschriften.* Leipzig.

Herrmann, Johann. 1912. *Friedrich Ast als Neuhumanist.* Diss. Phil., Munich.

Hertz, Deborah. 1988. *Jewish High Society in Old Regime Berlin.* New Haven: Yale University Press.

Hertz, Martin. 1851. *Karl Lachmann. Eine Biographie.* Berlin.

Herzfeld, Michael. 1992. *The Social Production of Indifference: Exploring the Symbolic Roots of Western Bureaucracy.* Chicago: Chicago University Press.

Hesse, Werner. 1879. *Beiträge zur Geschichte der früheren Universität in Duisburg.* Duisburg.

Hesse-Cassel. 1767–1802. *Sammlung Fürstlich Hessischer Landes-Ordnungen und Ausschreiben.* Edited by C. G. Apel. 7 vols. Cassel.

———. 1813–66. *Sammlung von Gesetzen, Verordnungen, Ausschreiben und sonstigen allgemeinen Verfügungen für die kurhessischen Staaten.* 17 vols. Cassel.

Hesse-Darmstadt. 1819–. *Großherzoglich Hessisches Regierungsblatt.* Darmstadt.

———. 1831. *Statistisch-topographisch-historische Beschreibung des Grossherzogthums Hessen. Bd. IV.* Edited by Georg W. J. Wagner. Darmstadt.

———. 1903 *Die Schulordnungen des Großherzogtums Hessen.* Edited by W. Diehl. 2 vols. Monumenta Germaniae paedagogica, 27–28. Berlin: Wiedmann.

Heun, Carl. 1792. *Vertraute Briefe an alle edelgesinnte Jünglinge, die auf Universitäten gehen wollen.* 2 vols. Leipzig.

Heyne, Christian G. 1772. *Einleitung in das Studium der Antike, oder Grundriß einer Anführung zur Kenntniß der alten Kunstwerke.* Göttingen.

Hinschius, Paul. 1869–97. *System des katholischen Kirchenrechts mit besonderer Rücksicht auf Deutschland.* 6 vols. Berlin.

Hirsching, Friedrich K. G. 1786–91. *Versuch einer Beschreibung sehenswürdiger Bibliotheken Teutschlands nach alphabetischer Ordnung der Städte.* 4 vols. in 5 pts. Erlangen.

Hocke, Gustav René. 1978. *Das europäische Tagebuch.* Wiesbaden: Limes.

Hoffbauer, Johann Christoph. 1805. *Geschichte der Universität Halle.* Halle.

Hoffmann, Max. 1901. *August Böckh.* Leipzig: Teubner.

Hoffmann, S. F. W., ed. 1837. *Lebensbilder berühmter Humanisten.* 1st ser. Leipzig.

Höflechner, Walter. 1991 "Zum Einfluß des deutschen Hochschulwesens auf Öster-reich in den Jahren 1875–1914." In Brocke 1991, 155–83.

Hofmann, Erich. 1969. "Philologie." In University of Kiel 1965–69, V/2, 103–275.

Hofmann, Johannes, ed. 1926. *Stammbuch aus vier Jahrhunderten.* Leipzig.

Hofstaetter, Walther. 1908. *Das Deutsche Museum (1776–1788) und Das Neue Deutsche Museum (1789–1791). Ein Beitrag zur Geschichte der deutschen Zeitschriften im 18. Jahrhundert.* Probefahrten, 12. Leipzig: Voigtländer.

Holborn, Hajo. 1959. *A History of Modern Germany: The Reformation.* Princeton: Princeton University Press.

———. 1964. *A History of Modern Germany:1648–1848.* Princeton: Princeton University Press.

Holmes, Frederic L. 1988. "The Formation of the Munich School of Metabolism." In Coleman and Holmes 1988, 179–210.

———. 1989. "The Complementarity of Teaching and Research in Liebig's Labora-tory." In Olesko 1989, 121–64.

Hölscher, U. 1885. "Urkundliche Geschichte der Friedrichs-Universität zu Bützow." *Jahrbücher des Vereins für Mecklenburgische Geschichte und Alterthumskunde* 50:1–110.

Holy Roman Empire. 1737. *Neue und vollständige Sammlung der Reichs-Abschiede.* 4 pts. in 2 vols. Frankfurt a.M.

———. 1886–. *Monumenta Germaniae historica.* Legum sectio, I–IV, Hanover/Leipzig.

Hont, Istvan and Michael Ignatieff, eds. 1983. *Wealth and Virtue: The Shaping of Polit-ical Economy in the Scottish Enlightenment.* Cambridge: Cambridge University Press.

Horn, Ewald. 1893. *Die Disputationen und Promotionen an der deutschen Universität.* Centralblatt für Bibliothekswesen, Beiheft 11. Leipzig.

———. 1895/96. "Ueber den Philosophischen Magister und Doktortitel." *Academische Revue* 2:573–81, 650–56.

———. 1897. *Kolleg und Honorar.* Munich.

———. 1901. "Zur Geschichte der Privatdozenten" *Mitteilungen der Gesellschaft für deutsche Erziehungs- und Schulgeschichte* 9:26–70.

Horn, Franz. 1808. *Friedrich Gedike, eine Biographie.* Berlin.

Horowitz, Helen Lefkowitz. 1994. *The Power and the Passion of M. Carey Thomas.* New York: Knopf.

Hoskin, Keith. 1979. "The Examination, Disciplinary Power and Rational Schooling." *History of Education* 8/2:135–46.

Houben, Heinrich. 1965 [1924]. *Verbotene Literatur von der klassichen Zeit bis zur Gegenwart.* 2 vols. Hildesheim: Olms.

Hradil, Hannelore. 1980. "Der Humanismus an der Universität Ingolstadt (1477–1585)." In Boehm and Spörl 1972–80, 2:37–63.

Huber, Victor A. 1843. *The English Universities.* 2 vols. London.

Hufbauer, Karl. 1982. *The Formation of the German Chemical Community (1720–1795).* Berkeley: University of California Press.

Hufen, Fritz. 1955. *Über das Verhältnis der deutschen Territorialstaaten zu ihren Lan-desuniversitäten im alten Reich.* Diss. Phil., Munich.

Hugo, G. 1828. *Beyträge zur civilistischen Bücherkenntniß der letzten vierzig Jahren.* Berlin.

Humboldt, Wilhelm von. 1960–81. *Werke in fünf Bänden.* Edited by A. Flitner and K. Giel. Darmstadt: WBG.

————. 1993. *Schriften zur Politik und zum Bildungswesen.* Vol. 4 of 4th ed. of *Werke in fünf Bänden* [1964]. Edited by A. Flitner and K. Giel. Darmstadt: WBG.

Hummel, Gerhard. 1940. *Die humanistische Sodalitäten und ihr Einfluß auf die Entwicklung des Bildungswesens der Reformzeit.* Inaugural Dissertation. Leipzig: Edelmann.

Hunter, Michael. 1981. *Science and Society in Restoration Cambridge.* Cambridge: Cambridge University Press.

Huter, Franz, ed. 1971. *Die Fächer Mathematik, Physik und Chemie an der philosophischen Fakultät zu Innsbruck.* Veröffentlichungen der Universität Innsbruck, 66 (Forschungen zur Innsbrucker Universitäts-Geschichte, 10). Innsbruck: Österr. Kommissionsbuchhandlung.

Hyde, Thomas. 1674. *Catalogus impressorum librorum Bibliothecae Bodleianae in Academia Oxoniensi. . . .* Oxford.

Impey, Oliver and Arthur MacGregor, eds. 1985. *The Origins of Museums: The Cabinets of Curiosities in Sixteenth- and Seventeenth-Century Europe.* Oxford: Clarendon Press.

Ijsseling, Samuel. 1976. *Rhetoric and Philosophy in Conflict: An Historical Survey.* The Hague: Nijhoff.

Itter, Johann. 1698 [1679]. *De honoribus sive gradibus academicis liber . . . editio nova.* Frankfurt a.M.

Jacob, Ludwig Heinrich (appeared anonymously). 1798. *Ueber die Universitäten in Deutschland besonders in den Köngl. Preußischen Staaten.* Berlin.

Jacobs, Wilhelm G. 1998 [1984]. *Johann Gottlieb Fichte.* 3rd ed. Reinbeck: Rowholt.

James, Thomas. 1605. *Catalogus librorum Bibliothecae publicam quam vir orantissimus Thomas Bodleius . . . in Academia Oxoniensi nuper instituit. . . .* Oxford.

————. 1620. *Catalogus universalis librorum in Bibliotheca Bodleiana. . . .* Oxford.

Jebb, John. 1774a [1772]. *Remarks upon the Present Mode of Education in the University of Cambridge to Which is Added a Proposal for Its Improvement.* 4th ed. Cited from Jebb 1807, 2:255–335.

————. 1774b. *A Proposal for the Establishment of Public Examinations in the University of Cambridge with Occasional Remarks.* Cited from Jebb 1807, 2:337–70.

————. 1807. *The Works Theological, Medical, Political and Miscellaneous.* 3 vols. London.

Jeserich, Kurt and Hand Pohl and Georg-Christoph von Unruh, eds. 1983–88. *Deutsche Verwaltungsgeschichte.* 6 vols. Stuttgart: Deutsche Verlags-Anstalt.

Jöcher, Christian G. 1750. *Allgemeines Gelehrten Lexikon.* 4 vols. Repr. Hildesheim, 1961.

————. 1784–1819. *Allgemeines Gelehrten Lexikon. Fortsetzung und Ergänzungen,* by J. C. Adelung. 7 vols. Repr. Hildesheim, 1960–61.

Johag, Helga. 1977. *Die Beziehung zwischen Klerus und Bürgerschaft in Köln zwischen 1250 und 1350.* Rheinisches Archiv, 103. Bonn.

Johns, Adrian. 1998. *The Nature of the Book: Print and Knowledge in the Making.* Chicago: Chicago University Press.

Johnson, Hubert C. 1975. *Frederick the Great and his Officials.* New Haven: Yale University Press.

Johnson, Jeffrey. 1989. "Hierarchy and Creativity in Chemistry, 1871–1914." In Olesko 1989, 214–40.

Jones, Peter. 1983. "The Scottish Professoriate and the Polite Academy, 1720–46." In Hont and Ignatieff 1983, 89–117.

Jordak, Karl. 1965. *Die Universität Wien, 1365–1965*. Vienna: Bergland.

Jugler, Johann F. 1909. *Leipzig und seine Universität . . . aus dem Jahre 1779*. Edited by Friedrich Zarncke. Leipzig.

Jung, Horst-Wilhelm. 1966. *Anselm Franz von Bentzel im Dienste der Kurfürsten von Mainz*. Beiträge zur Geschichte der Universität Mainz, 7. Wiesbaden: Steiner.

Jungnickel, Christa and Russell McCormmach. 1986. *Intellectual Mastery of Nature: Theoretical Physics from Ohm to Einstein*. 2 vols. Chicago: University of Chicago Press.

Just, Leo and H. Mathy, eds. 1965. *Die Universität Mainz: Grundzüge ihrer Geschichte*. Mainz: Mushake.

Justi, Johann Heinrich von. 1755. *Staatswirthschaft, oder systematische Abhandlung aller Oekonomischen und Cameral-Wissenschaften*. 2 vols. Leipzig.

———. 1758. *Staatswirthschaft, oder systematische Abhandlung aller Oekonomischen und Cameral-Wissenschaften*. 2 vols. 2nd ed. Leipzig.

———. 1760. *Scherzhafte und Satyrische Schriften*. 3 vols. Berlin, 1760.

———. 1760–61. *Die Grundfeste zu der Macht und Glückseeligkeit der Staaten; oder ausführliche Vorstellung der gesamten Policey-Wissenschaft*. 2 vols. Königsberg.

———. 1761–64. *Gesammelte politische und Finanzschriften*. 3 vols. Leipzig.

———. 1775. *Anweisung zu einer guten deutschen Schreibart*. Leipzig.

———. 1782. *Grundsätze der Policeywissenschaft*. Comm. by J. Beckmann. 3rd ed. Göttingen.

Kahn, Charles. 1996. *Plato and the Socratic Dialogue: The Philosophical Use of a Literary Form*. Cambridge: Cambridge University Press.

Kangro, Hans. 1957. "Zur Geschichte der Physik an der Universität Freiburg i. Br." In Zentgraf 1957, 9–22.

Kant, Horst. 1996. "Albert Einstein, Max von Laue, Peter Debye und das Kaiser-Wilhelm Institut für Physik in Dahlem (1917–1939)." In Brocke and Laitko 1996, 227–43.

Kant, Immanuel. 1798. *Streit der Fakultäten*. Königsberg.

———. 1968–77 [1902–23]. *Werke*. 9 (+2) vols. Berlin: de Gruyter.

Kantorowicz, Ernest H. 1957. *The King's Two Bodies: A Study in Medieval Political Theology*. Princeton: Princeton University Press.

Karady, Victor. 1986. "Les universités de la Troisème République." In Verger 1986, 323–65.

Karlsruhe, Latin Society. 1767–70. *Acta Societatis Latinae Marchio-Badensis inauguralia*. 2 vols. Edited by G. A. Tittel. Karlsruhe / Tübingen.

Kaufmann, Georg. 1894. "Zur Geschichte der academischen Grade und Disputation." *Centralblatt für Bibliothekswesen* 11:201–25.

———. 1888–96. *Die Geschichte der deutschen Universitäten*. 2 vols. Stuttgart.

Kayser, Albrecht. 1790 *Ueber die Manipulation bey der Einrichtung einer Bibliothek und der Verfertigung der Bücherverzeichnisse. . . .* Bayreuth.

Kearney, Hugh. 1970. *Scholars and Gentlemen: Universities and Society in Industrial Britain, 1500–1700*. London: Faber.

Keck, Theodor. 1965. *Verfassung und Rechtsstellung der Churfürstlich-Bayerischen Landesuniversität Ingolstadt (1472–1800)*. Diss. Jur., Erlangen-Nuremberg.

Kehrbach, Karl et al., eds. 1886–. *Monumenta Germaniae paedagogica*. 62 vols. Hamburg / Berlin.

Keil, Robert and Richard Keil. 1858. *Geschichte der Jenaischen Studentenlebens. . . (1548–1858)*. Leipzig.

————(eds.). 1859. *Deutsche Studenten-Lieder des siebzehnten und achzehnten Jahrhunderts*. Lahr.

————1893. *Die deutschen Stammbücher des sechzehnten bis neunzehnten Jahrhunderts*. Berlin.

Kekulé, Reinhard. 1880. *Das Leben Friedrich Gottlieb Welcker*. Leipzig.

Keller, Ludwig. 1895. "Comenius und die Akademien der Naturphilosophen des 17. Jahrhunderts." *Geisteskultur. Monatshefte der Comeniusgesellschaft* 4:1–28, 69–96, 133–84.

————. 1903. "Gottfried Wilhelm Leibniz und die deutschen Sozietäten des 17. Jahrhunderts." *Vorträge und Aufsätze aus der Comenius-Gesellschaft* 11/3:2–15.

————. 1909. "Die Sozietäten des Humanismus und die Sprachgesellschaften." *Vorträge und Aufsätze aus der Comenius-Gesellschaft* 17/4:3–60.

————. 1912. "Akademien, Logen und Kammern des 17. und 18. Jahrhunderts." *Vorträge und Aufsätze aus der Comenius-Gesellschaft* 20/2:5–41.

Kelly, Michael. 1994. "Foucault, Habermas, and the Self-Referentiality of Critique." In Kelly 1994, 365–400.

Kelly, Michael, ed. 1994. *Critique and Power: Recasting the Foucault/Habermas Debate*. Cambridge, MA: Harvard University Press.

Kelter, Edmund, ed. 1908. *Jenaer Studentenleben zur Zeit des Renommisten von Zachariae. Nach Stammbuchbildern aus dem Besitz des Hamburgischen Museum für Kunst und Gewerbe geschildert*. Hamburg: Gräfe & Sillem.

Kempf, Thomas. 1991. *Aufklärung als Disziplinierung. Studien zum Diskurs des Wissens in Intelligenzblättern und gelehrten Beilagen des zweiten Hälfte des 18. Jahrhunderts*. Cursus, Texte und Studien zur deutschen Literatur, 2. Munich: Iudicium.

Kenney, Martin. 1986. *Biotechnology: The University-Industrial Complex*. New Haven: Yale University Press.

Ker, N.R. 1985. *Books, Collectors and Libraries*. Edited by Andrew Watson. London: Hambledon.

————. 1986. "The Provision of Books." In McConica 1986, 441–519.

Kern, Bärbel and Horst Kern. 1990 [1988] *Madame Doctorin Schlözer. Ein Frauenleben in den Widerspruchen der Aufklärung*. Munich: Beck.

Keussen, Hermann. 1934. *Die alte Universität Köln. Grundzüge ihrer Verfassung und Geschichte; Festschrift zum Einzug in die neue Universitaet Köln*. Cologne: Creutzer.

Kibre, Pearl. 1962. *Scholarly Privileges in the Middle Ages*. Medieval Academy of America, 72. Cambridge, MA: Mediaeval Academy of America.

Kiefhaber, Johann K.S. 1827. *Grundlinien einer Anleitung zur Archivs- und Registratur-Wissenschaft zum Gebrauch bey den Vorlesungen über dieselbe*. Munich.

Kink, Rudolf. 1854–55. *Geschichte der kaiserlichen Universität zu Wien*. 2 vols. Vienna.

Kirchner, Joachim. 1928. "Zur Entstehung- und Redaktionsgeschichte der Acta Eruditorum." *Archive für Buchgewerbe und Gebrauchsgraphik*. Pressa-Sonderheft, 4, 75–88.

————. 1928–31. *Die Grundlagen des deutschen Zeitschriftenwesen*. . . . 2 vols. Leipzig: Hiersemann.

————. 1958–62 [1942]. *Das deutsche Zeitschriftenwesen*. 2nd ed. 2 vols. Wiesbaden: Harrassowitz.

Kirsten, Johann (*auct. et resp.?*). 1785. *Dissertatio de Praestantia Magistrorum, eorumque dignitate, jure absus et transmissione in Doctores devoluta . . .*, Henricus Posse (*praeses?*). Göttingen.

Kistner, Adolf. 1930. *Die Pflege der Naturwissenschaften in Mannheim zur Zeit Karl Theodors*. Mannheim Altertumsverein, 1. Mannheim.

———. 1937. "Die Anfänge der Experimentalphysik in Heidelberg." *Zeitschrift für Geschichte des Oberrheins*, n.s. 50:110–34.

Kittler, Friedrich. 1985. *Aufschreibesysteme 1800/1900*. Munich: Fink.

Kius, Otto. 1865 "Das Stipendiumwesen in Wittenberg und Jena im 16. Jahrhundert." *(Ilgens) Zeitschrift für die historische Theologie* 35:96–159.

Klant, Michael, ed. 1984. *Universität in der Karikatur*. Hanover: Fackelträger.

Klausen, Rudolf H. 1837. "A. Böckh's Biographie." In Hoffmann 1837, 29–62.

Kloß, Alfred. 1916 *Die heidelbergischen Jahrbücher der Literatur in den Jahren 1808–1816*. Diss. Phil., Leipzig.

Kluge, Alexander. 1958. *Die Universitäts-Selbstverwaltung. Ihre Geschichte und gegenwärtige Rechtsform*. Frankfurt a.M.: Klostermann.

Knigge, Adolph Freiherr von. 1922 [1788]. *Ueber den Umgang mit Menschen*. Hanover: Hahn.

Knowles, David. 1966. *From Pachomius to Ignatius: A Study in the Constitutional History of the Religious Orders*. Oxford: Oxford University Press.

Knox, Dilwyn. 1991. "*Disciplina*. The Monastic and Clerical Origins of European Civility." In Monfasani and Musto 1991, 107–35.

———. 1995. "Erasmus' *De Civilitate* and the Religious Origins of Civility in Protestant Europe." *Archiv für Reformationsgeschichte* 86:7–55.

Köchly, Hermann. 1874. *Gottfried Hermann. Zu seinem hundertjährigen Geburtstage*. Heidelberg.

Koenig, Fredrick. 1985. *Rumor in the Marketplace: The Social Psychology of Commercial Hearsay*. Dover: Auburn House.

Koerner, Lisbet. 1999. *Linnaeus: Nature and Nation*. Cambridge, MA: Harvard University Press.

Kohfeldt, G. and W. Ahrens, eds. 1919. *Ein Rostocker Studenten-Stammbuch von 1736/37*. Rostock: Leopold.

Kolde, Theodor. 1910. *Die Universität Erlangen unter dem Hause Wittenbach (1810–1910)*. Erlangen/Leipzig: Deichert.

Koldeway, Friedrich. 1895. *Geschichte der klassischen Philologie auf der Universität Helmstedt*. Brunswick.

Koller, Heinrich. 1977. "Stadt und Universität im Spätmittelalter." In Maschke and Sydow 1977, 9–26.

König, René. 1935. *Vom Wesen der deutschen Universitäten*. Berlin: Die Runde.

Kopitzsch, Franklin, ed. 1976. *Aufklärung, Absolutismus und Bürgertum in Deutschland. Zwölf Aufsätze*. Munich: Nymphenburger Verlagshandlung.

Köpke, Rudolf. 1860. *Die Gründung der Königlichen Friedrich-Wilhelms Universität zu Berlin*. Berlin.

Körte, Wilhelm. 1833. *Leben und Studien Friedrich August Wolfs, des Philologen*. 2 vols. Essen.

Kortum, Carl Arnold. 1910. *Des Jobsiadendichters Carl Arnold Kortum Lebensgeschichte von ihm selbst erzählt*. Edited by K. Diecke. Dortmund: Ruhfus.

Kosegarten, Johann G. L. 1856–57. *Geschichte der Universität Greifswald*. 2 vols. Greifswald.

Koser, Reinhold. 1904. *Die Neuordnung des preussischer Archivwesens durch den Staatskanzler Fürsten von Hardenberg*. Mitteilungen der K. Preussischer Archivverwaltung, 7. Leipzig.

Krause, Peter. 1979. '*O alte Burschenherrlichkeit.' Die Studenten und ihr Brachtum*. Graz/Vienna: Stryria.

Krebs, Manfred. 1949. "Das badische General-Landesarchiv. Grundriß seiner Geschichte und seiner Bestände." *Zeitschrift für die Geschichte des Oberrheins* 97 (n.s.
58): 248–331.

Kreittmayr, Freiherr Wigulaeus X. A. von, ed. and comm. 1756–68. *Codex Maximilianeus Bavaricus civilis.* 4 vols. Munich.

Kremer, Richard. 1991. "Between *Wissenschaft* and Praxis: Experimental Medicine and
the Prussian State, 1807–1850." In Schubring 1991, 155–70.

———. 1992. "Building Institutes for Physiology in Prussia, 1836–1846: Contexts, Interests and Rhetoric." In Cunningham and Willams 1992, 72–109.

Kreußler, Heinrich G. 1810. *Geschichte der Universität Leipzig.* Dessau.

Krones, Franz von. 1886. *Geschichte der Karl-Franzens Universität in Graz.* Graz.

Kundtmann, Johannes (*auct. et resp.*). 1644. *Dissertatio de Academia,* Johannes Seldius
(*praeses*). Wittenberg.

Kunoff, Hugo. 1982. *The Foundation of the German Academic Library.* Chicago: American Library Association.

Kurras, Lotte, ed. 1987. *Zu gutem Gedenken: Kulturhistorische Miniaturen aus der Ger-
manischen Nationalmuseum (1570–1770).* Munich: Prestel.

Lackmann, Heinrich. 1966. "Leibniz' bibliothekarische Tätigkeit in Hannover." In
Totek and Haase 1966, 321–48.

Laitko, Hubert. 1991. "Friedrich Althoff und die Wissenschaft in Berlin. Konturen
und Strategie." In Brocke 1991, 69–85.

———. 1996. "Persönlichkeitszentrierte Forschungsorganisation als Leitgedanke der
Kaiser-Wilhelm-Gesellschaft: Reichweite und Grenzen, Ideal und Wirklichkeit."
In Brocke and Laitko 1996, 583–632.

Lampe, Hermann, ed. 1975. *Die Entwicklung und Differenzierung von Fachabteilungen
auf den Versammlungen von 1828 bis 1913. Bibliographie zur Erfassung der Sek-
tionsvorträge mit einer Darstellung der Entstehung der Sektionen und ihrer Pro-
blematik.* Schriftenreihe zur Geschichte der Versammlung deutscher Naturforscher
und Ärtze, Dokumentation und Analyse, 2, Hildesheim: Gerstenberg.

Lampe, Hermann, Hans Querner, and Ilse Gärtner, eds. 1972. *Die Vorträge der allgemeinen Sitzungen auf der 1.-85. Versammlung 1822–1913.* Schriftenreihe zur
Geschichte der Versammlung deutscher Naturforscher und Ärtze, Dokumentation und Analyse, 1. Hildesheim: Gerstenberg.

Lansius, Thomas. 1666. *Commentatio historico-politico-juridica de Academiis.* Helmstedt.

Latour, Bruno. 1987. *Science in Action.* Cambridge, MA: Harvard University Press.

———. 1990. "Drawing Things Together." In Lynch and Woolgar 1990, 19–68.

———. 1999. *Pandora's Hope: Essays on the Reality of Science Studies.* Cambridge, MA:
Harvard University Press.

Latour, Bruno and Steve Woolgar. 1986 [1979]. *Laboratory Life: The [Social] Construction of Scientific Facts.* Rev. ed. Princeton: Princeton Unversity Press.

Laukhard, Friederich C. 1792–1802. *Leben und Schicksale von ihm selbst geschrieben.* 5
vols. Halle.

Lauterbach, Wolfgang A. 1728–29. *Dissertationes Academicae.* 4 vols. Tübingen.

Lawrence, C. H. 1984a. *Medieval Monasticism.* London: Longmann.

———. 1984b. "The University in State and Church." In Catto 1984, 97–150.

Leader, Damian R. 1988. *A History of the University of Cambridge, Vol. 1: The University to 1546* (in Brooke 1988–2004). Cambridge: Cambridge University Press.

Leclercq, Jean. 1957. *L'Amour des lettres et le désir de Dieu: Initiation aux auteurs monastiques du moyen âge*. Paris: Édition du Cerf.

Le Goff, Jacques. 1957. *Les intellectuals au Moyen Age*. Paris: Éditions du Seuil.

———. 1977. *Pour un autre Moyen Age: Temps, travail et culture en Occident*. Paris: Gallimard.

Lehmann, Hartmut and Anne-Charlotte Trepp, eds. 1999. *Im Zeichen der Krise. Religiosität im Europa des 17. Jahrhunderts*. Göttingen: Vandenhoeck & Ruprecht.

Leibniz, Gottfried Wilhelm. 1923–. *Sämtliche Schriften und Briefe*. Multiple series and volumes in progress. Berlin: Akademie.

———. 1996 [1875–90]. *Die Philosophische Schriften*. Edited by C. I. Gerhardt. 7 vols. Hildesheim: Olms.

Leigh, Johann G. (*praeses*). 1715. *Dissertatio historico-philosophica de origine et causis disputationum academicarum*, J. H. Deterding (*resp.*). Rinteln.

Lemon, Lee and Marion Reis, eds. and trans. 1965. *Russian Formalist Criticism: Four Essays*. Lincoln: University of Nebraska Press.

Lenauderius, Petrus. 1583. "De privilegiis Doctorum," pp. 3–21 in vol. 18 of *Tractatus illustrium in utraque . . . iuris . . . .* Venice.

Lenoir, Timothy. 1988. "Science for the Clinic: Science Policy and the Formation of Carl Ludwig's Institute in Leipzig." In Coleman and Holmes 1988, 139–78.

———. 1992a. "Laboratories, Medicine and Public Life in Germany, 1830–1849: Ideological Roots of the Institutional Revolution." In Cunningham and Willams 1992, 14–71.

———. 1992b. *Politik im Tempel der Wissenschaft. Forschung und Machtausübung im deutschen Kaiserreich*. Translated by Horst Brühmann. Frankfurt: Campus.

———. 1997. *Instituting Science: The Cultural Production of Scientific Disciplines*. Stanford: Stanford University Press.

Lessing, Gotthold Ephraim. 1979 [1747]. *Der junge Gelehrte*. Stuttgart: Reclam.

Leube, Martin. 1921–54. *Die Geschichte der Tübinger Stift im 16. und 17. Jahrhundert*. 2 vols. Stuttgart: Steinkopf.

Leventhal, Robert. 1986. "The Emergence of Philological Discourse in the German States, 1770–1810." *Isis* 72:243–60.

Lévi-Strauss, Claude. 1969 [1949]. *The Elementary Structures of Kinship*. Translated by James Bell, Rodney Needham and John Sturmer. Rev. ed. Boston: Beacon Press.

Lexis, Wilhelm, ed. 1893. *Die deutschen Universitäten*. 2 vols. Berlin.

———. 1904. *Des Unterrichtswesen im Deutschen Reich*. 4 vols. Berlin: Asher.

Leyh, Georg. 1957. "Die deutsche Bibliotheken von der Aufklärung bis zur Gegenwart." In Bömer et al. 1957–61, 2:1–491.

Lhotsky, Alphons. 1965. *Die Wiener Artistenfakultät 1365–1497*. Österreichische Akademie der Wissenschaften, Phil.-hist. Kl., Sitzungsberichte, 247/2. Vienna.

Lichtenberg, Georg Christoph. 1983–92 *Briefwechsel*. Edited by Ulrich Joost and Albrecht Schöne. 4 vols. Munich: Beck.

Liess, Albrecht. 1980. "Die artistische Fakultät der Universität Ingolstadt 1472–1588." In Boehm and Spörl 1972–80, 2:9–35.

Lilienthal, Michael (*praeses*). 1712. *Schediasma critico-literarum de philothecis . . . vulgo von Stamm-Büchern*, Johann Balth. Charisius (*resp.*). Königsberg. Repr. in Fechner 1981, 237–98.

———. 1713. *De Machiavellismo litterario*. Königsberg / Leipzig.

Limnaeus, Johann. 1616. *Disputatio de academiis*. Jena.

———. 1629–34. *Juris publici Imperii Romano-Germanici*. 3 vols. Strasbourg.

Lindberg David and Robert Westman, eds. 1990. *Reappraisals of the Scientific Revolution*. Cambridge: Cambridge University Press.

Lindemann, Margot. 1969. *Deutsche Presse bis 1815*, vol. 1 of *Geschichte der deutsche Presse*. Abhandlungen und Materialien zur Publizistik, 5. Berlin: Colloquium.

Lindroth, Sten. 1976. *A History of Uppsala University 1477–1977*. Uppsala: Almqvist & Wiksell.

Lipsius, Justus H. 1909. "Das philologische Seminar, Proseminar, Institut." In University of Leipzig 1909b, IV/1, 1–27.

Locher, Johann J. 1773. *Speculum Academicum Viennense*. Vienna.

Locke, David. 1992. *Science as Writing*. New Haven: Yale University Press.

Lodge, David. 1995 [1984]. *Small World: An Academic Romance*. New York: Penguin.

Loen, Johann Michael von. 1742. *Der redliche Mann am Hofe*. Frankfurt a.M.

Loewe, Hans. 1917. *Die Entwicklung des Schulkampfs in Bayern bis zum vollständigen Sieg des Neuhumanismus*. Monumenta Germaniae paedagogica, Beiheft 2. Berlin: Wiedmann.

———. 1925. *Friedrich Thiersch. Ein Humanistenleben im Rahmen der Geistesgeschichte seiner Zeit*. Munich: Oldenbourg

Loggan, David. 1675. *Oxonia illustrata*. Oxford.

———. 1694. *Cantabrigia illustrata*. Cambridge.

Loose, Wilhelm, ed. 1880. "Briefe eines Leipziger Student [Paul Behaim] aus den Jahren 1572–1574." *Deutsche Schulprogramme 1880*, Nr. 480, Beigabe zum Jahresbericht der Realschule zu Meißen.

Lorey, Wilhelm. 1940. "Die Physik an der Univesität Gießen im 17. und 18. Jahrhundert." *Nachrichten der Gießener Hochschulgesellschaft* 14:14–39.

———. 1941. "Die Physik an der Universität Gießen im 19. Jahrhundert." *Nachrichten der Gießener Hochschulgesellschaft* 15:80–132.

Luca, Ignatz de. 1782. *Journal der Literatur und Statistik*. Vol. 1. Innsbruck.

Luscombe, D. E. 1969. *The School of Peter Abelard. The Influence of Abelard in the Early Scholastic Period*. Cambridge: Cambridge University Press.

Lutius, Horatius. 1582. *De privilegiis Scholarium*, pp. 257–434 in *Tractatus de privilegiis quator . . . jure consultorum*. Cologne.

Lynch, Michael and Steve Woolgar, eds. 1990 [1988]. *Representation in Scientific Practice*. Cambridge, MA: MIT Press.

Lyotard, Jean-François. 1979. *La condition postmoderne. Rapport sur le savoir*. Paris: Minuit.

———. 1988. *Le Postmoderne expliqué aux enfants*. Paris: Galilée.

Maack, Heinrich. 1956. *Grundlagen des studentischen Disziplinarrechts*. Beiträge zur Freiburger Wissenschafts- und Universitätsgeschichte, 10. Freiburg im Br.: Albert.

Macey, David. 1995 [1993]. *The Lives of Michel Foucault: A Biography*. New York: Vintage.

Mackensen, Wilhelm F. A. (appeared anonymously). 1791. *Letztes Wort über Göttingen und seine Lehrer*. Repr. Göttingen: Vandenhoeck & Ruprecht, 1987.

Macray, William, ed. 1890. *Annals of the Bodleian Library*. 2nd ed. Repr. in History of Libraries, Collection 1. Oxford: Clarendon.

Mahn, Jean-Berthold. 1951. *L'Ordre Cistercien et son gouvernement des origins au milieu du XIII$^e$ siècle*. 2nd ed. Paris: de Boccard.

Mallet, Charles E. 1924–27. *A History of the University of Oxford*. 3 vols. London: Methuen.

Mandonnet, Pierre F. 1938. *St. Dominique, l'idée, l'homme, et l'oeuvre*. Rev. ed. by M. H. Vicaire. 2 vols. Paris: Desclée de Brouwer.

Manheim, Ernst. 1979. *Aufklärung und öffentliche Meinung. Studien zur Soziologie der Öffentlichkeit im 18. Jahrhundert*. Edited by Norbert Schindler. Kultur und Gesellschaft. Neue historische Forschungen, 4. Stuttgart-Bad Cannstatt: frommann-holzboog.

Mann, Thomas. 1974 [1960]. *Gesammelte Werke in dreizehn Bänden*. 2nd ed. Fischer: Frankfurt.

Maravall, José. 1986 [1975]. *Culture of the Baroque: Analysis of a Historical Structure*. Translated by Terry Cochran. Minneapolis: University of Minnesota Press.

Marback, Richard. 1999 *Plato's Dream of Sophistry*. Columbia: University of South Carolina.

Marcus, Steven. 1985. "Freud and Dora: Story, History, Case History." In Bernheimer and Kahane 1985, 56–91.

Marino, Luigi. 1995. *Praeceptores Germaniae. Göttingen 1770–1820*. Göttingen: Vandenhoeck & Ruprecht.

Markus, Gyorgy. 1987. "Why Is There No Hermenutics of Natural Sciences? Some Preliminary Theses." *Science in Context* 1/1:5–51.

Marx, Karl. 1981 [1962; 1890; 1867]. *Das Kapital. Kritik der politschen Ökonomie*. 3 vols. 4th ed. In Marx and Engels 1956–, vol. 1/1–3.

Marx, Karl and Friedrich Engels. 1956–. *Karl Marx und Friedrich Engels Werke*. 36 vols. Berlin: Dietz.

———. 1966. *Studienausgabe*. 4 vols. Frankfurt a.M.: Fischer.

———. 1970–. *Gesamtausgabe (MEGA)*. Multiple volumes in progress. Berlin: Dietz.

Maschke, Erich and Jürgen Sydow, eds. 1977. *Stadt und Universität im Mittelalter und in der frühen Neuzeit*. Stadt in der Geschichte, 3. Sigmaringen: Thorbecke.

Matthaeus, Gottlob (*auct. & resp.*). 1705a. *Dissertatio historico-moralis de malis eruditorum uxoribis, (vulgo) von den bösen Weibern der Gelehrten [Sectio I]*, Gottfried Boettnerus (*praeses*). Leipzig.

———(*auct. & resp.*). 1705b. *Dissertatio historico-moralis de malis eruditorum uxoribis, (vulgo) von den bösen Weibern der Gelehrten [Sectio moralis]*, Gottfried Boettnerus (*praeses*). Leipzig.

Matthews, George. 1959. *News and Rumor in Renaissance Europe (The Fugger Newsletters)*. New York: Capricorn.

Mauss, Marcel. 1989 [1950]. *Sociologie et anthropologie*. 3rd ed. Paris: PUF.

Mayer, Andreas, ed. 1791–93. *Thesaurus novus juris ecclesiastici potissimum Germaniae*. 3 vols. Regensberg.

Mayer, Hermann. 1892–94. *Die Universität Freiburg in Baden in der ersten Hälften des 19. Jahrhundert*. 3 vols. Bonn.

———. 1926. *Die alten Freiburger Studentenbursen*, Zeitschrift der Gesellschaft für Beförderung der Geschichts-, Altertums-, und Volkskunde von Freiburg, dem Breisgau und den angrenzenden Landschaften, 3rd supp. vol. Freiburg im Br.

Mayer, Otto. 1924 [1896]. *Deutsches Verwaltungsrecht*. 2 vols. 3rd ed. Berlin: Duncker & Humblot.

McCarthy, John. 1995. "Reviewing Nation: The Review and the Concept of Nation." In Rowland and Fink 1995, 151–68.

McClellan, James E. 1985. *Science Reorganized: Scientific Societies in the Eighteenth Century*. New York: Columbia University Press.

McClelland, Charles E. 1980. *State, Society, and University in Germany 1700–1914*. Cambridge: Cambridge University Press.

———. 1988. "'To Live for Science': Ideals and Realities at the University of Berlin." In Bender 1988, 181–97.

McConica, James. 1986. "The Rise of the Undergraduate College." In McConica 1986, 1–68.

McConica, James, ed. 1986. *The Collegiate University* (vol. 3 in Aston 1984–). Oxford: Clarendon Press.

McKenzie, Donald F. 1986. *Bibliography and the Sociology of Texts. The Panizzi Lectures, 1985*. London: British Library

McKitterick, David. 1986. *Cambridge University Library. A History: The Eighteenth and Nineteenth Centuries*. Cambridge: Cambridge University Press.

McLaughlin, Terence P. 1935. *Le très ancien droit monastique de l'Occident*. Diss. Jur., Strasbourg/Poitiers.

McLuhan, Marshall. 1969 [1962]. *The Gutenberg Galaxy: The Making of Typographic Man*. New York: New American Library.

———. 1966 [1964]. *Understanding Media: The Extensions of Man*. 2nd ed. New York: New American Library.

McNeill, William. 1984 [1982]. *The Pursuit of Power: Technology, Armed Force and Society since A.D. 1000*. Chicago: University of Chicago Press.

Mecklenburg. 1848–59. *Gesetzsammlung für die Mecklenburg-Schwerin'schen Lande*. Edited by H. F. W. Raabe. 6 vols. Wismar et al.

Meinel, Christoph. 1988. *"Artibus Academicis Inserenda:* Chemistry's Place in Eighteenth and Early Nineteenth Century Universities." *History of Universities* 7:89–115.

Meiners, Christoph. 1775–76. *Vermischte philosphischen Schriften*. 3 vols. Leipzig.

———. 1802–6 *Geschichte der Entstehung und Entwicklung der hohen Schulen unsers Erdtheils*. 4 vols. Göttingen.

Meisner, Heinrich O. 1969. *Archivalienkunde vom 16. Jahrhundert bis 1918*. Göttingen: Vandenhoeck & Ruprecht.

Meister, Richard. 1958. *Geschichte des Doktorats der Philosophie an der Universität Wien*. Oesterreichische Akademie der Wissenschaften, Phil.-hist. Kl., Sitzungsberichte, 232/2. Vienna: Rohrer.

———. 1963. *Entwicklung und Reform der Österreichischen Studienwesens*. Österreichische Akademie der Wissenschaften, Phil.-hist. Kl. Sitzungsberichte, 239:1/1–2. Vienna: Boehlau.

Melanchthon, Philipp. 1843. "Oratio de gradibus in Theologia . . . in promotione trium Doctorum, anno MDXXXIII. die Iunii XVIII," pp. 227–31 in vol. 11 of *Philippi Melanthons Opera quae supersunt omnia (Corpus Reformatorum)*. Edited by C. G. Breitschneider. Halle.

Mencken, Johann B. 1715. *De charlataneria eruditorum*. Leipzig.

Mendus, Andreas. 1668. *De iure academico*. Leiden.

Menze, Clemens. 1966. *Wilhelm von Humboldt und Christian Gottlob Heyne*. Ratingen: Henn.

Merian, Matthäus. 1959–67 [1643–54]. *Topographia Germaniae*. 16 vols. Cassel/Basel.

Merton, Robert K. 1970 [1938]. *Science, Technology, and Social Change in Seventeenth-Century England*. New York: Harper.

Mettler, Werner. 1955. *Der junge Friedrich Schlegel und die griechische Literatur*. Züricher Beiträge zur deutschen Literatur und Geistesgeschichte, 11. Zurich.

Metzger, Johann David (appeared anonymously). 1804. *Aeußerungen über Kant, seinen Character und seine Meinungen*. Königsberg.

Meusel, Johann G. 1796–1834. *Das gelehrte Teutschland, oder Lexikon der jetzt lebenden teutscher Schriftsteller*, with G. C. Hamburger. 35 vols. Lemgo.

———. 1802–16. *Lexikon der vom Jahre 1750 bis 1800 verstorbenen teutscher Schriftsteller*. 15 vols. Repr. Hildesheim, 1968.

Meyer zu Ermgassen, H. 1977. "Tisch und Losament." In Heinemeyer 1977, 101–246.

Meyerhoff, Ecbert (*praeses*). 1670. *Doctores bullati*, Johann G. Simon (*resp*.). Jena.

Meÿfart, Johann M. 1636. *Christliche und aus trewen Herzen wolgemeinte auch demütige Erinnerung von der Erbawung und Fortsetzung der Academischen Disciplin auff den Evangelischen Hohen Schulen in Deutschland*. . . . Erfurt.

Mezger, Werner. 1981. *Hofnarren im Mittelalter. Vom tieferen Sinne eines seltsamen Amts*. Constance: Universitätsverlag.

Mezger, Werner et al. 1984. *Narren, Schellen und Marotten*. Kulturgeschichtliche Forschungen, 3. Remschied: Kierdorf.

Michaelis, Johann Daniel. 1768–76. *Raisonnement über die protestantischen Universitäten in Deutschland*. 4 vols. (vols. 1–3 appeared anonymously). Frankfurt a.M./ Leipzig.

Michalsky, Helga. 1978. *Bildungspolitik und Bildungsreform in Preussen*. Weinheim/ Basel: Beltz.

Michel, Willy. 1982. *Ästhetische Hermeneutik und frühromantishe Kritik. Friedrich Schlegels fragmentarische Entwürfe, Rezensionen, Charakteristiken und Kritiken (1795–1801)*. Göttingen: Vandenhoeck & Ruprecht.

Middendorp, Jacob. 1594. *Academiarum celebrium universari terrarum orbis* . . . . Cologne.

Milkau, Fritz and Georg Leyh, eds. 1952–61. *Handbuch der Bibliothekswissenschaft*. 3 vols. 2nd ed. Wiesbaden: Harrassowitz.

Miller, Edward. 1967. *Prince of Librarians: The Life and Times of Antonio Panizzi of the British Museum*. London: Deutsch.

Mitchell, W. J. T. 1986. *Iconology: Image, Text, Ideology*. Chicago: Chicago University Press.

Mitchell, W. J. T., ed. 1981. *On Narrative*. Chicago: University of Chicago Press.

Mittler, Elmar. 1971. *Die Universitätsbibliothek Freiburg i.Br. 1795–1823. Personal, Verwaltung, Übernahme der säkulierisierten Bibliotheken*. Beiträge zur Freiburger Wissenschafts- und Universitätsgeschichte, 35. Freiburg: Albert.

Mocek, Reinhard, ed. 1990. *Die Wissenschaftskultur der Aufklärung*. Halle: Martin-Luther- Universität Halle-Wittenberg.

Moeller, Bernd. 2001. "Adolf von Harnack—der Außenseiter als Zentralfigur." In Nowak and Oexle 2001, 9–22.

Monfasani, John and Ronald Musto, eds. 1991. *Renaissance Society and Culture: Essays in Honor of Eugene Rice, Jr*. New York: Italica.

Moorhouse, E. Hallam. 1909. *Samuel Pepys: Administrator, Observer, Gossip*. London: Chapman and Hall.

Moorman, John R. 1968. *A History of the Franciscan Order*. Oxford: Clarendon.

Morgan, Victor. 2004. *A History of the University of Cambridge, Vol. 2: 1546–1750* (in Brooke 1988–2004). Cambridge: Cambridge University Press.

Morreal, John. 1994. "Gossip and Humor." In Goodman and Ben-Ze'ev 1994, 56–64.

Morrell, J. B. 1997. *Science, Culture and Politics in Britain, 1750–1870*. Aldershot: Variorum.

Morrell Jack and Arnold Thackray. 1981. *Gentleman of Science: Early Years of the British Association for the Advancement of Science*. Oxford: Clarendon Press.

Mörsdorf, Klaus. 1964–67. *Lehrbuch des Kirchenrechts*. 3 vols. Vol. 1: 11th ed., vol. 2: 12th ed., vol. 3: 10th ed. Munich: Schoeningh.

Mühl, Werner A. 1961. *Die Aufklärung an der Universität Fulda*. . . . Quellen und Abhandlungen zur Geschichte der Abtei und der Diözese Fulda, 20. Fulda.

Müller, Johannes. 1883–1917. *Die Wissenschaften-Vereine und Gesellschaften im neunzehnten Jahrhundert*. 2 vols. in 3 pts. Repr.: Hildesheim: Olms, 1965.

Müller, Karl Otfried. 1843. *Archäologische Mittheilungen aus Griechenland*. . . . Edited by Adolf Schöll. Frankfurt a.M.

Müller, Petrus. 1715. *Tractatio juridica de gradu doctoris*. Jena.

Müller, Willibald. 1883. *Gerhard van Swieten. Biographischer Beitrag zur Geschichte der Aufklärung in Österrich*. Vienna.

Münster, Sebastian. 1598 [1592]. *Cosmographey; das ist/Beschreibung Aller Länder*. . . . Basel.

Murray, A. Victor. 1967. *Abelard and St. Bernard: A Study in Twelfth Century 'Modernism.'* Manchester: Manchester University Press.

Müsebeck, Ernst. 1918. *Das preussische Kultusministerium vor hundert Jahren*. Stuttgart/Berlin: Cotta.

Musserlus, Jacob. 1533. *De titulus et dignitatibus*. Leipzig.

Myers, Greg. 1988. "Every Picture Tells a Story." In Lynch and Woolgar 1988, 231–66.

Myres, J. N. L. 1958. "Oxford Libraries in the Seventeenth and Eighteenth Centuries." In Wormald and Wright 1958, 236–55.

Naudé, Gabriel. 1644. *Advis pour dresser une biblioththèque*. . . . 2nd ed. Paris.

———. 1661. *Instructions Concerning Erecting of a Library*. . . . Translated by J. Evelyn. London.

Neudegger, Max J. 1881. "Zur Geschichte der bayerischen Archiv [I]." *Archivalische Zeitschrift* 6:115–58.

———. 1882. "Zur Geschichte der bayerischen Archiv [II]." *Archivalische Zeitschrift* 7:57–119.

———. 1904. *Geschichte der bayerischen Archive. IIIa. Die organische Umgestaltung der drei Haupt-Archive in München seit 1799*. Munich: Ackermann.

Neumeister, Sebastian and Conrad Wiedemann, eds. 1987. *Res Publica Litteraria. Die Institutionen der Gelehrsamkeit in der frühen Neuzeit*. 2 vols. Wolfenbütteler Arbeiten zur Barockforschng, 14/1–2. Wiesbaden: Harrassowitz.

Newman, L. M. 1966. *Leibniz (1646–1716) and the German Library Scene*. Library Association Pamphlet No. 28. London: Library Association.

Neyffer, J. C. and L. Ditzinger. 1626. *Illustrissimi Wirtembergici ducalis novi collegii quod Tubingae* . . . . n.l.

Nicolai, Friedrich. 1783–96. *Beschreibung einer Reise durch Deutschland und die Schweiz im Jahre 1781*. 12 vols. Berlin.

Niebuhr, Hermann. 1983. *Zur Sozialgeschichte der Marburger Professoren, 1653–1806*. Quellen und Forschungen zur hessischen Geschichte, 44. Darmstadt: Hess. Hist. Kommission.

Nietzsche, Friedrich. 1986 [1974–84]. *Sämtliche Briefe*. Edited by Giorgio Colli and Mazzino Montinari. 8 vols. Frankfurt a.M.: dtv.

———. 1999 [1988/1967–77]. *Sämtliche Werke*. Edited by Giorgio Colli and Mazzino Montinari. 15 vols. 2nd ed. Frankfurt a.M.: dtv.

Nockles, P. B. 1991. "An Academic Counter-Revolution: Newman and Tractarian Oxford's Idea of a University." *History of Universities* 11:137–97.

Noel-Tod, Alex. 1980. *The Bodleian Library in the Eighteenth Century with Reference to Oxford College Libraries and the Radcliffe Library.* Aberystwyth: College of Librarianship Wales.

Nowak, Kurt and Otto Gerhard Oexle, eds. 2001. *Adolf von Harnack. Theologe, Historiker, Wissenschaftspolitiker.* Veröffentlichungen des Max-Planck-Instituts für Geschichte, 161. Göttingen: Vandenhoeck & Ruprecht.

Oates, J. C. T. 1958. "The Libraries of Cambridge, 1570–1700." In Wormald and Wright 1958, 213–35.

———. 1986. *Cambridge University Library. A History: From the Beginnings to the Copyright Act of Queen Anne.* Cambridge: Cambridge University Press.

Oegg, Josef A. 1804. *Ideen einer Theorie der Archivwissenschaft.* Gotha.

Oelrichs, Johann. 1758. *De duarum ac trium et quidem superiorum atque omnium Facultatum Doctoribus commentatio.* Rostock.

Ohnsorge, Werner. 1962. *Zweihundert Jahre Geschichte der Königlichen Bibliothek zu Hannover (1665–1866).* Veröffentlichungen der Niedersächsischen Archivverwaltung, 14. Vandenhoeck & Ruprecht: Göttingen.

Olesko, Kathryn. 1988. "Commentary: On Institutes, Investigations, and Scientific Training." In Coleman and Holmes 1988, 295–332.

———. 1991. *Physics as a Calling: Discipline and Practice in the Königsberg Seminar for Physics.* Ithaca: Cornell University Press.

Olesko, Kathryn, ed. 1989. *Science in Germany: The Intersection of Institutional and Intellectual Issue. Osiris.* 2nd ser., 5. Canton, MA: History of Science Society.

Ong, Walter. 1959. "Latin as a Renaissance Puberty Right." *Studies in Philology* 56:103–24.

———. 1983 [1958]. *Ramus, Method, and the Decay of Dialogue: From the Art of Discourse to the Art of Reason.* Cambridge: Cambridge University Press.

———. 2003 [1982]. *Orality and Literacy: The Technologicizing of the Word.* London: Routledge.

Oppermann, Heinrich. 1844. *Die Göttinger gelehrten Anzeigen.* . . . Hanover: Kius.

Ornstein, Martha. 1928. *The Role of Scientific Societies in the 17th Century.* Chicago: University of Chicago Press.

Outram, Dorinda. 1980. "Politics and Vocation: French Science, 1793–1830." *British Journal for the History of Science* 13:27–43.

———. 1983. "The Ordeal of Vocation: The Paris Academy of Sciences and the Terror, 1793–95." *History of Science* 21:251–73.

———. 1988. "Military Empire, Political Collaboration, the Cultural Consensus: The *Université Impériale* Reappraised: The Case of the University of Turin." *History of Universities* 7:287–303.

Overfield, James H. 1984. *Humanism and Scholasticism in Late Medieval Germany.* Princeton: Princeton University Press.

Ozment, Steven, ed. and trans. 1990. *Three Behaim Boys: Growing Up in Early Modern Germany.* New Haven: Yale University Press.

Paré, Gérard M. and A. Brunet. and P. Tremblay. 1933. *La renaissance du XII$^e$ siècle: Les écoles et l'enseignement.* Publications de l'institut d'études médiévales d'Ottawa, 3. Paris/Ottawa: Inst. d'études médiévales.

Parkes, M. B. 1992. "The Provision of Books." In Catto and Evans 1992, 407–83.

Parkes, M. B. and Andrew G. Watson, eds. 1978. *Medieval Scribes, Manuscripts & Libraries: Essays Presented to N.R. Ker.* London: Scholar Press.

Parsons, Talcott. 1949 [1937]. *The Structure of Social Action: A Study in Social Theory with Special Reference to a Group of Recent European Writers.* Glencoe: Free Press.

Paschius, Johann. 1701 [1686]. *Gynaeceum doctum; sive dissertatio historico-literaria, vom belehrten Frauenzimmer.* Wittenberg.

Passow, Franz. 1839. *Leben und Briefe.* Edited by A. Wachler. Breslau.

Paul, Harry. 1991. "The Role of German Idols in the Rise of the French Science Empire." In Schubring 1991, 184–97.

Paulsen, Friedrich. 1896–97. *Geschichte des gelehrten Unterrichts.* 2 vols. 2nd ed. Leipzig: Veit.

———. 1919–21. *Geschichte des gelehrten Unterrichts.* 2 vols. 3rd ed. Leipzig: Veit.

Pauntel, Eugen. 1965. *Die Staatsbibliothek zu Berlin . . ., 1661–1871.* Berlin: de Gruyter.

Peck, Harry T., ed. 1897. *Harper's Dictionary of Classical Literature and Antiquities.* New York: Harper.

Pfannensteil, Max, ed. 1958. *Kleines Quellenbuch zur Geschichte der Gesellschaft Naturforscher und Ärzte. Gedächtnisschrift für die hunderste Tagung der Gesellschaft.* Berlin: Springer.

Pfetsch, Frank. 1974. *Zur Entwicklung der Wissenschaftspolitik in Deutschland 1750–1915.* Berlin: Duncker & Humblot.

Philip, Ian. 1983. *The Bodleian Library in the Seventeenth and Eighteenth Centuries.* The Lyell Lectures, Oxford, 1980–1981. Oxford: Clarendon Press.

———. 1986. "Libraries and the University Press." In Sutherland and Mitchell 1986, 725–55.

———. 1997. "The Bodleian Library." In Brock and Curthoys 1997, 585–97.

Philip, Ian and Paul Morgan. 1997. "Libraries, Books and Printing." In Tyacke 1997, 659–85.

Philoparchus, Germanus [Ch. H. Schweser]. 1701–52. *Der Kluge Beamte. . . .* 7 vols. Nuremberg.

Plachta, Bodo. 1994. *Damnatur-Toleratur-Admittitur. Studien und Dokumente zur literarischen Zensur im 18. Jahrhundert.* Studien und Texte zur Sozialgeschichte der Literatur, 43. Tübingen: Niemeyer.

Plöchl, Willibald M. 1953–60 [1953–59]. *Geschichte des Kirchenrechts.* 5 vols. 2nd ed. of vols 1–2: 1960. Vienna: Herhold.

Pollard, Graham. 1978. "The Pecia System in the Medieval Libraries." In Parkes and Watson 1978, 145–61.

Pölnitz, Götz von, ed. 1942. *Denkmale und Dokumente zur Geschichte der Ludwig-Maximilians-Universität Ingolstadt-Landshut- München.* Munich: Callway.

Pommerania. 1765–1802. *Sammlung gemeiner und besonderer Pommerscher und Rügischer Landes-Urkunden.* Edited by Johann C. Dähnert. 8 vols. in 2 ser. (ser.1, vols. 1–4 and ser. 2, vols. 1–4). Stralsund.

Porter, Roy. 1996. "The Scientific Revolution and the Universities." In Ridder-Symoens 1996, 531–62.

Porter, Roy, ed. 2003. *The Cambridge History of Science: Volume 4, Eighteenth-Century Science.* Cambridge: Cambridge Univerity Press.

Porter, Roy and Mikulàs Teich, eds. 1992. *The Scientific Revolution in National Context.* Cambridge: Cambridge University Press.

Post, Robert. 1994. "The Legal Regulation of Gossip: Backyard Chatter and the Mass Media." In Goodman and Ben-Ze'ev 1994, 65–71.

Prantl, Karl von. 1872. *Geschichte der Ludwigs-Maximilians-Universität in Ingolstadt, Landshut, München.* 2 vols. Munich.

Probst, Jacob. 1869. *Geschichte der Universität in Innsbruck . . . 1860.* Innsbruck.

Propp, V. 1968 [1927]. *Morphology of the Folktale.* Translated by L. Scott. Rev. by A. Wagner. 2nd ed. Austin: University of Texas Press.

Prutz, Hans. 1894. *Die Königliche Albertus-Universität zu Königsberg i. Pr. im neunzehnten Jahrhundert.* Königsberg.

Prutz, R. E. 1845. *Geschichte des deutschen Journalismus.* Hanover.

Puschner, Johann G. n.d. [ca. 1710–20]. *Amoenitates Altdorfinae.* Nuremberg.

———(appeared by "Dendrono"). 1725a. *Natürliche Abschilderung des academischen Lebens.* Nuremberg. Repr. in Altnürnberger Landschaft Mitteilungen, Sonderheft 11. Nuremberg, 1962.

———. 1725b (circa). *Abschilderung des academischen Lebens.* Nuremberg.

Pütter, Johann. 1765. *Anleitung zur juristischen Praxi.* 3 pts. 3rd ed. Göttingen.

———. 1770. *Institutiones juris publici germanici.* Göttingen.

Pütter, Johann Stephan and F. Saalfeld and G. H. Oesterle. 1765–1838. *Versuch einer academischen Gelehrten-Geschichte der Georg-Augustus Universität zu Göttingen.* 4 vols. Göttingen/Hanover.

Raabe, Paul. 1988. "Gelehrtenbibliotheken in der Zeitalter der Aufklärung." In Arnold and Vodosek 1988, 103–22.

Raabe, Paul, ed. 1977. *Öffentliche und Private Bibliotheken im 17. und 18. Jahrhundert. Raritätenkammern, Forschungsinstrumente oder Bildungsstätten?* Wolfenbüttler Forschungen, 2. Bremen/Wolfenbüttel: Jacobi.

Rabiosus, Anselm (a.k.a. Andreas G. F. Rebmann). 1796. *Wanderungen und Kreuzzüge durch einen Teil Deutschlands.* 2 vols. 2nd ed. Altona.

Raeff, Marc. 1983. *The Well-Ordered Police State: Social and Institutional Change through Law in the Germanies and Russia, 1600–1800.* New Haven: Yale University Press.

Rashdall, Hasting. 1936 [1895]. *The Universities in Europe in the Middle Ages.* Rev. ed. by F. M. Powicke and A. B. Emden. 3 vols. Oxford: Oxford University Press.

Ratjan, Henning. 1870. *Geschichte der Universität Kiel.* Kiel.

Ray, William. 1990. *Story and History: Narrative Authority and Social Identity in the Eighteenth-Century French and English Novel.* Cambridge, MA: Blackwell.

Rebuffus, Petrus. 1585 [1540]. *Privilegia Universitatum, Collegiorum, Bibliopolarum. . . .* Frankfurt a.M.

Renn, Jürgen and Giuseppe Castagnetti and Simone Riegger. 2001. "Adolf von Harnack und Max Planck." In Nowak and Oexle 2001, 127–55.

Rethwisch, Conrad. 1886. *Der Staatsminister Freiherr von Zedlitz und Preussens höherens Schulwesen in Zeitalter Friedrichs des Grossens.* 2nd ed. Strasbourg.

Reuter, Hans. 1966. "Das Gebäude der Herzog-August-Bibliothek zu Wolfenbüttel und ihr Oberbibliothekar Gottfried Wilhelm Leibniz." In Totek and Haase 1966, 349–60.

Ribbeck, Otto. 1879–81. *Friedrich Wilhelm Ritschl.* 2 vols. Leipzig.

Richarz, Monika. 1974. *Der Eintritt der Juden in die Akademischen Berufe.* Tübingen: Mohr.

Richter, Gottfried. 1936. *Das anatomische Theater.* Abhandlungen zur Geschichte der Medizin und der Naturwissenschaften, 16. Berlin: Ebering.

Ridder-Symoens, Hilde de. 1996. "Management of Resources." In Ridder-Symoens, ed. 1996, 155–209.

Ridder-Symoens, Hilde de, ed. 1992. *Universities in the Middle Ages.* Cambridge: Cambridge University Press.

————. 1996. *A History of the University in Europe.* Vol. 2, *Universities in Early Modern Europe.* Cambridge: Cambridge University Press.

Rinck, Christoph F. 1897. *Studienreise 1783/84, unternommen im Auftrage des Markgrafen Karl Friedrich von Baden.* Edited by Moritz Geyer. Altenburg.

Ringer, Fritz. 1969. *The Decline of the German Mandarins: The German Academic Community, 1890–1933.* Cambridge, MA: Harvard University Press.

Ritschl, Friedrich. 1829. *Schedae criticae.* . . . Diss. Phil., Halle.

Ritter, Gerhard. 1922. *Via antiqua und via moderna auf den deutschen Universitäten des XV. Jahrhunderts.* Sitzungsberichte der Heidelberger Akademie der Wissenschaften, Phil.-hist. Kl., 1922:7. Heidelberg: Winters.

Roche, Daniel. 1978. *Le siècle des lumières en province. Académies et académiciens provinciaux, 1680–1789.* 2 vols. Civilisations et Sociétes 62. Paris: École des Hautes Études en Sciences Sociales.

Rodenberg, Carl and Volquart Pauls. 1955. *Die Anfänge der Christian-Albrechts Universität Kiel.* Quellen und Forschungen zur Geschichte Schleswig-Holsteins, 31. Neumünster: Wachholtz.

Roethe, Gustav. 1901. "Göttingische Zeitungen von gelehrten Sachen." In University of Göttingen 1901, 567–688.

Rohr, Julius B. von. 1730. *Einleitung zur Ceremonial-Wissenschaft der Privat-Person.* Berlin.

Roloff, Heinrich. 1961. "Die Katalogisierung." In Milkau and Leyh 1952–61, 1:242–366.

Roman Catholic Church. 1879. *Corpus iuris canonici.* Edited by A. L. Richter and A. Friedberg. 2 vols. 2nd ed. Leipzig.

————. 1901–27 [1758–98]. *Sacrorum conciliorum nova et amplissima collectio.* Edited by J. D. Mansi. 31 vols. Repr. as 53 vols. in 58 pts. Paris.

————. 1914. *The Rule, Statutes and Customs of the Hospitallers, 1099–1310.* Translated and comm. by Edwin J. King. London: AMS Press.

————. 1935–65. *Dictionnaire de droit canonique.* Edited by R. Naz et al. 7 vols. Paris.

————. 1973. *Conciliorum Oecumenicorum decreta.* Edited by J. Albergio et al. 3rd ed. Bologna: Inst. per le Scienze Religiose.

Roman Empire. 1872–95. *Corpus iuris civilis.* Edited by P. Krueger, T. Mommsen, R. Schoell, and W. Kroll. Berlin.

Rönne, Ludwig Moritz Peter von. 1840–41. *Das Polizeiwesen des preussischen Staates.* 2 vols. Breslau.

Rosenberg, Hans. 1958. *Bureaucracy, Aristocracy and Autocracy: The Prussian Experience 1660–1815.* Cambridge. MA: Harvard University Press.

Rosenberg, Werner. 1930/31. *Das Recht der akademischen Grade in Preußen.* Diss. Rechts- u. Staatswissenschaft, Breslau.

Rosnow, Ralph and Gary Fine. 1976. *Rumor and Gossip: The Social Psychology of Hearsay.* New York: Elsevier.

Ross, Ludwig. 1834–45. *Inscriptiones Graecae ineditae.* 3 vols. Nauplia/Athens/Berlin.

————. 1855–61. *Archäologische Aufsätze.* 2 vols. Leipzig.

————. 1863. *Erinnerungen und Mittheilungen aus Griechenland.* Berlin.

Rössler, Emil, ed. 1855. *Die Gründung der Universität Göttingen.* 2 pts. Göttingen.

Rössler, Helmuth and Günther Franz, eds. 1970. *Universität und Gelehrtenstand 1400–1800.* Deutsche Führungsschichten in der Neuzeit, 4. Limburg/Lahn: Starcke.

Rothblatt, Sheldon. 1974. "The Student Sub-culture and the Examination System in Early Nineteenth Century Oxbridge." In Stone 1974, 1:247–304.

————. 1981 [1968]. *Revolution of the Dons.* Cambridge: Cambridge University Press.

————. 1988. "London: A Metropolitan University?" In Bender 1988, 119–49.

Rousseau, G. S. and Roy Porter, eds. 1990. *The Ferment of Knowledge: Studies in the Historiography of Eighteenth-Century Sciences.* Cambridge: Cambridge University Press.

Rowland, Herbert. 1995. "The Physiognomist Physiognomized: Matthias Claudius's Review of Lavater's *Physiognomische Fragmente.*" In Rowland and Fink 1995, 17–29.

Rowland, Herbert and Karl J. Fink, eds. 1995. *The Eighteenth Century German Book Review.* Beiträge zur neueren Literaturgeschichte, 3rd ser., 135. Heidelberg: Winter.

Roy, Ian and Dietrich Reinhart. 1997. "Oxford and the Civil Wars." In Tyacke 1997, 687–731.

Rubenow, Heinrich. 1867. "Oratio pro datione insigniorum (sic) . . ., anno 1460 recitata (Greifswald)." Edited by T. Pyl. *Pommersche Geschichtsdenkmäler* 2:129–50.

Rückbrod, Konrad. 1977. *Universität und Kollegium. Baugeschichte und Bautyp.* Darmstadt: Wiss. Buchgesellschaft.

Rufus, Mutianus. 1885. *Der Briefwechsel des Mutianus Rufus.* Edited by Carl Krause. Zeitschrift des Vereins für hessische Geschichte und Landeskunde, n.s. 9, Supplement. Cassel.

Rupke, Nicolaas, ed. 2002. *Göttingen and the Development of the Natural Sciences.* Göttingen: Wallenstein.

Russack, Hans H. 1942. *Deutsche bauen in Athen.* Berlin: Limpert.

Russell, Colin. 1983. *Science and Social Change 1700–1900.* London: MacMillian.

Rybczynski, Wittold. 1986. *Home: The Short History of an Idea.* New York: Penguin.

Sabean, David W. 1984. *Power in the Blood: Popular Culture and Village Discourse in Early Modern Germany.* Cambridge: Cambridge University Press.

————. 1990. *Property, Production and Family in Neckarhausen, 1700–1870.* Cambridge: Cambridge University Press.

————. 1996. "Soziale Distanzierungen. Ritualisierte Gestik in deutscher bürokratischer Prosa der Frühen Neuzeit." *Historische Anthropologie* 4/2:216–33.

————. 2001. "Peasant Voices and Bureaucratic Texts: Narrative Structure in Early Modern German Protocols." In Becker and Clark 2001, 67–94.

Sackur, Ernst. 1892–94. *Die Cluniacenser in ihrer kirchlichen und allgemeingeschichtlichen Wirksamkeit bis zur Mitte des elften Jahrhunderts.* 2 vols. Halle.

Sagittarius, Thomas. 1615. *Oratio de privilegiis Magistrorum.* Jena.

Salzmann, Christian G. 1783–88. *Carl von Carlsberg, oder über das menschliche Elend.* 6 vols. Leipzig.

Samurin, E. I. 1977 [1964–67]. *Geschichte der bibliothekorisch-bibliographischen Klassification.* Translated by Willi Hoepp. 2 vols. in 1. Munich: Verlag Dokumentation.

Sauerbrei, Johann (*praeses*). 1671. *Diatribe academica de foeminarum eruditione posteriorem,* Jacobus Smalcius (*resp.*). Leipzig.

Saxony. 1724. *Codex Augusteus.* 2 vols. Leipzig.

————. 1772. *Codex Augusteus . . . Fortgesetzt.* Leipzig.

————. 1805-6. *Codex Augusteus . . . Zweite Fortsetzung.* 3 pts. Leipzig.

————. 1824. *Codex Augusteus . . . Dritte Fortsetzung.* Dresden.

Schaefer, Karl Heinrich. 1965 [1903]. *Pfarrkirche und Stift im Deutschen Mittelalter.* Kirchenrechtliche Abhandlungen, 3. Amsterdam.

Schaff, Josef. 1912. *Geschichte der Physik an der Universität Ingolstadt.* Diss. Phil., Erlangen.

Schaffer, Simon. 1980. "Natural Philosophy." In Rousseau and Porter 1980, 55–91.

————. 1983. "Natural Philosophy and Public Spectacle in the Eighteenth Century." *History of Science* 21:1–43.

————. 1988. "Astronomers Mark Time: Discipline and the Personal Equation." *Science in Context* 2/1:115–45.

————. 1990. "Genius in Romantic Natural Philosophy." In Cunningham and Jardine 1990, 82–98.

————. 1992. "Self Evidence." *Critical Inquiry* 18:327–62.

————. 1993. "The Consuming Flame: Electrical Showmen and Tory Mystics in the World of Goods." In Brewer and Porter 1993, 489–526.

————. 1999. "Enlightened Automata." In Clark, Golinski, and Schaffer 1999, 126–65.

Schalscheleth, Samuel P. 1795 *Historisch-geographische Beschreibung Wittenbergs.* Frankfurt a.M./Wittenberg.

Schauf, Karl. 1904. *Studien zur Geschichte der Wiener Universität im Mittelalter.* Vienna.

Scheel, Günter. 1973. "Leibniz as Direktor der Bibliotheca Augusta in Wolfenbüttel." In *Akten des II. Internationalen Leibniz-Kongresses, Hannover, 17.-22. Juli 1972.* Studia Leibnitiana Supplementa, XII, I, 71–83.

Scheicher, Elisabeth. 1979. *Die Kunst- und Wunderkammern der Habsburger.* Vienna: Molden.

————. 1985. "The Collection of Ferdinand II at Schloss Ambrao. . . ." In Impey and MacGregor 1985, 29–38.

Schein, Sylvia. 1994. "Used and Abused: Gossip in Medieval Society." In Goodman and Ben-Ze'ev 1994, 139–53.

Schelsky, Helmut. 1971 [1963; 1960]. *Einsamkeit und Freiheit. Idee und Gestalt der deutschen Universität und ihrer Reform.* 2nd ed. Düsseldorf: Bertelsmann-Universitäts-Verlag.

Schiebinger, Londa. 1989. *The Mind Has No Sex? Women in the Origins of Modern Science.* Cambridge, MA: Harvard University Press.

————. 1993. *Nature's Body: Gender and the Making of Modern Science.* Boston: Beacon.

Schieffer, Rudolf. 1976. *Die Enstehung von Domkapiteln in Deutschland.* Bonner Historische Forschungen, 43. Bonn.

Schiffler, Horst and Rolf Winkeler, eds. 1985. *Tausend Jahre Schule. Eine Kulturgeschichte des Lernens in Bildern.* Stuttgart/Zurich: Belser.

Schindling, Anton. 1977. "Die reichstädtische Hochschule in Straßburg 1538–1621." In Maschke and Sydow 1977, 71–83.

Schipperges, Heinrich. 1976. *Weltbild und Wissenschaft. Eröffnungsreden zu den Naturforscherversammlungen 1822 bis 1972.* Schriftenreihe zur Geschichte der Versammlung deutscher Naturforscher und Ärtze, Dokumentation und Analyse, 3. Hildesheim: Gerstenberg.

Schleiermacher, Friedrich D. 1808. "Gelegentliche Gedanken über Universitäten in Deutschland." In Weischedel 1950, 106–92.

————. 1959. *Hermeneutik. Nach den Handschriften.* Edited by Heinze Kimmerle. Heidelberg: Winter.

Schleswig-Holstein. 1832. *Systematische Sammlung der für die Herzogthümer Schleswig und Holstein erlassenen . . . Verordnungen und Verfügungen, Bd. IV.* Kiel.

Schlosser, Julius von. 1908. *Die Kunst- und Wunderkammern der Spätrenaissance.* Monographien des Kunstgewerbes, n.s. 9. Leipzig: Seemann.

Schluchter, Wolfgang. 1979. *Die Entwicklung des okzidentischen Rationalismus. Eine Analyse Max Webers Gesellschaftsgeschichte.* Tübingen: Mohr.

Schmack, Wilhelm. 1975 [1914]. *Ein Jahrhundert Berliner philologischer Dissertationen (1810–1910)*. Hildesheim: Olms.

Schmid, Achatius. 1772. *Zuverläßiger Unterricht von der Verfassung der Herzoglich Sächsischen Gesamtakademie zu Jena*. Jena.

Schmid, Christian (*praeses*). 1734. *De Fanaticis academiarum hostibus*, Godofred Bauer (*resp.*). Leipzig.

Schmid, Karl Adolf, ed. 1859–78. *Enzyklopädie des gesamten Erziehungs- und Unterrichtswesens*. 11 vols. Gotha.

Schmidt, Hermann J. 1969. *Nietzsche und Sokrates. Philosophische Untersuchungen zu Nietzsches Sokratesbild*. Meisehnheim a. Glan: Hain.

Schmidt, Oswald G. 1867. *Petrus Mosellanus. Ein Beitrag zur Geschichte des Humanismus in Sachsen*. Leipzig.

Schmidt-Schönbeck, Charlotte. 1965. *300 Jahre Physik und Astronomie an der Kieler Universität*. Kiel: Hirt.

Smith, Crosby and M. Norton Wise. 1989. *Energy and Empire: A Biographical Study of Lord Kelvin*. Cambridge: Cambridge University Press.

Schmitz, Rudolf et al. 1978. *Die Naturwissenschaften an der Philipps-Universität Marburg, 1527–1977*. Marburg: Elwert.

Schneider, Eugen. 1891. "Zur Geschichte des württembergischen Staatsarchiv." *Archivalische Zeitschrift*, n.s. 2:54–77.

Schneider, Phillipp. 1885. *Die Bischöflichen Domkapitel, ihre Entwicklung und rechtliche Stellung im Organismus der Kirche*. Mainz.

Schneider, Ute. 1995. *Friedrich Nicolais Allgemeine Deutsche Bibliothek als Integrationsmedium der Gelehrtenrepublik*. Wiesbaden: Harrassowitz.

Schnurrer, Christian F. 1798. *Erläuterungen der Württembergischen Kirchen-Reformation und Gelehrten-Geschichte*. Tübingen.

Schoeman, Ferdinand. 1994. "Gossip and Privacy." In Goodman and Ben-Ze'ev 1994, 72–82.

Schöler, Walter. 1970. *Geschichte des naturwissenschaftlichen Unterrichts im 17. bis 19. Jahrhundert*. Berlin: de Gruyter.

Scholes, Robert. 1974. *Structualism in Literature: An Introduction*. New Haven: Yale University Press.

Scholes, Robert and Robert Kellogg. 1966. *The Nature of Narrative*. New York: Oxford University Press.

Schöne, Albrecht, ed. 1976. *Stadt-Schule-Universität-Buchwesen und die deutsche Literatur im 17. Jahrhundert*. Barock-Symposion, 1974. Munich: Beck.

Schönert, Jörg, ed. 1991. *Erzählte Kriminalität. Zur Typologie und Funktion von narrativen Darstellungen in Strafrechtspflege, Publizistik und Literatur zwischen 1770 und 1920*. Tübingen: Niemeyer.

Schönfuß, Walther. 1914. *Des erste Jahrhundert der Allgemeinen Literatur-Zeitung*. Diss. Phil., Leipzig.

Schormann, Gerhard. 1982. *Academia Ernestina. Die schaumburgische Universität zu Rinteln an der Weser (1610/21–1810)*. Academia Marburgensis. Beiträge zur Geschichte der Philipps-Universität Marburg, 4. Marburg: Elwert.

Schorske, Carl. 1988. "Science as Vocation in Burckhardt's Basel." In Bender 1988, 198–209.

Schrader, Wilhelm. 1894. *Geschichte der Friedrich-Universität zu Halle*. 2 vols. Berlin.

Schreiber, Heinrich. 1857–60. *Geschichte der Stadt und Universität Freiburg im Breisgau*. 2 vols. Freiburg im Br.

Schröder, Konrad. 1964. *Vorläufiges Verzeichnis der in Bibliotheken und Archiven vorhandenen Vorlesungsverzeichnisse deutschsprachiger Universitäten aus der Zeit vor 1945.* Saarbrücken: Anglistisches Institut der Universität des Saarlandes.

Schroeder, Matthaeus G. (*praeses*). 1717a. *Dissertatio historico-moralis de misanthropia eruditorum, von mörosen Gelehrten,* Adamus F. Traeiner (*resp.*). Leipzig.

————. 1717b. *Dissertatio historico-moralis de misogynia eruditorum, von übelgesinnten Gelehrten gegen das weibliche Geschlecht,* Gottlieb S. Holtzmüller (*resp.*). Leipzig.

————. 1717c. *Dissertatio historico-moralis de misocosmia eruditorum, vulgo von schmutzigen Gelehrten,* Ehrenfried Ebelt (*resp.*). Leipzig.

Schroll, Sister Mary Alfred. 1941. *Benedictine Monasticism as Reflected in the Warnefrid Hildemar Commentaries on the Rule.* New York: Columbia University Press.

Schubart, Georg. 1678. *De Comitibus Palatini Caesaris exercitatio historica.* In *De palatio Lateranensi . . . commentatio primam edita,* pp. 85–366. Edited by T. Reinesius. Jena.

Schubring, Gert. 1989. "The Rise and Decline of the Bonn Natural Sciences Seminar." In Olesko 1989, 57–93.

————. 1991. "Spezialschulmodell versus Universitätsmodell: Die Institutionalisierung von Forschung." In Schubring, ed. 1991, 276–326.

Schubring, Gert, ed. 1991. *'Einsamkeit und Freiheit' neu Besichtigt. Universitätsreformen und Diziplinenbildung in Preussen als Modell für Wissenschaftspolitik im Europa des 19. Jahrhunderts.* Boethius, 24. Stuttgart: Steiner.

Schulte-Albert, Hans. 1971. "Gottfried Wilhelm Leibniz and Literary Classification." *Journal of Library History* 6:133–52

Schultz, Uwe. 1965. *Immanuel Kant.* Hamburg: Rowohlt.

Schulze, Johann D. 1810 [1802]. *Abriss einer Geschichte der Leipziger Universität.* Leipzig.

Schulze, Johann. 1827. Review of Friderich Thiersch's *Über gelehrte Schulen. Jahrbücher für wissenschaftliche Kritik* 1:86–107.

Schulze, O. F. A. 1927. "Zur Geschichte des physikalischen Instituts." In Hermelink and Kaehler 1927, 756–63.

Schwartz, Paul. 1910–11. *Die Gelehrtenschulen Preussens unter dem Oberschulkollegium.* Monumenta Germaniae paedagogica, 46, 48, 50. Berlin: Weidmann.

————. 1925. *Die erste Kulturkampf in Preussen um Kirche und Schule (1788–1798).* Monumenta Germaniae pedagogica, 58. Berlin: Weidmann.

Schwedt, Georg, ed. 1983. *Zur Geschichte der Göttinger Universitätsbibliothek. Zeitgenössische Berichte aus drei Jahrhunderten.* Göttingen: Verlag Goettinger Tageblatt.

Schwimmer, Johann M. 1672. *Tractatus politicus de academicis omnium facultatem professoribus academia et studiosus.* Jena.

Schwinges, Rainer. 1986. *Deutsche Universitätsbesucher im 14. und 15. Jahrhundert.* Veröffentlichungen des Instituts für Europäische Geschichte Mainz: Abteilung Universalgeschichte, 123. Stuttgart: Steiner.

Searby, Peter. 1997. *A History of the University of Cambridge, Vol. 3: 1750–1870* (in Brooke 1988–2004). Cambridge: Cambridge University Press.

Seckendorff, Veit L. von. 1678 [1656]. *Teutscher Fürsten-Staat.* Frankfurt a.M.

Sehling, Emil. 1893. *Daniel von Superville. Das Kanzleramt an der Universität Erlangen.* Leipzig.

Seidel, Werner. 1953. *Baugeschichte der Niedersächsischen Staats- und Universitätsbibliothek in Göttingen.* Hainbergschriften, 11. Göttingen: Haentzschel.

Seidemann, Karl. 1843. *Die Leipziger Disputation im Jahre 1519. . . .* Dresden.

Seifert, Arno. 1971. *Statuten- und Verfassungsgeschichte der Universität Ingolstadt (1472–*

*1586)*. Ludovicio Maximilianea, Universität Ingolstadt-Landshut-München, Forschungen, 1. Berlin: Duncker & Humblot.

———. 1972. "Das Georgianum (1494–1600)." *Ludovicio Maximilianea. Universität Ingolstadt-Landshut-München. Forschungen* 4:147–206. Berlin: Duncker & Humblot.

Selle, Götz von. 1944. *Geschichte der Albertus-Universität zu Königsberg in Preussen.* Königsberg: Kanter.

———. 1953. *Universität Göttingen. Wesen und Geschichte.* Göttingen: Vandenhoeck & Ruprecht.

Seuffert, Johannes M. 1793. *Von dem Verhältnisse des Staats und der Diener des Staats gegeneinander im rechtlichen und politischen Verstande.* Würzburg.

Seybolt, R. F., ed. and trans. 1921. *The Manuale Scholarium.* Translation of Anon 1476. Cambridge, MA: Harvard University Press.

Shapin, Steven. 1974. "The Audience for Science in Eighteenth Century Edinburgh." *History of Science* 12:95–121.

———. 1994. *A Social History of Truth: Civility and Science in Seventeenth-Century England.* Chicago: University of Chicago Press.

Shapin, Steven and Simon Schaffer. 1989 [1985]. *Leviathan and the Air-Pump: Hobbes, Boyle, and the Experimental Life.* Princeton: Princeton University Press.

Shapiro, Barbara. 1983. *Probability and Certainty in Seventeenth-Century England: A Study of the Relationships between Natural Science, Religion, History, Law, and Literature.* Princeton: Princeton University Press.

Sehling, Emil. 1893. *Daniel von Superville. Das Kanzleramt an der Universität Erlangen.* Leipzig.

Shils, Edward. 1988. "The University, the City, the World: Chicago and the University of Chicago." In Bender 1988, 210–30.

Siefert, Helmut. 1967. *Das naturwissenschaftliche und medizinische Vereinswesen im deutschen Sprachgebiet (1750–1850).* Inaugural Dissertation, Marburg.

Simon, Joan. 1966. *Education and Society in Tudor England.* Cambridge: Cambridge University Press.

Simpson, Renate. 1983. *How the Ph.D. Came to Britain.* Research into Higher Education Monographs, 54. Guilford, Surrey: Society for Research into Higher Education.

Sinemus, Volker. 1976. "Stilordnung, Kleiderordnung, Gesellschaftsordnung im 17. Jahrhundert." In Schöne 1976, 22–43.

Slee, Peter. 1988. "The Oxford Idea of a Liberal Education 1800–1860: The Invention of Tradition and the Manufacture of Practice." *History of Universities* 7:61–87.

Small, Albion. 1909. *The Cameralists, the Pioneers of German Social Polity.* Chicago: University of Chicago Press.

Smith, Adam. 1976 [1776]. *An Inquiry into the Nature and Causes of the Wealth of Nations.* Edited by E. Cannan. 2 vols. Chicago: University of Chicago Press.

Snoblen, Steve. 2000. *William Whiston: Natural Philosopher, Prophet, Primitive Christian.* Diss. Phil., Cambridge.

Society of Jesus. 1887–94. *Ratio Studiorum et Institutiones Scholasticae Societatis Jesu per Germaniae olim vigentes.* Monumenta Germaniae paedagogica, 2, 5, 9, 16. Edited by G. M. Pachtler. Berlin.

———. 1896. *Rheinische Akten zur Geschichte des Jesuiten-Orden 1542–1582.* Edited by Joseph Hansen. Publicationen der Gesellschaft für Rheinische Geschichtskunde, 14. Bonn.

————. 1919. *Exercitia spiritualia Sancti Ignatii de Loyola.* 8 pts. Monumenta historica Societatis Jesu, 57, Monumenta Ignatiana, ser. 2. Rome.

————. 1934–38. *Constitutiones Societatis Jesu.* Monumenta historica Societatis Jesu. 3rd ser., 1–3 (1st ser., 63–65). Rome.

————. 1965–. *Monumenta paedagogica Societatis Jesu.* Rome: Monumenta Historica Soc. Iesu.

Sohm, Rudolf. 1949. *Institutionen. Geschichte und System des römischen Privatrechts.* 17th ed. by L. Mitteis and L. Wenger. Munich/Leipzig: Duncker & Humblot.

Solerius, Anselm (a.k.a. Theophil Raynaud). 1671 [1655]. *Tractatus de pileo.* Amsterdam.

Sonnenfels, Joseph von. 1771–77. *Grundsätze der Policey-, Handlungs-, und Finanz-Wissenschaft.* 3 vols. 3rd ed. Vienna.

————. 1782. *Grundsätze der Policey, Handlung, und Finanz.* 2 vols. 5th ed. Vienna.

————. 1785. *Über den Geschäftstil.* 2nd ed. Vienna.

Southern, R. W. 1970. *Western Society and the Church in the Middle Ages.* New York: Penguin.

Spacks, Patricia. 1985. *Gossip.* New York: Knopf.

Specht, Thomas. 1902. *Geschichte der ehemaligen Universität Dillingen (1549–1804).* Freiburg im Br.: Herder.

Spengel, Leonard. 1854a. *Das philologische Seminarium in München und die Ultramontanen.* Munich.

————. 1854b. *Das philologische Seminarium in München und die Ultramontanen. Fortsetzung.* Munich.

Spieß, Philipp E. 1777. *Von Archiven.* Halle.

Spinner, Helmut. 1991. "Das 'System Althoff' und Max Webers Kritik, die Humboldtsche Universität und die Klassische Wissensordnung: Die Ideen von 1809, 1882, 1914, 1919, 1933 im Vergleich." In Brocke 1991, 503–63.

Staehelin, Andreas. 1957. *Geschichte der Universität Basel 1632–1818.* Studien zur Geschichte der Wissenschaften in Basel, 4 and 5/1–2. 2 vols. Basel: Helbig & Lichtenhahn.

Staehelin, Andreas, ed. 1960. *Professoren der Universität Basel aus fünf Jahrhunderten. Bildnisse und Würdigungen.* Basel: Reinhardt.

Staël (Holstein), Germaine (Madame) de. 1968 [1813]. *De l'Allemagne.* 2 vols. Paris: Garnier.

Stafford, Barbara. 1994. *Artful Science: Enlightenment Entertainment and the Eclipse of Visual Education.* Cambridge, MA: MIT Press.

Stählin, Otto. 1928. *Das Seminar für klassische Philologie an der Universität Erlangen.* Erlangener Universitätsreden, 1. Erlangen.

Stahlmann, Wilhelm. 1899–1900. "Das Herzogliche philologisch-pädagogische Institut auf der Universität zu Helmstedt (1779–1810)." *Jahresbericht über das Herzogliche Gymnasium zu Blankenburg am Harz.* Blankenburg am Harz.

Stein, Friedrich. 1891. *Die akademische Gerichtsbarkeit in Deutschland.* Leipzig.

Steinen, Wolfram von den. 1958/59 "Monastik und Scholastik. Zur Dom Jean Leclercq *L'Amour des lettres et le désir de Dieu.*" *Zeitschrift für deutsches Altertum und deutsche Literatur* 89:243–56.

Steinmaurer, Rudolf. 1971. "Die Lehrkanzel für Experimental-physik." In Huter 1971, 55–119.

Stephanus, Matthaeus. 1611. "De Academiis." Lib. III, par. ii, in *Tractatus de jurisdictione.* Frankfurt.

———. 1617. *De nobilitate civili.* Frankfurt a.M.

Stern, Fritz. 1990. "Freunde im Widerspruch: Haber und Einstein." In Vierhaus and Brocke 1990, 516-51.

Stichweh, Rudolf. 1991. *Der frühmodene Staat und die europäische Universität: Zur Interaktion von Politik und Erziehungssystem im Prozeß ihrer Ausdifferenzierung (16.-18. Jahrhundert).* Frankfurt: Suhrkamp.

Stieda, Wilhelm. 1934. *Erfurter Universitätsreformpläne im 18. Jahrhundert.* Sonderschriften der Akademie gemeinnütziger Wissenschaften zu Erfurt, 5. Erfurt: Villaret.

Stollberg-Rilinger, Barbara. 1986. *Der Staat als Maschine. Zur politischen Metaphorik des absoluten Fürstenstaats.* Historische Forschungen, 30. Berlin: Duncker.

Stolleis, Michael. 1988-92. *Geschichte des öffentlichen Rechts in Deutschland.* 2 vols. Munich: Beck.

Stone, Lawrence, ed. 1974. *The University in Society.* 2 vols. Princeton: Princeton University Press.

Storey, R. L. 1992. "University and Government 1430-1500." In Catto and Evans 1992, 709-46.

Stözel, A. 1889. "Die Berliner Mittwochsgesellschaft über Aufhebung oder Reform der Universitäten (1795)." *Forschungen zur Brandenburgischen und Preußischen Geschichte* 2:201-22.

Strauss, Gerald. 1978. *Luther's House of Learning: Indoctrination of the Young in the German Reformation.* Baltimore: Johns Hopkins University Press.

Streich, Gerhard. 1977. "Die Büchersammlungen der Göttinger Professoren im 18. Jahrhundert." In Raabe 1977, 241-99.

Sturdy, David. 1995. *Science and Social Status: The Members of the Académie des Sciences, 1666-1750.* Bury St Edmunds: Boydell.

Sturm, L. C. (appeared anonymously). 1704. *Die geöffnete Raritäten- und Naturalien-Kammer.* Hamburg.

Stutz, Ulrich. 1955 [1895]. *Die Eigenkirche als Element des mittelalterlich-germanischen Kirchenrechts.* Darmstadt.

———. 1972 [1895]. *Geschichte des kirchlichen Benefizialwesens von seinem Anfängen bis auf die Zeit Alexanders III.* 3rd ed. Aalen: Scientia-Verlag.

Sudhoff, Karl, ed. 1922. *Hundert Jahre Deutscher Naturforscher-Versammlungen. Gedächtnisschrift zur Jahrhundert-Tagung der Gesellschaft Deutscher Naturforscher und Ärzte, Leipzig, im September 1922.* Leipzig: Vogel.

Süß, Wilhelm. 1928-30. *Karl Morgenstern (1770-1852). Ein kulturhistorisches Versuch.* 2 vols. Eesti Vabariigi Tartu Ülikooli, Acta et commentationes Universitatis Tartuensis (Dorpatensis), B. Humaniora, 16 & 19. Dorpat.

Sutherland, L. S. 1986a. "The Curriculum." In Sutherland and Mitchel 1986, 470-91.

———. 1986b. "The Administration of the University." In Sutherland and Mitchel 1986, 205-25.

Sutherland, L. S. and L. G. Mitchell, eds. 1986. *The Eighteenth Century* (vol. 5 in Aston 1984-). Oxford: Clarendon Press.

Sviedrys, Romualdus. 1970. "The Rise of Physical Science at Victorian Cambridge." *Historical Studies in the Physical Sciences* 2:127-51.

———. 1976. "The Rise of Physics Laboratories in Britain." *Historical Studies in the Physical Sciences* 7:405-36.

Talbot, C. H. 1958. "The Universities and the Mediaeval Library." In Wormald and Wright 1958, 66-84.

Taylor, Archer. 1966. *General Subject-Indexes Since 1548.* Philadelphia: University of Pennsylvania Press.

———. 1986. *Book Catalogues: Their Varieties and Uses.* 2nd ed. Bury St. Edmunds: St Paul's Bibliographies.

Taylor, Gabriele. 1994. "Gossip as Moral Talk." In Goodman and Ben-Ze'ev 1994, 34–46.

Teufel, Waldemar. 1977. *Universitas Studii Tuwingensis. Die Tübinger Universitätsverfassung in vorreformatorischer Zeit (1477–1534).* Contubernium. Beiträge zur Geschichte der Eberhard-Karls-Universität Tübingen, 12. Tübingen: Mohr.

Theiner, Augustin. 1835. *Geschichte der geistlichen Bildungsanstalten.* Mainz.

Thiele, Gunnar. 1938. *Geschichte der preussischen Lehrerseminare.* Monumenta Germaniae paedagogica, 62. Berlin: Weidmann.

Thiersch, Friedrich. 1826–38. *Ueber gelehrte Schulen.* 3 vols. Stuttgart.

———. 1833. *De l'état actuel de la Grèce.* . . . 2 vols. Leipzig.

———. 1838. *Ueber den gegenwärtigen Zustand des öffentlichen Unterrichts.* 3 vols. Stuttgart.

———. 1846. *Apologie eines Philhellenen wider den Fürsten Hermann L. G. von Pückler Muskau.* Munich.

Thiersch, Heinrich W. J. 1866. *Friedrich Thierschs Leben.* 2 vols. Leipzig.

Tholuck, August. 1853–54. *Das akademische Leben des siebzehnten Jahrhunderts.* 2 vols. Halle.

Thomasius, Christian. 1724. *Programmata Thomasiana.* Halle/Leipzig.

Thomasius, Jacob. 1670. *Erotemata Logica . . . Acceßit pro adultis processus disputandi.* Leipzig.

Thomasius, Jacob (*praeses*). 1671. *Diatribe academica de foeminarum eruditione priorem,* Johann Sauerbrei (*resp.*). Leipzig.

Thommen, Rudolf. 1889. *Geschichte der Universität Basel, 1532–1632.* Basel.

Thompson, James W., ed. 1939. *The Medieval Library.* Chicago: University of Chicago Press.

Thorndike, Lynn, ed. and trans. 1949 [1944]. *University Records and Life in the Middle Ages.* New York: Columbia University Press.

Titius, Gottlieb. 1701. *Ein Probe des deutschen Geistlichen Rechts.* Frankfurt.

———. 1724. *Juris privati Romano-Germanici.* Leipzig.

Todorov, Tzvetan. 1978 [1971]. *Poétique de la prose.* Paris: Seuil.

Tomashevsky, Boris. 1965. "Thematics." In Lemon and Reis 1965, 62–95.

Tomek, Wenzel W. 1849. *Geschichte der Prager Universität zur Feier der 500 jährigen Gründung.* Prague.

Torquatus, Alexander. 1666. *Inauguarati Chr.-Albr. Academiae Kiloniae.* Kiel.

Totok, Wilhelm and Carl Haase, eds. 1966. *Leibniz. Sein Leben—Sein Wirken—Sein Welt.* Hanover: Verlag für Literatur und Zeitgeschehen.

Tschanterus, Johann C. (*resp. et auct.*). 1704. *De eruditis studiorum intemperie mortem sibi accelerantibus, dissertatio I, eaque historica,* Gottfried Boettnerus (*praeses*). Leipzig.

——— (*praeses*). 1705. *De eruditis studiorum intemperie mortem sibi accelerantibus, dissertatio II, eaque physica,* Johann C. Wolff (*resp.*). Leipzig.

Tuchman, Arleen. 1988. "From the Lecture to the Laboratory: The Institutionalization of Scientific Medicine at the University of Heidelberg." In Coleman and Holmes 1988, 65–99.

———. 1991. *Science, Medicine, and the State in Germany: The Case of Baden, 1815–1871.* New York: Oxford University Press.

Turner, Roy Steven. 1971. "The Growth of Professorial Research in Prussia, 1818 to 1848–Causes and Context." *Historical Studies in the Physical Sciences* 3:137–182.

———. 1973. *The Prussian Universities and the Research Imperative.* Diss. Phil., Princeton.

———. 1974. "University Reformers and Professional Scholarship." In Stone 1974, 2:495–531.

———. 1980. "The Prussian Universities and the Concept of Research." *Internationales Archiv für die Sozialgeschichte der deutschen Literatur* 5:68–92.

———. 1982. "Justus Liebig versus Prussian Chemistry: Reflections on Early Institute-Building in Germany." *Historical Studies in the Physical Sciences* 13/1:129–62.

———. 1991. "German Science, German Universities: Historiographical Perspectives from the 1980s." In Schubring 1991, 24–36.

Twigg, John. 1990. *The University of Cambridge and the English Revolution 1625–1688.* The History of the University of Cambridge: Texts and Studies, 1. Cambridge: Boydell Press / Cambridge University Library.

Tyacke, Nicholas, ed. 1997. *The Seventeenth Century* (vol. 4 in Aston 1984–). Oxford: Clarendon Press.

Uffenbach, Zacharius Conrad von. 1753–54. *Merkwürdige Reisen durch Niedersachsen, Holland and Engelland.* 3 vols. Ulm.

Ullmann, Walter. 1954. "The Medieval Interpretation of Fredrick I's Authentica 'Habita.'" In *L'Europa e il diritto Romano. Studi in Memoria di Paolo Koschaker,* pp. 99–136. Vol. 1. Milan: Giuffrè.

Ulrichs, Carl Ludwig. 1886. *Die philosophische Fakultät an der Universität Würzburg.* Festrede, Würzburg Universitätsreden. Würzburg.

University of Altdorf. 1912. *Die Matrikel der Universität Altdorf, 1576–1809.* Edited by E. Steinmeyer, 2 vols. Veröffentlichungen der Gesellschaft für fränkische Geschichte, 4th ser., 1/1–2. Würzburg.

———. 1970. *Die Personalbibliographien des Lehrkörpers der philosophischen Fakultaet zu Altdorf von 1578 bis 1809.* By Magda Weigert. Diss. Med., Erlangen-Nuremberg.

University of Bamberg. 1923–24. *Die Matrikel der Akademie und Universität Bamberg, 1754–1803.* Edited by W. Hess. 2 vols. Bamberg: Kirsch.

———. 1971. *Personalbibliographien der Professoren der Philosophischen Fakultät der Academia Ottoniana und Universitas Ottoniana-Fridericiana Bambergensis von 1646–1664 und 1770–1803.* By Irene Pauler von Hofer. Diss. Med., Erlangen-Nuremberg.

University of Basel. 1907. *Die Statuten der philosophischen Fakultät der Universität Basel [ca. 1465].* Edited by C. C. Bernoulli. Basel.

———. 1951–80. *Die Matrikel der Universität Basel, 1460–1818.* Edited by H. G. Wackernagel. 5 vols. Basel: Verlag der Universitätsbibliothek.

———. 1960. *Professoren der Universität Basel aus fünf Jahrhunderten. Bildnisse und Würdigungen.* Edited by Andreas Staehelin. Basel: Reinhardt.

University of Berlin. 1899 *Verzeichnis der Berliner Universitätsschriften 1810–1885.* Berlin.

———. 1955. *Gesamtverzeichnis des Lehrkörpers der Universität Berlin. Bd. I: 1810–1945.* Edited by Johannes Asen. Leipzig: Harrassowitz.

University of Bonn. 1897. *Verzeichnis der Bonner Universitätsschriften 1818–1885.* Edited by Fritz Milkau, Bonn.

University of Breslau. 1905. *Verzeichnis der Breslauer Universitätsschriften 1811–1885.* Edited by Karl Pretzsch. Breslau: Korn.

University of Cambridge. 1796–. *Cambridge University Calendar.* Cambridge.

University of Cologne. 1919–81. *Die Matrikel der Universität Köln, 1389–1797.* Edited by H. Keussen et al. 7 vols. Publikationen der Gesellschaft für Rheinische Geschichtskunde, 8/1–7. Bonn/Düsseldorf: Behrendt.

University of Dillingen. 1909–15. *Die Matrikel der Universität Dillingen, 1551–1695.* Edited by T. Specht et al. 3 vols. Archiv für Geschichte des Hochstifts Augsburg, 2 & 3/1–2. Dillingen.

University of Dorpat. 1820. *Statut der Kaiserlichen Universität Dorpat.* Dorpat.

———. 1822 *Reglement für das nach §§ 93–100 des Allerhöchst bestätigten Statuts der Kaiserlichen Universität zu Dorpat daselbst eröffnete Pädagogisch-philologische Seminarium.* Dorpat.

———. 1889. *Album Academicum der Kaiserlichen Universität Dorpat, 1802–1889.* Edited by A. Hasselblatt et al. Dorpat.

———. 1973. *Tartu Ülikoolis Kaitstud Väitekirjad, 1802–1918, Bibliographia.* Edited by E. Oissar. Tartu.

University of Duisberg. 1938. *Die Matrikel der Universität Duisburg, 1652–1818.* Edited by W. Rotscheidt. Duisburg: Rheinische National-Druckerei.

University of Erfurt. 1881. *Acten der Erfurter Universität.* Edited by J. C. H. Weissenborn. 3 vols. Halle: Hendel.

University of Erlangen. 1777a. *Auspicia Seminarii philologici indicit et de eius forma.* By T. C. Harles. Erlangen.

———. 1777b. "Einrichtung des neuen Seminarii philologici zu Erlangen." *Acta historico-ecclesiastica nostri temporis* 4:608–22.

———. 1778. "Philologisches Seminarium zu . . . Erlangen: Aussichten über die Pflanzeschulen von Schulleuten." *Ephemeriden der Menschheit* 7:110–18.

———. 1843. *Personalstand der Friedrich-Alexander Universität Erlangen in ihrem ersten Jahrhundert.* Erlangen.

———. 1918. *Register zur Matrikel der Universität Erlangen, 1743–1843.* Veröffentlichungen der Gesellschaft für fränkische Geschichte. 4th ser., 4. Munich/Leipzig.

———. 1968. *Die Personalbibliographien des Lehrkörpers der philosophischen Fakultät zu Erlangen von 1743 bis 1806.* By Tankred Gastauer. Diss. Med., Erlangen-Nuremberg.

———. 1973. *Personalbibliographien von Professoren und Dozenten der philosophischen Fakultät zu Erlangen . . . 1806 bis 1856.* By Heinrich Kraft. Diss. Med., Erlangen-Nuremberg.

University of Frankfurt a.d.O. 1887–1965. *Ältere Universitätsmatrikeln der Universität. I. Frankfurt a.d.O.: Die Matrikel, 1649–1811.* Edited by E. Friedländer et al. 3 vols. Publicationen aus den Königlichen Preußischen Staatsarchiven, 32, 36, 49. Leipzig.

———. 1897–1906. *Akten und Urkunden der Universität zu Frankfurt a.O.* Edited by G. Kaufmann et al. 6 vols. Breslau: Marcus.

———. 1898–99. *Statuta facultatis philosophicae in academia Francofurtana.* Edited by P. Reh. Jahres-Bericht des Königlichen Gymnasiums zu Gross-Strehlitz f. d. Schuljahr 1898/99. Gross-Strehlitz.

University of Freiburg im Br. 1830a. *Statut für das philologische Seminarium.* Freiburg im Br.

————. 1830b. *Betrachtung über die Wichtigkeit und Bedeutung des Studiums der classischen Literatur . . . nebst Nachricht über das an der hiesigen Universität neu begründete philologische Seminar.* Programm by Carl Zell. Freiburg im Br.

————. 1830c. *De studio graecarum latinarumque literarum . . . Oratio quam in seminario philol. inaugurata.* By Carl Zell. Freiburg im Br.

————. 1907–57. *Die Matrikel der Universität Freiburg im Br., 1460–1806.* Edited by H. Mayer and F. Schaub. 4 vols. Freiburg im Br.: Herder.

————. 1957. *Statuta Collegii Sapientiae: Sätzungen des Collegiums Sapientiae zu Freiburg im Breisgau, 1497. Faksimile Ausgabe.* By Johannes Kerer. Edited by J. F. Beckmann and R. Feger. 2 vols. Lindau/Konstanz: Thorbecke.

————. 1964. *The Medieval Statutes of the Faculty of Arts of the University of Freiburg in Breisgau.* Edited by H. Ott and J. M. Fletcher. Texts and Studies in the History of Medieval Education, 10. Notre Dame: The Medieval Institute.

University of Gießen. 1812. "[On the Seminar]." *Jenaische Allgemeine Literaturzeitung.* Intelligenzblatt, 23 Mai, Nr. 33:257–58.

————. 1827. "Bekanntmachung, die Statuten des philologischen Seminars zu Gießen." In Hesse-Darmstadt 1819–, 26 Sept., Nr. 45:425–30.

————. 1881. *Die ältesten Privilegien und Statuten der Ludoviciana.* Edited by H. Wasserschleben. Programm, Universität Gießen.

————. 1890–1957. *Die Matrikel der Universität Gießen, 1608–1807.* Edited by E. Klewitz et al. 2 pts. Pt. 1: Mitteilungen des Oberhessischen Geschichtsvereins, n.s. 2–6, Gießen, 1890–96. Pt. 2: Bibliothek familiengeschichtlicher Quellen, 11. Neustadt a.d. Aisch: Degener.

————. 1907. *Die Universität Gießen von 1607 bis 1907: Beiträge zu ihrer Geschichte.* Festschrift zur dritten Jahrhundertfeier. 2 vols. Gießen: Toeplemann.

————. 1971. *Katalog der Dissertationen und Habilitationsschriften der Universität Gießen von 1801–1884.* By Franz Kössler. Berichte und Arbeiten aus der Universitätsbibliothek Gießen, 22. Gießen: Universitäts-Bibliothek.

————. 1976. *Die Dissertationen und Habilitationsschriften der Universität Gießen im 18.Jahrhundert.* Edited by Hermann Schüling. Berichte und Arbeiten aus der Universitätsbibliothek Gießen, 26. Gießen: Universitäts-Bibliothek.

————. 1982. *Statuta Academiae Marpurgensis deinde Gissensis de anno 1629. Die Statuten der Hessen-Darmstädtischen Landesuniversität Marburg 1629–1650/Gießen 1650–1879.* Edited by H. G. Gundel. Veröffentlichungen der Historischen Kommission für Hessen, 44. Marburg: Elwert.

University of Göttingen. 1737. "Programma . . . in scholis seminarii philologci. . . ." In Gesner 1743–45, 1:59–76.

————. 1738. "Seminarium Philologicum zu Göttingen." In Hanover 1738, 209–22. Also in Vormbaum 1860, 3:358f, 426–31.

————. 1901. *Festschrift zur Feier des hundertfünfzigjährigen Bestehens des Königlichen Gesellschaft der Wissenschaften zu Göttingen. . . .* Berlin: Weidmann

————. 1937. *Die Matrikel der Georg-August-Universität zu Göttingen, 1734–1837.* Edited by G. von Selle. 2 vols. Veröffentlichungen der Historischen Kommission für Hannover, 9/1–2. Hildesheim/Leipzig: Lax.

————. 1961. *Die Privilegien und ältesten Statuten der Georg-August-Universität zu Göttingen.* Edited by Wilhelm Ebel. Göttingen: Vandenhoeck & Ruprecht.

————. 1962. *Catalogus professorum Gottingensium 1734–1962.* Edited by Wilhelm Ebel. Göttingen: Vandenhoeck & Ruprecht.

University of Greifswald. 1893–94. *Ältere Universitätsmatrikeln der Universität. II.*

*Universität Greifswald (1456–1700).* Edited by E. Friedländer et al. 2 vols. Publicationen aus den Königlichen Preussischen Staatsarchiven, 52 & 57. Leipzig.

———. 1956. *Festschrift zur 500-Jahrfeier der Universität Greifswald.* 2 vols. Greifswald: Verlag der Volksstimme.

University of Halle-(Wittenberg). 1736. "Conspectus legum societatis latinae generalium." *Pierides sive Latium literatum continens selectum elaborationum a membris societatis latinae exhibitam.* Edited by Martin Heinrich Otto. Halle.

———. 1778. *Nachricht von der bey dem königl. theologischen Seminarium zu Halle neuerrichteten Erziehungsanstalt.* By Christian Gottfried Schütz. Halle.

———. 1779. "[On the *Erziehungsinstitut*]," *Neue Hallische Gelehrte Zeitungen,* 719.

———. 1779. *Plan und Gesetze der Naturforschenden Gesellschaft zu Halle.* Halle.

———. 1781. "[On the *Erziehungsinstitut*]." *Hallische Gelehrte Zeitung,* 62.

———. 1783. *Abhandlungen der Hallischen Naturforschenden Gesellschaft,* 1. Halle.

———. 1809. *Neue Schriften der Naturforschenden Gesellschaft zu Halle,* 1. Halle.

———. 1879. *Festschrift zur Feier des 100 jährigen Bestehens der Naturforschenden Gesellschaft in Halle a.d.S.* Halle.

———. 1952. *450 Jahre Marin-Luther Universität Halle-Wittenberg.* Edited by L. Stern. 3 vols. Halle-Wittenberg: Verlag der Universität Halle-Wittenberg.

———1953. *Bibliographie der Universitätsschriften von Halle-Wittenberg 1817–1885.* Edited by Wolfram Suchier. Arbeiten aus der Universitäts- und Landesbibliothek Sachsen-Anhalt in Halle a.d.S., 3. Halle: Deutscher Verlag der Wissenschaften.

———. 1960–94. *Matrikel der Martin-Luther Universität Halle-Wittenberg (1690–1741).* Edited by F. Zimmermann et al. 2 vols. & in progress. Arbeiten aus der Universitäts- und Landesbibliothek Sachsen-Anhalt Halle a.d.S., 2 & 40. Halle: Univ.- u. Landesbibliothek.

University of Heidelberg. 1807. "[On the Seminar]." *Allgemeine Literaturzeitung.* Intelligenzblatt, 29:227.

———. 1884–1916. *Die Matrikel der Universität Heidelberg, 1386–1870.* Edited by G. Toepke et al. 7 vols. Heidelberg: Winter.

———. 1886. *Urkundbuch der Universität Heidelberg.* Edited by Eduard Winkelmann. 2 vols. Heidelberg.

———. 1891. *Statuten und Reformationen der Universität Heidelberg von 16. bis 18. Jahrhundert.* Edited by August Thorbecke. Leipzig.

———. 1961. *1386–1961. Ruperto-Carola. Sonderband. Aus der Geschichte der Universität Heidelberg und ihrer Fakultäten. 575 Jahre Ruprecht-Karl Universität Heidelberg.* Heidelberg: Brausdruck.

University of Helmstedt. 1779. "Ordnung des philologisch-pädagogischen Instituts zu Helmstedt, 1779-1780." In Hanover 1886, 2:463–77.

———. 1780. "Nachricht von dem auf der Julius-Carls-Universität zu Helmstedt errichteten philologisch-pädagogischen Institut." By Friedrich August Wideburg. In *Gelehrte Beyträge zu den Braunschweigischen Anzeigen* 79–81:617–36.

———. 1788. "Nachricht von der Einrichtung des philologisch-pädagogischen Seminariums auf der Julius Karl Universität." By Friedrich August Wideburg. In *Humanistisches Magazin* 2 [?]:289–97.

———. 1797. *Verfassung und Methode des philologisch-pädagogischen Instituts.* By Friedrich August Wideburg. Helmstedt.

———. 1963. *Die Statuten der Universität Helmstedt.* Edited by P. Baumgart and E. Pitz. Veröffentlichungen der Niedersächsischen Archivverwaltung, 15. Göttingen: Vandenhoeck & Ruprecht.

—————. 1979. *Die Matrikel der Universität Helmstedt, 1685–1810.* Edited by H. Mundhenke. Veröffentlichungen der Historischen Kommission für Niedersächsen und Bremen. 4th sect., 3. Hildesheim: Selbstverlag der Historischen Komm.

University of Ingolstadt/Landshut/Munich. 1782–1809 *Annales Ingolstadiensis Academiae.* Edited by Valentin Rotmar, Johann Engerd, and Johann N. Mederer. 5 vols. Ingolstadt/Munich.

—————. 1812–29. *Acta philologorum Monacensium.* Edited by Friedrich W. Thiersch. 3 vols. Munich.

—————. 1872–73. *Das Matrikelbuch der Universität Ingolstadt-Landshut-München, 1472–1872.* Edited by Franz Freninger. 2 pts. Munich.

—————. 1970. *Die Personalbibliographien der Mitglieder des Lehrkörpers der medizinischen und philosophischen Fakultät zu Landshut . . . 1800 zur 1826.* By Günther Werk. Diss. Med., Erlangen-Nuremberg.

—————. 1971. *Personalbibliographien der Mitglieder der philosophischen Fakultät zu München von 1826 bis 1850.* By Rainer Glosauer. Diss. Med., Erlangen-Nuremberg.

—————. 1973. *Die Universität Ingolstadt im 15. und 16. Jahrhundert. Texte und Regesten.* Edited by A. Siefert. Ludovicio Maximilianea, Universität Ingolstadt-Landshut-München, Quellen, 1. Berlin: Duncker & Humblot.

—————. 1975–77. *Verzeichnis der Doktoren und Dissertationen der Universität Ingolstadt-Landshut-München 1472–1970.* Edited by Lieselotte Resch and Ladislaus Buzas. 7 vols. Munich: Universitätsbibliothek.

University of Jena. 1737. "Nachricht von der Lateinischen Gesellschaft in Jena." In *Götten 1735–41,* 3:625–28.

—————. 1741–43. *Exercitationes Societatis Latinae.* Edited by F. E. Hallbauer. Jena.

—————. 1752–56. *Acta Societatis Latinae Jenesis.* Edited by J. E. Walch. 5 vols. Jena.

—————. 1767. *Anzeige eines Instituts zur Beförderung des Studiums der Mathematik und Physik besonders für künftige Ärtzte.* By Johann E. B. Wiedeburg. Jena.

—————. 1793. *Nachricht von der Gründung einer naturforschenden Gesellschaft zu Jena.* Jena.

—————. 1794. *Nachrichten von den Fortgang der naturforschenden Gesellschaft zu Jena.* Jena.

—————. 1800a. *Neue Statuten der naturforschenden Gesellschaft zu Jena.* Jena.

—————. 1800b. *Acroasis pro Societatis Latinae Jenensis instauratione.* By Heinrich C. A. Eichstädt. Jena.

—————. 1806. *Nova acta Societatis Jenensis.* Edited by Heinrich C. A. Eichstädt. Leipzig.

—————. 1823. "Plan zum philologischen Seminarium bey der Universität Jena." Edited by H. C. A. Eichstadt. *Annales academiae Ienensis* 1:121–22, 179–82. Jena.

—————. 1829. *Statuten der Universität Jena.* Jena.

—————. 1858. *Lebensskizzen der Professoren der Universität Jena seit 1558 bis 1858.* By Johann Günther. Jena.

—————. 1900. "Die Statuten der Universität Jena von 1591." Ed. by G. Mentz. *Mitteilungen der Gesellschaft für deutsche Erziehungs- und Schulgeschichte* 10/1:56–68.

—————. 1944–86. *Die Matrikel der Universität Jena, 1548–1764.* Edited by G. Mentz et al. 3 vols. & in progress. Jena/Weimar/Halle: Fischer.

—————. 1958a. *Geschichte der Universitätsbibliothek Jena.* Claves Jenensis, 7. Weimar: Boehlau.

—————. 1958b. *Geschichte der Universität Jena 1548/58–1958. Festgabe zum vierhundertjährigen Universitätsjubiläum.* 2 vols. Jena: Fischer.

University of Kiel. 1666 *Inauguratio Christiano-Albertinae Academiae Kiloniae*. Edited by Alexander Torquatus. Kiel. [Bound with other documents at E:GöttUB, 4° H.i.p. V 110/2.]

————. 1856. "Das philologische Seminar." *Chronik der Universität Kiel*. Kiel.

————. 1915. *Das Album der Christian-Albrechts-Universität zu Kiel 1665–1865*. Edited by F. Grundlich. Kiel: Lipsius & Tischer.

————. 1956. *Professoren und Dozenten der Christian-Albrechts-Universität zu Kiel 1665–1954*. Edited by Friedrich Volbehr et al. 4th ed. Kiel: Hirt.

————. 1965–69. *Geschichte der Christian-Albrechts-Universität Kiel, 1665–1965*. 6 vols. Neumünster: Wachholtz.

University of Königsberg. 1836. *Erster Bericht über das naturwissenschaftliche Seminar bei der Universität zu Königsberg*. Edited by Ernst Meyer. Königsberg.

————. 1837. *Zweiter Bericht über das naturwissenschaftliche Seminar bei der Universität zu Königsberg*. Edited by Ernst Meyer. Königsberg.

————. 1838. *Dritter Bericht über das naturwissenschaftliche Seminar bei der Universität zu Königsberg*. Edited by Heinrich Rathke. Königsberg.

————. 1839. *Vierter Bericht über das naturwissenschaftliche Seminar bei ber Universität zu Königsberg*. Edited by Ludwig Moser. Königsberg.

————. 1908–17. *Die Matrikel und die Promotionsverzeichnisse der Albertus-Universität zu Königsberg, 1544–1829*. Edited by G. Erler. 3 vols. Leipzig: Duncker & Humblot.

————. 1999. *Vorlesungsverzeichnisse de Universität Königsberg (1720–1804)*. Edited by Michael Oberhausen and Riccardo Pozzo. 2 vols. Stuttgart: frommann-holzboog.

University of Leipzig. 1799. *Nachricht von der am 31 Jannuar 1799 gestifteten natur-forschenden Privatgesellschaft zu Leipzig*. Leipzig.

————. 1801–4. *Commentarii Societatis philologicae Lipsiensis*. Edited by Christian D. Beck. 4 vols. Leipzig.

————. 1809. *De consiliis et rationibus seminarii philologici. . . .* By Christian D. Beck. Leipzig.

————. 1810. "[On the seminar in] Beilage: Neuen allgemeine Intelligenzblatt." *Neue Leipziger Literaturzeitung* 49–56.

————. 1811–13. *Acta seminarii Regii et Societatis philologicae Lipsiensis*. Edited by Christian D. Beck. 2 vols. Leipzig.

————. 1836–40. *Acta Societatis Graecae*. Edited by A. Westermann et al. 2 vols. Leipzig.

————. 1857. *Die urkundlichen Quellen zur Geschichte der Universität Leipzig in den ersten 150 Jahren ihres Bestehens*. Edited by Friedrich Zarncke. Abhandlungen der königlichen sächsischen Gesellschaft der Wissenschaften, 3. Leipzig.

————. 1861. *Die Statutenbücher der Universität Leipzig aus den ersten 150 Jahren ihres Bestehens*. Edited by Friedrich Zarncke. Leipzig.

————. 1879. *Urkundbuch der Universität Leipzig von 1409 bis 1555*. Edited by Bruno Stübel. Codex diplomaticus Saxoniae regiae. 2nd sect., 11. Leipzig.

————. 1897–1902. *Matrikel der Universität Leipzig [1409–1559]*. Edited by G. Erler. 3 vols. Codex diplomaticus Saxoniae regiae, 2nd sect., 16–18. Leipzig: Giesecke & Devrient.

————. 1909a. *Die jüngere Matrikel der Universität Leipzig 1559–1809*. Edited by G. Erler. 3 vols. Leipzig: Giesecke & Devrient.

————. 1909b. *Festschrift zur Feier des 500 jährigen Bestehens der Universität Leipzig*. 4 vols. Leipzig: Hirzel.

University of Mainz. 1743–68. *Codex diplomaticus exhibens anecdota ab anno DCC-*

*CLXXXI ad MCCC Moguntiaca*. . . . Edited by F. de Gudenus. 5 vols. Göttingen/ Frankfurt a.M.

———. 1907. "Antiquissima statuta bursalia domum Schenckenbergicae et Algesheimensis." Edited by F. Hermann. *Archive für hessische Geschichte*, n.s. 5:109– 124.

———. 1952. "Professoren der kurfürstlichen Universität Mainz, 1477–1797." Edited by Otfried Praetorius. *Familie und Volk* 1:90–100, 131–39.

———. 1977a. *Die ältesten Statuten der Universität Mainz*. Edited by Heinz Duchhardt. Beiträge zur Geschichte der Universität Mainz, 10. Wiesbaden: Steiner.

———. 1977b. "Jesuiten als Lehrer an Gymnasium und Universität Mainz und ihre Lehrfächer . . . 1551–1773." By Fritz Krafft. In *Beiträge zur Geschichte der Universität Mainz* 2:259–350. Wiesbaden: Steiner.

University of Marburg. 1811. "[On the Philology Seminar]," *Jenaische Allgemeine Literaturzeitung*. Intelligenzblatt, 28. Sept., Nr. 64:506–07.

———. 1848. *Urkundensammlung über die Verfassung und Verwaltung der Universität Marburg*. Edited by Bruno Hildebrand. Marburg.

———. 1927. *Catalogus Professorum Academiae Marburgensis 1527–1910*. Edited by Franz Grundlach. Veröffentlichungen der Historischen Kommission für Hessen, 15/1. Marburg: Elwert.

———1977. *Die Statuten der Universität Marburg von 1560*. Edited by H. G. Gundel. Academia Marburgensis. Beiträge zur Geschichte der Philipps-Universität Marburg, 1:111–79. Marburg: Elwert.

University of Münster. 1825. "Einrichtung eines philologisch-pädagogischen Seminars in Münster." *Allgemeine Schulzeitung* 2/3:211–13.

University of Olmouc. 1962. *Die Professoren der k.k. Franzens-Universität zu Olmütz (1828–1855)*. Edited by Richard Zimprich. Steinheim/Main: Quellenverlag Diwisch.

University of Paderborn. 1931–32. *Die Matrikel der Universität Paderborn, 1614–1844*. Edited by J. Freisen. 2 vols. Paderborn: Thiele.

University of Paris. 1889–92. *Chartularium Universitatis Parisiensis*. Edited by H. Denifle and E. Chatelain. 4 vols. Paris.

———. 1894–97. *Auctarium chartularii Universitatis Parisiensis*. Edited by H. Denifle and E. Chatelain. 2 vols. Paris.

University of Prague. 1830–48. *Monumenta historica Universitatis Carlo-Ferdinandeae Pragensis*. Edited by A. Dittrich et al. 3 vols. Prague.

———. 1970a. *Personalbibliographien von Professoren der philosophischen Fakultät zu Prag . . . von 1800 bis 1860. Vol. 1*. By Uta Egert. Diss. Med., Erlangen-Nuremberg.

———. 1970b. *Personalbibliographien von Professoren der philosophischen Fakultät zu Prag . . . 1800 bis 1860. [Vol. 2]*. By Isolde Hienstorfer. Diss. Med., Erlangen-Nuremberg.

———. 1971. *Personalbibliographien der Professoren und Dozenten der philosophischen Fakultät der Karl-Ferdinand-Universität Prag im ungefahren Zeitraum von 1700– 1800*. By Gerhard Weiss. Diss. Med., Erlangen-Nuremberg.

University of Rinteln. 1879–80. "Statuta, leges et privilegia illustris et magnificae Academiae Holsato-Schawenburgiicae in oppido Rinteln . . . anno MDCXXI." Edited by H. F. Suchier. *Jahresbericht über das Königliche Gymnasium zu Rinteln*. Rinteln.

———. 1971. *Catalogus Professorum Rinteliensium . . . (1610–1810)*. By Willy Hänsel. Schaumburger Studien, 31. Rinteln: Boesendahl.

University of Rostock. 1829. *Statuten für das Grossherzogliche philologische Seminarium zu Rostock.* Rostock.

———. 1889–1922. *Die Matrikel der Universität Rostock [1419–1831].* Edited by A. Hofmeister and E. Schäfer. 6 vols. Rostock: Nusser.

———. 1969. *Die Universität Rostock, 1419–1945. Festschrift zur Fünfhundertfünfzig-Jahrfeier der Universität.* 2 vols. Rostock: Deutscher Verlag der Wissenschaften.

University of Salzburg. 1972. *Festschrift: Universität Salzburg, 1622–1962–1972.* Salzburg: Pustet.

University of Strasbourg. 1876. "Statuta Academiae Argentinensis." Edited by J. Rathgeber. *Zeitschrift für die Geschichte des Oberrheins* 28:195–286.

———. 1890–94. *Les statuts et privilèges des universités français depuis leur fondation jusqu'en 1789.* Edited by Marcel Fornier. 4 vols. Paris.

———. 1892. *Annales des professeurs des académies et universitaires Alsaciennes 1523–1871.* By Oscar Berger-Levrault. Nancy.

———. 1897–1907. *Die Alten Matrikeln der Universität Straßburg 1621–1793.* Edited by G. Knod. 3 vols. Urkunden und Akten der Stadt Straßburg. 3rd sect. Strasbourg.

University of Trier. 1917–26. *Akten und Urkunden zur Geschichte der Trierer Universität.* Edited by L. Keil. 2 vols. Trier: Lintz.

University of Tübingen. 1838. "Bekanntmachung, die Einrichtung von Seminarien für Lehramts-Candidaten an der Universität betreffend." *Staats- und Regierungsblatt für das Königreich Württemberg,* 332–35.

———. 1877. *Urkunden zur Geschichte der Universität Tübingen aus den Jahren 1476 bis 1550.* Edited by Rudolf Roth. Tübingen.

———. 1906–54. *Die Matrikel der Universität Tübingen [1477–1817].* Edited by H. Hermelink et al. 3 vols. in 5 pts. Tübingen: Kohlhamer.

———. 1960. *Die Lehrstühle der Universität Tübingen und ihre Inhaber 1477–1927.* By Ernst Conrad. Diplomarbeit für das Lehramt. Unpublished, in *Lesesaal.* Tübingen Universitätsbibliothek, Paed. E 301.

———. 1977. *500 Jahre Eberhard-Karls-Universität Tübingen. Beiträge zur Geschichte der Universität Tübingen.* Edited by H. Decker-Hauff et al. 3 vols. Tübingen: AT-TEMPTO.

University of Vienna. 1693. *Calendarium academicum . . . Universitatis Viennensis.* Vienna.

———. 1850. "Statuten des philologisch-historischen Seminars zu Wien." *Zeitschrift für die österreichischen Gymnasien* 1:855–61.

———. 1956–75. *Die Matrikel der Universität Wien [1377–1689].* Publikationen des Instituts für österreichische Geschichtsforschung. 6th ser., 1st sect., 1–5. Vienna/Graz/Cologne: Boehlau.

———. 1963. *Acta facultatis artium Universitatis Vindobonensis 1385–1416.* Edited by P. Uiblein. Publikationen des Instituts für österreichische Geschichtsforschung. 6th ser., 2nd sect. Graz/Vienna.

———. 1970 [1966]. *Die philosophische Fakultät der Universität Wien von 1740–1800 mit besonderer Berücksichtigung der Humaniora.* By Godehard Schwarz. Diss. Phil. Vienna.

———. 1971. *Personalbibliographien von Professoren der philosophischen Fakultät zu Wien . . . von 1787 bis 1820.* By Günter Bräu. Diss. Med., Erlangen-Nuremberg.

———. 1972. *Personalbibliographien von Professoren der philosophischen Fakultät zu Wien . . . 1820 bis 1848.* By Gerhard Will. Diss. Med., Erlangen-Nuremberg.

University of Wittenberg. 1768. "Von der Wittenbergischen Universität und Stadt." *Wittenbergisches Wochenblatt*. . . .15 April, 1:15:130–32.

———. 1806. "Das hiesige akademische Seminarium nach seiner neuen Organisation." *Neues Wittenbergisches Wochenblatt*. . . . 2 August, 31:243–50.

———. 1841–1966. *Album Academiae Viteburgensis [1502–1812]*. Edited by K. E. Förstemann et al. 3 ser. in 7 vols. Leipzig/Magdeburg/Halle.

———. 1867. *Die Wittenberger Universitaets- und Facultaets-Statuten vom Jahre MDVIII*. Halle.

———. 1926–27. *Urkundenbuch der Universität Wittenberg*. Edited by Walter Friedensburg. 2 vols. Historische Kommission für die Provinz Sachsen und für Anhalt, n.s. 3/1–2. Magdeburg: Selbstverlag der Historischen Kommission.

University of Würzburg. 1922–82. *Die Matrikel der Universität Würzburg [1582–1830]*. Edited by S. Merkle et al. Veröffentlichungen der Gesellschaft für fränkische Geschichte. 4th ser., 5/1–2. Munich/Leipzig: Duncker & Humblot.

———. 1966. *Lehre und Forschung in Mathematik und Naturwissenschaften, insbesondere Astronomie, an der Universität Würzburg von der Gründung bis zum Beginn des 20. Jahrhunderts*. By Maria Reindl. Quellen und Beiträge zur Geschichte der Universität Würzburg, Beiheft 1. Würzburg.

———. 1970. *Personalbibliographien von Professoren der philosophischen Fakultät der Alma Mater Julia Wirceburgensis . . . 1582–1803*. By Karl-Heinz Logermann. Diss. Med., Erlangen-Nuremberg.

———. 1971. *Personalbibliographien der Professoren der philosophischen Fakultät zu Würzburg von 1803–1852*. By Peter Langhans. Diss. Med., Erlangen-Nuremberg.

———. 1972. *Die Personalbibliographien der Professoren der aristotelischen Physik in der philosophischen Fakultät der Alma Mater Julia Wirceburgensis von 1582–1773*. By Winfried Stosiek. Diss. Med., Erlangen-Nuremberg.

———. 1973. *Personalbibliographien von Professoren der philosophischen Fakultät der Alma Mater Julia Wirceburgensis von 1582 bis 1803*. By Gudrun Uhlenbrock. Diss. Med., Erlangen-Nuremberg.

———. 1982. *Vierhundert Jahre Universität Würzburg: Eine Festschrift*. Edited by P. Baumgart. Quellen und Beiträge zur Geschichte der Universität Würzburg, 6. Neustadt a.d. Aisch.

University of Zurich. 1832. *Gesetze und Verordnungen für die Hochschule in Zürich*. Zurich: Ulrich.

Utley, Francis L., ed. 1961. *The Forward Movement of the Fourteenth Century*. Columbus, Ohio: Ohio State University Press.

Van der Laan, James. 1995. "Nicolai's Concept of a Review (Journal)." In Rowland and Fink 1995, 95–111.

Van Houdt, Toon and Jan Papy, Gilbert Tournoy and Constant Matheeussen, eds. 2002. *Self-Presentation and Social Identification: The Rhetoric and Pragmatics of Letter Writing in Early Modern Times*. Supplementa Humanistica Lovaniensia, 18. Louvain: Leuven University Press.

Vandermeersch, Peter. 1996. "Teachers." In Ridder-Symoens 1996, 210–55.

Varrentrapp, Conrad. 1889. *Johannes Schulze und das höhere preussische Unterrichtswesen in seiner Zeit*. Leipzig.

Vaughan, Roger. 2000. *Listen to the Music: The Life of Hilary Koprowski*. New York: Springer.

Verger, Jacques, ed. 1986. *Histoire des universités en France*. Toulouse: BhP.

Verne, Jules 1986 [1879]. *Les 500 millions de la Bégum*. Paris: Livre de Poche.

Versammlung [Gesellschaft] deutscher Naturforscher und Ärzte. 1828–. *Amtlicher Bericht.* Title and place varies.

Versammlung deutscher Philologen und Schulmänner. 1838. *Verhandlungen der ersten Versammlung deutscher Philologen und Schulmänner in Nürnberg 1838.* Nuremberg.

————. 1840. *Verhandlungen der zweiten Versammlung deutscher Philologen und Schulmänner in Mannheim 1839.* Mannheim.

————. 1841. *Verhandlungen der dritten Versammlung deutscher Philologen und Schulmänner in Gotha 1840.* Gotha.

Veysey, Laurence. 1965. *The Emergence of the American University.* Chicago: University of Chicago Press.

Vicaire, Marie-Humbert. 1957. *Histoire de Saint Dominique.* 2 vols. Paris: Éditions du Cerf.

Vierhaus, Rudolf. 1984. *Deutschland im Zeitalter des Absolutismus (1648–1763).* Göttingen: Vandenhoeck & Ruprecht.

————. 1990. "Adolf Harnack" in Vierhaus and Brocke, 463–85.

————. 1996 [1989]. "Bemerkungen zum sogennanten Harnack-Prinzip. Mythos und Realität." In Brocke and Laitko 1996, 129–38.

————. 2001. "In Großbetrieb der Wissenschaft. Adolf Harnack als Wissenschaftsorganisator und Wissenschaftspolitiker." In Nowak and Oexle 2001, 419–441.

Vierhaus, Rudolf and Bernhard vom Brocke, eds. 1990. *Forschung im Spannungsfeld von Politik und Gesellschaft. Geschichte und Struktur der Kaiser-Wilhelm-/Max-Planck-Gesellschaft. Aus Anläß ihres 75jährigen Bestehens.* Stuttgart: Deutsche Verlags-Anstalt.

Virgil. 1997 [1697; ca. 19 BCE]. *The Aeneid.* Translated by John Dryden. Edited by Frederick Keener. London: Penguin.

Vischer, Wilhelm. 1860. *Geschichte der Universität Basel von der Gründung 1460 bis zur Reformation 1529.* Basel.

Vogt, Ernst. 1979. "Der Methodenstreit zwischen Hermann und Böckh und seine Bedeutung für die Philologie." In Flashar et al. 1979, 103–21.

Volkmann, Richard. 1874. *Geschichte und Kritik der Wolfischen Prolegomena zu Homer.* Leipzig.

————. 1887. *Gottfried Bernhardy.* Halle.

Voltaire. 1964 [1734]. *Lettres philosophiques.* Paris: Flammarion.

Vormbaum, Reinhold, ed. 1860–64. *Evangelische Schulordnungen.* 3 vols. Gütersloh.

Walther, Georg. 1641. *Tractatus de Statu, Juris, & Privilegiis Doctorum facultatum Doctorum omnium.* Nuremberg.

Wangerin, Albert. 1907. *Franz Neumann und sein Wirken als Forscher und Lehrer.* Brunswick: Vieweg.

Ward, W. R. 1997. "From the Tractarians to the Executive Commission, 1845–1854." In Brock and Curthoys 1997, 306–36.

Warwick, Andrew. 2003. *Masters of Theory: Cambridge and the Rise of Mathematical Physics.* Cambridge: Cambridge University Press.

Watson, Richard. 1818. *Anecdotes of the Life of Richard Watson . . . .* Edited by Richard Watson [Jr.]. 2 vols. 2nd ed. London.

Watt, Ian. 1987 [1957]. *The Rise of the Novel: Studies in Defoe, Richardson and Fielding.* London: Hogarth.

Wattenbach, Wilhelm. 1864. "Petrus Luder, der erste humanistische Lehrer in Heidelberg." *Zeitschrift für die Geschichte des Oberrheins* 22:33–127.

Weber, Heinrich. 1880–82. *Geschichte der gelehrten Schulen im Hochstift Bamberg vom 1007–1803.* 3 vols. Bamberg.

Weber, Max. 1956 [1921]. *Wirtschaft und Gesellschaft. Grundriß einer verstehenden Soziologie.* Edited by J. Winckelmann. 4th rev. ed. 2 vols. as 1. Tübingen: Mohr.

———. 1976a [1921]. *Wirtschaft und Gesellschaft. Grundriß der verstehenden Soziologie. Studienausgabe.* Edited by J. Winckelmann. 5th rev. ed. (also published in 1976c, vols. 1–2). Tübingen.

———. 1976b [1958; 1904–5]. *The Protestant Ethic and the Spirit of Capitalism.* Translated by Talcott Parsons, New York: Scribner.

———. 1976c [1921]. *Wirtschaft und Gesellschaft. Grundriß der verstehenden Soziologie.* Edited by J. Winckelmann. 3 vols. [vols. 1–2 as 1; vol. 3 as notes]. 5th rev. ed. Tübingen.

———. 1984–. *Gesamtausgabe.* Edited by Horst Baier et al. Kommission für Sozial- und Wirtschaftsgeschichte der Bayerischen Akademie der Wissenschaften. Multiple vols. in progress. Tübingen: Mohr.

———. 1988a [1922]. *Gesammelte Aufsätze zur Wissenschaftstheorie.* Tübingen: Mohr.

———. 1988b [1920]. *Gesammelte Aufsätze zur Religionssoziologie.* 3 vols. Tübingen: Mohr.

———. 2001. *Religiöse Gemeinschaften, Teilband 2, Wirtschaft und Gesellschaft. Die Wirtschaft und die gesellschaftlichen Ordnungen und die Mächte. Nachlaß.* Edited by Hans Kippenberg with Petra Schilm and Jutta Niemeier. Sect. 1, vol. 22/2. In Weber 1984–.

Wegele, Franz X. von. 1882. *Geschichte der Universität Würzburg.* 2 vols. Würzburg.

Weijers, Olga. 1987. *Terminologie des universités au XIIIe siècle.* Lessico intellettuale Europeo, 39. Rome: Ed. dell'Ateneo.

Weiller, Cajeten. 1824. "Geschichte der Akademie. Jahresberichte der königlichen bairischen Akademie der Wissenschaft in München (1824)." *Denkschriften der Bayerischen Akademie der Wissenschaft* 9:1–76.

Weindling, Paul. 1992. "Scientific Elites and Laboratory Organization in *fin de siècle* Paris and Berlin: The Pasteur Institute and Robert Koch's Institute for Infectious Diseases Compared." In Cunningham and Willams 1992, 170–88.

Weischedel, Wilhelm, ed. 1960. *Idee und Wirklichkeit einer Universität. Dokumente zur Geschichte der Friedrich-Universität zu Berlin.* Berlin: de Gruyter.

Weisz, George. 1983. *The Emergence of Modern Universities in France, 1863–1914.* Princeton: Princeton University Press.

Wendt, Bernhard. 1937. *Der Versteigerungs- und Antiquariats-Katalog im Wandel dreier Jahrhunderte . . . .* Leipzig: Liebisch.

Werner G. and E. Schmidt-Herrling. 1937. *Die Bibliotheken der Universität Altdorf.* Beiheft zum Zentralblatt für Bibliothekswesen, 69. Leipzig: Harrassowitz.

Werner, Michael. 1991. "Die Auswirkungen der preussischen Universitätsreform auf das französische Hochschulwesen (1850–1900) unter besonderer Berücksichtigung der Geisteswissenschaften." In Schubring 1991, 214–26.

Westfall, Richard. 1980. *Never at Rest: A Biography of Isaac Newton.* Cambridge: Cambridge University Press.

Westman, Robert. 1980. "The Astronomer's Role in the Sixteenth Century." *History of Science* 18:105–47.

Whewell, William. 1845. *Of a Liberal Education in General; with Particular Reference to the Leading Studies of the University of Cambridge.* London.

White, Hayden. 1981. "The Value of Narrativity in the Representation of Reality." In Mitchell 1981, 1–24.

————. 1987. *The Content of the Form: Narrative Discourse and Historical Representation*. Baltimore: Johns Hopkins University Press.

————. 1990 [1978]. *Tropics of Discourse: Essays in Cultural Criticism*. Baltimore: Johns Hopkins University Press.

Wiegand, Fritz. 1967. "Die Vermögenswerte der ehemaligen Universität Erfurt um das Jahr 1816." *Beiträge zur Geschichte der Universität Erfurt* 13:149–92.

Wiener, Otto. 1909. "Das physikalische und theoretisch-physikalische Institut." In University of Leipzig 1909b, 4/2:24–69.

Will, Georg A. 1801. *Geschichte und Beschreibung der Nürnbergischen Universität Altdorf*. Altdorf.

Williams, Penry. 1986. "Elizabethan Oxford: State, Church and University." In Mc-Conica 1986, 397–440.

Willison, I. R. 1977. "The Development of the British Museum Library to 1857 in its European Context." In Raabe 1977, 33–61.

Wilpert, Paul, ed. 1964. *Beiträge zum Berufsbewusstsein des mittelalterlichen Menschen*. Miscellanea Mediaevalia, 3. Berlin/New York: de Gruyter.

Winstanley, D. A. 1935. *Unreformed Cambridge: A Study of Aspects of the University in the Eighteenth Century*. Cambridge: Cambridge University Press.

————. 1947. *Later Victorian Cambridge*. Cambridge: Cambridge University Press.

————. 1955 [1940]. *Early Victorian Cambridge*. Cambridge: Cambridge University Press.

Wissel, Rudolf, ed. 1971–88. *Des alten Handwerks Recht und Gewohnheit*. 2nd ed. Edited by E. Schraepler and H. Reissig. 7 vols. Einzelveröffentlichungen der Historischen Kommission zu Berlin, 7:1–7. Berlin: Wasmuth.

Wolf, Ernst. 1952. "Zur wissenschaftlichen Bedeutung der Disputationen an der Wittenberger Universität im 16. Jahrhundert." In University of Halle 1952, 2:335–44.

Wolf, Friedrich August. 1831. *Encyclopädie der Philologie*. Edited by G. H. Stockman. Leipzig.

————. 1833. *Darstellung der Alterthumswissenschaft. . . .* Edited by S. F. W. Hoffmann. Leipzig.

————. 1835. *Über Erziehung, Schule, Universität (consilia scholastica). Aus Wolfs literarischen Nachlass*. Quedlinburg/Leipzig.

————. 1908 [1795]. *Prolegomena zu Homer*. Translated by Hermann Muchau. Leipzig: Reclam.

————. 1935. *Friedrich August Wolf; ein Leben in Briefen*. 3 vols. Stuttgart: Metzler.

————. 1985 [1795]. *Prolegomena to Homer*. Translated and comm. by Anthony Grafton, Glenn Most and James Zetzel. Princeton: Princeton University Press.

Wolf, Gerson. 1871. *Geschichte der K. K. Archive in Wien*. Vienna.

Wolff, Christian. 1841. *Christian Wolffs eigene Lebensbeschreibung*. Edited by H. Wuttke. Leipzig.

Wood, Paul. 1994. "Science, the Universities, and the Public Sphere in Eighteenth-Century Scotland." *History of Universities* 13:99–135.

Worden, Blair. 1997. "Cromwellian Oxford." In Tyace 1997, 733–72.

Wordsworth, Christopher. 1877. *Scholae Academicae: Some Account of the Studies at the English Universities in the Eighteenth Century*. Cambridge.

Wormald, Francis and C. E. Wright, eds. 1958. *The English Library Before 1700: Studies in Its History*. London: University of London Press.

Wotke, Karl. 1905. *Das Österreichische Gymnasium im Zeitalter Maria Theresias*. Monumenta Germaniae paedagogica, 30. Berlin: Hofmann.

Wright, J. M. F. (appeared anonymously). 1827. *Alma Mater; or, Seven Years at the University of Cambridge. By a Trinity-Man.* 2 vols. London.

Württemberg. 1843. *Sammlung der würrtembergischen Schul-Gestze. Dritte Abtheilung, enthaltend die Universitäts-Gestze bis zum Jahr 1843.* Edited by T. Eisenlohr. In *Vollständige, historisch und kritisch bearbeitete Sammlung der württembergischen Gesetze,* II/3. Edited by A. L. Reyscher. Tübingen.

Wuttke, Heinrich. 1842–43. "Ueber das Doktorat." *Jahrbuch der deutschen Universität* 2:109–25.

Yates, Frances. 1966. *The Art of Memory.* London: Routledge.

Zarncke, Friedrich, ed. 1857. *Die deutschen Universitäten im Mittelalter.* Leipzig.

Zedler, Gottfried. 1896. *Geschichte der Universitätsbibliothek zu Marburg von 1527–1887.* Marburg.

Zeeden, Ernst. 1957. "Die Freiburger philosophische Fakultät im Umbruch des 18. Jahrhunderts." In Bauer et al. 1957, 1–139.

Zentgraf, E., ed. 1957. *Aus der Geschichte der Naturwissenschaften an der Universität Freiburg im Breisgau.* Beiträge zur Freiburger Wissenschafts- und Universitätsgeschichte, 18. Freiburg im Br.

Ziegler, Caspar (*praeses*). 1679. *De visitatione ecclesiasticae et procuratio jure,* Georg Heber (*resp.*). Wittenberg.

Ziegnerus, Friedrich (*praeses*). 1671. *De magistris,* A. Francus (*resp.*). Leipzig.

Zimmermann, Albert, ed. 1971. *Der Begriff der Repraesentatio im Mittelalter.* Miscellanea Mediaevalia, 8. Berlin / New York.

———. 1974. *Antiqui und Moderni. Traditionsbewusstsein im späten Mittelalter.* Miscellanea Mediaevalia, 9. Berlin / New York.

Zincke, Georg H. 1742–43. *Grundriß einer Einleitung zu den Cameral-Wissenschaften.* 2 vols. Leipzig.

Zindel, Johann C. 1791. "De ecclesiis cathedralis. Dissertatio canonico-juridicae." In Mayer 1791–93, 1:33–88.

Ziolkowski, Theodore. 1990. *German Romanticism and Its Institutions.* Princeton: Princeton University Press.

Zloczower, Awraham. 1981 [1966]. *Career Opportunities and the Growth of Scientific Discovery in Nineteenth Century Germany with Special Reference to Physiology.* New York: Arno.

Zoepfl, Heinrich. 1860–61. *Altherthümer des deutschen Reichs und Rechts.* 3 vols. Leipzig.

Zormbala, Konstantina. 1991. "Die Gründung der Universität Athen 1837 durch Bayern—nach welchem 'deutschen' Modell?" In Schubring 1991, 268–73.

# Illustration Credits

Gustav Seeberger's *Vorhalle der Münchener Universität, 1846,* now Geschwister-Scholl-Platz, University of Munich, from Münchener Stadtmuseum. Reproduced with permission.

## FIGURES

1.1 An academic lecture, from Sebastian Münster, *Cosmographey; das ist / Beschreibung Aller Länder* . . . , Basel, 1598 [1592], dccclxiii and dcccclxxii. Reproduced with permission of the Universitätsbibliothek Göttingen.

1.2 Corpus Christi College, Oxford, from David Loggan, *Oxonia illustrata,* Oxford, 1675. Reproduced with permission of the Universitätsbibliothek Göttingen.

1.3 Jesuit College, Munich, from Matthäus Merian, *Topographia Germaniae,* 16 vols., Frankfurt a.M., 1643-54, vol. 11. Reproduced with permission of the Universitätsbibliothek Göttingen.

2.1 The order of academic precedence and costumes, University of Cambridge, from *Cantabrigia illustrata,* by David Loggan, Cambridge, 1694. Reproduced with permission of the Universitätsbibliothek Göttingen.

2.2 *Catalogus Professorum,* University of Basel, 1690/91. Reproduced with permission of Universitätsbibliothek Basel.

2.3 *Catalogus Professorum,* University of Basel, 1712/13. Reproduced with permission of Universitätsbibliothek Basel.

2.4 *Professorenzettel* of Michael Mästlin, University of Tübginen, 1607, at Hauptstaatsarchiv Stuttgart, A274.17, fol. 107. All rights reserved by the Hauptstaatarchiv Stuttgart. Reproduced with permission.

2.5 *Professorenzettel* of Andreas Osiander, University of Tübginen, 1607, at Hauptstaatsarchiv Stuttgart A274.17, fol. 110. All rights reserved by the Hauptstaatarchiv Stuttgart. Reproduced with permission.

2.6 *Vorlesungsverzeichnis,* University of Berlin, Summer Semester 1822, pg. 3. Reproduced with permission of the Universitätsbibliothek Göttingen.

2.7 *Vorlesungsverzeichnis,* University of Berlin, Summer Semester 1822, pg. 4. Reproduced with permission of the Universitätsbibliothek Göttingen.

2.8 *Index lextionum,* University of Berlin, Summer Semester 1821, pg. 12. Reproduced with permission of the Universitätsbibliothek Göttingen.

2.9 *Index lextionum*, University of Berlin, Summer Semester 1821, pg. 15. Reproduced with permission of the Universitätsbibliothek Göttingen.

3.1 Heinrich the German's lecture hall by Laurentinus de Voltolina (SMPK, Inv.-Nr. Min. 1233), circa. 1380. At the Bildarchiv, Preussischer Kulturbesitz, Berlin. Reproduced with permission.

3.2 Title page of Johann M. Meÿfart, *Christliche und aus trewen Herzen wolgemeinte auch demütige Erinnerung von der Erbawung und Fortsetzung der Academischen Disciplin auff den Evangelischen Hohen Schulen in Deutschland. . .*, Erfurt 1636. Reproduced with permission of the Universitätsbibliothek Göttingen.

3.3 Lecture and disputation hall at the Collegium Illustre, University of Tübingen, from J. C. Neyffer and L. Ditzinger, *Illustrissimi Wirtembergici ducalis novi collegii quod Tubingae . . . delineatio*, n.l. 1626. Reproduced with permission of the Universitätsbibliothek Göttingen.

3.4 Lecture and disputation hall from *Speculum Cornelianum*, containing illustrations by Jacob van der Heyden from 1618 and others in his style, Strasbourg, 1879. Reproduced with permission of the Institut für Hochschulkunde, Universität Würzburg.

4.1 A doctoral oral and subsequent celebration, University of Jena, circa 1740, from Edmund Kelter, ed., *Jenaer Studentenleben zur Zeit des Renommisten von Zachariae*, Hamburg 1908, frontispiece. Reproduced with permission of the Universitätsbibliothek Göttingen.

4.2 A senate or faculty council sentencing a standing student to a three year suspension, University of Jena, circa 1740, from Edmund Kelter, ed., *Jenaer Studentenleben zur Zeit des Renommisten von Zachariae*, Hamburg: Gräfe & Sillem, 1908, 24 (detail). Reproduced with permission of the Universitätsbibliothek Göttingen.

4.3 "Der Theologe im Exam," 1770 (A. Göhner), University of Tübingen, from Tübingen Städtisches Museum. Reproduced with permission.

4.4 Model grading table for the County of Waldeck, 1704, reprinted in Reinhold Vormbaum, ed., *Evangelische Schulordnungen*, 3 vols., Gütersloh 1860–64, 3:123. Reproduced with permission of the Universitätsbibliothek Göttingen.

4.5 Model grading table for Württemberg, 1729, reprinted in Reinhold Vormbaum, ed., *Evangelische Schulordnungen*, 3 vols., Gütersloh 1860–64, 3:315. Reproduced with permission of the Universitätsbibliothek Göttingen.

4.6 F. A. Wolf's grades for his seminar students, University of Halle, 1805, from Geheimes Staatsarchiv, Preußischer Kulturbesitz, Berlin, I. HA. Rep. 76. alt II. Nr. 102. fol. 121v–22r. Photograph reproduced with permission.

4.7 F. A. Wolf's grades for his seminar students, University of Halle, 1806, from Geheimes Staatsarchiv, Preußischer Kulturbesitz, Berlin, I. HA. Rep. 76. alt II. Nr. 102. fol. 133v–34r. Photograph reproduced with permission.

4.8 R. W. Buss's "Examination of Candidates for the Degree of Bachelors of Arts," University of Oxford, from Victor A. Huber, *English Universities*, London, 1843, II/2, 524. Reproduced with permission of the Universitätsbibliothek Göttingen.

4.9 Oral exam in the law faculty, University of Tübingen, circa 1850, from *Illustrationen zum Burschenleben*, Eßlingen a.N., n.d. [1853?] (UAT S 161/808). Reproduced with permission of the Universitätsarchiv Tübingen.

5.1 Informal disputation at the Collegium Sapientiae, University of Freiburg im Br., from Johan Kerer's *Statuta Collegii Sapientiae* (A 105/8141), circa 1497, 41r. Reproduced with permission of the Univsitätsachiv Freiburg im Br.

5.2 Domestic disputation at the Collegium Sapientiae, University of Freiburg im

Br., from Johnan Kerer's *Statuta Collegii Sapientiae* (A 105/8141), circa 1497, 39r. Reproduced with permission of the Univsitätsarchiv Freiburg im Br.

5.3 Dining hall, Collegium Illustre, University of Tübingen, from J. C. Neyfferand and L. Ditzinger, *Illustrissimi Wirtembergici ducalis novi collegii quod Tubingae . . .* , n.l., 1626. Reproduced with permission of the Universitätsbibliothek Göttingen.

5.4 Collegium in the home of Julius F. Höpfner a lecturer in the law faculty, University of Gießen, from Höpfner's *Studentenstammbuch* (Hs 1217d), circa 1764. Reproduced with permission of the Handschriftenabteilung, Universitätsbibliothek, Gießen.

5.5 Ludwig E. Grimm's "Vorlesung in der Wohnung an der Allee in Göttingen, 28.5.1830," depicting Jacob Grimm's private collegium in summer semester 1830, University of Göttingen, from Städtisches Museum Göttingen. Reproduced with permission.

6.1 Title page of Johann Stier's *Praecepta metaphysicae,* Erfurt , 1641 [O 71.4° Helmst. (1)]. Reproduced with permission of the Herzog-August-Bibliothek, Wolfenbüttel.

6.2 Title page of Friedrich Bierling's (*praeses*), *De causis cur nonulli eruditi nihil in lucem emiserint,* Gerhard F. Werkamp (*resp.*), Rinteln, 1702. Reproduced with permission of the Universitätsbibliothek Göttingen.

6.3 Title page of Johann C. Tschanter's (*resp. et auct.*), *De eruditis studiorum intemperie mortem sibi accelerantibus, dissertatio I, eaque historica,* Gottfried Boettnerus (*praeses*), Leipzig, 1704. Reproduced with permission of the Universitätsbibliothek Göttingen.

6.4 Title page of Johann C. Tschanter's (*praeses*), *De eruditis studiorum intemperie mortem sibi accelerantibus, dissertatio II, eaque physica,* Johann C. Wolff (*resp.*), Leipzig, 1705. Reproduced with permission of the Universitätsbibliothek Göttingen.

6.5 Title page of Gottlob Matthaeus's (*auct. et resp.*), *Dissertatio historico-moralis de malis eruditorum uxoribis, (vulgo) von den bösen Weibern der Gelehrten,* Gottfried Boettnerus (*praeses*), Leipzig, 1705. Reproduced with permission of the Universitätsbibliothek Göttingen.

6.6 Title page of Matthaeus G. Schroederus's (*praeses*) *Dissertatio historico-moralis de misogynia eruditorum, von übelgesinnten Gelehrten gegen das weibliche Geschlecht,* Gottlieb S. Holtzmüller (*resp.*), Leipzig, 1717. Reproduced with permission of the Universitätsbibliothek Göttingen.

6.7 Adolf Neumann's drawing of Friedrich Ritschl, from Otto Ribbeck, *Friedrich Wilhelm Ritschl,* 2 vols., Leipzig, 1879–81, vol.1 , frontispiece. Reproduced with permission of the Universitätsbibliothek Göttingen.

6.8 Title page of Friedrich Ritschl's *Schedae criticae . . . ,* Diss. phil., Halle, 1829. Reproduced with permission of the Universitätsbibliothek Göttingen.

6.9 "Sententiae Controversae" from Friedrich Ritschl's *Schedae criticae . . . ,* Diss. phil., Halle, 1829. Reproduced with permission of the Universitätsbibliothek Göttingen.

7.1 Ludwig E. Grimm's "Thee Schlapps, Mittwoch Abend beim Blumenbach" (BGM GR. Slg. HZ. 606), circa 1830, from Brüder Grimm Museum, Cassel. Copyright 2001 by Brüder Grimm Museum Cassel. Reproduced with permission.

7.2 Letter from the Königsberg Rector and Academic Senate to the ministry, 1670, from Geheimes Staatsarchiv, Preußischer Kulturbesitz, Berlin, I. HA. Rep. 7. Nr. 190. 1566–1689, fol. 286r. Reproduced with permission.

7.3 Letter of reference for Christian Wolff by Leibniz, 1706, from Geheimes

Staatsarchiv, Preußischer Kulturbesitz, Berlin, I. HA. Rep. 52. Nr. 159n, 3d, 1691–1724, fol. 364. Reproduced with permission.

7.4 Letter of reference for Christian Wolff by Leibniz, 1706, from Geheimes Staatsarchiv, Preußischer Kulturbesitz, Berlin, I. HA. Rep. 52. Nr. 159n, 3d, 1691–1724, fol. 366. Reproduced with permission.

8.1 The library, University of Altdorf, from Johann G. Puschner, *Amoenitates Altdorfinae*, n.d. (circa 1710–20), Nuremberg. Reproduced with permission of the Universitätsbibliothek Göttingen.

8.2 The library, University of Göttingen, from Georg D. Heumann, *Wahre Abbildung der Köngl. Groß-Britan. u. Churfürstl. Braunschweigisch-Lüneburgische Stadt Göttingen*, Göttingen, 1747, (GöttUB, gr. 2° H.Hann. V, 29 *rara*.). Reproduced with permission of the Universitätsbibliothek Göttingen.

8.3 Floor plan to the library, University of Göttingen, from Johann Stephan Pütter, F. Saalfeld, and G. H. Oesterley, *Versuch einer academischen Gelehrten-Geschichte der Georg-Augustus Universität zu Göttingen*, 4 vols., Göttingen/Hanover, 1765–1838, vol. 1. Reproduced with permission of the Universitätsbibliothek Göttingen.

8.4 Key to the floor plan to the library, University of Göttingen, from Johann Stephan Pütter, F. Saalfeld, and G. H. Oesterley, *Versuch einer academischen Gelehrten-Geschichte der Georg-Augustus Universität zu Göttingen*, 4 vols., Göttingen/Hanover, 1765–1838, vol. 1. Reproduced with permission of the Universitätsbibliothek Göttingen.

# Acknowledgments

Jeffrey Alexander, Amos Funkenstein, Robert Westman, and M. Norton Wise supported me and the original research. In addition to continued help from the above, the work and I have enjoyed the support, individually, of Jane Caplan, Lorraine Daston, Nick Jardine, Peter Reill, Hans-Jörg Rheinberger, David Sabean, Simon Schaffer, and Rudolf Vierhaus, and, institutionally, of Bryn Mawr College, the Society of Fellows in Humanities at Columbia University, the Max-Planck-Institut für Geschichte in Göttingen, and the Max-Planck-Institut für Wissenschaftsgeschichte in Berlin. Further intellectual stimulus and support came from Peter Becker, Hans Erich Bödeker, Marina Frasca-Spada, Heidrun Friese, Martin Gierl, Michael Hagner, Ernst Hamm, Anke te Heesen, Klaus Hentschel, Isabel Hull, and Ulinka Rublack. David Sabean read and commented on the antepenultimate revision, and Simon Schaffer and Nick Jardine on the penultimate. Catherine Rice brought the book through its ultimate revision. Mara Naselli made the book more readable and more correct in form.

Chapter 1 was read and commented on by Simon Werrett.

Chapter 2 was read and commented on by Alix Cooper. This is a revision of "Parades académiques: Contribution à l'économique politique des livrets universitaires," translated by Marielle Aujollet, *Actes de la recherche en sciences sociales*, December 2000, 135: 6–24, based on a paper presented at *Inconscients adacémiques,* organized by Pierre Bourdieu, Olivier Christin, and Franz Schultheis, 3–4 December 1999, Université Neuchâtel.

Chapter 3 was read and commented on by Martin Gierl.

Chapter 4 was read and commented on by Jane Caplan and John Gascoigne. This is a revision of "On the Table Manners of Academic Examination," pp. 33–67 in *Wissenschaft als kuturelle Praxis*, edited by Hans Erich Bödeker, Peter Reill, and Jürgen Schlumbohm (Vandenhoeck & Ruprecht, 1999), based on a paper presented at *Wissenschaft als kulturelle Praxis*, organized by the three editors in honor of Rudolf Vierhaus, 13–15 November 1997, Max-Planck-Institut für Geschichte, Göttingen.

Chapter 5 was read and commented on by Peter Reill and Mary Terrall. This is a revision of "On the Dialectical Origins of the Research Seminar," *History of Science,* 1989, 27:111–54.

Chapter 6 is revision of "On the Ironic Specimen of the Doctor of Philosophy," *Science in Context,* 1992, 5:91–137, drawn from my dissertation.

Chapter 7 was read and commented on by Peter Becker and André Wakefield. This is a revision of "On the Ministerial Archive of Academic Acts," *Science in Context,* 1996, 9/4:421–86, drawn from a paper presented at *The Prose of Objectivity,* co-organized by Peter Becker and me, 16–20 August 1994, Lessing Akademie, Wolfenbüttel.

Chapter 8 was read and commented on by Marina Frasca-Spada and Nick Jardine. This is a revision of "On the Bureaucratic Plots of the Research Library," pp. 190–206 in *History of the Book/History of the Sciences,* edited by them, Cambridge University Press, 2000.

Chapter 9 was read and commented on by Isabel Hull. This is a revision of part of "On the Ministerial Registers of Academic Visitations," pp. 95–140 in *Little Tools of Knowledge: Historical Essays in Academic and Bureaucratic Practices,* edited by Peter Becker and me, University of Michigan Press, 2001, based on a paper presented at *The Rhetoric of Bureaucratic & Academic Prose,* organized by David Sabean, 13–14 May 1994, Clark Library, Los Angeles.

Chapter 10 was read and commented on by Lisbet Rausing and Nick Hopwood. This is a revision of part of "On the Ministerial Registers of Academic Visitations," pp. 95–140 in *Little Tools of Knowledge: Historical Essays in Academic and Bureaucratic Practices,* edited by Peter Becker and me, University of Michigan Press, 2001, based on a paper presented at *The Rhetoric of Bureaucratic & Academic Prose,* May 1994.

Chapter 11 was read and commented on by Lorraine Daston and Florence Vienne. This is a revision of "On the Professorial Voice," *Science in Context,* 2003, 16 (1/2): 43–57, specially edited by Lorraine Dason and Otto Sibum, based on a paper presented at *The Persona of the Scientist,* organized by the editors, 4–6 June 1999, Max-Planck-Institut für Wissenschaftsgeschichte, Berlin. Thanks to Florence for letting me to listen to her tapes of Michel Foucault's lectures at the Collège de France.

Chapter 12 was read and commented on by Simon Werrett and Michael Hagner.

4 April 2005, San Marcos, California
www.academiccharisma.net

Ah! j'en ai trop pris:—Mais, cher Satan, je vous en conjure, une prunelle moins irritée! et en attendant les quelques petites lâchetés en retard, vous qui aimez dans l'écrivain l'absence des facilté descriptives ou instructives, je vous détache ces quelques hideux feuillets de mon carnet de damné.

Arthur Rimbaud, *Une saison en enfer* (1873)

# Index

Abelard, Peter, 75, 420

*Abitur*, 124–26, 441

Abraham, 357

Academic calendar. *See* academic year

Academic canon: battle of the books (late medieval *via antiqua versus via moderna*), 73–74, 106–7, 410; as classic texts, 410; as crystallized charisma, 17; in general, 18; medieval texts, 17, 44, 410; versus charismatic figures or prophets, 17–18. *See also* academic year lecture catalogue; lectures

Academic degrees: and the dead, 198, 201; and the emperor's authority, 193; juridical and physical conditions for candidacy, 197–202; as setting precedence, 34–35, 40. *See also* academic persona; bachelors; doctors; masters

Academic labor: as alienated, 7–8; as artisanal, 211–12; as artistic, 203, 210–11; as entrepreneurial, 13–14, 17; fees for, 44–45; graphorrhea, 213; Oxbridge as utopia, 22–24; and the philology seminars, 169–79; policed by the disciplinary lecture catalogue, 55; regulated as professorial, 50–52; and teaching at home, 153–56; work ethic forged in German lands, 86; and writing, 158. *See also* bureaucracy; home; lecture catalogue; ministry; office; publication; writing

Academic persona: as agonistic, 15, 74–80, 523n1; "Amerikanization," 464–65; and anonymity, especially in reviews, 287, 373, 375–76, 424, 475, 558n66; Apollonian versus Dionysian, 399–401; as artistic bureaucrat, 203, 210–11, 443–44; as authorial, 179, 202, 203, 207–11, 237; babble as protean, 372; and the bathrobe, 155; and "Big Business," 468–69, 473; as bureaucratic or a

civil servant, 10, 202, 290, 534n51; celibacy, clerical attire, and the study, 155, 213; charisma of the name, 370, 374; charisma and sex appeal from conferences, 474; as charismatic Führer, 469–70, 473; as charismatic generally, 3, 8, 296; the chorus, 411–12; as Christian (or not), 197, 199–201; conflated with "paperwork," 363; and the conversation, 422; coquetry, 420; cream puffs, handshakes, and the scholarly racket, 381; cult of personality, 437, 452, 466–67, 469–71; *deus ex machina*, 397, 404–5; as disinterested professional, 6–7; in *dissertationes eruditorum*, 214–18; and the dossier, 289–95; *Eigenthümlichkeit* and *Erfindungsvermögen*, 211; and endogamy, 241–43; *ex cathedra*, 409–11; as Fichtean-Romantic, 210; in Gedike's hearing, 385–90; and Germanic irony, 211, 542n66; as German Protestant, 3–4; and a good whipping, 379; gossip (and coffee), 395–96, 415–19; as Gothic or Neo-Gothic, 183–84, 186, 197, 210–11; the Harnack Principle, 466–71; heroic like a crowned athlete, 74, 95, 187; impact of grading on, 95, 130, 139–40; and Jesuiticism, 13, 21, 26, 436–37, 517n40; and the juridical generally, 97, 197–202; lapidary style, 262–63, 264–65; the Little Big Men, 451–52; lording over bookshelves, 301, 312; making noise, 373–74; as male (or not), 197, 199–201; managed through envy, 379; managed through vanity, 13; man with a "big name" or reputation, 374, 377, 378; as martial, 15; as meritocratic, 7; ministry induces cacophony and irrationality, 267–68; ministry suppresses cacophony and dissonance, 369; minting